$225.00
4-14-11

Judaism and Islam

The Library of Essays on Sexuality and Religion
Series Editor: Stephen Hunt

Judaism and Islam

Edited by

Stephen Hunt

University of the West of England, UK

ASHGATE

Published by
Ashgate Publishing Limited
Wey Court East
Union Road
Farnham
Surrey GU9 7PT
England

Ashgate Publishing Company
Suite 420
101 Cherry Street
Burlington
VT 05401-4405
USA

www.ashgate.com

British Library Cataloguing in Publication Data
Hunt, Stephen.
    Judaism and Islam. – (The library of essays on sexuality
    and religion)
    1. Sex–Religious aspects–Judaism. 2. Sex in rabbinical
    literature. 3. Sex–Religious aspects–Islam. 4. Sex
    customs–Islamic countries.
    I. Title II. Series III. Hunt, Stephen, 1954-
    296.3'66-dc22

Library of Congress Control Number: 2010928860

ISBN 9780754629214

Mixed Sources
Product group from well-managed
forests and other controlled sources
www.fsc.org Cert no. SGS-COC-2482
© 1996 Forest Stewardship Council
FSC

Printed and bound in Great Britain by
TJ International Ltd, Padstow, Cornwall

Contents

JUDAISM

PART I   JUDAISM AND SEXUALITY: EXPLORING HISTORICAL VIEWPOINTS

PART II   JUDAISM AND SEXUALITY: THE TRADITIONAL–MODERNIST DIVIDE

ISLAM

PART III   ISLAM AND SEXUALITY: SEXUALITY IN HISTORICAL CONTEXT

PART IV   ISLAM AND SEXUALITY IN GLOBAL PERSPECTIVE

Acknowledgements

The editor and publishers wish to thank the following for permission to use copyright material.

Anthropological Quarterly for the essay: Janet L. Bauer (1985), 'Sexuality and the Moral "Construction" of Women in an Islamic Society', *Anthropological Quarterly*, **58**, pp. 120–29. Copyright © 1985 by The Catholic University of America Press.

Berghahn Books Ltd for the essay: Abdessamad Dialmy (2005), 'Sexuality in Contemporary Arab Society', *Social Analysis*, **49**, pp. 16–33.

Brill Academic Publishers for the essay: A.E. Souaiaia (2007), 'She's Upright: Sexuality and Obscenity in Islam', *Hawwa*, **5**, pp. 262–88. Copyright © 2007 Koninklijke Brill NV, Leiden.

Equinox Publishing for the essay: Jerome Gellman (2006), 'Gender and Sexuality in the Garden of Eden', *Theology & Sexuality*, **12**, pp. 319–35. Copyright © 2006 SAGE Publications.

Institute of Southeast Asian Studies for the essay: Lily Zakiyah Munir (2002), '"He Is Your Garment and You Are His ...": Religious Precepts, Interpretations, and Power Relations in Marital Sexuality among Javanese Muslim Women', *Sojourn: Journal of Social Issues in Southeast Asia*, **17**, pp. 191–220.

Jewish Action for the essay: Marc Angel, Hillel Goldberg and Pinchas Stolper (1992), 'Homosexuality and the Orthodox Jewish Community', *Jewish Action*, **53**, pp. 54–9.

Francis Landy for the essay: Francis Landy (1979), 'The Song of Songs and the Garden of Eden', *Journal of Biblical Literature*, **98**, pp. 513–28.

Oxford University Press for the essay: Javaid Rehman (2007), 'The Sharia, Islamic Family Laws and International Human Rights Law: Examining the Theory and Practice of Polygamy and Talaq', *International Journal of Law, Policy and the Family*, **21**, pp. 108–27. Copyright © 2007 Javaid Rehman.

Palgrave Macmillan for the essay: Shahnaz Khan (2003), '*Zina* and the Moral Regulation of Pakistani Women', *Feminist Review*, **75**, pp. 75–100. Copyright © 2003 *Feminist Review*.

Sage Publications for the essays: Hagar Lahav (2007), 'The One: God's Unity and Genderless Divinity in Judaism', *Feminist Theology*, **16**, pp. 47–60. Copyright © 2007 SAGE Publications; Tova Hartman and Naomi Marmon (2004), 'Lived Regulations, Systemic Attributions: Menstrual Separation and Ritual Immersion in the Experience of Orthodox Jewish Women', *Gender & Society*, **18**, pp. 389–408. Copyright © 2004 Sociologists for Women in Society.

Series Preface

For professional and personal reasons, I chose 'sexuality and religion' as my primary research area when I embarked on my postgraduate training and later academic career in Britain about two decades ago. For many years during this journey, I was often frustrated with – and intimidated by – a sense of professional loneliness, most acutely experienced when 'sexuality' scholars asked me why I bothered with 'religion'; and 'religion' researchers raised their eyebrows about my interest in the intersection of these two phenomena. Well, as many readers must have observed, a lot has changed since then – and for the better. There is no denying that, in recent years, the intersection between sexuality and religion has been mainstreamed into the agenda of theoretical and empirical research, thanks not only to the strenuous efforts of boundary-pushing scholars, but also increasing awareness of its importance among funders.

This collection of essays is a landmark testament to – and celebration of – the achievement thus far. It also showcases the fertile ground on which more fruits of labour could be harvested. The breadth and depth of this collection – organised into five volumes, focusing respectively on Christianity; Judaism and Islam; Religions of the East; Indigenous Religions; and finally New Religions – is indeed breathtaking. As someone who often complains (primarily to my poor students, my captive audience) about the entrenched ethnocentric character of 'sociology of religion' – more accurately (and indeed more truthfully) – 'sociology of Western institutional Christianity', I am delighted with Stephen Hunt's open-mindedness and broad field of vision in the design of this collection and the selection of essays. Drawing on theoretical and empirical material from sociology, theology, anthropology, religious studies, cultural studies, and history (to name but a few), the collection demonstrates that the manifestations of the intersection between sexuality and religion are varied and multi-faceted, with enabling and constraining potentials, mediated through a variety of power structures. Therefore, their relationship should not be essentialised (e.g. religions are inherently sex-negative; sexuality can only flourish in secular – and assumed liberal and democratic – spaces).

I congratulate Stephen Hunt and Ashgate for having had the vision and perseverance to produce this indispensible collection which will undoubtedly inspire scholars in this area for many years to come. This collection educates us about the complexity and diversity in the scholarly and everyday understandings of 'lived' sexuality and religion. We owe them a huge debt of gratitude.

ANDREW KAM-TUCK YIP
University of Nottingham, UK

Introduction

At first glance the enterprise of this volume in bringing together Judaism and Islam, by way of comparing their respective views of human sexuality, may appear at least ambitious and tortuous at best. There is much that differentiates the two faiths besides their well-publicized and frequently exaggerated mutual animosities. Perhaps most obvious are matters of scale and historical progression. While Islam, in terms of the number of adherents, constitutes the second largest faith in the world, Judaism is to be found much further down the list of so-called 'World Religions'. Partially this is because Judaism relates to a single ethnic group, namely, the Jews. Notwithstanding the Jewish diaspora, Islam has wider global resonance, especially given the earnest mission of evangelization that renders it truly 'universalistic'. Although both religions may be counted among the 'historically predominant religious culture[s]' (Norris and Inglehart, 2006, pp. 43–4), their particular histories by no means occupy the same time line. While the definitive date for the formation of Judaism remains a matter of speculation (by most approximations deemed to have originated in at least 1500 BCE), Islam has a self-assigned exact dating for its founding in 622 CE when the prophet Muhammad led the embryonic Muslim community to Medina (*Hijra*).

Despite the contrasts, there are commonalities that unite Judaism and Islam in their moral tenets, including attitudes towards and engagement with the subject of sexuality. To a degree these commonalities denote the intersection between the two religions in that the latter derives a sizable number of its beliefs and practices from the former. Thus Dirks (2006) uses the analogy of a tree, noting that each of the three Abrahamic faiths – Judaism, Christianity and Islam – claim to be the one, true vertical extension of a trunk of primary divine revelation, with the last two religions interpreted as lateral branches deviating from the verticality of the original trunk. Thus the holy scriptures of each – the Judaic Torah, the Christianity Bible and the Islamic Qur'an – are not identical. Nonetheless, the younger two religions acknowledge God's truth as founded in the previous religion(s).

The dominant form of Judaism today (rabbinic Judaism) matured in the eastern Greco-Roman world and partially through one of its sectarian derivatives, namely Christianity, proved to have a profound impact on the later rise of Islam. Given that both Judaism and Islam are monotheistic faiths, they have observably forged distinct but comparable outlooks towards sexuality. The shared faith in the single God has fashioned their foundational religious dispositions with an emphasis on holy writings as divinely inspired, thus creating similarities in structure, practice and jurisprudence, which permit no distinction between the religious and the secular world. As the creator and source of all that exists, God concerns himself with human activities in this world, providing complex regulations for spiritual life. This includes dress and dietary codes, alongside the strict regulation of sexual behaviour, whose contravention justly brings divine judgement. Hence, there are not dissimilar prohibitions against cultural exogamy, pre-marital sex, adultery and homosexuality. Nevertheless, Judaism and Islam, to varying degrees within each faith, have been enculturated by localized cultural mores, in addition to being profoundly challenged by the modern world. Historically and cross-culturally, then, there are complex attitudes towards sexuality to be unearthed both between and within the respective faiths.

Matters of the comparison of beliefs and practice, beside dimensions of enculturation and engagement with modernity, illuminate the similarities and differences between Judaism and Islam. In surveying their orientations towards sexuality this volume will give scope to these variations and sometimes transformative outlooks by engaging with the work to be found in several scholarly disciplines: religious studies, theology, psychology, sociology and anthropology among them. Part I connects with the conventional Judaic view of sexuality, tracing its origins through the relevant holy scriptures, together with supplementary written and oral traditions, and how these have been variously interpreted. Part II focuses on more contemporary themes including the contestation and defence of traditional Jewish attitudes towards sexuality via orthodox and liberal renderings of the faith. As a counterpoint, Part III includes contributions examining Islamic views of sexuality from a historical and conventional perspective. Traditional Islam (both Sunni and Shi'ite), however, faces its own trials, some in parallel with Judaism, others in stark contrast. Hence, Part IV presents essays from a localized perspective pertaining to Islamic customary teachings of sexuality including their adaptations and transformations by Islamic communities in discrete cultural contexts.

JUDAISM

Judaism and Sexuality: Exploring Historical Viewpoints

The Jews, as a distinct ethnic group, have identified divine providence at work through every stage of their collective existence. Yahweh (God) chose Abraham to father an elect nation of destiny. Through the prophet of the Exodus, Moses, and subsequent prophets he asserted his goodness, providence and judgement. The account of this dispensation is related in the Judaic Torah ('teaching' or 'instruction', occasionally translated as 'law'), which pertains sometimes to the Five Books of Moses (the Pentateuch) or sometimes to the totality of Judaism's original ethical and legal religious text. The Ten Commandments and associated detailed laws established the moral foundations for a chosen people but also established the measure by which all nations would ultimately be judged. The Torah constitutes the first three sections of the *Halakha* (composed by Rabbi Yosef Karo in the sixteenth century) and guides religious practices and beliefs, contouring numerous aspects of day-to-day life. 'Halakha' is often literal rendered as 'the path' and is derived from the Hebrew root meaning 'to go' or 'to walk', not dissimilar to Muslim Law, the Shari'ah, which stems from the Arabic 'road' or 'path'.

Through its holy writings and rabbinic tradition Judaism has come, like Islam and indeed Christianity, to stress the interconnectedness between sexuality, procreation and marriage. However, the relationship is more ambiguous in Judaism. The Torah does not prohibit pre-marital sex for a man in a consensual relation with any woman he could potentially marry. The only parameters placed on sexual activities in the Torah are prohibitions against adultery, homosexuality, sex with any relative (whether blood-related or otherwise), with a woman during her menstrual cycle and bestiality (Lev. 18:6–23). Pre-marital sex nonetheless has come to be considered a gross violation of custom and considered sinful by rabbinic scholars of the Talmud. To a great extent this was due to cultural traditions that highly valued female virginity, subsequently justified by aspects of the law including the principles of modesty (*zenut*) that forbid female sexual immorality as part of a code prohibiting depraved thoughts, gaping at members of the opposite sex, adopting modest attire, viewing images that are sexually arousing and animals copulating, transvestism and erotically embracing (*chibuk*) or kissing (*nishuk*) one's spouse in public.

Rules related to chastity and modesty might suggest a tradition of sexual asceticism. To be sure, Judaism has not been without its ascetic streams. For example, the life of the ancient Ḥasidim or Perushim (Pharisees) and Ẓenu'im (Essenes) was regulated by *askesis* (the practice of fortitude), leading to a view of sensual life as defiling. The call to sexual abstinence, however, proved to be historically exceptional due to the weight placed on the virtues of marriage. Indeed, the matter of marriage and sexuality became a source of boundary conservation between Christian and Judaic communities as the former grew in influence. In this regard, the Persian Christian sage Aphrahat wrote in 344 CE justifying his faith's emphasis on chastity, thus counteracting the Jewish claim for a greater holiness and superiority identified with marriage and procreation (Koltun-Fromm, 2000).

A life of chastity has also proved to be rare given that the conventional Judaic view of sexuality would appear to be a positive and affirming one. In Jewish law, sex is not considered shameful, sinful or obscene, but pleasurable, while its reproductive aspect emulates the works of a creator God. Although sexual desire is derived from *yetzer ra* (the evil impulse), it is not a necessary vice for the mere purpose of procreation. In Chapter 1 of this volume, Daniel Boyarin confirms this Judaic view of sexuality by engaging with the scholarship of Michel Foucault and his insistence that there was no autonomous realm of sexuality in the ancient world. Foucault insisted that the intrinsic quality of sex was absent within classical cultures given that desire and pleasure were inextricably bound up with the relations of power and domination. Permitted and tabooed sexual behaviour was connected to function of status: the world was divided into males as dominators of sexual activity and females as the dominated. Boyarin points out, however, that no parallel research has been conducted into a historical view of sexuality in Judaism, which displays a far more positive attitude towards the subject than commonly supposed.

Such a viewpoint would seem to be vindicated by the reading of the celebrated poetic work of King Solomon (ruling approximately from 967 BCE) in the Tanakh, Song of Songs, which has traditionally been portrayed as the ideal for heterosexual relationships and is infused with the passionate language of desire and longing of a couple in love (Crawford, 2008). Several poems include eloquent but scarcely vulgar praises of the physical features of both the male and female, including the line 'Your stature is like a palm tree, and your breasts are like its clusters' (7:7). While the work can be said to constitute a Jewish theology of sexuality, it has come to have a rather curious place in the history of sexuality (Moore, 2001) given that its rich narrative is open to varied allegorical interpretation and images of heterosexual attraction including a portrayal of God and Israel as male lover and female beloved. Illustrating the variety of interpretations of the Song of Songs, in Chapter 2 Francis Landy relates a more psychological interpretation and explores the work in the context of the garden of paradise of Eden.

The mutual male–female compatibility and egalitarianism of sexual relations is seemingly reflected in idealized Judaic marriage. Historically speaking, the institution has been advanced as the only acceptable outlet for expressions of the sexual impulse, but not judged as merely a matter of sexuality and reproduction. Marriage is informed by its alleged spiritual and companionship qualities. In the Torah, the word employed for sex between husband and wife is derived from the root *Dalet-Ayin-Tav*, connoting 'to know' (*yada*), which lucidly illustrates that appropriate sexuality involves both the heart and the mind, in conjunction with the spiritual dimension. The need for physical compatibility between spouses is recognized in Jewish law, where sexual desire is satisfied by them out of mutual love and desire, sex being designated *mitzvah* – a mandate associated with an act of kindness. The Talmud, through the laws of *onah*, confirms sex as one of the wife's three basic rights (the others being food and clothing), specifying both the quantity and the quality of sex that a man provides for 'performing the conjugal duty' and, although debated, whenever his wife has the desire.

Despite the apparent egalitarian nature of sexual relations, from a scriptural standpoint in ancient Israel wives were considered the property of their husbands: 'A man takes a wife and possesses her. If she fails to please him because he finds in her something unseemly, he shall then write her a bill of divorcement, hand it to her and send her away from his house' (Deut. 24:1). Sexual metaphors of subjection also resonate in rabbinic literature and where cultural fear of the female as a temptress has led to the boundary separation between men and women. Therefore rabbinical Judaism has historically consigned women largely to domestic roles and forged a gender division especially notable in the realms of public worship and ecclesiastical leadership, alongside regulations such as men being forbidden to walk behind women, males and females being separated on festive occasions and even having separate days for visiting cemeteries. Women are often discouraged from the obligation to study Torah, which is commonly viewed in rabbinical theology as the apex of religious devotion. For such reasons Orthodox Judaism is often depicted as being essentially patriarchal in nature.

The matter of patriarchy has recently attracted academic attention, noting particularly that studies in early Judaism had initially tended to overlook women and retain their isolation from the larger narrative of Jewish history. In this respect they seemed to share considerable overlap with other distorted presentations of the ancient world (Archer, 1990). Today, the field of Jewish gender studies has been enhanced by scholarship focusing on Jewish women, which has promoted a radical rethinking of traditional narratives. Exemplifying such trends, in Chapter 3 Hagar Lahav examines the cultural ways in which Judaism has historically comprehended the relationship between the individual and divinity, showing that this understanding has deeply engendered dimensions with repercussions related to perceptions of sexuality. Grounded in feminist critiques of theology, as well as in Jewish and cultural studies, the essay deconstructs the conceptualization of the God–person relationship in both Orthodox and Kabbalic Jewish streams as based on a hierarchical division into different spaces: the *Mitzvah* (Commandment, Duty, Law) is perceived to be the highest space and represented as 'manly'; the intermediate space – Grace – is represented as a 'good woman' or as 'mother'; the lowest space is that of desire and personal will, culturally represented by a child or a whore-woman, a place characterized by an attitude of disregard, opposition and fear.

Some feminist writings have also attempted to bring a reinterpretation of Judaic scripture that renders the matter of sexuality as more conducive to gender equality. This includes the essential meaning of the story of the Garden of Eden in Genesis 2–3, which describes the sexual relationships between Adam and Eve. However, in Chapter 4 Jerome Gellman questions this radical interpretation of the relationship between the original couple, arguing that male sexual dominance is clearly rooted deep in Judaic religious text. Gellman suggests that these feminist arguments are not convincing and are hard to square with the biblical rendering if four central elements in the story are considered: the sexual nature of *ha'adam*, Adam/the earthling at the start of the creation narrative; God's 'curse' of Eve; the meaning of the woman as a 'helper' to Adam; and Adam's naming of the woman. Gellman concludes that the most plausible meaning of these chapters is that Adam dominates Eve sexually and otherwise from the very moment of her creation.

Sexuality, given its strong natural drive, has led to broader aspects of control and regulation within Judaism. Reflecting an inherent sanctity, sexuality has strong boundaries and guidelines in relation to endorsement and taboo. There are, however, areas of contention. For instance, the faith has struggled with disagreements over what conduct is permitted within a marriage. Rabbi Huna, a third-century Babylonian teacher, is believed to have counselled his daughters on how to exercise sexual techniques, including different positions during intercourse, with the purpose of 'arousing their husbands' desire'. On the other hand, the superstition grew up that children were born lame because the husband 'inverted the table' in regard to the conventional sexual posture. Clearer prohibitions nonetheless endure in the Orthodox tradition. In principle, birth control is permitted so long as the couple are committed to eventually fulfilling the *mitzvah* to be fruitful and multiply. In addition, Jewish law clearly prohibits male masturbation – 'secreting semen in vain' (*hotza'at zera levatala*). This law is derived from the story of Onan (Gen. 38:8–10), who practised coitus interruptus as a means of birth control to evade fathering a child for his deceased brother. It follows that methods that destroy the seed or block the passage of the seed are not permitted, including the use of condoms. However, the contraceptive pill is well recognized as an acceptable form of birth control under Jewish law.

Traditional Jewish sexual practices also include the law of *niddah*, separation of husband and wife during the woman's menstrual period, prohibiting intercourse. The ruling is part of the laws also known as *taharat ha-mishpachah*, family purity, as recorded in the *Torah* (Lev. 15:19–24). The time of separation begins at the first sign of blood and ends in the evening of the woman's seventh 'clean day' (Talmudic scholars extended the period of separation to last a minimum of 12 days). At the end of the *niddah*, as soon as possible after nightfall after the seventh clean day, the woman must immerse herself in a kosher *mikvah*, a ritual pool. The *mikvah* was traditionally used to cleanse a person of various forms of ritual impurity. Today, it is used almost exclusively for the period of *niddah*.

The complexities of *nidda*, as well as other aspects of Judaic sexuality, are often misunderstood outside the faith. This is illustrated in Chapter 5 by David Ribner and Peggy Kleinplatz who consider how, for more than two millennia, Jewish communities around the world have found themselves the focus of speculation, misinformation, fear, derision and at times envy regarding their sexual beliefs and practices. Some of these perceptions have become sufficiently influential as to reciprocally induce Jewish perceptions of sexuality. This chapter sheds light on some of the better and lesser well-known myths that circumscribe the subject in Judaism. The authors commence, however, by offering a representative view of sexuality, intimacy and related gender expectations as debated in conventional Jewish sources such as the Torah, Talmud and Midrash.

Judaism and Sexuality: The Traditional–Modernist Divide

For traditional Jews the commandments and law that govern numerous aspects of life are still binding. However, since the second-century codification of the *Mishnah* (the first major written redaction of the Jewish oral traditions) the rabbinic authorities have endeavoured to temper a number of scriptural regulations. In this task they have been aided by the fact that the oral Torah is not regarded as complete, given that with changes in human society there are always fresh and unique situations to which it has to be appropriated. This has proved to be so in relation to laws of marriage and divorce, which have been adjusted to enhance the status of women. At the same time, Orthodox Judaism has retained other conventions such as a strong prohibition regarding interfaith sexual relations and marriage.

Conservative Judaism stands midway between the divide of liberal and Orthodox opinion on sexual matters, affirming that *Halakha* is an obligatory guide to Jewish life but nonetheless subject to periodic revision by the Rabbinate. Consequently, a number of conventional rulings followed by Orthodox Judaism have been eroded. Arising in the nineteenth century in order to accommodate the modern world while at the same time acknowledging the worth of tradition, the Conservative variant maintains a diversity of formal teachings including the laws of *niddah* and a general prohibition regarding non-marital heterosexual conduct. However, it has in recent years adapted a policy of being more accommodating of interfaith couples in an attempt to retain the loyalty of future generations to the faith. This reflects the fact that more traditional strands of Judaism in North America and many European countries have declined rapidly in synagogue membership, with much of the deficiency going to the Reform Responsa (Reformed Judaism) with its more liberal views of sexuality. The latter still discourages sex before marriage, but its more tolerant attitudes (along with Reconstructionist Judaism) towards both sexual diversity and interfaith marriage may have contributed to the increasing attractiveness of less conventional expressions of the faith during the 1990s.

The essays in Part II of this volume engage with some of these changing attitudes and explore how contrasting movements within Judaism have dealt with the matter of sexuality, including theological reflection, while casting light on lay perspectives. In Chapter 6 Tova Hartman and Naomi Marmon, by way of illustrating the implications of Judaic sexual regulation, overview the lived experiences of *mikvah* for Orthodox Jewish women. They consider the regimen of ritual purity by examining the ways in which the women live and experience this custom. The authors show how the experiences range further than the conventional schematic abstractions of the integral gender/sexuality oppression–empowerment dichotomy to display a multitextured range of sentiments and experiences. Similarly, in Chapter 7 Mark Guterman explains how among Modern-Orthodox Jews, measured by a list of 'strict' and 'lenient' prohibited behaviours, sexual laws are frequently refined, violated or even ignored. In Chapter 8 Judi Keshet-Orr explores the impact that Jewish laws and teachings continue to have upon Jewish women. Sexual practices are examined in the light of twentieth-century influences and the advent of psychosexual therapy. Some contemporary literature is also discussed and the views of prominent figures within the Jewish community are permitted a voice in this essay.

In Chapter 9 Rachel Rosenthal provides further insights into the past and present regulation of sexuality. She argues that Halakhic conceptions of sexuality in Jewish texts, which promote the expression of heterosexual desire through marriage, form the foundation of the rendering of sacred texts that disenfranchise women in the process of divorce and rebuff homosexuality as a permissible sexual identity. Located in the family, where struggles between authority and the expression of sexuality frequently occur, these two issues exemplify how changes in social norms in the USA may impact interpretations and implementation of *Halakha* by rabbinical authorities of modern Jewish movements. Because Orthodox, Reform, Conservative and Reconstructionist Judaism each approach Jewish texts and traditions differently, their viewpoints are tempered by their varying theological assumptions about the divine authority of sacred works.

In recent years, at least in a number of Western societies, Conservative and Reformed Judaic variants have, to varying degrees, relaxed more stringent views of sexual variants including homosexuality and lesbianism. In the USA, for example, neither observe conventional sexuality rules and they have welcomed non-married and homosexual couples and even endorsed homosexual commitment civil unions. Even conservative Judaism has liberalized allowing individual rabbis, congregations and rabbinical schools to instigate their own policy on homosexual conduct. Nevertheless, lesbian women who consider themselves traditional or conservative in the context of religious practice often experience tremendous conflicts regarding the integration of same-sex emotional and sexual feelings with their religion and spirituality (Glassgold, 2008) and are forced to reconcile seemingly discordant elements by utilizing texts that portray them as role models in a newly constructed cultural canon (Alpert, 1997).

The dilemma is still generated by a historical prohibition of homosexual acts grounded in a world-view that sees heterosexuality as natural and heterosexual marriage as the only route to religious and personal fulfilment (Kaghn, 1989). In Chapter 10 Marc Angel, Hillel Goldberg and Pinchas Stolper make this clear and defend the conventional Judaic position on homosexuality. Their argument is not against the laws that give homosexual citizens protection equal to that given to heterosexuals. Rather, they contend that all citizens have a right not to be involuntarily exposed to overt sexual behaviour or preferences, whatever the nature. In their view the rights of homosexuals really amount to a campaign to legitimize homosexuality to obtain society's approval of immoral behaviour. For the authors the real issue is not individual rights for homosexuals, but collective coercion of everyone else to subscribe to the legitimization of homosexuality. They contend that it is in the best interests of Judaism to support the continued granting of basic civil rights to all, while making clear the moral opposition to the underlying conduct of those who exercise their freedom in violation of basic ethical norms of Judaism.

ISLAM

Islam and Sexuality: Sexuality in Historical Context

According to Islam, God's revelation to humankind has proceeded through various dispensations. Allah revealed the Ten Commandments by means of the prophet Moses, the Golden Rule (codes of ethical behaviour) through the prophet Īsā (Jesus) and his final revelation via the exemplary life and utterances of the prophet Mohammed. The holy scripture, the means by which God finally revealed his will to man, is the Qur'an and it is the Qur'an, whose tenets are coded in the Shari'ah, that ultimately shapes attitudes towards sexuality.

The Sunnah of the prophet Mohammed presents the articulated dispositions on matters of sexuality conforming to the sacred word, while his sayings (*Ahadith*) are endorsed by Sunni, but not Shia Muslims. All such divine inspirations are supplemented by the rulings (*fatwa*) of religious leaders (*Imams*) over several centuries.

While Islam undoubtedly carries a number of influences also central to Judaism and Christianity, in its disposition towards sexuality some of its own distinct attributes can be discerned. Certainly the regulation of sexuality encompasses a way of life integrated with matters of gender difference and modesty (*hijab*) not dissimilar to Orthodox Judaism. Beyond this observation, as Shahidian (2007) points out, delineating criteria for an 'Islamic sexuality' is arduous given that no uniform code for sexual behaviour or relations exists. There are, for Shahidian, a multitude of Islamic 'sexualities'. Even so, he suggests, we may deduce certain relative constants and one such revealed in the Qur'an (13:3) is that just as plants and animals are created 'in pairs' (*azwaj*) – each has a *qarin* who is the mate of the opposite sex – so male and female sexuality reflects bivalence and the dual relations of contraries.

Similarly to Judaism, Islam considers sexual desire a natural aspect of human relationships. Several Qur'anic verses (for example 2:183–7; 4:1; 53:45) refer to the heterosexual act and resultant reproduction as part of the divine design for establishing a harmonious family, leading to the spiritual equilibrium of the *Ummah* (community). As instructed in the Qur'an, 'Your Lord created you of a single soul and from it created its mate, and from the pair of them scattered abroad many men and women' (4:1) and 'So now lie with them, and seek what Allah has prescribed for you' (2:187). In subsequent verses the demise of the first male and female in Eden is recounted; where Satan led them astray to perceive their 'shameful parts which had been hidden for them … and they hurried to cover themselves with leaves' (7:19–22). Thus, in Islam, sexuality, subsequently tainted by aspects of sinful transgression, is comprehended as heterosexual in nature and contained within the divinely sanctioned institution of marriage (*nikâh*) which elevates intercourse from an act of lust to a sacred undertaking, thus demarcating legitimate and prohibited forms of sexual activity.

According to Islam, the sex drive is to be purified and refined in a wholesome way by codified regulations if it is not to result in dishonourable acts. Every functioning bodily part, including sexual organs, has a specific purpose. Nonetheless, it is human determination that must curb and control primal cravings. That said, the fact that the natural sex drive is God-given militates against its ascetic suppression, although a certain ambiguity remains. According to a hadith, Muhammad stated 'whoever cannot afford to establish a family, he must fast from desiring sex, for abstention in that case will protect him from sin' (Ibn Abbas). This explains the condemnation of sexual self-stimulation. While the Qur'an does not mention masturbation overtly, it is firmly discouraged as *makruh* (detestable) and this is enforced in most traditions of Islamic rulings: the Shia forbid masturbation without qualification, while some Sunni jurisprudence takes a weaker condemnatory position with the rationale that it encourages lust. Another restriction is that it is considered *haram* for a woman to have intercourse during her menstrual period, for forty days after childbirth, during the daylight hours of Ramadan and while on pilgrimage. Sexual hygiene is a prominent topic in Islamic jurisprudence (*fiqh*) due to its practical application in everyday life. Thus Muslims are advised to avoid sexual intercourse during menses so as not to cause discomfort to the woman (Qur'an, 2:222). The Qur'an says of sexual intercourse during the month of Ramadan 'It is made lawful to you to go into your wives on the night of the fast' (2:187) and thus it is prohibited in the daylight hours.

Through emulation of the actions of Muhammad, this same type of prohibition is applied also to voluntary fasts.

It is the fear of unrestrained sexual desire that dictates the Islamic emphasis on modesty. The word '*hijab*' is used in the Qur'an in its literal rendering as denoting a barrier that separates two things from one another. Thus the Prophet's wives were commanded to observe *hijab* in the sense of not facing any adult male who could legitimately marry them. Over time the term came to indicate the dress of a woman in accordance with Islamic requisites. This is supplemented by the belief that Allah created males to be more attracted to the female body than vice versa. It follows that women should not display their bodies in a manner that brings temptation. Beyond that generalized command there exist no specific rules determining the details of how to dress accordingly. Nevertheless, it is expected that neither males nor females should be attired or act in a sexually provocative way in the company of the opposite sex.

For Muslims, based on an understanding of the Qur'an and the Ahadith, sexual relations are confined to marriage between a wife and husband (with polygamy permissible under rare and unique circumstances). Adultery (*Zina*) is strictly forbidden in the Qur'an (17:32); *Sura* 24:13 ensures that the act must be viewed before four eye-witnesses to justify punishment being meted out. While the strictest forms of Sunni law can prescribe the death penalty for adultery, in Shia law pre-marital sex is considered a lesser offence and might be punishable by a maximum of 100 lashes to the male. Even this may be interpreted to denote the gravity of the wrongdoing.

When a person is sufficiently mature, can survive independently and is prepared to conform to the responsibilities of marriage, he or she can undertake what constitutes a civil contract, witnessed first by God and thereafter by the community. The main terms of an Islamic marriage are, formally at least, the free consent of both spouses (usually restricted to parents' agreement of suitability), the dowry of the wife and the respect of terms that either spouse may opt to contain in the marriage contract (most often the woman's insistence on being the only wife or the right to divorce without the consent of her husband and void of stating any reason). The Qur'an (4:22) declares the conditions for men with regard to marriage. Marriage to a range of close relatives is prohibited, while temporary marriage (*muta*) is not allowed by the majority of Sunni schools, but permitted by Shia traditions. Qur'anic verses make it legal for Muslim men to marry women from other Abrahamic religions (that is, Jews and Christians), provided that the women are faithful to their own religious beliefs, but such interfaith marriage is generally deemed unwise.

The above simplistic and rather archetypal overview of Islamic views of sexuality has, however, to be tempered by cultural and historical variants by which the notion of 'sexualities' might be justified. Such complexities are explored in the third and fourth parts of this volume, which present essays placing attitudes towards sexuality in diverse contexts, exploring both constants and variations. In Chapter 11 Ahmed Souaiaia considers some of the continuities by exploring the concepts of sexuality and obscenity in Islamic traditions and the way in which culture shapes and refines notions of attractiveness, propriety and legality. Souaiaia concludes that societal values are preserved in emerging religious teachings of expanding categories for acts, rules and values that rely on practice-based consensus, rather than negotiated consensus. In Islam, reiterating the observation above, obscenity and profanity become dysfunctions that disturb individuals' spiritual balance and subsequently that of the community. In Chapter 12 As'ad AbuKhalil also identifies enduring aspects of the specific construct of sexual and gender images. While a static Islam heritage (*Turath*) is observable, it is supplemented by systematic socialization, education and indoctrination, which transmit cultural values and attitudes from one generation to another regarding the realm of sexuality.

The notion of a consistent continuity has to be modified. In a good number of interpretations part of the Islamic heritage relating to sexuality is viewed as essentially linked to the matter of patriarchy and has been so from its foundations, thus establishing an unchanging hegemony. Within this framework, as frequently claimed by feminist scholars, the dominant partner is the male, thus forming the basis of a hierarchy with females, boys, slaves, servants and maids descending in an order of sexual submissiveness. Moreover, it is frequently asserted that Islam from the beginning founded a dominant sexual relationship, where regarding women as men's 'tilth' is tantamount to permitting men to enter the female sexual 'fields' as they please. In this respect, Sabbah writes that 'The ideal of female beauty in Islam is obedience, silence, and immobility, that is, inertia and passivity' (1984, p. 4). 'This woman is depicted as an omnisexual woman, a creature whose most prominent attribute, which determines her whole personality and behavior, is her sexual organs' (Sabbah, 1984, p. 24). The female would also appear to be the temptress. Muhammad, by way of warning in a hadith, is reported to have stated that 'There is nothing left after I go more dangerous to men than the temptations of women' (Al-Bukhaari). Arguably, this hadith exemplifies Islamic beliefs regarding extramarital and pre-marital sex.

That Islam itself is not the source of female suppression and that the fuel that keeps the flames of patriarchy alive is essentially man-made has been famously advanced by the fictional work of Alify Rifaat (1987). In Chapter 13 Javaid Rehman attempts to throw academic light on this assertion by assessing the compatibility of the Shari'ah and Islamic family laws with international human rights law, especially in relation to polygamy and the *Talaq* (unilateral divorce given by the husband) within Islam. It is evident that while the Qur'an and Sunna remain the principal foundations of the Shari'ah, the formulation of a legally binding code from primarily ethical and religious sources has not been an uncontested matter. It is also submitted that the Shari'ah and Islamic family laws that eventually emerged during the second and third centuries of the Muslim calendar were heavily influenced by the socio-economic, political and indigenous tribal values of the prevailing times. During the development phases of the classical legal schools, the Islamic jurists frequently adopted male-centric approaches towards women's rights and family laws. Attempts to rectify the injustices built into the prevailing system of polygamous marriages and unilateral *Talaq* procedures have resulted in some, albeit limited, success through the process of directly appealing to the primary sources of the Shari'ah.

In similar vein, in Chapter 14, Elizabeth Shlala Leo also constructs a counterpoint to the feminist interpretation of Islam as *inherently* patriarchal. She sees sexuality, gender and patriarchy as modern concepts that Western feminist scholars have uncritically utilized in their historical inquiry into women in Islam without ample consideration of periodization. This has led to scholarship that superimposes modern conceptual frameworks upon earlier time periods. As we have seen, the revelation of the Qur'an insists that the sexes were ordered in relation to each other in a reflection of their physical and biological complementarity. There was not, however, the construction of sexuality and gendering that is evident in the patriarchal society of the modern world. In this essay, the author attempts to trace the historiographical evolution of female sexuality from the time of the Prophet until the Middle Ages, particularly through the development of the female gendered roles of wifehood and motherhood as found in the Qur'an, hadith and fiqh.

Also complicating the subject of female sexuality is the matter of how women interpret and give meaning to Islamic teachings. Thus recent academic works have considered the mediation of female sexual identity in different cultural contexts. Ozyegin (2009), for instance, demonstrates that in the process of negotiating often contradictory expectations of their sexual behaviour in Turkey young women cultivate purposefully ambiguous identities related to their state of virginhood. She highlights an important normative shift from a focus on the physical reality of virginity to an emphasis on the moral expression of virginity. In much the same vein Khan *et al.* (2002) provide a qualitative study of the sexual behaviour of married women in Bangladesh from both rural and urban areas, indicating that, despite normative restrictions, many women reveal considerable variation in their sexual behaviour with respect to sexual negotiation, sex during menstruation and forced sex. Similarly, male sexual identity may also vary considerably. Thus Ouzgane (2003) outlines the great complexity, variety and difference of male identities in Islamic societies – from the Taliban orphanages of Afghanistan to the cafés of Morocco, to Iraqi military conscripts – showing how the masculine gender is constructed and negotiated in the Islamic Ummah, often eschewing the notion that the male identity is inseparable from the control of women.

In addition, recent works indicate that, like Judaism, Islam has responded to and negotiated the contemporary world (Rohit, 2009). The Islamic diaspora in the Western context presents perhaps the most radical challenge to the Ummah. This might suggest recourse to traditional values as part of the boundary maintenance established against the incursion of permissive norms. However, there is contrary evidence: as Nader Ahmadi indicates in Chapter 15 in relation to Sweden, the encounter with a more permissive sexual culture seems to have influenced Iranian migrants' views on sexuality. The traditional authoritarian patriarchal sexual relationship among Iranian migrants is giving way to more egalitarian relationships and a relatively strong tendency towards a similarity of views between males and females regarding sexuality. The important change noted in regard to sexuality is the evolving of individualism in regard to both sexual decision-making and forms of relationships.

Islam and Sexuality in Global Perspective

A range of Islamic sexualities have been observable from a historical viewpoint, but also continue to be observed cross-culturally in Muslim homelands where cultural norms have shaped beliefs, attitudes and behaviour. In Chapter 16 Lily Zakiyah Munir considers sexuality in Java as a cultural construct, pointing out that the teachings of the Qur'an on sexual equality and reciprocity may not always apply. This is because there are at least two factors that determine a Javanese Muslim's attitude to sexuality. First, diversity in religious texts lends itself to varied interpretations and emphasis, which results in the wide range of experiences found in Muslim communities across the world. Second is the influence of local Javanese culture, which is patriarchal in nature and has consequently assigned asymmetrical power relations in marriage with all their ramifications regarding women's sexuality. This patriarchal ideology has been sustained by the Javanese stereotypical concept of womanhood and further perpetrated by the political structure through the institutionalization of familial ideology.

With reference to a very different cultural context, in Chapter 17 Abdessamad Dialmy suggests that Arab scholarship regarding sexuality is currently contending with many obstacles. This essay provides a contentious preface to the current state of knowledge in the area. After briefly sketching a typology of Arab sexuality, especially its peculiar form of phallocracy, Dialmy reviews fresh sexual trends, some of which adapt current practices to Shari'ah law (for example visitation marriages), while others break with it altogether (for example prostitution). He then discusses three distinctive areas of public and policy concerns in Arabic culture, namely honour killings, impotence and Viagra use, and sex-education programmes that are precipitated by concerns over HIV/AIDS.

In Chapter 18 Shahnaz Khan discusses the cases of women who have been incarcerated under the *Zina* (illicit sex) Ordinance in Pakistan. This leads to an examination of women's moral regulation by their families, a process in which the state is apparently complicit. Khan argues against relativist explanations of this process that view Pakistani culture or notions of timeless Islam as the reason for women's incarceration. Instead, she examines the interconnection of morality with the legal/judicial structures, the relationship between the state and patriarchy within families, and the plight of impoverished women in Pakistan within an era of globalization. In her analysis, Khan links economic development and human rights to globalization and the continuing price of militarization. Such connections allow feminists to target the structural conditions that sustain the laws in Pakistan and feasibly construct an environment that will bring about their repeal.

There are often distinct attitudes displayed towards sexuality by the regime in a fundamentalist Islamic state, but even in Iran the situation may be changing. A core component of the Islamic Revolution's ideology appears to be the reformulation of gender discourse expressed as an Islamic hypermasculinity (Gerami, 2003). Attention has thus been drawn towards women's roles and rights in the Islamic Republic, and men are assumed to have benefited universally from the regime's policies. The young men who bide the dictates of the mullahs and sacrifice themselves for the Republic are martyrs. Then there are the ordinary men whom the Shari'at favours as the mainstay of the family and civil society. Mahdavi (2007), however, found that the sexual and social practices of young people in contemporary Iran are surprisingly liberal. The regime may attempt to restrict social freedoms such as pre-marital heterosexual contact, homosexual encounters, dancing, alcohol consumption and large group gatherings, but such policies are not always followed. Many young adults use their 'rebellious' social behaviour to make political statements against a regime that dissatisfies them, stating, in their own words, that they are enacting and bringing about a 'sexual revolution'. Sexuality thus becomes a site of resistance. By way of complementing such findings, in Chapter 19 Janet Bauer also shows that in Iran shortly after the Islamic Revolution women learned to adapt to what is morally acceptable according to their social class. As in other societies the female construct of sexuality is more important in communicating moral standards and regulating sexual conduct than the male. However, within certain confines women are able to indicate preferences for alternative interpretations.

Varying cultural attitudes towards sexuality have also been extended to same-sex relationships. Homosexuality is forbidden in Islam and explicitly punishable by death, enforced in Iran, Saudi Arabia, the United Arab Emirates, Yemen, Sudan and Mauritania, in accordance with the story of Lot in the Qur'an (7:80–84,11:69–83, 29:28–35), a rendering of the story similar to that in the biblical Book of Genesis. It is not always clear, however, whether or not the Qur'an specifically refers to lesbianism. The verse that begins 'if any of your women commit a lewd act' has been interpreted to refer to female homosexuality, but it has also been rendered to refer to a more general prohibition on sexual activity.

The reality is that Islam has historically displayed a complex attitude towards same-sex relationships, changing according to time and place. Irrespective of historic prohibition, there were always accommodations to pederasty and to gender-variant individuals, and there are claims that Islam has been far less hostile to homosexuality as long as those penetrated were young and effeminate (Murray and Roscoe, 1997). As a cultural expression, homosexuality has been traced through literary works including interpretations of Islamic mythical literature (Wafer, 1997). In medieval Islamic societies sex was organized to conform to social and political hierarchies and homosexual activity was related to gender, with those penetrating reflecting male superiority: the boys who were penetrated took on the subordinate female role and in countries such as Morocco were often prostitutes (Nicole, 2007).

The subject of homosexuality is now a matter of some concern in Islamic communities across the world. In the Netherlands, as elsewhere, Muslim leaders have been particularly outspoken on homosexuality in relation to the wider tolerance of it in Western societies (Hekma, 2002). The struggle of Muslim homosexuals for recognition within their own community, where homosexuality is prohibited, is compounded by the so-called 'Clash of Civilisations'. As Abraham (2009) has shown, in the case of Australia at least, the sexuality of Muslims has been impacted by the wider cultural and political milieu. In particular, the xenophobic appraisal of Muslim males as sexual predators has enhanced the view that Islamic communities constitute 'the other'.

Some evidence suggests that the views of individual Muslims towards homosexuality are as condemning as those of their leaders (Lunsing, 2003). However, Gelbal and Duyan (2006) found that the attitudes of educated young Muslim people in Turkey towards lesbians are seemingly more positive than their attitudes toward gay men, indicating a slow acceptance of wider liberal values. A general animosity, however, has led to gay Muslims in the West seeking their own unique identity forged by religion, ethno-cultural attributes and colour (Minwalla *et al.*, 2005). Andrew Yip (2007, 2008) has shown how gay, lesbian and bisexual Muslims in the Western context have often found their sense of belonging eroded because of the attitudes of their religious and cultural communities. In the final chapter of this volume Yip suggests that this 'minority within minority' status underlines their quest for the right to accurate representation, maintenance of identity/lifestyle, freedom from discrimination based on sexual orientation, practice of religious faith in harmony with sexuality, participation in religious/community life and simply to be different. They achieve this through the 'queering' of religious texts and traditions and grassroots support networks. While this might be a wholly new development in Islam, the matter of homosexuality, albeit in a marginalized constituency, exemplifies once again that while certain constants remain, Islamic 'sexualities', in the same way as Judaic 'sexualities', are as diverse as they have ever been.

References

Abraham, I. (2009), '"Out to Get Us": Queer Muslims and the Clash of Civilisations in Australia', *Contemporary Islam*, **3**, 1, pp. 79–97.

Alpert, R. (1997), *Like Bread on the Seder Plate: Jewish Lesbians and the Transformation of Tradition*, New York: Columbia University Press.

Archer, L.J. (1990), 'Her Price is Beyond Rubies: The Jewish Woman in Greco-Roman Palestine', *Journal for the Study of the Old Testament*, Supplementary Series 60, Sheffield: Sheffield Academic Press.

Crawford G.L. (2008), *In Celebration of Love, Marriage, and Sex: A Journey Through the Song of Solomon*, Longwood, FL: Xulon Press.

Dirks, J.F. (2006), *Abrahamic Faiths: Judaism, Christianity, Islam: Similarities and Contrasts*, Beltsville, MD: Amana.

Gelbal, S. and Duyan, V. (2006), 'Attitudes of University Students towards Lesbian and Gay Men in Turkey', *Sex Roles*, **55**, 7/8, pp. 573–79.

Gerami, S. (2003), 'Mullahs, Martyrs, and Men: Conceptualizing Masculinity in the Islamic Republic of Iran', *Men and Masculinities*, **5**, 3, pp. 257–74.

Glassgold, J.M. (2008), 'Bridging the Divide: Integrating Lesbian Identity and Orthodox Judaism', *Women & Therapy*, **31**, 1, pp. 59–72.

Hekma, G. (2002), 'Imams and Homosexuality: A Post-gay Debate in the Netherlands', *Sexualities*, **5**, 2, pp. 237–48.

Kaghn, Y. (1989), 'Judaism and Christianity: The Traditional–Modernist Debate', *Journal of Homosexuality*, **18**, 1–2, pp. 47–82.

Khan, M.E., Townsend, J.W. and D'Costa, S. (2002), 'Behind Closed Doors: A Qualitative Study of Sexual Behaviour of Married Women in Bangladesh', *Culture, Health & Sexuality*, **4**, 2, pp. 237–56.

Koltun-Fromm, N. (2000), 'Sexuality and Holiness: Semitic Christian and Jewish Conceptualizations of Sexual Behavior', *Vigiliae Christianae*, **54**, 4, pp. 375–95.

Lunsing, W. (2003), 'Islam versus Homosexuality? Some Reflexions on the Assassination of Pim Fortuyn', *Anthropology Today*, **19**, 2, pp. 19–21.

Mahdavi, P. (2007), 'Passionate Uprisings: Young People, Sexuality and Politics in Post-revolutionary Iran', *Culture, Health & Sexuality*, **8**, 5, pp. 445–57.

Minwalla, O., Rosser, S., Feldman, J. and Varga, C. (2005), 'Identity Experience among Progressive Gay Muslims in North America: A Qualitative Study within Al-Fatiha', *Culture Health and Sexuality*, **7**, 2, pp. 113–28.

Moore, S.D. (2001), *God's Beauty Parlor and Other Queer Spaces in and around the Bible*, Contraversions: Jews and Other Differences, Stanford, CA: Stanford University Press.

Murray, S.O. and Roscoe, W. (1997), *Islamic Homosexualities: Culture, History, and Literature*, New York: New York University Press.

Nicole, K. (2007), 'Homosexuality in Islam: A Difficult Paradox', *Macalester Islam Journal*, **2**, 3, pp. 52–64.

Norris, P. and Inglehart, R. (2006), *Sacred and Secular: Religion and Politics Worldwide*, New York: Cambridge University Press.

Ouzgane, L. (2003), 'Islamic Masculinities: Introduction', *Men and Masculinities,* **5**, 3, pp. 231–35.

Ozyegin, G. (2009), 'Virginal Facades: Sexual Freedom and Guilt among Young Turkish Women', *European Journal of Women's Studies,* **16**, 2, pp. 103–23.

Rifaat, A. (1987), *Distant View of a Minaret and Other Stories*, London: Heinemann.

Rohit, D. (2009), 'Mumtaz Bibi's Broken Heart: The Many Lives of the Dissolution of Muslim Marriages Act', *Indian Economic & Social History Review,* **46**, pp. 105–30.

Sabbah, F. (1984), *Woman in the Muslim Unconscious*, New York: Pergamon.

Shahidian, H. (2007), 'Islamic Sexual Culture', in G. Ritzer (ed.), *Blackwell Encyclopaedia of Sociology*, London and New York: Blackwell.

Wafer, J. (1997), 'Muhammad and Male Homosexuality', in S.O. Murray and W. Roscoe (eds), *Islamic Homosexualities: Culture, History, and Literature*, New York: New York University Press.

Yip, A.K.T. (2007), 'Changing Religion, Changing Faith: Reflections on the Transformative Strategies of Lesbian, Gay, and Bisexual Christians and Muslims', *Journal of Faith, Spirituality and Social Change*, **1**, 1, at: http://www.fsscconference.org.uk/journal/1-1.htm.

Yip, A.K.T. (2008), 'The Quest for Intimate/Sexual Citizenship: Lived Experiences of Lesbian and Bisexual Muslim Women', *Contemporary Islam*, **2**, 2, pp. 103–29.

Bibliography

Adang, C. (2003), 'Ibn Ḥazm on Homosexuality: A Case-Study of Ẓāhirī Legal Methodology', *Al-Qantara*, **24**, 1, pp. 5–31.

Anderson, G. (1989), 'Celibacy or Consummation in the Garden? Reflections on Early Jewish and Christian Interpretation of the Garden of Eden', *Harvard Theological Review*, **82**, 2, pp. 121–48.

Archer, L.J. (1983), 'The Role of Jewish Women in the Religion, Ritual, and Cult of Graeco-Roman Palestine', in A. Cameron and A. Kuhrt (eds), *Images of Women in Antiquity*, Detroit, IL: Wayne State University Press.

Archer, L.J. (1990), 'Bound by Blood: Circumcision and Menstrual Taboo in Post-Exilic Judaism', in J.M. Soskice (ed.), *After Eve: Women, Theology and the Christian Tradition*, London: Marshall Pickering.

Archer, L. (2001), 'Muslim Brothers, Black Lads, Traditional Asians: British Muslim Young Men's Constructions of Race, Religion and Masculinity', *Feminism & Psychology*, **11**, 1, pp. 79–105.

Ariel, Y. (2006), 'Can Adam and Eve Reconcile? Gender and Sexuality in a New Jewish Religious Movement', *Nova Religio*, **9**, 4, pp. 53–78.

Atasoy, Y. (2006), 'Governing Women's Morality: A Study of Islamic Veiling in Canada', *European Journal of Cultural Studies*, **9**, 2, pp. 203–21.

Boellstorff, T. (2005), 'Between Religion and Desire: Being Muslim and Gay in Indonesia', *American Anthropologist*, **107**, 4, pp. 575–85.

Boellstorff, T. (2006), 'Domesticating Islam: Sexuality, Gender, and the Limits of Pluralism', *Law & Social Inquiry*, **31**, 4, pp. 1035–53.

Carr, Lloyd G. (1984), *The Song of Solomon: An Introduction and Commentary*, Tyndale Old Testament Commentaries, Downers Grove, IL: InterVarsity Press.

Chave, P. (1998), 'Towards a Not Too Rosy Picture of the Song of Songs', *Feminist Theology*, **6**, pp. 41–53.

de Munck, V.C. (2005), 'Sakhina: A Study of Female Masculinity in a Sri Lankan Muslim Community', *South Asia Research*, **25**, 2, pp. 141–63.

Diamond, E. (2004), *Holy Men and Hunger Artists: Fasting and Asceticism in Rabbinic Culture*, Oxford: Oxford University Press.

Diamond, J.A. (2007), 'King David of the Sages: Rabbinic Rehabilitation or Ironic Parody?', *Prooftexts: A Journal of Jewish Literary History*, **27**, 3, pp. 323–26.

Dillow, J.C. (1977), *Solomon on Sex*, Nashville, TN: Thomas Nelson.

Duits, L. and van Zoonen L. (2006), 'Headscarves and Porno-Chic: Disciplining Girls' Bodies in the European Multicultural Society', *European Journal of Women's Studies*, **13**, 2, pp. 103–17.

Erdreich, L. (2006), 'Marriage Talk: Palestinian Women, Intimacy, and the Liberal Nation-State', *Ethnography*, **7**, 4, pp. 493–523.

Eron, L.J. (1991), 'That Women Have Mastery Over Both King and Beggar' (Tjud. 15.5) – the Relationship of the Fear of Sexuality to the Status of Women in Apocrypha and Pseudepigrapha: 1 Esdras (3 Ezra)

3–4, Ben Sira and the Testament of Judah', *Journal for the Study of the Pseudepigrapha*, **5**, pp. 43–66.

Falk, M. (1982), *Love Lyrics from the Bible: A Translation and Literary Study of the Song of Songs*, Sheffield: Almond Press.

Fortier, C. (1997), 'Blood, Sperm and the Embryo in Sunni Islam and in Mauritania: Milk Kinship, Descent and Medically Assisted Procreation', *Body & Society*, **13**, pp. 15–36.

Fuerst, W.J. (1975), *The Song of Songs*, Cambridge Bible Commentary, Cambridge: Cambridge University Press.

Goldberg, H.G. (1998), 'Coming of Age in Jewish Studies, or Anthropology is Counted in Minvan', *Jewish Social Studies*, **4**, 3, pp. 29–64.

Gressgård, R. (2006), 'The Veiled Muslim, the Anorexic and the Transsexual: What Do They Have in Common?', *European Journal of Women's Studies,* **13**, 4, pp. 325–41.

Hakak, Y. (2009), 'Youthful Bodies Rebel: Young Men in Israeli Haredi Yeshivas Today', *Young*, **17**, 3, pp. 221–40.

Harris, C. (2005), 'Desire versus Horniness: Sexual Relations in the Collectivist Society of Tajikistan', *Social Analysis*, **49**, 2, pp. 78–95.

Inhorn, M.C. (2007), 'Masturbation, Semen Collection and Men's IVF Experiences: Anxieties in the Muslim World', *Body & Society*, **13**, 3, pp. 37–53.

Killoran, M. (1998), 'Good Muslims and "Bad Muslims", "Good" Women and Feminists: Negotiating Identities in Northern Cyprus (Or, the Condom Story)', *Ethos*, **26**, 2, pp. 183–203.

Lieu, J. (1999), 'The "Attraction of Women" in/to Early Judaism and Christianity: Gender and the Politics of Conversion', *Journal for the Study of the New Testament*, **21**, 72, pp. 5–22.

Longman, C. (2007), '"Not Us, But You Have Changed!" Discourses of Difference and Belonging among Haredi Women', *Social Compass,* **54**, 1, pp. 77–95.

Mernissi, F. (1987), *Beyond the Veil: Male-Female Dynamics in Modern Muslim Society*, Bloomington: Indiana University Press.

Murphy, R.E. (1990), *The Song of Songs*, Hermeneia Commentary Series, Philadelphia: Fortress Press.

Noorani, Y. (2004), 'Heterotopia and the Wine Poem in Early Islamic Culture', *International Journal of Middle Eastern Studies*, **36**, 3, pp. 345–66.

Obermeyer, C.M. (2000), 'Sexuality in Morocco: Changing Context and Contested Domain', *Culture, Health and Sexuality*, **2**, 3, pp. 239–54.

Ramji, H. (2007), 'Dynamics of Religion and Gender amongst Young British Muslims', *Sociology,* **41**, 6, pp. 1171–89.

Rashkow, I. (2000), *Taboo or Not Taboo: Sexuality and Family in the Hebrew Bible*, Minneapolis, MN: Fortress Press.

Rowson, E.(1991), 'Categorization of Gender and Sexual Irregularity in Medieval Arabic Vice Lists', in J. Epstein and K. Straub (eds), *Body Guards: The Cultural Politics of Gender Ambiguity*, New York: Routledge.

Satlow, M.L. (1994), '"They Abused Him Like a Woman": Homoerotocism, Gender Blurring, and the Rabbis in Late Antiquity', *Journal of the History of Sexuality*, **5**, 1, pp. 1–25.

Schmitt, A. and Sofer, J. (eds) (1992), *Sexuality & Eroticism Among Males in Moslem Societies*, New York: Haworth Press.

Schnoor, R.F. (2006), 'Being Gay and Jewish: Negotiating Intersecting Identities', *Sociology of Religion*, **67**, 1, pp. 43–60.

Siraj, A. (2009), 'The Construction of the Homosexual "Other" by British Muslim Heterosexuals', *Contemporary Islam*, **3**, 1, pp. 41–57.

Stein, D. (2001), 'A Maidservant and Her Master's Voice: Discourse, Identity, and Eros in Rabbinic Texts', *Journal of the History of Sexuality*, **10**, 3/4, Special Issue: *Sexuality in Late Antiquity*, pp. 375–97.

Stone, K. (ed.) (2001), 'Queer Commentary and the Hebrew Bible', *Journal for the Study of the Old Testament*, Supplement Series 334, London: Sheffield Academic Press.

Svensson, J. (2007), 'HIV/AIDS and Islamic Religious Education in Kisuma, Kenya', *International Journal of Qualitative Studies on Health and Well-Being*, **2**, 3, pp. 179–92.

Toor, S. (2007), 'Moral Regulation in a Post-Colonial Nation State: Gender and the Politics of Islamization in Pakistan', *Interventions*: *International Journal of Post-Colonial Studies*, **9**, 2, pp. 255–75.

Yip, A.K.T. (2003), 'Reflections on Islam and Homosexuality', *Anthropology Today*, **19**, 5, pp. 19–20.

Yip, A.K.T. (guest ed.) (2009), Special Issue, *Islam and Sexuality*, *Contemporary Islam*, **3**, 1 (entire issue).

Further Reading

Archer, Leonie J. (1990), 'Gender and Ritual in the Judaeo-Christian Tradition', in A. Joseph (ed.), *Through the Devil's Gateway: Women, Religion and Taboo*, London: SPCK.

Marmon, S. (1995), *Eunuchs and Sacred Boundaries in Islamic Society*, New York: Oxford University Press.

Pope, M.H. (1977), *Song of Songs*, Anchor Bible 7c, Garden City, NY: Doubleday & Sons.

Westheimer, R.K. and Mark, J. (1995), *Heavenly Sex: Sex in the Jewish Tradition*, New York: New York University Press.

Wouk, H. (1974), *This Is My God: The Jewish Way of Life*, New York: Pocket Books.

JUDAISM

Part I
Judaism and Sexuality:
Exploring Historical Viewpoints

[1]

Are There Any Jews in "The History of Sexuality"?

DANIEL BOYARIN

Department of Near Eastern Studies
University of California, Berkeley

INTRODUCTION: HOMOPHOBIA BEFORE SEXUALITY?

PERHAPS THE most solid conclusion of Michel Foucault's last research and the scholarship that has followed in its wake has been that there was no autonomous realm of "sexuality" within classical cultures at all; desire and pleasure were inextricably bound up with the relations of power and domination that structured the entire society.[1] Permitted and tabooed sexual behavior was completely a function of status. The world was divided into the screwers—all male—and the screwed—both male and female. No parallel research has been done for either biblical

This text has been presented in various avatars. It was first lectured to the undergraduate honors program at Tel-Aviv and Ben-Gurion Universities, then to the Comparative Literature department at the Hebrew University, at the University of California, Berkeley, and the University of Michigan, to the Gay and Lesbian Students' Group at the Hebrew University, and finally at the School of Criticism and Theory at Dartmouth. From each of these forums it gained. I thank also Gerard F. Beritela, Carolyn Dinshaw, Erich Gruen, Diana Fuss, Geoffrey Galt Harpham, Chana Kronfeld, Menahem Lorberbaum, Christopher Newfield, Amy Richlin, Froma Zeitlin, Noam Zion, and an anonymous reader for the *Journal of the History of Sexuality*. I wish especially to thank David M. Halperin, who spent an inordinate amount of time and energy helping me with this text. No one of them, of course, is responsible for the opinions or errors contained here. This text was prepared while I was enjoying a leave provided by a President's Research Fellowship in the Humanities of the University of California.

[1] David M. Halperin, *One Hundred Years of Homosexuality: And Other Essays on Greek Love* (New York, 1990); David M. Halperin, John J. Winkler, and Froma I. Zeitlin, eds., *Before Sexuality: The Construction of Erotic Experience in the Ancient Greek World* (Princeton, NJ, 1990); John Winkler, *The Constraints of Desire: The Anthropology of Sex and Gender in Ancient Greece* (New York, 1989). See, however, n. 18 below.

or talmudic culture. At first glance, these cultures seem to be cultures within which the category of homosexuality, at least as a taxonomy of practices if not of persons, exists with a vengeance. After all, these cultures and their offshoots are taken to be the very origin of the deep-rooted homophobia within "our culture."[2] This would seem, then, to raise significant problems for Foucault's notion that "homosexuality" as a category only appears in the modern European culture. Foucault's total neglect of biblical and Jewish culture in his historical work thus produces a crucial gap in his work and in our knowledge, one that threatens the whole edifice. In this article I will suggest that analysis of biblical and talmudic cultural materials, far from being counterevidence, provides some crucial evidence to flesh out Foucault's speculation that the category of sexuality of which we know is special to our modern Euro-American culture. The alleged prohibitions on "homosexuality" in Judaism can be plausibly interpreted as being fully comprehended by the workings of gendering in this culture without any category of sexuality being either necessary or even probable to understand them.

THE BIBLE BEFORE SEXUALITY

A Different Taxonomy

"Do not lie with a man a *woman's lyings* [*miškəbei 'iššā*]; that is *to'ēbā*" (Lev. 18:22).[3] This verse is usually taken in both scholarly and popular parlance to prohibit "homosexuality" *tout court*, a conclusion that, if correct, would provide a serious counterexample to Foucault's historiography. In this article, I hope to be able to show that another approach to understanding this verse is at least as plausible as the assumption that "homosexuality" is at issue.[4] Let me clarify the structure of the argument that follows. I begin with the assumption that there is no more reason to assume that ancient Jewish culture does have a system of sexuality than

---

[2] And as I am writing this (in early February 1993), we are once more reminded to our horror and alarm just how little progress has been made.

[3] The word *to'ēbā*, usually translated "abomination" or "detestable," means something like "transgression of borders." It is used biblically for many types of ritual transgressions that are not sexual. In any case, there is no warrant whatever for the accepted renderings, which are obviously loaded with later cultural meanings and would quite beg the current question.

[4] As I was completing work on this article, Saul M. Olyan, "'And with a Male You Shall Not Lie the Lying Down of a Woman': On the Meaning and Significance of Leviticus 18:22 and 20:13," *Journal of the History of Sexuality* 5 (1994): 179–206, which arrives at partially converging conclusions, came to my attention. The two articles partially complete each other's arguments and partially dissent from each other.

to assume the opposite. Indeed, given Foucault's work and the work of historians who have shown how "sexuality" develops at a particular moment in history,[5] it becomes equally plausible to begin by assuming that Jewish culture of the biblical and talmudic periods was not organized around a system of sexual orientations defined by object choice (or for that matter in any other way), in other words, to put the burden of proof, as it were, on the other party. I know of no evidence that would support the claim for a system of sexual orientations (there is no talmudic equivalent even for the *cinaedus*).[6] Any positive evidence, therefore, that militates against the production of a category of sexuality in the culture becomes highly significant.

There is one further methodological point.[7] The base of data on which I describe late antique Jewish culture is highly skewed in that it includes the expression of one very limited social group within the culture, a learned, hegemonic, male rabbinic elite (and even within that I am almost exclusively concentrating on its Babylonian variety). In fact, I know almost nothing, aside from what I can read between the lines or against the grain of the Talmud, of what the rest of the (Jewish) world was doing or thinking.[8] This is particularly significant, because from the much more variegated remains of Greek culture we learn of a heterogeneous cultural situation, wherein certain types of texts—medical texts, for example—have an entirely different ideology of sex than do the high cultural literary artifacts of, for example, Hesiod. This is even more the case in the later Greek and Hellenistic worlds than in the archaic period. There might very well have been an analogous cultural situation in late antique Jewish culture. A partial control is provided by the fact that the Talmud, while the product of an elite, is not elitist in structure in that its modes of expression are often enough vulgar—in the highest sense of that term, and some have claimed that there are even female voices to be discovered there. Furthermore, one would expect that this type of religious elite would be, if anything, more stringent than other segments of the society, although this would be a particularly weak form of argu-

[5] Arnold Davidson, "Sex and the Emergence of Sexuality," *Critical Inquiry* 14 (Autumn 1987): 16–48, reprinted in *Forms of Desire: Sexual Orientation and the Social Constructionist Controversy*, ed. Edward Stein (London, 1992), pp. 89–132.

[6] Although the Talmud does enjoin the use of perfumes for men "in places where male intercourse is common," because this would lead people to suspect him of such behavior. Generally, as in this instance, when the Talmud speaks of a predilection for anal intercourse, it attributes such tastes to geographical or ethnic groups—not to individual proclivities.

[7] Initially brought to my attention by Marion Bodian when I presented an early version of this article at the University of Michigan.

[8] For examples of such against-the-grain reading, see Daniel Boyarin, *Carnal Israel: Reading Sex in Talmudic Culture* (Berkeley, 1993).

ment from silence. These considerations should serve as a caution against any essentializing or totalizing statements about Jewish culture, which I do not claim, in fact, to be making. What I am investigating then are particular discursive practices, not whole cultures—whatever that might even mean—and claiming that these discursive practices are fully comprehensible without assuming a cultural subsystem of sexuality.[9] Even more to the point, perhaps, my claim is not to have found proof positive for the Foucaultian hypothesis but, rather, to be disputing what might have been otherwise taken as a body of counterevidence by suggesting what I hope will be accepted as a convincing alternative reading of it.

My first argument in demonstrating the lack of a binary opposition of hetero/homosexuality in talmudic culture (with the above qualifications and strictures) will be a text that shows that the Talmud did not read such a category into the biblical prohibitions on male intercourse, understanding that only anal intercourse and no other male-male sexual practices were interdicted in the Torah. In the Babylonian Talmud Niddah 13b, we find the following colloquy:

> Our Rabbis have taught: Converts and those who sport with children, delay the Messiah.
>
> I understand "converts," for Rabbi Helbo has said that converts are as difficult for Israel as *sappaḥat* [a skin disease]! But what is this about those who sport with children? If I will say it refers to male intercourse [*miškāb zākor*, a technical term referring to male-male anal penetration], they are subject to stoning! Rather, [shall we say] it refers to intercrural [between the thighs; *dérĕk 'ēbārim* (Hebrew), *diamêrizein* (Greek)] intercourse? But that is like the children of the flood [i.e., masturbation—Rashi]. Rather it refers to those who marry minor girls who are not of child-bearing age, for Rabbi Yossi has said that the son of David will not come until all of the souls in the "body" are finished [i.e., until all of the souls that were created at the Beginning of the universe have been born into bodies, the Messiah will not arrive].

The Talmud quotes an earlier text (tannaitic, i.e., Palestinian and prior to the third century of the Christian era) that condemns converts to Judaism and pedophiles in what seems to be rather extreme language. The Talmud (Babylonian and post–third century) asks what is meant by sporting with children. From the answer that the Talmud suggests to its

---

[9] By using the term "culture," then, I mean to be asserting that the textual practices that I analyze are not mere language but are a significant cultural practice, however widespread their acceptance or not.

question, it is quite clear that the Talmud sharply distinguishes male-male anal intercourse from other same-sex practices, arguing that only the former is comprehended by the biblical prohibition on male intercourse. This point already establishes the claim that this culture, insofar as we can know it, does not know of a general category of the homosexual (as a typology of human beings) or even of homosexuality (as a bounded set of same-sex practices).

Sporting with Children

It is important to understand the intricate cultural coding of this passage. Rabbinic discourse frequently uses exaggerated language to inculcate prohibitions and inhibitions that are not forbidden in the Torah. There is, accordingly, an inner-cultural recognition that such prohibitions, precisely because they are expressed in extreme language, are not as "serious" as those that are forbidden in the Bible. It is as if there is a tacit cultural understanding that the more extreme the rhetoric, the less authoritative the prohibition. Thus, just as in the case of masturbation, where there is no biblical text indicating that it is forbidden, and it is therefore designated hyperbolically as being like "the children of the flood," so also for "sporting with children," the text finds highly hyperbolic language with which to express itself.[10] "Preventing the Messiah" has about the same status of hyperbole as being one of "the children of the flood," and neither of them is taken as seriously as those prohibitions for which the Torah explicitly marks out an interdiction and a punishment.

Thus, since male anal intercourse is forbidden by the Torah explicitly and a punishment marked out for it, there is no need to utilize obviously hyperbolic language like that of delaying the coming of the Messiah. Far from strengthening the case, it only would weaken it. As the canonical commentary of Rashi has it: "*Only* delaying the Messiah? But it is forbidden by the Torah and punishable by stoning!" (emphasis added). Therefore, claims the Talmud, this cannot be what is meant by "sporting with children" in the text. The Talmud then suggests that what is being spoken of here is the practice of intercrural intercourse between men and boys, according to some authorities the standard sexual practice of Greek

---

[10]The Onan story in the Bible itself has, of course, nothing to do with masturbation at all. Onan's "sin" was coitus interruptus for the purpose of preventing the mandated conception of a child by his brother's widow. "Onanism" for masturbation is thus, as Amy Richlin points out to me, just as much a misnomer as "sodomy" for homosexual intercourse is (for the latter see below).

pederasty.[11] This, however, is "merely" a type of masturbation, for which another axiological category exists. Masturbators are not Messiah delayers but children of the flood.[12] All that is left, therefore, for our category of delaying the Messiah is intergender pedophilia, forbidden because it is antinatalist.

The tannaitic text itself will bear, however, some further analysis. The term I have translated "sport with" means variously "to play" and "to laugh" but frequently is used as an explicit term for sexual interaction, as it undoubtedly is meant here. The term for "children" here is a gender-indeterminate word that refers to anyone from infancy to puberty. The first question to be asked of the original statement is, What is the association between converts and those who sport with children? I would suggest that at least a plausible answer is that Greco-Roman converts are taken to be those who sport with children or even tempt other Jews into such sport. If that be granted, it would seem clear that it is pederasty that is being spoken of. The third interpretation that the Talmud offers, then, for the earlier text, namely, that intergender pedophilia is referred to, seems highly implausible. On the other hand, the Talmud's refusal to understand anal intercourse as being the intention of the original text seems well founded, for it would be, as I have indicated above, highly unusual to use hyperbolic language such as that of Messiah prevention to refer to that for which an explicit biblical reference could be cited. It seems, therefore, that some other pederastic sexual practice is connoted by "sporting with children," and intercrural intercourse seems as good a candidate as any. In other words, my hypothesis is that the second suggestion that the Talmud makes in order to interpret the original source seems the most likely one, namely, that "those who sport with children" refers to pederasts who practice forms of sexual behavior that do not include anal intercourse. If this reading is accepted, it would follow that both levels of the talmudic discourse, that is, the original Palestinian tannaitic statement and its later Babylonian talmudic interpretations, understood the Torah's interdiction to be limited only to the practice of male anal intercourse, of use of the male "as" a female. If this interpretation is deemed finally implausible, then the tannaitic evidence falls by the wayside. Whether or not my reading of the tannaitic text is accepted, it is clear that this is how the Babylonian Talmud understood the Torah, as we see, I repeat, from the explicit distinction made between anal intercourse, forbidden by the Torah, and intercrural intercourse, which the

[11] K. J. Dover, *Greek Homosexuality, Updated and with a New Postscript* (1978; Cambridge, MA, 1989), pp. 98, 106.
[12] Because the flood was caused by those who "destroyed their way upon the ground," taken by the rabbinic commentaries to refer to spilling of the seed.

Torah has permitted. At the very least, we have positive evidence that late antique Babylonian Jewish culture did not operate with a category of the "homosexual" corresponding to "ours." As the Talmud understood it, male-male sexual practices other than anal intercourse are not prohibited by the Torah and only fall under the category of masturbation, which is the same, whether solo or in concert.[13] This provides strong evidence within the Talmud for the absence of a category of homosexuals or even of homosexual practices isomorphic with that of modern Euro-American culture.

Female Homoerotic Practice

Further evidence for the absence of a category of the "homosexual" in talmudic culture may be found in (the admittedly very rare) discussions of female same-sex genital practices, for instance, Babylonian Talmud Yevamoth 76a:

> Rav Huna said: "Women who rub each other may not marry priests," but even Rabbi Eliezer who said that "an unmarried man who has intercourse with an unmarried woman without intending to marry her makes her a *zōnā* [and thus unfit to marry a high priest]," his words only apply to a man [who lies with a woman] but as for a woman [who lies with a woman], it is mere lasciviousness.[14]

Also Babylonian Talmud Shabbat 65a–b:

> Shmuel's father did not allow his daughters to lie with each other. . . . Shall we say that this supports the view of Rav Huna, for Rav Huna said: "Women who rub each other may not marry priests"? No, he forbad it in order that they should not learn [the feel] of another body [and they would then lust to lie with men (Rashi)].

The only reason, according to this text, that unmarried women should not excite each other sexually is because it might lead to immorality— that is, sex with men![15] Female same-sex practices just do not belong to

---

[13]To be sure, the text does not mention other types of homoerotic practice, so it is impossible to determine even normative, let alone actual and popular, dispositions toward them.

[14]The term *zōnā* refers to a category of women forbidden to priests because of past sexual practices. I am leaving it untranslated here, because it is precisely its definition that is at stake here.

[15]I will argue below that this does not reflect a general lack of interest in what women do as long as they do not do it with men. The prohibition on female cross-dressing is every bit as severe as that on male cross-dressing, just to take one highly salient example. Further,

the same category as male anal intercourse any more than other forms of male same-sex stimulation. We see from here, moreover, that the notion that the Talmud, like Queen Victoria, just did not believe in the possibility of female homoeroticism is not a true assumption. It was understood that women could pleasure each other, but this did not form a single category with male intercourse. Male anal intercourse is sui generis, and its genus is clearly not in any way identical to "our" category of homosexuality.

This provides us then with further evidence that not only is there no category, no "species of human being," of the homosexual, there is, in fact, no category formed by same-sex acts per se either. Neither people nor acts are taxonomized merely by the gender of the object of genital activity. Male-male anal intercourse belongs to a category known as "male intercourse," while other same-sex genital acts—male and female—are subsumed under the category of masturbation, apparently without the presence of another male actor introducing any other diacritic factor into the equation.[16]

Anal Intercourse as Cross-Dressing

A thousand years (and in the case of the Babylonian Talmud, several thousand kilometers) separate the Torah sources and their talmudic interpreters. While it is impossible, therefore, to use the Talmud as direct evidence for biblical culture, it nevertheless provides highly significant indirect evidence, since it is counterintuitive to assume that in the biblical period, the category of homosexuality existed and later disappeared in the same *Kulturgebiet*. Still, such an assumption, while implausible, is not impossible. In any case, however, at the very least the talmudic testimony suggests that the "homosexuality" interpretation of the biblical material is not ineluctable and that other options should be considered.[17] If it is not same-sex eroticism per se that worries Leviticus, what cultural force is it that could have produced the powerful interdiction on

---

there is little reason to assume that the point here is that they will turn to men because sex with women is an inadequate substitute as modern male chauvinists would have it, but simply that once acquainted with the joys of sexual stimulation, they might very well seek it with men also, and that is forbidden.

[16] It nevertheless remains the case that having intercourse with a nonfertile girl or woman or having anal, intercrural, or oral intercourse with a woman does not constitute masturbation, while having oral or intercrural intercourse with a man does. This difference will have to be examined further in later chapters of this research.

[17] Olyan (n. 4 above) has also argued on inner-biblical philological grounds alone that "male intercourse" comprises solely anal penetration.

Judaism and Islam 13

Are There Any Jews in "The History of Sexuality"? 341

male anal intercourse? Cross-cultural comparison points us in a promising direction here. David Halperin contends that for the Romans (the contemporaries, roughly speaking, of the Rabbis), as for the earlier Greeks, the relevant distinction between sexual practices was not between same-sex and other-sex desire but between status positions.[18] Adult free males penetrated. Some preferred boys and some women, and many liked both. There was something pathological and depraved, however, in the spectacle of an adult male allowing his body to be used as if it were the body of a person of penetrable status, whether the man did so for pleasure or for profit.[19] "It is sex-role reversal, or *gender-deviance,* that is problematized here."[20] In other words, the fulfillment of the pleasure of the penetrating male involved either an appropriate ascription of lower status to the passive partner or an inappropriate degradation to that status. I would like to suggest that in the biblical culture—at least as received by the Talmud—also, "sexuality," rather than being the controlling figure of other subsidiary discourses, is subsumed under larger cultural structures. If in the Greco-Roman formation sexual patternings were subordinated to larger structures having to do with power and status, in biblical culture also I will claim sexual taboos were subsidiary to another cultural structure. Here, I suggest, also penetration of a male constituted a consignment of him to the class of females, but, rather than a degradation of status, this constituted a sort of a mixing of kinds, a generally taboo occurrence in Hebrew culture. Just as in Greece, then, the prohibited forms of sexual practice were parts of entire cultural systems. There violating the body of the free, adult male sexually constituted one offense within a category of many against such a body. As Halperin has demonstrated, other such offenses included even placing a hand on his body without his consent. "It was an act of *hybris,* or 'outrage,' which signified the violation of a status distinction, the attempted reduction of a person to a status below the one he actually occupied ('using free men as slaves,' Demosthenes loosely but vividly defined it)."[21]

[18] For studies critical of Halperin's position (and of the Foucaultian stance generally), see Bruce Thornton, "Constructionism and Ancient Sex," *Helios* 18 (1991): 181–93; and Amy Richlin, "Zeus and Metis: Foucault, Feminism, Classics," *Helios* 18 (1991): 160–80. I continue to find the evidence for the thesis compelling in spite of some difficulties and occasional seeming counterevidence.

[19] Halperin (n. 1 above), pp. 22–24 and 88–112; and Winkler (n. 1 above), pp. 45–70. See also Amy Richlin, "Not before Homosexuality: The Materiality of the *Cinaedus* and the Roman Law against Love between Men," *Journal of the History of Sexuality* 3 (1993): 523–73.

[20] Halperin, p. 23.

[21] Ibid., p. 96. See also Dover (n. 11 above), pp. 34–39; and David Cohen, "Sexuality, Violence, and the Athenian Law of *Hubris,*" *Greece and Rome* 38, no. 2 (1991): 171–88.

I would like to suggest the following hypothesis: In biblical culture
as well the sexual taboo enters into an entire system of forbidden practices, but one of a completely different nature—not of *hybris,* but of *hy-
brids.* In that system, one may not hybridize or even plant two species
together, mate a horse to a donkey, weave linen and wool into linsey-
woolsey. God-given categories must be kept separate. Anthropologist
Mary Douglas already made this point with regard to sexual prohibitions
in general in ancient Israel:[22]

> Other precepts extend holiness to species and categories. Hybrids
> and other confusions are abominated.
> ### *Lev. xviii*
> And you shall not lie with any beast and defile yourself with
> it, neither shall any woman give herself to a beast to lie with
> it; it is perversion
> The word perversion is a significant mistranslation of the rare He-
> brew word *tebhel, which has as its meaning mixing or confusion.*[23]

I suggest that the interdiction on male-male anal intercourse as well enters in the biblical cultural system into the subsystem of such violations
of the symbolic realm. In its immediate literary context, the verse just
cited that prohibits male anal intercourse follows immediately on the
verse that prohibits "bestiality" within which the word "confusion" (of
kinds) is emphasized, hinting that there may be a connection between
the two prohibitions on this level as well. A much stronger argument for
this point is derived from the parallelism in language and form to the
taboo on cross-dressing. This prohibition is phrased in the following
fashion: "The woman shall not wear that which pertains unto a man,
neither shall a man put on a *woman's garment* [*śimlat 'iśśā*], for all that
do so are *to'ēba* unto the Lord thy God" (Deut. 22:5).[24] The latter appears as: "Do not lie with a man a *woman's lyings* [*miškəbei 'iśśā*]; that is
to'ēba" (Lev. 18:22).[25] Both the usage of the term *to'ēba* and the
semantic/syntactic parallelism of "a woman's garment" and "a woman's

---

[22]It has been brought to my attention that Thomas Thurston has already suggested
the possible pertinence of Mary Douglas's work to our question (Thomas M. Thurston,
"Leviticus 18:22 and the Prohibition of Homosexual Acts," in *Homophobia and the Judaeo-
Christian Tradition,* ed. M. L. Stemmeler and J. M. Clark [Dallas, 1990]). Unfortunately,
I have not been able to obtain this text in Jerusalem. From secondary discussions, I gather
that the thesis is less developed in Thurston than here, but, nevertheless, priority is his.

[23]Mary Douglas, *Purity and Danger: An Analysis of Concepts of Pollution and Taboo*
(1969; London, 1978), p. 53 (emphasis added).

[24]See n. 3 above.

[25]I have somewhat tortured English syntax to reproduce the parallelism that is obvious in the Hebrew. To be sure, Deuteronomy and the "Holiness" Code of this portion
of Leviticus are generally considered different documents according to modern biblical

lyings" are common to the two prohibitions, suggesting a cultural relation between them. (The seeming lack of parallelism, in that the first verse is gender symmetrical while the second only mentions men, forms a key argument for my thesis below.)

Thus when one man "uses" another man as a female, he causes a transgression of the borders between male and female, much as by planting two species together he causes a transgression of the borders of species. Now at first glance this explanation seems somewhat paradoxical, because the other cases of levitically prohibited category crossing involve the keeping apart of things that are different. Thus, one does not mix wool with linen in a garment. One might have thought, therefore, that if anything, homoerotic relations would be more consistent with the idea of keeping the different separate. This paradox is, however, only apparent. What we must think of, in order to understand the levitical system, is the "metaphysics" underlying it. These prohibitions belong to the Priestly Torah that emphasizes over and over in its account of the Creation in Genesis 1 that God has created from the beginning the separate kinds of creatures.[26] Male and female are among the kinds that were created at the very beginning (Gen. 1:27). Now if we understand that it is the kinds that have to be kept separate, that is, the categories or types, because confusing their borders (*tebhel*) is an abomination—as opposed to a mere necessity to keep physically separate the tokens of the categories—then we can understand the specifics of the Torah's interdiction of male anal intercourse. The Torah's language is very explicit; it is the "use" of a male as a female that is *to'ēba*, the crossing of a body from one God-given category to another, analogous to the wearing of clothes that belong to the other sex, by nature as it were. Moving a male body

criticism. However, Deuteronomy also interdicts "mixtures of kinds." Whatever its subcultures, biblical culture certainly showed degrees of coherence as well.

[26]This connection was realized by the Rabbis. In the Palestinian Talmud, Tractate Kil'aim (Forbidden Mixtures) 27a, Rabbi Shim'on ben Lakish remarks: "Everywhere that it says 'according to its kind,' the laws of forbidden mixtures apply." The phrase "according to its kind" appears no less than five times in the verse immediately preceding the verse that describes the creation of humankind in separate sexes, called also in Hebrew "kinds." Technically, biblical critics assign the laws of forbidden mixtures to a source known as the Holiness Code (H), produced, as was the Priestly Code (P), according to them in temple circles. According to the latest scholarly opinion, H is a secondary elaboration of P, and the "authors" of H were the redactors of P in its current form (Israel Knohl, *The Sanctuary of Silence: A Study of the Priestly Strata in the Pentateuch* [Jerusalem, 1992; Minneapolis, 1994], whose conclusions have been accepted by Jacob Milgrom, *Leviticus 1–16*, Anchor Bible [Garden City, NY, 1992]). Even, however, according to older critical views according to which H is older than P, there has never been a doubt as to their common provenience in priestly circles such as those that produced Genesis 1 as well and no reason to assume, therefore, major cultural differences between them. See also n. 25 above.

across the border into "female" metaphysical space transgresses the categories in the same way as putting on a female garment, for both parties,
since both participate (presumably willingly) in the transgressive act.

Now it is clear why only male anal intercourse and not other homoerotic practices are forbidden by the Torah. The issue is gender (as the
verse of the Bible explicitly suggests) and not "homosexuality," and gender is conceived around penetration and being penetrated. The lack of a
prohibition on female homoerotic behavior, a fact about which "there
has been considerable speculation" according to the latest interpretations of biblical law, now receives a fresh explanation.[27] Up until now,
this omission has generally been explained as the sign of a general lack
of interest in what women do when it does not lead to possible illicit
pregnancy and thus confusion in the realm of the Name-of-the-Father.[28]
However, as we have seen from the above-quoted verse from Deuteronomy, it is simply not the case that female behavior is not controlled by
this system, nor that the Torah is uninterested in what women do. For
cross-dressing, the male and female are equally controlled. The same
point holds for intercourse with animals as in the verse quoted above.
We see, therefore, that female sexual behavior is every bit as much of
interest to the Torah as male sexual behavior, even in situations where
illicit pregnancy could not possibly result. Were there a category of the
homosexual whose activities are condemned per se, there is no reason
that only the males would be included in it, nor any reason that only
one male-male genital practice would be forbidden. It follows, then, that
there was no such category in either biblical or talmudic culture and that
some other explanation than a horror of "homosexuality" must be advanced for the taboo on male anal intercourse. The explanation for this
taboo generally accepted among biblical scholars is that "homosexuality," being allegedly a regular practice of the Canaanites, or even part of
their cult, the Bible abjected it as part of its project of differential production of Israelite culture. There is very little (or no) evidence that I
know of to support such a view; indeed, there is virtually none that the
Canaanites were especially given to homosexual practices. I submit that
it is a reasonable hypothesis to subordinate the sexual practice under the
category of gender-crossing and conclude that only male anal intercourse was considered as a kind of cross-dressing owing to the penetration of one body by another. The Rabbis (in contrast apparently to the

[27] Baruch Levine, *Leviticus*, JPS Torah Commentary (Philadelphia, 1989), p. 123.

[28] Compare the opposite but structurally similar explanation that Foucault gives for the
differential treatment of male-male sex and female-female sex in Artemidorus, where only
the latter is considered as "contrary to nature" (Michel Foucault, *The Care of the Self*, vol.
3 of *The History of Sexuality*, trans. Robert Hurley [New York, 1986], pp. 24–25).

Romans)[29] did not imagine female-female sexual contact as involving any form of penetration that they recognized as such.[30]

Penetration as constituting the female. The very word for female, *nəqēbā* in both biblical and talmudic Hebrew, as well as talmudic Aramaic, means "orifice bearer," as if male bodies did not possess orifices. A talmudic text emphasizes to what extent gender was constituted by penetration and being penetrated within this cultural system. The Talmud is trying to determine what sorts of jealousy on the part of a husband will invoke the ceremony of the Waters of Curse—that is, the biblical ritual whereby a wife suspected of adultery drinks water in which

---

[29] Judith Hallett, "Female Homoeroticism and the Denial of Roman Reality in Latin Literature," *Yale Journal of Criticism* 3 (Fall 1989): 209–28. Some of Hallett's evidence is, however, questionable, especially her interpretation of Phaedrus's Fable in which he accounts for "tribadic females and effeminate males" by recounting that Prometheus got drunk when making human beings and attached some male genitals to female people and some female genitals to male people by mistake. Hallett interprets this to mean that lesbians are women with male genitalia (p. 210), a contradiction of biological reality that she understandably finds quite unsettling. To me it seems quite patent that the purport of the fable is that tribads are the men who got female genitals by mistake, and the *molles* are the women with male genitals attached to them. This actually provides beautiful evidence for Halperin's definition of sexuality as that modern cultural entity whose chief conceptual function "is to distinguish, once and for all, sexual identity from matters of gender—to decouple, as it were, *kinds* of sexual predilection from *degrees* of masculinity and femininity" (Halperin [n. 1 above], p. 25; see also below). For Phaedrus it was impossible to imagine a woman loving women, so a lesbian must "really" be a man in a woman's body "by mistake," and this was, in one version or another, the most common way in Euro-America of accounting for same-sex eroticism until the early twentieth century. Even Krafft-Ebing toward the end of the nineteenth century still conceived of lesbians as men with female bodies, i.e., as male souls in bodies with female genitalia (George L. Mosse, *Nationalism and Sexuality: Middle-Class Morality and Sexual Norms in Modern Europe* [Madison, WI, 1985], p. 106). For "us," the situation is precisely reversed. Monique Wittig notwithstanding, lesbians are in our contemporary culture clearly women, thus explaining Hallett's misreading—if I am correct. The best (in fact, for me, the only cogent) evidence that Hallett cites for her claim that tribadism was understood as involving penetration is the text by Martial that describes a tribad who penetrates boys (anally) as well as women (pp. 215–16). In any case, the very etymology of the Greek loan word *tribas* suggests that at least at one time female same-sex eroticism was understood to involve only rubbing and not penetration, just as in the Talmud.

[30] This can be demonstrated philologically. The term that is used, and which I have translated as "rubbing," is used in another sexual context as well: "Our Rabbis have taught: One who is rubbing with her son and he enters her, Bet Shammai say that he has rendered her unfit to marry a priest, and Bet Hillel say that she is fit to marry a priest" (Babylonian Talmud, Sanhedrin 69b). From this context we learn clearly two things: "Rubbing" involves contact of external genital with external genital, and it does not include penetration, for the rubbing here is contrasted with the entering. We also learn, by the way, of a fascinating sexual practice that, as long as it did not include penetration, was apparently hardly even disapproved of, to judge from the tone of this passage.

a passage from a Torah scroll has been dissolved. If she is "guilty" God causes certain bodily diseases, and, if "innocent," God leaves her alone (and promises her progeny):[31]

We have learned, "sexual intercourse"—excluding something else.

The verse says that the husband suspects his wife of having had sexual intercourse with another man, and the midrashic passage quoted indicates that this is to exclude a situation in which he suspects her of "something else":

> What is "something else"? Rav Sheshet said: "It excludes anal intercourse [lit., not according to her manner]."

For Rav Sheshet, anal intercourse does not constitute intercourse at all and therefore it is not adultery, so if a husband suspects his wife of this, she does not undergo the "test" for adulteresses, but Rava dissents:

> Rava said to him: "But with reference to anal intercourse, it is written 'a woman's lying'!" Rather Rava said: "It excludes a case where he suspected her of intercrural intercourse."[32]

Rava argues from the verse that treats of male anal intercourse. His argument is that since that practice is defined, as we have seen, as "a woman's lyings," it follows that anal intercourse with women is indeed defined as intercourse. Crucial in the context of the present inquiry is Rava's proof that male-female anal intercourse counts as full intercourse for the purpose of definitions of adultery from the fact that male-male anal intercourse is defined by the Torah as "a woman's lyings [i.e., as intercourse in the fashion of lying with women]"! From the verse prohibiting this behavior between men, we learn that it is appropriate when practiced between a man and a woman. The exact talmudic term for male-female anal intercourse is "penetration not according to her way," which we might be tempted to gloss as penetration that is not natural to her, but this is precisely the interpretation that the Talmud denies us by assuming that such intercourse is natural to women, indeed can be defined by the Torah, as "a woman's lyings"![33] Moreover, in a further passage (Babylonian Talmud Sanhedrin 54a), the Talmud argues explicitly that with reference to women there are two kinds of intercourse, that is, vaginal and

---

[31] Surprisingly little work has been done on this important site for understanding both biblical and talmudic gender politics. In another part of the present research, I hope to do much more with this. Certainly by the time of the Talmud—if not actually much earlier—the practice itself had fallen into complete desuetude.

[32] Interestingly enough, according to Dover (n. 11 above), representations of male-female intercrural intercourse are unknown from the vase paintings (p. 99).

[33] Compare Herodotus i 61.1f., cited in Dover, p. 100.

anal, because the verse that deals with male-male anal intercourse indicts it as "a woman's lyings [plural *miškəbei*]"; thus two kinds of lying with women exist. "According to her way" means, then, simply something like in the more common or usual fashion and a discourse of natural/ unnatural is not being mobilized here. It follows, then, that the manner of lying with women is penetration *simpliciter* and no distinction of anal/ vaginal is intended by the Torah but only a distinction between penetrative and nonpenetrative sex.[34] Men penetrate, women are penetrated; so for a man to be penetrated constitutes a "mixing of kinds" analogous to cross-dressing.

A contemporary temptation would be to reverse the relation that I have suggested and propose that the reason that cross-dressing is forbidden is because it leads to, simulates, or somehow is associated with "homosexuality." Indeed, some have gone so far as to suggest that the entire system of forbidden "mixtures"—and especially, of course, the taboo on cross-dressing—is to support the prohibition on so-called homosexuality. As Terry Castle has remarked, "The implication . . . that sodomy follows from transvestism—became a standard notion in the eighteenth century."[35] I am, as it were, turning this notion upside down—leaving it for the eighteenth century and ours—and interpreting that male anal intercourse is for the biblical culture not the result of cross-dressing, nor is transvestism an index of deviant sexual practice, but rather anal intercourse with a man is an instance of cross-dressing.[36]

Note then both the similarity and the enormous difference between this explanation of the biblical culture and the interpretations of Greek culture of the Foucaultian school. In both, that separate realm that we identify as sexuality is subsumed under larger cultural structures and discourses.[37] In the latter, since the issues involved are social status and power, there is no shame in (or taboo against) an appropriately higher-status male penetrating a lower-status male.[38] In the biblical culture, on

[34] I owe this last formulation to David Halperin.

[35] Terry Castle, *Masquerade and Civilization: The Carnivalesque in Eighteenth-Century English Culture and Fiction* (Stanford, CA, 1986), pp. 46, 47, as cited in Marjorie Garber, *Vested Interests: Cross-Dressing and Cultural Anxiety* (New York, 1992), p. 381.

[36] Note that this is entirely different from the (false) association between cross-dressing (transvestism) and homosexuality in contemporary folk culture, on which see Garber, p. 130. I avoid the term "sodomy" as anachronistic for the biblical culture, although not, of course, for the culture of the eighteenth century.

[37] Indeed, it is highly symptomatic that in the talmudic analogue of Artemidorus, sexual dreams are taken as symbolic of other activities, just as in the Greek text, while, of course, in "our" formation the opposite is the case.

[38] There was, paradoxically enough, some shame attached to the status of the *erômenos* if he grants his favors to the *erastês*. See Dover, p. 42 and esp. pp. 81–84. See also his simple comparison between this situation and the discourse of heterosexual "seduction" in

the other hand, where the issue does not seem to have been status so much as an insistence on the absolute inviolability of gender dimorphism—since such violation would constitute a mixing of categories—any penetration of a male by another male constitutes a transgression of this boundary for both parties. In either case, we now understand why other male-male sexual practices are not mentioned in the Torah at all and need to be subsumed by the Talmud under the rubric of masturbation. We also understand why female-female sexual practices are not spoken of by the Torah and are treated very lightly indeed by the Talmud. It is because they are not perceived as simulacra of male-female intercourse. They do not confuse the dimorphism of the genders, because they are not conceptualized in this culture around penetration.[39]

Were the Men of Sodom Sodomites?

It is important at this point to discuss the story of the Destruction of Sodom, since this text has often been interpreted as encoding a condemnation of—and therefore production (or presupposition) of—a category of homosexuality.[40]

The story is as follows (Gen. 19:1–12). God, having become aware of the evil of the people of Sodom, has determined to destroy the city and has sent angels in the form of men to announce this to Lot, so that he and his family can be saved. In the evening the people of Sodom come to the door of the house and demand access to the strangers, desiring to "know them." Lot offers instead his two virgin daughters. The people are very angry: "This one has come to dwell among us, and he is judging us. Now we will do more evil to you than to them" (Gen. 19:9). At this point a miracle is produced, the people are struck blind, and Lot and his family escape.

Both writers who want to insist that the Bible condemns homosexuality and writers who wish to argue against this proposition have operated

---

twentieth-century English society (pp. 88–89). Although it has been said before, it is worth once more remarking on Dover's exemplary quiet good sense and taste.

[39]There is even a slight bit of evidence, but very inconclusive, that might indicate that solo masturbation with a dildo was more blamable for women than mutual nonpenetrative rubbing (TB Avodah Zara 44a), where a certain female ruler is disparaged for having had made for herself an imitation penis that she used every day. Since this is, however, in a nonlegal discursive context, it is impossible to determine what the normative status of such activity would have been. Were this evidence more conclusive, it would provide strong confirmation for my interpretation.

[40]Eva Cantarella, *Bisexuality in the Ancient World* (1988; New Haven, CT, 1992), p. 195 (further references in text).

with the assumption that if this is a story about homosexuality then it provides strong support for the idea that the Bible operates with a category of homosexuality that it violently condemns. Typical is Eva Cantarella, who in arguing against Robin Scroggs's claim that the Leviticus verses are totally isolated in biblical literature and probably late,[41] writes, "The proof of how forced this interpretation is comes from the celebrated story of the people of Sodom" (p. 195). Rightly dismissing interpretations that deny the sexual nature of the Sodomites' intentions, she concludes, "It seems very difficult to deny that the biblical account should be taken to mean that homosexuality is an execrable type of behaviour" (p. 197). Difficult or no, this is precisely what I intend to do.

I begin by stating that there is no possibility of denying that the intention of the Sodomites was to rape the strangers. Commentators who attempt to interpret "know" here in a nonsexual sense are ignoring the simple and clear fact that Lot "offers" his daughters as sexual substitutes for the strangers. Does he do so because he condemns their "homosexuality" and is trying to convert them to "heterosexuality"? Some interpreters would have us believe this proposition, but the story makes absolutely clear why he is protecting the men: "Only to these men do nothing, seeing that they have come under the protection of my roof." The offer of his daughters in exchange is simply because, as his "property," he has the right to do so, while he is obligated to protect guests from all harm. Far from a rebuke, Lot is simply offering them an alternative to protect his honor, and one that he expects, moreover, that they will accept. (One could, of course, query why he offers his daughters and not himself, and two answers could be given. Either he expects the daughters to be more attractive to the men than he himself would be or women are generally dispensable in his culture. This question will be further addressed below.) The rejection of his proffer is not portrayed in terms of a homosexual preference on the part of the Sodomites but as a furious response to Lot's judgmental stance toward them. This is, after all, the stated reason for their anger: "This one has come to dwell among us, and he is judging us!" Any "hermeneutics of suspicion" here that suggests some other reason for the fury runs the serious risk of anachronism, of simply filling in a gap where there is none and doing so, moreover, with our own cultural expectations. Their expressed intention, moreover, to do worse to him than they intended to do to the strangers is not at all erotic in its implications. There is, accordingly, no warrant whatever for Eva Cantarella's conclusion that "the Sodomites do not want Lot's daughters: they want the foreign visitors. This is their sin"

[41] Robin Scroggs, *The New Testament and Homosexuality: Contextual Background for a Contemporary Debate* (Philadelphia, 1983), p. 73.

350   DANIEL BOYARIN

(p. 195). Had they taken Lot's daughters, they would have been equally sinful—a proposition that will be further verified from a parallel text immediately below.

The point has been made that in the myriad references to the Sodomites in later biblical writing, not once is their alleged "homosexuality" even mentioned. Scroggs has collected eleven such allusions (p. 74). Where they make mention at all of the nature of the Sodomite sin, it is always violence that is at issue, not sexual immorality. Typical is Isa. 1:10–17, where the "officers of Sodom" are addressed and their sin is described as "their hands being full of blood" (1:16), and their atonement is to do justice with the orphan and the widow (1:17). He argues from this that these writers either did not know of or did not accept the "homosexual dimension of the story of Sodom." On the other hand, there is a parallel story—almost surely modeled on the Sodom narrative—in which the sexual aspect is clearly presupposed (I shall presently be returning to this text), and therefore, Scroggs writes, "Contrary to later references, the homosexual dimension of the story of Sodom is accepted" (p. 75). It seems to me that Scroggs has missed the point, although he is tending in the right direction. There is no reason to assume that the prophetic writers did not know of the homosexual rape aspect of the Sodom story, but it was considered by them a synecdoche for the violence of the Sodomites, not an issue of sexual immorality.

The same point ought to be made about rabbinic interpretations of this story. As Scroggs correctly points out, there is nothing in the rabbinic readings of the Sodom story that indicates that their particular sinful nature was "homosexuality." The emphasis is always on their violence and murderousness (p. 80). Scroggs, however, draws the wrong conclusion from this premise. Thus he writes, "The Palestinian Targum's clear statement of the sin as sexual does not, perhaps surprisingly, seem to have informed rabbinic midrash of this time" (p. 81). Scroggs has been misled by the modern category of sexuality to assume that the Rabbis would certainly have marked off sexual inclination as a separate and unequal determiner of human moral status. There is no reason whatever to assume that the Rabbis, assiduous readers of the Bible with no reason to apologize for the Sodomites, denied the sexual nature of their intention toward the "men." They almost certainly did understand it this way, as did everyone else in the ancient world. It was not understood by them, however, as it was not understood by the inner-biblical interpretative tradition, as being the essence of the Sodomite sinfulness or the point of the story. Indeed, judging from this Jewish interpretative tradition, the homosexual aspect of their violence was hardly worth remarking; it did not add to the heinousness of their brutality. For the interpretative tradition that locates the sin of Sodom in their "unnatural" sexuality, we look neither to the inner-biblical allusions nor to rabbinic midrash, but to first-century Hellenistic (Greek-speaking) Jewish texts, whether Palestinian or otherwise. Not surprisingly, here as elsewhere, the New Testament is closest to these other Hellenistic Jewish traditions.[42] The crucial element that enters, it seems, with Hellenistic culture is the notion of nature and the possibility of an act being *contra naturam*, as opposed to being merely forbidden. This is a peculiarly Greek idea, whether or not Greeks applied it in the same way—obviously they did not—as Hellenized Jews were to.[43] For the ancient Near East, and ancient Israel among them, acts were taboo or permitted, abhorred or praiseworthy, but never consonant with or against nature itself. Consequently, the notion that a type of desire was "unnatural" and the people who possessed it were somehow monstrous had to wait for the grafting of Greek thinking onto biblical culture that took place among Hellenistic Jews.[44] This story in the Bible and in the (Hebrew/Aramaic speaking) Rabbis is no more a condemnation of homoerotic desire than a story about a heterosexual rape would be a condemnation of heteroerotic desire, and the parallel text from Judges, to which I turn now, makes this clear.

In the story in Judges 19 the account is similar to the Sodom story. This is also a story of inhospitality and violence toward strangers. The inhospitality of the men of Gibeah is focused on right at the beginning of the story. The Levite, his concubine, and his servant are wandering in the town at nightfall, and, contrary to the customs of Israel, no one of these Israelites takes them into their home for the night (19:15). An elderly foreigner, not one of the natives of the place—like Lot—finally takes them in and exhibits the appropriate friendliness and generosity toward strangers (19:21). The wicked inhabitants of the place surround the house and make exactly the same demand that was made of Lot, that he bring out the stranger to be raped. Once more, the host pleads with

[42] Cantarella, pp. 200–201. In the New Testament, as in first-century Jewish literature and not in the Bible nor the Rabbis, the Sodomites' sin is identified as homosexual (contrast Jude 1:7, where the sin of Sodom is identified as sexual immorality and perversion, to Ezek. 16:49–50, where it is referred to as arrogance and lack of concern for the poor and the needy). See Daniel Boyarin, "Brides of Christ: Paul and the Origins of Christian Sexual Renunciation," in *The Ascetic Dimension in Religious Life and Culture*, ed. Vincent Wimbush (New York, in press), for other examples in which the New Testament's discourse of sex is closest to that of such texts as the *Testaments of the Twelve Patriarchs* and different from that of the Rabbis.

[43] Helmut Koester, "ΝΟΜΟΣ ΦΥΣΕΩΣ: The Concept of Natural Law in Greek Thought," in *Religions in Antiquity: Essays in Memory of Erwin Ramsdell Goodenough*, ed. Jacob Neusner (Leiden, 1968), pp. 521–41.

[44] The Rabbis themselves, as I have argued at length in *Carnal Israel* (n. 8 above) and elsewhere, resisted and rejected Hellenistic philosophy, although they were heavily influenced in other ways by Hellenistic culture.

them, "because this man has come into my house" (19:23), and offers
his virgin daughter and the concubine as "substitutes." The man pushes
his concubine out, and she is gang-raped and abused all night, until in
the morning she is found dead with her hand on the doorstep, having
died trying desperately to get in. This is an absolutely horrifying story
of violence toward women, and, while the men of Gibeah are punished
terribly for their murder of the woman (20:4 ff.), the Levite who threw
her to the dogs to save his skin is let off scot-free by the text.[45] A story
of primitive male privilege of the most repulsive sort, this is not in any
way, however, a discourse about homosexuality. Indeed, here, the acceptance of a "heterosexual" substitute shows that the people of Gibeah are
not being anathematized as "homosexuals." Their punishment is explicitly owing to their violence toward the woman and not to their supposed
homoeroticism. In both of these stories we find, then, a representation,
perhaps with some historical basis, of a tradition of aggression toward
strangers, acted out as "homosexual" rape (and murder—the Levite expected that he was to be killed as well [20:5]).[46] These accounts have
nothing whatever to do with either legal or discursive practices related
to same-sex desire.

We should indeed be appalled by both of these narratives, but not for
an alleged condemnation of homosexuality, which they do not inscribe,
but, rather, for the callous indifference to the fate of women that they

[45] As Phyllis Trible has remarked, "These two stories show that the rules of hospitality
in Israel protect only males. Though Lot entertained men alone, the old man also has a
female guest, and no hospitality safeguards her. She is chosen as the victim for male lust.
Further, in neither of these stories does the male host offer himself in place of his guests"
(Phyllis Trible, *Texts of Terror: Literary-Feminist Readings of Biblical Narratives*, Overtures
to Biblical Theology [Philadelphia, 1984], p. 75). Trible's further suggestion, however,
that the woman was not dead, and the husband's dismemberment of her to call for revenge
was a sacrifice of a living victim, is totally insupportable. Her claim (pressed at least as a
question) that "the cowardly betrayer [is] also the murderer" and that "no mourning becomes the man" (p. 80) seems to me just plain wrong. She is certainly already dead; this is
what the Bible tells us when it says that she did not answer him, and the dismemberment
is pursued in a sort of extravagance of mourning and desire for revenge for the violence
done her—to be sure engendered by his cowardice and callous domination of her. He was
willing for her to be sexually abused; the violence done her that causes her death appalls
even him.

[46] Dover (n. 11 above), p. 105. A more modern analogue can be found in James Dickey's
Deliverance, where a group of "hillbillies" attack and rape one of a party of middle-class
canoers who have "invaded" their territory. For anal rape described as formalized or official
aggression, see also Mekilta derabbi Ishmael Amaleq 1, where a foreign conqueror punishes the king of Israel by "standing before him ruffians who had never known woman in
their lives and they tortured him with anal intercourse." (Incidentally, this does not mean
that they were "homosexuals" but that they were virgins and very randy.) See also Amy
Richlin, *The Garden of Priapus: Sexuality and Aggression in Roman Humor,* rev. ed. (New
York, 1992), passim.

do. The final conclusion is that there is no evidence in the Hebrew Bible for a category of homosexuals or homosexuality at all, and whatever explanation is adopted for the prohibition of male anal intercourse, there is as little reason to believe that it extended to other forms of homoerotic practice.[47] The hypothesis offered here, namely, that male anal intercourse was understood as a category violation, a kind of cross-dressing, while not provable, certainly seems to me to be a plausible one.

Epilogue: Gender versus Sexuality

Neither the Bible nor, as I hope to have shown here, the Talmud knows of such a typology—of that entity called by us "sexuality," whose "chief conceptual function," according to Halperin, "is to distinguish, once and for all, sexual identity from matters of gender—to decouple, as it were, kinds of sexual predilection from degrees of masculinity and femininity." And as Halperin further observes, "That is what makes sexuality alien to the spirit of ancient Mediterranean cultures."[48] This is as true for the biblical/talmudic Jewish culture of the ancient Mediterranean as it is for the Greek. Both biblical and talmudic texts confirm rather than refute Foucault's general hypothesis of the "history of sexuality." Neither of them divides off sexual practices from the general categories of forbidden and permitted. Precisely because there is no separate realm of sexuality with all its definitional fraughtness for self-identification and that of others, there is also no separate realm of the sexually forbidden. Of course, I do not mean that forbidden genital practices do not form distinct corpora within either biblical or talmudic law codes. Where a man put his penis was categorized as a separate area of experience than what he put in his stomach, for instance. What I mean is that it does not have a separate ontological, axiological, or even moral status. As opposed to our culture where violating the rules against homoeroticism provokes an entirely different set of reactions from the violation of other moral taboos—including sexual ones such as adultery—there is no evidence in biblical/talmudic culture that suggests that that was the case there. Tabooed practices may have been ranked according to severity, but they did not at any time constitute different "species" of human beings. Violating

---

[47]Contra Cantarella who is still speaking of "homosexuality" as a transhistorical category (p. 198), ten years after Foucault's work (which she cites but neither accepts nor contests). My point is not, of course, that Foucault has become some sort of received doctrine that must be acknowledged but that he has opened questions that must be addressed whenever we speak of "sexuality." Whether or not he is explicitly brought in, we simply cannot assume a category of homosexuality for any and every cultural formation and text; it must be argued for.

[48]Halperin (n. 1 above), p. 25.

the Sabbath, for instance, produced precisely the same category of transgression (punishable by death) as did male intercourse.

The element common to both classical culture (with all of its variations) and biblical culture (with all of its variations), is that the taboos and tolerances of the cultural vis-à-vis same-sex genital practice were tied precisely to structures of maleness and femaleness, to gender and not to a putative sexuality. The absence of "sexuality" does not obviously preclude violence against those who engaged in male anal intercourse, although it should be emphasized that there is not the slightest bit of evidence to suggest that such violence was actually practiced in talmudic times.[49] It seems, however, to permit a much greater scope for other forms of male intimacy, eroticized and otherwise. "Who is a friend?" a midrash asks. "He that one eats with, drinks with, reads with, studies with, sleeps with, and reveals to him all of his secrets—the secrets of Torah and the secrets of the way of the world."[50] "Sleeps with" does not have the metaphorical value that it has in English or German, but the text is certainly reaching for a very intense and passionate level of male-male physical intimacy here. The "way of the world" is a somewhat ambiguous metaphorical term that can refer to several areas of worldly life, including business, but especially sex.[51] Male intimacy, it seems, for the talmudic culture includes the physical contact of being in bed together, while sharing verbally the most intimate of experiences, a pattern not unknown in other cultures. The image of two men in bed together talking of their sexual experiences with women is reminiscent of ethnographic descriptions of Barasana (Colombian) tribesmen, lying in hammocks, fondling each other and talking about sex with women.[52] Another way of saying this would be to claim that precisely because biblical and talmudic cultures did not have, according to my reading, a category of the homosexual, they therefore allowed for much greater normative possibilities for the homoerotic. The break in categorical continuity between anal intercourse, which did threaten gendered male identity in that culture as in ours, and other same-sex intimate practices,

[49] In the Mishna, Makkot, chap. 1, the point is explicitly made that the death penalties of the Bible are no longer operative, except possibly for murder.

[50] Solomon Shechter, ed., *Aboth de Rabbi Nathan* (Vienna, 1887; New York, 1967).

[51] As indicated by the following text, among others: "When his wife died, Rabbi Tarfon said to her sister during the mourning period: Marry me and raise your sister's children. And even though he married her, he did not behave with her according to the way of the world until after thirty days" (Kohellet Rabba, 9). See also Bereshit Rabba 22. Now although the sexual meaning is not the most frequent one for this collocation it is certainly a readily available one. Thus while it is a meaningless claim (because unfalsifiable) that this is what the author of this text "intended," it is hard to escape concluding that the sexual association would have been present for any recipient of this text.

[52] David F. Greenberg, *The Construction of Homosexuality* (Chicago, 1988), p. 71.

both erotic and not, which did not, allowed for such practices to be engaged in, more or less normatively, without calling up the specter of a threatened masculinity.[53] Eve Kosofsky Sedgwick has perhaps best captured the oddness of our present system: "It is a rather amazing fact that, of the very many dimensions along which the genital activity of one person can be differentiated from that of another (dimensions that include preference for certain acts, certain zones or sensations, certain physical types, a certain frequency, certain symbolic investments, certain relations of age or power, a certain species, a certain number of participants, etc. etc. etc.), precisely one, the gender of object choice, emerged from the turn of the century, and has remained, as *the* dimension denoted by the now ubiquitous category of 'sexual orientation.'"[54] It is only after the production of a category of sexuality per se, of a sexual identity determined by object choice, that any form of physical intimacy between men and indeed almost any form of intimacy at all becomes so problematic for our culture. In this sense the ancient cultures of the Mediterranean are more like each other—for all their differences—than any of them are like our own.

[53] Of course, I do not know and cannot speculate precisely what expressions of intimacy the actual talmudic rabbis permitted themselves. Precisely one point of this study is, however, to suggest that the borders of erotic experience were not nearly as sharply defined then as now.

[54] Eve Kosofsky Sedgwick, *The Epistemology of the Closet* (Berkeley, 1990), p. 8.

[2]

THE SONG OF SONGS AND THE GARDEN OF EDEN

FRANCIS LANDY

UNIVERSITY OF SUSSEX, FALMER, SUSSEX, ENGLAND

I. *Critics and Techniques*

UNDERSTANDING a text is always a work of comparison, both with our own experience, of love for instance, and with other texts, within the same literary tradition or beyond it. In this article I will suggest that a particularly useful comparison can be made between the Song of Songs and the myth of the Garden of Eden in Genesis, whose preoccupations it shares, and of which it is an inversion, since it portrays Paradise in this world, rediscovered through love. The Song transforms the images and motifs of the story of the Garden of Eden, so that it can be seen as a commentary on it, as a participant in a debate, whose subject is the emergence of culture from nature. Each of the texts, moreover, has secret correspondences with the other; the narrative of the loss of Eden anticipates its survival in the union of man and woman, while in the Song of Songs love is protected from society and returns to origins. There is an interplay of concord and opposition, a fourfold structure:

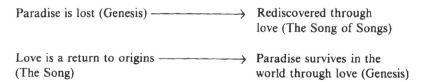

Paradise is lost (Genesis) ⟶ Rediscovered through love (The Song of Songs)

Love is a return to origins (The Song) ⟶ Paradise survives in the world through love (Genesis)

The relationship of the Song with Genesis 2 has been remarked upon at length by Karl Barth, in his immensely comprehensive *Church Dogmatics,*[1] from a theological perspective; for him they sanctify sexual love, in contrast with the repressive attitude towards eroticism in the rest of the OT. Daniel Lys,[2] too, points to the parallel with the garden of Eden in discussing the function of the Song in the Bible. He writes "Le Cantique n'est rien d'autre qu'un commentaire de Gen.2," without substantiating the relationship. By far the most detailed comparison is that constructed by Leo Krinetski,[3] for whom the Song is an allegory of the Christian dramas of sin and redemption, a view conditioned by the need to find a Christian relevance for it. All these writers

are preoccupied with theological considerations, the charge that a love song is
an anomaly in the Bible, a strange if fortunate intrusion. For the literary critic,
however, the Song, like all poetry, transcends simple categories such as
secular and sacred. "Man loves because God loves and as God loves."[4] It is a
human love poem, and for that reason it is sacred.

More recently, Phyllis Trible has affirmed that "Canticles is a commentary
on Genesis 2-3. Paradise Lost is Paradise Regained."[5] In particular, both
counter the dominant patriarchalism of the Bible with a vision of a world
where the sexes are equal, where indeed the woman takes the initiative. By and
large, this perception is justified, but distorted by Trible's ideological need to
reconcile Women's Liberation and the Bible. It abstracts a particular
comparison from the texts in their totality; and all that they say—that
tremendous complex of multiple suggestions—is implicitly valued only
according to that perspective. It is characterized by perhaps roguish special
pleading, e.g. "If the woman (in Genesis) be intelligent, sensitive, and
ingenious, the man is passive, brutish and inept,"[6] but the fun masks a failure
of sensitivity. This undermines many of her insights, even with regard to her
chosen subject. For instance, "Male dominance is totally alien to Canticles";[7]
in my view, the poet shows himself very aware and bitterly critical of
prevailing sexual mores.[8] The relationship between the two texts is both wider
and subtler than Trible suggests.

The Song largely consists of metaphors, and there can be no analysis of it
without an attempt to interpret them; through the images one comes to the
meaning. They are at the same time extremely lucid and extraordinarily
refractory—lucid as communicators of feelings, of what it is like to be lovers,
difficult only if one struggles to rationalize them. There have been many
unconvincing attempts, well summarized in an article by Richard Soulen;[9] the
latter's own suggestion, that they are objective correlatives of emotions,[10] is
just, provided that the range of emotions is expanded to include aesthetic
correlatives, such as woman and flower. But I think we can go further than
that: the images are the symbolic metalanguage of the poem; like dream-
imagery, packed with meanings, infinitely suggestive. They have the

---

[4]Franz Rosenzweig, *The Star of Redemption* (London: RKP, 1971) 199.

[5]Phyllis Trible, "Depatriarchalizing in Biblical Interpretation" *JAAR* 41 (1973) 30–48, esp.p.
47

[6]"Depatriarchalizing in Biblical Interpretation," 40.

[7]"Depatriarchalizing in Biblical Interpretation," 46.

[8]I have found Julian Pitt-Rivers, *The Fate of Shechem and the Politics of Sex* (Cambridge,
1977) to be a fascinating discussion of the Mediterranean code of honor in relation to the Bible,
and especially the Song of Songs. The girl is far more vulnerable to shame than the man, and all
the references to shame come from her mouth. For instance, in chap. 5 the watchmen beat her
when she shamelessly goes out at night in search for her lover; but when he whispers through her
door (5:2) he suffers no such opprobium. Young men are expected to be daring and to take the
initiative.

[9]Richard Soulen, "The *Wasfs* of the Song of Songs and Hermeneutic," *JBL* 86 (1967) 183–90.

[10]T. S. Eliot, "Hamlet," *Selected Essays* (London: Faber, 1961) 145.

associations that we bring to them from our own lives, and those that are assigned to them within the poem. For instance, the fawn becomes a symbol for the Lover (2:8–9, 2:17, 8:14), and for the breasts (4:5, 7:4); the Lover and the breasts are thus linked in an associative cluster, an insight confirmed by contemporary psychoanalysis.[11] The poem is a communications center, finding equivalents between the most disparate objects, as T. S. Eliot argued.[12] The associations develop along two planes, two axes:

    (i) the *syntagm*, the axis of combination

    (ii) the *paradigm*, the axis of selection.[13]

The former refers to the sequence of words as they are combined to form a sequence or story; associations develop through proximity, through sharing the same context. A good example is the dialogue of 2:1–3, where the image of the Lover as apple tree caps that of the Beloved as lily.[14]

A paradigm, however, refers to the class from which a word is selected. For instance, the fawn belongs to the paradigm of wild creatures, represented in the Song also by lions, leopards, foxes, and doves. Most images, of course, participate in several paradigms.

A related distinction is that between metonymy and metaphor. Metonymy is the naming of something by its attributes, for instance the person by the parts of his face. All these—eyes, nose, lips etc.—are associated through proximity. Through metaphor, on the other hand, resemblances are discovered between the most distant objects; they are associated through similarity.

In Roman Jakobson's classic formulation, poetry projects the principle of equivalence from the axis of selection into the axis of combination.[15] In other words, different, even distant, syntagms are found to be paradigmatically related. We get refrains or parallel stories. Equally, metaphor collaborates with metonymy; for instance, in the portraits of the lovers, meticulous metonymy is combined with outrageous metaphor. The most unlikely correlates, from the far parts of the earth, meet together on the human face and body.[16] The resulting pairings or couplings are the fabric of poetry. Nevertheless, the images do not merely signify hermetically within the poem; they have a public meaning, a reference to our common heritage of signs and senses. Thereby we come to perceive ourselves, to understand our own experience, through that of literature. The work of interpretation combines the elucidation of the image through its relevant general meaning in context

[11]In particular, the school of Melanie Klein.

[12]T. S. Eliot, "Tradition and the Individual Talent," *Selected Essays*, 18.

[13]Cf. Roman Jakobson, "Linguistics and Poetics: A Concluding Statement," *Style in Language* (ed. T. Sebeok; Cambridge: MIT, 1960) 350–78; Samuel Levin, *Linguistic Structures in Poetry* ('s-Gravenhage: Mouton, 1962); and Nicolas Ruwet, *Langage, Musique, Poesie* (Paris: Seuil, 1972), for the background to this part of the article.

[14]Throughout the article, except in translations, I use the Lover as conventional term for the hero, and the Beloved for the heroine, of the poem.

[15]"Linguistics and Poetics," 358.

[16]For the relation of metonymy and metaphor, cf. "Linguistics and Poetics," 370.

with its particular meaning in the symbolic dialect of the poem. In this article I will investigate one image from the Song in this fashion, together with its paradigmatic equivalents. The image is that of the garden; I will relate it to its mythological prototype in the garden of Eden and plot their correlations and differences.

One presupposition of mine must, I think, first be considered. Many critics affirm that the Song is an anthology, a hodgepodge of originally discreet lyrics. So it might be; but the literary critic is concerned with the text as he finds it. Furthermore, the very concept of poetic unity is questionable, and certainly ethnocentric.[17] No text is isolated, self-sufficient; none can be understood without reference to others. Thus the question of unity is not relevant, for each component in the discourse—whether it is genre, cycle, or single composition—is related to every other, more or less, sooner or later. It is the critic's task to follow the threads wherever they take him, without artificially isolating formal units.

II. *The Garden*

The garden functions as a setting and a fully-worked image in three episodes in the Song, of which the most important is 4:12–5:1:

> (The Lover): A locked garden is my sister, my bride, a locked fountain, a sealed spring. Your shoots are pomegranate paradise, with precious fruits, cypress and nard. Nard and saffron, sweet cane and cinnamon, with every incense-bearing tree; myrrh and aloes, with all species of spices. A fountain of gardens, a well of living waters, flowing from Lebanon (4:12–15).

> (The Beloved): Awake, O north wind, and come, O south; breathe on my garden that its spices may flow, let my love come into his garden, and eat his precious fruits (4:16).

> (The Lover): I have come into my garden, my sister, my bride, I have gathered my myrrh with my spice, I have eaten my comb with my honey, I have drunk my wine with my milk; eat, O friends, drink and be drunken, O lovers (5:1).[18]

---

[17]Cf. the work of Roland Barthes, that literature consists of codes, that there is no such thing as an autonomous piece of literature, e.g., *S/Z* (London: Cape, 1970) or "Style and its Image," *Literary Style: A Symposium* (ed. S. B. Chatman; London: Oxford University, 1971) 3–10. Better still, Jacques Derrida, *L'Ecriture et la Différence* (Paris: Seuil, 1967). For a spirited defense of the unity of the Song, cf. S. D. Goitein, *Iyyunim BaMiqra* (Jerusalem, 1957) 283–89.

[18]The rough-and-ready translation is my own. There are only a few points that require comment:

(i) Several critics emend *gal, pool/fountain*, in 4:12, to *gan, garden*, to conform to the first stich. This is the reading in the Versions. On the other hand, *gal* is a superb paranomasia, as has been pointed out by Robert Gordis, (*The Song of Songs and Lamentations* [New York: KTAV, 1974] 87–88), Keith Schoville, (*The Impact of the Ras Shamra Texts on the Study of the Song of Songs* [Ph.D. dissertation, University of Wisconsin, 1969] 80–81) and Daniel Lys, (*Le Plus Beau Chant*, 188).

(ii) *šĕlāḥayik, your shoots*, in 4:13 is a difficult and uncertain word. *Your shoots* is perhaps the most commonly accepted interpretation. Marvin Pope (*The Song of Songs* [AB 7c; Garden City: Doubleday, 1977] 490) adopts a frequent alternative, *conduit, groove*, which allows him some pleasant puns on *groovy groves*.

Here the garden is the garden of love, which the Lover enters and whose fruit he enjoys (4:16; 5:1); it is both identified with the Beloved (4:12–14) and distinguished from her, since she is the spring that waters the garden (4:12, 15) and owns it (4:16).[19] The garden is the Lover's also (4:16; 5:1); in the last words of the passage he invites friends to come and share in its delights. The closed garden becomes ever more open.

The next passage that uses the image of the garden (chap. 6) is in the form of a chiasmus:

(The Daughters of Jerusalem): Whither did your lover go, O fairest among women? Whither did your lover turn, that we may seek him with you? (6:1).

(The Beloved): My beloved went down to his garden, to the beds of spices, to feed in the gardens, and to cull lilies. I am my beloved's and my beloved is mine, who feeds among the lilies (6:2–3).

(The Lover): You are beautiful, my love, as Tirzah, lovely as Jerusalem, terrible as constellations. Turn your eyes away from me, for they dazzle me; your hair like a flock of goats trailing down from Gilead. Your teeth are like a flock of ewes who have come up from the washing; each of them twinned/perfect, and none of them bereaved. Like a slice of pomegranate is your temple behind your veil. There are sixty queens and eighty concubines, and maidens without number. One is my dove, my perfect one, one to her mother, choice/marvelous for the one who gave her birth; the daughters saw her and called her happy, the queens and concubines praised her.

Who is this who peers forth like the dawn/the Morning Star, fair as the moon, brilliant as the sun, terrible as constellations. I went down to the nut garden, to look at the verdure by the brook, to see whether the vine was in flower, the pomegranate had blossomed. I did not know, my soul set me . . . chariots of my princely people (6:4–12).[20]

(iii) The translation *paradise* for *pardēs* in 4:13 is a little extravagant, perhaps, for a word which simply means *orchard, grove,* but I wished to refer to its subsequent history.

(iv) The identity of the spices is somewhat uncertain.

(v) The Beloved's speech may begin either at the beginning of 4:15, 4:16, or 4:16b. This creative ambiguity cannot be reproduced in English.

[19]*Garden* or *gardens,* both singular and plural. There is no need to emend the plurals to singulars, as does Gordis (*The Song of Songs,* 83, 90). The garden is the prototype of all gardens; it is, as it were, all gardens.

[20](i) *nidgālôt* occurs only in this chapter (6:4, 10). Interpretations vary from the traditional *an army with banners* to Marvin Pope's *trophies* (*The Song of Songs,* 560), citing Anat's grisly hoard of heads and hands in the Ugaritic epics. Gordis (*The Song of Songs,* 93, 94; and "The Root DGL in the Song of Songs" *JBL* 88 [1969] 203–4) proposes *wondrous sights,* from the root *dgl, see,* but this seems altogether too vague in context. The present reading follows that of Wilhelm Rudolph (*Das Buch Ruth; Das Hohe Lied; Die Klagelieder* [KAT 17/1–3, Gütersloh: Mohn, 1962] 162). Very similar is that of S. D. Goitein ("'*Ayumma Kannidgalot,*' Song of Songs VI. 10," *JSS* 10 [1965] 221): *the brilliant stars.* This could both parallel the celestial phenomena in 6:10 and complement the terrestrial capitals in 6:4.

(ii) *bārâ, choice/marvellous,* in 6:9 is echoed immediately in 6:10, where I have translated *brilliant.* Its wide range of connotations include *pure , bright, select, excellent.*

(iii) In Job 8:12 *ʾib, verdure,* denotes rushes in marshland. Accordingly, *NEB* translates "the rushes by the stream." Here, however, the reference appears to be to the flourishing of trees in the spring.

(iv) 6:12 has defeated most commentators, myself included.

The Beloved asserts that the Lover cannot be found, because he has gone down to his garden (6:2). In 6:11–12, this descent is racapitulated by the Lover; there love surprises him. He goes to appraise the progress of the spring (6:11), as in 6:2–3 he goes to browse among scents and flowers. 6:4 and 6:10, like 6:2 and 6:11, are chiasmic echoes, complementary comparisons of the Beloved with objects of splendor, luminaries of earth and heaven. Both end with the same mysterious simile "terrible as constellations." Inset in this curiously wrought framework is a fragment of a *wasf*[21]to the Beloved, itself a variant of 4:1–3, and a meditation on her uniqueness. Thus the passage begins with the loss of the Lover; it turns to his thoughts in the garden, and concludes with a triumphant reconciliation. We may schematically summarize the structure of this passage:

6:2–3 = 6:11–12   The Lover's descent to the garden—inaccessible

6:4 = 6:10   Comparison with terrestrial capitals, concluding "terrible as constellations"

Wasf 6:5–7 ‖ 4:1–3   Beloved too dazzling

6:8–9   Her brilliant uniqueness

6:10 = 6:4   Comparison with celestial rulers, concluding "terrible as constellations"

6:11–12 = 6:2–3   The Lover's descent to the garden—surprised by love

There is another reference to the garden in the Song:

(The Lover): You who sit among gardens, friends listening to your voice, let me hear (8:13). (The Beloved): Flee, my beloved . . . (8:14).[22]

In an interesting inversion of 6:2, then, here it is the Lover who is excluded; the Beloved sits and sings.

Those critics who have commented on this image have for the most part considered it merely as a euphemism for the genitalia of the Beloved.[23] This

---

[21]The conventional term for the formal descriptions of the lovers.

[22]Several critics are reluctant to accept this phrase at its face-value, and propose reinterpretations, such as Gordis (*The Song of Songs*, 102) who suggests that it is a quotation, the song that the Lover wants to hear, or Lys (*Le Plus Beau Chant*, 308) that it is a flashback. Most ingenious of all is Marvin Pope's suggestion (*The Song of Songs*, 699) that there is a *double-entendre* with *bĕriaḥ, bolt,* analogous to the colloquial usage of *screw* in English. Indeed *bolt* translates the pun perfectly; but apart from the lack of concrete evidence to support this proposal, one wonders what could possibly be its meaning in context.

[23]E.g. Gordis, *The Song of Songs*, 88; Lys, *Le Plus Beau Chant*, 232; E. Levinger *Shir Hashirim* (Jerusalem, 1973) 68.

has necessitated considerable emendation; for instance, of *gannîm, gardens*, to *gannî, my garden*, in 4:15 and 8:13;[24] and created difficulties over the interpretation of "Eat, friends, drink and be drunken, O lovers" in 5:1, and the descent to the garden in chap. 6. As these critics point out, it is inconceivable that the Lover should make the Beloved common property, or that the absent Lover, sought in 5:8–6:1, should be found in the Beloved's private parts. Hence there is a proliferation of emendations and grammatical ingenuities: that *dôdîm* and *rēᶜîm* are substantives, meaning *love, friendship*,[25] or plural for singular;[26] that 6:2 is only coincidentally an answer to 6:1, and was originally the beginning of a separate lyric.[27]

This insistence that the garden can only be a sexual euphemism ignores the one certainty of poetry, that it is polysemantic, as Jakobson says,[28] that it is meaningful on many levels. To put it crudely, the image of the garden is as much about the garden as about sex; about the cycle of fertility in nature as well as in man. The vagina may be one of its connotations; that the Beloved is an enclosed garden may mean among other things that she is chaste; but to confine it to that signification is to equate womanhood with maidenhead. For the vagina itself is a symbol, admittedly a powerful one, of woman in her relation to man; it is only one of the signs in human discourse.

To understand the various configurations of the image in the poem, I may begin with a definition. A garden is an area enclosed and cultivated, for delight as well as necessity, where man collaborates with nature and transcends it, liberating himself from the struggle for subsistence to exploit it aesthetically. It is constantly endangered, by wild growth, drought, hostile irruption, and consequently has to be protected; within it, wild nature is tamed and harnessed. Thus it generates, historically, the opposition between wild and tame nature, as well as that between the cycle of seasons and perpetual flourishing, since it is watered by the perennial springs, "flowing from Lebanon" (4:15). It combines process in time with vulnerable immortality, ever repeated change with changelessness.

The identification of the Beloved with a locked garden (4:12) provides us with our first equivalence: that of the garden and Woman, of whom the Beloved is the idealized representative. Like the garden, the woman is the source of delights, olfactory and delicious seductions; likewise, in her, nature is tamed and humanized. People are themselves paradigms of the garden, products of a cultural process, manifesting itself, above all, in the sense of oneself, as distinct from all others. She is enclosed in her person, protected by the defenses that preserve her identity, her unique privacy. At the same time, as "a sealed spring" (4:12) ". . . A fountain of gardens, a well of living waters"

---

[24] Schoville (*The Impact of the Ras Shamra Texts*, 110), for instance, suggests that the *m* of *gannîm* is enclitic.

[25] M. Dahood, "Hebrew-Ugaritic Lexicography X," *Biblica* 53 (1972) 393.

[26] Gordis, *The Song of Songs*, 88.

[27] E. Levinger, *Shir Hashirim*, 68, 73.

[28] "Linguistics and Poetics," 370.

(4:15), she is a spring distinct from the garden, that is created, that flourishes through her. The garden (the body, the personality) becomes, as we know through psychoanalysis, an object, inhabited, animated, tended by us, its informing spirit. Finally, the garden is possessed by her "Awake, O north wind, and come, O south, breathe on *my* garden . . ." (4:16). But its fruit ripens and its spices become redolent only for the sake of the Lover, that she should become his garden, that she should be absorbed in him. "Let my love enter *his* garden . . ." (4:16): paradoxically the garden fulfills itself through self-surrender. The invitation to the Lover to "enter his garden" is, as most commentators have said, an image of the sexual act; it is also a return to the womb, where he is entirely enclosed in her. At the same time, the Beloved's presence becomes ever more diffused; the winds are commanded to spread abroad her perfumes, to entice *friends* and *lovers*. Her universality is already suggested by the phrase "Awake, O north wind, and come, O south" (4:16); she nonchalantly controls the winds, awakening them from opposite ends of the earth.

In chap. 6, the garden is essentially private, secluded in a river valley (6:11). It is an index of wealth, especially since the Lover possesses more than one garden, and has planted them with spices (6:2). Elsewhere in the poem, he is identified with King Solomon,[29] the supremely gifted and fortunate man; this is one of his *Travestien*, or conventional *personae*.[30] The king goes down to his garden, where he must not be disturbed, "to cull lilies";[31] *lilies* in the Song symbolize the Beloved, and thus, paradigmatically, all women. Similarly, the refrain in 6:3—"I am my beloved's and my beloved is mine, who feeds among the lilies"—introduces another image for the Lover, taken from the animal kingdom: the *fawn*, with which he is compared in 2:8–9, 17 and 8:14. "I am my beloved's and my beloved is mine, *who feeds among the lilies*" (6:3 = 2:16) echoes "Your two breasts are like two fawns, twins of a doe, *who feed among the lilies*" in 4:5. The association of fawns and lilies is further established by the syntagmatic conjunction of the refrain in 2:16 with the equivalence *fawn* = *lover* in 2:17.[32] King, fawn, and lover feed off lilies (= women). The human and natural orders are tightly interwoven, as throughout the Song. The fawn feeding off lilies parallels the king having the pick of women in the sexual garden or harem, as in 1:3–4. This is the theme of one of the meditations from

[29] 1:1, 2–4, 5–6, 9–13; 3:6–11; 7:6; 8:11–12. These are the passages in which Solomon is either explicitly referred to, or indirectly, through royal imagery. Of course, other passages are related to them through refrain, e.g. 3:6 = 8:5

[30] Gillis Gerleman, *Ruth. Das Hohelied* (BKAT 18; Neukirchen-Vluyn: Neukirchener, 1965) 60–62. Gerleman argues that *king* and *shepherd* were conventional images for lovers, like *knight* and *shepherd* in Medieval Romance.

[31] *Lilies* is the most conventional translation of *šôšannîm*, whose exact identity is uncertain. Marvin Pope (*The Song of Songs*, 368) proposes *lotus*.

[32] ". . . who feeds among the lilies. Until the day blows and the shadows flee, turn, my beloved, and be like a deer or a young gazelle on the cleft (?) mountains." There is another link between the two passages: like 2:17a, 4:6a reads "Until the day blows and the shadows flee. . . ." Thus 2:16–17 and 4:5–6 form parallel units.

the garden: "There are sixty queens, and eighty concubines, and maidens without number. One is my dove, my perfect one . . ." (6:8–9). The garden is aesthetic and sexual; even among the flowers, and among the women, he cannot stop thinking of his beloved. Although he is the one "who feeds among the lilies," nevertheless their love is perfect and reciprocal—"I am my beloved's and my beloved is mine."

In 8:13, the garden is that of the singer, whose song expresses the love of the lovers and their garden, and is its image in words. In the poem, as in the garden, language is cultivated, it organizes, tries to make an artistic whole out of experience, refining and perfecting for a moment man's unending self-reflection, out of which he creates his own image and identity. Through the friends (i.e., us) who listen to the Song and participate in its emotions the love becomes eternal. Thereby it loses its immediacy, is distanced by language. Throughout the book, in talking to each other, the lovers are in fact talking about each other.[33] Paradoxically, the Lover, who in the guise of Solomon is also the composer of the Song, is separated from his love by the very act of its expression. One is reminded of Edmond Jabès's definition of the relationship of the writer to his work: "Are you in the book? My place is on the threshold."[34]

III. *The Paradigm of the Garden*

The most obvious paradigmatic equivalents of the garden are the city and the palanquin (3:6–11). Both are enclosed and protected, products of the culture in which nature is perfected. Like the garden, they are compared with the lovers, and are pervaded with their presence; they are their outward manifestation, and consequently alien to them.

The city is as beautiful as the Beloved—"You are beautiful, my love, as Tirzah, lovely as Jerusalem" (6:4)—and parts of her body are compared with parts of cities—"Your eyes are pools of Heshbon at the gate of Bat-Rabbim" (7:5), for example, or "Your neck is like the Tower of David" (4:4). Two parallel "dream sequences" (3:1–4; 5:2–7) have an urban setting—in each the Beloved, restless, searches for her Lover through the city at night: in the first she finds him; in the second she fails and is beaten by the watchmen. However, it is also the home of the daughters of Jerusalem, friends of the Beloved throughout the poem, and the capital of Solomon's kingdom, the focus of all his wealth and power. The city only lives through its inhabitants, and its center is the king, the Lover in the poem.

The palanquin (3:6–11) is made by the king, for the sake of the Beloved; it is constructed out of the most costly materials—silver, gold, purple—but its

---

[33]For example, in the wasfs.
[34]Edmond Jabès, *Le Livre des Questions* (Paris: Gallimard, 1963) 15.

center is "paved with the love of the daughters of Jerusalem";[35] by implication, this is its most precious substance, without which it would be merely a useless frame, just as the garden could not exist if the Beloved did not water it.

The king is at the head of a hierarchical society, most intricately organized in cities for mutual protection and aid; in society, as in the citizen himself, anarchic human nature is ordered and disciplined, the savage tamed. The attitude of the poem and the lovers to this civilized achievement is ambivalent, however; on the one hand, it is a celebration of the magnificence of Solomon's kingdom, a cultured Golden Age; on the other, it insists that love is worth all pleasures and riches; for the king, the Beloved is worth the entire kingdom.[36] Thus it is subversive of the assumptions on which society is based, that sexual desire must be controlled for its preservation, through institutions such as marriage and the incest taboo and that a king who valued his Beloved more than his kingdom would be irresponsible, as was the Solomon of tradition. Love is very powerful in the Song, as in life; a king is its subject—"A king is caught in the tresses thereof" (7:6)—is one of its most suggestive images. Therefore society is inimical to love, tainting the lovers with shame—the watchmen of the city beat the Beloved (5:7), lovers cannot kiss publicly (8:1). Shame intrudes into the relationship of the lovers at many points, of which these are two of the most apparent. Therefore, love retreats from society into its private world, into an enclosed garden; the Beloved brings her Lover back to her mother's house, "to the room of the one who conceived me" (3:4), from the terrors of the nocturnal city. Through political organization and ethical codes man protects himself from perils, from the environment and from his own nature, but they too are experienced as hostile; politics is ruthless, moral codes are repressive.

At the same time, like the nature which is tamed and flourishes in the garden, on which man lives, love is the generative force through which society perpetuates itself, and is its supreme value. All the arts in the Song are dedicated to the pursuit of love—the arts of love-poetry and perfumery, for example. From one point of view, the Song may be seen as a search for value, like Ecclesiastes, in which love is compared with and found to be superior to all pleasures and riches—it is worth all civilization. "How beautiful and how pleasant is love among delights" (7:7).[37] The construction of equivalences

---

[35] Many of the older critics found the image difficult and proposed ingenious emendations or alternative translations, e.g. *ʾhbh* = leather. Among the critics who defend the MT and the normative reading of *ʾahăbāh* as *love* (in the context of the Song it can have hardly any other meaning), cf. Lys, *Le Plus Beau Chant*, 160–61; Levinger, *Shir Hashirim*, 48–49; and most recently, Marvin Pope, *The Song of Songs*, 445.

[36] For instance, the Beloved is as beautiful as the royal capitals, Jerusalem and Tirzah; in 7:5–6 she is compared systematically with parts of the land of Israel.

[37] The *NEB* translates "my loved one, daughter of delights," and Pope (*The Song of Songs*, 632) argues for "O Love, daughter of delights," following the Syriac and Aquila. The LXX and most other versions agree with the MT, however. From the point of view of poetic comprehensibility there seems little to choose between the one and the other.

engenders a mutual dependence: the lovers express themselves and surround themselves with objects of beauty and delight, such as wine and love poetry, and they seek correlatives for their beauty in the natural world, in the exuberant imagery; on the other hand, they are at the fecund center of the spring, whose beauty is only appreciated, only acquires human significance, in their eyes. When the Lover goes "to see if the vines were in flower, the pomegranates had blossomed" (6:11), one remembers that it was for his sake that the garden was planted.

The garden was enclosed to preserve it from intrusion, a danger illustrated in connection with the vineyards by 2:15—"Catch us the foxes, the little foxes, who raid vineyards." Similarly, the city is guarded by the watchmen on the walls (5:6) against surprise attack; they also patrol the streets against subversion within (3:3; 5:6). Sixty men-at-arms guard the palanquin of love, "all of them gripping swords, expert in war, each with his sword by his side, for fear in the night" (3:7).[38]

In each case the fear is that of destruction in time, the knowledge that all man's achievements perish. Perhaps the glories of Solomon's kingdom were legendary, even when the poem was written down. Only Love is as strong as Death, and is therefore of supreme value; Death destroys all but Love— "Many waters cannot quench Love, and the Floods will not overwhelm her" (8:7).[39]

Through love, too, man develops and realizes his full potential as a human being; in the love of the lovers all relationships are consummated, both with nature—since through metaphor Man represents Creation—and with the nuclear family—the lovers see each other as brother and sister, mother and son, and reenact those relationships, at least in fantasy. They become a divine

---

[38]Schoville (*The Impact of the Ras Shamra Tablets*, 71), M. Dahood (*Psalms* [*AB* 17; Garden City: Doubleday, 1968] 2.227) and Gordis (*The Song of Songs*, 85) hold that *ʾāḥuzê* means *skilled* in this context, from the Akkadian *aḥazū, learn*. On the other hand, J. Greenfield ("Ugaritic MDL and its Cognates," *Bib* 45 [1964] 527–34) argues that *ʾāḥuzê* is deponent and means *girded with (weapons)* while *mēlumdê* is related by metathesis to Ugaritic *MDL, saddle, bind*. Both these meanings are possible.

Little can be said in favor of the view that *paḥad, fear*, means *a pack (of wild dogs*, etc.) propounded by Schoville (*The Impact of the Ras Shamra Tablets*, 71) and Dahood (*Ugaritic-Hebrew Philology* [Rome: Pontifical Institute, 1965] 69). Pope (*The Song of Songs*, 437) comments: "Fearsome as a pack of wild dogs may be, it does not seem likely that this alleged meaning is appropriate or adequate to the degree of dread . . ." in this or related contexts. In any case it only interpolates a metaphor between the fear and its source, makes concrete "la terreur nocturne étant toujours à l'affût comme le monde du Néant menaçant celui de l'Etre," as Lys, (*Le Plus Beau Chant*, 157) remarks. Philological argument against this view is presented by D. R. Hillers ("Paḥad Yiṣḥaq," *JBL* 91 [1972] 92n. 18).

[39]Pope (*The Song of Songs*, 210–29) argues at considerble length that the Song of Songs emanates from a funeral feast for precisely this reason.

flame (8:6);[40] the splendor of the lovers is that of man transformed, literally transfigured through love; through it he becomes once more king of the garden, entrusted with the care of all nature—"all things under his feet" (Ps 8:7).

IV. *The Garden of Eden*

At this point comparison with the garden of Eden may be profitable. As an etiological myth it is extraordinarily comprehensive. It explains the creation of vegetation, man, animals, and woman; the origin of language; the prohibition of incest; the beginning of history and the necessity for culture, as well as lesser details, such as the cause of pain in childbirth and the enmity between serpents and women. Other consequences of the fall are the subservience of women to men, the hostility of the earth, and, most important of all, human morality; its concomitants are moral awareness and sexual shame, and hence the origin of clothes. The impulse that causes the catastrophe is man's ambition, his wish to be like God. The myth idealizes prehistory, when nature spontaneously provided man with all his needs; his emergence into history and culture is forced on him by the withdrawal of nature's bounty, the loss of Paradise.

In the Song of Songs, through culture man tries to recreate Paradise, cooperating with, as well as exploiting, nature. The attempt is similar to that of the author of Ecclesiastes (2:3-11), who surrounds himself with delights, only to find that they too are devoid of significance, a wasted effort. In the Song, as we have seen, civilization is vulnerable; it survives only through love, and only love is of ultimate value. For in love the natural impulse is humanized, undergoes a cultural process, manifested in the language of courtship or in love-play; in turn it stimulates the development of culture, such as the arts of poetry or perfumery. Thus the Song of Songs inverts the story of the garden of Eden; man rediscovers Paradise.

The relationship, however, is not simply oppositional. In the Song, Paradise is limited by the fallen world; Death is undefeated, society imposes shame on the lovers, time inevitably separates them. Thus the garden is enclosed; the lovers, while reenacting the primordial situation, playing the parts of brother and sister, mother, son and daughter, can never actually be so; language separates them as well as unites them. Similarly, the ideal harmony of "I am my beloved's and my beloved is mine" disappears on the last appearance of the formula: "I am my beloved's and his desire is for me."[41] It is clear that the verse indicates more than mere reciprocity. The echo of God's

---

[40]The divine reference here is extremely controverted. Nevertheless, in the context of the declaration that Love is as strong as Death, as powerful as Sheol, the possibility that it is "the flame of Yah" is very suggestive. Its immediate association is with the fire of the altar, that is never extinguished, through which man communicates with God. Indeed the metaphor of fire frequently signifies God in the OT (e.g., Deut 4:24 or the burning bush).

[41]Chaim Rabin, "Some Etymological Notes," *Tarbiz* 33 (1963) 114-17, makes the interesting suggestion that *tĕšûqâ* means *loyalty/fealty*, not *desire*.

words to Eve: "And to your husband shall be your desire, and he shall rule over you" (Gen 3:16) is very striking; it both parallels that imbalance and inverts it, since it is now man whose *těšûqâ* is for woman.

Some aspects of the Genesis myth are not echoed in the Song of Songs; in particular, the image of the serpent does not appear there. In the serpent, nature is already hostile to man; his very existence is a sign of the impending fall. Comparable images in the Song are the lions and leopards of 4:8, or the foxes of 2:15. The latter, apparently, may be easily caught, and are minimized: "Catch us foxes, little foxes." In 4:8 "With me from Lebanon, O bride, with me from Lebanon come, hurry/look down from the summit of Amana, from the summit of Senir and Hermon, from the dens of lions, from the mountains of leopards," man is still miraculously lord of nature, unharmed and unafraid, like Enkidu.[42] We feel a tension, however, because we know that the Beloved is really alien to Lebanon, the beasts truly dangerous, that there is a conflict between the recaptured mythical harmony and the historical estrangement.

The interrelation of the two texts may be illustrated by two examples: the first is the image of the tree. In Genesis, alongside the procreative tree[43] that produces death is the tree of life. They promise the fulfilment of man's deepest wishes: for knowledge, "at the price of all that a man hath,"[44] even if the price is death; and for immortality, rooted in the fear of death, which is also a fear of life as a creative and destructive process. These two desires contradict each other in this world, and also in the Garden of Eden. For there the tree of life is permitted when that of knowledge is forbidden; but once Adam and Eve have broken the injunction and eaten the fruit, the tree of life is guarded and man sent out into the world. There is thus an inversion:

	Pre	*Post*	
Tree of Knowledge	–	+	– = Forbidden
Tree of Life	+	–	+ = Permitted

The trees are emblematic of the difference between God and man: God can combine knowledge and immortality; he is changeless but is responsible for, and participates in, the process of life and death. In the Song of Songs, there is

---

[42]There may be a mythological allusion here, as was suggested by W. F. Albright ("Archaic Survivals in the Text of Canticles," *Hebrew and Semitic Studies Presented to G. R. Driver* [ed. D. Winton-Thomas and W. McHardy; Oxford: Clarendon, 1963] 3). He considered this verse to be a fragment of a poem dedicated to Adonis, who invited his Beloved, a goddess whom the Greeks identified with Aphrodite, to accompany him on his ill-fated hunt in the mountains of Lebanon; the Lebanon was sacred to Asherah. Schoville (*The Impact of the Ras Shamra Tablets*, 75–78) remarks that she was called "Mistress of the Lions." Thus the safety of the heroine among ferocious beasts is part of the mythological background of the passage, as well as being a well-known motif in pastoral poetry, evidence of the Beloved's magical innocence and charm.

[43]The serpent, the tree, and God are overlapping images of the same generative power. God himself is the tempter, since he planted the temptation, and the serpent is its spokesman, who merely puts it into words. And the temptation is God's secret, creative knowledge, enshrined within the tree.

[44]William Blake, "The Four Zoas," *The Portable Blake* (New York: Viking, 1946) 384.

only one tree, that is a tree of knowledge and of life: the apple-tree that is identified with the Lover in 2:3, and under which the Beloved awakens him in 8:5.

In 2:3, however, she is under the apple-tree: "Like an apple-tree among the trees of the wood, so is my love among sons; in his/its shadow I sat and took pleasure, and his/its fruit was sweet to my palate."

The apple-tree symbolizes the Lover, the male sexual function in the poem; erect and delectable, it is a powerful erotic metaphor. It provides nourishment and shelter, traditional male roles—the protective Lover, man the provider—that originate, in a far more powerful form, in the mother, to whom the child clings and who gives it suck. Through the metaphor, we perceive the common identity that, according to Genesis, urges lovers to seek each other and become "one flesh." Instead of bringing death into the world, the tree curses sickness: "Sustain me with raisin-cakes, stay me with apples, for I am lovesick" (2:5).

In 8:5 the Lover is under the apple-tree: "Who is this who comes up from the wilderness, leaning on her beloved? Under the apple-tree I awakened you (m.); there your mother travailed with you, there she who gave birth to you travailed."

His Beloved, wakening him to consciousness, plays the role of his mother, who wakened him to the world. In the Song, wakening has the connotation of becoming aware, finding true knowledge, through love (cf. especially 5:2; 7:10). This knowledge is that love is as strong as death, it confers immortality. In Eden, however, waking, "opening one's eyes" (Gen 3:5,7), precipitates the fall; the traumatized lovers hide their bodies from each other. However, the Song celebrates nakedness; it is only decent shame that is ignorant. Constantly, it interposes itself between the lovers and prevents the fulfilment of their love.[45] But in the Song nakedness can only be spoken of through language: through the tissue of metaphors and metonymies that replaces the genitals with secondary sexual features (e.g., eyes, breasts) and by remote and unlikely objects. The formal descriptions are in fact exercises in frustration.[46] This brings to us the central pun of the Genesis narrative: *ᶜārūm—nakedness* and *subtlety* (2:25; 3:1). Outside the garden, nakedness can only be expressed through subtlety, through lovers' subterfuges, elaborate metalanguage; or indeed, through clothing.

[45]This takes various forms. For example, lovers cannot kiss openly in the street (8:1); the Beloved wishes her lover were like a brother, with whom physical affection was publicly accepted precisely because sexual consummation is prohibited. A girl who is shameless in love is beaten by the guardians of public morality (5:7). A man who gives all for love is despised (8:7). The metalanguage of lovers is like a camouflage; for example, in 2:10-13 the Lover invites the Beloved to go for a walk to see the spring, as if the spring were the main object of the walk, as if they were indifferent to each other and only united by their pleasure in the season. At other times, shame ensures the failure of their love, as in the opening of the dream sequence of 5:2-7, when it is the Beloved's qualms that banish the Lover and ironically lead to her humiliation.

[46]This is because poetry attempts the impossible, to merge the *signifiant* and the *signifié*, the word and the experience it tries to express. "What expresses itself in language we cannot express by means of language"; L. Wittgenstein, *Tracatus Logico-Philosophicus* 4. 1. 21.

Moreover, in 8:5 the recollection of birth and love's awakening is in astonishing contrast to its context: "Who is this who comes up from the wilderness, leaning on her Beloved?" In the desert, as in Genesis after the fall, the ground is cursed, nature is barren. The couple support each other as they climb towards their homes in the settled regions, coming into view of the onlookers. Paradigmatically, their journey is paralleled by that of the palanquin (3:6), through the refrain. "Who is this who comes up from the wilderness?" (3:6 = 8:5). The palanquin is a microcosm of civilization, surrounded by terror and animated by love; the equivalence of the palanquin and the lovers is striking and significant, for man survives the hostility of nature through love and cooperation, and through his efforts nature is no longer cursed. On this journey he remembers his origins; Paradise accompanies him.

The second instance of the mutual illumination of the texts is the problem of incest and human origins. In Genesis, man is created out of the union of dust and spirit, earth and sky, and woman is formed out of him; in the Song of Songs, it is woman who is associated with images of earth and sky—the sun, moon and constellations, and the land of Israel—with the constituents of man, whose mother she is. It is a strangely fatherless poem, that stresses man's human parentage, his birth from his mother. Incest is a very persistent motif in the Song. The Lover calls his Beloved "my sister, my bride" (4:9, 10, 12; 5:1, 2—where it is "my sister, my friend"); she imagines him as her brother in 8:1; and their love recalls, is superimposed on that of the mother. At several of the most intimate moments there is a reversion to maternal imagery. The Beloved enacts the role of the mother in 8:5; in 3:11 the mother crowns the king's wedding; in 6:9 his love is as total as that of her mother. In 3:4 (= 8:2), the Beloved takes her lover "to my mother's house, to the chamber of the one who conceived me," to the site of conception, both genital and social. We realize that the lovers repeat their parents' consummation, their own procreation; the sequence of generations is abolished by the act that sustains it. Love in the Song, as in life, symbolically reenacts all relationships and fulfills incestuous wishes through sublimation. The Beloved is only metaphorically a sister, can only play the mother, and at one point in particular, this unreality is felt as painful: "Who would make you like a brother to me, suckling my mother's breasts; I would meet you outside, I would kiss you, and none would despise me" (8:1). The simile here distinguishes terms apparently alike; she does not wish him to be her brother, only a quasi-brother, since otherwise she could not make love with him (8:2–4); she wishes to return to a time before the prohibition of incest.

The Garden of Eden was such a time, before the promulgation of laws, before shame intervened between the lovers. The relationship of Adam and Eve cannot be categorized because they precede family. Eve is man's split self, his double, separated from him so that he should not be alone; paradoxically, the two halves perpetually strive to reunite and erect the barriers of shame, clothing etc. to prevent this catastrophic fusion. "For this reason (that Woman is 'bone of my bone') man shall forsake his father and his mother"

(Gen 2:22); in search of a primordial unity, that precedes incest and family. Incest is the condition of this world, while man's true home is in Eden. "And he shall cleave to his wife, and they shall be one flesh" (Gen 2:22). In a sense. incest is forbidden because it is not truly incestuous, it leaves us stranded in the cycle of human generation. In the Song, however, where the Beloved attracts to herself all the images of spring and nature, love for her emanates from and focuses the love of the earth, man's true parent, in Genesis. There, likewise, as well as being a secondary creature, derivative of man, Eve is "the mother of all that live" (Gen 3:21).

V. *Conclusion*

In this article, I have been trying to compare the myth of the garden of Eden and the Song of Songs, to suggest that the latter is a comment on the former, from within the historical process, but not to establish a direct, conscious dependence, nor a unique relationship. They use the same terms to discuss the same themes; these can be traced through other books of the Bible and beyond it. A nostalgic return to Paradise characterizes the pastoral; elements of the myth of Paradise are found in many parts of the Bible. Other images in the Song will be found to belong to different paradigms, to have different references. To give a straightforward example, incestuous desire in the lovers recalls the prohibitions in Leviticus and the history of the forefathers with their tangled sexual relations. Legal, genealogical, and etiological codes are correlated. Each word, image, poem, is a nexus of relationships, a bundle of distinctive features, radiant in the light of others. The reader parts them, gives them individuality; hence their opacity.

[3]

The One:
God's Unity and Genderless Divinity in Judaism

Hagar Lahav
hagarla@012.net.il

ABSTRACT

This article examines the cultural ways in which traditional Judaism understands the relationship between an individual and Divinity. The article shows that this understanding has deep gendered dimensions. Grounded in feminist critiques of theology, as well as in Jewish studies and cultural studies, the article shows that the conceptualization of God-person relationship, in both Orthodox and *Kaballic* Jewish streams, is based on a hierarchical division to three different spaces. These spaces are: *Mitzvah* (Commandment, Duty, Law), Grace, and Desire or Will. The *Mitzvah* is perceived to be the highest space and is represented as 'manly'. The intermediate space—Grace—is represented as a 'good woman' or as 'mother'. This space is characterized by a sacred yearning, as well as by lack of stability and continuity, paralysis, and even death. The lowest space is the space of Desire and personal will, which is culturally represented by a child or a whore-woman. This space is characterized by an attitude of disregard, resistance and fear. The article demonstrates how this cultural division of Divinity in to three, contradicts the declared Jewish position that God/Divinity is 'One, Sole and Unique' (*Echad, Yachid ve-Meuchad*), and points at the inherent need of genderless conceptualization of Divinity in Judaism.

Keywords: Divinity, faith, gender, genderless, God, Hebrew, Jewish culture, Judaism, Kaballa, Mitzvah

Introduction

Judaism is generally defined by its monotheistic perception of Divinity as One, United, and Indivisible Force.[1] A deeper cultural and linguistic analysis such as that presented in this article reveals that this concep-

---

1. M. Idel, 'Nishmat Eloah', in S. Arzy, M, Fachler and B. Kahana (eds.), *Life as a Midrash* (Tel Aviv: Yediot Achronot, 2004), pp. 339-80 (in Hebrew).

tion of the Divine is really fragmented by the patriarchal in at least two basic ways: first is God-language, including male images. This well-known critique, discussed widely in Jewish as well as Christian feminist theology,[2] is part of the background but not at the centre of this paper. The second gender fragmentation of the supposedly indivisible God in Judaism can be found in looking at the traditional conceptualization of the relationship between the Divine and a person. I claim that such an approach reveals that—Divinity is divided into three different aspects or spaces that correlate two basic patriarchal images: the image of the patriarchal family (i.e., a hierarchical, genealogical structure that includes one father, one mother and a child or children) and the dualistic perception of the woman as either a mother or a whore. This paper aims to illuminate the latter form of cultural fragmentation of the indivisible Deity in Judaism and to propose a new conceptualization, one that re-unites the existing fragments in a free, equal, un-hierarchical, a-gender, and liberating manner.

Linguistic Gendering of the Divine

Although Judaism is a complex composite of perceptions and beliefs, one might argue that Jewish thinking is characterized by the perception of Divinity as an all inclusive, indivisible whole.[3] Whether the Divine is conceived of as an essence, an existence, a being, a system, an energy, or the like, it is always one and inclusive: *Eyn od mil'vado*—'There is nothing but him', and also 'there is no one else but him'.

   In order to preserve the notion of such Divinity—One as an all inclusive, indivisible Unity, Judaism affirms that it is impossible—indeed forbidden—to describe Divinity in human terms; as stated in the commandment 'Thou shalt not make unto thee a graven image, nor any manner of likeness' (Exod. 20.4).[4] Accordingly, one might assume that such a conception of non-human Divinity, one that resists anthro-

---

2.   For this critique from the Jewish perspective, see especially R. Adler, *Engendering Judaism: An Inclusive Theology and Ethics* (Boston: Beacon Press, 1999); Judith Plaskow, *Standing Again at Sinai: Judaism from a Feminist Perspective* (San Francisco: Harper & Row, 1990); Judith Plaskow and Donna Berman (eds.), *The Coming of Lilith* (Boston: Beacon Press, 2005); Tamar Ross, *Expanding the Palace of Torah: Orthodoxy and Feminism* (Waltham, MA: Brandeis University Press, 2004). Similarly, from the general monotheistic perspective, see P.S. Anderson, *A Feminist Philosophy of Religion* (Oxford: Blackwell, 1998).

3.   See, for example, M. Halbertal, D. Kuzweil and A. Sagi (eds.), *On faith* (Jerusalem: Keter, 2005, in Hebrew).

4.   *A Hebrew-English Bible*, According to the Masoretic Text and the Jewish Publication Society 1917 Edition (Mamre: Mechon Mamre, 2005).

pomorphic visions of God, cannot be gendered. Yet, in Judaism, as in other religions, God is gendered and described as male.

This paradoxical situation has not escaped the eyes of feminist Jewish scholars who have concentrated their critique on three complementary linguistic forms that gendered the Divine.[5]

The first is the totalizing domination of male, hierarchical, and patriarchal images of God in Judaism; such as Father, King, Lord, Warrior, Hero, and so forth, and referring to God as 'he' or 'him'. These verbal images incorporate assumptions about manhood, and concomitantly about womanhood, as well as about the hierarchical, patriarchal relationship between men and women. Here one can easily relate, for example, to the oft-repeated description of the Divine as One who relates to the disobedient/devoted people of Israel as husband does to his whoring/loyal wife.[6] This very well-known critique by feminist theologians, together with the understanding that religious language does not merely create a certain social pattern but also grants its legitimacy,[7] led one of the most important Jewish Orthodox feminist theologians to ask herself, as well as her readers, 'Can we still pray to "Our Father in Heaven"?'[8]

The second linguistic form that is the subject of critique, in a way stronger than the first, relates to the fact that Hebrew speech about—and to—God is always performed in the masculine. Such a form of denotation is a-priori masculine as it is rooted securely and substantively in the structure of the Hebrew language, which is among the most gendered of languages. The entire world is gendered in Hebrew and so it is impossible to relate to any essence—be it an object, a living entity, a person, or the Divine—in a genderless manner. Since Divinity must be gendered linguistically and since according to patriarchal principles it cannot be defined as a female, which represent the inferior, then all forms of reference to God must be in the masculine.

The third complementary linguistic form critiqued is that the universal is referred to in Hebrew, as in other languages, only in the masculine. For example, in Hebrew the word *adam* means a person. In doing so, it

---

5.   See Adler, *Engendering Judaism*; Plaskow, *Standing Again at Sinai*; Plaskow and Berman (eds.), *The Coming of Lilith*; and Ross, *Expanding the Palace of Torah*. See also T. Ross and Y. Gellman, 'The Implications of Feminism for Orthodox Jewish Theology', in M. Mautner, A. Sagi and R. Shamir (eds.), *The Multi-cultural in a Democratic-Jewish State* (Tel Aviv: Ramot, 1998), pp. 443-65 (in Hebrew).

6.   See, for example, the book of Hosea.

7.   Ross, *Expanding the Palace of Torah*, p. 113.

8.   T. Ross, 'Can we still speak to God the Father?', in M. Ilan (ed.), *Ayin Tovah: Dialogue and Polemic in Israeli Culture* (Tel Aviv: Hakibbutz Hameuchad, 1999), pp. 264-78 (in Hebrew).

refers not only to a particular historic/mythic (male) figure but also to all human beings (a phrase that in itself identifies the universal with the masculine).[9] In Simone de Beauvoir's words, the language itself defines maleness as normative and femaleness as the Other.[10] From this perspective, it is impossible to relate to the Divine as feminine and still keep the notion of One, because any feminine reference (such as referring to the Goddess, for example) automatically implies, linguistically, that there is also a second, male, existence. In other words, 'God' can exist for itself, as a universal One, but 'Goddess' obligates the linguistic existence of (at least) two Divines — one male and one female.

As noted above, this linguistic critique is well established in feminist theology, from both Jewish and Christian perspectives.[11] However, the patriarchal attribution of the conception of God in Judaism does not begin and end with the a-priori gender linguistic identification. From here on, I would like to focus on a less obvious aspect of the patriarchal notion of the Jewish God — descriptions of God's nature through a denotation of characteristics that result in a division of what I claim is, in essence, indivisible.

Dividing the Divine

Traditional Judaism claims that God can be realized, touched, or connected to humans in their lives via three different personal aspects that complement one another:[12]

- *Mitzvah* (Commandment, Duty, Law) — What must a person do to satisfy the will of Divinity?
- *Chessed* (Grace) — What has a person been given by the Divine? What are the capabilities with which God blesses a person? And accordingly, what is a person capable or incapable of doing in order to satisfy the Divine will?
- *Yetzer* (Desire, Will, Lust) — What does a person want? What does a person desire from the Divine? Does a person desire to satisfy God's will? Does a person have other desires, stronger that this desire?

9.   This linguistic pattern creates, of course, an illogical relation in which B (woman) is being described as totally different from — and as inferior to — A (man), and at the same time, as being a part of A (universal = man).

10.   Simone de Beauvoir, *The Second Sex* (trans. to Hebrew by S. Perminger; Tel Aviv: Bavel, 2001).

11.   See nn. 2 and 5.

12.   See, for example, Y. Caspi, *Inquiring of God* (Tel Aviv: Yediot Achranot, 2002, in Hebrew).

A critical reading of Judaic texts reveals that these three components reflect two basic complementary patriarchal conceptions in mainstream Judaism. The first is the structure of the family and relations between its members—father, mother and child, as perceived in the patriarchal-heterosexual conception of the world. The second are the roles allocated to women according to the patriarchal conception of their relations with males—as a mother or as a whore.[13] Those two polar extremes are represented in the *Midrash* in the figures of Lilith (the demon, the temptation, Adam's first wife who refused to surrender to him and left the Garden of Eden)[14] versus Eve (the mother of all living beings who is created from Adam's body to be his helper) (Gen. 2.18, 21-24; 4.1).

Also, it is worth noting the similarity between these two complimentary perceptions of the three Divine components—the *Mitzvot/*Law, Grace and Desire—and the Freudian psychic structures—super-ego, ego, and id.[15] The table below summarizes these four relations:

Jewish terms	*Family Position*	*Gender Position*	*Freudian concepts*
'Mitzvah' (Duty, Commandment, Law)	Father	Man (normative, universal)	Superego
'Chessed' (Grace)	Mother	Mother (good woman)	Ego
'Yetzer' (Desire, Will, Lust, Sin)	Child	Whore (bad woman)	Id

According to this patriarchal conception, 'Desire' (*Yetzer*)—representing childishness or prostitution—has the lowest ranking and is least valued. It is defined principally in negative terms as narcissism, on the one hand, and social threat, on the other hand. As such, Desire is perceived along a spectrum from fear to disregard. Many times it is predefined as sin. These are the threatening depths of the subconscious, as well as the body, which disrupt mature adults' attempts to control their lives.[16]

'Grace' (*Chessed*) is attributed a middle ground, one located in the maternal world. This is the space of forgiveness, embodiment, love,

---

13. D. Lemish, 'The Media, the Whore and the Madonna', in *Panim* 22 (2002), pp. 84-92 (in Hebrew).

14. See, for example, Plaskow and Berman (eds.) *The Coming of Lilith,* pp. 23-35, 81-86.

15. B. Kahana, '*Hatzimtzum kemafthach*', in Arzy, Fachler and Kahana (eds.), *Life as a Midrash,* pp. 412-47.

16. See, for example, M. Ankori and O. Ezrachi, *The Secret of Leviathan* (Ben-Shemen: Modan, 2004, in Hebrew).

and the understanding of the limited nature of human life in the face of the temptations of Desire and difficulties of obligation. However, it is perceived to be the place of 'non-action', 'non-progression', and in certain ways is a place of paralysis and even death. Accordingly, in some Jewish traditions, Grace is represented as being achievable only in the next world.[17]

The highest status is reserved for *Mitzvot* (duties, laws); actions taken to fulfil God's plan. This is assumed to be the essence of existence and responsible for the quality of a person's life. Accordingly, a person is rewarded for performance of a *Mitzvah* and punished for its non-performance. And, of course, it is masculine. This masculinity manifests itself, for example, in the fact that *Mitzvot* are directed mostly to men. More over, some claim that men's *Mitzvot* are designed to reflect the 'special relationship' between men and God.[18]

Orthodox Conceptualization

According to this triangular patriarchal conceptualization, these three essential components are portrayed existing in a strict hierarchical order. This order assigns the *Mitzvot*, the laws, a privileged position and, thereby weakens God's Grace, as well as, human Desire. In Orthodox-*Halachic* Judaism, belief in 'Our Father in heaven' has been preoccupied for hundreds of years with the *Mitzvot*.[19] For example, the Orthodox claims that there are 613 obligatory *Mitzvot* (only three of which are directed solely to women). Volumes have been written about each *mitzvah* in order to

---

17. The gendered conceptions of maternity and desired spaces stand in the center of both Luce Irigaray's and Julia Kristeva's works. See Anderson, *A Feminist Philosophy of Religion*; Luce Irigaray, *This Sex which is Not One* (New York: Cornell University Press, 1985); M. Whitford (ed.), *The Irigaray Reader* (Oxford: Blackwell, 1991); Luce Irigaray, *An Ethics of Sexual Difference* (New York: Cornell University Press, 1993); Luce Irigaray, *Je, Tu, Nous: Toward a Culture of Difference* (London: Routledge, 1993); Luce Irigaray, *Thinking the Difference: Toward a Peaceful Revolution* (London: Athlone Press, 1994); *I Love to You*, London: Routledge; Luce Irigaray, *Democracy Begins Between Two* (New York: Routledge, 2000); M. Toril (ed.), *The Kristeva Reader* (Oxford: Blackwell, 1986); J. Kristeva, *In the Beginning was Love: Faith and Psychoanalysis*, (New York: Columbia University Press, 1987); J. Kristeva, *Black Sun: Depression and Melancholia* (New York: Columbia University Press, 1989); J. Kristeva, *New Maladies of the Soul* (New York: Columbia University Press, 1995). However, these two scholars write from within Christian symbolization, that differs significantly from Jewish symbolization, and thus remain beyond this paper's borders.

18. R. Weiss-Goldman, 'I want to bind you in *tefillin*: Women adopting *mitzvahs* of men', in D. Ariel, M. Leibowitz and Y. Mazor (eds.), *Baruch Sheasni Isha? The Woman in Judaism* (Tel Aviv: Yediot Achronot, 1999), pp. 105-25 (in Hebrew).

19. See, for example, M. Wyschogrod, *The Body of Faith: Judaism as Corporeal Election* (San Francisco: Harper & Row, 1983).

explain and to interpret its deepest meanings and the *Halachic* (Law) literature constitutes the largest body of Jewish writing.

At the same time, Orthodox Judaism seems driven to suppress human desire for the Divine. In relating to the family structure, presented earlier, where Desire is ascribed to the child, an associated form of this symbolization, the demand to repress Desire is represented by the repeated sacrifice of children by their fathers in biblical accounts, either in a symbolic or in an historic act: for example, the near sacrifice of Isaac (Genesis 22) and the symbolic sacrifice of Ishmael (Genesis 21) by Abraham; the symbolic sacrifice of Esau by Isaac (Genesis: 27); the actual sacrifice of Jephthah's daughter by her father (Judges 11); and the symbolic sacrifice of Michal by King Saul (1 Sam. 18.20-21, 1 Sam. 25.44, 2 Sam. 3.13-16).

And, in a complementary way, the mother-whore perception associates Desire with the 'bad woman:' the Bible continually compares 'the sons of Israel' who desired to worship gods or goddesses others than YHWH with a whoring wife who prostitutes herself. Such a conceptualization, for example, is the key conception in the Book of Hosea. From this conception one can easily understand the almost obsessive way in which the *Mishnah* and the *Talmud*[20] are preoccupied with the control of sexuality, in general, and women's sexuality in particular.[21]

At the same time, Grace / Motherhood is both glorified and trivialized in the patriarchal conception that is the foundation of Orthodox Judaism. It is glorified as the source of life, as the essence of life, as God's presence: 'Return YHWH, rescue my soul, save me for your grace',[22] pleads the biblical writer(s) to God (Ps. 6.5). However, at the same time in Orthodox Jewish praxis, Grace is trivialized in all manner of rhetorical and practical forms. It is articulated either as marginal to the obligation of the law (private instead of public, imaginary instead of real, passive instead of active, concrete instead of transcendental, emotional instead of rational etc.), or as unreachable in 'this world'.[23]

However, in my point of view, in seeking to preserve the integrity of this complex of mutual conceptualizations, traditional Orthodox Judaism fights a losing battle by attacking the inner forces of a person's soul. Furthermore, it loses the power of the non-masculine components of both the Divine and its creation, for the following reasons:

20. Texts, which are not included in the Bible, but are considered to be sacred.

21. For a deep discussion of this phenomena from feminist perspective, see Plaskow, *Standing Again at Sinai*, pp. 170-210. See n. 2 for details.

22. *'Shuvah Yah' chaktzah nafshi hoshieni lemaan chasdecha'*.

23. For further elaboration of this subject see the *Kabbalistic* perceptions of the *Shechinah* in the next section.

1. *Desire* is not solely a craving and a drive that represses responsibility; it is also the source of belief in other, better options. It is not only a source of danger and threat, but also an opportunity for growth and progress; it is a source of creativity and hope.
2. *Grace* does not belong solely to the next world. Love and forgiveness can—indeed should—be realized first and foremost in the here and now.[24] It is the essence of existence, no less reasonable than action and obligation. It has the capability of connecting past—present—future, will and action, and the other dichotomist categories referred to previously.
3. *Mitzvot* are not only 'obligations', accompanied by 'reward' and 'punishment'. They are also expressions of responsibility and choice whose acceptance or rejection has consequences. As such *Mitzvot* are not only undertaken on behalf of a commanding, all-knowing Father. They exemplify a person's right, ability, and desire to *act* and to take responsibility for the outcomes of such actions.

Historically, alternative forms of religious Jewish discourse have attempted to restore a balanced inter-relationship between these three approaches to the Divine. However, rather than undermining the hierarchical order, such attempts end up preserving it. For example, Hasidism and the Kabbalah (see the next section) tried to reform the hierarchical conceptualization, but eventually surrendered to the supremacy of the law in Judaism (at least until the mid-20th century).[25] Other reformist attempts that refused to surrender to this strict priority of the Jewish law were banished from Judaism (such as, Christianity, on one hand; and Gnosticism and the Sabbatean movement and on the other hand).[26]

Kabbalistic Revision

Critical and mystical approaches within Judaism, including the *Kabbalah* and the *Hasidism*, have long been aware of the consequences that Orthodox Judaism suffers for domination by *Mitzvah* of Desire and Grace.[27]

---

24. I cannot resist citing Irigaray's insightful words: 'Hell appears to be a result of culture that has annihilated happiness in earth by sending love, including divine love, into a time and place beyond our relationships here and now' (Irigaray, *Thinking the Difference*, p. 112. See n. 17 above for details).

25. J. Garb (2005), *'The Chosen will Become Herbs': Studies in Twentieth Century Kabbalah* (Jerusalem: Hartman Institute, 2005) (in Hebrew).

26. S.G. Shoham, *'Nitschon Hmuvasim'*, in *Life as a Midrash*, pp. 271-312.

27. This section is based primarily on my understanding of the important *Kabalist* Rabbi Yehudah Ashlag (See: Y. Ashlag, *Sefer Hahakdanot* [Jerusalem: Press of the

They do so by re-conceptualizing Desire and Grace in a manner that enhances their value. For example, Kabbalistic approaches added feminine aspects to the masculine references to the Divine by reserving the masculine to the transcendental parts of Divinity and assigning the feminine to the *Shechinah*, the Divine presence. In calling for restoration of what they call 'the lost honour' of the *Shechinah*-femininity in the Jewish tradition, they reduce the difference in value between the Law and Grace; and by talking about Desire for God's presence (the Desire for *Geula* = salvation from the *Galut* = exile), they reduce the differences in value between Grace and Desire.

In doing so, the Kabbalistic reformation does not undermine the traditional philosophical perspective, but rather *preserves* it in three important ways:

The first preservation is of the notion of hierarchy. Even if the gaps between the ranks are diminished, they still remain. The gap between *Mitzvah* and Grace, between God and the *Shechinah*, is hierarchical in many ways: The *Shechinah* is God's *Shechinah*. She belongs to him. She is God's wife. God can exist without *Shechinah*, but God's *Shechinah* cannot exist without God. She is weak, can be exiled, can be lost, and cannot be trusted. An example is the phrase 'Kiss of the *Shechinah*' which is a euphemism for death. He, on the other hand, is always the All-Good, the Almighty.

The gap between Grace and Desire presents itself in different ways in the works of different writers. In general, it can be summarized as a perception that sees Desire (*Yetzer*) as the basic drive of creation (*Yetzi-rah*).[28] In its raw state, however, Desire represents temptation, a great

---

Research Center of Kabbalah, 1978]); *Sefer Matan Torah* (Jerusalem: Press of the Research Center of Kabbalah, 1982); A. Ashlag, *Or Habahir* (Jerusalem: Or Yehodah Yeshiva, 1990); A. Ashlag, *Pirush Hasulam Lesefer Ha'Zohar* (Bnei-Brak: Or Hasulam, 1999). All of these books are in Hebrew. Ashlag, along with Rabbi A.I. Kook, is considered to be one of the two most important writers in 20th century *Kabbalah* (see Garb, 'The Chosen will Become Herbs'. For secondary understanding of his writing, see also B. Ashlag, *Shamati* [Bnei-Brak: Derech Emet, 2003] [in Hebrew]) and the teaching of Rabbi M. Lithman in www.kaballha.info.org. For more general approaches to *Kabbalah* literature see, among others: M. Idel, *Kabbalah: New Perspectives* (Tel Aviv: Schocken, 1993 [in Hebrew]); M. Idel, *Absorbing Perfections: Kabbalah and Interpretation* (New Haven: Yale University Press, 2002); G. Scholem, *Mechkarey Kabbala* (Tel Aviv: Am Oved, 1998); G. Scholem, *Pirkay Yesod Behavanat Ha'Kabbalah Usmalia* (Jerusalem: Bialik Institute, 1976) (both in Hebrew). For special gender-sensitive studies of *Kabbalic* thinking see D. Abrans, *Haguf Haelohi Hanashi Ba'Kabbalah* (Jerusalem: Magnes, 2004 [in Hebrew]); O. Ezrachi and M. Gafni, *Mi Mefached Mi'Lilith* (Ben Shemen: Modan, 2004 [in Hebrew]); Ankori and Ezrachi, *The Secret of Leviathan*, pp. 182-210; Plaskow, *Standing Again at Sinai*, pp. 211-24.

28. See M. Rutenberg, *The Yetzer: A Kabbalistic Psychology of Eroticism and Human Sexuality* (Northvale: Aronson, 1997); M. Rutenberg, 'Jewish psychology', in *Life as a Midrash*, pp. 484-514.

danger to the bodily, bestial and unstable nature of 'this world' (*Olam ha-zeh*). Only a transformation of Desire from a 'will to accept' (id, lower ego) to a 'will to give' or the 'will to influence (good)', is capable of transforming people from the bodily existence of raw Desires to the spiritual loving world of the *Shechinah*, and from there — onto God. Only such transformation can bring people from the state of 'this world' to the 'next world'.[29]

The second preservation of the traditional perspective lies in the retention of the gender assumptions included in each component, as can be seen in the last paragraphs. In other words, narrowing the gaps is accomplished without opposing the gender identity associated with these different aspects of Divinity. God remains only male; the *Shechinah* remains only female, his bride; and Desire remains as either the bad woman or the immature parts of the male personhood. From this perspective, for the mature Jewish male, Desire is a drive to attain unification that is achieved by pairing with the female-*Shechinah*, in order to reach the ultimate male — God.

There is almost no Kabbalistic writing about how the Jewish woman reaches either God or the *Shechinah*. Unsurprisingly, the very few extant references are only to 'good women' — the mothers, and not to 'bad women' — the whores. Generally, the common suggestion is for them to pair with their husbands, who in parallel pair with the *Shechinah*, which in turn pairs with God. This pairing will enable 'good women' to fulfil their role in the creation, which is, of course, the role of wifehood and motherhood.

This articulation of the Divine-human relationship obviously preserves patriarchal, dualistic, and hierarchical conceptions of gender. Women fulfill themselves through their bodies, men — through their spirituality; men can reach God by themselves, women need men; the only worthwhile sexual relations are heterosexual relations that should take place only within an official family, one that has received its 'blessing from Heaven'; the only purpose of pairing is creation; and, of course, in doing so there is a total unification between sex and gender.

The third Kabbalistic preservation of the traditional perspective is that of divisibility itself. Here, as in the Orthodox perception, the supposedly un-divided, stays, in effect, divided. Unlike the Orthodox vision, in the Kabbalah the parts of the One can be paired with each other, but they remain nevertheless substantively different from one another. Those parts can never truly dissolve entirely into one another, and the strict boundaries between them are retained. And thus complete unity of the One remains unattainable.

29. See Ashlag's writing, n. 27.

Genderless Divinity

Based on this critique, I claim that the Kabbalistic gender revision is far from sufficient. In my view, not only does the understanding of each component, their application to gender, their assumed values, and the nature of their inter-relationship need to be revised in order to retrieve a less patriarchal conception of the Jewish God, but more fundamentally — the actual conception of the divisibility of the Divine must be reformed. In other words, the conception of unity needs to be reaffirmed based on the axiomatic notion with which I started this discussion; namely that Divinity in Judaism is One. As One, it is neither human nor divisible, neither familial nor gendered.

All forms of patriarchal thinking disguise and in doing so prevent us from experiencing God's unity. Thus, the spirit of the Divine, the holy — in which will, capabilities, and responsibilities are unified — becomes inconceivable. Since these components are presented in patriarchy as separate entities — and even as contradictory to one another — it becomes impossible to conceive of, let alone believe in, such unity.

Accordingly, in my view the feminist project includes a reconceptualization of the Jewish God. As such, this project involves both of the two meanings of the Hebrew word *drash:* it is both a demand and a process of interpretation.

The result of such a process should be a reinterpretation and a reclaiming of a genderless Divinity. In this notion, I do not mean that Divinity does not have different faces. I do mean, however, that these faces of the Divine should not be contradictory, nor even conceived to be complementary to each other. Instead, they are different aspects of the same force that manifests itself through all of its aspects, throughout each one of us. Such a conceptualization does not include an indispensable connection to gender and/or to sex.

Moreover, this notion should not be understood to exist only at the declarative level, as denotation, but primarily as essence. In other words, this return to the universal must resist strongly and openly the patriarchal tendency to identify the universal with the masculine. It should insist that the non-human Divinity manifests itself in hu-wo/man life in all of these aspects. In the patriarchal conception criticized above, some of these aspects are articulated as feminine and others as masculine; some as mature and others as childish; some as spirit and some as body: and so forth. However, according to the reconceptualization they exist indivisibly within the One, as part of the Unity. Not only is there no hierarchical division between components, there is actually no division whatsoever.

Though there is continuous unity of all aspects of the Divine, some can be dominant, just as certain aspects are dominant in a particular society, in a particular personality, in a particular moment of an individual's life. Similarly, all aspects always exist together, admitted or not, in women as well as in men, in adults as well as in children; in all of us. All these different articulations co-exist within Divinity, and accordingly the Divine can neither be conceived of as a human/man being, nor be symbolized, as such.

In my view, such a project of a genderless conceptualization of the Divine does not contradict the principles of Judaism. On the contrary, it restores it to an original path that has been lost. Only a genderless Divinity preserves, truthfully, the principle of unity. Such a conceptualization not only exists beyond the differential value of masculinity and femininity and maturity and childishness in patriarchal thinking, but also beyond the dichotomies that characterize such thinking. In such a conception, there would be no division by gender, nor any of the other types of divisions referred to throughout this essay. Furthermore, worship through such a conceptualization of Divinity may bring a person to the point where Mitzvah, Grace, and Desire are unified/one; in which the mother, father, and the child are one within it.

Such a project is not unique *to* Judaism. Similar attempts have been undertaken in other religions. However, such an effort is unique *in* Judaism in two ways. In a positive direction, two principles support advancement of this feminist conceptualization. The first is the emphasis in Judaism on God as non-human existence and the prohibition of representation in human form, as discussed earlier. The second is the tradition of investigating Divine intentions. Within this tradition the 'meaning' of the sacred is considered to be greater, richer, and more dynamic than the strict literal interpretation, and thus the evolution of ideas is considered to be a cumulative manifestation of God's divine providence in itself. From this perspective, novelty in God-perception is not only accepted, but encouraged.[30] These two principles make the attempt to fashion a genderless Divinity through the use of Jewish resources relatively 'user-friendly'.

In a negative direction, it is impossible to escape the gendered nature of the Hebrew language, discussed earlier. These linguistic forms, along with the longstanding, strict patriarchal practices of the religious establishment, which lie outside the purview of this dissertation,[31] are a difficult challenge for this project.

---

30. For a brilliant analysis and use of this tradition from a feminist perspective see Ross, *Expanding the Palace of Torah*, pp. 197-212. See n. 2 above.

31. The subject of the patriarchal practices of the Jewish religious establishment is

Personal Epilogue

I wish to conclude on a personal note. As a feminist believer who is not attached to the religious establishment, prayer (in Hebrew) is my most difficult challenge today. In my view, one of the basic reasons for believing in the existence of a system, energy, a law that is greater than myself, and in which I have a place, is that such a belief brings into my life a force that I can turn to and from which I can receive. Belief such as this requires the existence of prayer—as a medium of communication between a person and the Divine. Yet, how can one pray to a genderless Divinity if the language employed does not include words that enable any form of genderless expression?

'God *is* my answer', I said to myself when I chose to believe in the Divine. However, there is no Hebrew expression, such as the English 'is', that conceals gender, only HIM. And, thus, this one embryonic sentence presents the challenge with which I am struggling today: the challenge to close the verbal gap between myself—a feminist woman—and my genderless Divinity.

I still do not have an answer to this challenge. At the end of the day I still have to speak of the Divine in Hebrew, a language in which God only can be referred to in the masculine form. Yet, when I speak in such a manner now, my *kavanah*[32]—my intention, as well as my direction—is to something else. Given my language's limitations, I am incapable of speaking, indeed even thinking, of the Divine in the most ultimate of senses—as a unity—in genderless terms. But while it seems that this may be the case forever, I have succeeded recently in creating a complete prayer—in Hebrew—to a genderless Divinity. Speech in this prayer is directed neither to a Female nor to a male. This may seem a minor achievement, as it is only one short prayer. Yet, it has taken me three years to articulate.

Is the effort to refashion a Genderless-One-Divinity worthwhile? And, if so, why? My answer is yes, most definitely. First, I have in my life Divinity in which I can participate, with all of the strength, hope, and affirmation that this concept has for me. Such belief is a primary

---

the key consideration of most Jewish-feminist thinking, which tends to neglect theological questions in favor of practical concerns that are assumed to be more urgent. See H. Lahav, 'Reviewing Plaskow's "The Coming of Lilith"', in *Nashim* 12 (Fall 2006), pp. 301-308.

32. The Hebrew word *kavanah*, meaning both direction and intention, is a key notion in Kabbalistic thinking. It symbolizes, on the one hand, the inner changes that a person must undertake in order to reach divinity; and, on the other hand, the attempt to repair oneself as well as the world.

aspect of my personal development. Second, I see a similarity between belief in such Divinity and my feminist belief. Both differ, significantly, from the hegemonic secular-liberal belief surrounding me. In proposing an alternative to it, they fracture it and thus allow new options to present themselves. Both offer a vision, a dream, a belief in the possibility of a better existence, on both personal and social levels. Both suggest *tikun*,[33] – a repairing of the world and of the individual. Hope is the essence of my belief both in the Divine and in Feminism.

And thus I say to my *Divinity: Bruchi Eti El'Yha, Ruach Ha'Olam.*[34]

33. The Hebrew word *tikun*, meaning renewal, repair or fixing, is a key notion in Kabbalistic thinking. It symbolizes the human ability to reach not only expiation, but to *repair* the world, as well as, themselves through devotion to Divinity.

34. This phrase is a deliberate distortion of the traditional Jewish blessing 'Baruch ata Adonay melech ha'olam' that can be translated as 'Blessed be you (in masculine) Lord, king of the world'. 'Bruchi' is a non-existent word: neither Baruch (masculine) nor Brucha (feminine) but a non-gendered form which is not possible in the Hebrew. The ending 'ei' applies to First Person Singular. So Bruchi means, 'blessed genderless-you/ me', referring to the genderless nature of Divinity and its ability to blur the boundaries between first, second and third person. The same applies to 'Ati'. El is 'God', but also 'to' or 'towards'. Yha is one of the names of the Jewish God (referring to the explicit name Y-H-W-H). Putting together those two words I create the word elyah, which means 'to/towards her'. So there is a game of words here, creating a feminine figure out of two masculine manes of God. Also El-Yha refers to the biblical story of Hagar, how was the only woman in the Bible who gave God a name, El-Hay (God-is-alive or Living-God). 'Ruach' – spirit or wind. This is one of the rare words in Hebrew that can be used both in masculine and feminine forms. And of course, it represents different power relations from the traditional 'king'. 'Ha'olam' is the world or the universe. The resulting blessing is, 'Blessed be (the genderless) you/me, El-Yah (named God/to her), the (genderless) Spirit of the Universe'.

[4]

Gender and Sexuality in the Garden of Eden

Jerome Gellman

gellman@bgu.ac.il

Abstract

Various attempts have been made to argue that the plain meaning of the story of the Garden of Eden in Genesis 2–3 supports a feminist, or at least a woman-friendly, understanding of the gender and sexual relationships between Adam and Eve. I counter that these arguments are not convincing and are hard to square with the biblical text, by considering four central elements in the story: (1) The sexual nature of *ha'adam*, Adam/the earthling at the start of our story; (2) God's 'curse' of Eve; (3) The meaning of the woman being a 'helper' to Adam; and (4) Adam's naming of the woman. I conclude that the most plausible meaning of these chapters is that Adam dominates Eve sexually and otherwise from the very moment of Eve's creation.

Keywords: Garden of Eden, Adam, Eve, patriarchy in the Bible, feminist interpretation, sexuality in the Bible, Phyllis Trible, Phyllis Bird

Feminist theologians who wish to retain some manner of commitment to Hebrew Scriptures have an intimidating task. One way of dealing with that task has been to seek out neglected counter-trends in the Hebrew Bible, highlighting relevant passages or stories against the prevailing patriarchal ethos.[1] Within that mode lies the attempt to take hitherto

---

1.   A paradigm of this method is Ilana Pardes. In an intriguing argument, Ilana Pardes contends that Genesis 4 contains a counter tradition to Genesis 2–3. According to Pardes, in the former, Eve usurps the male prerogative of naming, creation, and power-over. See *Countertraditions in the Bible, A Feminist Approach* (Cambridge, MA: Harvard University Press, 1992).

regarded severely androcentric passages and to contend that a correct reading of them reverses or at least ameliorates their androcentric nature. Paramount in this genre has been the treatment by some feminists of the biblical story of Adam and Eve in the Garden of Eden.

The story of Adam and Eve in Genesis, chs. 2–3, has historically been taken to endorse male normativity, especially in sexuality. There have been some exceptions, in medieval times in particular, which had little impact over time:[2] Adam is the normative sexual being to whom Eve is subordinate. This, in turn, has helped shaped gender attitudes for the Western religious tradition.[3]

Consequently, some feminist thinkers have pounced on the story as evidencing severe patriarchy at the very heart of Western civilization.[4] Other feminists, however, disagree. The most influential of these is Phyllis Trible, with Mieke Bal, Phyllis Bird, and Carol Meyers having written important revisionist articles on the topic as well. In her richly argued and highly influential work on Genesis 2–3, Phyllis Trible aims to establish that, 'Rather than legitimating the patriarchal culture from which it comes, the myth places that culture under judgment.'[5] Her basic thesis is this: Originally, the woman and the man enjoyed an egalitarian relationship. Things were supposed to be this way. When this relationship was corrupted, the patriarchal arrangement came into being. Our story, then, records the severe androcentric social reality that came about because of the 'fall' from gender equality. Hence, our story does not see the severe androcentrism of the Hebrew Bible as an ideal, but as an aberration from the ideal.

Mieke Bal has a more moderate agenda than Trible. Her 'interpretation of Eve's position shows her in a more favorable light than do the common uses of the text,' yet, unlike Trible she says, 'I do not want to suggest that this is a feminist, feminine, or female oriented text.'[6] Rather,

2.   For some of these exceptions see David Clines, *What Does Eve Do to Help? And Other Readerly Questions to the Old Testament* (Sheffield: JSOT Press, 1990).

3.   For a detailed history of this influence see Pamela Norris, *Eve: A Biography* (New York: New York University Press, 1999) and John A. Phillips, *Eve: The History of an Idea* (New York: Harper and Row, 1984).

4.   See, for example, Elisabeth Schlusser Fiorenza, *In Memory of Her* (New York: Crossroad, 1986), Kate Millett, *Sexual Politics* (New York: Doubleday, 1970) and Eva Figes, *Patriarchal Attitudes* (Greenwich, CT: Fawcett, 1970).

5.   Phyllis Trible, 'Eve and Adam: Genesis 2-3 Reread,' in Carol P. Christ and Judith Plaskow (eds.), *Womanspirit Rising: A Feminist Reader in Religion* (San Francisco: Harper's, 1979), p. 81.

6.   Mieke Bal, *Lethal Love: Feminist Readings of Biblical Love Stories* (Bloomington, IN: Indiana University Press, 1987), p. 110.

Bal hopes to reveal the 'problematization' of male ideology in the story. Her reading of the Garden of Eden is meant to be more 'woman-friendly' than hitherto.

Phyllis Bird contends that while the story of Adam and Eve in Genesis 2–3 does center on Adam, it does so only in treating him as 'representative of the species.' The story is not about gender and sexuality, but about the 'place of humans within the created order.'[7]

Carol Meyers is after a nuanced understanding of the complexities of gender relations in Ancient Israel and how these complexities surface in Genesis 2–3. She wishes to look at the text when 'the barriers of traditional perspectives are removed,' so as to 'place the Eve and Adam tale in the context of ancient Israelite life.'[8] Her purpose is to critique a monolithic understanding of male domination of women.

These feminist thinkers, and others like them, wish to convince us that *their* readings are true to the original intent of the biblical author rather than the severe patriarchal interpretation that grew up, on their view, only afterward. Just as workers in the Sistine Chapel uncovered Michelangelo's true colors below the accumulated grit of history, so these writers mean to uncover the true, original non-androcentrism of the story of Adam and Eve below the accretion of tradition.

Susan Lancer has critiqued the revisionist understanding of Genesis 2–3, from the vantage point of speech-act theory.[9] Unlike Lancer, in what follows I wish to focus on the language of the text itself to raise serious difficulties with these woman-friendly readings of the story of Adam and Eve. In addition, in order to critique what I take to be the strongest argument in favor of the revisionist readings, namely that male domination, including sexual domination, entered only with the 'curse' on Eve, I will provide a new, severely androcentric understanding of the 'curse' on Eve, that is at least *as plausible* as the revisionist argument. I will conclude, to my sorrow, that a case for the new feminist reading of the Adam and Eve story is very difficult to defend. Feminist theology cannot discover its message buried in the text of this story in the Bible.

The central elements in the revisionist readings of the story of the Garden of Eden are: (1) The true sexual nature of הָאָדָם (*ha'adam*), Adam/ the earthling at the start of our story; (2) God's curse of Eve; (3) the

7.   Phyllis A. Bird, 'Bone of My Bone and Flesh of My Flesh,' *Theology Today* 50 (1993), pp. 521-34.

8.   Carol Meyers, *Discovering Eve: Ancient Israelite Women in Context* (New York: Oxford University Press, 1988), p. 79.

9.   Susan S. Lancer, '(Feminist) Criticism in the Garden: Inferring Genesis 2-3,' *Semeia* 41 (1988), pp. 67-84.

meaning of the woman being a 'helper' to Adam; and (4) Adam's naming of the woman.

The Earthling

Phyllis Trible claims the earthling, אדם *adam*, to have been androgynous or sexually undifferentiated at the start. In her earlier treatment of our story she writes:

> Ambiguity characterizes the meaning of *'adham* in Genesis 2–3. On the one hand, man is the first creature formed (2:7).... On the other hand, *'adham* is a generic term for humankind. In commanding *'adham* not to eat of the tree of the knowledge of good and evil, the Deity is speaking to both the man and the woman (2:16-17). Until the differentiation of female and male (2:21-23), *'adham* is basically androgynous: one creature incorporating two sexes.

Later Trible took a different view:

> Although the word *ha-adam* acquires ambiguous usages and meanings – including an exclusively male reference – in the development of the story, those ambiguities are not present in the first episode. Instead, the earth creature here is precisely and only the human being, so far sexually undifferentiated.[10]

Bal echoes the latter view:

> First, a sexless creature is formed. The first body, *the* body, unique and undivided, is the body of the earth creature, the work of Yahweh the potter. From 2:7 to 2:20 this creature has no name, no sex, and no activity. It emerges as a character-to-be, showing by what it has not, how a character should be. This first step is nothing more than the positing of existence of a potential character.[11]

Similarly Meyers:

> Certain words may be rendered as masculine in places where they are not meant to specify gender. Perhaps the best example is the generic word for 'human,' *'adam*, which permeates the creation tales and appears frequently elsewhere in the Bible. This word is usually, if not universally, translated as 'man.' In most cases the gender specific value of the word 'man' is thereby erroneously attached to a collective singular Hebrew word designating 'human' life, as a category to be distinguished from God on the one hand and animals on the other.[12]

---

10. Phyllis Trible, *God and the Rhetoric of Sexuality* (Overtures to Biblical Theology; Philadelphia: Fortress Press, 1978), p. 80.
  11. Bal, *Lethal Love*, pp. 112-13.
  12. Meyers, *Discovering Eve*, p. 81.

These authors' claim of an initial androgyny or undifferentiated sexuality is meant to ground an original equality of man and woman in our story. This original equality is meant to support the view that male domination of women arose only from a corruption of the ideal. Male domination allegedly arises only in God's curse to Eve at 3.16 after the sin of eating from the Tree of Knowledge.[13]

However, neither androgyny nor sexual neutrality fit the Bible's description of the creation of the woman or what takes place subsequently. Androgyny does not fit the description of the woman being made from a *side* of the earthling. This implies that the woman's body was shaped from there and not somehow separated out from the intermixed body. God 'fashioned,' ןביו (*va'yiven*), literally, 'built' the woman out of the earthling. The implication is clear that God shaped the woman out of a piece of the earthling, rather than separating the two from one another. Similar considerations count against the original earthling having been sexually undifferentiated. While God 'fashions' the woman, we can deduce from Scriptures that God does not have to 'fashion' the earthling in any way.

More convincingly, perhaps, that the earthling was originally sexually a male is verified by its retention of its name and the consciousness of its own continued identity after the forming of the woman. The earthling had been called האדם (*ha'adam*), 'the *adam*,' as a play on the word אדמה (*adamah*), earth, from which it had been formed. The name *adam*, however, remains the name of the male earthling who survives the emergence of the female. It is this male alone who is referred to as *ha'adam* after the formation of the woman in 3.23, 9, 12, and 20. (The name also quite clearly refers only to the man in v. 22 where God frets that *ha'adam* will now eat from the Tree of Life, and therefore expels *ha'adam* from the garden to till the soil, a male occupation. Previously the woman is referred to explicitly 13 times. This includes when both the man and the woman are mentioned separately as hiding together. It does not say that '*ha'adam*' hid. Therefore, there is no basis for thinking that the word '*ha'adam*' here includes the woman.) Were '*ha'adam*' the name of an androgynous or undifferentiated earthling, we should expect that there would now be new names for each of the *new* male and female beings that emerged. But there aren't.

It is not only the earthling's name that continues after the emergence of the woman. After the creation of the woman, the original earthling's

13. Lancer concurs with this understanding of the linguistic meaning of *ha'adam*, arguing only that the writer *expected* the audience to assume that the earthling was male. See Lancer, '(Feminist) Criticism,' p. 72.

self-consciousness remains exactly as it had been before. Upon awakening, the earthling retains its previous self-identity and consciousness of self when he declares that he has found what he had been looking for previous to the creation of the woman. His post-operative consciousness is thus *the same* as that of the earthling who preceded the creation of the woman. This shows that the earthling was exclusively sexually a male all along.

The considerations I have brought here invalidate the allegation that the word שׁיא (*ish*), the Hebrew word for 'man' occurs first only after the creation of the woman, implying that previously the earthling had not been a man. If we contend that only *then* does maleness arise together with femaleness, the problems I have raised remain unsolvable. On the other hand, if we assume that the earthling was male from the start, we will be able to explain the earthling's speech as no more than an etymological confirmation that the woman gets her life as an extension of the man, just as her name is an extension of his.

The claim of original equality of man and woman, however, does not rest solely on the alleged non-maleness of the earthling. It also rests on God's address to Eve.

God's Address to Eve

That God's address to Eve states that 'He shall rule over you,' clearly intimates that until then man was not destined to dominate woman, or so Trible reasons:

> Of special concern are the words telling the woman that her husband shall rule over her (3:16). This statement is not license for male supremacy, but rather it is condemnation of that very pattern. Subjugation and supremacy are perversions of creation. Through disobedience, the woman has become slave. Her initiative and her freedom vanish. The man is corrupted also, for he has become master, ruling over the one who is his God-given equal.

Phyllis Bird takes a view similar to Trible's:

> The woman's dependence on the man gives a social dimension to her pain that is lacking in the man's. A hierarchy of order is introduced into the relationship of the primal pair. Mutuality is replaced by rule. Patriarchy is inaugurated as the sign of life alienated from God. The rule of man over woman, announced in Genesis 3:16, is the Bible's first statement of hierarchy within the species, and it is presented as the consequence of sin.[14]

If we assume equality from the start, we can make good sense of male domination being invoked subsequently upon the woman. But if there was no equality to begin with, as I am claiming, how can we understand

14. Bird, 'Bone of My Bone,' p. 527.

Eve's subordination to the man to have come about as the result of her sin? My reply begins by noting two characteristics of God's announcement to the woman in 3.16 that the man shall rule her:

1. It is only God's addresses to the snake and to man that mention a curse. In v. 14 the snake is declared ארור (*arur*) or accursed, and in v. 17 the earth is declared ארורה (*arura*) because of man. Although the curse does not apply directly to the man, clearly he is being cursed by way of the curse put on the land 'because of' him. However, the language of curse does not appear in God's address to the woman in 3.16.
2. God's addresses to both the snake and the man begin by alluding to the sin each had done. Verse 3.14 begins in this way: 'And the Lord God said to the snake, "because you have done this..."' And 3.17 opens with these words, 'And to the man he said, "Because you listened to the voice of your woman, and ate from the tree...."' In God's address to the woman in 3.16, in contrast, there is no reference to her sinful act, but simply, 'To the woman he said, "I will increase your pain..."'.

Trible is aware of (1) and (2) and takes them to indicate that God is not giving a punishment to the woman. God's saying 'And he shall rule over you,' is but a remark on the change that has taken place from equality to male domination. I suggest a different interpretation of 3.16: harmonious with an originally intended patriarchal relationship between the man and the woman. My interpretation, an unalloyed patriarchal one, is *at least as plausible* as this revisionist contention that 3.16 proves that there was no original intent of male domination. If my proposed interpretation is at least as plausible as the other, then 3.16 cannot stand as a proof of the revisionist interpretation. My interpretation of 3.16 requires backing up to an understanding of Eve's sin with the Tree of Knowledge.

Eve's Sin

On my alternative reading, intended to be at least as plausible as the revisionist one, the story of the Tree of Knowledge is about Adam's sin of eating from the Tree of Knowledge. Eve is but an auxiliary to the story. In Gen. 3.1-6, shrewdly, cunningly, the snake works through the woman to get *Adam* to eat from the tree. It speaks to the woman, gets her to eat from the tree, counting on her getting carried away and then giving the fruit to Adam. The snake's shrewdness works. It succeeds in getting *Adam* to eat from the forbidden tree. Let's see how this story takes form.

Since she was created after God had given the prohibition on the tree to Adam, Eve did not know of the forbidden tree (remember that in this version Adam is exclusively male all along!). God is not recorded as repeating the command to Eve after her creation. So Adam was the one to declare the prohibition to Eve (perhaps adding the prohibition himself on touching the tree, which God nowhere decreed, in order to paternally keep Eve away from trouble[15]). We should not be surprised that the Bible does not record Adam conveying the prohibition to Eve. In the Pentateuch typically God speaks to men, and it is understood that the men convey God's words to women, without that ever being mentioned. For example, when God changes Sarai's name to Sarah and blesses her, the news is not given to Sarah, but to Abraham (Gen. 17.5). Nowhere does the Bible record Abraham's passing on God's word to Sarah, though we are supposed to believe he did. Another example: When the Israelites prepare to receive the Torah at Mt Sinai, Moses speaks to the 'people' (Exod. 19.15), which turns out to be to the men only: 'And he said unto the people: "Be ready against the third day; come not near a woman."' We are supposed to assume that the men convey the Word to the women, without that being mentioned.[16]

Why did Adam think that the divine prohibition applied to Eve as well as to him? After all, the original command was given to Adam in second person singular. The answer is that Adam sees the woman as an extension of himself, 'flesh of his flesh,' spirit of his spirit (Gen. 2.23), and therefore obligated by the command in a derivative way. Eve seems to have internalized her derivative status when to the snake she quotes God as saying, 'You,' in the plural, meaning her and Adam, must not eat from the tree (Gen. 3.3). She does not say, 'I' may not eat from the tree. She does not perceive the prohibition to apply to her directly and individually. In fact, Adam may even not have told her of nature of the tree.[17] When speaking to the snake, in 3.3, the woman refers to the Tree of Knowledge simply as 'the tree in the middle of the garden.' Adam may have simply issued an authoritative stricture, in the name of God, without explanation of the nature of the tree.

My point is that Adam figures as the authority and Eve as subject to him. Indeed, it is this that gets him in trouble. For where is Adam when Eve meets the snake? We may assume that he is not present, since no mention is made of his presence. Furthermore, it is hard to imagine that were he present he would not have been engaged in the goings on in one

15. This paternal attitude toward the woman appears in rabbinic literature in *Avot D'Rabbi Natan*, ch. 1: 'How do we know that Adam made a boundary to [God's] words? For God told him that he must not eat from the tree of good and bad. But from Eve's words we learn that Adam put a boundary on her.'

16. This situation is the reason for Judith Plaskow's, *Standing Again at Sinai: Judaism from a Feminist Perspective* (San Francisco: HarperCollins, 1990).

17. This is Gunkel's view. See Hermann Gunkel, *Genesis* (Macon, GA: Mercer University Press, 1997), p. 16.

way or another, either to protest or acquiesce.[18] The snake deals with Eve in the absence of Adam, getting Adam to eat through her. No significant dialogue then passes between Adam and the woman when she hands him the fruit (see Gen. 3.6). The woman is not *a temptress*. She does not tempt him to eat from the tree. She simply gives it to him in her enthusiasm. ('Women are like that!')

Since the man was not present at the scene of her eating, we can suppose that he was unaware that this fruit was forbidden. Neither did he inquire as to the fruit's origin; he thought he didn't even have to ask from where she picked the fruit. He was extremely impressed with his own authority and by the boundaries he had placed on the woman. He need not worry, he thought, that she would defy his command to her.

Adam knew that he had eaten from the tree of knowledge of good and evil when immediately after eating its fruit he had undergone a magical change of consciousness, of embarrassment at being naked. So, when God comes walking through the garden Adam hides, with 'his woman.' That the story is about Adam eating from the tree, and that Eve figures only as an auxiliary to the main event, is well testified in Gen. 3.9 by God's now calling to Adam and Adam only, 'Where are you,' when both Adam and Eve hide from God. God is not concerned with the woman's whereabouts.

Adam blames God for not having put an obedient enough personality into the woman: 'The woman *you* gave me, she gave me from the tree, and [that's why] I ate,' (3.12). The woman, that is *God*, who created her defective, is to blame. God, on the other hand, blames Adam. Adam thought he could just give Eve instructions about the tree and sit back and relax. Adam thought his authority could carry the day. God's punishment to Adam, therefore, is not directly for *eating* from the tree, but for heeding the woman's offer to eat the fruit, which then resulted in his eating from the tree. (My reading happens to agree with the *Standard Revised Version of the Bible* that inserts a comma between the heeding of the woman's voice and eating from the tree: 'Because you have listened to the voice of your wife, and have eaten of the tree, etc.' I note this as an interesting fact, not as support!)

Bear in mind that at this point in our story, which has heavily anthropomorphic features (such as God walking through the garden and making

---

18.   Adam's absence is an accepted position in rabbinic literature. According to Rabbi Aba bar Kuriah, in *Genesis Rabbah*, 19.3, Adam had fallen asleep, after intercourse, and according to the 'Rabbis' there, God had taken Adam on a tour of the world. Also, when Christian art depicts Eve's sin, it typically portrays Adam as absent or meanwhile preoccupied with other matters. See Norris, *Eve: A Biography*.

clothes for the couple), God appears as not knowing, or at least as pretending not to know, what had transpired. God knows, or pretends to know, only what he learns from God's interrogation of the man and the woman. When Adam reports (3.12), 'The woman you put at my side she gave me of the tree, and I ate,' God immediately turns to the woman accusingly, 'What is this you have done!'? God accepts Adam's testimony completely! She is given no chance to offer her version of the story. Male testimony determines reality. So far, no mention has been made of the woman eating from the tree. God had not known (or pretended not to have known) that Adam had eaten from the tree. God also does not know (or pretends such) that the woman ate from the tree. Hence, God's question can refer only to her having given the fruit to her man.

The woman then gives a defense of her having given the fruit to the man: 'The serpent duped me, and I ate.' God learns for the first time that she ate from the tree. She is saying to God that hers was not a vicious, premeditated act of trying to corrupt the man. Her giving him the fruit was part of an episode in which the snake worked on her to get carried away and taste the fruit. She then gave it to Adam in a moment of loss of self-control. Surely, God would have mercy on her.

We might have expected God to reply to her now, 'What! You *too* ate from the tree!?' God does not do so. *Nowhere in this story does God reprimand the woman for eating from the tree!* That is because her cardinal transgression, and what she was held accountable for, was not her eating the forbidden fruit, but her causing 'her man' to eat![19] And that came about because she failed to heed Adam's decree.

Now we can understand why God's address to the woman, 'And he shall rule over you,' in v. 16, after the sin, is not called a curse and why in that verse no mention is made of her sin. When first fashioning the woman from the man, she was subordinate to Adam, but God had not taken sufficient care to make her in such a way that she would be obedient to her man. Although Adam had told her not to eat from the tree, she was persuaded to do so. God must now rectify matters, to add into the women a mechanism to guarantee that she will obey her husband. The mechanism is this: she will have such a strong sexual desire for him that she will then have a self-serving reason to want to obey his wishes. That the woman will have great pain in childbirth is an indication of how strong will be her sexual desire for the man. It will be so strong as to overshadow her fear of the consequences should she conceive and give birth. (My interpretation fits the translation of the *Standard Revised*

---

19. Could it be that Adam was wrong and that the prohibition on eating did not apply to the women?

Version of the Bible with the word 'yet:' 'To the woman he said, "I will greatly multiply your pain in childbearing; in pain you shall bring forth children, *yet* [my emphasis] your desire shall be for your husband, and he shall rule over you."') The result: He will rule over you.

The weakness of woman will be corrected for in this way. God now sees to it that Adam will rule over her, especially in sexual domination, not only *de jure* but also *de facto*. This is not a punishment for her sinful act, but a corrective to her character for the sake of man. And neither is it a curse. The instigator and the transgressor, the snake and the man, are involved in curses. The intermediary, the weak link in the chain, the woman, requires *correction*.

Am I certain that this version of the story is the correct one? No. But that is not the issue. I claim only that it is at least as plausible as the version in which man and woman are originally equal. And when we add the difficulties I have noted with thinking the earthling was not sexually male to start with, this is especially so. But on my reading of the story, that God tells the woman only now after the sin that the man is to rule her, does not imply that she was not fashioned for this station from the very start. I conclude that a case has not been made for the evidence that man and woman were equal to begin with and that male domination, including sexual domination, entered only as a curse over the woman.

The Woman as 'Helper'

Trible contends that the woman was an equal 'helper' to the man:

> The phrase needing explication is 'helper fit for him.' In the Old Testament the word *helper* (*'ezer*) has many usages…. In our story, it describes the animals and the woman. In some passages, it characterizes Deity…. Thus *'ezer* is a relational term; it designates a beneficial relationship; and it pertains to God, people, and animals. By itself, the word does not specify positions within relationships; more particularly, it does not imply inferiority. Position results from additional content or from context. Accordingly, what kind of relationship does *'ezer* entail in Genesis 2:18, 20? Our answer comes in two ways: (1) The word *neged*, which joins *'ezer*, connotes equality: a helper who is a counterpart. (2) The animals are helpers, but they fail to fit *'adham*. There is physical, perhaps psychic, rapport between *'adham* and the animals, for Yahweh forms (*yasar*) them both out of the ground (*'adhamah*). Yet their similarity is not equality. *'Adham* names them and thereby exercises power over them. No fit helper is among them. And thus the narrative moves to woman…. God is the helper superior to man; the animals are helpers inferior to man; woman is the helper equal to man.

And:

> The Hebrew word *ezer* … has been traditionally translated 'helper' — a translation that is totally misleading because the English word *helper* suggests an

330   *Theology & Sexuality*

assistant, a subordinate, indeed, an inferior, while the Hebrew word *ezer*
carries no such connotation.... In our story the accompanying phrase,
'corresponding to it' (*kenegdo*), tempers this connotation of superiority to
specify identity, mutuality, and equality.[20]

Meyers concurs. She asks, 'How does 'one who helps' or 'helper' stand
in relationship to the one receiving help?' and replies:

Traditional interpretations of this story would have us believe that a helper
is an assistant or subordinate, who renders aid to a master or superior. Yet,
in the Hebrew Bible the noun 'helper' can refer to just the opposite, namely,
to a superior.... The noun 'helper' can thus indicate either a superior or a
subordinate. How can one resolve this ambiguity in any given case?... In
fact, [in Genesis 2] the answer is neither of the possibilities suggested above:
the helper stands neither higher nor lower than the one being helped.
[There is] a nonhierarchical relationship between the two; it means
'opposite,' or 'corresponding to,' or 'parallel with,' or 'on a par with.'[21]

Now, surely 'helper' by itself implies neither subordination nor equality.
Does then כנגדו (*k'negdo*) imply equality as Trible claims? Does the context
of the story imply this, as Meyers claims?

K'negdo need not imply equality between the helper and the helped.
Here's an alternative possibility: The Bible is accounting for the existence
of sedentary social arrangements, wherein men were freed from other
tasks in order to devote themselves to the occupation of farming, or
'tilling the soil.' (No such division of labor exists among animals. Thus,
the human arrangement requires explanation.) Men were peculiarly
marked for farming with the domestication of large animals and their
use in plowing and harvesting. Men were best suited physically to control
the beasts. The biblical text may therefore reflect the understanding that
for the new arrangement to work it was not enough for the animals to
come under man's control. It was also necessary that man have a person
who will assist him by undertaking tasks from which man was to be
relieved. The assistant will be 'opposite him' in the sense of performing
tasks from which he is to be relieved. Thus, the woman is created for the
sake of the success of the man's occupation. Whatever intimacy is to be
between them, the relationship is destined to be defined as one between a
simply 'created' person (the man) and a 'created-for' person (the woman).[22]

Whether the context of the story disambiguates 'helper' as an equal, as
Meyers wishes, depends on how one reads other elements of the story,
particularly whether the earthling was originally a man and whether the
man's twice naming of the woman, once as אשה (*ishah*) and once as חוה

20. Trible, *God and Rhetoric*, p. 90.
21. Meyers, *Discovering Eve*, p. 85.
22. On this point see Clines, *What Does Eve Do to Help?*, pp. 25-48.

(*havva*) implies male domination of the woman. I have already discussed the original nature of the earthling, and now turn to the theme of naming in our story.

Adam's Naming of the Woman

Standardly, scholars maintain that in the ancient world, giving a name implied domination or power over that which was named. I can do no better than to quote von Rad, who writes that, 'Name-giving in the ancient Orient was primarily an exercise of sovereignty, of command.'[23] Hence, Adam's giving names to the animals and to the woman implies his mastery over them. Trible, though, denies that Adam's naming of the woman '*ishah*' fits the biblical naming motif of domination of the name giver over the named:

> Some read into the poem a naming motif. The man names the woman and thereby has power and authority over her.... [However] neither the verb nor the noun *name* is in the poem. We find instead the verb *gara'*, to call: 'She shall be called woman.' Now, in the Yahwist primeval history this verb does not function as a synonym, parallel, or substitute for *name*. The typical formula for naming is the verb *to call* plus the explicit object *name*. This formula applies to Deity, people, places, and animals. [Examples in Gen. 4.17, 25, 26].... Genesis 2:23 has the verb *call* but does not have the object *name*. Its absence signifies the absence of a naming motif in the poem. The presence of both the verb *call* and the noun *name* in the episode of the animals strengthens the point.... In calling the animals by name, *'adham* establishes supremacy over them and fails to find a fit helper. In calling woman, *'adham* does not name her and does find in her a counterpart. Female and male are equal sexes.

And:

> The noun 'name' is strikingly absent from the poetry. Hence, in calling the woman, the man is not establishing power over her but rejoicing in mutuality.[24]

Trible is calling our attention to the fact that when in 2.20 Adam gives names to the animals it says that he called 'names' to them. However, in 2.23, in the first naming of the woman, Adam does not give a 'name' to the woman. He only says what she is to be 'called.' The latter kind of

23.   G. von Rad, *Genesis: A Commentary* (Philadelphia: Westminster Press, 1972), p. 83. See also Claus Westermann, *Genesis 1–11* (Minneapolis: Augsburg, 1984), pp. 228-29, and Herbert Marks, 'Biblical Naming and Poetic Etymology,' *JBL* 114 (1995), pp. 29-50.

24.   Trible, *God and the Rhetoric*, p. 100.

performance, calling and not name-giving, does not entail domination, in Trible's eyes. Not so Adam's second naming of Eve in 3.20, after the sin and consequent corruption of the egalitarian relationship. Says Trible of this event of naming:

> At this place of sin and judgment, 'the man calls his wife's name Eve' (3:20), thereby asserting his rule over her. The naming itself faults the man for corrupting a relationship of mutuality and equality.

And even more strongly, Trible writes:

> Now, in effect, the man reduces the woman to the status of an animal by calling her a name. The act itself faults the man for corrupting one flesh of equality, for asserting power over woman, and for violating the companion corresponding to him.[25]

For Trible, that Adam after the sin *names* the woman, and does not just *call* her something is a tip-off that things have changed. For the first time a hierarchal relationship is installed. A primal egalitarian relationship has been broken.

However, in opposition to Trible, it is a striking fact that when the woman is first brought to the man following her creation she is entirely passive and silent before him. She has no say in the proceedings and there is no hint of mutuality between her and the man. It is a classic naming ceremony, if not by naming terminology, then surely by form.[26] (This was noticed in 1 Tim. 2.11-13, which declares: 'Let the woman learn in silence with all subjection... For Adam was first formed.')

More importantly, the terminological distinction between 'giving a name' and 'calling' faces difficulties. The fact is that we find in the Pentateuch instances of 'calling' alone, without a word for 'name' or 'naming,' in which domination or power-over is clearly implied. Here are three examples: In Gen. 21.31 (which source-criticism assigns to the same source as our story), it says of Abraham that 'he called the place "Beer-Sheva,"' without a word for 'name' or 'naming' appearing. The name sticks and the place becomes a cultic center for Abraham. In Gen. 26.33 once again concerning Beer-Sheva, we are told that Abraham only *called* it שבעה (*shiv'a*), from which came the name 'Beer-Sheva.' And in Num. 32.41, we read that 'Yair son of Menashe went and captured their farms and he called them "Yair's farms."' He then works those farms. The name sticks, as we find in 1 Chron. 2.23 that G'shor and Aram later capture

---

25. Trible, *God and Rhetoric*, p. 133.

26. See Lancer, '(Feminist) Criticism,' p. 73 for a similar argument dependent on speech-act theory.

farms by that name. In all three cases, the calling alone, without a 'naming,' creates a power or dominion of the caller over the called.

On the other side, the explicit giving of a *name* is not always a sign of mastery. In Gen. 16.13 (which source-criticism assigns to the same source as our story), it says of Hagar that 'she called the *name* of God "the God of seeing."' Surely the verse does not imply Hagar's mastery of God. And according to Gen. 22.14, when Abraham's sacrifice of Isaac is inter-rupted, 'Abraham called the *name* of the place א-דוני יראה (*Adonai-yir'eh*), "God will see."' Abraham, however, gains no 'mastery' over the place or the sacred mountain. Indeed, as far as we are told, Abraham never returned to that locale again.

So the meaning Trible makes of the distinction between calling and naming does not hold. Any difference there might be between calling and naming does not affect the way of seeing the relationship between the man and the woman.[27]

On the contrary, what indicates Adam's dominion over the animals is not how he gives them names, by calling or by name giving. What indi-cates dominion is that Adam's names *stick* — whatever name Adam gave, *that would be its name*. Biblical names have semantic meaning, and are not mere designators. Thus an act of naming expresses the meaning that some-thing has for the name-giver. Abraham, for example, when conferring a name on the mountain gives expression to what the place means to him. When the name giver's subjective perspective of the named becomes the accepted name, the name giver's subjective viewpoint has become objec-tified for others, indicating a degree of control or power of the namer over the named. Thus, Abraham's name does not become the mountain's *name* (For example, it is called the 'mountain of Moriah' in 2 Chron. 3.1), but only the source of a *saying*: 'whence the present saying, "On the mount of the Lord there is vision (Genesis 22:14)."'

Adam's name for the woman sticks, too. She is henceforth called by the names he bestowed upon her. Both names confer upon the woman the man's point of view of her. First, she is אשה (*ishah*), simply a 'woman,' derived from איש (*ish*), a 'man.' Secondly, he names her a second time, reasserting his dominion over her after the failure of her obedience with the forbidden fruit. Whereas in the first naming, Adam named her directly in relation to him, for she was taken from man, here he names her חוה (*havvah*) in recognition of her bearing children. It is her sexual

27. See George W. Ramsey, 'Is Name-Giving as Act of Domination in Genesis 2:23 and Elsewhere?' *CBQ* 50 (1988), pp. 24-35, and Lanser, '[Feminist] Criticism in the Garden,' who maintain that calling is no different from naming, on grounds other than those I have given.

desire for her husband and for bearing children that will insure her obedience and thus the stability of the patriarchal arrangement.

Ronald Simkins claims that naming as an act of domination, 'is foreign to the Yahwist's narrative' in our story, since in our story 'name-giving is placed in the context of finding a suitable helper for man.'[28] However, that this is the context does little to mitigate the domination theme. This is especially so since it is the man who names the woman, twice, and that the man's naming determines the names of women for all times. The woman nowhere names the man. His names are givens in the story, outside of human reach. Our narrator is not only telling a local story, but looking ahead to the gender relations created by our story.

Bal has a more complex understanding of Adam's conferring a proper name on the woman, in the second naming. Bal interprets Genesis 2–3 as recounting the development of character in both the man and the woman. At this point in the story, 'Since the characters are completed now, they can receive the label that makes them memorable: proper name.' And, 'The man, in giving her this particular name [*hawwa*], determines the character further: Eve is imprisoned in motherhood.'[29] Yet, there is another side to the naming:

> The fact that she is appointed as the future creator/provider of 'all living,' may very well be signified in the resemblance between her name and Yahweh's, HW being the phonetic actant that opposes the creators to the creatures, signified by DM. Again, this argument is not meant to imply a female superiority but a functional analogy between the two creative forces. Adam, by giving the woman that name, is the very character who stresses this creative function. In his address to the man, Yahweh in his turn highlights Adam's functional relationship to the earth, which, presented both as an antagonistic and as a sympathetic force, is endowed with the actantial position of the opponent. Hence the four are cross-determined: Adam relates Eve to Yahweh; Yahweh relates Adam to earth. The characters are now completed.[30]

Bal's intriguing explanation of the second naming of the woman does not contradict the interpretation I have given it. It is consistent with her proposal that we have here a recognition by Adam of the mechanism by which the woman will wish to be obedient to him: her desire for children. Bal goes further, though, to portray both an imprisonment of the woman in motherhood and an appreciation by Adam of the life-giving

28. Ronald A. Simkins, 'Gender Construction in the Yahwist Creation Myth,' in Athalya Brenner (ed.), *Genesis: The Feminist Companion to the Bible (Second Series)* (Sheffield: Sheffield Academic Press, 1998), p. 45.

29. Bal, 'Lethal Love,' p. 128.

30. Bal, 'Lethal Love,' p. 129.

powers of the woman that the man no longer will have. This sorrow lives together with his celebration of women's motherhood.

To conclude, I believe that the attempt to read Genesis 2–3 as woman-friendly, and to neutralize the theme of male sexual domination, does not and cannot succeed. We are doomed to understand this story as androcentric in nature. Hence, this story cannot serve us as a source for a primal ideal of gender and sexual egalitarianism between men and women. Then what becomes of feminist theology? It can proceed only by boldly declaring independence from its being able to read this biblical text in a favorable light. Feminist theology, if it wishes to remain within a circle of faith, would do better to opt for one of two mechanisms, or both. The first is the creation of 'midrashic' alternatives to scriptural literacy of the story of the Garden of Eden, 'women's midrash.'[31] The second would be openness to the possibility of new revelational moments in our time, including of the full humanity of women, which supplement the old revelation that did not have that teaching.[32, 33]

31.   On woman's midrash see Peninah Adelman, *Miriam's Well: Rituals for Jewish Women Around the Year* (Fresh Meadows, NY: Biblio Press, 1986); Sharon Cohen, 'Reclaiming the Hammer: Toward a Feminist Midrash,' *Tikkun* 3.2 (1988), pp. 55-57; 94-95; Naomi Graetz, 'Response to Popular Fiction and the Limits of Modern Midrash,' *Conservative Judaism* 54.3 (2002), pp. 106-10; Jennifer Gubkin, 'If Miriam Never Danced ... A Question for Feminist Midrash,' *Shofar* 14.1 (1995), pp. 58-65; N. Rosen, *Biblical Women Unbound: Counter-Tales* (Philadelphia: The Jewish Publication Society, 1996). A striking genre of women's midrash is presented in Rivkah Lubitch, *Creative Feminist Midrash* (Ramat-Gan: Bar-Ilan University, n.d.) which speaks of the 'Torah of Miriam' as independent of and complementary to the 'Torah of Moses.'

32.   A feminist view of 'progressive revelation' can be found in Tamar Ross, *Expanding the Palace of Torah, Orthodoxy and Feminism* (Hanover: Brandeis University Press; University Press of New England, 2004).

33.   I am indebted to Charlotte Katzoff, Rakefet Levkovich, Yair Lorberbaum, Yuval Lurie, Ilana Pardes, and Tamar Ross for their valuable comments, and to Naomi Graetz for information on women's midrash.

[5]

The hole in the sheet and other myths about sexuality and Judaism

DAVID S. RIBNER[1] & PEGGY J. KLEINPLATZ[2]

[1]*Sex Therapy Training Program, School of Social Work, Bar Ilan University, Israel,*
[2]*Faculty of Medicine and School of Psychology, University of Ottawa, Canada*

ABSTRACT *For more than two millennia, Jewish communities around the world have found themselves the focus of speculation, misinformation, fear, derision and, at times, envy regarding the sexual beliefs and practices of its members. Over the centuries, some of these perceptions have become powerful enough to reciprocally influence how Jews perceive themselves. This paper seeks to shed light on some of the better and lesser well-known myths which surround sexuality and Judaism. The initial concentration is on a representative view of sexuality, intimacy and related gender expectations as discussed in traditional Jewish sources such as the Bible, Talmud, and Midrash. We then examine a number of myths which have become part of the legends surrounding Jewish sexuality, and look at the origins, where available, of this "common wisdom" and provide source material supporting more accurate information. While this paper focuses on the stigma and preconceived notions regarding Jewish sexuality, our point has application whenever we as sexual health professionals are called upon to educate or practice in the value-laden realm of human intimacy.*

KEYWORDS: *sexual myths; Judaism; culture; religion*

Introduction

As sex therapists and educators we are advised to be culturally sensitive, attuned to our own cultural biases and to be literate about differences in sexual practices among various ethnic, minority and religious groups. We are to understand sexual values in context and to avoid inserting prevailing cultural ethnocentrism into our own interpretations of others' beliefs. As ethical sexual health professionals, we are to be wary of sexual myths about minority groups and to ensure that we do not perpetuate stereotypes, no matter how common they may be. It is in this spirit that we wish to add to the growing literature on sexual diversity by focusing on sexuality and Judaism.

Correspondence to: David S. Ribner, Sex Therapy Training Program, School of Social Work, Bar Ilan University, Ramat Gan 52900, Israel. E-mail: matzeel@hotmail.com

446   *D. S. Ribner & P. J. Kleinplatz*

For more than two millennia, Jewish communities around the world have found themselves the focus of speculation, misinformation, fear, derision and, at times, envy regarding the sexual beliefs and practices of its members. Jews have been accused of such widely divergent practices as sexual witchcraft, forbidding all foreplay or desiring only gentile women. Over the centuries, some of these perceptions have become powerful enough to reciprocally influence how Jews perceive themselves. This paper seeks to shed light on some of the better and lesser well-known myths, which surround sexuality and Judaism.

The initial concentration will be on a representative view of sexuality, intimacy and related gender expectations as discussed in traditional Jewish sources such as the Hebrew Bible (i.e., what Christians refer to as "The Old Testament"), Talmud (i.e., discussion and interpretation of Jewish law), and Midrash (i.e., further elaboration and illustration of Jewish values and beliefs). We then examine a number of myths which have become part of the legends surrounding Jewish sexuality, and look at the origins, where available, of this "common wisdom" and provide source material supporting more accurate information.

The classic prejudice

In January, 2005, I (P.K.) was teaching an undergraduate class in Human Sexuality at the University of Ottawa and covering the history of sexuality in Western civilization. As I covered the laws, mores and traditions of the ancient Hebrews, I mentioned that sexuality was considered holy and sexual desire seen as a gift from God (Genesis, 2:24). Within marriage, sex was regarded as a wife's privilege and husband's responsibility, to be enjoyed by both (Exodus, 21:10). (I asked them to make a particular note of this point as they would see that in later Western history, it would be the other way around, e.g., during the Victorian era.) Traditional sources were cited to indicate that contrary to popular belief, in Judaism sex was intended for purposes of pleasure – equally the wife's pleasure – and not only for procreation (Friedman, 1996). I continued to cover the basics, for example, the notion that sexual relations were so sacred that they were encouraged particularly on the Jewish Sabbath, in order to heighten the marital bond and thereby bring the proper atmosphere of harmony into the home on this holy day.

A student identifying herself as Rebecca stated that although these laws may have been the case thousands of years ago, certainly they did not apply today. I explained that modern Judaism was still governed by Biblical and Talmudic law, even if many Jews were currently unaware of these sex-positive traditions. Rebecca, sure that I was mistaken, added that she knew many Orthodox Jews and that none of them spoke openly about their sex lives in such glowing terms. I assured Rebecca that most young people across different religions often had little accurate information about the religious beliefs of their own heritages; as one who teaches Sex Therapy at Saint Paul University, I had noticed that many of the lay pastoral counselors had little knowledge of Canon law; similarly, many Jews had minimal understanding of Jewish teachings; and many Moslems, and others, were poorly versed in Sharia law, thus enabling injustice and prejudice against Moslems to flourish. Rebecca continued however, emphasizing that she actually knew many Orthodox Jews quite well and that none of the sex-positive material I had covered about Judaism was apparent in her discussions with such Jews.

I responded that Rebecca was directly on point when she drew conclusions based on her observations. However, if she were at all familiar with Jewish traditions, she would know that Jews are not inclined to display openly that which is cherished most. For example, the holiest of Jewish religious objects, the parchment of the Torah scroll, is not normally readily visible. It is not hidden as if it were an object of shame, but rather protected from casual observation. In the course of an ordinary week, it is covered and kept tucked away until the time is right. However, on the Sabbath and on Jewish holy days, the scroll is unwrapped and revealed with the majesty appropriate to the reading of the Torah. Similarly, the "many religious Jews" she knew, if they were truly as observant as she claimed, would not be inclined to discuss their sexuality openly with her any more than they would display a Torah scroll for no particular reason on an ordinary, weekday afternoon. They would be reserving their sexuality to be shared with their husbands or wives, even if that choice might result in misleading interpretations of the part of the casual observer.

Rebecca, still incredulous, explained that as a Jew, albeit a non-observant Jew, she "knew" that ancient Jewish law had been reformed and done away with the restrictiveness of Jewish tradition. I responded that on the contrary, apparently, the Judaism in which she had been raised had conveyed little of the traditional, sex-positive value system that was her heritage. Again, she corrected me, explaining that in her social circle, "all knew that religious Jews only have sex through the hole in the sheet." I suggested that she investigate for herself the origins of that particular, anti-Semitic myth intended to marginalize Jews for most of the last millennium, but asserted that it is most certainly a myth. On the contrary, Jews are prohibited from any barriers during sex (Shulhan Arukh, Even Ha-Ezer 76:13); whatever lingerie the couple might be wearing to entice one another should be substantially removed prior to sex. Nothing is permitted to interfere with the full intimacy of the union of couples during sex; thus, the hole in the sheet is the antithesis of deep Jewish belief in unrestricted sexual intimacy.

Understanding the problem

Rebecca is hardly unique. On the contrary, she is prototypical of individuals, Jewish and otherwise, who believe without question the little they have heard about sexuality and religion and whom we have encountered as sex therapists and educators. The appalling lack of accurate information about sexuality in Judaism has come to be normative. Combined with the myths that thrive in the resulting vacuum, problems are inevitable for Jewish individuals/couples and the clinicians who work with them.

Why is so little known? Historically, Jewish families were to teach their children about sexuality as they matured and especially in preparation for marriage. Sexuality was seen as an intimate and private matter, appropriate for discussion within the home and family and in the context of other Jewish studies but with little public

448   *D. S. Ribner & P. J. Kleinplatz*

discussion. But the politics and context of Jewish education per se were interrupted dramatically by the European Enlightenment and the Shoah, in combination with American "melting pot" values and secular sexual values. Jews who immigrated to the United States in the early decades of the 20th century were encouraged to become Americans first and to assimilate into American culture. Day school Jewish education became the exception rather than the norm for American Jewish children.

By the time the next wave of Jewish immigration hit North America in the late 1940s and early 1950s, the bulk of American Jewry had been out of touch with its roots for almost 50 years. As such, the sex-negative values, which flourished in Christian society during those years, had enveloped American Jews, who lacked the basic Jewish literacy, let alone sophisticated Jewish philosophy, with which to counteract the prevailing American sexual values and beliefs. Given that open discussion of sexuality was frowned upon in American society, and neither Jewish homes nor schools were equipped with the educational tools to teach young Jews about sexuality and Judaism, myths, some transferred from European origins, grew amidst ignorance.

Soon, the phrase "Judeo-Christian tradition" – an oxymoron if ever there was one – came to be popular. Although this phrase is found in secular parlance and even sometimes in Christian theological circles, it has rarely been used in Jewish scholarship. The abundant differences between the traditional, sex-positive, Jewish beliefs and practices as compared to those of neighboring societies have been too discrepant for such a phrase to be valid. The phrase reflects an assumption so embedded in the surrounding cultures that it is beyond question. Nonetheless, it illustrates precisely the lack of knowledge of traditional Jewish sexual values and observances. Whereas there may be some few areas where Jewish and Christian values coincide (e.g., Thou shalt not kill), sexuality is not among them. Nonetheless, in the absence of Jewish literacy within American communities, it was all too easy for the distinctive character of Jewish sexual teachings to be lost. Christian/secular sexual values had begun to infiltrate the thinking of American Jews who did not even know enough to distinguish between their own traditions and those surrounding them. For example, the little known about Jewish sexual laws and traditions focused on the "Thou shalt not"s rather than the "Thou shalt"s.

Strikingly, the little that is communicated was taught or learned selectively. Most Jews – and non-Jews – are convinced, erroneously, that sex is intended for procreation alone in Judaism and as such, the use of birth control is forbidden, as is sex for pleasure. They have heard that some archaic and arcane laws still prohibit Jewish men from touching their "dirty" wives while they menstruate and until their wives wash in a special cleansing bath. On the other hand, they are incredulous when told that Jewish men vow publicly during their wedding ceremonies to provide sexual pleasure to their wives, in addition to providing for their physical wellbeing. Disturbingly, it is news to them that sexual fulfillment is considered essential for the marital bond and is so fundamental to creating happiness and harmony in the Jewish home that it is an intrinsic element of keeping the Sabbath holy.

Furthermore, the current trend in many observant Jewish circles is to put a premium on laws governing the relationship between the individual and God rather than emphasizing the laws governing interpersonal conduct. To the extent that Jewish teachings underplay the value of how Jews treat one another as essential within traditional Jewish values and beliefs, the rich legacy around sexuality has been overlooked and at times distorted.

These laws and traditions have not been lost; they are kept alive in sacred texts and among those who were fortunate enough to have escaped Eastern Europe alive and conveyed their traditions to their children and within the school systems they established in the post-war years. The differences in Canadian immigration patterns versus those of their American neighbors should be dealt with elsewhere. Suffice it to say that the demographic differences were such that a much higher proportion of young Canadian Jews growing up as first-generation Canadians in the 1950s and 1960s received Jewish day schooling at both primary and secondary levels from the outset. Thus, many of the myths that took root so readily in the United States were less likely to take hold in Canada's newer, better-educated, Jewish communities.

Traditional conceptions of sexuality in Judaism

Whereas in Christianity sex has historically held a rather central role as sin and as a source of guilt, in Judaism sex has traditionally been viewed as one of God's gifts, to be appreciated as a form of devotion through joy. There is a rejection of asceticism and celibacy; neither is seen as a virtue although there are times of abstinence (to be discussed below).

Sexual connection provides an opportunity for spirituality and transcendence. When approached with the appropriate intent, it can mean intimate contact with the partner and a glimpse of the heavenly. The appropriate intent is crucial. In Hebrew it is referred to as "kavannah." There is no English equivalent for this term. In Jewish philosophy, it refers to the way one performs what might otherwise be a mundane act (e.g., eating, drinking, studying, washing) so as to imbue it with spiritual significance and sanctity.

The kind of kavannah that partners are to bring to sex is suggested by the Biblical language for sexual relations. Many have joked about the Biblical verb "to know" as if it were a euphemism for sex but on the contrary, there is no prudery here; the term captures, conveys and teaches precisely the nature of the spiritual intent Jews are to bring to lovemaking. Jews are to approach lovemaking so as to deepen their knowledge of themselves, one another, and the sacred in the universe. This is not to deny the purely physical pleasure of sex, but rather to intend this pleasure to be mutual. This physical, emotional and spiritual joining creates sanctity within the marital relationship (Bulka, 1986). According to some traditions, when the partners unite in lovemaking, they are illuminating the emanations of God. It is as though wisdom and understanding/insight come together, thus revealing knowledge. That is, by making love with the appropriate spiritual intent, they are centered in and simultaneously transcending bodily experience and touching the ineffable.

Given this perspective, choice and awareness are integral to sexuality in Judaism. One must be fully mindful during sexual relations lest they be trivialized. As such, there are prohibitions against sex, even within marriage, when one or the other is

450   *D. S. Ribner & P. J. Kleinplatz*

drunk, angry or too tired to be fully engaged and present. In other words, not only is rape forbidden by Jewish law, it is the antithesis of the full, mutual desire, consent and kavannah required to make lovemaking transformative and holy (Friedman, 1996).

This kind of sexuality presupposes a committed, intimate relationship. Technically, in early pre-Biblical Jewish history, there were no laws against premarital sex in that the act of intercourse formalized the partners' commitment to one another. By definition, once a couple had engaged in intercourse, they had, in essence, declared that they would be spending the rest of their lives together. (Deut.24:1 and Shulhan Arukh, Even Ha-Ezer 26:4). Obviously, more public wedding ceremonies have been the norm in Jewish communities for thousands of years. Nonetheless, this obscure piece of history indicates just how seriously sexual relations were regarded in Jewish thinking and belief.

The sexual relationship

Traditional Jewish observance expressly forbids sexual contact between spouses during the days of menstruation and for a week thereafter. These laws governing sexual relations (i.e., Taharat Hamishpacha) represent an inviolate and integral aspect of identity as an Orthodox Jew (Donin, 1972). It has been said that this practice represents "primitive blood taboos" and indicates that menstruating women are unclean, impure, or forbidden from religious observance (e.g., the oft-repeated myth that they are not allowed to come in contact with a Torah scroll). Such notions demonstrate a fundamental ignorance of the meaning of Jewish ritual. The practice, "like all Jewish laws, concerns a spiritual concept outlined by a physical boundary" (Weidman Schneider, 1985, p. 204). We will deal with the complexity of this spiritual/physical dynamic in an upcoming article.

This "two weeks on/two weeks off" pattern of contact characterizes marital life until menopause, with two notable time frame exceptions, pregnancy and nursing (until post-partum menstruation resumes), when uninterrupted contact is permitted. Some potential benefits (e.g., heightened sexual interest after a two-week abstinence) or challenges (e.g., the tension of no physical contact for two weeks) have been the focus of considerable attention (Burt & Rudolph, 2000; Ostrov, 1978; Petok, 2001).

When touch is permitted it is strongly encouraged and the partners are to create an atmosphere in which it is safe to be physically, emotionally and spiritually open and to be known intensely. The tone is of loving-kindness (Bulka, 1986) and the guiding principle is, "Love your neighbor as yourself." The focus is on an intense connection with the person within rather than on superficial characteristics such as appearance. Traditional Jewish teachings about sexuality offer a play on words to communicate the nature of the intimacy to which the couple aspires: The Hebrew word "panim" is translated literally as "face" and figuratively as "what is on the surface." However, when one adds as a prefix the Hebrew letter "bet," meaning "in," before "panim," this creates the word "befnim" meaning "within." The Talmud tells us that this word shift symbolizes the way we are to make love, that is, to move from attending to superficial characteristics, whether in terms of appearance or otherwise, and to direct one's focus on the special person within. Only when one can truly grasp and appreciate the uniqueness of the partner that one is making love with the appropriate kavannah (as described above), is it safe for the partner to let go and be vulnerable on every level simultaneously. (This is in marked contrast to much of North American society in which rates of plastic surgery are skyrocketing and in which one is seeking this actress' nose or that celebrity's breasts.) Thus, although the Talmud encourages men and women to put some care and attention into making oneself appealing and desirable for one's partner, the nature of this desirability is hardly limited to one's looks. In other words, the Talmud articulates what is later translated by Jewish philosopher Martin Buber as the "I-Thou" relationship in contrast to the more objectifying "I-it" relationship (1958). Similarly, it is later encapsulated by Viktor Frankl (1955) as the enduring "loving attitude" which deepens with age and wrinkles, as opposed to mere infatuation, which is inclined to be more transitory.

Myths about sex and Jews

Stereotypes about Jews' sexuality stand in stark contrast with the reality of Judaism's traditional perspectives on sexuality. Historically, images and stereotypes of Jews' sexuality have reinforced the construct of Jew as other; that is, the content of such stereotypes have varied cross-culturally and historically, but in each instance served to maintain the image of the Jew as alien and often evil. Some images have been so bizarre – and effective – that they have persisted and become ubiquitous. For example, the myth that Jews are not permitted direct skin-to-skin contact, let alone sexual pleasure, and as such, must procreate via a hole in a sheet, first appeared in the late Middle Ages. It has kept the image of Jew as foreign alive wherever Jews were found throughout the Diaspora and thus preserved the social order. Other myths have varied over time and place in keeping with the sexual values of the surrounding communities.

Myth #1 – In 19th-century and early 20th century Poland, where Jews made up 10% of the otherwise Roman Catholic population, Jewish women were often depicted as sexually ravenous temptresses. Within that environment, the image of Jew as nymphomaniac helped to maintain the belief that it was best to keep one's physical distance from Jews, while at the same time firmly implanting them in the images of sexual fantasy (Boyarin, 1997). This belief corresponded with Goebel's images of the Jewish man as uncontrollable, sexual animal (Varga, 1981). In contrast, in 1960s to 1970s American pop culture, a period of alleged "sexual liberation," Jews were portrayed as sexually awkward and undesirable. Jewish women were depicted as sexually passive, aggressive, passive-aggressive, demanding yet unresponsive and excessively concerned with their appearances. Jewish men were depicted as intelligent yet emotionally immature, anxiety-ridden, sexually inept and ineffectual. (See *Private Benjamin, Dirty Dancing, Goodbye Columbus, The Heartbreak Kid, Portnoy's Complaint*, Woody Allen's early works, etc.) Intriguingly, now that American Jewish inter-marriage rates hover at 50%, the sexuality of Jews seems to be less of an issue

452   *D. S. Ribner & P. J. Kleinplatz*

(see *The OC, Friends, Dharma and Greg, Beverly Hills 90210,* and *American Pie*). Sexual propaganda as a mechanism of social control has been better documented around stereotypes of black people in the American south than around Jews (Bederman, 1995; Royster, 1997).

Myth #2 – Perhaps no myth regarding sexuality in traditional Judaism has been more pervasive than that of the requirement to have sex through a hole in a sheet. As we have presented above, this is an anathema to the very essence of the place and purpose of sexuality within normative Judaism. The endurance and strength of this myth has influenced not only the non-Jewish world, but Jewish perceptions as well. Rebecca's view, presented in the introduction to this paper, reflects a troubling level of Jewish ignorance about Jewish laws, traditions and practices. In addition, on exceedingly rare occasions we have heard of individual couples, usually the newly observant, who have learned of this myth, assumed it to be true and tried to implement it as part of their sex lives. The newly religious present a particularly fertile soil in which such false practices can take root, erroneously assuming, as they often do, that ascetism is essential to orthodox religiosity, a notion much more Christian than Jewish.

As sexual health practitioners and academics of long standing, we have learned from and enquired among many Jewish communities around the world. We have never encountered any group or sub-group of religious Jews who tolerated, let alone advocated, the practice of sex through a hole in a sheet, nor have we seen any text permitting or even encouraging such a practice. The extent that full skin-to-skin contact represents the norm of marital sexuality is reflected in a Talmudic ruling (Babylonian Talmud, Ketubot 48a, which asserts in part that "...he not follow the custom of the Persians who engage in marital relations with their clothes"), later codified into Jewish law (Shulhan Arukh, Even Ha-Ezer 76:13), stating that if either spouse declares that he or she can only have sex if clothed, this is immediate grounds for divorce.

Other than the need to ridicule or belittle, what, then, is the source of this myth? We offer the following possibilities, aware that none is entirely convincing:

- In the film "Like Water for Chocolate," set in early 20th century Mexico, a newly married couple, about to consummate their marriage, places an embroidered sheet with a hole in it between their two bodies. We have no firm information as to the extent this accurately depicts a common cultural norm for that time and place. However, it is certainly possible that other traditional ethnic groups may have adopted this practice for some or all sexual occasions. That Orthodox Jews, as a traditional ethnic group, would also advocate this practice may be a logical, albeit mistaken assumption.
- Visitors to Jerusalem's Ultra-Orthodox neighborhoods have remarked on sheets with diamond-shaped holes in them hanging from clothes lines. Travelers to Europe, particularly Eastern Europe, may have seen something similar. These are decorative duvet (quilt) covers, with holes only in the top layer of two, in which the duvets are inserted. The embroidery and monogramming on them, particularly around the decorative cutouts, may

not be noticeable from a distance. In addition to being quite useless for any sexual activity – one partner would need to be placed within the two layers, making breathing a problem – hanging a symbol of marital intimacy in public view would violate strong Jewish communal norms regarding modest behavior.

- The Jerusalem Talmud, a somewhat less authoritative source for the codification of Jewish law and custom than the Babylonian Talmud, relates (Yevamot 1b) that Rabbi Yosi ben Halafta had sexual intercourse 5 times "through a sheet." He did this as a way of dealing with a seeming contradiction between two biblical phrases regarding levirate marriages, the practice of marrying a sister-in-law whose husband has died childless. We quote this as an act of intellectual honesty, because this rather obscure source does not appear as a precedent for encouraged behavior in any canon of Jewish law or compilation of communal custom.

- Apparently, this form of denigrating and differentiating between "us" and "them" is hardly unique to Jews. Some mainline Protestants have been said to claim that "everyone knows" that the Amish have sex through a hole in the sheet, just as historically, Southern Baptists "knew" that Roman Catholics "did it" through a hole in the sheet.

Myth #3 – Rebecca's flawed understanding of sexuality in Judaism also included another commonly heard myth, that for Jews, sex is forbidden on the Sabbath and holidays. For generations, Friday night, the Sabbath eve, has also been referred to as "mitzvah night," the night for fulfilling a commandment. While this time of the week engenders a variety of practices associated with Sabbath observance, in this case the specific adjuration is for the married couple to culminate their evening with sexual intercourse.

The range of textual justifications for this practice is broad, however the central themes focus on a parallels between the sanctity of the Sabbath and the sanctity of marital intimacy, and between the spiritual and physical joys of the Sabbath and those of sexual union. The warm, inviting, family atmosphere of the celebratory Friday night meal, including lit candles, flowers, a festive menu and some wine as integral components, functions, in part, as preparatory experiences later leading to sexual activity for the spouses. Both are expected to attain a feeling of desire for one another, so that intercourse results from mutual attraction and not the requirement to fulfill a commandment. The Jewish view of the Sabbath, quite parallel to its view of marital intimacy, seeks to integrate the physical with the spiritual, thereby elevating the naturally mundane to the potentially sacred. Forbidding sex on the Sabbath would be a clear contradiction of this belief.

In addition to the cycle of Taharat Hamishpacha as explained earlier, the Jewish calendar indeed contains days in which sexual contact is forbidden:

- Yom Kippur – The Day of Atonement – a time of introspection, purification, prayer and forgiveness during which each member of the community seeks to accentuate the spiritual and minimize the physical;

454   *D. S. Ribner & P. J. Kleinplatz*

- The Ninth of the month of Av – when the community remembers a series of historical tragedies.

Other than these days, however, no yearly dates mandate restrictions as to otherwise legitimate sexual activity.

Myth #4 – A popular myth holds that the only acceptable justification for sexual relations in Judaism is procreation. From Talmudic times (Babylonian Talmud, Yevamot 12b), learned discussions as to the permissibility of birth control fill literally hundreds of pages in Jewish legal volumes, taking such a topic beyond the range of this paper. Primarily, the debates have centered, not only on the permissibility of birth control, but on when and through which methods as well. As indicated earlier in this paper, marital intimacy is predicated on the dual obligations of procreation and providing the opportunity for sexual pleasure. While the minimum procreative obligation finds fulfillment with two children, one of each sex, strong traditional support exists for the position that every pregnancy is a God-given miracle of creation and thus precludes human interference (Zimmerman, 2005). Indeed, there are those within the Ultra-Orthodox community who live this belief, but observation of family size gives ample evidence to the wide-spread use of birth control, sanctioned or not. If a couple has had six children, from a purely functional perspective, they probably could have had sixteen, and most do not. Reports from our clients and others involved in this area indicate a growing tendency toward leniency in using birth control. We speculate that three factors contribute to this change: a growing awareness of issues regarding women's health, the impact of economic concerns on family size and the availability of birth control options more consistent with traditional Jewish law. Feldman (1968) presents a detailed analysis of this last highly complex and evolving topic.

Myth #5 – Another popular myth is that women's primary role in Jewish sexual traditions is utilitarian or instrumental; that is, she is to produce as many children as possible. There is no consideration for her as sexual subject but only as object. (This myth tends to be articulated differently depending on the speaker's politics.) The evidence demonstrates otherwise. Notwithstanding the commandment to "be fruitful and multiply," the value of making love per se, for both parties, is not to be underestimated. If it is a "mitzvah" to make love to one's spouse in general, it is especially so with a wife who is infertile, post-menopausal or already pregnant (Feldman, 1968). Obviously, no woman in these categories is liable to become pregnant under these circumstances. The importance within Jewish tradition of sexual relations in such situations signifies to the couple, and the wife in particular, that her inherent worth as a sexual being goes beyond her ability to procreate and that she is entitled to pleasure.

In fact, further evidence as to the importance of the wife's pleasure surfaces in several key sources. In a lengthy Talmudic debate about which sexual acts are permitted, forbidden or ideal (Babylonian Talmud, Nedarim, 20a), the guiding consideration emerging from this discussion is whether or not these acts bring satisfaction to the wife. Almost anything that a loving couple might need to do to bring about her sexual fulfillment is deemed acceptable, even if it might not be perceived as ideal in the abstract. In the Iggeret Hakodesh (i.e., "The Holy Letter," typically attributed to Nachmanides though the author is more likely unknown), husbands are encouraged to arouse their wives and bring them to orgasm before they ejaculate themselves. Thus, given the emphasis on female sexual pleasure in Jewish law and tradition, it is evident that the notion that women are merely second-class sexual beings is erroneous.

Conclusion

Simpson and Ramberg (1992) have noted that "Professionals in the field of sex therapy must develop a set of personal values that is both respectful and non-judgmental" (p. 512). Taking this a step further, Bhugra (2002) wrote "Relationships and sexual therapies have to be seen and delivered in the context of an individual's culture and society as well as of prevalent norms when the therapies are being offered. Furthermore, the clinician must be aware of specific cultural and ethnic patterns of relationship behaviors and social mores" (p. 99). While this paper has focused on the stigma and preconceived notions regarding Jewish sexuality, our point has application whenever we as sexual health professionals are called upon to educate or practice in the value-laden realm of human intimacy.

While sensitivity to another's ethnic context stands as a marker of any educational or therapeutic model, experience has taught that cultural blindness may be a greater risk in one's own backyard. The certainty that individuals/couples bring to assumptions about their own families and communities may prove an even more difficult obstacle to surmount. Examining one's own prejudices, "common knowl-edge" and belief systems may cause unpleasant tremors in the foundations of clients' and students' worldviews. Denying the importance of such open-minded self-exploration for sexual health professionals, too, runs the risk of failing to understand those we have undertaken to help. As no ethnic group holds a monopoly on prejudice, so no ethnic group holds a monopoly on honesty.

Acknowledgement

We would like to thank Rabbi Reuven P. Bulka, Ph.D. for his constructive sug-gestions on an earlier draft of the manuscript.

References

BEDERMAN, G. (1995). *Manliness and civilization: A cultural history of gender and race in the United States, 1880 – 1917.* Chicago: University of Chicago Press.

BOYARIN, D. (1997). *Unheroic conduct: The rise of heterosexuality and the invention of the Jewish man.* Los Angeles: University of California Press.

BHUGRA, D. (2002). Literature update: A critical review. *Sexual and Relationship Therapy, 17,* 99 – 106.

BUBER, M. (1958). *I and Thou.* New York: Charles Scribner & Sons.

BULKA, R.P. (1986) *Jewish Marriage: A Halakhic Ethic.* New York: Ktav.

456   *D. S. Ribner & P. J. Kleinplatz*

BURT, V.K. & RUDOLPH, M. (2000). Treating an Orthodox Jewish woman with obsessive-compulsive disorder: Maintaining reproductive and psychologic stability in the context of normative religious rituals. *American Journal of Psychiatry, 157*, 620–624.

DONIN, H.H. (1972). *To be a Jew*. New York: Basic Books.

FELDMAN, D.M. (1968). *Birth control in Jewish law*. New York: New York University Press.

FRANKL, V.E. (1955). *The doctor and the soul*. USA: Vintage Books.

FRIEDMAN, A.P. (1996). *Marital intimacy: A traditional Jewish approach*. Northvale, NJ: Jason Aronson.

OSTROV, S. (1978). Sex therapy with orthodox Jewish couples. *Journal of Sex and Marital Therapy, 4*, 266–278.

PETOK, W.D. (2001). Religious observance and sex therapy with an Orthodox Jewish couple. *Journal of Sex Education and Therapy, 25*, 22–27.

ROYSTER, J.J. (1997). *Southern horrors and other writings: The anti-lynching campaign of Ida B. Wells, 1892–1900*. Boston: Bedford Books.

SIMPSON, W.S. & RAMBERG, J.A. (1992). The influence of religion on sexuality: Implications for sex therapy. *Bulletin of the Menninger Clinic, 56*, 511–523.

VARGA, W.P. (1981). *The number one Nazi Jew-baiter: A political biography of Julius Streicher, Hitler's chief anti-Semitic propagandist*. New York: Carlton Press.

ZIMMERMAN, D.R. (2005). *A lifetime companion to the laws of Jewish family life*. Jerusalem: Urim Publications.

Contributors

DAVID S. RIBNER, D.S.W., *Director, Sex Therapy Training Program, School of Social Work, Bar Ilan University.*

PEGGY J. KLEINPLATZ, Ph.D., *Faculty of Medicine and School of Psychology, University of Ottawa, Ottawa, Ontario, Canada.*

Part II
Judaism and Sexuality:
The Traditional–Modernist Divide

[6]

LIVED REGULATIONS, SYSTEMIC ATTRIBUTIONS
Menstrual Separation and Ritual Immersion in the Experience of Orthodox Jewish Women

TOVA HARTMAN
NAOMI MARMON
Hebrew University of Jerusalem

The rules that govern Jewish Orthodox women's bodies, in particular those of ritual purity and immersion, are often criticized as patriarchal and an expression of oppression or domination. This study challenges the structuralist analysis of the regimen of ritual purity by examining how religious women themselves live and experience this system. The authors interviewed 30 Orthodox Jewish women living in Israel who observe these rituals in an effort to hear their experiences. The women's expression of their experiences moved beyond the conventional, schematic abstractions of the oppression-empowerment dichotomy into a multitextured range of responses. This article presents the ways in which they voiced this multiplicity of feelings and experiences.

Keywords: women's ritual; niddah, mikveh, *oppression, Jewish religious rites*

The demonization and regulation of women's bodies within religious patriarchies has been well documented in various cultures. Women have been subjected to a range of negative characterizations (e.g., as polluting, dangerous temptresses; Douglas 1966), and their bodies have been accused of being "inherently different from men's [bodies] in ways that made them both defective and dangerous" (Weitz 1998, 3). As a result, women have been systematically overdressed and undressed, locked indoors and exposed to public humiliation, and even burnt at the stake to placate men's fears about the hyperbolized, often mythologized, dangers their bodies are purported to pose (Arthur 1999; Daly 1999; Eilberg-Schwartz 1995; Polhemus 1978; Sanday 1982; Turner 1996). Menstruation in particular, an almost universal

AUTHORS' NOTE: *We wish to thank Shira Wolosky and Charles Buckholtz for their generous help and insightful comments.*

REPRINT REQUESTS: *Naomi Marmon and Tova Hartman, Hebrew University, School of Education, Mount Scopus, Jerusalem, Israel.*

390   GENDER & SOCIETY / June 2004

taboo, has been studied extensively from a range of perspectives: Psychological, sociological, anthropological, and comparative religious. Feminist analysis has highlighted the extent of the oppression the various strictures surrounding the menstrual taboo effect—spoken and unspoken, encoded in texts, and transmitted orally.

Religious codes, which tend to reify these attitudes into explicit catalogues of restrictive norms, can be pointed to as obvious agents in this systemic silencing of women. The Jewish laws of modesty and *niddah* (the system of ritual purity and immersion) would seem to serve as Judaism's version of this familiar patriarchal device. Jewish feminists claim that these laws oppress and degrade women and their bodies because their restrictions imply that women are a "potential source of pollution and disorder whose life and impact on men must be regulated" (Baskin 1985, 14; see also Baum, Hyman, and Michel 1976; Biale 1984; Priesand 1975; Swidler 1976). Judith Plaskow (1990, 184-85) maintained that based on Jewish sources about women, "It is difficult to conclude anything other than that women are a source of moral danger and an incitement to depravity and lust." "It is precisely in this area [of sexual regulation]," said Paula Hyman (1976, 110), "that the second-class status of women within Judaism is highlighted."

This systemic or structural critique of patriarchal systems in general and Jewish religious law as a salient case in point—particularly the negative valuations attributed to menstruation and the oppressive practices that arise therefrom—has unquestionable force. We certainly concur with the basic insight that as a *mitzvah* (commandment) that is specifically incumbent on women yet governs and regulates the sexual relationships of married couples, *mikveh* immersion, like the menstruation rites of other cultures, "is a fecund symbol for both condensing and expressing a complex set of notions about women, life, and the world" (Delaney 1988, 76). At the same time, it is our claim that the theoretical power of this account leaves unanswered—perhaps unasked—just how religious women themselves live and experience their regimens and commitments: How they both see and do not see the disciplinary structures (see Foucault 1979) in which they reside and through which they, in very complex and countering ways, define themselves.

Foucaultian discipline structure is extremely relevant and powerful in analyzing these practices. Niddah, in fact, is a highly complex structure of what Foucault (1979) called "micropractices." In niddah, these would include awareness of beginning and end of menstruation as well as the postures of the body during this period of taboo, which can include cooking, sleeping arrangements, dress, and a very detailed range of regulations of intimate contacts. The discipline is there; however, it is not just punishment. There are certainly coercive penetrating elements. Yet how it is practiced becomes a medium of expression for the women who practice it, according to their own interpretation and voice.

The stark dichotomy often posited in structuralist thinking between rule on one hand and its interpretation/attribution on the other (including psychological attitudes and behavioral practices) is something we wish to challenge with what might be called a more hermeneutic approach. Just as in hermeneutics, a text cannot be uncoupled from its interpretation—the interpretation is in some way constitutive of the text—a structuralist approach that attempts to separate rules from the women who live them seems inherently flawed. This is particularly salient in the Jewish context, where rules are in fact manifest in text. The text is read; the rule is lived. The hermeneutic frame opens what might appear in structuralist thinking as a rigid, oppositional dichotomy, toward the more nuanced realities of experiential life, and therefore applies to the women we interviewed.

It is indeed an unintended irony of structuralist analysis that precisely because the models themselves are so compelling, the necessity to listen closely to the voices of actual people seems, on some level, to be obviated. If such voices are sought out and solicited, there is a strong temptation to theorize them into preexisting categories and systemic abstractions rather than to place them in a dynamic relationship with theory, allow them to call the categories into question, or force us to recalibrate our understanding of the system itself. Thus, when one comes to rely too heavily on structuralist methods for understanding cultures, the nuances of individual lives are often obscured. In fact, as potent as the systemic critique of religious patriarchy admittedly is, it has not yet managed to articulate a multivocal account of the experiences of women living within these systems (for exceptions, see Kandiyoti 1991; Kaufman 1993).[1] This absenting of actual women's voices constitutes a conspicuous gap in knowledge and, consequently, a theoretical weakness.

This article examines case studies (Stake 2000) of Orthodox Jewish women vis-à-vis the practice of niddah. Our intention here is primarily cartographic: To map out the lived landscape of niddah observance in all its provocative complexity and in doing so convey something of the richness and sophistication of the women who are constantly negotiating its marked trails and hidden passes, its contours and its cliffs. "Social reality is characterized by discontinuities in which plurality and the coexistence of opposite meanings take place. To reduce those to a two-dimensional picture is to flatten and constrain the field of knowledge" (Perelberg 1990, 45). What emerges, then, is a picture of niddah practice as viewed from the perspective of the women who live within the Jewish legal (*halakhic*) system that looks very different from the characterizations of those lives as deduced or inferred from systemic analyses.

When thinking about the observance of niddah, we kept in mind that ritual acts can be conceptualized in terms of two constituent parts: Regulation and attribution. *Regulation* refers to the behavioral aspects of the ritual, *attribution* the reasons given for the behaviors. Steinberg (1997) pointed out that Orthodox Jewish tradition, and especially niddah observance, require fealty to ritual praxis irrespective of one's attributions or understanding thereof. He also noted, along with Yanay and Rapoport (1997), that while the practice of niddah has remained relatively constant among traditional Jewish women over many centuries, the attributions have varied radically at different times and in different places.

As discussed above, the rules that govern religious women's bodies are often criticized as oppressive methods of domination. In fact, a self-conscious discourse of oppression figured prominently in our informants' descriptions of their experience observing the niddah laws. This, however, was only part of the picture: They also had many positive attributions with regard to the ritual and uplifting things to say about the effects and implications of niddah in their lives. What was most striking about the accounts these women gave was the ease and willingness with which they made distinctions: Among elements of these practices they found meaningful and/or beautiful, those they found neutral or unmeaningful, and those they found burdensome, unsavory, offensive, or oppressive. As we will show, it is the simultaneous validity of this multiplicity of responses—so often set in opposition—which in fact constitutes the vibrant discourse of observance.

METHOD

The authors conducted one-to-one, in-depth personal interviews with 30 Orthodox Jewish women in Jerusalem during the course of the year 2001. The interviews centered around the women's experiences with the rituals of niddah and *mikveh* immersion, including what these observances mean to them and how they affect their relationships with self, spouse, community, and God. An initial group was cultivated through informal contacts, which led to other contacts (snowballing). The women ranged in age from 25 to 57 and have been married between 4 months and 35 years.

All of the interviews were conducted in the mother tongue of the interviewee (either Hebrew or English). The majority were conducted in Hebrew and translated by the interviewer to English when transcribed from the audio recording. Each participant was interviewed once, with interviews lasting up to three hours. Interview sessions were conducted in the homes of the interviewees, at a time that was deemed comfortable and private. While similar topics were covered in each interview, an open format was employed, allowing the flow of conversation to follow the interviewee's lead. This meant that not every topic was discussed with each participant. The quotes below are representative of the reactions garnered.

In analyzing the interviews, we used the process of grounded theory development (Charmatz 1983, 1995) as well as elements of Gilligan et al.'s (1988) voice-centered analysis, which sensitized us to thematic patterns and the significance of linguistic cues. The strengths of the grounded theory method (Denzin and Lincoln 1994) were particularly appropriate for the goals of this study. This methodology allowed us to ground our analytical work firmly and concretely within both cultural context (Bruner 1990) and real-life situations (Mishler 1979; Tappan 1990). Thus, we utilized grounded theory not to prove or disprove hypotheses but rather to generate categories for theorizing our informants' experiences (Strauss and Corbin 1994).

While these observations can only be said to apply to the specific group of women interviewed (Altheide and Johnson 1998), it is our hope that their voices will help to illuminate the feelings of the larger population to whom they belong. This work can also serve as a jumping-off point for further research into the experiences of different groups of modern women living within traditional valuative frameworks (Geertz 1966).

THE BURDENS OF OBSERVANCE

The basis for niddah practice is found in Leviticus (chap. 15, 18, 20). According to rabbinic tradition, a woman remains in niddah for a minimum of 12 days—5 for the period of the menstrual flow and 7 "clean" days thereafter. During this time, sexual intercourse and any physical intimacy is forbidden. At the end of the 7 clean days, a woman must immerse in the mikveh; husband and wife are then free to resume sexual relations.

An Awareness of Oppression

Throughout our interviews, there could be detected an undercurrent of these women's grappling with the notion of oppression and its relevance to their lives. Often, they raised the issue unprompted, reflecting a general awareness of feminist claims regarding women's roles in patriarchal religious structures. Deborah, for example, was clearly responding to this implicit discourse when, without our having asked her anything about oppression, she offered that "[the niddah laws are] not something that's oppressive to me."

These women's awareness of feminist discourse and their desire not to think of themselves, or be viewed by others, as oppressed deeply informed their responses to the questions we posed. Once again without external prompting, in discussing how she and her husband moderate their intimacy during the times of niddah, Yael, the wife of a rabbi, first raised and then attempted to exorcize the specter of oppression: "[Niddah] shouldn't be very oppressive. But every time, it's true—there's no doubt, there are. We go more covered, we try to go with pajamas . . . or all kinds of things that cover—there are all these things." Despite her suggestion that "it shouldn't be oppressive," there is nonetheless the implicit concession that although perhaps ideally these laws should not be oppressive, that is nonetheless an unavoidable dimension of how they are experienced.

Although these women seem familiar in a general way with feminist vocabulary—familiar enough, for example, to appropriate the use of the term "oppression" to certain elements of their experience—ultimately we must ask if they are speaking the same language. To formulate an answer, we must first ask, What do these women mean when they use the term "oppression"? We suggest deconstructing the term into three subcategories, ranging in magnitude from (1) the imposition of severe inconvenience (e.g., a job with long hours or an "oppressive" commute), to (2) the stifling of ambitions and drives (e.g., career tracking), to (3) more literal and direct forms of subjugation (e.g., sexual harassment and exploitation, systemic wage discrimination). These are, of course, soft categories, with plenty of overlap among them. Still, for heuristic purposes, they are useful in untangling some of the threads of our informants' discourse of oppression.

"Particularly Difficult": The Unique Challenges Surrounding Niddah

Some of our informants reported experiencing the laws of niddah differently from other religious obligations. They found it "particularly difficult," and this distinction can be accounted for by a number of factors. Leah depicted her difficulties with niddah as stemming from a combination of the newness of the mitzvah, the newness of the relationship it circumscribes, and the area of the relationship on which it lays claim:

> This is really the first time that you have to deal with something that is really hard. What—do you struggle over transgressing Shabbat? . . . Things that are new for us we learn, we deal, we try, we improve . . . but these are really difficult. . . . I am sure that I am not the only person who is struggling with this difficulty . . . mainly in that a relationship is new and everything is new.

By contrasting this mitzvah with those surrounding Sabbath observance, she distinguishes between areas of observance that have become second nature through a lifetime of acculturation and the hardship of a new mitzvah to which she has become obligated through marriage.

Other women named different aspects of niddah observance as annoying or onerous. Chana, a mother of teenage children, spoke of the burdensome rigor of the internal checks required twice daily on the cessation of bleeding:

> Well, I can say that it is certainly a burden! And the seven clean days are very difficult because you always feel that you have to be connected to the clock and see if it's time to do another check, and make sure that it doesn't get too late. That is a real pain.

While Chana discussed the burdens connected to time pressures, Rivka disdained the physically intrusive aspect of the obligation: "The checks are not pleasant. . . . It annoys me that I have to shove something into my body."

These women's complaints about the niddah ritual fall roughly into the category of inconvenience as outlined above. This is not to dismiss or belittle their grievances, only to highlight the fact that they are framed more in terms of logistical annoyances than as threats to identity.

"A Horrible Feeling": Niddah, Marriage, and Distortions of the Self

Yael felt differently. She also related directly to the particular difficulty of taking on niddah observance at the time of marriage, and her complaint begins with the characterization of niddah as an inconvenience or burden. However, the context in which she understands this burdensomeness expands and becomes tied to other marriage-related identity hardships, which taken together become emblematic for her of a deeper form of oppression:

> It's a certain burden, and we don't always love it. . . . At the beginning it's a horrible feeling because *they* are changing this for *you* and that for *you*—*they* change your family name, things that are difficult; that is, they do reduce a certain essence/identity (*mahut mesuyemet*). . . . *She* has to leave the family that gave her an identity and change *her* name, *she* has to cover *her* hair—and *she* already doesn't belong to everyone as *she* did before. (emphasis added)

Yael notes that the "burden" and "difficulty" of taking on niddah observance at this particular juncture of the life cycle is exacerbated by the constellation of other changes imposed on women at this time. Cumulatively, these changes brought about a "horrible feeling." Unlike Leah, she relates to her observance not as a positive choice but as a series of abuses "they" are imposing on "you," "she," and "her"—absenting herself completely as a first-person voice from her own discourse (Brown and Gilligan 1992; Gilligan et al. 1988). This dissociation bespeaks an acute inner dissonance vis-à-vis the nexus of niddah and marriage that, for Yael, is far from resolved.

Yosefa's displeasure with niddah was not limited to its effect on her life immediately following marriage:

> My problem is not just how hard it is to do the checks twice a day—not just that I can't have intercourse—it's that I can't be touched. My needs for being touched are not just sexual; they're human.

Yosefa expressed a profound sadness at the denial of nonsexual contact during niddah, which she experiences as a basic human need. After giving birth, she "stained" continuously for three and a half months, which, according to *halakha*, assigned her the status of niddah for that entire period. During that time, she underwent frequent and acute emotional crises, which she attributed to the denial of physical contact with her husband. She was aware that in cases of extreme emotional duress, halakha allows for leniencies. She also knew that to procure such an exemption would require petitioning a rabbi. "I know if I called my rabbi, told him I was crying all the time, he'd say okay; but why do I have to be mentally ill before I can get permission?" Yosefa felt that to enter into the legal fiction of mental illness would represent a compromise to her integrity even more damaging that the ordeal she was currently suffering. She related to the niddah laws as dehumanizing for the manner in which they disregarded her basic emotional needs.

Shifra was even more strident in her condemnation of niddah: "Not being able to touch each other is torture. . . . It's hard enough that you don't have sex when you want; but the touching. . . . To go to bed in a separate bed is just . . ." Shifra's speech became halting, her tone increasingly livid, as she described the intense frustration and inner turmoil of feeling bound inextricably to a ritual that is a source of unremitting personal torment.

To say that these women felt stifled by the niddah requirements would be a grave understatement; "suffocated" comes closer to encapsulating their responses. They experienced the ritually imposed cycle of separation and closeness as a series of deprivations and degradations in violent opposition to their psychological and emotional health. Knowing that they could be touched in the near future did nothing to relieve this distress; on the contrary, the absence of a sexually neutral space within which to relate to their husbands was a key deprivation and common complaint.

Legal Impotence: The Requirement to Ask a Rabbi

In addition to the significant emotional and physical difficulties presented by niddah observance, our informants also expressed frustration with its authoritarian structure. If a woman observing niddah sees a blood stain, either while she is not menstruating or on the cloth of one of the internal checks during the seven clean days before immersion, she is instructed to ask a rabbi whether this stain renders her unclean. She (or her husband) brings the cloth or her undergarments to the rabbi, who examines them and makes a ruling about her status. In this dynamic, our informants described feeling demoralized, divested of personal power—deprived not only of authority as a passive heir to this legal code but of an education sufficient to grant an understanding of its arcane bylaws.

Many of their accounts resonated with the third category of oppression—systemic subjugation—and thus with the feminist claim that religious women's obligations, and the control of the body and sexuality, constitute a patriarchal exercise of domination and social control (Turner 1996).

> I spoke to my husband, and then I asked a Rabbi. I didn't really like that. To tell the truth, that was always something that really put me off in this whole matter because it's very personal and private. And to go take your physiological evidence to someone—I was never comfortable with it. (Deborah)

Deborah's words conveyed a sense of dehumanization in life's most delicate sphere, such that she felt reduced to a kind of medical exhibit. Her humiliation was exacerbated by having to petition a man for menstrual validation and sexual permission—which in addition to being viscerally repellant reminded her that these obligations were part of a system in which men dominate women's sexuality. Tina also expressed her experience of violation and domination in an almost physical way:

> What really bothers me are the checks that I have to do inside my body: I sometimes have this feeling that it is the long hands of the rabbis of hundreds of years literally entering my body to check me.

Responses to Rabbinic Authority

Our informants described a range of responses to this sense of rabbinic subjugation. Deborah maintained her observance of the niddah ritual itself while eventually factoring out the rabbinic component. "I decided I had enough sense to make these decisions on my own." Yertl made a similar decision—although hers can be viewed as somewhat more subversive and extreme, given that her husband is a rabbi who regularly answers niddah questions from women in their community. "Don't you think it's strange that during 25 years of marriage he never asked me, 'Don't you have a question?' But I would never ask him or anyone." Like Deborah, Yertl can be seen as practicing a kind of civil disobedience, appropriating authority where she feels authority has been traditionally misplaced.

Another informant expressed her hostility toward this aspect of niddah observance by manipulating the system to the point of mockery. Whenever she would have a stain that required consultation, she would "shop around" to see who would offer her the most lenient opinion, playing the power of the rabbinic authorities against one another. While her story added a cynical twist to a common frustration, and expressed her personal rebellion against this part of the system, it is important to note that at the end of the day she remained within the system—continuing to observe the laws and ultimately accepting rabbinic authority (albeit the most lenient version of it she could find) rather than casting off the system as a whole or even this particular ritual.

Tina noted that during the course of history, male impurity faded as a practical halakhic category, and men's mikveh immersion was deemed obsolete. She related the story of a friend, strictly religious in all other aspects of her life, who ceased observing niddah as an act of resistance against this historical bias. "Well, too bad," Tina quoted her friend as saying. "I'm stopping."

BEARABLE TO BENEFICIAL, AUTHORITY TO POWER: POSITIVE RESPONSES TO OBSERVANCE

Our informants accept the obligations of halakha in their lives even when they personally dislike them and had little hesitancy acknowledging this difficulty. At the same time, many of them spoke at length of the benefit and value that the observance of *mitzvot* in general brings to their lives and extolled the importance of upholding them. Using terms such as "beauty" and "enhancement," they stressed not only the voluntary and at times enthusiastic nature of their participation in halakhic ritual but a sense of value and benefit in the particular halakhic realm of niddah. Some had to search to find these benefits, while others claimed to experience them naturally and vividly. Some found that they made other, unsavory aspects of niddah observance bearable, some made no attempt to connect the two realms, and others spoke exclusively of empowerment and beauty.

Ritual as Rote: Commitment to Halakha as the Basis for Observance

One dominant strain in our interviews placed the value of niddah observance not locally within this particular set of rituals but rather as a component of halakhic observance as a whole. Many of these women spoke openly about the negative elements of niddah observance, but in the final analysis, they all concluded that the value of halakha as a way of life, and the benefits of membership within the religious Jewish community, outweighed these concerns. They related to the halakhic lifestyle as a whole greater than the sum of its parts.

Chava, who has been married for almost 35 years, made it clear that it was only because of her commitment to a religious way of life that she observed this mitzvah and that she did so despite profoundly negative feelings toward the ritual itself: "I hated the whole thing—from beginning to end. I only did it because I had to, but my life would've been much better without it."

Similarly, Deborah "accepted [niddah] from the point of view that it is halakha," maintaining, "I certainly do not see the logic in it." She has a strong enough voice to state unequivocally that she feels burdened by what to her are incomprehensible strictures; yet ultimately, she chooses to subsume that voice to the goal of maintaining a religious lifestyle. In such an encompassing system, spiritual meaning and value are not necessarily to be found in every particularity of observance. Rather, the primary source of value is drawn from the fact of adhering to a lifestyle and deferring to a system in which, on the whole, one believes. Deborah articulated this position very clearly:

> Why do I wait a certain number of hours between meat and milk, and why do I refrain from turning on the electricity on Shabbat, and why do I do lots of other things? From my point of view, it all belongs to the same category. It's halakha. . . . It's the way I live my life. . . . Do I feel a fantastic rush every time I do something? No!

Likewise, Rachel, who has seven children, noted that when she took on the obligations of the laws of niddah upon marriage, she felt "a great amount of happiness because I knew I was doing the right thing." This sentiment recurred in many of the interviews.

A number of our informants placed even less stock in the niddah ritual per se. For us as observers, who prefer to place ritual activity—especially rituals as seemingly charged as niddah and mikveh—in contexts of valence and meaning, these women's voices are important to keep in mind inasmuch as they resist placement on even a nuanced axis of oppression/empowerment. For them, niddah is simply internalized as one among many halakhic rituals, which themselves are indistinguishable from the other rituals of daily life. For example, Jane said, "I do not feel oppressed; for me it is not intrusive, it is a vestige of something. It is one of the things that do not have that much meaning, but I do them anyway."

Despite her indifference vis-à-vis meaning, Jane did claim to find benefit in the niddah ritual:

> I find no meaning in the ritual per se, but I do find benefit in the constant renewal of
> sexual interest. And there is a positive effect in having to find other means of commu-
> nication [aside from sex]. This was not the reason for it, but it is a happy side effect.
> The point could've been made in less than two weeks a month, but still there is some-
> thing to be gained.

Interestingly, Jane feels no need to translate these "happy side effects" of her
niddah observance into sites of religious meaning, much less project them back into
the ritual's initial intent, that is, transform them into a form of apologetics. The ritual justifies itself: One divine commandment among many. No other explanation or
justification is required.

Halakhic Enfranchisement: Subjective Authority in the Legal Sphere

One form of benefit many of our informants claimed from their niddah observance was a sense of halakhic enfranchisement, which translated for them into feelings of personal and collective efficacy (Bandura 1997; Weissberg 1999). As an
encompassing legal system consisting of not only prescribed activities but commandments to perform, halakhic authority is constituted through the assignment of
responsibility over mitzvot governing different spheres of life. The vast majority of
these mitzvot, and certainly those invested with particular significance, are placed
largely or wholly in the hands of men.

Not so niddah—women are the sole arbiters of this central mitzvah. This responsibility and authority gave many of our informants a sense of being valued and
appreciated as subjects and agents in religious life. Being fully responsible for both
their own and their husbands' compliance with the laws was understood by some of
our informants as a form of authority and respect. For example, Yael stated,

> You are checking, you are doing the checks every time, and only you and God know
> what's going on there—not even your husband. It's all the responsibility of the
> woman! You can say it came out clean, you can say all these things, and no one will
> know if it's true or it's not true, but it's up to you. It's a truthfulness that you have to
> know (with) yourself. You have to get there really clean.

On one hand, it is somewhat striking that Yael would recognize and allow for the
possibility that someone else would have control over her most intimate bodily
sphere. It can be seen as a testament to the extent to which she has internalized the
patriarchal dominance of the halakhic system that she takes this possibility for
granted. Nonetheless, the fact that within this system she does maintain authority
over the interface of her body with a critical facet of religious law is understandably
seen, within its lived context, as an important locus of religious authority. When
they decide how to apply a given injunction, or when they choose to alter their
observance in a way that better suits their psychological makeup or emotional
needs or not to follow a given bylaw to the letter, these decisions evince individual
expression and personal control for many of our informants. Inherent in the system,

they feel, is an esteem for woman as halakhic arbiter and actor, faith in her honesty and decision-making ability. Being entrusted with the reigns of observance in this important mitzvah imbues them with a sense of empowerment and halakhic consequence, significance and worth (Staples 1990; Weissberg 1999).

Essential Validation: The Niddah Period and Respect for Women's Needs

A number of our informants appreciated the niddah cycle's legislation of a nonsexual sphere within married life. Shoshana framed this appreciation in terms of the ritual's intrinsic "intent":

> The meaning of the separation is that during a woman's cycle, during those two weeks, a woman might be feeling more sensitive/delicate (*adin*), and involvement in sexual relations bothers/disturbs (*mafria*) during this period. It is a period of quiet with myself.

Sara added that in addition to respecting a woman's biological-emotional needs, the laws of niddah also place welcome limitations on spousal discourse. Noting that women sometimes have difficulty refusing their husbands' sexual advances, she described as an intended benefit the imposition of an external, impartial, and inherently legitimate separation that obviates the need to rebuff a husband's desire for sex. She felt this advantage especially keenly after giving birth:

> You know, I think about couples who don't observe, and you have to start saying, 'It's good for me now or it's not so comfortable.' It's good in my view that there is time. It's not nice. At that time the woman is so concentrated on herself, and you don't want sex.

This separation allowed Sara to focus her energies internally in this time of transition and tumult, without feeling bad about doing so. It gave her the time she needed while menstruating or recuperating after birth, which perhaps her husband would not be sensitive to or need for himself.

Rachel felt similar benefits. "I usually enjoy sex. But there are times when *a woman* needs the physical and times when she doesn't want it. It's good that the laws respond to that" (emphasis added). Her account presents an interesting contrast to those of Yosefa and Shifra above, who complained precisely of the absence of a nonsexualized space within the niddah cycle's on/off sexual dialectic. Rachel's speech pattern was interesting inasmuch as it reflected an unwillingness, inability, or possibly obliviousness to this alternate perspective: She began by describing her enjoyment in the first person, but moved to an inclusive third person as she related to a feeling she assumed is common to all women.

Like Rachel, Rivka spoke of the benefit of this separation in facilitating her ability to be more of an individual within the relationship: "I needed the space. . . . I think that the mitzvot and the world of Torah are built with a lot of contemplation about the nature of people." By respecting her in this way, Rivka said, the laws affirm her inherent feminine sensibilities and encourage her to relate more deeply to herself and her preferences.

Among our informants who expressed sentiments consonant with those quoted above, Bruria was the most unequivocal. She felt that the niddah cycle enhances her marriage:

> The mikveh gives me a wonderful feeling, when I go, I feel like my husband is waiting for me like an honored guest, like he waits Friday night for the Sabbath angels. . . . It makes me feel like our relationship moves to a higher level.

She claimed that it also enhances her sense of inner peace and self-esteem:

> Every time, there is this feeling of renewal, and I feel that I enter the water as a religious person who is accepted for who I am, without makeup, without colors: I have an intrinsic net worth, without any props.

Bruria introduced novel interpretations of the meaning and purpose of niddah, openly acknowledging that these interpretations were her own and engaging in an inner dialogue as to whether "there is intellectual honesty in giving this modern meanings that perhaps were not the original intent." She concluded, "I think there is."

It would be possible to interpret the above characterizations as variations on the theme of patriarchal apologetics, or even false consciousness—an internalization of patriarchal demands that is so deep that it results in total identification, which is then formulated using a rhetoric that draws on feminist language. It is equally possible, though, that the resonance these women express with the halakhic system's take on women's life cycles emerges from a sense of identification that is genuine and profound, based primarily on their experience of their biological and emotional rhythms. These informants feel that their tradition embodies a feminist voice in that it responds to needs of women's bodies, minds, and souls, that it is not merely prescriptive, telling them what they can and cannot do with their bodies, but descriptive of their own deepest understanding and experience of themselves.

The truth of these women's consciousness is, of course, impossible to know. Whether somewhere on the spectrum between oppression and validation or simply unique to each individual woman, what was most interesting to us was the manner in which these informants use the tradition to articulate their needs to their partners in an authoritative way. Whether the needs themselves are essential or constructed—if this distinction is still relevant—what is clear is that their assertion and articulation are facilitated greatly by tradition's definitive imprimatur. Halakha has given these women legitimation for a "no" voice within their sexual relationships— a voice that within both traditional and modern patriarchies, has to varying degrees been silenced and denied. The law gives the only voice that can possibly counter the irresistible authority and power of men's sexual desire, granting women the power of an oppositional patriarchal voice: The power of the rabbis/God negotiating with the power of their male partners. Those women who do feel the need to refrain from sexuality feel that they come to the negotiating table with the only voice that can counter the voice of men's desire, that is, the more powerful men's voice of tradition. Their "no" voice, then, becomes a voice that bears rabbinic affirmation.

This appeal to tradition to articulate women's needs with patriarchal authority constitutes an interesting, even novel, form of resistance. It is a resistance that is limited inasmuch as it operates within the assumptions of a patriarchal context and reflects the acceptance of the paradigm of silencing women. Nonetheless, its practical efficaciousness in establishing sexual boundaries resonant with the needs of our informants is a palpable benefit for which they express profound appreciation.

Possessing a Voice in Sexuality

In addition to respecting their desire to be nonsexual, the halakhic framework, according to many of our informants, sanctions women's sexual desires within the framework of marriage. The Torah (Ex 21:10) charges every married man with the mitzvah of *onah*, that is, the commandment to provide his wife with her conjugal rights. Thus, the halakhic system establishes a sexual sphere within marriage that is distinct from procreation and encourages women to expect, demand, and enjoy an active and vital sexual relationship with their spouses.

Although the mitzvah of onah is separate from the directives of niddah, they overlap inasmuch as part of the husband's onah requirement obliges him to sexual relations on the night of mikveh immersion and encourages women to communicate to their husbands (either symbolically or verbally) when they are sexually available.

> A woman can also initiate physical things. It's good to say that I want this or that, especially because the woman is supposed to enjoy. In fact, the husband is not fulfilling his commandment of onah if you don't enjoy. So that means that if you want sex, or whatever, then he has to agree, and you have the right to ask for it. (Yael)

Contrary to Freud's (1963) image of the silent and passive woman sexual partner, because of the mitzvah of onah, Yael feels as though "she has the right to ask" when she wants sex.

Sara echoed this sentiment: "Whatever the woman wants is the obligation of the husband. I remember that they spoke to us about how important it is that a woman should also enjoy." This halakhic premium on women's sexual fulfillment can be seen as a stark challenge to broad-based claims that religion represses women sexually and that women's pleasure is achieved through surrender, passivity, and recognition of themselves as sexual objects (Nicholson 1994).

Jane concurred that this element of niddah affirms, very practically and directly, her own needs within the sexual relationship and validates a woman's rights to sexual fulfillment and desire more generally:

> The general feeling of the mitzvah of onah makes me feel that the tradition goes against the idea that sex is all about him and his needs.... The mikveh joins the larger value of what does *she* need, what does the woman deserve.

Just as our informants above felt that the tradition speaks with them in validating their "no" voice within their sexual relationships, similarly, these women felt that it "joins" their "I want/I need/I desire" voice—another voice traditionally silenced by men's power. Their sexual fulfillment is validated and underwritten by a patriarchal tradition that in this instance stands and speaks unequivocally with them, demanding of its men participants, as a requirement of membership in good standing, that they listen.

Postponing Immersion: Halakhic Authority and Sexual Power

Because women are the arbiters of niddah observance, it also functions as a locus of women's power. By, for example, refusing to go to the mikveh or delaying their immersion, they command the *halakhically* sanctioned authority to withhold sex from their husbands. This authority is significant in that it turns on its head the general Western construction that "heterosexual sex means that men enact their social power over women" (Choi and Nicholson 1994, 22). Because Orthodox women are conscious of the potential to delay immersion and thereby halt sexual relations, this awareness serves as an instrument of power even when they choose not to act on it.[2] Accordingly, these laws imbue women with a sexual standing that counters the Foucaultian notion "that the discourses associated with female sexuality specifically act to regulate and control women, and to maintain men's position of power" (Ussher 1994, 148). The women we interviewed clearly perceive themselves as, to a large extent, regulating and controlling their sexual relationships and, as such, as occupying positions of power not only within the discourses associated with their sexuality but within their actual sexual practice. A number of our informants cited instances when communities of women banded together, refusing (as a group) to go to the mikveh until an injustice done by one of the men in the community against a woman peer was rectified. The historicity of these stories is far less important than what they reveal about the sense of not only individual but communal influence with which Orthodox women feel empowered by the laws of niddah.

Miriam, a Chassidic woman and mother of eight, delayed going to the mikveh as a form of birth control. Having evaluated her sexual and emotional needs and decided that she "didn't want to have children too quickly," she found herself unable to get a rabbinic sanction to use contraceptives. She then took matters into her own hands, utilizing the power invested in her by the halakhic system to subvert rabbinic authority, determine her own sexual destiny, and curb her husband's sexual activity by simply waiting an extra day or two before she went to the mikveh.

Mikveh can be used as an overt tactic of power, a sexual weapon.

> There was one time that I thought not to go to the mikveh. There was something that
> was bothering me, something that was bothering us, that we hadn't resolved, so I
> didn't feel like going. But then I realized that that is not right. (Yael)

Despite the fact that she decided against it, that she consciously thought about
delaying means that she is aware of the power she wields.

The knowledge of the subversive potential held by this aspect of niddah observance is something some of these women came to on their own. For others, it was
inherited knowledge, passed down to them by their mothers to help them find more
maneuverability and negotiability—and ultimately a kind of power—within the
patriarchal system than may first seem apparent.

The type of power these women described resonates with Perelberg's (1990)
concept of "the power of the weak." This power is distinguished, first of all, from an
idea of authority (Bendix 1973, cited in Perelberg 1990), which is "linked to the
idea of legitimization, the right to make particular decisions, and to command obedience." Power, on the other hand, "lies in the possibility of imposing one's will
upon the behavior of other persons" (Bendix 1973, cited in Perelberg 1990, 290).
Perelberg emphasized that these " 'oblique' or peripheral power strategies" are in
no way equivalent to direct forms of authority, but insisted equally that

> The fact that power can be exercised from a subordinate position is fundamental to
> both the way in which gender roles are constructed in different societies and the
> respective positions from which men and women perceive themselves (see also
> McCormack and Strathern 1980, who have pointed out that most societies tend to
> present a more complex pattern of interaction between men and women than one
> would perceive by examining the 'official' system of rights, duties, and authority). (P. 45)

DISCUSSION AND CONCLUSION

The women we interviewed reported a range of attributions to the niddah ritual,
as well as a range of responses to the same attributions and the basic niddah regulations. Some women felt oppressed by the practice of niddah. There were those who
felt vehemently that the regulatory aspect of niddah itself impinged on their psychological and emotional well-being in ways damaging and profound. They felt
subjugated, harassed, and in some cases abused by a rabbinic authority that
intruded in the most private aspect of their lives, put their excretory functions on
display, and exposed their sexuality for patriarchal supervision and control. Others
also described the regulatory element of niddah as oppressive but seemed to mean it
as a term of inconvenience rather than the more penetrating and severe connotations
implied by the systemic critique.

Complicating the picture, however, were those among our informants for whom
regulation per se was not inherently oppressive. The fact that their sexuality was
regulated was not a significant categorical distinction from the other requirements
of their halakhic lifestyle. In fact, some expressed appreciation for the sexual

regulations affected by niddah, the structure that it gave to their sexual practice (which they felt was deeply consonant with essential biological and emotional needs), and the cycle of abstinence and desire, of individuality and coupling, that it facilitated in their relationships with their husbands. Yet others resisted attribution altogether, relating to niddah strictly as a behavioral phenomenon, a series of acts to be accomplished—a "checklist," as one put it—and expressed disinterest, indifference, and even hostility vis-à-vis attempts to imbue it with different meanings.

With few exceptions, the interviewees did not relate to the fact that these regulations have been couched within a discourse of defilement. While aware of these voices, our informants dismissed them as antiquated remnants of a premodern consciousness. They did not see themselves as second-class citizens being segregated from a fearful or disdainful society or from husbands skittish at the potential ill effects of menstrual blood; nor does observance provoke feelings of degradation or shame.[3] Indeed, many of our informants have maintained ancient practices while abandoning the ancient or medieval classifications and valuations. It seems that for these women, defilement has largely evaporated as an attribution for niddah, following its evaporation from modern consciousness as a whole. What is left is a system of sexual regulations that itself elicits a wide range of alternative attributions and diverse emotional responses.

Among this wide range of accounts, some resonated with elements of the systemic analysis, some challenged it, and others seemed to hover outside of its purview altogether. It is possible to view all of these as "resistances," in the broad Foucaultian sense of responses to power (Foucault 1980, 95-96). It should be noted, of course, that the phenomenon of the oppressed identifying and collaborating with the oppressor is not new and certainly could be presented as a plausible explanation for some of these women's affirmation and justification with niddah as nonoppressive, beneficial, and essentially correct. These women could be interpreted as suffering from a range of cognitive-emotional disorders—for example, false consciousness, Uncle Tom–style oppressor identification, and patriarchal collaboration. We felt, however, that privileging systemic analysis in this way would constitute an abstraction and flattening of their experience. Overvoicing them in these ways would inevitably sacrifice a more nuanced and inclusive appreciation of their experiences.

By listening in this way, we could hear the women's thoughts and experiences move beyond the schematic abstractions of prevailing concepts and into a highly textured range of responses. By refusing to implicate them on an axis of collaboration-resistance, or to locate them within a simple oppression-empowerment dichotomy, we were better able to hear the ways in which they manage a broad range of voices at times in concert, at times in conflict, and at times content merely to coexist. We were able to hear not only hidden "knots of resistance" (Foucault 1980) but knots of experience more broadly. We find Gruenbaum (2000, 57) to be instructive and appropriately cautionary in this regard:

> For the most part, Western feminists have found themselves in a dilemma. . . . To label women of a different culture as having a false consciousness . . . sounds like a deligitimization of the culture or belief of others . . . and thus too often the result has been a pedagogy of missionizing, telling others what they ought to do differently for reasons justified only by the enlightened outsiders' beliefs.

Following Irvine (1995), we were able to hear clear voices of oppression and regret alongside the benefits, positive attributions, and pockets of power our informants described, without feeling compelled to justify the former and explain away the latter. Like Kaufman (1993), we found that women's lived experience of niddah incorporates not only diverse reactions but a sophisticated weaving of responses vis-à-vis this patriarchal practice. While we cannot discount the possibility that our interviewees spoke through voices laden with forms of false consciousness, collusion, and apologetics (both calculated and naive), we wish to affirm the possibility of a ritual performativity that is deeply and authentically integrated with alternative attributions of meaning. It must be emphasized that such alternative attributions cannot themselves be reified into inherent, systemic truths about the nature and/or intent of niddah. The depths of sadness, frustration, and anger experienced and expressed by these women cannot be underestimated or dismissed. Just as the positive responses of women who feel held and spoken with by the tradition fall outside the purview of an analysis that focuses primarily on structures and texts, so too those who feel abused and demoralized in ways not systemically obvious are unwittingly ignored. Further studies concentrating on the accounts of women living within highly structured patriarchal systems will contribute to a deepening appreciation of the complex negotiations and nuanced responses that constitute these women's experiences of their own lives, in their own words.

NOTES

1. Kandiyoti's (1991) structural analysis examines the differences between the lived experiences of Islamic women in different Muslim countries and their roles and position in the modern nation-states of the Middle East. Unlike the present work, her focus is on the effects of the political projects of states on women's lives. Kaufman (1993) gave voice to the experiences of newly religious Jewish women, individuals who have chosen to reject their upbringing in a feminist and secular environment and move to a life of commitment to religious teachings. Similar to our work, she spoke to them about how they understand their lives within the context of what is considered an oppressive patriarchal system and gave voice to their wide range of experiences. However, she assumed a dichotomy between their lives before becoming religious (with an emphasis on individual freedom and feminist opportunity) and their lives after the choice to live in a closed and patriarchal system, asking questions of how and why they chose to embrace this way of life rather than simply allowing them to speak in their own categories of meaning.

2. The use of the laws of *niddah* as a source of women's power is consistent with Rahel Wasserfall's (1992) findings in an ethnographic study of niddah in the Israeli-Moroccan community. She noted, "*Niddah* is also a symbolic site where the division of power between husband and wife is enacted" (p. 309). In the Moroccan society, it is the man's duty to send his wife to the *mikveh*. As an assertion of their power, women sometimes demand that their husbands "beg" them to go.

Women tell of putting off their visits to the *miqve* [*sic*] and not paying heed to the constant demands of their husbands to go to the ritual bath. Indeed, delaying the *miqve* and thereby sexual relations seem in the eyes of these women to be the principle source of feminine power. (P. 322)

3. This can be contrasted with Shweder's (1991) account of Oriya Brahman society, in which "menstruating women . . . share with men the belief that during menstruation they are unclean and untouchable."

REFERENCES

Altheide, David L., and John M. Johnson. 1998. Criteria for assessing interpretive validity in qualitative research. In *Collecting and interpreting qualitative materials*, edited by N. Denzin and Y. Lincoln. Thousand Oaks, CA: Sage.

Arthur, L. 1999. *Religion, dress and the body.* Oxford, UK: Berg.

Bandura, A. 1997. *Self-efficacy: The exercise of control.* New York: W. H. Freeman.

Baskin, J. 1985. The separation of women in rabbinic Judaism. In *Women, religion, and social change*, edited by Y. Haddad and E. Findly. Albany: State University of New York Press.

Baum, C., P. Hyman, and S. Michel. 1976. *The Jewish women in America.* New York: New American Library.

Biale, R. 1984. *Woman and Jewish law.* New York: Schocken Books.

Brown, L. M., and C. Gilligan. 1992. *Meeting at the crossroads.* Cambridge, MA: Harvard University Press.

Bruner, J. 1990. *Acts of meaning.* Cambridge, MA: Harvard University Press.

Charmaz, K. 1983. The grounded theory method: An explication and interpretation. In *Contempory field research*, edited by R. M. Emerson. Prospect Heights, IL: Waveland Press.

———. 1995. Grounded theory. In *Rethinking methods in psychology*, edited by J. A. Smith, R. Harre, and L. Van Langenhove. London: Sage.

Choi, P., and P. Nicolson. 1994. *Female sexuality.* London: Harvester Wheatsheaf.

Daly, C. 1999. The "Paarda" expression of Hejaab among Afghan women in a non-Muslim community. In *Religion, dress and the body*, edited by L. Arthur. Oxford, UK: Berg.

Delaney, C. 1988. Mortal flow: Menstruation in Turkish village society. In *Blood magic: The anthropology of menstruation*, edited by T. Buckleyand and A. Gottlieb. Berkeley: University of California Press.

Denzin, N., and Y. Lincoln, eds. 1994. *Handbook of qualitative research.* Thousand Oaks, CA: Sage.

Douglas, M. 1966. *Purity and danger.* London: Routledge and Kegan Paul.

Eilberg-Schwartz, H., ed. 1995. *People of the body.* Albany: State University of New York Press.

Foucault, M. 1979. *Discipline and punish: The birth of the prison.* Translated by Alan Sheridan. Harmondsworth: Penguin.

———. 1980. *History of sexuality.* New York: Vintage.

Freud, S. 1963. *Sexuality and the psychology of love.* New York: Macmillan.

Geertz, C. 1966. Religion as a cultural system. In *Anthropological approaches to the study of religion*, edited by M. Banton. London: Tavistock.

Gilligan, C., B. Miller, D. Osborne, J. Ward, G. Wiggins, D. Wilcox, C. Brown, D. Argyris, J. Attaunucci, B. Bardige, and G. Johnston. 1988. *A guide for the reader.* Boston: Harvard Press.

Gruenbaum, E. 2000. *Female circumcision controversy: An anthropological perspective.* Philadelphia: University of Pennsylvania Press.

Hyman, P. 1976. The other half: Women in the Jewish tradition. In *The Jewish woman*, edited by E. Koltun. New York: Schocken Books.

Irvine, J. 1995. *Sexuality education across cultures.* San Francisco: Jossey-Bass.

Kandiyoti, D. 1991. *Women, Islam and the state.* Philadelphia: Temple University Press.

Kaufman, D. 1993. *Rachel's daughters.* New Brunswick, NJ: Rutgers University Press.

408   GENDER & SOCIETY / June 2004

Mishler, E. 1979. Meaning in context: Is there any other kind? *Harvard Educational Review* 49:1-19.

Nicholson, P. 1994. Anatomy and destiny: Sexuality and the female body. In *Female sexuality*, edited by P. Choi and P. Nicolson. London: Harvester Wheatsheaf.

Perelberg, R. J. 1990. Quality, asymmetry, and diversity: On conceptualization of gender. In *Gender and power in families*, edited by R. J. Perelberg and A. Miller. London: Routledge.

Plaskow, J. 1990. *Standing again at Sinai*. San Francisco: Harper.

Polhemus, T. 1978. *The body reader: Social aspects of the human body*. New York: Pantheon.

Priesand, S. 1975. *Judaism and the new woman*. New York: Behrman House.

Sanday, P. 1982. *Female power and male dominance*. Cambridge, UK: Cambridge University Press.

Shweder, R. 1991. *Thinking through cultures*. Cambridge, MA: Harvard University Press.

Stake, R. 2000. Case studies. In *Handbook of qualitative research*, 2d ed., edited by N. Denzin and Y. Lincoln. Thousand Oaks, CA: Sage.

Staples, L. 1990. Powerful ideas about empowerment. *Administration in Social Work* 14:29-42.

Steinberg, J. 1997. From a "pot of filth" to a "hedge of roses" (and back): Changing theorizations of menstruation in Judaism. *Journal of Feminist Studies in Religion* 13:2.

Strauss, A. L., and J. Corbin. 1994. Grounded theory methodology: An overview. In *Handbook of qualitative research*, edited by N. K. Denzin and Y. S. Lincoln. Thousand Oaks, CA: Sage.

Swidler, L. 1976. *Women in Judaism*. Metuchen, NJ: Scarecrow Press.

Tappan, M. B. 1990. Hermeneutics and moral development: Interpreting narrative representations of moral experience. *Developmental Review* 10:239-65.

Turner, B. 1996. *The body and society*. London: Sage.

Ussher, J. 1994. Theorizing female sexuality: Social constructionist and post-structuralist accounts. In *Female sexuality*, edited by P. Choi and P. Nicholson. London: Harvester Wheatsheaf.

Wasserfall, Rahel. 1992. Menstruation and identity: The meaning of *niddah* for Moroccan women immigrants to Israel. In *People of the body*, edited by Howard Eilberg-Schwartz, 309-27. Albany: State University of New York Press.

Weissberg, R. 1999. *The politics of empowerment*. New York: Praeger.

Weitz, Rose. 1998. *The politics of women's bodies*. New York: Oxford University Press.

Yanay, N., and T. Rapoport. 1997. Ritual impurity and religious discourse on women and nationality. *Women's Studies International Forum* 20:5-6.

Tova Hartman is a lecturer at the Hebrew University of Jerusalem, School of Education. Her research concentrates on gender, sexuality, and culture. Her recent book, Appropriately Subversive: Modern Mothers in Traditional Religions, *was published by Harvard University Press in 2002.*

Naomi Marmon is a doctoral candidate at the Hebrew University of Jerusalem. Her research includes work on Jewish religious women's identity, gender construction, and ritual practice. Her current focus revolves around the lived experiences of members of this community in constructing identity in light of the Jewish laws regulating sexuality.

[7]

Observance of the Laws of Family Purity in Modern–Orthodox Judaism

Mark A. Guterman

Abstract This research is a follow-up to a previous study measuring the observance of the ritually unclean period (*Niddah*) among Modern–Orthodox Jews. A total of 267 participants completed an online questionnaire comprised of a list of 16 "strict" and "lenient" forbidden behaviors. Participants reported whether they had engaged in these behaviors during Week 1 (the actual menstrual period) and during Week 2 (the "clean days" following the cessation of bleeding). Results showed that laws were being violated, with more transgressions during the second week than the first week. Additionally, more "lenient" laws were being broken than "strict" ones. Level of religious observance was significantly negatively correlated to the number of transgressions. However, there was no significant correlation between the number of transgressions and the age at marriage, sex, or how long one had been married.

Keywords Sex · Judaism · Jewish law · Orthodox Judaism · Orthodox Jews · Purity · Ritual

Introduction

Orthodox Judaism holds that the observance of the Jewish code of law, *Halakha*, goes hand-in-hand with rabbinical interpretation of these laws, teachings, and rules, and that both have been part of Jewish life and tradition since its inception (Keshet-Orr, 2003). However, due to the Enlightenment and the emancipation of Jews, a split divided the

M. A. Guterman (✉)
Department of Psychology, School of Psychology (T-WH1-01), Fairleigh Dickinson University, Metropolitan Campus, 1000 River Road, Teaneck, NJ 07666-1914, USA
e-mail: guterman.m@gmail.com

Jewish community. On one side, there was a movement towards embracing modernity through religious reformation and assimilation. On the other side (as a reaction to this idea of reformation), Ultra-Orthodoxy materialized, struggling to maintain traditional beliefs and practices by totally rejecting modernity. During the nineteenth century, Modern–Orthodoxy was presented as a solution to this split. It sought to adhere to traditional religious commitments (such as the observance of *Halakha*) while, at the same time, embracing many aspects of modern culture (Kaplan, 1979; Kurzweil, 1985; Leibman, 1982). This type of dialectical approach seems to offer a harmonistic identity: these Jews are both religious and modern (Schachter, 2002).

The *Halakha* details strict rules governing every aspect of the daily lives of Jews, including the sexual lives of married couples. Jewish law expressly forbids any physical contact between spouses during the days of menstruation and for a week thereafter. In addition, there are *Harchakot*, which are laws set up by the Rabbis to prevent anyone from getting close to violating *Niddah* (Eider, 1999; Y. Lehrfield, personal interview, August 22, 2006). These *Harchakot*, along with all rabbinical interpretation, carry the same weight of transgression as the original laws, and should be viewed as such (Eider, 1999; Keshet-Orr, 2003).

According to stipulated ritual, an Orthodox Jewish wife is responsible for ensuring that she is no longer exhibiting vaginal bleeding by swabbing herself carefully with a linen cloth for each of the seven days following the overt cessation of the menstrual flow (Burt & Rudolph, 2000; Eider, 1999). The seven clean days after menstruation culminate with the wife's obligation to immerse that night in the *Mikvah*, the ritual bath. This entire period of time, from the beginning of the "bleeding days," until the end of the seven "clean days," when the woman immerses herself in the ritual bath, is called the "*Niddah* (ritually unclean)" period.

Arch Sex Behav (2008) 37:340–345   341

It is only at the end of the *Niddah* interval, after the ritual bath, that spouses are permitted to physically touch one another. This "two weeks on/two weeks off" pattern of contact characterizes marital life until menopause, with two notable time frame exceptions: pregnancy and nursing (until postpartum menstruation resumes), when uninterrupted contact is permitted (Eider, 1999; Ribner, 2003). These "Laws of Family Purity" represent an integral aspect of identity as an Orthodox Jew (Donin, 1972; Wasserfall, 1992).

The Laws of Family Purity provide some potential benefits (e.g., heightened sexual interest following a two-week abstinence) as well as some challenges (e.g., the tension of no physical contact for two weeks) to Jewish couples, and have been the focus of some attention (Burt & Rudolph, 2000; Guterman, 2006; Hartman & Marmon, 2004; Ostrov, 1978; Petok, 2001; Wenger, 1998/1999).

Hartman and Marmon (2004) conducted interviews with Orthodox Jewish women. During these interviews, several observations were made. Many of the interviewed women found *Niddah* to be "particularly difficult," as compared to other religious obligations. One interviewee described her difficulty with *Niddah* as, "My needs for being touched are not just sexual; they're human." This lack of distinction between sexual and platonic touching during *Niddah* is the cause of much controversy amongst Jews (Hartman & Marmon, 2004) and critics of Judaism. In fact, some have referred to the laws of *Niddah* as "primitive blood taboos" (Wenger, 1998/1999). While these complaints are certainly not permissions to transgress, they may help to understand why so many couples choose to decide for themselves which aspects they will (and will not) follow (i.e., the laws that prohibit certain types of sexual contact).

Religion has long been considered an important influence on sexuality, defining the normative and penalizing the deviant. Research across disciplines has explored the relation between religiosity and sexual behavior (Davidson, Darling, & Norton, 1995). Previous studies have used a number of diverse methodologies (e.g., surveys, interviews, meta-analyses), and have studied the relation between religion and sexual behaviors (e.g., premarital sex, cohabiting, sexual behaviors while dating). Studies have found that women who more often attended religious services were less likely to have had premarital intercourse (Sack, Keller, & Hinkle, 1984; Thornton & Camburn, 1989). Other studies have found that this correlation persists through adulthood (Barkan, 2006). Studies have also reported that college students reporting higher levels of religiosity were less likely to give or receive oral sex or to participate in intercourse (Francis, 2006; Mahoney, 1980). Significant differences have been found regarding the degree of religiosity and the age of the beginning of sexual intercourse (Davidson et al., 1995; Hardy & Raffaelli, 2003). Women with religious beliefs reported fewer premarital sexually active friends

(Sack, Keller, & Hinkle, 1984). All told, well over 40 studies have found that increased levels of religiousness significantly correlate with lower levels of sexual activity (Murray-Swank, Pargament, & Mahoney, 2005). The main factor at the root of these findings is that different religions attempt to regulate sexual behavior and, to an extent, they are successful. Therefore, one would expect that, within Judaism, higher levels of religion would correlate with lower numbers of transgressions of the laws of *Niddah*.

While attention has been given to the emotions and thoughts of Jews observing the laws of *Niddah*, and studies have examined the relation between religiosity and sexual behavior, there is very limited research in exploring the actual adherence to these religious guidelines for sexual activity.

Of the American Jewish population of 5.2 million adults and children, 46% belong to a synagogue. Among those who belong to a synagogue, 22% are Orthodox, meaning that over 526,000 Jews in America are dealing with these Laws of Family Purity (Kotler-Berkowitz et al., 2004). Given the importance of religion to so many people's sexual decisions, as well as the fact that therapists must deal with many issues among Jews regarding *Niddah* (Keshet-Orr, 2003), empirical studies are needed to examine how well religious Jews adhere to their laws. The first study to look at the observance of Modern–Orthodox Jewish couples found that many laws were being broken overall and that more "lenient" laws were being broken than "strict" ones. In addition, the study found that older congregants were more likely to break the laws than younger ones (Guterman, 2006). This study was intended as a follow-up, to examine more closely, and in greater detail, the observance (or lack thereof) of *Niddah* among Modern–Orthodox Jews. Specifically, this study examined the difference in observance between the two weeks of *Niddah*.

Method

Participants

Participants were married, self-identified Modern–Orthodox Jews who filled out an online questionnaire survey. They were recruited via popular Modern–Orthodox online communication methods (see below). Participants were asked to complete the survey only if they defined themselves as Modern–Orthodox on the Internet. The survey was available worldwide on the Internet.

The final sample consisted of 119 men (44.57%) and 148 women (55.43%). It is not known whether any of the participants were couples, though this is doubtful as all responses were obtained from separate IP addresses (i.e., no one used the same computer).

Arch Sex Behav (2008) 37:340–345

The men were, on average, 35.45 years old (SD = 10.83; range, 21–70). The women were, on average, 33.53 years old (SD = 10.40; range, 19–61). The reported age at marriage for men was, on average, 24.57 years old (SD = 3.48; range, 20–38). The reported age at marriage for women was, on average, 23.48 years old (SD = 5.04; range, 18–64).

Measures

Demographic questions included age, sex, age married, and a "religious observance" section (see below). These demographic questions were included because they logically seem to be the most important factors that may influence which types of behaviors are transgressed during the ritually unclean period. The "religious observance" section contained four questions. The participants were instructed to rate, on a scale from 1 (very poor) to 6 (excellent), their religious observance of the following: eating kosher, Sabbath, daily prayers, and blessings on food. These items were taken from a previous religiosity scale (Rettinger & Jordan, 2005). In this study, the four items had a Cronbach's alpha of .78.

The questionnaire included a list of 16 behaviors, divided into two categories. The "lenient" (*Harchakot*) items were composed of four behaviors: passing items to each other, sleeping in joined (not separated) beds, sitting on the same cushion on a couch, and tapping each other on the shoulder, with a Cronbach's alpha of .85 for Week 1 and .87 for Week 2. The "strict" (actual *Niddah*) items were composed of 12 behaviors: holding hands in private, holding hands in public, kissing not on lips, kissing on lips without tongue, kissing passionately (with tongue), heavy petting (rubbing/squeezing/etc.), orgasm-directed caresses for the man (hand-job), orgasm-directed caresses for the woman (fingering), oral sex for the man (fellatio), oral sex for the woman (cunnilingus), anal intercourse, and vaginal intercourse, with a Cronbach's alpha of .91 for Week 1 and .95 for Week 2. These categories were supported by Rabbi Y. Lehrfield, who pointed out that there were two main categories of items: those which were strictly forbidden by the Torah (categorized as "strict"), and *Harchakot*, those laws instituted by the Rabbis to prevent the community from violating the Torah-forbidden laws (categorized as "lenient"). It should be mentioned, however, that all these behaviors (whether "strict" or "lenient") are expressly forbidden by Jewish law (Eider, 1999; Y. Lehrfield, personal interview, June 19, 2005).

These 16 items were listed twice—once under the heading of "Week 1" (the actual menstrual period) of the *Niddah* (ritually unclean) time of each month, and again under the heading of "Week 2" (the "clean days" following the cessation of bleeding) of the *Niddah* (ritually unclean) time of each month. Items were scored as either 0 ("no") or 1

("yes"). Menopausal women were instructed to note how they acted during their years of menstruation.

Procedure

Modern–Orthodox Jews were targeted for this online questionnaire survey using popular online communication methods (newsgroups [e.g., soc.culture.jewish.moderated, Rational Judaism], Yahoo! Groups [e.g., JewsTalk, TeaneckShuls, EdisonHighlandParkBulletinBoard], and other message boards [e.g., Hashkafah]). This allowed access to a large sample of the Modern–Orthodox Jewish community.

Potential participants were asked to complete a quick, four-minute survey. Participants were given an explanation of the survey, emphasizing how important it was to be completely honest, and guaranteeing the participant's anonymity several times.

Results

Descriptive statistics of frequencies were carried out on the data. During Week 1 (the actual menstrual period), an average of 3.76 behaviors were transgressed (SD = 4.08; range, 0–16). During Week 2 (the seven "clean days" following the cessation of bleeding), an average of 4.83 behaviors were transgressed (SD = 5.17; range, 0–16). The breakdown of participants performing each type of transgression is displayed in Table 1.

A 2 (Sex) × 2 (Behavior Type: proportion of "lenient" vs. proportion of "strict") × 2 (Time: Week 1 vs. Week 2) repeated measures analysis of variance was conducted to test for any main effects or interactions. Mean proportions of transgressed behaviors are displayed in Table 2.

Two significant main effects were found. First, a main effect of Time was found, $F(1, 265) = 46.45$; $p < .001$, eta^2 = .15, indicating that more behaviors were transgressed during the second week of *Niddah* than during the first week. Second, a main effect of Behavior Type was found, $F(1, 265) = 352.24$; $p < .001$, eta^2 = .57, indicating that there were a significantly larger proportion of "lenient" behaviors transgressed than "strict" behaviors. In addition, two interaction effects were found. First, Time interacted with Behavior Type, $F(1, 265) = 11.33$; $p < .01$, eta^2 = .04. Specifically, there was a larger increase in the proportion of "strict" behaviors, compared to "lenient" behaviors, being committed (see Table 2). Second, Sex interacted with Time, $F(1, 265) = 8.38$; $p < .01$, eta^2 = .03. Specifically, men, compared to women, showed a larger increase in the overall behaviors being committed from Week 1 to Week 2 (see Table 3).

Correlations between religious observance and number of transgressions during each week were performed. For

Arch Sex Behav (2008) 37:340–345   343

Table 1 Participants performing each type of transgression

	Men				Women				Combined			
	Week 1		Week 2		Week 1		Week 2		Week 1		Week 2	
	N	%	N	%	N	%	N	%	N	%	N	%
"Lenient" Behaviors												
Pass Items	97	36.33	101	37.83	82	30.71	86	32.21	179	67.04	187	70.04
Joint Beds	43	16.10	44	16.48	35	13.11	49	18.35	78	29.21	93	34.83
Same Cushion	78	29.21	81	30.34	63	23.60	73	27.34	141	52.81	154	57.68
Tap Shoulder	66	24.72	68	25.47	58	21.72	63	23.60	124	46.44	131	49.06
"Strict" Behaviors												
Hold Hands (Private)	51	19.10	54	20.22	44	16.48	50	18.73	95	35.58	104	38.95
Hold Hands (Public)	41	15.36	44	16.48	34	12.73	41	15.36	75	28.09	85	31.84
Kiss (Not on Lips)	50	18.73	51	19.10	44	16.48	52	19.48	94	35.21	103	38.58
Kiss (No Tongue)	42	15.73	45	16.85	31	11.61	44	16.48	73	27.34	89	33.33
Kiss (with Tongue)	20	7.49	35	13.11	14	5.24	29	10.86	34	12.73	64	23.97
Heavy Petting	17	6.37	31	11.61	18	6.74	36	13.48	35	13.11	67	25.09
Hand-job	13	4.87	24	8.99	13	4.87	30	11.24	26	9.74	54	20.22
Fingering	6	2.25	19	7.12	10	3.75	26	9.74	16	5.99	45	16.85
Fellatio	8	3.00	17	6.37	7	2.62	19	7.12	15	5.62	36	13.48
Cunnilingus	2	0.75	15	5.62	2	0.75	17	6.37	4	1.50	32	11.99
Anal Intercourse	3	1.12	3	1.12	2	0.75	6	2.25	5	1.87	9	3.37
Vaginal Intercourse	4	1.50	13	4.87	6	2.25	23	8.61	10	3.75	36	13.48

Table 2 Mean proportions of transgressed behaviors

	Week 1				Week 2			
	Lenient		Strict		Lenient		Strict	
	M	SD	M	SD	M	SD	M	SD
Men	0.50	0.39	0.16	0.24	0.57	0.42	0.26	0.34
Women	0.48	0.40	0.14	0.23	0.50	0.40	0.20	0.30
Combined	0.49	0.40	0.15	0.23	0.53	0.41	0.23	0.32

Table 3 Mean proportions of total transgressed behaviors

	Week 1		Week 2	
	M	SD	M	SD
Men	0.33	0.29	0.42	0.35
Women	0.31	0.29	0.35	0.33
Combined	0.32	0.29	0.38	0.34

Week 1, results showed a moderate negative correlation ($r = -0.57$; $p < .01$; $n = 267$). In other words, as one's religious observance score increased, the number of transgressions during Week 1 decreased. For Week 2, results also showed a moderate negative correlation ($r = -0.53$; $p < .01$; $n = 267$). Overall, these two correlations show that the scoring of the religious observance questions can be used as

a predictor of number of transgressions during the *Niddah* period.

Two more correlations were tested. The first determined that there was no significant correlation between age at marriage and number of transgressions across weeks (Week 1: $r = .01$; Week 2: $r = .05$). The second showed that there was no significant correlation between how long one had been married, and the number of transgressions across weeks (Week 1: $r = .16$; Week 2: $r = .16$).

Discussion

Based on the above analyses, it is concluded that, despite the prohibitions, nearly every participant reported transgressing at least once during the taboo period (with an average of 3.76 behaviors during Week 1 and 4.83 behaviors during Week

344   Arch Sex Behav (2008) 37:340–345

2). This supports the previous study which reported that, over the course of the two-week period, 3.34 behaviors were transgressed, on average (Guterman, 2006). One may wonder why 3–4 violations constitute nonobservance; after all, a score of 3.4 (out of 16) is fairly observant. However, the reader is reminded that performing any one of these behaviors is a sin according to Jewish law. Therefore, while it may be better than committing 16 sins, each of the 3 or 4 behaviors was still a transgression.

The interviews conducted by Hartman and Marmon (2004) may shed some light as to why these transgressions are taking place. One woman found the laws "dehumanizing" in that they disregarded her emotional needs. Another described her "intense frustration and inner turmoil" and felt "bound inextricably" to a ritual which caused her so much "personal torment." In fact, a number of women expressed frustration about the absence of a sexually neutral space wherein they could relate to their husbands. Specifically, they wanted to have platonic physical contact with their husbands, which would not lead to sexual activity. Many interviewees did "not see the logic in [*Niddah*]" and stated that their lives "would've been much better without it."

The most important finding of this study was that, despite the *Halakha* seeing no difference between weeks one and two, there was a significant difference in the amount of transgressions being committed during the two weeks; participants were more ready to ignore the *Halakha* during the second week of *Niddah*. These data seem to reveal that it is not necessarily the Laws of Family Purity that are being observed; rather, it may be that the restrictive nature of the laws is simply convenient when a woman is actually menstruating. Once she has stopped menstruating, however, the stringency of the laws may seem too great (or may seem unimportant in the first place), and are therefore disregarded. The reasons for abstaining from sexual behaviors during the actual menstruation are still unclear: is it due to religion or is it due to fear of menstrual blood? Future studies should compare the "clean days" of *Niddah* to the permitted weeks (following immersion in the *Mikvah*), so as to further assess whether this increase in Week 2 is a full return to normal activity or whether there is still some restraint. This will help clarify if these religious Jews are following the common pattern of many non-religious individuals, who limit their sexual behavior during the menstrual period itself and increase their frequency in the weeks thereafter.

The reason for the difference in adherence between "lenient" and "strict" laws may also be better understood by referring back to the women interviewed by Hartman and Marmon (2004). In the absence of a sexually neutral place for these couples, many seem to have drawn their own lines, and decided that the "lenient" laws (which are of a more platonic nature) are not as important. This certainly follows the logic of the complaint quoted above, "My needs for

being touched are not just sexual; they're human." Following the same logic, couples may have felt that they can decide for themselves, without the rabbinical guidelines, what "comes close to violating *Niddah*," and therefore ignored the "lenient" laws across weeks.

Finally, it is important to note that the "religious observance" section, a Likert scale rating one's religious observance of eating kosher, Sabbath, daily prayers, and blessings on food, correlated well with transgressive behavior. This supports the reliability of the scale (Rettinger & Jordan, 2005), and allows for future studies to include this new, shorter version (containing only four items) to help determine religiosity.

These results fit well with the previous literature on the subject. As mentioned earlier, over 40 studies have demonstrated that higher levels of religiosity correlate with lower levels of sexual behavior (Murray-Swank et al., 2005). Although this study looked at a different religion (i.e., Judaism), the results remained. That is, religious observance was inversely correlated with the total number of sexual behaviors. This suggests that these effects are not religion-specific, and can be applied to Judaism as well.

The replication of the results of Guterman (2006), coupled with this study's much larger sample size (and evenly sexed sample), makes the findings of these two studies hard to ignore. Certain laws are simply disregarded in the Modern–Orthodox Jewish community. The fact remains: public rules, whether they are of a religious or social nature, are often broken.

The main strengths of this study lie in its straightforwardness and anonymity. Very little research like this has been conducted within the Jewish community, and it would be interesting to have comparative data of adherence and transgression in other ritual realms within Judaism. Furthermore, this is the first Internet-based study of this topic among this group, yet it reports similar results to the previous study, in which the sample was recruited through a synagogue (Guterman, 2006). This suggests that future studies in this area can make use of the advantages that Internet research has to offer.

Being a survey, there were some inherent problems with the design. For one, it is hard to ensure that the participants told the entire truth. Repeated guarantees of anonymity probably helped, but there is no way to know for sure. Trying to reach a representative sample of the population is always difficult. It was for this exact reason that the survey was conducted online. However, this may have led to some complications in the sample (i.e., a response bias); one does not know how typical of Modern–Orthodox Jews the sample was. Yet, the results showed that there were both participants who transgressed none, or few, of the laws, as well as participants who transgressed many of the laws. This seems to suggest that this study obtained a representative sample of

Arch Sex Behav (2008) 37:340–345

the Modern–Orthodox Jewish community, since there were participants from both ends of the spectrum. Additionally, there is room for speculation as to whether the same results would have emerged had the sample been recruited through Orthodox synagogues, rather than the Internet. However, the previous study (Guterman, 2006) used the recruiting method and obtained extremely similar results. Of course, an even larger sample size may tell us more information. Further research in this area is strongly recommended. Research should focus on other denominations of Judaism, and how well the laws are followed within these sects.

Acknowledgment The author would like to thank Orit Avishai, Stephen Armeli, Robert McGrath, Winnie Eng, J. Kenneth Davidson, Sr., and David Moore for their comments on earlier drafts of this article.

References

Barkan, S. (2006). Religiosity and premarital sex in adulthood. *Journal for the Scientific Study of Religion, 45,* 407–417.
Burt, V. K., & Rudolph, M. (2000). Treating an Orthodox Jewish woman with obsessive-compulsive disorder: Maintaining reproductive and psychologic stability in the context of normative religious rituals. *American Journal of Psychiatry, 157,* 620–624.
Davidson, J. K., Darling, C. A., & Norton, L. (1995). Religiosity and the sexuality of women: Sexual behavior and sexual satisfaction revisited. *Journal of Sex Research, 32,* 235–243.
Donin, H. H. (1972). *To be a Jew.* New York: Basic Books.
Eider, S. D. (1999). *Sefer Hilkhot Niddah = Halachos of Niddah.* Jerusalem: Feldheim Publishers.
Francis, L. (2006). Attitude toward Christianity and premarital sex. *Psychological Reports, 98,* 140.
Guterman, M. A. (2006). Identity conflict in Modern-Orthodox Judaism and the laws of family purity. *Method & Theory in the Study of Religion, 18,* 92–100.
Hardy, S., & Raffaelli, M. (2003). Adolescent religiosity and sexuality: An investigation of reciprocal influences. *Journal of Adolescence, 26,* 731–739.
Hartman, T., & Marmon, N. (2004). Lived regulations systemic attributions: Menstrual separation and ritual immersion in the experience of Orthodox Jewish women. *Sex & Society, 18,* 389–408.
Kaplan, L. (1979). The ambiguous Modern-Orthodox Jew. *Judaism, 28,* 439–448.
Keshet-Orr, J. (2003). Jewish women and sexuality. *Sexual and Relationship Therapy, 18,* 215–224.
Kotler-Berkowitz, L., Cohen, S. M., Ament, J., Klaff, V., Mott, F., & Peckerman-Neuman, D. (2004). *The National Jewish Population Survey 2000-01: Strength, challenge and diversity in the American Jewish population.* New York: United Jewish Communities.
Kurzweil, Z. E. (1985). *The modern impulse of traditional Judaism.* Hoboken, NJ: Ktav Publishing House.
Leibman, C. (1982). The evolvement of neo-traditionalism among Orthodox Jews in Israel. *Megamot, 27,* 231–249.
Mahoney, E. R. (1980). Religiosity and sexual behavior among heterosexual college students. *Journal of Sex Research, 16,* 97–113.
Murray-Swank, N., Pargament, K., & Mahoney, A. (2005). At the crossroads of sexuality and spirituality: The sanctification of sex by college students. *International Journal for the Psychology of Religion, 15,* 199–219.
Ostrov, S. (1978). Sex therapy with Orthodox Jewish couples. *Journal of Sex and Marital Therapy, 4,* 266–278.
Petok, W. D. (2001). Religious observance and sex therapy with an Orthodox Jewish couple. *Journal of Sex Education and Therapy, 26,* 22–27.
Rettinger, D. A., & Jordan, A. E. (2005). The relations among religion, motivation and college cheating: A natural experiment. *Ethics & Behavior, 15,* 107–129.
Ribner, D. S. (2003). Determinants of the intimate lives of Haredi (Ultra-Orthodox) Jewish couples. *Sexual & Relationship Therapy, 18,* 53–62.
Sack, A. R., Keller, J. F., & Hinkle, D. E. (1984). Premarital sexual intercourse: A test of the effects of peer group, religiosity, and sexual guilt. *Journal of Sex Research, 20,* 168–185.
Schachter, E. P. (2002). Identity constraints: The perceived structural requirements of a 'good' identity. *Human Development, 45,* 416–433.
Thornton, A., & Camburn, D. (1989). Religious participation and adolescent sexual behavior and attitudes. *Journal of Marriage & the Family, 51,* 641–653.
Wasserfall, R. (1992). Menstruation and identity: The meaning of Niddah for Moroccan women immigrants to Israel. In H. Eilberg-Schwartz (Ed.), *People of the body* (pp. 309–327). Albany, NY: State University of New York Press.
Wenger, B. S. (1998/1999). Mitzvah and medicine: Sex, assimilation, and the scientific defense of 'family purity'. *Jewish Social Studies, 5,* 177–202.

[8]

Jewish women and sexuality

JUDI KESHET-ORR

Whittington Hospital NHS Trust, London, UK

ABSTRACT *This paper sets out to explore the effect that Jewish laws and teachings have, and continue to have, upon Jewish women. Sexual practice are examined in the light of twentieth century influences and the advent or psychosexual therapy in conjunction with an integrative approach to psychotherapy are included. Some twentieth century literature is discussed and prominent figures within the Jewish community were approached and their views incorporated within the text. The results of the research are distilled from a MSc dissertation which the author undertook in 1995. Professionals implications are highlighted and conclusions are drawn. This work is specific to Jewish women and is in no way intended to be a comparison with other ethnic groups.*

Introduction

'Nothing makes religious people as nervous as sex, or at least unregulated sex'
Berne (1993).

Love, intimacy, sensuality, relating, communication and sexuality are some of the positive words used when describing the process of psychosexual therapy and what it attempts to provide, enhance and encourage with and for the client(s). Words less often used are shame, guilt, disappointment, secrecy, anger and rage. Psychosexual and relationship therapy offered from a Humanistic Integrative orientation approaches the work from a perspective which, whilst acknowledging the value of the more traditional cognitive behavioural, psychodynamic or medical viewpoints also emphasises the empowerment and equality of the individual or couple. Humanistic therapy does not talk in terms of 'cure' rather that the therapist and client(s) together seek out a variety of new awarenessess and insights which the client can utilize and employ if they wish. The need to identify and work with the family of origin constructs which have informed the couple or individual, in addition to the effects of gender, ethnicity and cultural belief system of the therapist upon the therapeutic relationship are all part of this complex therapeutic alliance. Sexuality and the increased awareness of woman has impacted on many communities; however those from minority groups

Correspondence to: Judi Keshet-Orr, 181 Hampstead Way, London, NW11 7YA, UK, Tel: 020 8455 4511; Fax: 020 8455 4514; Email: judiko@ulfie.demon.co.uk; Website: www.partnertherapy.com

216   *Judi Keshet-Orr*

who may have clear and strict rulings regarding their sexual practices and behaviour have largely been ignored within current literature and within approved psychosexual training environments. To understand the complex nature of any difficulties presented by Jewish women, the genesis of the belief system and the historical context must be understood. In 1970 Masters and Johnson introduced 'sensate focus' which, it could be argued has become the backbone of sex therapy in the UK. It could be suggested that this system fails to address, with any level of depth, is the past and present emotional, spiritual, social and cultural reality of the client(s). Furthermore, it does not address the cultural mores of many minority groups. However Masters and Johnson also stated that 'there is no such thing as an uninvolved partner in any marriage in which there is some form of sexual inadequacy' and whilst we may consider the language outdated, the tenet is something which could be considered to be as accurate today as it was when written. This article focuses on sexuality and Jewish women and how to perform psychosexual therapy from a humanistic perspective with this client group. In considering the difficulties inherent in any such task, we need to address aspects of Jewish law, which has both a written and oral tradition. Thus far then, we are congruent with humanistic therapy. However the oral and written traditions within Jewish law do not always appear to be in harmony and therefore contradictions may be found.

The Talmud is the central text; within it are found the Gemara and Mishna. Gemara is the Talmudic commentary on the Mishna, which is the second century rabbinic legal code and forms the basis of the Talmud and its oral code. Halakah—'the way' is Jewish law, these have specific rulings, and are both oral and written traditions. The Torah contains the whole body of religious teaching and laws and specifically the five books of Moses. Rabbinical discourse over the interpretation of these laws, teachings and rules has been part of Jewish life and tradition since the creation of these documents. Broadly speaking Jews are divided into two ethnic groups; Sephardic Jews are generally accepted as those who originate from Spain, Portugal, Iran, Iraq, North Africa and India. Ashkenazie Jews are those who originate from Germany, and are of Eastern European decent. A lesser used term is that of Mizrahim that specifically denotes those who originate from Asia and North Africa. Other definitions include Masorti, Liberal, Reform and Orthodox; within the orthodox tradition there are several sub divisions. Thus, there are many complexities within these labels and divisions and it is not within the scope of this paper to develop these in any depth.

In my work as a psychosexual and relationship therapist I am often presented with, and confronted by, the beliefs with which Jewish women were brought up and their current life styles. Techniques, methods and philosophy within Humanistic therapy, can often be at variance with these beliefs. Individuals and couples' work using integrative methods is a creative and challenging way of working where almost inevitably there are some profound disclosures, and where the meaning for the client forms the foundation of the therapeutic contract.

Within the work of a psychosexual and relationship therapist it is openly acknowledged that sexuality and sexual/sensual functioning and the capacity to be intimate plays an important role in all our lives. Looking holistically at the issues we are not only confronted by what is commonly regarded as the biological drive, our libidinal energy, but also by that of sexual attraction which may have nothing or very little to do with availability or compatibility. Sex may be experienced as power with or over. Thus, work within this domain contains endless components and curiosities for the practitioner and client alike.

Looking historically at psychotherapy, which is often labelled 'the Jewish science,' Brewer (1986:2) suggests that Jews outweigh non-Jews in the profession. Her suggestion that:

'within the past ten years women have turned to women therapists with their problems. Within the Jewish community, there is now a greater number of female sex therapists, in a field which has traditionally been dominated by males'.

I would add, however that Jewish women cannot be seen as a single collective; they come self-labelled, from different backgrounds and cultures and with different belief systems. 'Onah' describes the conjugal rights of a woman who is married, including the marital obligations of the husband. Briefly, the husband is instructed to ensure that his wife has sufficient sexual and sensual enjoyment and activity within the marriage. Whilst instruction or prescription may be a part of the more conventional approach to sexual therapy, it is, in essence contra-indicated when working with an egalitarian and integrative approach to therapy. Clearly, it is difficult to work freely and holistically within a community, which in some parts, is controlled by a strict adherence to Jewish law. Additionally, within Jewish law, a man is obliged to produce at least two children, preferably one of each sex; should his wife prove to suffer with infertility difficulties and the husband cannot fulfil this requirement a divorce can be legitimized. A woman who is unable to become pregnant may bring forth a multitude of sexual and social difficulties, which can attack the very foundations of her gender role.

For Jewish women the fact that sexuality is a social and historical construction is particularly obvious, there existing a religious and historical tenet in Talmudic law. Same sex or multiple relationships are not addressed other than to attach critical and damming rules to these. One of the difficulties in succinctly defining sexuality is the lack of precise and uniform vocabulary. It is also true that many social symbols are based on sexuality. Thus many people when describing sexuality talk in symbolic language, vague terms or with a clinical and political distance which does not reflect the totality of the human experience of sexuality.

Despite over two decades in practice I am still reminded by many clients of their difficulties when invited to talk through their sexual and intimate issues. This often coupled with either lack of information or misinformation and can lead to a position where folklore or opinions become fact; and it is then a source of great distress to the individual or couple. This difficulty appears to have no respect for age or orientation.

There is a wealth of information on Jewish law and its application to life, equally there is a wealth of information on offering sex therapy from a traditional and often medicalized and pathologized belief system. Sadly, there is little written about the application of sexual and relationship therapy from a Humanistic integrative bias. Perhaps it is true to say that one of the first integrative sex therapists was Wilhelm Reich followed by Alexander Lowen and the neo-Reichians and more recently the Gestaltists and body therapists. A fundamental issue is that psychosexual therapists spend a great

218   *Judi Keshet-Orr*

deal of time learning by doing; each session is potentially an experiential learning arena and informs the practice of the therapist. I suggest that it is vital that we do not become theory bound and continue to appreciate that it is the relationship and not necessarily the theory which enhances and encourages the work. We, as therapists need to confront working at times contradictory system. Thereby we use that which is valuable to the client. This would mean that issues of 'purity' can be lost; our exploration of other methodologies can enhance our work and we would be congruent to life by abandoning a linear system working with an openly dialogic environment which respects the level of energy and awareness of the client. As therapists, we work with what is alive for us and meaningful for the client.

This style would in itself create some difficulties when working with more orthodox women within the Jewish community who adhere to the traditional teachings on sexuality. These would include only having sexual intercourse in the 'missionary position', with the lights off at predetermined times within the middle portion of the woman's menstrual cycle whilst at the same time putting the responsibility on the husband to ensure his wife's sexual pleasure and gratification.

From an integrated perspective, this is clearly untenable, and unless the psychosexual therapist comes from the same or similar traditions, therapy, which is full of richness, exploration, innovation and experimentation, is largely unworkable. The constraint placed on any sexual therapists would be so great as to encourage a prescriptive and advice giving environment.

Authors such as Jong, Miller, Roth and Potok achieved popularity in part, through their description of Jewish life as a conglomeration of mythology and caricature, no less effective for encompassing the kernel of truth apparent in all stereotyping. It could be argued that this demonstrates a form of internalized anti-Semitism, perhaps disguised as another Jewish stereotype—self-deprecation.

Portrayal of Jewish women in these part autobiographical novels range from Jong's rapacious sexual being to the archetypal matriarch. Jeffrey Weeks in his essay 'Questions of Identity' (Kaplan 1987: 31) says:

'Sexual identity and sexual desire are not fixed and unchanging. We create boundaries and identities for ourselves to contain what might otherwise threaten to engulf or dissolve into formlessness'.

As therapists, this is a notion we can and do work with. However, this is juxtaposed by a traditional Jewish perception, which might be that rigid boundaries are both necessary and essential to preserve their intrinsic Jewishness. Plaskow (1991: 179) states:

'The heart of Jewish ambivalence toward sexuality is roughly this: The sexual impulse is given by God and thus is a normal and healthy part of Jewish life. Sexual relations are appropriate only within the framework of heterosexual marriage, but within marriage, they are good, indeed, commanded. Yet sexuality—even within marriage—also requires careful, sometimes rigorous control, in order that it not transgress the boundaries of marriage or the laws of *niddah* [a menstruating woman] within it'.

The idea that civilization requires sublimation of the sexual drive runs through the work of many writers. For Jewish woman it may well be that adherence to traditional mores and values are a means of ensuring the continuing identity of the Jewish people. Judaism has always acknowledged that women are sexual beings and the 'Madonna/whore' dichotomy prevalent in Christian belief has therefore not existed for Jewish women. Furthermore, Judaism has never welcomed celibacy as having any religious or spiritual worth.

The growth of Western psychotherapy and its relationship with Eastern traditions over the last 100 years has taken a particular interest in sexuality. Freud's name is inextricably linked with the concept of sex, despite much of this being associated with repression, fixation and anxiety. One may be forgiven for thinking that Freud's beliefs and theoretical understanding of sexuality was largely governed by his relationship to his mother, a Jewish woman. If we look at the notion of penis envy and the concept that the clitoris is inferior, we must also address the serious ramifications that this belief supports. Within the world of established Freudian psychotherapy (and no doubt within some areas of Judaism), the notion that the vaginal orgasm is 'mature' whereas the clitoral one is 'immature' can have great influence. Orthodox Jewish women who may only experience penetrative sex in the missionary position, with an absence of foreplay, are unlikely to experience a clitoral orgasm. Denied that which is commonly regarded as the more intense orgasmic experience they then may be asked if they comfort themselves that they experience the more 'mature' sexual pleasure as described by Freud, a Jewish man, thus making congruent the traditional orthodox teachings surrounding sexual practice.

Humanistic therapy also has many Jewish exponents. Wilhelm Reich, Fritz Perls, Jack Rosenberg and Abraham Maslow have in common what could be described as a more life affirming view of female sexuality; their belief being that women have a powerful and energetic sexual drive, which they have a right to develop, pursue and enjoy. They do not see sexual activity as a purely procreative or physical activity. It may also be true that many men have been raised to believe that unless they are in control sexually then the experience is a negative or humiliating one and the sexually liberated woman poses an inevitable threat. One way of dealing with this possible or supposed threat is to demonize women. Judaism is no exception to this. Lileth, the folkloric figure who predates Eve as Adam's companion, is described as a long-haired temptress insisting on the woman superior position in sexual activity; she also has murderous tendencies. The man who is tempted by this figure risks all, including, as the sins of the father are visited on the children, the continuation of the race.

Clearly there is much therapeutic work to be done when working with this original template. During the formative years of psychosexual therapy, the emphasis was placed on behavioural techniques not on psychotherapeutic longer-term involvement. During the last 20 years this original form of sex therapy has moved into areas that are more diverse; these rely on the motivation, inter-action and communication skills of both therapist and client. Any sexual therapist does, however, need to be appropriately conversant with the physiology, anatomy and organic causes of sexual difficulties.

In an earlier research study, which I undertook in 1995, I asked Jewish women about their experiences in psychotherapy and psychosexual therapy. All these women ($n = 36$) had to a lesser or greater degree, at some time within their therapeutic process explored the relevance of sexuality, its impact on their lives and to what degree being Jewish had affected them. All the women spoke about the way in which therapy had given them a language to understand and express their sexuality in ways that had previously been denied. At its simplest level, the therapeutic alliance had given these women accurate and factual information regarding anatomy and physiology, bodily functioning and a safe environment in which to explore their issues. The women who I interviewed had diverse experiences of Psychosexual therapy both medium and long term. They had experienced behavioural, psychodynamic and humanistic therapists; no school or modality of therapy had been used more than any other. I therefore had to surmise that it was the therapy in itself and not the school or method which had allowed for a more openly dialogic environment where a commonality of language was created, that each woman's choice was validated and thereby enhanced the fluidity of their sexual, sensual and intimate language. Additionally it allowed some of these Jewish women to confront issues about monogamy, orientation confusion and divorce. An important factor for these women was that they were able to undertake a depth exploration of the meaning of their Jewishness and its relationship to their sexuality.

The paradox of healthy sexuality is that its very liberation and openness creates potential vulnerability. Simply, in order to experience the excitation of vulnerability a woman needs to feel safe enough in her environment to have access to her full emotional and expressive world. Some of the comments which I received from respondents included:

> 'being Jewish is me, therefore it must effect my sexuality',
> being Jewish is a fundamental part of my identity, it informs me physically and emotionally',
> 'being Jewish informs my sexuality, I idealise family values',
> 'I feel bad and guilty for not wanting or taking pleasure in sex at the 'right' times',
> 'how do I as a Jewish woman teach my sons and daughters about sex and how do I teach them to have views which are open and consistent with Judaism?'.

The essence of these women's Jewishness ran through these statements and cannot, I believe, be dissassociated from them being sexual women. Judaism and its teachings and relevance to woman are full of contradictions. Whilst women are seen as sexual beings with rights and needs, they are seen as people who will be sexually available at prescribed times, heterosexuality is assumed. Links between sexuality, fertility and femininity are also issues, which are present and create challenges within the therapeutic environment.

Working with a Jewish woman, either in a couple or as an individual raises additional questions, not least the one of ethnotherapy. Weinstein Klein says:

> 'Ethnotherapy seeks to move people from conflicts in their identity to a more secure and positive grounding in their group, as well as more positive self-esteem. Personal problems are then seen through an ethnic lens in their defining social context'.

One must question: can we truly fit the client with the therapist? We need to address not only the gender of the therapist but also the religious and political background of both client and therapist. None of us are free of folklore, myth and anecdotal tales; I suggest that when working and within supervision we need to identify and work towards resolution of these lest we contaminate and taint the process.

Jewish therapists working with Jewish clients may have an exacting task within their internal and external supervision process; this is fertile ground for transferential issues. Clearly early sexual information and education play an important part in determining later sexual attitudes and practices. Within formal Jewish education, there appears to be little or no formal sex education, furthermore there is very little data on Jewish women. With this in mind, the Chief Rabbi commissioned a survey in 1993. Within this study the questionnaire was entitled 'Survey of Attitudes' although many of the questions asked were factual and included issues such as income, education, kosher food and family issues. Sexuality was omitted from this major piece of work.

During my own research study I spent some time asking the women what effect, if any, Jewish law had on their sexuality. When considering the effect of Feminism on their sexuality these women recognized the gulf between traditional Jewish law and twentieth century feminist politics. They fell into two distinct camps, half choosing effectively to opt out of tradition whilst holding on to what they perceived as part of their essential Jewishness and birthright and the remainder choosing to find a way through the dilemmas. All the women I had spoken to brought these issues to therapy. Hershal writing in Jewish Women in Therapy (Siegel & Cole, 1990: 39) states:

'For Jewish women who do not see themselves reflected in the images and roles set forth by classical Judaism, the task is to develop an identity that will combine the values of feminism with those of Judaism. Feminist therapists can be crucial in making women aware that the negative stereotypes regarding femaleness they have internalized are derived from classical male authored Jewish texts'.

Thus, personal challenges may confront family norms leading to the potential for an inter-familial re-evaluation of what it means to preserve Judaism. Part of the therapeutic process may be to consider whether the relationship between the conscious denial of certain aspects of Jewish law and the acceptance of the general assumption, which affirms the rights of women, is congruent with integrative therapy.

Sexuality with all its fluidity and variation must also be seen in the context of self-esteem, body image, environmental, personal and social security. Therefore, how safe Jewish women feel in Britain today is a question, which is worthy of asking. Second generation women often dealing with, and confronted by, the holocaust may have specific psychosexual issues to examine. Did Jewish women change after this relatively recent trauma? Perhaps given that Jews had never, in modern times, had a 'home land' until the creation of Israel, the issues contained within assimilation, particularly for the non-orthodox, are issues that have to be dealt with in some form or other. This may have been through denial or keeping themselves in what could be regarded as modern time 'shtetle' (small Jewish towns or villages) enclaves.

There is little doubt that the children and grand children of holocaust survivors and refugees have passed on to them a set of values and beliefs, which have caused much confusion, anxiety and pain. There is a commonly understood notion that the one and a half million children who died in the concentration camps need to be replaced, and families rebuilt. A Jewish psychotherapist documented in Baker's (1993: 158) work states:

> 'You know, I've got no family; my mother came to this country as a child and all her family perished; my father's parents died, too, when he was little and he was separated from his only sister. The most important thing for me to do was to become a mother, a Jewish mother'.

I have little doubt that marriage and producing children is seen as a fundamental part of being Jewish and, thus, that the continuation and preservation of Jewish people within society is guaranteed. Another important aspect of the holocaust experience in which six million people died was the brutalization of the racial psyche. Thus Jewish women must not only ensure the continuation of the line but also ensure that they are never again so vulnerable. This coupled with the guilt of the survivor who when so many died, and whose grief at whole chapters of families disappearing could been seen as leading to a calcification of any experiences, sexual, racial or inter-personal, which could then lead to further vulnerability. The holocaust continues to have a profound impact on attitudes to children and family values. The significance of relationships and having a Jewish partner who understands these values and cultural norms appears to be of similar concern. The continuation of the Jewish line is carried through the mother, even if the father is a non Jew. Jews do not seek converts; however, the orthodox community does not truly accept those who do convert to Judaism.

Judaism and its teachings and relevance to women is full of contradictions. Whilst women are seen as sexual beings with rights and needs, they are also seen as people who will fulfil their husband's needs both sexually and as mother and home maker. The woman is the reason that the husband remains faithful. Single men are often viewed with suspicion, they are obliged to marry and produce children. Exclusive relationships are deemed essential; in reality we know that this is not always the practice. One of the many contradictions is that in written Jewish law a woman may remain unmarried and childless, however, in oral law this is not the case. Rabbinical interpretation carries a great deal of weight. Woman may be ordained as rabbis within the Liberal and Reform but not in the Orthodox movement.

When working in the domain of Jewish women and sexuality it is important to attempt to define sexuality. There would also be some distinction to examine between that which is generally understood to be healthy or unhealthy sexuality coupled with the notion that in order to have sex you need to have love. This would clearly be important when working with any client from any culture.

The duality of function focused on women's genitalia is also an important issue; sexual pleasure and reproduction may not always go in parallel. Whilst some people will take this for granted others may not only see these two functions as inextricably linked and inseparable but also find the notion of pure sexual pleasure, with no attention or desire placed upon reproduction, as one that is almost unthinkable.

As therapists working within this complex field, we need to have some understanding and cognisance of the multi-faceted issues involved when working with Jewish women and their sexuality. To address specifically the objectives and aims of the psychosexual and relationship domain within any client group we must address our fundamental task and mandate that is offered by the client. As therapists, we need to be of service to our clients, many of whom present with poor or diminished communication skills, difficulties in resolving conflict, anger management, sexual confusions and difficulties, inhibition and psychogenic dysfunction. Many clients will attend seeking pharmacological answers and treatments; for some there may be a place within their therapeutic process where these treatments are appropriate, for others, there is no such 'quick fix'.

Jewish psychosexual and relationship therapists working with Jewish clients need to confront and explore their own internalized messages and their degree of comfort with their own form of Jewishness. From the outside Jews may be seen as a homogenous group, from within there are many divisions and sub sections. On a simple level, it may not be possible to offer or perform integrative sexual and relationship therapy with some of the more orthodox branches of Jews and indeed they may not seek intervention from a therapist. In the event that they do, the Jewish therapist is faced with some dilemmas. According to Jewish law there are some relationships which are not sanctioned, these would include an incestuous relationship, a mixed or trans-religious relationship, adulterous relationships, a relationship with anyone who is the product of a defined forbidden relationship, and same sex relationships. Transgender or gender dysphoric work or the use of surrogates is also forbidden. Thus, a large population may be excluded from therapeutic work. For the therapist this may raise ethical issues should any of these excluded or forbidden relationships come to light within the process of therapy. In essence, the therapist is faced with only three choices: they may terminate therapy, they may be critical of the client and move into a 'critical parent' figure; or they may do nothing. Jews, within the law, must not support or collude with any transgressions. Issues about menstruating women and the prohibition of sexual intimacy during this period of the month abound. If, as Jewish law prescribes sexual activity must take place in an environment of holiness, the spontaneous, free and more experimental forms of intimacy and sexuality are by this very guiding rule excluded.

Clearly not all Jewish clients present with the more orthodox or conventional forms of Judaism, however it is my experience that many clients carry with them these beliefs and mores into their therapy, it may be from these emotional places within that of an environment of criticism and frustration or perhaps regret and confusion form the basis for the therapy.

As integrative therapists we need to be aware of our own introjects when working with this client group. Furthermore, a solution focused form of sexual therapy will not I believe work with the more religious or observant Jewish women and we are therefore invited to construct a form of therapeutic alliance which will honour both our own beliefs and ethics and support the client in her desire to change and heal. It is incumbent upon us to be sufficiently well informed about any cultural group and Jewish women are certainly no exception to this.

224   *Judi Keshet-Orr*

References

BAKER, A. (1993). *The Jewish woman in contemporary society*. London: Macmillan Press Ltd.
BERNE, E. (1993). *Sex and human loving*. London: Penguin Books.
BREWER, J.S. (1986). *Sex & the modern Jewish woman—an annotated bibliography*. New York: Biblio Press.
KAPLAN, P. (1987). *The cultural construction of sexuality*. London: Routledge.
PLASKOW, J. (1991). *Standing again at Sinai—Judaism from a feminist perspective*. New York: Harper Collins.
SIEGEL, R. & COLE, E. (1990). *Jewish women in therapy—seen but not heard*. New York: Harrington Park Press.

Contributor

JUDI KESHET-ORR, UKCP reg. BASRT Accred. BASRT Recognised Supervisor. MAHPP BRCP. UPA Clinical member, *Consultant Psychosexual and Relationship Psychotherapist*

[9]

OF PEARLS AND FISH: AN ANALYSIS OF JEWISH LEGAL TEXTS ON SEXUALITY AND THEIR SIGNIFICANCE FOR CONTEMPORARY AMERICAN JEWISH MOVEMENTS

RACHEL SARA ROSENTHAL*

Analyzing *halakhic* texts provides insights into the past and present regulation of sexuality under *Halakhah*.[1] This Article argues that halakhic conceptions of sexuality in Jewish texts, which promote the expression of heterosexual desire through marriage, form the basis of modern strategic readings of sacred texts that disenfranchise women in the process of divorce and reject homosexuality as a permissible sexual identity. Located in the family,[2] where struggles between authority and the expression of sexuality commonly occur, these two issues illustrate how changes in American social norms may, or should, affect the interpretations and implementation of Halakhah by the rabbinical authorities of the modern Jewish movements.

Because Orthodox, Reform, Conservative, and Reconstructionist Judaism each approach Jewish texts and traditions differently, however, their decisions are tempered by their varying theological assumptions about the divine authority of sacred works. Nonetheless, each movement's approach to sexuality has practical effects on the lives of American Jews who follow Halakhah. Consequently, Part II analyzes halakhic texts from past and present rabbinical perspectives that exemplify the laws regulating sexuality, focusing on the rabbinic preference for heterosexual desire as properly expressed in marriage. This Article examines the underlying

---

* Candidate for J.D., Columbia Law School, 2006; B.A., Duke University. I would like to thank Professors Eric Meyers, Carol Meyers, Jean Fox O'Barr, and Eric Zakim for their support. All errors, of course, are attributable only to me.

[1] This Article employs the term Halakhah, that is, the Hebrew word for Jewish law, to signify the corpus of Jewish texts that introduces and expands laws rather than those works that engage in exegesis of certain sacred texts. The plural of Halakhah is *Halakhot* and the adjective is halakhic. In this Article, halakhic is generally equivalent to sacred because many Jewish movements consider Jewish legal texts to have some relationship to God and to holiness, although the degree differs substantially.

[2] Of course, the effects of power dynamics in the family depend on the individuals involved; within the family unit, the woman may in fact have more influence. This Article, however, looks at Jewish legal positions, that is, the "official" regulations that do not reflect reality in every family.

486 *Columbia Journal of Gender and Law* [Vol. 15:2

normative assumptions of differences between men's and women's sexuality. In this context, the discussion of heterosexuality also addresses the modern Jewish attitudes regarding the purpose of marriage between a man and a woman from traditional and liberal perspectives.

Parts III and IV explore the influence of halakhic conceptions of sexuality on divorce and homosexuality. These issues have been chosen because they are matters regulated by Jewish legal institutions. Part III addresses the legal intricacies of divorce in the Jewish tradition and the difficult situation of the *agunah*, a woman whose husband has refused to grant her a *get*, or a Jewish writ of divorce. The issue of divorce is located in a larger textual discussion of the position of women in marriage. The section explains how, in the rabbinic materials, the assumptions underlying the halakhic regulation of a woman's sexuality conflict with contemporary social norms. This Article also explores the respective American Jewish movements' responses to this issue. Part IV begins with an analysis of halakhic verses that prohibit homosexual sex in contrast to those texts that suggest the possibility for alternative genders and sexualities. It also addresses the halakhic and social implications of these texts for modern Jewish movements, examining the official reactions of traditional and liberal Jewish movements to the increased visibility and participation of gay, lesbian, bisexual, and transgender Jews ("GLBT Jews") in their respective Jewish communities. It also incorporates GLBT Jews' articulations of their relationships to, and with, the larger Jewish communities in the search for positive Jewish identity.

Part V concludes with an analysis of whether the modern American Jewish movements are consistent in their manner of interpreting and implementing halakhic texts in their respective developments of Halakhah. While the modern Jewish movements are actively responding to the difficulties posed by topics such as divorce and homosexuality, Orthodox, Reform, Conservative, and Reconstructionist Judaism approach each controversial matter strategically, in accordance with their respective theological beliefs. It is important, then, to recognize both how these contemporary authorities apply halakhic texts, as well as how their decisions considerably affect the many people today who value Jewish legal traditions. This Article argues that the Reconstructionist approach to halakhic texts is the most consistent in terms of its internal logical reasoning, even though it departs furthest from the traditional rabbinical constructions of sexuality.

I. MODERN JEWISH MOVEMENTS: A PARALLEL LEGAL SYSTEM IN AMERICA

The focus of this work is on modern American Jewish movements and their dependence on, or departure from, past halakhic texts in their development of contemporary Halakhah. Specifically, this Article analyzes how older halakhic texts regulated marriage, divorce, and homosexuality and how these texts formed the basis for the dominant paradigm of heterosexual marriage in Judaism. Halakhah regulates life in a way that is different from, but just as important as, secular law. The scope of this Article is restricted to Jewish law. Religious law is important to individuals and to society in its own right. While secular law may sometimes act as a reference point, religious law can, and does, stand alone as a parallel system. Indeed, breaking these religious laws can lead to sanctions for the offender.

Just as other religions contain a variety of perspectives, Jewish beliefs and practices are not monolithic. It is important to identify the major streams of Judaism in America and their varying attitudes towards the sacred texts, as their theological perspectives certainly shape their positions on contemporary gender issues.

The most traditional movement is Orthodox Judaism, which upholds the divine and immutable authority of the Hebrew Bible and the Oral Law, including the *Midrashim*, the *Mishnah* and *Gemara* of the *Talmud*, works of the *Rishonim* and *Aharonim*, and decisions by rabbinical scholars today.[3] For Orthodox Jews,[4] "Halakhah is the essence" of Jewish belief, and their "version [of Jewish law] is the only correct interpretation of Judaism."[5] There do exist "liberals in the [Modern] Orthodox camp who recognize the human factor and espouse the need for Halakhic development" and reject the opinions of rabbis who do not "[allow] for [any] economic, sociological, or psychological factors in Halakhah,"[6] as well as those who disallow this approach. It is important to note the possibility for internal disagreement, as it has a considerable impact on the implementation of halakhically-based decisions.

---

[3] 17 ENCYCLOPEDIA JUDAICA 1486-94 (1971).

[4] There are two distinct movements within this traditional version of Judaism: Modern Orthodoxy and Ultra-Orthodoxy. Although Orthodox Jews claim to represent "Torah-true" Judaism, Modern Orthodoxy more accurately reflects one response to the *Haskalah*, or Jewish Enlightenment of the eighteenth and nineteenth centuries. *Id.* This was a period when Jewish leaders advocated limited secularization with the expectation that fundamental beliefs in one God and Halakhah as promulgated by the rabbis would remain constant. *Id.* Jewish leaders encouraged Jews to leave the ghettos of Europe and take advantage of the rights the state accorded to them by enjoying secular cultural pursuits and learning the national languages of the countries in which they lived. This endorsement eventually led to Jewish reformers advocating changes in Jewish liturgy and practice, both in Orthodoxy and Reform Judaism. Ultra-Orthodoxy, in part, was another reaction to that freedom, and Jews in Ultra-Orthodox sects continue to reject the secular world. *Id.*

[5] GILBERT S. ROSENTHAL, CONTEMPORARY JUDAISM: PATTERNS OF SURVIVAL 65-66, 84 (1986).

[6] *Id.* at 63.

In contrast, Reform Judaism promotes a more pluralistic attitude. Ethical teachings of the Jewish tradition guide Reform theology, and thus "Halakhah is valuable, but is not to be accepted on blind faith as coming from Heaven."[7] In this context, Jewish practice changes more readily in response to modernity because the goal is to maintain guiding principles, such as compassion, rather than enforce specific laws that are now considered to compromise moral actions.[8] This does not mean, however, that Jewish law is totally irrelevant.[9] Decisions by the Central Conference of American Rabbis, the national organization for Reform rabbis, as well as other Reform thinkers, take into account halakhic norms and their historical background, even as these Reform rabbis are willing to consider non-halakhic factors, especially values, that militate against traditional arguments.[10]

Conservative Judaism's views lie between the religious ideologies of Reform and Orthodox Judaism. Conservative Judaism recognizes Jewish texts and traditions as authoritative and, to a limited extent, divine in origin, but also realizes the need for change "when specific *mitzvot* [commandments] seem to be outmoded or arbitrarily unethical."[11] These Jews emphasize the binding nature of Jewish practice while using historical and philosophical insights into the development of Judaism to evaluate the modern application of Halakhah. [12] The Rabbinical Assembly, the professional organization to which Conservative rabbis belong, has granted the Committee on Jewish Law and Standards "the responsibility for recommending revisions in religious practice on the basis of Halakhic interpretation."[13]

---

[7] *Id.* at 147. Indeed, Reform Jews do not have one standard conception of God; rather "Reform believes in a varied interpretation . . . with wide latitude for naturalists or mystics, supernaturalists or religious humanists." *Id.*

[8] 14 ENCYCLOPEDIA JUDAICA, *supra* note 3, at 23.

[9] The Columbus Platform in 1937 "assumed a considerably more affirmative approach toward traditional observance and practice" than had been historically present in Reform Judaism. DAVID RUDAVSKY, MODERN JEWISH RELIGIOUS MOVEMENTS: A HISTORY OF EMANCIPATION AND ADJUSTMENT 312 (1967).

[10] 14 ENCYCLOPEDIA JUDAICA, *supra* note 3, at 26.

[11] ROSENTHAL, *supra* note 5, at 211.

[12] "Conservative Judaism admits that change and renewal, as people . . . gain new ethical sensitivities, or no longer share a particular observance's social assumptions, are necessary." MARC LEE RAPHAEL, PROFILES IN AMERICAN JUDAISM: THE REFORM, CONSERVATIVE, ORTHODOX, AND RECONSTRUCTIONIST TRADITIONS IN HISTORICAL PERSPECTIVE 101 (1984).

[13] RUDAVSKY, *supra* note 9, at 342.

Originally an offshoot of Conservative Judaism, and now a Jewish movement in its own right, Reconstructionism does not recognize the divine origin of Jewish texts or traditions. The ancient works of Judaism instead represent "man's attempt to discover God as the power of self-fulfillment or salvation."[14] Halakhah is not binding: "Jews should voluntarily choose to observe those customs that are personally meaningful and socially valuable for group survival."[15] This community uses Jewish laws and traditions as guidelines for a religiously evolving civilization. From this perspective, ethical issues in Judaism can be readily solved outside, while still referencing, the halakhic framework. Unlike Orthodox Judaism, where authority is decentralized, or Reform and Conservative Judaism, where decision-making is generally by official committee (while granting individual rabbis some freedom), Reconstructionism encourages "congregational committees, under rabbinic leadership" to determine community practices.[16]

A. Analyzing Halakhah

This Article analyzes those halakhic works that are most representative of rabbinic legal positions[17] on issues of sexuality, especially those texts that modern Jewish legal authorities continue to refer to today. It evaluates Halakhah in a variety of time periods. The Hebrew Bible, mostly written (though not standardized) by the first century C.E., serves as the basis for explanations in later texts, and this Article examines biblical laws in the historical context of the Ancient Near East. From the third century, the *Mishnah* is a concise collection of legislation, organized by topic, whose authors often refer to the biblical verses as support for their halakhic innovations. Many works of halakhic *Midrash*, texts that generally follow the order of the Bible, also come from the first centuries C.E. The *Tosefta*, a body of legal literature contemporaneous with the *Mishnah*, but not included in its final redaction, extends the Mishnaic rulings. Rabbis from the *Mishnah*, *Midrash*, and *Tosefta* are called *Tannaim* and material from this time period is called *tannaitic*. There are two Talmuds that consist of the *Mishnah* and commentary on the *Mishnah*, called the *Gemara*. The

---

[14] ROSENTHAL, *supra* note 5, at 255.

[15] *Id.*

[16] RAPHAEL, *supra* note 12, at 186.

[17] It is important to note that all of these sources are collected works, meaning that redactors gathered, edited, and re-edited the sources and previous editions. This Article interprets the positions as they appear in modern printed editions, with the acknowledgement that other, hidden voices may have shaped the texts. *See, e.g.*, RICHARD ELLIOTT FRIEDMAN, WHO WROTE THE BIBLE? (1987); 15 ENCYCLOPEDIA JUDAICA, *supra* note 3, at 15.

Jerusalem Talmud, also known as the *Yerushalmi*, was set down around the fourth century C.E. in the land of Israel. The Babylonian Talmud, also known as the *Bavli*, was compiled from the third century until the sixth century C.E. in Babylonia. Most of the people from this period are called *Amoraim*.

Most of the sources from later than the sixth century date from the eleventh century C.E. onward. Rabbi Shlomo Yitzchak, otherwise known as Rashi, wrote his commentary on the Torah during this time. Rabbi Moses ben Maimon, also known as *Rambam* or Maimonides,[18] compiled halakhic rulings in the *Mishneh Torah*. Finally, in the fifteenth century, Joseph Caro wrote the *Shulchan Arukh*. He evaluated three major works of legal rulings written in earlier centuries, including the *Mishneh Torah*, and chose what he considered the most definitive rulings. This Article also includes halakhic scholars who lived from the Renaissance until modern times.[19]

While this analysis covers a broad spectrum of works, an examination of every text relating to sexuality in the Jewish tradition is neither practicable nor feasible. Because the major movements of Judaism use the full corpus of sacred texts in their contemporary interpretations of sexuality, however, it is important to evaluate these halakhic texts in their proper historical contexts. This Article analyzes those texts that best illuminate the consequences of Jewish understandings of sexuality for contemporary Orthodox, Reform, Conservative, and Reconstructionist Judaism.

B. Sexuality

Scholars have historically differentiated between sex and gender. Sex suggests a person's biological makeup—whether she or he has female or male reproductive organs, respectively—and gender refers to a societal construction that expects certain behaviors from women and men in a culturally assembled context. Sexuality, to a limited extent, is the bridge between these two terms: "the physical and emotional grounding of an individual's capacity to love, [including] the physical and psychological dimensions of the human person."[20] Certainly, "sex, sexuality, and reproduction are all closely woven into the fabric of living things. All relate to the propagation of the race and the survival of the species. Yet there can

---

[18] Rabbi Moses ben Maimon was born in Spain and lived in Egypt during the twelfth century. 11 ENCYCLOPEDIA JUDAICA, *supra* note 3, at 754-55.

[19] These more recent texts are called *responsa* because each *responsum* generally responds to a legal problem in Jewish law.

[20] Michael A. Hayes, *Sexuality and Spirituality: Embattled Enemies or Kissing Cousins?*, *in* RELIGION AND SEXUALITY 240, 244 (Michael A. Hayes et al. eds., 1998).

be sex without sexuality, and reproduction need not [but can] be sexual."[21] While different cultures may recognize a variety of sexualities and genders, most societies, including the Jewish community, assign gendered sexual scripts to men and women. Babies are not born with innate knowledge of these expectations; rather they "are given an assigned gender based on anatomical appearance . . . [which] is significant because it tells *others* how to respond."[22] Learned over time, expressions of sexuality reflect a sexual identity strongly tied to a person's perceived sex and gender. When this Article refers to sexuality, this means the full range of bodily and emotive responses to sexual arousal, including a variety of sexual activities that may sometimes culminate in sexual intercourse. This definition of sexuality does not consist only of sex; it also refers to all the reactions a person has when attracted to another. These are, however, modern, secular conceptions that are certainly not incorporated in ancient texts and are not necessarily included in modern Jewish legal approaches. Sexuality is a tool for analysis and critique.

II. HALAKHIC CONCEPTIONS OF (HETERO)SEXUALITY

Halakhah overwhelmingly prescribes one legitimate option of sexual expression for Jews: heterosexual intercourse between a man and a woman legally married to each other. The rabbis and redactors of halakhic texts, in their legislation about marriage and other relationships between Jews, work from the normative assumption of heterosexual desire and behavior for men and women. As they note similarities and differences with regard to men's and women's sexuality, the rabbis set the standards for the physical expression of desire. Their laws reach far beyond marriage and divorce to include everyday interactions between men and women. For example, rabbis instituted laws of modesty to control perceived sexual tension and presumably to aid people in avoiding sexual sins, namely sexual relations outside of marriage. Today, halakhic constructions of sexuality are the repositories of the rabbis' assumptions concerning sexuality. Their interpretations' continuing authority contributes to the emphasis on marriage between men and women and on procreation in the Jewish community.

This section argues that the rabbis of the texts identify particular characteristics of sexuality and that these attributes support the halakhic ideal of heterosexual marriage for the expression of sexual desire. They differentiate between the sexual roles of men and women in detailed

---

[21] *Sex, in* ENCYCLOPÆDIA BRITANNICA ONLINE (2005), http://search.eb.com/eb/article-9109533.

[22] BRYAN STRONG ET AL., HUMAN SEXUALITY: DIVERSITY IN CONTEMPORARY AMERICA 121 (4th ed. 2002).

discussions in order to reinforce that heterosexual model. The extent to which men and women develop and exhibit these sexual feelings, in the rabbis' opinions, differs substantially[23] and subsequent legislation reflects that assumption, albeit with a double standard. The rabbis explain that men actively pursue and engage in sexual intercourse as evidenced by their easy, likely arousal by women, their overt expression of desire, and their dominant position during sexual intercourse. On the other hand, they contend that women suppress explicit articulation of their sexual desires, unless they are vigorously seducing men and leading the entire Jewish

---

[23] Indeed, differences begin and are established early. The rabbis contest when sexual desire and desirability begin in boys and girls. On the surface, it appears that the legal distinction would correlate with the age of responsibility and eligibility for marriage: around twelve years old for a girl and thirteen years old for a boy. There is, however, halakhic awareness that no one can quantify sexual development on the basis of age, simply because children physically mature at different rates. In a legal commentary from the last century, Rabbi Abraham Yeshayashu Karelitz explained that the regulation of a girl's sexual expression was "a measure against erotic thought and distraction and should not apply to girls too young to have such an effect. One would suppose it applies only where temptation lurks, i.e., that it is not a matter of age but of physical form and appearance." GETSEL ELLINSON, II WOMAN AND THE MITZVOT: THE MODEST WAY 191, 350 (Raphael Blumberg trans., 1992) (quoting *Hazon Ish, Orah Hayyim* 16, letter 8).

This position finds support in many of the earlier halakhic sources. In the Babylonian Talmud, for example, *Berakhoth* 24a addresses the question of whether a man may recite the *Shema* in bed in front of his children and other minors. *Id.* at 191 n.54. R. Hisda said that a man may do so "until a young girl is three years and one day old and until a young boy is nine years and one day old," after which age it is likely he will be aroused by those children. HEBREW-ENGLISH EDITION OF THE BABYLONIAN TALMUD: BERAKOTH 24a (Isidore Epstein ed., Maurice Simon trans., Soncino Press 1972) [hereinafter BERAKOTH]. The dialogue continues: "Others say until a young girl is eleven years and one day old and until a young boy is twelve years and one day, each up until when 'your breasts were established and your hair had grown.'" *Id.* (author's translations).

The signal for when a child has reached adulthood, therefore, is not age alone but rather the onset of puberty, a phenomenon of which the rabbis were well aware. They realized that puberty affected the two sexes differently: "[T]he two indicators [of puberty], the first of which applies to both boys and girls, whereas the second is gender-specific, are the appearance of pubic hair and the growth of a girl's breasts." CHARLOTTE ELISHEVA FONROBERT, MENSTRUAL PURITY: RABBINIC AND CHRISTIAN RECONSTRUCTIONS OF BIBLICAL GENDER 143 (2000). Fonrobert includes several textual references with regard to the physical onset of puberty: mNid 6:11; mNid 5:9, 6:1, 6:11-12; tNid 6:2-7; mNid 5:8; tNid 6:4 (mNid refer to *Mishnah Niddah*, and tNid refers to the related *Tosefta*). *See generally* HEBREW-ENGLISH EDITION OF THE BABYLONIAN TALMUD: NIDDAH (Isidore Epstein ed., Israel Slotki trans., Soncino Press 1989) [hereinafter NIDDAH]. Practically, this varying development had few effects on the application of modesty conventions. Girls and boys who have not reached puberty by age twelve or thirteen, respectively, or for some authorities, even younger children, are held to the same standards of modesty as are men and women who have reached physical maturity, because their adherence to these laws serves to educate them about the proper ways of relating to members of the opposite sex. According to the rabbis, boys and girls, clearly differentiated in their youth, grow up to be adult men and women with distinctive sexual expressions and responsibilities.

community to sin. Expressed within those roles are halakhic admonitions and advice meant to prevent illicit sexual relations that come about from sexual tension between men and women seeking to express their desires. The rabbis limit contact between unmarried men and women, but for men, Torah study is promoted as a way, in part, to prevent extramarital sexual intercourse. Their regulations address nearly every possibility of sexual arousal, prohibiting those actions that might contribute to a permissive atmosphere. Recognizing the limitations of those guidelines, Halakhah decrees that matrimony, by satisfying sexual desires with the goal of procreation, is the natural and proper resolution of sexual tension.

The next section explores contemporary reactions to this halakhic structure; all of the modern Jewish movements have, within the last ten years, if not before, affirmed the central role of marriage in Jewish practice, emphasizing in particular its role in procreation, and have only recently reevaluated the position of the traditional heterosexual family in Judaism. Together, the halakhic construction of sexuality and the situating of that heterosexual paradigm in the modern context provide the background for the analysis of divorce and homosexuality in Jewish tradition.

A. Male Sexuality

Encouraging marriage is the halakhic way of regulating men's sexual needs that would otherwise lead to aggressive and unchecked pursuit of intercourse. First, this section explains the rabbis' concern for men's sexual desires and the possibility of Torah study as the solution to this problem. Second, it explores how the rabbis viewed and regulated sexual intercourse within marriage. It is crucial to note that the rabbis write from their own experiences and observations, and thus their laws reflect heterosexual male perceptions of sexual identity.

For the rabbis of the texts, male sexual desire threatened men's physical lives as well as the basic structure of society. Halakhah considers men more likely to seek satisfaction of their sexual desires. The male is always at the mercy of his *Yetzer HaRa*, the evil inclination that, with women, "present[s] a particular threat to male sexual self-control."[24] Men are easily aroused: Babylonian Rabbi Sheshet[25] exclaims, "[A]ll who see a woman's little finger, it is as if he is seeing her secret place."[26] Lest one

---

[24] Michael Satlow, *"Try To Be A Man": The Rabbinic Construction of Masculinity*, 1996 HARV. THEOLOGICAL REV. 37, 89.

[25] Rabbi Sheshet lived during the late third century in Babylonia. GUNTER STEMBERGER, INTRODUCTION TO THE TALMUD AND MIDRASH 92 (Markus Bockmuehl ed. and trans., 2d ed. 1996).

[26] HEBREW-ENGLISH EDITION OF THE BABYLONIAN TALMUD, *supra* note 23, at 24a (author's translation).

think that this statement is merely an aberration, the redactor(s) included this rabbi's statement again in *Shabbat* 64b.[27] The rabbis also realized that visual stimulation was not the only action that causes arousal, concluding, for instance, that "a woman's voice constitutes an erotic stimulus."[28] In the Babylonian Talmud, *Ketuboth* 64b offers evidence for this strong desire and its inevitable relief, in a sinful sexual liaison if not within the context of marriage:

> R[abbi] Hiyya bar Yosef[29] said to Shmuel,[30] what is the difference between a rebellious husband and a rebellious wife? He said to him [i.e. Shmuel said to Rabbi Hiyya bar Yosef]: Go [and] learn from the market of prostitutes: who hires who? Another explanation: his [urge/desire] is [lit. formed] external, [and] hers is internal.[31]

This text suggests that, because men take the initiative in illicit sexual relations, the "male sexual drive is stronger than the female sexual drive."[32] This passage does not confer its approval on men who hire prostitutes, but

---

[27] ELLINSON, *supra* note 23, at 79.

[28] *Id.* at 100, 355 (citing the *Kol Bo* 45, a halakhic work from before the fourteenth century).

[29] According to Stemberger, this third century rabbi, a second-generation member of the *Amoraim*, "migrated from Babylonia to Palestine." STEMBERGER, *supra* note 25, at 87.

[30] Probably from the first generation of *Amoraim*, Shmuel lived in the third century in Babylonia. *Id.*

[31] MICHAEL SATLOW, TASTING THE DISH: RABBINIC RHETORICS OF SEXUALITY 286 (1995) [hereinafter SATLOW 1995]. I verified Satlow's translation using the text from the HEBREW ENGLISH EDITION OF THE BABYLONIAN TALMUD: KETUBOTH 24a (Isidore Epstein ed., Samuel Daiches trans., Soncino Press 1989) [hereinafter KETUBOTH]. *See also* Ketuboth 24a, Ma'agar Sfirat HaQodesh/Store of Holy Texts, http://kodesh.snunit.k12.il/b/l/l3201.htm (last visited Oct. 16, 2005) [hereinafter Store of Holy Texts]. Because the halakhic texts examined in this Article are Jewish holy texts originally written in Hebrew or Aramaic and because English-translated editions of the texts may not be easily accessible to readers, I have provided two separate sources for the same halakhic texts. In writing this Article, I read, translated in the first instance, or verified translation of halakhic texts by examining them exclusively in Hebrew or Aramaic, relying mostly on the original versions of the halakhic texts located online at the Store of Holy Texts. In the process of editing, I have reviewed the Soncino Press editions, which have the texts in both languages, and verified the Store of Holy Texts' Hebrew/Aramaic editions. Consequently, in each place where I cite a halakhic text, or a chapter within that work, I have provided these two parallel sources in an effort to best accommodate my audience's needs as dictated by their knowledge of Hebrew and Aramaic.

[32] SATLOW 1995, *supra* note 31, at 286.

rather shows that the rabbis feared male sexual desire was so strong that most men, even moral men, would engage in immoral sex.[33]

For the creators of Halakhah, all of these factors come together to threaten men's physical lives as well as the basic structure of society. According to a story in *Sanhedrin* 75a in the Babylonian Talmud,

> [a] man once cast his gaze upon a woman and became so aroused that his life was imperiled. Upon examining him, physicians pronounced that his only hope was to have intercourse with her, but the rabbis said that they would let him die before permitting such a thing. It was then suggested that she stand before him naked, but the rabbis' response was the same. When it was suggested that she talk to him from behind a wall, they were again opposed.[34]

This man's intense reaction to seeing a woman indicates the strength of these feelings and the danger that ensues when he cannot relieve them. The doctors advocate what they consider most reasonable: erotic contact between the two. The word used for intercourse has the root *baal*, which also means "to be master of" or "to take possession of." Here, the woman is the object of this "taking." The rabbis, perhaps using the word "baal" for this reason, see the woman as literally an object of his affections of which he alone requests possession:

> And why did he not marry her? It would not have satisfied him. As R. Yitzchak said, "Since the day the Temple was destroyed, the desire for intercourse has been transferred to sinners: Stolen waters are sweet and bread eaten in secret is pleasant" (*Prov.* 9:17).[35]

---

[33] Importantly, the prostitutes to whom this section refers are female. The use of the word "*zonot*," that is, the feminine plural for prostitutes, underscores the direction of that male desire toward women and heterosexual sex. The passage does not leave room for sexual intercourse to happen between people of the same sex within the halakhic framework. This omission probably indicates the inconceivability for legitimate homosexual desire or homosexual identity for at least some of the rabbis. Of course, this does not mean that men and women did not engage in homosexual activity.

[34] ELLINSON, *supra* note 23, at 49. Ellinson's translation was verified with the HEBREW ENGLISH EDITION OF THE BABYLONIAN TALMUD: SANHEDRIN 75a (Isidore Epstein ed., Jacob Shachter trans., Soncino Press 1994). *See also* Sanhedrin 75a, Store of Holy Texts, http://www1.snunit.k12.il/kodesh/bavli/snhd075a.html (last visited Oct. 16, 2005).

[35] ELLINSON, *supra* note 23, at 79. Given that the other rabbis in related sections of this discussion are *Tannaim*, I surmise that Rabbi Yitzchak lived in the early third century and agree with Stemberger that he was one of Rabbi's contemporaries. STEMBERGER, *supra* note 25, at 79.

In this passage, the rabbis do not consider the possibility that this relationship might involve two willing partners. The physicians and rabbis disagree whether sexual contact between this man and woman would actually relieve *his* desire or promote more aggressive, sinful sexual behavior by him, considering that "some people's sexual pleasure depends on the experience being adventurous and illicit."[36] A man's sexual desire wrongly channeled leads to inappropriate sexual contact outside the approved framework of marriage; the rabbis respond to this challenge by legislating conditions for contact between men and women.[37]

So far, this section has shown that Halakhah presumes that strong male sexual desires for women, so intense that they potentially threaten an unmarried man's ability to function normally in the world, necessitate resolution through expression of those feelings. It has also indicated that the rabbis considered it likely that sexually unsatisfied men would seek out illicit sexual liaisons in order to relieve their feelings. This is not, however, limited to unmarried men. Within the context of a heterosexual marriage, this trend of male aggression in matters of sexuality continues: Halakhah proposes that men initiate intercourse, perhaps recognizing that men's desires are stronger. In other words, "a man requests sexual relations" outright by "showing his wife extra affection and love before nightfall, speaking to her of love and embracing her."[38] In *Baba Metsia* 83a/84b, a discussion of marital sexuality and its connection to procreation "sports unusually graphic representations of maleness and the question of maleness as figured through the body":

> [t]here are those who say that this they said to her: "As the man, so is his virility." And there are those who say that thus did they say to her: "Love compresses the flesh." . . . Said Rabbi Yohanan,

---

[36] *Id.* at 50 n.16.

[37] Not surprisingly, the above passage ignores masturbation as a means to resolution, probably because it is forbidden. Masturbation is roundly condemned in the ancient sources, including multiple places in the Babylonian Talmud. *See* NIDDAH, *supra* note 23, at 13a, 13b; *Even HaEzer* 23:1-3, *in* SHULCHAN ARUKH (Shneur Zalman ed., Kehot Publication Society 2002). *See also* Walter Jacobs, CCRA Responsa: ARR/153.Masturbation (1979), http://data.ccarnet.org/cgi-bin/respdisp.pl?file=153&year=arr/. The most important factor regarding this prohibition was the problem of *hash-hatat zera*, or the "destruction of seed," that could have been used to procreate. *See* DAVID M. FELDMAN, BIRTH CONTROL IN JEWISH LAW: MARITAL RELATIONS, CONTRACEPTION, AND ABORTION AS SET FORTH IN THE CLASSIC TEXTS OF JEWISH LAW 109 (1998). In any case, masturbation seemingly allows men to satisfy their desires outside of the marital context; this concept troubles the rabbis because, in their opinion, it does not resolve the problem. For example, the man above craved a particular woman, and autoeroticism would not have satisfied his desire.

[38] Hannah Rockman, *Sexual Behavior among Ultra-Orthodox Jews: A Review of Laws and Guidelines, in* JEWISH EXPLORATIONS OF SEXUALITY 191, 199 (Jonathan Magonet ed., 1995) [hereinafter JEWISH EXPLORATIONS].

"Rabbi Ishma'el the son of Yose's member was like a wineskin of nine *kav*; Rabbi El'azar the son of Rabbi Shim'on's member was like a wineskin of seven *kav*." Rav Papa said, "Rabbi Yohanan's member was like a wineskin of three *kav*." And there are those who say: like a wineskin of five *kav*. Rab Papa himself had a member which [sic] was like the baskets of Hipparenum.[39]

This text links male sexual desire for his wife to the size of a man's penis. The mere occurrence of this narrative suggests that rabbis had little difficulty illustrating how men were quite explicit about their sexual desires within marriage.

Assuming that mere contact with women erotically stimulated men, Halakhah prescribes marriage for every man for the relief of sexual urges. Generally the mandate that "marriage per se is a requirement of the law, and even its deferral must be justified"[40] is connected to the duty of procreation. However, the texts go further than procreation. Maimonides explains that an unmarried man may continue studying Torah "providing his sexual drive does not get the better of him; if it does he is required to marry even if he already has children, in order that he not come to thoughts of sin."[41] Later rabbis codified this principle in the Middle Ages.[42]

While they recognized that the institution of marriage controls male sexuality, the rabbis generally encouraged moderation for unmarried and married men by the active limiting of sexual thoughts through dedicated religious study. As Feldman summarizes R. Abraham ben David, "the husband's intention [regarding sex] is a meritorious one if . . . he wants to avoid 'thoughts of sin.' . . . [M]oderation in sex, food, and drink should be *his* goal."[43] Halakhah situates Jewish textual study in opposition to the expression of sexuality, whether marital or otherwise. Because men were considered easily aroused, a *responsum* suggests that

[39] DANIEL BOYARIN, UNHEROIC CONDUCT: THE RISE OF HETEROSEXUALITY AND THE INVENTION OF THE JEWISH MAN 95 (1997). Boyarin's translation was verified with the HEBREW ENGLISH EDITION OF THE BABYLONIAN TALMUD: BABA MEZIA 84a (Isidore Epstein ed., Salis Daiches trans., Soncino Press 1994) [hereinafter BABA MEZIA]. *See also* Mezia 84a, Store of Holy Texts, http://www1.snunit.k12.il/kodesh/bavli/bbam084a.html (last visited Oct. 16, 2005).

[40] FELDMAN, *supra* note 37, at 27.

[41] *Id.* at 32 (citing the MISHNEH TORAH: ISHUT 15, 3). *See generally* MISHNE TORAH: RAMBAM (Moshe ben Shaltiel ed., Ma'or Publication Society 1975).

[42] FELDMAN, *supra* note 37, at 32 (noting that this principle can be found in the *Tur* and the *Shulhan Arukh, Even HaEzer* 1, 4).

[43] *Id.* at 69 (stating that ben David is a "contemporary and official critic of Maimonides' Law Code").

498   *Columbia Journal of Gender and Law*   [Vol. 15:2

> if a man knows [that traveling next to women] will lead to erotic
> thought, he should avoid travel then unless essential. If he must
> reach work, he should strive to divert himself with Torah thought.
> As *Rambam* advises, "If it will lead to erotic thought, he should
> turn his heart from banalities to Torah, that 'lovely hind and
> graceful doe'" (*Prov.* 5:19).[44]

The above example may also emphasize Halakhah's realization that there
are appropriate and inappropriate contexts for the expression of sexual
feelings; however, it is important to note that the avoidance of erotic
thoughts associated with women without the intention of marital sex is
seemingly accomplished by religious study.

Interestingly, though, the explanation given by Rabbi Simon ben
Azzai[45] for the justification of his continued bachelorhood implies that he
transfers his erotic thoughts, explained as "love," to Torah study, rather than
negating those feelings completely. He defends himself: "What can I do?
My soul is in love with [the study of] Torah. It is possible that the world
will be perpetuated by others."[46] Ben Azzai's connection of his love for
Torah with the commandment to have children is significant because it
highlights the relationship between sexual desire and procreation. He rejects
the obligation to reproduce by choosing to continue his Jewish learning; this
refusal is perhaps recognition of the mechanics of procreation. More likely,
it is a declaration that he, unlike other men, can direct his erotic feelings
toward the texts and therefore does not present a risk to the society at large:
he will not lose control of his emotions and pursue illicit sexual relations.
Furthermore, the root *hšk*, meaning "to be in love with," which Ben Azzai
used to denote his love of Torah, is not unique in this context. Later
halakhic works use similar sexual vocabulary to show their approval of this
lifestyle choice: "One whose soul is in love with the Torah and studies it as
Ben Azzai did, and cleaves unto it all his days commits no sin thereby."[47]
The word "cleaves," from the root *dbk*, implies marital sex, as it is the same
root used in *Genesis* 2:24 in the explanation of marriage: "Therefore a

---

[44] ELLINSON, *supra* note 23, at 64-65 (citing Moshe Feinstein, IGROT MOSHE: EVEN
HAEZER, 14) (quoting *Hilkhot Isurei Biah* 21:19).

[45] For Ben Azzai's biographical information, see STEMBERGER, *supra* note 25, at
74.

[46] FELDMAN, *supra* note 37, at 31. The translation of the Hebrew here is my own.
See also HEBREW ENGLISH EDITION OF THE BABYLONIAN TALMUD: YEBAMOTH 63b (Isidore
Epstein ed., Israel W. Slotki trans., Soncino Press 1994) [hereinafter YEBAMOTH]. This text
may also be transliterated as "Y'vamot"; *see also* Y'vamot 63b, Store of Holy Texts,
http://www1.snunit.k12.il/kodesh/bavli/ibmu063b.html (last visited Oct. 16, 2005).

[47] *Id.* at 31-32 (author's translation). *See generally Mishneh Torah Ishut* 15:3,
supra note 41. *See also* Mishneh Torah: Ishut 15:13, Store of Holy Texts,
http://kodesh.snunit.k12.il/i/4115.htm (last visited Nov. 6, 2005).

man/husband leaves his father and his mother and cleaves (*dabak*) with his woman/wife and they become one flesh."[48] The language makes it clear that Ben Azzai satisfies his sexual desires by having an intimate connection with Torah.[49]

The rabbis' discussion of male sexuality continues into a detailed exposition of marital intercourse. Indeed, Maimonides advises in the *Mishneh Torah, Deot* 4:19 that "[s]exual expression [in marriage] for the relief of physical pressures is both morally and physically salutary."[50] While some would argue that Maimonides's suggestion is not necessarily halakhic because there are no punishments associated with its breach, such moral judgments may eventually gain the force of law because they are contained within legal texts.

Thus, aggressive in his pursuit of erotic fulfillment, a man takes control during the actual sex act. As *Niddah* 31b, from the Babylonian Talmud, explains: "And why does the man lie face downward [during sexual intercourse] and woman face upward towards the man? He [faces the elements] from which he was created and she [faces the elements] from whom she was created." [51] This explanation of positions in sexual intercourse reinforces the man's higher status as compared to the woman's inferior status: she is below him literally and figuratively. This does not imply that, in reality, women did not have active roles during sex, but only that the Halakhah encourages the man's control of the act of penetration.

A discussion of sexual positions in the *Shulchan Arukh* illustrates how this explanatory section of the *Niddah* was later used to delineate what constituted proper marital sexual intercourse:

> He underneath and she above him is considered an impudent act; both at the same level is considered a perverted act. It is told of Rabbi Eliezer that he used to have cohabitation with such awe

---

[48] *Genesis* 2:24 (Biblia Hebraica Stuttgartensia (Rudolf Kittel et al. eds., 1997)) (author's translation).

[49] Unfortunately, writers after Maimonides condemned Ben Azzai for his choice. FELDMAN, *supra* note 37, at 32. This disapproval does not, however, take away from the role that studying Jewish texts fulfills for men.

[50] *Id.* at 70 (paraphrasing R. Isaac Aboab).

[51] JUDITH R. BASKIN, MIDRASHIC WOMEN: FORMATIONS OF THE FEMININE IN RABBINIC LITERATURE 15 (2002). Baskin's translation was verified with *Niddah* 31b, *supra* note 23. *See also* Niddah 31b, Store of Holy Texts, http://www1.snunit.k12.il/kodesh/ bavli/nidh031b.html (last visited Oct. 16, 2005).

and terror that it appeared as if a demon was forcing him to do it.[52]

This halakhic text emphasizes that the proper position in marital sexual intercourse set out in *Niddah* can sufficiently gratify a man's sexual appetite. Rabbi Eliezer was able to release his great sexual feelings, like a "demon,"[53] by following the rabbinical rules of cohabitating properly with, it is assumed, his wife. However, in the *Mishneh Torah, Issrei Biah* 21:9, Maimonides challenges this limitation on sexual positions: "But a man's own wife is permitted to him and, with her, he is allowed to do as he pleases. He may cohabit with her whenever he pleases, kiss her wherever he pleases, and cohabit naturally or unnaturally."[54] Nonetheless, even this permission for liberality in the sexual act reinforces the halakhic ideal: male control of marital sex. Halakhah grants the husband the prerogative to have sexual relations with his wife, albeit within the limits discussed below.

While attitudes toward sexual orientation are addressed in Part V, at this point it is important to note that the rabbis look with favor on heterosexual intercourse within marriage. There are instructions for the expression of sexual desires within marriage, and, as shown *infra*, sex is seen favorably with regard to the wife's marital rights and to the general purpose of procreation. However, there is a dearth of instruction or encouragement for male (or female, for that matter) homoerotic behavior. This omission emphasizes the primacy of heterosexuality: the legal advice to men assumes that the man engaging in sexual relations does so with a female partner, his wife.

B. Female Sexuality

Because they were male, the rabbis were able to regulate male sexuality based on understandings of their own sexual identities, as shown by the bulk of personal evidence used to support the laws. The regulating of

---

[52] EVELYN KAYE, THE HOLE IN THE SHEET: A MODERN WOMAN LOOKS AT ORTHODOX AND HASIDIC JUDAISM 124 (1987) (citing SOLOMON GANZFIELD, CODE OF JEWISH LAW: A COMPLILATION OF JEWISH LAWS AND CUSTOMS (1963)). Kaye does not detail what section and verse of Ganzfield's book she references.

[53] This "demon" may also be an expression of Rabbi Eliezer's *Yetzer HaRa*, or as discussed, *supra* note 24, his "evil inclinations."

[54] FELDMAN, *supra* note 37, at 89. Feldman suggests that "unnaturally" could have three meanings—"dorsal," "retro," and "a tergo"—and reflect a concern for semination outside procreation. *Id.* at 155 n.63. Chapter 8 of Feldman's work discusses this topic more generally. Although I am unsure what would consist of cohabitating "unnaturally," Maimonedes clarifies his position by stating that "the way of piety is not to be frivolous about this but to approach it with holiness and not deviate from the natural," which means, I assume, the standard sexual position suggested by the other sources. *Id.* (quoting *Issrei Biah* 21, II).

female sexuality, however, was a different process altogether; to construct female sexual identities as reflected by female experiences, the rabbis had to rely on anecdotal evidence from female relatives. As a result, Halakhah reflects male opinions of what sexual practices and feelings women ought to have, especially with regard to how female sexual expression should fit into the patriarchal legal structure perpetuated by the rabbinical system. Therefore, "discussion of women's sexuality is primarily confined to strategies of control of women's sexuality" as "recorded by a small elite group of male religious leaders."[55]

Certainly, the rabbis affirmed that both sexes had strong desires, noting that "all sexual prohibitions, whether involving intercourse or foreplay, apply equally to the man and woman involved."[56] As they did for men, the rabbis prohibited certain activities that would lead to the sexual arousal of women, stating that "a woman, like a man, is enjoined to avoid every act that will lead to her own sexual arousal, such as reading pornographic literature."[57] This text indicates that Halakhah strongly discourages any activity that arouses women outside of marital intercourse. However, the rabbis believed that sexual stimulation occurred less frequently in women; the majority rule was, for example, that "a woman may gaze upon a handsome man, and likewise, most authorities hold that she may hear a man sing [because] the sages gauged that women are not aroused by this."[58] Additionally, Rabbi Ovadiah Yosef writes: "Here is proof that we do not fear women will have erotic thoughts [when looking at a man's penis]. The reason is that they are not prone to sexual arousal."[59] This is an extreme statement, considering the level of visual stimulation. Certainly women can become sexually aroused; other halakhic texts warn of that possibility. However, the extreme character of this comment indicates the extent to which women were seen as resistant to arousal.

Halakhah presents two constructions of female sexuality. The seductress who arouses herself and threatens to lead men to sin is held in opposition to the married woman who shows modesty regarding her sexuality and sexual desire, reserving it only for her husband. First, the problem of the seductress stems from the rabbinical concern that "she violates a prohibition against 'approaching intercourse' [and] she leads men to sin."[60] Initially, it seems this concept of female sexuality acknowledges

---

[55] SATLOW 1995, *supra* note 31, at 13.

[56] ELLINSON, *supra* note 23, at 46.

[57] *Id.*

[58] *Id.*

[59] *Id.* at 85-86 (citing *Yabia Omer*, Part I, 6:5).

[60] *Id.* at 46.

502   *Columbia Journal of Gender and Law*   [Vol. 15:2

women's power to arouse and to be aroused. Unfortunately, the attitude of
Halakhah is less flattering: "[R]abbinic literature portrays women not only
as sexually attractive to men, but also as more sexually avid and as less able
to control their overwhelming desires"[61] once aroused. In other words,
although it is harder to sexually excite women, once sexual feelings are
initiated, women cannot control themselves.[62] Judith Baskin terms this
character flaw "light mindedness,"[63] words that conjure images of weakness
and fallibility. In contrast, the extramarital sexual feelings of men are
viewed as outside forces that threaten him, and he is advised that Torah
study will negate those thoughts and prevent his acting wrongly. For a
woman, the texts equate her inability to control sexual arousal with a defect
in her character. The rabbinic "solution" places the physical burden of
controlling sexual stimulation on women. Women are instructed to monitor
their appearance and limit their interactions with men. By dressing
modestly and avoiding being alone with men, women reduce the risk that
either sex will inadvertently cause the arousal of another. Unlike men,
women are not given advice on how to curb their sexual desires, for
example, with sacred study—the rules of modesty provide a sufficient
check on female sexuality.

With marriage, however, the Halakhah desexualizes the married
woman outside the narrow context of marital intercourse. On one hand, the
law insinuates that, to a limited extent, marriage restrains women's sexual
desires as it does for men: by providing a channel for sexual expression.
Indeed, with marital sex serving as an outlet for sexual expression, the
rabbis believed that women were not even aroused by examination of their
vaginas. *Taharat mishpachah*, also called the "Laws of Family Purity,"
encompasses a set of practices that restrict a married couple's physical
contact during the wife's menstrual period.[64] The woman checks herself
with her fingers in order to ascertain when her period has begun and then
ceased. *Niddah* 13a, in Ellinson's words, rationalizes that "we do not fear
that a woman's vaginal self-examination for menstrual blood will sexually
stimulate her."[65] The authors and redactors of *Niddah* 13a, it seems,
misunderstand the reason for a woman's ability to examine herself without
arousal. More likely, she performs this practiced task with an attitude that
reflects the seriousness of this duty rather than for satisfying sexual desires.

---

[61] BASKIN, *supra* note 51, at 30 (quoting SATLOW 1995, *supra* note 31, at 158-59).

[62] *Id.*

[63] *Id.*

[64] 15 ENCYCLOPEDIA JUDAICA, *supra* note 3, at 703.

[65] ELLINSON, *supra* note 23, at 85-86.

However, many rabbis, including Rabbi Ovadiah Yosef,[66] interpreted this theory to mean that the threshold for a woman's stimulation is incredibly high—so much so that only intercourse with her husband arouses her—in direct contradiction with the image of woman as seductress. In effect, that conclusion acknowledges one possibility for sexual fulfillment: heterosexual sex in the context of marriage. While this position contradicts the existence of laws against women masturbating (why prohibit an act that will not provide any satisfaction?), even those rules support the norm of marriage because, without masturbation, a married woman can only relieve her sexual desires lawfully by having intercourse with her husband.

This high threshold for a woman's sexual arousal contributes to the halakhic perception of the woman's role in initiating and engaging in sex. She is "essentially passive, [for] a female depends on male potency for everything, including the production of progeny"[67] and sexual fulfillment. A male's penis makes him the more important actor in sex: "to penetrate was to reaffirm, perhaps even assert, this power. To be penetrated was perceived as being as women were perceived, that is, weak and dominated."[68] A woman does not make the first obvious move; rather, she prepares subtly by wearing nice clothes and acting more lovingly than usual. Granted, as will be explained in more detail *infra*, the husband is obligated to fulfill the wife's right to sexual pleasure, but he initiates that contact when he wants to have sex and believes his wife will acquiesce.

This does not mean that women were unable to subvert the system and control when they had sex with their husbands. Halakhah very strictly condemns marital rape: "Never may you [the husband] force her."[69] There is an instance, repeated in both the Babylonian and Palestinian Talmuds, when a wife rejects her husband's advances in accordance with *taharat mishpachah* because she is menstruating, but the next day tells him that she is available to him.[70] The confused husband runs to his rabbi who encourages him to believe her.[71] Charlotte Fonrobert reads this instance as giving the woman control over her sex life and also

---

[66] *Id.*

[67] BASKIN, *supra* note 51, at 18.

[68] Michael Satlow, *"They Abused Him Like A Woman": Homoeroticism, Gender Blurring, and the Rabbis in Late Antiquity*, 1994 J. HIST. SEXUALITY 2, 5 [hereinafter Satlow 1994].

[69] FELDMAN, *supra* note 37, at 74 (citing Rabbi Moses ben Nahman).

[70] FONROBERT, *supra* note 23, at 26.

[71] *Id.*

as a symptom of the rabbis' or the redactors' anxiety about women making legitimate *halakhic* arguments to their own advantage. In such instances, women's discourse is curtailed by repeatedly framing it as an issue of their believability, even in a case such as this where a rabbi rules in favor of the woman.[72]

In reality, a wife undermines the halakhic system by manipulating the rules to her advantage, giving herself some element of control. Normally, *taharat mishpachah* constitutes a halakhic control on marital sexuality by establishing limits on intercourse, ostensibly as a way to increase the couple's sexual pleasure, but here the woman co-opts that regulation. Halakhah, however, responds to this possible usurpation by avoiding legislation that might shift the balance of marital power toward her. While marital rape is condemned, there are no legal "consequences for husbands who do not respect their sexual partners."[73] Such injunctions are "ethical guidelines,"[74] subject to the level of restraint the husband can achieve. In contrast, "although the wife has the right in principle to refuse sex on any occasion, her consent can be understood through silence and necessarily ambiguous signs."[75] She does not actively seek out or directly turn down intercourse because she could be subject to legal action, even divorce, if she rebuffs her husband's advances outright. This possibility will be discussed in Part III, *infra*. However, it is important to see that rabbinical understandings of female sexuality form the basis for laws regulating divorce.

Although Halakhah strongly recommends that the proper position of marital sexual intercourse is as described in *Niddah*,[76] and although this suggests that the man controls penetration, there are also halakhic possibilities for the woman's active participation. Hannah Rockman recounts:

The Talmud relates how Rabbi [H]isda . . . personally instructed his daughters how to prepare for sexual relations: When he wants to hold the pearl [a euphemism for the breast] with one hand and the little fish [vagina] in the other hand, offer the pearl to him, but

---

[72] *Id.*

[73] BASKIN, *supra* note 51, at 108.

[74] *Id.*

[75] BOYARIN, *supra* note 39, at 171.

[76] *See supra* notes 50-54 and accompanying text.

don't offer the little fish to him until he is aroused. Then offer it to him.[77]

The woman actively controls the progression of intercourse, although it could be said that she restrains her husband's initiative. The text's circumlocution seemingly considers a woman's body as property. However representative of actual body parts, the "pearl" and "fish" are objects that people own. Whether the language actually reflects a rabbinic perspective of women as property, it is significant that the man is compared to an owner who determines what happens with his chattel. Like the situation of a man who forces his wife, there are no legal penalties for a husband who, during intercourse, does something his wife does not want; his wife cannot appeal to a rabbinic authority for intervention:

> A woman once came before Rabbi and said, "Rabbi! I set the table before my husband, but he overturned it." Rabbi replied: "My daughter! The Torah has permitted you to him—what then can I do for you?" A woman once came before Rab and complained, "Rabbi! I set a table before my husband, but he overturned it." Rab replied: "Wherein does it differ from a fish?"[78]

The woman "set[s] the table," that is, ambiguously signals that she is sexually aroused and wants sex in a certain manner, but the husband proceeds in an ostensibly aggressive way, possibly ignoring the normal conventions for intercourse.[79] The woman complains but has no recourse; again, the text refers to her as a fish, the property of her husband.[80] This

---

[77] Rockman, *supra* note 38, at 199.

[78] Babylonian Talmud, *Nedarim* 20b, *in* BASKIN, *supra* note 51, at 107. I verified Baskin's translation. *See* HEBREW ENGLISH EDITION OF THE BABYLONIAN TALMUD: NEDARIM 20b (Isidore Epstein ed., H. Freedman trans., Soncino Press 1994); *see also* Nedarim 20b, Store of Holy Texts, http://www1.snunit.k12.il/kodesh/bavli/ndri020c.html (last visited Oct. 16, 2005).

[79] While it is clear that "overturns" means having sex in a non-standard manner, Boyarin argues that the man insisted that he be on the bottom and the woman on top during sex. However, Boyarin admits that there is not a consensus for this definition; in a footnote, he mentions that it could refer to anal intercourse. I disagree with the rest of his analysis of this passage; he argues that the rabbis mean that the couple can engage in any positions during sex. The rest of the texts do not bear this out. Daniel Boyarin, *Women's Bodies and the Rise of the Rabbis: The Case of Sotah, in* JEWS AND GENDER: THE CHALLENGE TO HIERARCHY, STUDIES IN CONTEMPORARY JEWRY XVI 88, 93, 98 (Jonathan Frankel ed., 2000).

[80] Boyarin argues, based on the Talmudic discussion surrounding this text, that the fish represents intercourse, not the woman's body. I disagree because I think it is possible to read those texts in a way that analogizes a woman's body to a possession. For example, Boyarin refers to preceding text with a similar theme: "Anything that a man wishes to do [together] with his wife, he may do, analogous to meat that comes from the shop. If he

relationship maintains the heterosexual connection between the two, albeit with an uneven balance of power with regards to the legalities involved.

Still, the rabbis recognize that a woman ought to have and enjoy sex with her husband. Halakhah legally enjoins a husband to respect his wife's right to *onah*. One of the three marital requirements of the husband to his wife, onah mandates the wife's pleasure. The husband's duty varies depending on his occupation:

> With regards to *Onah*, said in the Torah: those who are men of leisure, every day; those who are workers, twice; those who are donkey-drivers, once; those who are camel-drivers, once every thirty days; those who are sailors, once every sixth months, in the words of Rabbi Eliezer.[81]

In this way, the system respects a wife's sexual needs, while recognizing the realities of the working world in antiquity. Ostensibly the central point of onah is not procreation but the wife's enjoyment; however, to "reward" the husband, this pleasure is connected with successful procreation, the birth of a son. "If the woman emits her semen first she bears a male child; if the man emits his semen first she bears a female child, for it is said, 'When a woman brings forth seed and bears a male.' (*Lev.* 12:2)."[82] The traditional interpretation of onah "always describe[s] [it] in terms of the man's sexual obligation to his wife."[83]

Here, however, the man receives two benefits from his duty, gaining both temporary sexual satisfaction and a tangible prize, a son.[84]

---

wishes to eat it with salt, he may; roasted, he may; boiled, he may; braised, he may. And similarly fish . . . ." *Id.* at 92. Boyarin appears to say that the methods of cooking are the variety of positions added to intercourse. It is also possible to read the different methods of cooking as varying methods of intercourse done to the "meat" of a woman.

[81] KETUBOTH, *supra* note 31, at Ch. 5. *See also* Ketuboth, Store of Holy Texts, http://www1.snunit.k12.il/kodesh/bavli/ctub05.html (last visited Oct. 16, 2005).

[82] BASKIN, *supra* note 51, at 21 (quoting *Niddah* 31a).

[83] BOYARIN, *supra* note 39, at 171-72 n.58.

[84] In Genesis, God commands men several times to "be fruitful and multiply." *Genesis* 1:28; 9:1,7; 35:11. Halakhah does not directly include women in this obligation, stating, "'Increase and multiply, fill the earth and subdue it,' [which] is interpreted to apply to one whose business it is to subdue rather than to be subdued." FELDMAN, *supra* note 37, at 53-54 (construing *Yebamoth* 65b). I verified this translation. *See* YEBAMOTH, *supra* note 46, at 65b. *See also* Yebamoth 65b, Store of Holy Texts, http://www1.snunit.k12.il/kodesh/bavli/ibmu065d.html (last visited Oct. 16, 2005). Therefore, the connection between procreation and sexuality is apparent primarily in texts about men's sexuality, especially about their penises. This emphasis on the male role in procreative sex once more highlights the passivity of women in initiating and engaging in intercourse because "in the ancient world, virility and the physical parts that made it possible were accorded enormous reverence," whereas women were the medium by which that process happened. BASKIN,

This text creates a causal relationship between a husband's ability to give pleasure to his wife and the subsequent sex of his legitimate children—and in the process manages to devalue a female child as the result of an unsatisfactory performance. To be sure, another tractate of the Talmud states:

> Rabbi Benjamin bar Yapat said in the name of R. Eleazar, all who make themselves holy at intercourse will have male children, as it is written, "For I the Lord am your God: you shall sanctify yourselves and be holy, for I am holy . . . ." (Lev 11:44).[85]

This Talmudic text makes it obvious that, just as the pursuit of holiness is looked upon favorably, so, too, are male children preferred, and that this result is directly related to the man's performance during sex.

Lest this explanation not be considered seriously, the rabbis even tell about their personal experiences in order to verify the connection:

> When Rabbi Ishma'el the son of Yose and Rabbi El'azar the son of Rabbi Shim'on used to meet each other, an ox could walk between them and not touch them. A certain matron said to them, "Your [sons] are not yours." They said, "Their [penises] are greater than ours." "If that is the case, even more so!" There are those who say that this this they said to her: "As the man, so is his virility." And there are those who say that thus did they say to her: "Love compresses the flesh."[86]

The discussion between the woman and the rabbis is about whether the men's physical size, including both their girth and penis size, would interfere with intercourse. While it could be argued that penis size is only meant physically and not sexually, the men's argument connects the two: sexual desire increases penis size and does not get in the way of successful intercourse that both produces sons and relieves sexual tension. The emphasis on heterosexuality comes from the need for a male and female in marriage to achieve the optimum sexual satisfaction and to physically have

---

supra note 51, at 18. Of course, men need women to act as the vessel for developing children, leading once more to the necessity of heterosexual marriage. The reality is that without women, men cannot fulfill their procreative responsibilities, even if they supposedly contribute more to that process.

[85] BASKIN, *supra* note 51, at 20 (quoting Babylonian Talmud, *Shevuot* 18b). *See also* HEBREW ENGLISH EDITION OF THE BABYLONIAN TALMUD: SHEVUOTH (Isidore Epstein ed., A.E. Silverstone trans., Soncino Press 1987).

[86] BOYARIN, *supra* note 37, at 95 (quoting *Baba Metsia* 84a). The text inserted into Boyarin's translation are my corrections as a result of verification with BABA METSIA, *supra* note 39. *See also* Baba Metsia 84a, Store of Holy Texts, http://www1.snunit.k12.il/kodesh/bavli/bbam084a.html 25 (last visited Oct. 16, 2005).

508   *Columbia Journal of Gender and Law*   [Vol. 15:2

legitimate children: "[J]ust as marriage has two essential functions, the procreational and the relational, so the marital act has these two essential functions."[87] According to Halakhah, that requires the union of a man and a woman. Overall, the text devalues the women's orgasm by making it the requirement through which a man acquires certain perks, rather than asserting that her orgasm fulfills the requirement of onah.

Boyarin is correct to assert that, regarding onah, "by coding male sexuality as a form of service to women, a mystifying protection of male access to women's bodies is secured."[88] On the surface, it recognizes that women, supposedly unable to initiate sex, need some form of legalized access to sex. However, the husband's requirement to have sex a certain number of times with his wife confirms the legality of his sexual access to her, and in sources on divorce, is turned around: the woman is required to have intercourse with her husband or risk being called a *moredet*, a rebellious wife.[89] Halakhah bends over backwards to ensure the wife's sexual access to her husband both to acknowledge the woman's need to have her sexual desires satisfied and also to make certain that men have legal access to intercourse within marriage. Interestingly, if a husband refuses to have sex with his wife, the woman can approach the rabbinical court and the rabbis can force him to divorce her. In contrast, if a man makes the same complaint to the court, "a wife could be divorced without her marriage settlement," or, if she would not agree to the divorce, the man could request permission to divorce her anyway.[90] In any case, onah only partially ensures the right of the wife to have her sexual needs fulfilled; the husband's right to satisfy his sexual desires is never in question.

C. Marriage in Judaism Today

Given this halakhic framework that promotes the relief of sexual tension through heterosexual marriage, it is important to analyze how the American Jewish movements have responded to these texts. Perhaps not surprisingly, all but one of the four major movements advocate the centrality of heterosexual marriage in Jewish tradition. Procreation within the marital context makes Jewish continuity and existence possible. As Rabbi Eugene Borowitz explains, "the imperiled situation of the Jewish community as a minority [especially after the Holocaust] makes family

---

[87] FELDMAN, *supra* note 37, at 129.

[88] BOYARIN, *supra* note 39, at 171-72 n.58.

[89] SHLOMO RISKIN, WOMEN AND JEWISH DIVORCE: THE REBELLIOUS WIFE, THE AGUNAH AND THE RIGHT OF WOMEN TO INITIATE DIVORCE IN JEWISH LAW, A HALAKHIC SOLUTION 7-9 (1989).

[90] BASKIN, *supra* note 51, at 93.

unity a particularly important instrument of our survival."[91] For Orthodox, Conservative, and Reform Judaism, the connection of human sexuality to procreation in a sanctified male-female relationship serves to maintain the existence of the Jewish people. Reconstructionist Judaism, on the other hand, recognizes the equal legitimacy of heterosexual and homosexual marriages and challenges the opinion of the other groups that this position threatens Jewish continuity. This section examines these positions in order to establish the foundation of these movements' attitudes toward sexuality, which inform their stances on the modern issues of divorce and homosexuality.

Orthodox Judaism promotes marriage for a number of reasons. First and foremost, matrimony is a traditional Jewish institution: Halakhah provides the basic marital framework through the *ketubah*,[92] and Jews, with few exceptions, are obligated or at least highly encouraged to follow those dictates. This outline for marital life "include[s] the powerful group of laws clustered around the concept of taharat mishpachah, '"family purity,' laws of modesty, [and] restrictions on the social mixing of the sexes."[93] While "[t]hey amounted to a discipline of self-imposed segregation, and they are among the Jewish laws most at odds with the assumptions of a liberal, open society,"[94] those laws have also been praised as maintaining the stability of the Jewish family and providing a system of "boundaries in marital, familial, and sexual relationships" for the members of a household that promotes respect and rejuvenates monthly the couple's sex life. [95] Underscoring all of this discourse, however, is the realization that the "integrated [and religious] Jewish home" functions as "the best guarantee of the survival of the Orthodox Jewish family," especially after the Holocaust and with the advent of high levels of assimilation.[96] Orthodox Judaism reinforces the traditional views of sexuality exemplified in the sacred texts by connecting them to the perception of a modern Jewish need for an increased religious population.

---

[91] EUGENE BOROWITZ, EXPLORING JEWISH ETHICS: PAPERS ON COVENANTAL RESPONSIBILITY 279 (1990).

[92] Marriage contract. 10 ENCYCLOPEDIA JUDAICA, *supra* note 3, at 926.

[93] JONATHAN SACKS, TRADITION IN AN UNTRADITIONAL AGE: ESSAYS ON MODERN JEWISH THOUGHT 102 (1990).

[94] *Id.*

[95] Debra Renee Kaufman, *Better the Devil You Know . . . and Other Contemporary Identity Narratives: Comparing Orthodox to Reform Judaism, in* PLATFORMS AND PRAYER BOOKS: THEOLOGICAL AND LITURGICAL PERSPECTIVES ON REFORM JUDAISM 221, 225 (Dana Evan Kaplan ed., 2002).

[96] Gershon Kranzler, *The Changing Orthodox Jewish Family, in* DIMENSIONS OF ORTHODOX JUDAISM 359, 367 (Reuven P. Bulka ed., 1983).

Reform Judaism, usually at odds with Orthodoxy, generally agrees with the primacy of marriage between a man and a woman in Jewish tradition. The liberal attitude towards marriage generally emphasizes marital sexuality and subsequent procreation as significant in Jewish tradition.[97] Indeed, heterosexuality is normative: "[M]arriage was [and is] the only acceptable social setting for the sexual relationship."[98] Unlike Orthodox Judaism, however, the Reform movement acknowledges that the traditional laws of Jewish marriage have sustained the "stability of the Jewish marriage [that] was procured at the cost of subordinating a woman's life to that of her husband"[99] and actively pursues a policy of equality between spouses, sexual and otherwise. The emphasis on marriage is coupled with serious revisions of unequal institutional qualities in a way that leaves room for more liberal interpretations.[100] Only recently did Reform Jews question the primacy of heterosexuality in their version of Judaism and advocate for the acceptance of homosexual and non-traditional families on the basis of a different approach to Jewish tradition. It appears that experts of the Reform movement incorporate the more desirable values that heterosexual marriage embodies and eschews those values expressed in Halakhah with which they disagree.

Similarly, Conservative Judaism believes in the sole legitimacy of heterosexual marriage. By currently disavowing the authenticity of homosexual commitment while also pressing for a more equal relationship between husband and wife, the Conservative Movement continues its position between Orthodoxy and Reform Judaism with regard to Jewish practice. Marriage between a man and a woman represents the ultimate connection between people and God. In addition, "sexual experience is a major source of pleasure and well-being for men and women, and its successful functioning [only in marriage] is a proper objective."[101] One official publication on sexuality does not explicitly delineate characteristics of male and female sexuality; rather the emphasis is on principles appropriate for both sexes, like modesty, respect, and honesty.[102]

[97] BOROWITZ, *supra* note 91, at 265.

[98] *Id.*

[99] *Id.*

[100] For instance, while the Reform marriage ceremony emphasizes the religious nature of matrimony, "Reform Jews have generally discarded the use of Chupah, the Aramaic Marriage Contract [which articulates sexual and other rights], and the custom of breaking the glass at the end of the marriage ceremony . . . [and encouraged] the double-ring ceremony." WILLIAM B. SILVERMAN, BASIC REFORM JUDAISM 205 (1970).

[101] ROBERT GORDIS, LOVE AND SEX: A MODERN JEWISH PERSPECTIVE 251 (1978).

[102] ELLIOT N. DORFF, THIS IS MY BELOVED, THIS IS MY FRIEND: A RABBINIC LETTER ON INTIMATE RELATIONS 9-11 (1996).

Concerning the promotion of equality in marriage, the Conservative Movement adopted a new ketubah in 1987 that, to a limited extent, uses more egalitarian language and protects the woman's right to a divorce should the marriage dissolve.[103] Conservative Judaism also recognizes the significant impact the family has on the continuation of Jewish tradition, and, like Reform Judaism, has only just begun to challenge traditional concepts of marriage in the movement. This middle-of-the-road position emphasizes sexuality as a central feature of heterosexual marriage, but does not go so far as to challenge the assumptions upon which this element is based. With respect to the halakhic texts, then, the Conservative Movement modernizes Jewish understandings of sexuality and sexual expression without abandoning traditional parameters.

Although recently Orthodox, Conservative, and Reform Judaism have initiated dialogue on the changing structure of the family, these Jewish movements continue to discuss issues of sexuality within a "compulsory heterosexuality" framework, that is, where heterosexuality is preferred and supported by a society.[104] For instance, the recent changes in Reform Judaism that permit gay and lesbian rabbis do not address the fundamental preference of Jewish society for heterosexual marriage, because even "appeals to [the traditional] passages constitute a major strategy in *contemporary* efforts to enforce compulsory heterosexuality."[105] In contrast, Reconstructionist Judaism has accorded equal respect to both heterosexual and homosexual relationships by stating its support for equal access of homosexuals to civil marriage.[106] This position subverts the religious system by undermining the "modes of constructing and policing relationships between gender roles, obligatory heterosexuality, and the

---

[103] *A New Ketubah Text* (Elliot Dorff trans., 1987), *in* PROCEEDINGS OF THE COMMITTEE ON JEWISH LAW AND STANDARDS OF THE CONSERVATIVE MOVEMENT: 1986-1990, at 241, 241-43 (2001) (The couple agrees that, "should either contemplate dissolution of their marriage, or following dissolution of their marriage in the civil courts, each may summon the other to the Beit Din of the Rabbinical Assembly and the Jewish Theological Seminary of America, or its representative, and that each will abide by its instructions so that throughout life each will be able to live according to the laws of the Torah.").

[104] Judith Plaskow defines this paradigm as a "complex web of ideologies and institutions through which people learn and are made to be heterosexual." Judith Plaskow, *Sexual Orientation and Human Rights: A Progressive Jewish Perspective*, *in* SEXUAL ORIENTATION & HUMAN RIGHTS IN AMERICAN RELIGIOUS DISCOURSE 29, 36 (Saul M. Olyan & Martha C. Nussbaum eds., 1998).

[105] *Id.* at 38.

[106] RECONSTRUCTIONIST RABBINICAL ASSOCIATION, RESOLUTION IN SUPPORT OF CIVIL MARRIAGE FOR SAME-SEX COUPLES (2004), *available at* http://www.therra.org/resolution-Mar2004.htm [hereinafter RRA Resolution].

constraint of female sexuality."[107] Reconstructionist Judaism thus stands in opposition to the other movements.[108]

III. THE ROLE OF SEXUALITY IN JEWISH DIVORCE

As stated in Part I, this section analyzes how halakhic conceptions of sexuality, and more specifically female sexuality, have influenced the development of Jewish divorce law. It also analyzes the responses of the modern American Jewish movements to the legal inequalities for women inherent in the legal system of Jewish divorce. Legally, marriage in the Jewish tradition formalizes a man's acquisition of rights to a woman's sexuality. Divorce undoes that process by allowing him to repudiate his rights to sexual intercourse with his wife. The older halakhic texts set out, and today's legal authorities maintain, a halakhic framework that establishes and dissolves this contractual association between husband and wife. Only a man traditionally has the legal power to effectuate and terminate this contract. The rabbis recognize marriage as the proper forum for the sexual expression of men and women, deriving the legitimacy of matrimony from their opinions about heterosexual desire. However, despite mandating marriage for both sexes, it is women who are left without any meaningful exit from the contract.

This section argues that the husband's official disavowal of the rights to sexual intercourse with his wife forms the basis of the process of divorce. By examining the provisions regarding sexuality that the husband agrees to in the ketubah, this section describes the requirements for a divorce. It also explores the circumstances, set out by the rabbis, whereby divorce is proper or even encouraged. These halakhic texts, combined with an analysis of the stipulations of the *get*,[109] provide further evidence for the centrality of sexuality in divorce. Because only a man can bring about a divorce, his refusal to grant the get has the added effect of precluding the woman's assumption of rights to her own sexuality. A woman who has not yet received a get from her husband is called an *agunah*, literally a chained woman, because she is still legally married to this man and is not free to remarry. In modern times, Jewish movements have realized that this disparity causes immense suffering on the part of women who do not have the freedom to move on with their lives after the factual termination of their marriages. Reform, Reconstructionist, Conservative, and Orthodox legal authorities advocate different solutions to remedy the situation of the chained woman. However, their suggestions do not resolve the central

---

[107] Plaskow, *supra* note 104, at 37.

[108] Indeed, the Reconstructionist approach to marital sexuality greatly influences the movement's positions on the issues discussed *infra*.

[109] Writ of divorce; the plural is *gittim*.

difficulty. The unjust situation derives from the ancient locations of sexuality in marriage and divorce contracts, and it is this problem, in conjunction with the man's unilateral control, that must be solved.

A. The Marriage Contract

While there are sacred elements to Jewish matrimony, a man and a woman formally marry through contract. The earliest Jewish legal traditions on marriage "categoriz[e] it as a commercial transaction by which sexual chattel is acquired."[110] The Hebrew Bible refers to a bride price, or *mohar*: "If a man seduces a virgin [*betulah*; sometimes understood as a young woman] who is not engaged and lies with her, he will marry her for the marriage/bride price, as a wife."[111] Lest one think that this transaction is only a fine for this particular case of his sleeping with the woman, the verse continues: "If her father really refuses to give her to him, he will pay the marriage/bride price of a virgin."[112] When the young woman is no longer a virgin, ostensibly her father does not receive the bride price of a virgin and loses potential income. Therefore, if a man has sex with a woman and refuses to marry her, he must pay damages that are equivalent to the financial amount her father would have received had she married as a virgin. While it is not certain what the actual amount of the bride price was, as it depended on the sexual status of the woman about to be married, it is clear that when money changed hands, the transaction, that is, the man's acquisition of the woman, was complete.

The Mishnah upholds this method of financial exchange to ensure the legal formality of the marriage. According to Judith Wegner, the rabbis

> focus[ed] on such matters as the impact of virginity on bride-price, circumstances when a man can or cannot expect his bride to be a virgin, the bridegroom's right to redress if his bride is not intact, and the father's right to financial compensation from a man who violates his minor daughter.[113]

Regarding the third specification, Wegner notes that "having paid for his bride's virginity, an aggrieved bridegroom, just as any buyer of goods that fail to meet specifications, can bring suit."[114] These general topics, however,

---

[110] RACHEL ADLER, ENGENDERING JUDAISM: AN INCLUSIVE THEOLOGY AND ETHICS 172 (1998).

[111] *Exodus* 22:15 (Biblia Hebraica Stuttgartensia, *supra* note 48).

[112] *Id.*

[113] JUDITH ROMNEY WEGNER, CHATTEL OR PERSON? THE STATUS OF WOMEN IN THE MISHNAH 20 (1998).

do not evoke the directness of the comparison of women to property. *Mishnah Kiddushin* 1 directly compares the woman to objects that can be owned:

> (1) The woman is acquired in three ways and acquires herself [or her autonomy] in two ways. She can be acquired by money, by deed, and by sexual intercourse. . . . She acquires herself [autonomy] by a get and the death of her husband [literally master]. . . . (2) A Hebrew slave is acquired by money or by deed and acquires himself by years [of working] or by the Jubilee or by [paying] his reduced price [that is, buying his freedom]. . . . (3) A Canaanite slave is acquired by money, by deed, or by usucaption. . . . (5) Mortgaged property is acquired by money, by deed, or by usucaption . . . .[115]

Before discussing the resemblance of the treatment of women to that of property, it is important to point out that the language for the wife and husband in this passage is not parallel and suggests a power differential. The woman is called *isha*, but the man is not called *ish*. Instead, "the word for husband is *ba'al*, the general term for an owner, master, possessor of property, bearer of responsibility, or practitioner of skill." [116] This terminology points to the legally uneven relationship: the man owns the woman's sexuality. She can only take possession of her own sexuality through the get or her husband's death. Other aspects of the Mishnah reiterate that unequal relationship.[117]

---

[114] *Id.* at 22.

[115] *See* HEBREW ENGLISH EDITION OF THE BABYLONIAN TALMUD: KIDDUSHIN 1:1-5 (Isidore Epstein ed., H. Freedman trans., Soncino Press 1990). *See also* Kiddushin, Store of Holy Texts, http://www1.snunit.k12.il/kodesh/mishna/kidu01.html (last visited Oct. 16, 2005).

[116] ADLER, *supra* note 110, at 171.

[117] Wegner gives further contours to the Mishnah's treatment of the wife as property:

First the [sages] use the same technical term q-n-y ('to acquire ownership') as for other forms of property. Second, the same three modes of acquisition apply to wife, Canaanite slave, and real property. . . . Intercourse is the specific form of usucaption that applies to a wife. Third, after setting out the list, the Mishnah's framers drop the subject of property; espousal of wives occupies the entire tractate. Obviously the sages list all these kinds of property along with the wife to suggest both a formal and a substantive analogy between acquiring a wife and acquiring chattel.

WEGNER, *supra* note 113, at 43. Wegner cautions that "the inclusion of the wife does not necessarily imply that she is the husband's property in all respects," seeing as how a wife retains her independence with regard to the property she brings into the marriage. *Id.* The ownership is specific to her sexuality; the man does not own her but sexual access to her body. The right to sexual intercourse with his wife regulates the expression of his sexual

The *Gemara* of the Babylonian *Talmud* continues this trend of considering the woman's sexuality as a commodity in its commentary on the above *Mishnah, Mishnah Kiddushin* 1.[118] The rabbis of this time period call the process through which formal acquisition occurs *kinyan*. According to Adler, "monetary acquisition (*kinyan kesef*) is . . . the one approved method [in the Talmud] for appropriating wives," although usucaption does not necessarily invalidate the marriage.[119] However, Moshe Meiselman contends that there are "two types of contracts: the *kinyan issur*, a contract whose basic purpose is to effect a change in personal or ritual status, and the *kinyan mamon*, a contract whose basic purpose is to effect a monetary change."[120] Marriage, in his opinion, is the former, rather than the latter; the physical act of giving of an object marks the change in personal status.[121] Adler disagrees, stating that, "while the purchase of the bride may have dwindled to a mere formality in the rabbinic transformation of marriage, her *acquisition* is no formality."[122] Adler argues that the distinctions between types of kinyan are irrelevant, as "[w]hat all the legally acceptable transactions have in common is that they are *unilateral* acts . . . [that, according to the laws in Kiddushin,] the man must take, and the woman must be *taken*."[123] Certainly the woman's status is changed from unmarried to married. However, it is impossible to ignore that her personal transformation is effected through a financial transaction.

Another talmudic innovation delays payment of the monetary amount. The kinyan still occurs in a symbolic form by representing the real price, but the actual amount stipulated in the ketubah is not transferred. In the Babylonian Talmud, Rabbi Judah explains in *Ketuboth* 82b: "At first they wrote for a virgin 200 *zuz* and for a widow 100 but the men grew old and did not marry women [because they could not afford to] until Simon ben Shetah enacted that all the groom's property is responsible for the ketubah."[124] As Judith Hauptman points out, though, "once the ketubah was

---

desire; without this structure, as discussed *supra*, the rabbis fear the man will seek out other, though certainly heterosexual, outlets for satisfying his desire.

[118] ADLER, *supra* note 110, at 174.

[119] *Id.*

[120] MOSHE MEISELMAN, JEWISH WOMAN IN JEWISH LAW 96 (1978) (citing *Hidushei ha-Ramban* to *Kiddushin* 16a).

[121] *Id.* at 96-97.

[122] ADLER, *supra* note 110, at 176.

[123] *Id.*

[124] *Ketuboth* 82a, *supra* note 31. *See also* Ketuboth 30, Store of Holy Texts, http://www1.snunit.k12.il/kodesh/bavli/ctub082b.html (last visited Oct. 16, 2005).

transformed into . . . a way of providing a woman with some assets to tide her over into her next marriage, then . . . as a deferred payment, [it] was no longer a gauge of her sexual intactness."[125] Still, the marriage transferred rights to the woman's sexuality. While it is now more accurately a "negotiated relationship between a woman who is subordinate and a man who is dominant," the ketubah nonetheless affirms the principle of *kinyan*.[126]

Today, there are two phases to the agreement: *kiddushin* and *nissu'in*. The former, also known as *'erusin*, "sufficed to make the man and the woman legally bound so that sexual connection by her with another man was adultery punishable as such, and to dissolve the bond a bill of divorce was required."[127] This method of betrothal officially transfers the rights to woman's sexuality to her future husband. Moreover, kiddushin literally means sanctification, which is "a major rabbinic means of drawing boundaries and demarcations, a legal and ritual creation of the universe out of undifferentiated chaos."[128] In this way, marriage essentially sets aside a woman for a particular man. The marriage is formalized when nissu'in occurs, i.e., when the bride goes to her new husband's home. Interestingly, nissu'in is also called "taking" or *likkuhin*,[129] which implies male control;

---

[125] JUDITH HAUPTMAN, REREADING THE RABBIS: A WOMAN'S VOICE 66 (1998).

[126] *Id.* at 74. Several centuries later, Maimonides codified this process of acquisition. In *Hilkhot Ishut* 1:3, he explains:

Once a woman is acquired and thus betrothed, even if she has not had intercourse and has not entered her husband's house, she is still the wife of a man [a married woman], and one, who is not her husband, who has intercourse with her, is liable for the death penalty from the *bet din* [rabbinical court], and if her husband wants to divorce her, she needs a get.

MISHNEH TORAH: HILKHOT ISHUT, *supra* note 41, at 1:3. *See also* Mishneh Torah Hilkhot Ishut 1:3, Store of Holy Texts, http://www1.snunit.k12.il/kodesh/mtr/aisu001.html (last visited Oct. 16, 2005).

The Rambam uses the same language for acquisition and betrothal. Because the infraction is sexual, it is the act of intercourse between a man and a woman betrothed to another man which presumably violates her husband's rights. Of course, Maimonides recognizes that, through the ketubah, the man is obligated to fulfill the requirement of onah, but even that entitlement affirms the man's right to have sexual intercourse with her. Overall "the conception of marriage as a unilateral acquisition of property, analogous to the acquisition of slaves, animals, or fields, rather than embodying commitments on the part of two participants, dominates legal thinking in rabbinic texts" throughout the centuries. ADLER, *supra* note 110, at 157.

[127] GEORGE HOROWITZ, THE SPIRIT OF JEWISH LAW: A BRIEF ACCOUNT OF BIBLICAL AND RABBINICAL JURISPRUDENCE WITH A SPECIAL NOTE ON JEWISH LAW AND THE STATE OF ISRAEL 256 (1953).

[128] ADLER, *supra* note 110, at 172.

[129] HOROWITZ, *supra* note 127, at 265.

the man literally takes the woman home to become his wife.[130] It is with this framework in mind that this Article presents the halakhic texts on divorce.

B. Halakhic Texts on Divorce

The rabbinic process for divorce essentially reverses the marital contract. The man gives a get, specifically written for this transaction, to his former wife in front of witnesses and members of the *beit din.*[131] *Deuteronomy* 24:1 serves as the biblical basis for this procedure: "[I]f a man takes a wife and marries her, but she does not find favor in his eyes—because he finds in her something sexually unappealing—he writes for her a document of cutting off/divorce and gives it into her hands and sends her from his house."[132] Because, in this verse, the man "takes" the wife, the rabbis interpret that action to mean that only a man can affect the kiddushin at the beginning of the marriage. Likewise, because it says "he writes for her," it follows that the husband is the only one who can end the relationship.

The text of the get, established in the Mishnah, explicitly releases the rights to the woman's sexuality. *Mishnah Gittin* 9:3 states: "[T]he body of the get says you are permitted to every man . . . that you may go and marry any man you wish."[133] With the ketubah, the man legally acquires sexual access to his wife; with the get, he relinquishes that access by permitting her to remarry and to have sex with her new husband. In fact, the man is forbidden to stipulate any conditions on this right. Otherwise, he would not actually surrender his access to her. This failure to surrender access infringes upon both the woman's right to choose another husband and also her future husband's right to her sexuality. Without the get, the woman is still married to her husband; he continues to be the only man with whom she may have sex and with whom she may have children. Any sexual relationship she has with another man is adulterous, and any child from that liaison is a *mamzer.*[134]

---

[130] Today, this "taking" is symbolized by the bridal canopy, the *chuppah,* and the *yichud,* the time the couple spends alone immediately after the marriage.

[131] Rabbinical court. Generally, the rabbinical court has three rabbis.

[132] *Deuteronomy* 24:1 (Biblica Hebraica Stuttgartensia, *supra* note 48).

[133] *Mishnah Gittin* 9:3. (The Schottenstein Edition) (citing Yisroel Simcha Schorr & Hersh Goldwurm eds., Mesora Publications, Ltd. 1993). *See also* Mishnah Gittin 9:3, Store of Holy Texts, http://www1.snunit.k12.il/kodesh/mishna/giti09.html (last visited Oct. 16, 2005).

[134] Technical term for illegitimate. 11 ENCYCLOPEDIA JUDAICA, *supra* note 3, at 840.

The Mishnah sets out acceptable reasons and avenues for divorce for both husband and wife. Regarding *Mishnah Gittin* 9:10, Judith Wegner explains that "the common denominator is that all three [rabbis'] views treat the wife as chattel" and uphold divorce as the "disposition of a man's exclusive right to a woman's sexual function."[135] Each authority in this text defines the husband's rights with regard to his wife slightly differently. Wegner describes each tannaitic position:

> The Shammaites perceive the essence of marriage as a husband's exclusive right to his wife's sexuality; so he can divorce only if some other man has had sexual relations with her. This approach treats the wife as chattel when her sexual function is in issue, but it protects her when she is without moral fault. The school of Hillel, by contrast, permits her husband to divorce her for the least infraction . . . . Her role is to serve him generally. . . . Aqiba goes further still; he treats the wife as no person at all, permitting the husband to discard her without even the flimsiest excuse.[136]

The husband essentially has many legitimate reasons for divorce available to him, and the possibilities reflect his status as an unsatisfied purchaser. In addition, there are instances when the rabbis encourage the man to exercise his power and divorce his wife. Rabbi Meir, in *Tosefta Sotah* 5, criticizes

> the conduct of a wicked man [who] is untroubled by his wife's going out with hair uncovered or a sleeveless blouse, being overly familiar with her male or female servants, going out to spin in the market place, bathing and acting frivolously with other men . . . .[137]

He suggests that "in such cases it is a mitzvah to divorce her."[138] Those actions by the wife violate *Dat Yehudit*, the proper behavior of a religious woman, because each incident has sexual overtones. The rabbis consider hair and uncovered arms liable to arouse, while intimate contact with other men suggests promiscuity. Interestingly, Getsel Ellinson explains that the fear of the woman spinning in public is also sexual because "she holds the thread to draw attention to her private parts."[139] If the wife obstinately

---

[135] WEGNER, *supra* note 113, at 47.

[136] *Id.*

[137] ELLINSON, *supra* note 23, at 125-26.

[138] *Id.* at 126.

[139] *Id.* at 127. This is ironic considering that women skilled in spinning and weaving were highly regarded, especially since their work likely improved their families' financial status.

refuses to accept the husband's divorce, the man simply receives permission from the *beit din* or, according to some traditions, from one hundred rabbis, and he could remarry without giving the get. Access to his sexuality was not at stake; with rabbinic approval, he was free to remarry.

In contrast to her husband, a wife can only ask for a divorce on four grounds under Halakhah:

(1) When her husband is afflicted by physical conditions or undertakes an occupation deemed unendurable for the wife
(2) When her husband violates or neglects his marital obligations
(3) When there is sexual incompatibility or
[4] when there has been wife beating.[140]

All of these rationales have sexual implications. The woman's legitimate complaints were limited to protests over her husband's sexual performance or problems with her sexual desire for him. The rabbis had compassion for the woman who was not sexually attracted to her husband. For example, Maimonides rules:

A woman who refuses to have intercourse with her husband is called *moredet* [rebellious]. One asks for her reason. If she says, 'I dislike him and am unable to have sexual relations with him freely,' one compels the husband to divorce her. She is not like a prisoner to live with one whom she detests.[141]

It is important to note that the court can only "compel" the husband to give her the get, even if she requests it for sexual reasons. The husband is the only one who can terminate the marriage, and he must do it willingly. Such willingness could mean that the husband freely terminated the marriage or, as Maimonides permitted, that an injunction allowed others to beat the man until he agreed.[142] Without a get, the woman cannot lawfully remarry and have legitimate children.

Later authorities, however, questioned whether even these reasons are valid: is the woman believable when she makes claims about her sex life? In the thirteenth century, Rabbi Shlomo ben Aderet worried that "such a law would make it possible for a woman to form a liaison with another

---

[140] ADRIENNE BAKER, THE JEWISH WOMAN IN CONTEMPORARY SOCIETY: TRANSITIONS AND TRADITIONS 55 (1993).

[141] MISHNEH TORAH: HILKHOT ISHUT 14:8 (Moshe ben Shaltiel ed., Ma'or Publication Society 1975); ELIEZER BERKOVITS, JEWISH WOMEN IN TIME AND TORAH 49 (1990).

[142] MISHNEH TORAH: GERUSHIN 2:20 (Moshe ben Shaltiel ed., Ma'or Publication Society 1975).

man and then demand that her husband be compelled to divorce her."[143] An illicit sexual liaison threatens her husband's claim to her that, in turn, is the basic foundation for the legal institution of marriage. The Tosafot[144] and other Halakhists, however, decide her claim on the basis of evidence; that is, rather than determine that she is not sexually involved with another man, they investigate whether her complaint of sexual dissatisfaction is true.[145] Her current husband's right to her sexuality overrides the other factors.

Overall, "whenever a man owns, acquires, or disposes of a woman's sexuality, the law treats the woman as chattel for that purpose," especially "for rules governing marriage [and] divorce."[146] With regard to terminating the marriage, the man acts unilaterally, but the woman is dependent on her husband to relinquish his legal right to her sexuality. If he refuses, she is an agunah. She is without control over her own sexuality and unable to remarry. The ancient laws for divorce created this inequitable legal status for women and, as shown below, the contemporary Jewish movements maintain the possibility of this status in modern Jewish law.

1. A Contemporary Halakhic Problem: the Agunah

Today, the situation most likely to cause a woman to become an agunah is the husband's flat-out refusal, either out of spite or in anticipation of monetary gain, to give his wife a get. All of the modern Jewish movements acknowledge that this state of affairs negatively impacts the woman's quality of life; she is unable to move on from the failed marriage and begin life anew. On the whole, though, their respective solutions do not address the issue of sexuality, which constitutes the major problem with Jewish divorce. This failure is a problem because the root cause of the agunah's unfortunate situation comes from the quasi-ownership of the woman's sexuality and the inability (or unwillingness) of the community or its leaders to change the laws.

On the least complicated level, Reform Judaism in America "turn[s] the whole business over to civil authorities" by the "declar[ation] that civil divorce alone suffice[s] to dissolve its marriages." [147] The Reform Movement repudiates the halakhic system of divorce to negate the inequalities in the process, namely, those problems that derive from the husband's sole ability to terminate marriage. This course of action follows

---

[143] BERKOVITS, *supra* note 141, at 50. This is also known as the *Rashba*.

[144] 15 ENCYCLOPEDIA JUDAICA, *supra* note 3, at 1278.

[145] BERKOVITS, *supra* note 141, at 50 (citing *Ketubot* 63b s.v, abal amra). *See also* KETUBOT, *supra* note 31.

[146] WEGNER, *supra* note 113, at 45.

[147] ADLER, *supra* note 110, at 201.

essentially a similar pattern as the Reform attitude to marriage, in which Reform rabbis "permit an exchange of rings and vows by the two parties, in contrast to Talmudic law,"[148] thereby making the marriage more equal as well. This approach to marriage and divorce, however, only works when Jewish laws are not seen as externally binding. Other Jewish movements continue to view the woman who uses this approach as an adulteress and any children from that type of adulterous relationship as *mamzerim*. The Reform Movement thus rejects the approach of the halakhic texts when Halakhah undermines equality.

On the other hand, Reconstructionism combines the traditional framework for marriage and divorce with a better understanding of the role of sexuality in the process. In a case with an agunah, according to Blu Greenberg, "the Reconstructionist *beit din* simply will give her a *shtar piturin*, a document that declares her free to remarry, even though she has no get, nor has her marriage been annulled."[149] This approach recognizes that the consequences of a woman remarrying without a get threaten Jewish stability by driving people away from Judaism. The stigma placed on her and her children makes it difficult for her to remarry according to Jewish tradition, thus discouraging her from remaining a member of the Jewish community. Significantly, the shtar peturin reinforces the court's right to grant the woman the ability to remarry. The beit din's control of her sexuality is taken away from her husband, rather than being recognized as always having been her own. The woman's sexuality is still treated like a commodity, but in this instance, the court exercises compassion.

The Conservative Movement, with its emphasis on maintaining Jewish legal tradition, has suggested three possible solutions to the agunah problem. In the 1950s, Rabbi Saul Lieberman advocated the introduction of a clause into the ketubah that would serve as a contractual prenuptial agreement. It stipulated that, if the couple divorced, the husband and wife would go before an official Conservative beit din and "authorize[] the b[e]it din to impose such terms of compensation as it may see fit for failure to respond to its summons." [150] There were several problems with the Lieberman clause, as it came to be known.[151] First, though "there was an effort to enforce [these] rules" in secular American courts, such clauses were found "to run afoul of the principle of separation of church and

---

[148] RUDAVSKY, *supra* note 9, at 295.

[149] BLU GREENBERG, ON WOMEN AND JUDAISM: A VIEW FROM TRADITION 135 (1998).

[150] IRVING A. BREITOWITZ, BETWEEN CIVIL AND RELIGIOUS LAW: THE PLIGHT OF THE AGUNAH IN AMERICAN SOCIETY 96-97 (1993).

[151] *Id.*

state."[152] Also, it "was rejected by the Orthodox as being halakhically invalid because of [the] indeterminate nature" of its stipulations.[153]

Next, the Conservative Movement tried the "Berkovits t'nai in 1968" that stated that "if our marriage should end in a civil divorce and within six months thereafter I give you a get, our marriage will remain valid and binding; if, however, six months have passed and I do not give you a get, then our marriage will have been null and void."[154] This was not acceptable to traditionalist authorities because "marriage is an unconditional commitment and conditional marriages and divorces thereby are rendered invalid by consummation of the marriage."[155] Most recently, Conservative rabbis have been in favor of a solution that recognizes the power of the rabbinical courts to give legitimacy to marriage in the first place, and "if the rabbis remove their sanction because of certain conditions no longer operating, the original act of kiddushin (betrothal) is voided,"[156] meaning the marriage was not valid and the woman does not need a get. Again the Orthodox movement disallows this option "on the grounds that the power to annul marriages was used only in limited instances and in post-talmudic times the power to annul marriages has been constricted."[157] Here, too, the Conservative Movement does not challenge the traditional framework that treats woman's sexuality as a commodity. Its methodologies address the inequalities of divorce by instituting procedures undertaken by the husband and by the rabbinical court; the man must come before the beit din or the court acts to help the woman. The woman lacks legal control over her sexuality until she receives the writ of divorce.

With a similar approach as Conservative Judaism, Orthodoxy does not challenge the underlying halakhic framework of marriage and divorce; Halakhah, after all, is immutable in their authorities' opinion. The Orthodox Movement has looked for ways to increase the power of their rabbinical courts, again using the beit din to assert its authority over the marriage and essentially convince the husband to give the get. According to Seymour Cohen,

---

[152] Seymour J. Cohen, *The United States Constitution and the Jewish Community: The Recalcitrant Husband and the Chained Woman (Agunah)*, *in* 21 JEWISH LAW ASSOCIATION STUDIES VIII: THE JERUSALEM 1994 CONFERENCE 25 (Edward A. Goldman ed., 1996).

[153] GREENBERG, *supra* note 149, at 136.

[154] *Id.* at 136-37.

[155] *Id.* at 137 (citing MIESELMAN, *supra* note 110, at 103-08).

[156] *Id.*

[157] *Id.* at 138.

> the Rabbinical Council of America [a national Orthodox rabbinical organization] has urged its membership to use . . . the premarital agreement to be signed by both husband- and wife-to-be in which the husband agrees to [financially] maintain and support his wife [by providing a certain amount of money] until the marriage has been terminated.[158]

In addition, "both parties stipulate that, in case of disagreement, they agree to have their dispute adjudicated by a specified person acceptable to both parties," ostensibly an Orthodox beit din.[159] This prenuptial agreement supposedly makes the halakhic stipulations for marriage and divorce, including the husband's obligation to support his wife financially and his responsibility to give her a get when the marriage is terminated, legally enforceable in the secular courts. Sexuality is simply not an issue; perhaps this attitude reflects the Orthodox opinion that kinyan for marriage is really "ritualistic."[160]

It is impossible to overlook the fact that the halakhic texts on marriage and divorce treat a woman's sexuality as her husband's property. The solutions proposed by the four modern movements of Judaism have tried to address the legal inequalities created by the husband's unilateral power to effect divorce, but they have ignored the issue of what property he commands. Certainly their efforts should be admired and regarded as necessary. Nonetheless, "[w]here women's sexuality is seen as an object to be possessed, and sexuality is confined to heterosexual marriage and perceived as an impulse that can take possession of the self, the central issues surrounding sexuality will necessarily be issues of control."[161] These issues of control are the result of the underlying fact that marriage and divorce involve the legal transfer of a woman's sexuality. When the solution persists in regarding woman's sexuality as a commodity, the modern Jewish movements in effect maintain the inequalities because the woman must still rely on the beit din's benevolence for her sexual freedom. It is crucial to resolve this issue in a way that treats each woman as a complete person, rather than property.

---

[158] Cohen, *supra* note 152, at 35.

[159] *Id.*

[160] MEISELMAN, *supra* note 120, at 96.

[161] Judith Plaskow, *Toward a New Theology of Sexuality, in* TWICE BLESSED: ON BEING LESBIAN OR GAY AND JEWISH 141, 142 (Christie Balka & Andy Rose eds., 1989).

IV. THE ROLE OF TRADITIONAL CONSTRUCTIONS OF SEXUALITY IN MODERN JEWISH APPROACHES TO HOMOSEXUALITY

By calling into question the very substance of halakhic texts, GLBT Jews challenge the heart of traditional Jewish gender expectations: Jewish man meets Jewish woman, they establish a middle-class home, and they have at least two children who grow up to marry Jews of the opposite sex and have their own children. Jewish society's inherent privileging of that ideal does not allow GLBT Jews full access to and support within Jewish communal life. This tension becomes all the more complex due to the great esteem in which many Jews, including GLBT Jews, hold their legal and communal traditions. This Part begins with an analysis of several Jewish texts that address homosexuality,[162] either halakhically or socially. It then explains how the modern movements of Judaism use those writings in their conceptions of homosexuality and of the roles of GLBT Jews in their communities. It examines significant passages on homosexuality in order to illuminate the major difficulties homosexuality poses to the normative assumptions underlying the Jewish legal system's regulation of sexuality. Because modern arguments are based on interpretations of halakhic texts, it is important to identify and explain how these legal materials functioned in their own historical and philosophical contexts. It is with knowledge of this historical framework that modern Jewish movements evaluate the claims of GLBT Jews, approaching the issue from distinct theological positions concerning the authority of sacred works for contemporary Jews. At stake is an understanding of how shifting social conceptions of sexuality can affect the interpretation and implementation of Jewish law as well as an awareness of the impact Jewish legal decisions about homosexuality can have on the lives of GLBT Jews.

A. Male Homosexual Desire

The main proscription against male homoerotic sex comes from the Hebrew Bible, *Leviticus* 18:22:

---

[162] As discussed in Part II, *supra*, the halakhic materials presume a heterosexual norm in sexual relationships. However, Jewish texts on homosexuality usually address prohibitions on homoerotic behavior, not relationships. It is important to recognize that the ancient works never address "homosexuality [as] a sexual orientation"; rather, the primary concern is with certain sexual practices. Rodney Mariner, *The Jewish Homosexual and the Halakhic Tradition: A Suitable Case for Treatment*, *in* JEWISH EXPLORATIONS, *supra* note 38, at 83, 85. In the past, homosexual intercourse was seen as deviation from that standard model of behavior, and therefore not within the rabbis' contemplation as a category that required regulation. This analysis assumes that some Greco-Roman men and women, Jewish and non-Jewish, did partake in homosexual activities; the rabbis of that era would hardly condemn what was not occurring.

> With a male you are not to lie (after the manner of) lying with a woman, it is an abomination [to'evah]", and 20:13, "A man who lies with a male (as one) lies with a woman—abomination [to'evah] have the two of them done, they are to be put-to-death, yes death, their bloodguilt is upon them![163]

The biblical description of homosexual sex, "after the manner of lying with a woman," represents a standard male method of expressing sexual desire through intercourse. Forbidden homosexual intercourse stands in opposition to legitimate heterosexual intercourse. Surrounding these verses are lines about other prohibited sexual contact including incest, bestiality, and intercourse with a menstruant, which constitute a group of prohibitions collectively called *arayot*. The Bible does not mention female homosexual contact; only male homoerotic activity triggers the death penalty,[164] in part because the verses surrounding the prohibitions are solely addressed to men.

The biblical authors set up homoerotic and nonconsensual sexual acts in opposition to heterosexual, legal sex in order to define and maintain a behavioral and cultural line between Israelite society and the surrounding peoples. The problem with homosexual sex is that, in Rachel Adler's words, it "violat[es] the categories and statutes that define the various social actors."[165] Contemporary expressions of sexuality could be understood within a framework different from the biblical perspective because, of course, the historical context has evolved.

---

[163] EVERETT FOX, THE FIVE BOOKS OF MOSES: GENESIS, EXODUS, LEVITICUS, NUMBERS, DEUTERONOMY 599, 607 (1995).

[164] The prescription for capital punishment does not mean, however, that the death penalty was implemented in Biblical times for homosexual sex or even for other activities called *to'evah* (abomination).

[165] ADLER, *supra* note 110, at 129. Several scholars have expanded on this approach. Rebecca Alpert suggests that "*to'evah* is actually a technical term used to refer to a forbidden idolatrous act [and] that the references in Leviticus are specific to cultic practices of homosexuality, and not sexual relationships as we know them today." Rebecca T. Alpert, *In God's Image: Coming to Terms with Leviticus*, *in* TWICE BLESSED, *supra* note 161, at 52, 68. Rodney Mariner argues that the contexts of these Biblical verses point to "non-consensual sodomy" or "where 'consent' . . . is at best dubious," inferring from this that the proscriptions do not address loving homosexual relationships but rather coercive sexual acts. Mariner, *supra* note 162, at 86-87. Phyllis Bird argues that that *to'evah* "belongs to the language of separation and distinction from the nations that came to expression during the exile and was applied retroactively to earlier stages of Israelite history." Phyllis A. Bird, *The Bible in Christian Ethical Deliberation concerning Homosexuality: Old Testament Contributions*, *in* HOMOSEXUALITY, SCIENCE, AND THE "PLAIN SENSE" OF SCRIPTURE 142, 152 (David L. Balch ed., 2000). The biblical approach to homosexuality actually reflects ancient Near Eastern attitudes attested in the archaeological record, especially in Egyptian and Mesopotamian sources. *Id.* at 156-57.

The rabbis were most concerned about male homosexual activity because it involved penetration. This action violates the rabbinic conception of heterosexual intercourse that "an active male penetrates a passive female" and means that the penetrated male "sacrifice[d] [his] 'maleness'" and acted female.[166] Indeed, "to penetrate was to reaffirm, perhaps even to assert, this [male] power . . . [whereas,] to be penetrated was perceived as being as women were perceived, that is, weak and dominated." [167] Additionally, homoerotic intercourse not only defied gender expectations but also defied the procreative paradigm. The earliest examples illustrate the developing legitimacy of that claim: Pseudo-Phocylides, an Alexandrian Jew from around the first century, argues that "anal intercourse between men is 'against nature'" and Josephus criticizes homosexual activity as causing the "confusion of sexual roles."[168] These positions reflect Greek and Roman conceptions of sexuality, and suggest that Greco-Roman influence was later incorporated into rabbinic thought.[169]

Male homoerotic activity so distorted the expected gender roles for sexual intercourse that even the potential for erotic contact between men was troublesome. The rabbis recognized that a male could sexually arouse and could be sexually aroused by another male. In *Mishnah Kiddushin* 4:14, for example, Rabbi Yehudah forbids two bachelors from sleeping underneath the same blanket. [170] The proscription presumably could be intended to prevent unintentional sexual arousal, which could culminate in homosexual intercourse. However, in the *Mishnah Torah*,[171] Maimonides, while extensively referring to this scenario, cites *Hilkhot Issurei Bi'ah*, 22:2 (the Laws of Forbidden Sexual Relations) for the assertion that Jewish men were not likely to become aroused in this manner.[172] Later authorities also negated any possibility of sexual arousal because "homosexuality was so rare among Jews that such preventative legislation was considered unnecessary."[173] Consequently, the perception that men, especially Jews, were naturally attracted to women was perpetuated.

---

[166] SATLOW 1995, *supra* note 31, at 316; Satlow 1994, *supra* note 68, at 15.

[167] Satlow 1994, *supra* note 68, at 2.

[168] *Id.* at 7-8.

[169] *Id.* at 1.

[170] MISHNAH KIDDUSHIN, *supra* note 115, at 4:14. *See also* Mishnah Kiddushin 4:14, Store of Holy Texts, http://www1.snunit.k12.il/kodesh/mishna/kidu04.html (last visited Oct. 16, 2005).

[171] A code of Jewish Law from the twelfth century.

[172] Norman Lamm, *Judaism and the Modern Attitude to Homosexuality*, *in* CONTEMPORARY JEWISH ETHICS 375, 381 (Menachem Marc Kellner ed., 1978).

[173] *Id.* For example, see KIDDUSHIN, *supra* note 115, at 82a.

B. Female Homosexual Desire

Although the Torah does not specifically mention female homoerotic acts, the rabbis forbade them based on their interpretations of *Leviticus* 18:3, which states that "[w]hat is done in the land of Egypt, wherein you were settled, you are not to do; what is done in the land of Canaan, to which I am bringing you, you are not to do; by their laws you are not to walk."[174] Just as the prohibition of male homosexual acts was intended to define boundaries between Israelite and non-Israelite, this statement is also about separating Jews from their neighbors in a more general sense. It was not until later, however, that the rabbis connected lesbianism to this separation and thus derived the proscription for lesbianism. *Sifra, Aharei Mot* 9:8[175] "describes these 'doings' [in the biblical verse cited above] as including lesbianism."[176] Sifra, as Midrash, is a halakhic work that "stands in direct relationship to a fixed, canonical text, [Leviticus]."[177] Its prohibitions are reflective, then, of a different exegetical tradition, in which female homosexual activity ostensibly serves as a threat to the general society. This danger is thus in contrast to male homosexual desire, where "rabbinic anxiety about male penetration is crucial."[178]

Lesbianism receives comparatively more comprehensive treatment in the Babylonian Talmud. *Shabbat* 65a/b and *Y'vamot* 76a conclude that "sexual intimacy between women does not render the individual women concerned 'unfit'" for marriage.[179] The rabbis in these texts allow a woman to maintain whatever current sexual status she has—virgin or widow, for instance—because they do not consider lesbian sexual expressions to be sex: "[I]n terms of definitions, it is significant that sexual acts between women are not considered a violation of the law because no act of intercourse takes place—in other words, it is the male experience[,] which defines what is a sexual act."[180] Although certainly discouraged, then, this female homosexual activity does not have the same grave implications as

---

[174] FOX, *supra* note 163, at 597.

[175] This text was "edited no later than the fourth century CE." Elizabeth Sarah, *Judaism and Lesbianism: A Tale of Life on the Margins of the Text, in* JEWISH EXPLORATIONS, *supra* note 38, at 95, 96.

[176] Mariner, *supra* note 162, at 84.

[177] STEMBERGER, *supra* note 24, at 235 (quoting G. Porton, *Defining Midrash, in* THE STUDY OF ANCIENT JUDAISM 55, 60 (J. Neusner ed., 1981)).

[178] SATLOW 1995, *supra* note 31, at 187.

[179] Sarah, *supra* note 175, at 97.

[180] BAKER, *supra* note 140, at 166.

528   *Columbia Journal of Gender and Law*   [Vol. 15:2]

male homoerotic contact because no penetration of a penis into a vagina occurs. To a certain extent during this period, men—fathers, husbands, brothers, or other male relatives—legally controlled women's sexuality, and women, whether or not they engaged in lesbian sex, were still under their male relatives' power. Men were still able to use their legal authority to encourage or require marriage for their female relatives, regardless of these women's sexual preferences.

Further, *Hilkhot Issurei Bi'ah* 21:8 confirms the prohibition from ancient works: "[W]hat they used to do [in Egypt] was that men used to marry men and women used to marry women [but] there is no specific negative commandment about it and no sexual intercourse is involved."[181] He specifically reminds his audience, "it is forbidden for women to mutually masturbate [lit. 'rub each other']."[182] Moreover, the difficulty with lesbian sex is not simply grounded in the Jewish desire to distance itself from foreign, non-Jewish practice. Mutual masturbation or any other sexual acts between women challenge the notion that a woman can and should only fulfill her sexual desires through intercourse with her husband, and vice versa. While Maimonides does not explicitly raise a concern that a woman will be sexually satisfied from intimate contact with another woman, he refers to the need to "prevent women who are known for such lesbianism from coming in to [a man's wife] and [to] prevent her from going out to them," [183] implying that women would seek out these relationships.[184]

C. The Case of the "Androgyne" and *"Tumtum"*

The paradigm for appropriate avenues of sexuality, however, was problematic when it was unclear whether or not the person in question was male or female. In *Mishnah Bikkurim* 1:5, tannaitic Rabbi Eliezer ben Jacob the Elder[185] places the *tumtum* and androgyne in the same category of woman: "[T]he administrator, the agent, the slave, the woman, the tumtum, and the androgyne can bring the first fruits but they cannot say the blessing

---

[181] Alan Unterman, *Judaism and Homosexuality: Some Orthodox Perspectives, in* JEWISH EXPLORATIONS, *supra* note 38, at 71 (quoting *Hilkhot Issurei Bi'ah*).

[182] *Id.*

[183] *Id.*

[184] *Id.*

[185] *See* STEMBERGER, *supra* note 25, at 68. Stemberger explains that Rabbi Eliezer ben Jacob the Elder is known for teachings on Temple; this leads me to conclude that the Rabbi Eliezer discussing the first fruits for sacrifices is probably that *tannaitic* figure.

because they cannot say 'that you gave me, G-d.'"[186] Tumtum is a halakhic technical term for someone whose biological sex is indeterminate. Later in Chapter Four of the Mishnah Bikkurim, the rabbis discuss how the androgyne is like both a woman and a man.[187] There is considerable confusion regarding this person's status as a sexual being. Michael Satlow explains the halakhic tradition concerning these people of uncertain sexuality, noting that "when an androgunos is sexually passive in vaginal intercourse, the act is not a capital crime,"[188] that is, not homoerotic, because the androgyne is acting like a woman, and the intercourse is essentially heterosexual. However, "only when [the androgyne is] passive in anal intercourse does the act come perilously close to male homoeroticism, and is thus prohibited."[189] The case of the androgyne is important because it points to the possibility that there exists another avenue for sexual expression. There are people who do not fit the paradigm, and yet they are able to express their sexual identities. Granted, the rabbis try to fit the androgyne in the heterosexual model; but the Halakhah remains confused, sometimes equating this person with women and other times with men.

In the case of the tumtum and androgyne, Maimonides is considerably stricter:

> [The offender] is free from the death penalty for vaginal intercourse with an androgyne. The *tumtum* is a doubtful case and so for sexual intercourse with a *tumtum*, or for vaginal intercourse with an androgyne, one would be punished by a rabbinical beating. An androgyne is allowed to marry a woman.[190]

The risk that a person with a penis might choose to be sexually active as a woman, thereby accepting the "weaker" position, is unbearable. Maimonides arguably goes against earlier texts and recommends punishment, even though a sanction is not biblically based, because the uncertainty threatens established sexual norms and challenges the traditional, fixed assignment of sexual authority in a relationship.

---

[186] This translation from the Hebrew is the author's. *See also* 3 MISHNA – SEDER ZERA'IM: BIKKURIM 1:5, 10-11 (Pinhas Kehati, ed., Eliner Library Dep't for Torah Education and Culture in the Diaspora 1994). *See also* Bikkurim 1:5, 10-11, Store of Holy Texts, http://www1.snunit.k12.il/kodesh/mishna/bicu01.html (last visited Oct. 16, 2005).

[187] 1 HERBERT DANBY, THE MISHNAH 98 (1933).

[188] SATLOW 1995, *supra* note 31, at 187.

[189] *Id.*

[190] Unterman, *supra* note 181. at 71, quoting *Hilkhot Issurei Bi'ah* 1:14-15.

530   *Columbia Journal of Gender and Law*   [Vol. 15:2

As demonstrated above, the positions against homosexuality in the biblical and rabbinic halakhic works reflect the way in which the biological realities of heterosexual sex suggest the unnaturalness of homoerotic activity. The rabbis' condemnations, however, lay the foundation upon which criticism of the modern Jewish movements is grounded.

D. Modern Approaches to Homosexuality within the Jewish Community

The halakhic ideal of heterosexual marriage pervades the positions on homosexuality of most of the modern movements of American Judaism. Both Orthodox and Conservative Judaism accept the textual position on the grounds that Halakhah is flatly authoritative in this matter. In contrast, Reform Judaism and Reconstructionism reject the Halakhah that ostracizes GLBT Jews and welcome them into the community. Only the Reconstructionist Movement eschews the heterosexist ideal completely.

1. Traditional Approaches: Orthodox and Conservative Judaism

As described in Part I, Orthodox Judaism regards the Hebrew Bible as the ultimate authority of Jewish law, but in fact assigns great, if not greater, weight to post-biblical texts, especially halakhic works. As expected, then, the expression of a homosexual identity through homoerotic intercourse is completely forbidden as a sin and an abomination among the Orthodox community. For example, Rabbi Alan Unterman explains the situation directly:

> The commitment of the Orthodox community to Torah is not a consciously selective one, but relates to a whole tradition, parts of which may seem obvious and relevant and parts obtuse and irrelevant. . . . It does not seem [that there needs to be] tacit approval for [the] lifestyle [of GLBT Jews] from the Halakhah than among other dissatisfied sinners.[191]

He continues emphatically, "[a]s long as gays are simply regarded as males and females, homosexual acts are prohibited to them."[192] This statement leaves open the possibility that sexual identity may one day not be classified along male or female lines, and the abolishment of this dichotomy will allow a different approach to the appropriateness of different, non-heterosexual expressions of sexuality.

Moreover, Rabbi Jonathan Sacks, the current Chief Rabbi of England, believes that "the ideals of heterosexuality and above all fidelity,

---

[191] *Id.* at 72.

[192] *Id.*

summed up in the concept of marriage, are not merely part of Biblical ethics. They are written into the entire fabric of the Biblical vision."[193] Homosexuality has no place in his model for Jewish life. Sacks's argument does not account for other institutions regulating sexuality, such as polygamy and levirate marriage that are no longer practiced today but were important parts of biblical narrative and law. Finally, Rabbi Michael Gold summarizes the possible reasons for this legal stance, stating that "procreation is impossible" and "homosexuality . . . threatens the Jewish ideal of family life, of marriage and children, articulated in the Torah."[194] These reasons speak to the social standard of heterosexuality for the Jewish community and point to applications of Jewish Law that reinforce that paradigm. It is important to note that some Orthodox thinkers advocate a more inclusive stance. They liken those who disregard the proscription on homosexuality to those who break the laws of *Shabbat* or *kashrut*: they may still participate and even be leaders in communal Jewish life to a limited extent, but their sins remain inappropriate and discouraged by the rabbinical leadership.

Orthodox Judaism, however, has not been able to ignore the presence of active GLBT Jews in their communities and therefore strives to correct their sexual activity, much like a rabbi would encourage wayward Jews to keep the laws of Shabbat. In 1974, Rabbi Norman Lamm articulated four responses to homosexuality.[195] He rejected three of them, namely, sanctioning gay people,[196] stopping all social critiques of homosexuality, and recognizing the authenticity of a gay alternative lifestyle. As a fourth option, Lamm suggested that this preference for sexual intimacy with a person of the same gender represents psychological imbalance, "in orienting ourselves to . . . homosexuals as patients rather than criminals, we do not condone the act but attempt to help the homosexual."[197] In other words, Lamm views GLBT Jews as ill patients in need of cure. Halakhically, this argument means that the homosexual is a person who cannot control his or her sin, that is, who is compelled to engage in homosexual acts, and someday might repent—even as that person continues to bear responsibility for those actions. This approach is supposed to engender compassion for the gay person. On a practical level, however, the Orthodox leadership strongly

---

[193] SACKS, *supra* note 93, at 169.

[194] MICHAEL GOLD, DOES GOD BELONG IN THE BEDROOM? 139 (1992).

[195] Lamm, *supra* note 172, at 384.

[196] Lamm argues that "criminal laws requiring punishment for homosexuals are simply unenforceable in society" and will probably encourage those acts in prison, stigmatizing those who ought to be learning from their crimes. *Id.* at 386.

[197] *Id.* at 395.

and publicly condemns homosexual activity. Despite this, openly GLBT Jews are hesitantly welcomed into some Orthodox communities, but they are usually under pressure to undergo therapy and marry in hopes of one day being cured of their "illness."

This official position does not necessarily reflect the lives of all Orthodox GLBT Jews. Orthodox Rabbi Steve Greenberg,[198] in an article published under a pseudonym, explains, "[g]ay feelings are hardwired into our bodies, minds, and hearts . . . I do not believe that G-d would demand that I remain loveless and celibate [and] I have chosen to seek a committed love, a man with whom to share my life."[199] His statement challenges the fundamental belief that all men and women are heterosexual as well as the primacy of heterosexual marriage in Jewish law. Greenberg speaks to the halakhic concerns as well: "If the Torah expressly forbids only this one form of sexual fulfillment, could we articulate a possible "halakhic" form of gay loving that excludes anal intercourse but permits a loving physical and emotional relationship between two men or two women?"[200] This solution respects the letter of the law, which he recognizes is "unchangeable" in the framework of Orthodox Judaism, but welcomes a different, more modern understanding of sexuality at odds with the rabbinic and halakhic views. While GLBT Orthodox Jews reject their rabbis' interpretations of homosexuality, it often comes with a high cost in regards to their membership in the Orthodox Jewish community.

The official position of Conservative Judaism on homosexuality is strikingly similar to the Orthodox stance. This is surprising considering that this movement generally encourages change within the halakhic system; in fact, it approached the transformation of women's roles in Judaism from a perspective that used innovations in Halakhah in response to modern challenges to traditional gender roles. The arguments against giving legitimacy to GLBT Jews, however, appeal to the unchanging authority of the text. Rabbi Joel Roth "acknowledges that homosexuality cannot be considered *inherently* abominable, but asserts that the Torah simply *attributes* the quality of abominableness to homosexuality, placing the prohibition beyond the reach of any extra-legal concerns that would favour

---

[198] Greenberg also appears in *Trembling Before G-d*, a film that illuminates some of the complexities of being a religious Jew and gay in a successful "portrayal of the anguish faced by Jews who want to remain Orthodox but see themselves as homosexual." Avi Shafran, Dissembling Before G-d ¶ 1, http://www.jlaw.com/Commentary/dissembling.html (last visited Oct. 12, 2005).

[199] Yaakov Levado, *Gayness and God: Wrestlings of an Orthodox Rabbi*, TIKKUN, Sept./Oct. 1993, at ¶¶ 55, 57. Later, it became known that the author was Rabbi Steve Greenberg. *See* Steve Greenberg, *Gayness and God*, http://www.indegayforum.org/authors/greenberg/greenberg31.html.

[200] *Id.* ¶ 46.

its abandonment."[201] By relying on the influence of the text, Roth asserts that Jewish law cannot change or adapt to accommodate respect for homosexuality because its legal wrongness remains squarely based on halakhic texts. Because the Torah forbids anal intercourse, "Roth's last word to the gay person is that 'Jewish law would have you be celibate.'"[202] Conservative synagogues have traditionally had control over their own religious practices, so in effect this means that individual communities can decide whether to welcome GLBT Jews into their congregations.

Because the Conservative Movement has more flexibly defined standards of practice as compared to those of Orthodoxy, there is considerable and vocal disagreement over the status of GLBT Jews. According to Rabbi Eliott Dorff, "the results of Roth's reasoning [are] 'unbelievably cruel'" because they are essentially a "position of extreme and formalistic fundamentalism" which disregards the innovation possible in halakhic discourse.[203] Moreover, Rabbi Hershel Matt questions "whether . . . the ancient and modern significance and consequences of homosexuality are the same and whether homosexuality today is inherently idolatrous, immoral, and destructive of Jewish existence."[204] Conservative rabbis like Matt believe that there is a potential for halakhic adaptation to modern conceptions of sexuality, and they encourage that change on an institutional level. The changes in Jewish law are also part of a larger understanding of how the shifting nature of the family leaves the possibility for same-sex families to be equal to traditional nuclear families.

Institutionally, however, "the Committee on Jewish Law and Standards determined that commitment ceremonies should not be performed and that sexually active homosexuals should not be admitted to the Movement's rabbinical and cantorial schools."[205] This latter position essentially forces GLBT Jews to choose between their religious calling to serve the religious needs of the Jewish community as a rabbi or cantor and their needs for human companionship and personal fulfillment. As the rabbis' disagreement persists, the disqualification of GLBT Jews from ordination at the Jewish Theological Seminary and from admittance into the Rabbinical Assembly still has a profound effect on the opportunities of GLBT people within the Conservative Movement. Benay Lappe, a former student of the Jewish Theological Seminary, explains, "I have always seen

---

[201] Mark Solomon, *A Strange Conjunction, in* JEWISH EXPLORATIONS, *supra* note 38, at 80.

[202] *Id.*

[203] *Id.*

[204] GOLD, *supra* note 174, at 143.

[205] DORFF, *supra* note 102, at 40.

the seminary's refusal to ordain openly gay and lesbian rabbis as profoundly misguided, obviously rooted in homophobia, and certainly not a prejudice that should be honored."[206] There is a "don't ask, don't tell" policy in force.[207] The institutions' negative stance on homosexuality likely extracts a high emotional toll on GLBT Jews who realize that the stance of these schools institutionalize homophobia in the Conservative Jewish community at large.

Lappe emphasizes another element that makes the situation more complex: the relationship of Conservative Judaism to other Jewish movements and Jews worldwide. Since the Conservative Movement revised its policies towards women, it has had to reaffirm its commitment to Halakhah in order to maintain its authenticity. Homosexuality, then, "is the final remaining issue that keeps the movement from being lumped together with the Reform movement. It is what makes possible whatever legitimacy the movement is granted by the rabbinate in Israel."[208] This facet is particularly significant with regards to establishing a context for the Conservative decisions about GLBT Jews. The Conservative Movement has not yet determined the most coherent manner in which to apply its theology, and so it is remaining faithful to the traditional Jewish legal stance on homosexuality.

2. Liberal Approaches: Reconstructionist and Reform Judaism

In contrast to traditionalists who privilege Jewish texts in their interpretations of homosexuality, liberal streams of Judaism weigh ethical considerations against contextual and historical factors in developing their

---

[206] Benay Lappe, *Saying No in the Name of a Higher Yes, in* LESBIAN RABBIS: THE FIRST GENERATION 197, 204 (Rebecca Alpert et al. eds., 2001) [hereinafter LESBIAN RABBIS].

[207] Lappe spent her six years of rabbinical school "in the closet," and soon "it was nearly impossible to keep [her] lesbian head above water, so to speak, with such an enormous tide of homophobia and sexism washing over [her] every day." *Id.* at 206. Even though the rabbinical school has a policy of "don't ask, don't tell," the dean interrogated Lappe: "[H]e went even further and told [Lappe] that he would not ordain [her] if [she] continued to refuse to answer him" on whether or not she was a lesbian. *Id.*

Similarly, in another article in LESBIAN RABBIS, the experiences of an anonymous lesbian rabbi are referenced. She notes that, while she was in rabbinical school, she was "still not ready to stand up to the Conservative Movement and its Rabbinical Assembly and state that [she was] a lesbian." *In Hiding, in* LESBIAN RABBIS, *supra* note 206, at 226, 233. She states: "I have neither the security nor the courage to add my name to this page. . . . I will help bring about the day when no one will have to feel alone or torn during rabbinical school, and that no one will have to hide who they are." *Id.*

[208] Lappe, *supra* note 206, at 215.

responses to homosexuality. For instance, Mark Solomon rejects "this prohibition [as] not divine, but all too erringly human."[209] He explains:

> Whether the prohibition of homosexual intercourse [in Jewish texts] is motivated by a loathing of pagan cultic practices, disapprobation of the rape of defeated enemy warriors, or simply revulsion at the idea of a man being 'womanised' in a society where women were regarded as necessarily passive and submissive, it certainly has no claim whatever on the conscience of any gay person today[,][210]

and ought not on any Jew as well. Because progressive Jews believe that people wrote the Torah, perhaps as a response to Divine inspiration or will, they claim an imperative to change the Jewish understanding of homosexuality. Progressive "supporters reexamine the entire history of Jewish teaching from biblical times through the present in the light of contemporary scientific and humanistic teachings about human sexuality and homophobia," and this approach gives a Jewish framework in which to give legitimacy to homosexuals.[211] They see the denial of legitimacy inappropriate, as "[m]ost gays would reject the patronizing implications of being regarded as ill," especially since most psychology and psychiatry groups have stated that homosexuality is not a mental illness.[212] Within the halakhic framework, Rabbi Harold Schulweis similarly points out that "in the Talmud, a deaf-mute was considered to be retarded, mentally incompetent, and imbecile not able to serve or witness or to be counted in the *minyan* or able to affect marriage and divorce. But that ruling was based on empirically false data," just like the notion of homosexuality as a disease instead of a sexual orientation.[213] Progressives affirm the legitimacy of homosexuality when they argue that, "[f]or a gay it is part of the nature G[-]d gave him [or her] and must be used in His service."[214] With this new understanding of human sexuality, then, it is possible to recognize different sexual orientations as equally valid and develop a vocabulary in which to analyze them.

---

[209] Solomon, *supra* note 201, at 82.

[210] *Id.*

[211] Yoel H. Kahn, *Judaism and Homosexuality: The Traditionalist/Progressive Debate, in* HOMOSEXUALITY AND RELIGION 47, 66 (Richard Hasbany ed., 1989).

[212] Unterman, *supra* note 181, at 74.

[213] Harold Schulweis, Morality, Legality, and Homosexuality (1992), http://www.vbs.org/rabbi/hshulw/morality_bot.htm.

[214] Lionel Blue, *Godly and Gay, in* JEWISH EXPLORATIONS, *supra* note 38, at 117, 121.

With that attitude, the Reconstructionist Movement has rejected the Halakhah that forbids homosexual activity. The Reconstructionist Rabbinical College welcomed GLBT Jews as students in 1994, and the movement "issu[ed] a significant statement in support of gay and lesbian rabbis and teachers, and the performance of gay marriages, and encouraging synagogues to be 'welcoming congregations.'"[215] Rebecca Alpert explains that "same-sex marriage is understood as a religious value because it provides economic justice, creates stable, committed relationships, and fosters support for childrearing."[216] In other words, Reconstructionist Judaism does not see homosexuality as a threat to the Jewish family and thus Jewish survival; indeed, GLBT Jews enhance the Jewish community's perception of what it means to be a successful Jewish family.

The Reform Movement has only within the past few years permitted equal participation for gays in its various institutions and ceremonies, but its history of supporting rights for homosexuals extends back to 1977 when the Central Conference of American Rabbis ("CCAR") "encourage[d] legislation which [would] decriminalize[] homosexual acts between consenting adults and prohibit discrimination against [gays and lesbians]."[217] GLBT Jews attended the rabbinical and cantorial schools through the 1980s "in the closet" and then "came out" after ordination. In 1990, the CCAR supported equal rights for gays and lesbians even as they affirmed the Jewish ideal of heterosexuality, and they also openly welcomed GLBT rabbis into their ranks. GLBT synagogues are also members of the Union of American Hebrew Congregations. Although not every synagogue is welcoming to GLBT members, there have been significant improvements in the attitudes of Reform Jews towards them.

For the Reform Movement, the issue of same-sex marriage has been most troubling because, even outside of the halakhic system, the Jewish community upheld the Jewish principle of heterosexual marriage. The alteration of Jewish law and principles could not occur completely apart from Jewish tradition, as evidenced by the Responsa Committee of the CCAR in 1997, which affirmed the halakhic construction of marriage:

> *[K]iddushin:* that concept whether understood according to its traditional terms or its Reform interpretation, is a legal institution whose parameters are defined by the sexual boundaries that Jewish law calls the *arayot.* Homosexual relationships, however

---

[215] *See* Sue Levi Elwell & Rebecca T. Alpert, Introduction, *Why a Book on Lesbian Rabbis?, in* LESBIAN RABBIS, *supra* note 206, at 24.

[216] Rebecca T. Alpert, *Religious Liberty, Same-Sex Marriage, and Judaism, in* G-D FORBID: RELIGION AND SEX IN AMERICAN PUBLIC LIFE 124, 127 (Kathleen Sands ed., 2000).

[218] Judaism and Homosexuality: Reform Judaism, http://www.religioustolerance. org/hom_jref.htm (last visited Dec. 12, 2005) (quoting Central Conference of American Rabbis, Resolution Adopted by the CCAR: Rights of Homosexuals (1977)).

exclusive and committed they may be, do not fit within this legal category; they cannot be called kiddushin.[218]

The issue here is not whether homosexual partners can have legitimate, sanctioned relationships but whether they can have a religious marriage; in fact, Reform Judaism announced its support of civil commitments in 1996.[219] In June 1998, the CCAR's Ad-hoc Committee on Human Sexuality concluded that "kiddushah [holiness—the same root as kiddushin] may be present in committed, same gender relationships between two Jews, and that these relationships can serve as the foundation of stable Jewish families, thus adding strength to the Jewish community."[220] The organization formalized this decision in March 2000, stating that "the relationship of a Jewish, same gender couple is worthy of affirmation through appropriate Jewish ritual [though] we support the decision of those who choose [not] to officiate at rituals of union."[221]

Within a Jewish framework, these two movements address homosexuality much like they do with other laws from Judaism: by looking at the ethical implications of any decision and deciding whether it reflects "Judaism" accurately or needs further innovation. More eloquently, as Tikva Frymer-Kensky says: "Perhaps this is another instance in which the path upon which our ancestors set out now leads in a direction that invalidates and hurts members of the community and that the path must be redirected to be more appropriate to our vision of ourselves and God."[222]

E. Consequences of these interpretations for GLBT Jews and for the Jewish community

This Part has shown that interpretations of sacred texts about sexuality have a large impact on Jewish responses to homosexuality. The modern Jewish movements respond to homosexuality through the context of their respective positions on the authority of Halakhah by affirming their

---

[218] Moshe Zemer, *Progressive Halakhah and Homosexual Marriage, in* GENDER ISSUES IN JEWISH LAW: ESSAYS AND RESPONSA 166 (Walter Jacob & Moshe Zemer eds., 2001).

[219] *See* RRA Resolution, *supra* note 106.

[220] AD-HOC COMMITTEE ON HUMAN SEXUALITY, REPORT TO THE CCAR CONVENTION (1998), *available at* http://www.google.com/search?q=cache:KKUagRFFz_YJ:www.ccarnet.org/hs.html+&hl=en.

[221] CENTRAL CONFERENCE OF AMERICAN RABBIS, RESOLUTION ON SAME GENDER OFFICIATION, (2000), *available at* http://data.ccarnet.org/cgi-bin/resodisp.pl?file=gender&year=2000.

[222] Tikva Frymer-Kensky, *Toward a Liberal Theory of Halakha*, 10 TIKKUN 77 (1995).

commitment to either uphold traditional laws or encourage innovations with respect to Jewish ideals. Although it is important to realize how the Jewish texts have functioned historically, it is also useful to understand how Jews use these legal principles in making modern-day decisions that affect so many gay, lesbian, bisexual and transgender Jews. The Orthodox and Conservative leadership appeal to the authority of sacred texts in discouraging GLBT Jews from expressing their sexual orientations, while the Reconstructionist and Reform Movements welcome GLBT Jews into their communities and encourage them to celebrate their lives, however untraditional, with everyone.

As long as Orthodox, Conservative, and some Reform Jews, regardless of their attitudes towards Halakhah, fail to show compassion, GLBT Jews will seek out their own communities in the search for acceptance. The first GLBT synagogue, Beth Chayim Chadashim, was founded in Los Angeles in 1972, and, in 1974, Congregation Beth Simchat Torah in New York was organized as a response to the strong alienation these Jews felt in the mainstream heterosexual Jewish community. Although traditionalists decry these places of worship as breaking apart the Jewish community and are "reluctant to grant religious or communal recognition to [GLBT] Jews,"[223] GLBT Jews argue that these communities provide them a safe space to be Jewish and GLBT. "[B]ecause the [GLBT Jew] has not felt comfortable in existing religious institutions . . . these synagogues perform a vital religious function"[224] by accepting different sexual orientations as well as Jewishness. Once this homophobia subsides, whether by halakhic innovation or evolving compassion, it is likely that GLBT Jews will return to Reform, Conservative, and Orthodox synagogues because they feel accepted and welcomed as part of the community and do not feel pressured to fulfill heterosexual expectations. In preparation, Jewish communities should reevaluate their understanding of the familial structure's role with respect to Jewish survival and recognize that gay, lesbian, bisexual, and transgender Jews value and contribute to the Jewish experience as both Jews and as GLBT persons. It is important for modern day American Jewish society to encourage that involvement, as it benefits everyone.

V. CONCLUSION

The view of sexuality expressed in halakhic texts recognizes the legitimacy of heterosexual marriage only because it is based on the normative assumption of heterosexual desire. Examinations of these materials confirm that Jewish law distinguishes between the characteristics

---

[223] Kahn, *supra* note 211, at 58.

[224] *Id.* at 65.

of men and women's sexuality, portraying the man as rightfully sexually aggressive and the woman as sexually passive. As a result, because Halakhah promotes heterosexual norms and standards for heterosexual expression, it establishes laws on marriage and divorce that disfavor women and marginalize GLBT Jews. Modern American Jewish movements are thus left with the task of developing approaches to these issues that reflect both the legal tradition as well as contemporary sentiments.

The respective theological frameworks of the modern Jewish movements considerably shape communal positions on these issues, but do not preclude deviations from established patterns of interpretation. Reform, Orthodox, and Conservative Judaism are not always consistent in their respective halakhic decisions, i.e., they do not apply their theories of Halakhah consistently. Reform Jewish leaders contend that Jewish principles guide their movement's rabbinical rulings. The sole acceptance of a Jewish marriage only between a man and a woman, however, does not fit that paradigm, considering that Reform halakhists eschew the need for a specifically Jewish divorce. It is inconsistent to advocate certain standards for relationships, along with their attendant legal structures, such as kiddushin, while acknowledging that the solution to another problem of sexuality requires the repudiation of the institution of Jewish divorce. In addition, Orthodox thinkers claim that their halakhists give preference to certain texts for specific historical reasons; but it is clear that extra-halakhic reasons sometime play a role. Orthodox authorities go to great lengths to find ancient commentaries of comparatively lesser importance which support their positions. With regard to homosexuality, the representatives of official institutions in Conservative Judaism refer to the authority of the Jewish texts much like their Orthodox counterparts; their rhetoric calls into question the fundamental legitimacy and practical applicability of their approach to Halakhah.

All these inconsistencies have the secondary effect of devaluing men's and women's sexuality in discussions of marriage, divorce, and homosexuality. While the non-Orthodox positions mentioned above recognize sexual desire in both men and women, the movements themselves are noticeably quiet in defining the characteristics of sexuality. This silence suggests that the underlying assumptions, such as men's aggressive and woman's passive sexual natures, implicitly sway halakhic decision-making, at least with regard to these three issues. Additionally, the refusal to articulate acceptance or repudiation of traditional stereotypes undermines attempts to reconcile these matters within the halakhic system. It is, for instance, erroneous for Conservative Jewish leaders to claim that changes to the legal stipulations of the ketubah with regard to divorce will alter Jewish attitudes toward sexuality by granting a woman more control over the expression of her sexuality. The solution actually shifts responsibility for the woman's sexuality to the court system, thereby devaluing her ability to make choices concerning the expression of her sexual desire. Because

540   *Columbia Journal of Gender and Law*   [Vol. 15:2

contemporary attempts by the modern Jewish movements have focused on the husband's unilateral power, legal authorities have overlooked the profound imbalance on which the marriage is established, namely, the treatment of women's sexuality as a commodity. To resolve this problem, interpreters of Halakhah must address this underlying assumption. Otherwise, any legal suggestions leave the woman at the mercy of both her husband and the religious courts when she tries to reassert control over her sexuality in a divorce.

Additionally, by applying current knowledge about sexual orientation, contemporary Jewish movements have the opportunity to take into account modern understandings of homosexuality. The Reform and Reconstructionist Movements already embrace GLBT Jews as people with a different and legitimate sexual orientation; the Conservative Movement is currently embarking on that path at the writing of this Article. Orthodoxy persists in labeling homosexual activity morally wrong, but that too is slowly changing through grassroots advocacy in Jewish communities in America. In Orthodoxy, the maintenance of traditional assumptions about sexuality devalues sexual desire that does not fit the paradigm, including the sexual orientation of GLBT Jews and the expressions of sexual desire in which the woman is more aggressive and the man is more passive.

It appears that only Reconstructionist Judaism is consistent in its position on sexuality. This movement continues to regulate divorce and homosexuality within a developing halakhically-based system, but the approach to the issues as well as attendant solutions reflect an understanding of sexuality that values men's and women's sexual desire, whether it is homosexual or heterosexual in nature. By allowing a woman to grant a get and encouraging men and women to be married to partners of the same or different genders in order to form Jewish families, Reconstructionist Judaism affirms the legitimacy of sexuality defined differently from traditional constructions through the articulation and implementation of a changing conception of sexuality. Contradicting positions on sexuality also undermine community; consistency adds legitimacy not only to men's and women's expressions of sexuality but also to the religious community as a whole whereby all Jews feel valued rather than alienated. If the modern Jewish movements are to continue to regulate sexuality, it is important that they show consistency in their rulings; without it, mixed messages might destabilize the entire halakhic system and the Jewish communal world.

This critique, however, ought not to forget that these issues directly affect people's lives. There are religious women that remain trapped in marriages because their husbands refuse to give them gittim. Gay, lesbian, bisexual, and transgender men and women, members of all the Jewish movements, continuously face homophobia and discrimination in their communities. With each decision, halakhic authorities use their significant influence to promulgate old and new interpretations of Jewish law. It is with this in mind that this Article calls for more research into the connection between halakhic conceptions of sexuality and gender issues. Such a study could bring about a reckoning between these older assumptions about sexual expression as reflected in ancient laws and contemporary theories of human sexuality and contribute to the intellectual and spiritual growth of the Jewish community.

[10]

HOMOSEXUALITY AND THE
ORTHODOX JEWISH COMMUNITY

Rabbis Marc Angel, Hillel Goldberg and Pinchas Stolper

There is one fact that all Orthodox Jews accept implicitly: our minority status in *Klal Yisrael*. No part of the Orthodox Jewish community, no matter how isolated or outreaching, believes that most Jews are Torah observant. It is assumed that more Jews violate the Shabbat than honor it, that intermarriage is rampant, that *kashrut* and the like are observed mostly in the breach.

How did matters devolve to this point?

There were major lines of demarcation in the demographic decline of Torah Judaism. The processes may have been gradual, but, at least in retrospect, major transitions stand out. Almost no living Jew can remember the first transitions; we were not present when the majority of American Jews stopped observing such *mitzvot* as *Shabbat, mikvah* and *kashrut*. The deterioration of the Jewish people, taken as a whole, in these respects, was not our responsibility.

One major transition did come within the lifetime of many of us. This is when Jews stopped marrying Jews, and, separately, when an attitude of acceptance of intermarriage pushed aside an attitude of opposition. Intermarriage began to sky-rocket in the 1960's, and, as the late sociologist of the American Jewish community, Professor Marshall Sklare, observed, it was in about 1970 that surveys first began to show a major shift in attitude. Prior to 1970, intermarriage was rejected; after that, it was accepted, with regret, to be sure, but the impulse to fight it was replaced with the impulse to make peace with it. In the wake of that watershed compromise came "patrilineal descent" (1983), non-halachic conversions by the thousands, and, today, an actual welcoming of intermarriage by some assimilated Jews.

Now we face the possibility of another watershed, tragic transition: the would be division of the Jewish community into heterosexual and homosexual communities. The policies of much of the non-Orthodox rabbinic leadership would have the effect of dividing Jewish society in just this way, but the non-Orthodox laity has yet to follow the leadership. While tragedy looms, its prevention is possible. Orthodox Jewry has many allies in *Klal Yisrael* in preventing this tragedy. Furthermore, Orthodoxy can bring the painful lessons learned from the previous stages of decline to the present challenge.

We can bring valuable knowledge of how the Jewish community succumbs and how, on the other hand, it can successfully respond. We have acquired some sophistication through success in retaining our youth, in attracting *ba'alei teshuvah*, and through our new confidence and numbers in general. We need not assume a future when the Jewish community will take for granted another, major deviation from Torah. We have an opportunity to shape the community rather than merely respond to its decline; to stop the slippage rather than to resign ourselves to being a minority with reference to still another area of observance.

The primary lesson to be learned from slippages of the past is to know that if a major deviation from Torah is not faced early, it will assume overwhelming proportions with dizzying speed. The time to stop the legitimization and routinization of homosexuality in the Jewish community is now, as much of the non-Orthodox Jewish leadership would have us believe that homosexuality is nothing but a natural part of the moral order of creation. We need to act before this thinking strikes root among the laity.

Our primary knowledge about how the Jewish community succumbs is that before a major deviation from Torah sets in, the Jewish community really does not want it. No matter how unobservant, Jews really do want to hold on to what they keep. Most Jewish parents really don't want homosexuality for their children. They can't abide it and haven't accepted the rationalizations for it. If the Orthodox community is vocally supportive of this instinctive adherence to Torah, the wider Jewish community will not succumb. Despair ("nothing can be done, this is the way of the world") will not take hold.

At the very least, a vocal, principled stand can strengthen individual families and slow the easy decline into an "alternative lifestyle" legitimized by countless cultural signals – newspaper articles, television commercials, academic conferences, campus "sensitizations." At the most, we can halt, in the entire Jewish community, a major trend away from Torah, for the first time since the Jewish *Haskalah* (Enlightenment) some 200 years ago.

This is not a simple row to hoe, not least because a few Orthodox families have discovered homosexuality in their own midst. Although many of these families anguish over their plight, some manifest the same dynamic that led to the acceptance of intermarriage around 1970. This dynamic is a rejection of *bushah* (shame), in favor of indifference or justification. On the individual level, this rejection is understandable, and it is critical for the Jewish community to distinguish between compassion on the individual level and communal level. On the individual level, people and families deserve compassion, counseling and support. If, however, the need to strengthen Torah standards is outweighed by the fear of articulating them, lest individuals be offended, Jewry will be overtaken by homosexuality just as it has been overtaken by intermarriage.

To be sure, it is the non-Orthodox community that is most susceptible to rationalizing homosexuality, since this community has virtually banished the very notion of absolute Torah standards. Then too, homosexual activists and their sympathizers, including Jewish sympathizers, sometimes use distasteful and illegal tactics to promote their agenda. But none of this should overshadow the fact that most Jews await principled, articulate leadership against spurious claims set forth by homosexual activists and defenders. Spiritual revulsion against homosexuality, appropriate to the *Chumash's* characterization of it as *to'evah*, remains widespread. The black despair of acceptance has not materialized, as it has on intermarriage. The Orthodox community may confidently mount its outspoken opposition to homosexuality.

This article summarizes ten basic Orthodox perspectives, classified under two major headings, "public policy" and "philosophy." These perspectives are gleaned from Orthodox Jewish leaders and thinkers who have grappled with the issues in learned journals, in the political arena, and in counseling sessions. These perspectives are not exhaustive; they are meant to provide basic guidelines for the many fronts on which the battle is being waged.

Public Policy

1. Terminology. It is wise not to use the word "gay". Words count. Definitions shape debate. "Gay" legitimizes and routinizes proscribed behavior. In contemporary usage, "gay" somehow unites the tonalities of innocence, heroism, and neutrality. The terms "homosexual" and "homosexuality" keep the debate honed to reality, which is sexual deviance, not "alternative lifestyle."

A further refinement: whenever a context allows, it is wise to use "homosexuality" rather than "homosexual." Homosexuality is a philosophy, far larger than the behavior of an individual. Homosexual activists want to legitimate homosexuality per se, not just the behavior of individuals. The historic opportunity before us is to stop the legitimization of homosexuality, not just to treat individuals. Treatment is important (on which more below), but it is a private matter for a clergyman and a therapist. It is precisely the homosexual activists' attempt to turn private behavior into public discussion that needs to be countered. By using the term "homosexuality," the debate, again, is kept to reality.

2. The press. It is legitimate to object to newspaper reportage that is specifically labeled homosexual (or "gay"). A basic misconception about the First Amendment to the US Constitution is that newspapers must give equal space to all sides. The opposite is the case. The First Amendment guarantees total discretion to a publisher, who may legally refuse to print anything, with or without justification. Free Speech means that anyone may say anything, but also that no one else is obligated to disseminate it. Under the First Amendment, a publication has no free speech unless it is free to say no as well as to say yes. The so-called "fairness doctrine" applies to television and is, in fact, in direct contradistinction to both the letter and spirit of the First Amendment.

It is legitimate to point out to Jewish newspapers, in particular, that by either printing or refusing to print homosexual news, newspapers make a value judgment. If they made the judgment that they wish to promote homosexuality, this is their right; but editors should not be allowed the conceit that they are above the fray, that they can print homosexual news without legitimizing homosexuality and offending a preponderance of their readers. Newspapers promote values; it is appropriate to question their placing a positive value on homosexuality.

3. Jewish unity. Jewish solidarity is radically eroded by synagogues that are specifically labeled homosexual ("gay congregations") and by Jewish activities of any kind that are specifically for homosexuals. Free association, undertaken by homosexuals, is a fundamental right, but this does not mean that the Jewish community is required to accord it anything but legal respect. Put it to Jewish leaders this way: Would they feel supportive of Jewish unity if they gave their congregations names like "Temple Emanuel: A Heterosexual Congregation"? How about "The Heterosexual Men's Club" or "A Memorial Service for Heterosexual Victims of the Holocaust"? (A separate, Jewishly sponsored memorial service of homosexual victims of the Holocaust actually took place in a major American city.) Inane uses of "heterosexual" make as much sense as parallel uses of "homosexual". Both jettison Jewish unity.

A few Jewish homosexual activists concede as much. They replace "homosexual" with "outreach to gays," as in "a congregation with a special outreach to gays." This makes no more sense than "Temple Emanuel: A Congregation with a Special Outreach to Heterosexuals." Institutions or activities defined by sexual orientation are inherently divisive.

Under the guise of liberalism, those who sanction homosexual synagogues do more than undermine Jewish unity and morality. They evade their responsibility to homosexuals. Homosexual synagogues mark the religious acceptance of homosexuality and the religious inequality of the homosexual – just the opposite of what is required: rejection of homosexuality and acceptance of the homosexual. Acceptance of a homosexual does not mean accepting a status – a deviant sexual orientation – but accepting a person. All should be welcome to pray in the synagogue. This does not mean that the synagogue may accept a permanent spiritual attenuation as a condition for a homosexual's participation. The synagogue may not, for example, accept "homosexual family" membership, "marriage" rites for homosexuals, or homosexual clergy. To reach out to help heal a weakness is one thing; to sanctify it is something else. Distinctions by sexual preference sanctify weakness and thus defeat Jewish unity.

4. The political arena. It is critical to object to so-called gay-rights laws. They are paraded as innocent, indeed, heroic human-rights protection for individuals. In fact, any homosexual who does not identify himself by his sexual practices or preferences is, in both theory and practice, already protected under the law. The same laws that protect all citizens protect homosexual citizens equally. The underlying point is this: Citizens have a right not to be involuntarily exposed to overt sexual behavior or preferences, whatever their nature. Citizens have a right to ask of each other that their sexual lives and preferences be kept private. So-called rights for homosexuals really amount to a campaign to legitimize homosexuality – to obtain society's stamp of approval. This is the real issue and it must be vocalized. The real issue is not individual rights for homosexuals, but collective coercion of everyone else to bend to the legitimization of homosexuality. Homosexual activists' goal is to subvert all of society's laws that protect or promote normal marriage and morality.

5. Mixed rabbinic and synagogue boards. The homosexuality issue introduces a new dimension to the debate on formal Orthodox participation in pluralistic religious bodies; again, not only because of the seriousness of the breach that is homosexuality, but also because of the opportunity at hand. When a so-called homosexual congregation is proposed for admission to a synagogue or Jewish community council, or when a so-called homosexual rabbi is proposed for admission to a rabbinic board, the Orthodox synagogue and rabbi have the opportunity, by refusing to participate in such a council or board, to fortify the will of Jews to hold the line against homosexuality. Visible protest against the legitimization of homosexuality gives heart to the masses looking for leadership on the issue.

Of course, many Orthodox leaders have always opposed maintaining relationships on a formal basis in pluralistic religious settings. Many other leaders have favored it, but now see it as increasingly difficult on account of the adoption of patrilineality, widespread non-halachic conversions and, finally, the acceptance of homosexuality. This acceptance looms as the proverbial "straw that broke the camel's back" – a step symbolic of a steady erosion of commitment to Jewish values, a step that forces a reevaluation of the maintenance of formal relationships by many who have favored it. In any case, the non-Orthodox leadership is out of touch with its own constituency on homosexuality. We have an historic opportunity to succeed on a critical issue in the Jewish community by not sitting formally with homosexual rabbis or synagogues in religious or communal contexts.

And make no mistake. If homosexuality is given the communal sanction, Hebrew-Christian "Messianic" Judaism is next. The same philosophical, emotional and sociological dynamics that would legitimize homosexuality will also, if left unchecked, legitimize the Messianics and give them and their philosophy the Jewish community's public sanction.

To summarize the public policy perspective, we must never give homosexuality the public sanction. This means countering its every legitimizer and legitimization, within and without the Jewish community. We must also work in the general community because this is an issue of universal import, and because the Jewish community is influenced from without. The Jewish community is ready to listen, if only we do not abandon our Torah responsibility.

Philosophy

1. Judaism. There is not a single source in all of the disciplines of Jewish sacred literature – *halachah, aggadah*, philosophy, *musar*, mysticism – that tolerates homosexual acts or a homosexual "orientation". Jews who sanction homosexuality must do so either wholly without reference to Jewish sacred literature, in which case their justification has no Jewish standing; or with reference to Jewish sources, in which case they act with ignorance or intellectual dishonesty. The idea, set forth by some of the non-Orthodox leadership, that the Torah prohibited only coercive and non-loving same-sex relationships, thus allowing for a contemporary, voluntary and loving same-sex relationship, is wholly without basis in a single piece of Jewish sacred literature written in the last 3,000 years.

2. Sin and sinner. With reference to virtually every sin, Judaism distinguishes between the *sin*, whose doom is hoped for, and the *sinner*, whose "turning" is hoped for. Meanwhile, the sinner retains the right to participate in most aspects of Jewish life. With reference to homosexuality, the Torah opposition to homosexuality does not extend to repudiation of the homosexual as a person, except insofar as he or she flaunts homosexuality or teaches it to others. Rabbi Barry Freundel has observed that there is no noun in the Hebrew Bible for homosexual, only a verb for the act. He suggests that there is no such thing as a homosexual per se, but only a person who commits a particular sin and, like people who commit other sins, can and may, with work and effort, do *teshuvah*.

3. Genetics. Various hypotheses suggest that homosexuality has some biological basis. Some psychiatrists credit these hypotheses; others do not. Even if there were universal agreement on this, the conclusion drawn by homosexuals – homosexuality is morally neutral – is fallacious. If homosexuality is an inborn predisposition in some people, it does not follow that they cannot and need not change. *Teshuvah* is precisely the belief that one can and should alter inborn (and other) non-normative predilections. Everyone has some sort of deep-rooted biological or psychological challenge to deal with. Even granted that a given individual with an inborn predilection will change only minimally, it does not follow that the effort to change is morally valueless. Quite the contrary. The refusal to submit to an immoral impulse, even without the sublimation or transfiguration of that impulse, is, in Judaism a very high moral achievement.[*] The moral challenge remains, even if a biological basis to homosexuality were substantiated.

---

[*] *A fuller treatment of this and related issues is in Rabbi Hillel Goldberg's "Homosexuality: A Religious and Political Analysis", forthcoming in* Tradition.

4. Outreach. The Orthodox Jewish community has been reaching out to Jews whose non-observance includes violation of the Torah's moral laws. This has not been easy, as anyone in *kiruv* involved in marriage counseling and related areas can testify. For those homosexual violators of the Torah's moral laws, *kiruv* is even more difficult. Indeed the complexities seem overwhelming. Yet, in principle, if one maintains that every Jew has a *pintele Yid* (spark of Judaism), there has to be a way to reach, counsel and transform these violators too. The Torah can reach every Jew.

For homosexuals, the requisite methods of outreach are not all in place; many halachic and psychological issues remain to be sorted out. Generally, it is understand that this kind of outreach requires special discretion, for both the individual and the community in which he or she lives. This outreach must walk a tightrope: full retention of the visceral recoil appropriate to the Torah's labeling homosexuality a *to'evah* and full willingness to help people whose spiritual sensitivities have been so stunted that, to them, their behavior, far from *to'evah*, is routine. Not every *kiruv* worker can walk this tightrope. Much as outreach to Jews in Jewish-Christian "Messianic" cults is a specialization, outreach to homosexuals must be a specialization. The Rabbinical Council of America has established a committee to explore, under the guidance of its Beth Din, the restraints and imperatives in outreach to homosexuals.

5. AIDS. The physical cause of AIDS is relevant (in most cases, morally relevant) to the victim, but not to a Jew's obligation to tend to the ill. It makes no more sense to deny care and compassion to a person who has contracted AIDS through homosexuality, promiscuity or drug use, than to deny care and compassion to a person who has contracted lung cancer through chain smoking.

Divine judgment, a relevant theological category for any victim, may be invoked by the victim. A friend's obligation includes responding sensitively to whatever ruminations about Divine judgment a victim might entertain. Some extraordinarily poignant moments of *teshuvah*, however inarticulate, can flow from sensitive listening and response. But for an onlooker to introduce this subject is to miss the mark. Further, even if a victim avoids the issue altogether or justifies himself to the end, the obligation to show compassion is absolute. No one is free of sin as to be able to say that only the pious deserve care and compassion.

We have already alluded to *Berachot* 10a that distinguishes between sin and sinner. The Messianic ideal is the disappearance of the sin, not of the sinner. To counter homosexuality – to work for the disappearance of this sin – is manifold *chesed*. It can restore families and prevent the dissolution of families. It can alleviate the most profound psychological debility – loneliness – and reduce the incidence of the most recalcitrant physical disease – AIDS. It can save the Jewish community from another, fundamental deterioration, and through that can abet a resurgence of Torah leadership for restoring all that has been lost for so many Jews.

Let us not overlook the universal dimensions of this *chesed*. The integrity of the family and of the marital relationship is among the fundamental spiritual imperatives of mankind. As Rabbi J. David Bleich has observed, "It is incumbent upon society to examine the present day AIDS epidemic in order to determine what can be learned from it. From a global perspective, perhaps mankind is being taught a lesson. Were our societal standard in conformity with divinely mandated norms, the opportunity for individual contagion would simply not arise." It is usually the Jew through whom ultimate moral meaning is framed. Orthodox Jewry has a special role in exercising leadership both in compassionately doing *kiruv* with the individual homosexual and in passionately upholding the Torah's rejection of homosexuality.

Rabbi Marc Angel is the Rabbi of Congregation Shearith Israel, the Spanish-Portugese Synagogue of New York City. He was recently the President of the Rabbinical Council of America.

Rabbi Hillel Goldberg is the Executive Editor of The Intermountain Jewish News *and a contributing editor of* Jewish Action.

Rabbi Pinchas Stolper is the Executive Vice President of the OU.

ISLAM

Part III
Islam and Sexuality:
Sexuality in Historical Context

[11]

SHE'S UPRIGHT:
SEXUALITY AND OBSCENITY IN ISLAM

A. E. SOUAIAIA
University of Iowa

Abstract

This paper explores the concepts of sexuality and obscenity in Islamic traditions and the way cultures and society shape the value systems that judge beauty, propriety, and legality. I conclude that societal values are preserved in emerging religious teachings—by way of expanding categories for acts, rules, and values and by relying on practice-based consensus; not on negotiated consensus. As such, in Islam, obscenity and profanity become nuisances that disturb individuals' spiritual balance and unwanted variables that destabilize social equilibrium.

Keywords

Sexuality in Islam, Obscenity in Islam, Women in Islam, Propriety in Islam, Morality in Islam.

INTRODUCTION

As is the case with its antecedents, Judaism and Christianity, Islam continues the tradition of paradoxical images of women as the symbol of life and death, obscenity and uprightness, and the definition of other opposites.[1] In a tantalizing translation and correction of values, the Qur'ānic discourse takes its readers from censuring sexual acts to sanctioning them as a means to returning to Paradise if undertaken within the confines of propriety and outside the bounds of obscenity. Given the brevity of the Qur'ānic narratives, Muslim

---

[1] For background on the representations of the feminine in Christian traditions, see *Ezekiel* 16. Addressing Jerusalem as a woman, the biblical God describes a decadent lifestyle and wherein reference is made to spreading a "garment over" the female to cover her nakedness. This image is present in early practices of the Arabs along with the persistence of judging the woman's body as a source of shame.

SHE'S UPRIGHT   263

exegetes connect the loose ends of each story to provide a continuous story of the human struggle with ethical and legal prescriptions.[2]

The so-called Abrahamic religions—Judaism, Christianity, and Islam—share similar views on sexuality and obscenity.[3] However, they also have fundamental differences in determining what is appropriate and what is not. Both the similarities and differences begin and end with the stories of creation and procreation.

In this study, I explore the origins and development of words and behaviors whose characterization oscillates between obscenity and piety.[4] Needless to say that most of the words and behaviors that may be labeled as obscene are related to sexuality and body functions. As such, the Islamic discourse on obscenity and sexuality amounts to exerting control over the way human beings interact in public as well as in private settings. In order to simplify the examination of the concepts of obscenity and sexuality, I start by looking at some acts and practices that are seen by one or all of these three religions as obscene and determine the context of such a determination.[5] Since sexual behavior and related acts, if undertaken in specific contexts, might be deemed obscene in Islam, I

---

[2] Note: When referencing classical exegetical works, I will indicate the chapter and verse number of the Qur'ān on which the exegetes are commenting instead of page number to avoid the discrepancies associated with different editions of the same work more of which are appearing in large numbers these days. For this work, I relied on the carefully revised collections of *tafsīr* provided by Mu'assasat Al al-Bayt li-'l-Fikr al-Islāmī (*al-Mashrū' al-kabīr li-tafsīr al-qur'ān al-karīm*) also available in digital form and online (altafsir.com, 2006). If other editions are used in this work, it will be shown as the full citation.

[3] It should be noted that these three religions share some of the views because, at least in the case of Islam, Muslims are not supposed to reject a practice or belief of the Jews and the Christians unless such a practice or belief is explicitly rejected in the Qur'ān or in the Sunnah. See the commentary [Q7: V189] in *Tafsīr al-qur'ān al-karīm*, wherein it is stated that the Prophet said, "If the People of the Book tell you something, neither believe them nor disbelieve them." [*idhā haddathakum ahl al-kitāb, fa-lā tuṣaddiqūhum wa-lā tukadhdhibūhum*].

[4] In Islam, sexual relations within the confines of valid marriage contracts are strongly recommended if not mandatory as argued by some jurists. It is reported that the Prophet Muhammad said: "the worst of your deceased are the celibate ones. [*shirāru mawtākum al-'uzzāb*]. See Najm al-Dīn al-Ḥillī, *Sharā'i' al-islām* (Beirut: Dar al-Aḍwā', 1969): 266.

[5] While sexuality and obscenity are openly discussed in the Qur'ānic, exegetical, and legal texts, it must be noted that Rabbinic Judaism does not allow such an open discussion. See Mishna Hagigah 2:1 and Babylonian Talmud Hagigah 11b wherein it is stated, "One should not discuss illegal unions in front of three

A. E. SOUAIAIA

also examine the scripture and the exegetical and jurisprudential works in order to understand the basis of ethical and legal judgments of sexual behavior and controversial acts. In order to do so, and given the terseness and brusqueness of the Qur'ān even when telling stories, I rely heavily on the classical commentaries to contextualize Qur'ānic passages. The importance of commentaries is underscored by the fact that Muslim exegetes used biblical sources to fill in the missing information.[6] From providing names to borrowing definitions, Muslim scholars were able to provide a narrative about the origins and development of the human race, the changing values, and the evolving social and cultural practices. The most intriguing of these narratives is the one that deals with obscenity and sexuality.

In terms of methodology, I employ textual analysis of primary sources and apply a normative approach to jurisprudential literature. I focus on several words and behaviors that have been seen differently depending on the time frame, the cultures wherein they existed, and the social circumstances that required a change of attitude towards them. In doing so, I provide an explanation of the conflicted roles of religious practices in interrupting existing customs in some instances, while preserving those in others. I show that, in the Islamic civilization, the Qur'ānic and exegetical discourses served as semi-permeable filters of values and practices that bridged earlier Semitic and pagan societies with post-*jāhiliyyah* ones. This study begins by looking at some of the so-called obscene and profane acts and behaviors in the scriptural stories of creation, before the emergence of Islam, and during the formative period of Islamic civilization.

---

persons, nor creation in front of two, nor the divine chariot in front of a single person, unless he was a wise man and had much knowledge of his own."

[6] Muslim scholars' borrowing from Judaism and Christianity is not hypothetical; in fact, early Muslim scholars repeatedly indicated that their information is taken from biblical sources. Ibn Isḥāq, the renowned compiler of the stories of the prophets (*Qiṣaṣ al-anbiyā'*), uses the phrases "according to what has reached us from the People of the Book;" "as they [People of the Book] claim;" or "as they [People of the Book] mention" ["*fīmā balaghanā 'an 'ahli al-kitāb;*" "*fīmā yaz'amūn;*" "*fīmā yadhkurūn*"] as refrains in his writings. See Muhammad Ibn Isḥāq, *al-Mubtada' fī qiṣaṣ al-anbiyā'* (Beirut: Arab Diffusion Company, 2006): 58, 90, and 91. See also al-Ṭabarī, *Jāmi' al-bayān* (Egypt: Al-Ḥalabī Press, 1954): 230; and Ibn Kathīr, *Tafsīr al-qur'ān al-aẓīm* (Beirut: Dar Iḥyā' al-Turāth al-Arabī, 2004): 95.

Theoretically speaking, I examine the themes of this study against the backdrop of the established opinions of anthropologists and sociologists who see moral and legal controls as a reflection of the power and interests within any given society as well as a means by which organized religion and other social control agencies serve and preserve their own agendas. Although the religious discourse is cloaked in an altruistic purpose, namely to preserve all that is inherently sacred, it will be shown throughout this study that the rules governing sexuality and defining obscenity are in fact mirroring the dominant value system, which is that of the elite. In addition to the above theoretical context, I also draw on the approaches to the study of rituals, purity and profanity developed by some philologists and scholars of religious studies when necessary.

THE PARADOX OF KNOWING: DIFFERENTIATING SEXUALITY AND OBSCENITY

According to Qur'ānic and exegetical texts, God had created the first human (Adam) from earthly clay in the shape and form that is assumed by human beings today. Then, the deity breathed into the mass of clay from Its soul (*rūḥ*); and there emerged an extraordinary creature.[7] In order to honor Adam, God commanded all heavenly beings to bow in respect before Adam; so they did except Satan (*Shayṭān/Iblīs*) who refused to do so on account that he, who was created from fire, is superior to Adam who was created from dirt. God argued that it is not his origins that made Adam special; rather, knowledge is what made him so. Although Adam, like the angels, was divinely taught, Adam's knowledge went beyond what he was originally taught and that made him a marvel in the eyes of God.[8]

According to Islamic traditions, after the creation of Adam, God extracted Eve from him and made her his mate. Then they were ordered to enjoy life in Paradise (*Jannah*) and use all that is available in it but one tree.

---

[7] According to the Qur'ānic discourse, humans are superior to any other creatures. See [Q2: V30–8].

[8] See [Q2: V30–2] and the classical commentaries explaining these passages.

And We said to Adam, "Go you and your mate and live in Paradise
and eat all that you want but do not approach this tree; if you do
so, you will be transgressing. But Satan whispered to them so that
he would expose to them their private parts saying, "Your Lord forbade you to eat from this tree because if you do so you will turn
into angels and you will live forever." He swore to them both that
he is providing them with good advice; and so, with malice, he tricked
them and when they tasted the tree, their genitals were exposed to
them; they hurried covering themselves with the leaves of the garden . . . [Q7: V22–6].⁹

Ironically, for a species that already had access to extraordinary
knowledge that was not rivaled by the knowledge possessed by
angels and other heavenly creatures, the first act of disobedience
resulted in knowing more: knowing about their own genitals.
According to the exegetical works, Adam and Eve, while in Paradise,
were either unaware of their genitalia or their genitalia (*saw'ah;
'awrah*) were hidden from them.¹⁰ That unawareness disappeared
when they ate from the forbidden tree.

When Adam and Eve saw their private parts, they ran from tree
to tree, pulling leaves and covering themselves with them.¹¹ While
doing so, Adam's hair became entangled in a tree so he started to
plead with it to let go of him. Then the deity addressed Adam:
"Are you running away from Me, Adam?" Adam answered, "No
I am *ashamed*, my Lord."¹² With this myth, emerges the concept of

---

⁹ All translations are the author's unless otherwise indicated.

¹⁰ According to Ibn 'Abbās, the light that was covering Adam and Eve shrunk
and turned into nails in the fingers and toes. See al-Qurṭubī's commentary on
[Q7: V22] in *al-Jāmiʿ li-'aḥkām al-qur'ān*. According to some Shiʿite scholars, their
private parts were not "visible to them, that is, their private parts were inside
their bodies." See al-Qummī's commentary on [Q7: V22] in *Tafsīr al-qur'ān*.

¹¹ Adam is said to have tried to pull leaves from many trees but they refused
him any but the fig tree. He and Eve then used fig leaves to cover their genitals. See Ibn 'Abbās' tradition in al-Qurṭubī's commentary on [Q7: V22] in *al-
Jāmiʿ li-aḥkām al-qur'ān*.

¹² See commentary of Ibn Kathīr on [Q7: V22] in *Tafsīr al-qur'ān al-karīm*. Ibn
Kathīr also reports on the authority of Wahb Ibn Munabbih that Adam and Eve
were clothed by light and neither of them (Adam and Eve) were able to see the
private parts of the other until they ate from the tree. Al-Ṭabarī on the other
hand, says that Adam and Eve were covered by their nails (*azfārihimā*). See *Jāmiʿ
al-bayān fī tafsīr al-qur'ān* by al-Ṭabarī (in his commentary on [Q7:V22]). It is also
reported that Adam hid in the trunk of a tree after seeing his private parts exposed
and when God asked if he was hiding from Him he replied, "I am ashamed."

personal shame as a reaction to nudity which is the foundation of societal inclination to judge nudity as indecent and obscene behavior.

As a punishment for ignoring God's warning against eating from the forbidden tree, Adam and Eve were sent down to earth wherein they and their offspring are tested further and ultimately, they will be judged.[13] In addition to providing them with guidance in the form of sending prophets and scriptures regularly, the descendents of Adam and Eve were also provided with fancy clothes to cover their private parts. As an act of providence, God "descended for the children of Adam simple clothes to cover their genitals, and fancy clothes; but He recommended the shield of piety for those who wish to follow His signs."[14] Subsequently, nudity and sexuality became central themes in the Islamic discourse on religious and public morality since especially nudity was the cause of the fall of humans' forefathers and the preeminent source of anxiety and shame on earth. As such, it was necessary that the human body and behavior be governed by strict rules. In addition to nudity and exposing one's private parts, human sexuality and procreation too, as a means and a necessity to the preservation of the human species, became subjects of the discourse on obscenity and decency.

On earth, Adam and Eve began to procreate;[15] before they died they had twenty twins, each pair consisted of a male and female.[16] According to exegetes, each member of the twin siblings was allowed to marry from the other pair but not from within the same one. With time, and as the human community grew larger, that practice

---

See al-Ṭabarī's commentary on [Q2: V36] in *Jāmiʿ al-bayān fī tafsīr al-qurʾān.* Emphasis mine.

[13] See commentary of Ibn Kathīr on [Q7: V22] in *Tafsīr al-qurʾān al-karīm.* Reference to the prohibition on eating from the tree as a test (*ikhtibār; imtiḥān*) can be found in Ismāʿīl Ibn Kathīr, *Tafsīr al-qurʾān al-aẓīm* (Beirut: Dar Iḥyāʾ al-Turāth al-Arabī, 2004): 95.

[14] See [Q7: V26]. See, also, Ibn Kathīr's commentary on [Q7: V26] in *Tafsīr al-qurʾān al-karīm* wherein the word *al-rīsh* (normally, means feather) is explained as luxury items and fancy clothes.

[15] The Qurʾān states that human beings were created from a single soul, and from that single soul (breathed into Adam) God created its mate so that Adam may find calmness with her and have sexual intercourse with her. See [Q7: V189] and the commentary of al-Ṭabarsī on the same verse in *Majmaʿ al-bayān fī tafsīr al-qurʾān.*

[16] Muhammad Ibn Isḥāq, *al-Mubtadaʾ fī qiṣaṣ al-anbiyāʾ* (Beirut: Arab Diffusion Company, 2006): 69.

was proscribed and people were instead asked to marry cousins, distant relatives, and non-relatives. By the time Islam emerged, these practices were defined but not practiced and the Qur'ān took it upon itself to redefine sexual relations and practices.[17] In doing so, new categories of improper acts and behaviors were established and the concept of obscenity was defined anew as *al-fāḥishah*. Since the very existence of the human race is dependent on sexual intercourse, human sexuality is described in Islam as a double-edged sword that could lead to profound consequences depending on how it is actualized.

SEXUALITY AND OBSCENITY IN PRE- AND POST-ISLAMIC ERAS

Although an accurate reconstruction of Arab society from the pre-Islamic era is difficult to achieve for lack of written evidence, Islamic literature contains a substantial amount of information that would allow us to compare and contrast life styles of Arab societies before and after the rise of Islam. To begin with, there is the curious statement in the Qur'ān that states:

> Do not marry women who were married to your fathers, except what had already occurred; indeed such an action is obscenity (*fāḥishah*), repugnance (*maqtan*), and bad life style (*sā'a sabīlā*). (*al-Nisā'*; [Q4:V22]).

Qur'ānic statements such as the above, together with evidence collected from pre-Islamic poetry,[18] suggest that pre-seventh century Arabs did not see a person marrying a close relative as obscene or improper.[19] In fact, it seems that it was a common practice for one man to marry numerous women; some he chooses from relatively distant clans and tribes to foster solidarity, others are inherited when

---

[17] See Ibn Kathīr, *Tafsīr al-qur'ān al-aẓīm* (Beirut: Dar Iḥyā' al-Turāth al-Arabī, 2004): 97.

[18] See the *Mu'allaqāt* and the poetry of Imru' al-Qays, 'Antarah Ibn Shaddād, and the so-called Ṣa'ālīk poets and many others from the pre-Islamic era.

[19] See al-Tha'libī's commentary on [Q4:V22] in *al-Kashf wa-'l-bayān* wherein he states that this verse was revealed in response to a number of people marrying the wives of their fathers or to their sisters. He mentions some of these individuals including "Hiṣn Ibn Abī Qays who married his father's wife Kubayshah, al-Aswad Ibn Khalaf who married his father's wife, Ṣafwān Ibn Umayyah Ibn Khalaf, who married his father's wife Fākhitah Bint al-Aswad Ibn al-Muṭṭalib, Manṣūr Ibn Māzin who married his father's wife Malīkah Bint Khārijah, and al-'Adawī . . ."

a father, a brother, an uncle, or a cousin dies. Inherited wives were seen as either a burden requiring the support of the male of the family or a bonus that add to the material value and prestige of the heir. The prevalence of these kinds of marriages and sexual practices must be the reason the Qur'ān detailed new guidelines forbidding men from marrying their mothers, sisters, aunts, and other close relatives.[20]

Early historical and religious materials describe societal practices that are radically different from that recommended in Islam. Commenting on [Q4:V22], Ibn Kathīr (d. 774 H) reports on the authority of al-Bukhārī, on the authority of Muhammad Ibn Muqātil, on the authority of Asbāṭ Ibn Muhammad, on the authority of al-Shaybānī, on the authority of 'Ikrimah that Ibn 'Abbās said:

> In the past, when a man dies, his relatives would have the right over his wife: one of them could marry her, they could decide to offer her in marriage to someone else, or they could prevent her from marrying. They had full rights over her instead of her family until this verse was revealed.[21]

In a similar tradition, it is reported on the authority of Wakī' on the authority of Sufyān, on the authority of 'Alī Ibn Budhaymah on the authority of Muqsim that Ibn 'Abbās said:

> During the *Jāhiliyyah* era, when a man dies and leaves behind a wife, a man would approach her and would throw a piece of cloth over her and she becomes his; this was the practice until this verse was revealed.[22]

---

[20] Muslim jurists, by way of analogy, prohibit a man from marrying a woman and her maternal or paternal aunt at the same time citing [Q4:V23]. Furthermore, if a man were to marry a woman then he would divorce her before sexual intercourse (*qabla an yuṣībahā*), still, it would be illegal for him to marry her mother. See Sulaymān al-Bājī, *al-Muntaqā: Sharḥ Muwaṭṭa' Mālik* (Cairo: Maktabat al-Thaqāfah al-Dīniyyah, 2004): 78.

[21] Al-Shaybānī too mentions that Abū al-Ḥasan al-Siwā'ī might had heard this same tradition from Ibn 'Abbās.

[22] This tradition is reported in most exegetical works including that by al-Qurṭubī who adds that "during pre-Islamic era, when a man dies, his son from another wife throws a piece of his clothes over her which gives him more rights over her than her own family." See al-Qurṭubī's commentary on [Q4: V19] in *al-Jāmi' li-aḥkām al-qur'ān*. See, also, al-Ṭabarsī's commentary on the same verse in *Majma' al-bayān fī tafsīr al-qur'ān*.

A. E. SOUAIAIA

ʿAlī Ibn Abī Ṭalḥah quoted Ibn ʿAbbās as saying:

> When a man dies and is survived by concubine or slave girl, his clos-
> est relative would throw a piece of his clothes over her to forbid
> other people from approaching her. If she was beautiful, he would
> marry her; if she was ugly, he would imprison her at home until she
> dies so that he would inherit her.[23]

Zayd Ibn Aslam commented on the same verse saying:

> During *Jāhiliyyah* era, when a man from among the people of Yathrib
> (later known as Madīnah) dies, his wife will be inherited by the same
> relatives who generally inherit his estate. The heir would then treat
> her badly until she dies so that he inherits her or he offers her in
> marriage to whomever he wants. The people of Tuhāmah used to
> mistreat their wives until she is forced to give back her dowry in
> return for him divorcing her or her agreeing to marry someone he
> wants her to marry. This verse was revealed to stop such a practice.[24]

Muhammad Ibn Abī Umāmah commented on the same verse saying that his father said: "When Abū Qays Ibn al-Aslat died,[25] his
son wanted to marry his wife—which was acceptable in *Jāhiliyyah*—
this verse was revealed to stop it."[26]

If illicit sexual intercourse is the obscene act it is said to be, one
should expect it to invalidate marriage with a woman who was

---

[23] See Ibn Kathīr's commentary on [Q4: V22].

[24] See Ibn Kathīr's commentary on [Q4:V22].

[25] The *kunyah* of Abū Qays and the name of his wife are a subject of dispute
suggesting that later exegeses were simply copying from earlier notes rather than
relying on independent interpretation of the sources of law. For instance, while
al-Ṭabarsī, in his *Majmaʿ al-bayān fī tafsīr al-qurʾān*, identifies the deceased as Abū
Qays Ibn al-Aslat and his wife's name as Kubayshah, al-Fayḍ al-Kāshānī, in his
al-Ṣāfī fī tafsīr kalām allāh al-wāfī, identifies them as Ibn al-Ashlat and Kubayshah.
Al-Qummī, in his *Tafsīr al-qurʾān*, identifies them as Ibn al-Aslab and Kubaythah.
While Muqātil Ibn Sulaymān identifies the son as Muḥṣan and the widow as
Kabshah, al-Thaʿlibī identifies them as Haṣn and Kubayshah. This confusion about
the names seems to be caused by decoding the Arabic writing system (misreading letters that appear to be the same in the absence of the diacritics that were
not well developed in early Islam).

[26] See commentary of Ibn Kathīr (774 AH) on [Q4: V19] in *Tafsīr al-qurʾān
al-karīm*. Some Muslim exegetes (see commentaries of al-Qurṭubī and al-Ṭabarsī
on [Q5: V19]) seem to suggest that only the stepson (the son of the husband from
another wife; recall that polygyny is common in pre-Islamic Arabia) may claim
the wife of his father. However, the Qurʾānic prohibition on marrying mothers
(*ummāhātukum*) may suggest otherwise.

SHE'S UPRIGHT   271

involved in *zinā*. However, Muslim scholars argue that verse [Q4:
V22] prohibits the son's marriage to a woman who was previously
married to the father but it does not prohibit marriage to a woman
who committed an illicit sexual intercourse with the father. The
jurisprudential rule, as stated in *al-Risālah*, is that "*zinā* does not
proscribe what is otherwise legal [*lā yuḥarramu bi-'l-zinā ḥalāl*]."[27]
With this in mind, the notion of obscenity as a social ill that affects
society as much as it affects the individual becomes evident.

Moreover, and in order to underscore the function of the concept of obscenity as a means of preserving social order and protecting the interests of the elite, one should consider the fact that,
according to Sufi scholars, a follower (*murīd*) is not allowed to marry
the widowed or divorced wife of the master (*shaykh/ʿārif*).[28] This
expanding of legal rules to cover social protocols is a form of appropriation of religious teachings to preserve social status by way of
analogy and it is an important function of organized religions and
cultural customs.

Islamic literature, including the exegetical works of the most
influential scholars within Sufi, Shiʿite, Zaydī, and Ibāḍī tendencies,[29] is full of references to sexuality and obscenity as fluid concepts. Some sexual practices are deemed inappropriate, while others

---

[27] See al-Silmī's commentary on [Q2:V22] in *Ḥaqāʾiq al-tafsīr*.

[28] Sufi authorities argue that the laws concerning biological fathers apply to
spiritual fathers as well [*mā jarā fī ābāʾ al-bashariyyah yajrī fī ābāʾ al-rūḥāniyyah*].
Therefore, it is not allowed for a follower to marry the wife of his Shaykh. See
Ibn ʿAjībah's commentary on [Q2: V22] in his *al-Baḥr al-madīd fī tafsīr al-qurʾān
al-majīd*.

[29] See commentaries on [Q4:V15–6] in *Tafsīr kitāb allāh al-ʿazīz* (al-Huwwārī
(d. 3rd century H), Ibāḍī); *Jāmiʿ al-bayān fī tafsīr al-qurʾān* (al-Ṭabarī (d. 310 H),
Sunni); *Tafsīr al-qurʾān* (al-Qummī (d. 4th century H), Shiʿite); *al-Tibyān al-jāmiʿ
li-ʿulūm al-qurʾān* (al-Ṭūsī (d. 460 H), Shiʿite); *al-Kashshāf* (al-Zamakhsharī (d. 538
H), Sunni); *Majmaʿ al-bayān fī tafsīr al-qurʾān* (al-Ṭabarsī (d. 548 H), Sunni); *Mafātīḥ
al-ghayb: al-Tafsīr al-kabīr* (al-Rāzī (d. 606 H), Sunni); *al-Jāmiʿ li-aḥkām al-qurʾān*
(al-Qurṭubī (d. 671 H), Sunni); *Anwār al-tanzīl wa-asrār al-taʾwīl* (al-Bayḍāwī (d. 685
H), Sunni); *Tafsīr al-Aʿqam* (al-Aʿqam (d. 9th century H), Zaydī); *al-Ṣāfī fī tafsīr
kalām allāh al-wāfī* (al-Fayḍ al-Kāshānī (d. 1090 H), Shiʿite); *Rūḥ al-bayān fī tafsīr
al-qurʾān* (Ḥaqqī (d. 1127 H), Sufi); *Fatḥ al-qadīr* (al-Shawkānī (d. 1250 H), Sunni);
Rūḥ al-maʿānī (al-Alūsī (d. 1270 H), Sunni); *Taysīr al-tafsīr* (ʿAṭfīsh (d. 1332 H),
Ibāḍī); *Tafsīr bayān al-saʿādah fī maqāmāt al-ʿibādah* (al-Janābidhī (d. 14th century
H), Shiʿite); *al-Taḥrīr wa-'l-tanwīr* (Ibn ʿĀshūr (d. 1393 H), Sunni); and *Aḍwāʾ al-
bayān fī tafsīr al-qurʾān* (al-Shanqīṭī (d. 1393 H), Sunni).

are encouraged or mandated. Marrying a relative was described, at one point and in some contexts, as obscene although the pre-Islamic Arabs treated marrying one's step-mother or half-sister as a matter of honor and obligation. Furthermore, marrying the wife of one's father is described as obscene but so are the acts that may be undertaken by the wife in specific situation. In order to have a sound understanding of the range of obscenity in the Qur'ānic discourse, one could consider these social practices in the context of [Q4:V19] which states:

> O you who believe, it is not allowed for you to inherit women against their will nor is it permitted for you to mistreat them in order to force them to give back to you that which was given to them, unless they commit a proven act of obscenity (*fāḥishatin mubayyinatin*). Live with them in the best of manners and if you feel hatred towards them, remember that it might be the case that you hate something in which God has made great good. [Q4:V19]

Explaining this verse, the Sunni exegete, al-Bayḍāwī (d. 685 H), reports that, before the rise of Islam, when a man dies and is survived by male heirs, one of the heirs would spread a piece of his clothes over the widow and declares his right over her: he could then marry her with the same dowry that was given to her by the deceased or offer her to someone else and keep her dowry for himself. Alternatively, he could smother and mistreat her to force her to buy herself out with what she inherited from her husband. These acts were prohibited unless she commits acts of obscenity such as "her refusal of sexual intercourse (*nushūz*) and intimacy (*sū'al-ʿishrah*), or becoming promiscuous (*ʿadam al-taʿaffuf*)."[30]

In addition to restrictions of sexual practices in the name of morality, society imposes dress codes in the name of propriety or modesty. Even modern societies today continue to legislate laws and ordinances that prevent revealing private parts. Before Islam emerged in Arabia, the people of Mecca used to perform religious rituals naked.[31] Ibn Kathīr reports that "pagans used to perform

---

[30] See al-Bayḍāwī's commentary on [Q4: V19] in *Anwār al-tanzīl wa-asrār al-taʾwīl*.

[31] Commenting on [Q7: V31], Ibn Kathīr asserts that, according to Ibn ʿAbbās, "the pagans used to worship around the Kaʿbah naked: men during the day and women during the night." See his *Tafsīr al-qurʾān al-karīm*.

ritual circumvolutions naked and they claimed that they were doing it in the form in which their mothers gave birth to them." In another tradition, they are said to justify worshipping in the nude because "they don't want to worship God in clothes they were wearing when they had disobeyed Him."[32] But even in a context where nudity and worship are linked, women are held to different standards: men worshipped totally naked and in broad daylight while women were partially covered and worshipped in the darkness of the night. Furthermore, women were shown to justify their nudity and explain its purpose, but not men. To be sure, all Arab pagans, with the exception of the people affiliated with the tribe of Quraysh, worshipped naked. Women however, worshipped semi-naked at night while men performed their rituals during day time. Women used to partially cover their private parts and chant the following verse of poetry:

> Today some of it or all of it is showing ***** But any part of it I reveal I do not permit
>
> [al-yawma yabdū baʿḍuhu aw kulluhu ***** wa-mā badā minhu falā uḥilluh]

Muslim exegetes argue that such practices were invented by pagans who then claimed that it was the practices of their forefathers. The Qur'ān prohibited such practices and commanded that people be upright (al-istiqāmah).[33]

Another pre-Islamic practice that was rescinded by the Prophet and that is related to obscenity and sexuality is the treatment of menstruating women. According to Islamic exegetes, "the people of Madīnah, whose culture was influenced by the Jews, used to isolate themselves from menstruating women: they did not eat with them, they did not drink from the same container, they did not sit with them on the same seat, and they did not share the same room with them." On the other hand, "Christians used to engage in sexual intercourse with menstruating women." When the Prophet was

---

[32] Ibn Kathīr reports on the authority of Ibn ʿAbbās that "the people of Quraysh used to worship around the Kaʿbah naked, going around whistling and clapping. God revealed [Q7: V32] to order them to wear clothes." See Ibn Kathīr's commentary on [Q7: V32] in *Tafsīr al-qurʾān al-karīm*.

[33] For information about pre-Islamic Arabs worshipping naked, see Ibn Kathīr's commentary on [Q7:V28–30] in Ibn Kathīr, *Tafsīr al-qurʾān al-aẓīm* (Beirut: Dar Iḥyāʾ al-Turāth al-Arabī, 2004): 212–3.

274   A. E. SOUAIAIA

asked about the validity of these practices and received complaints about the lack of resources needed to provide separate dwelling for women while menstruating, he pointed to the newly revealed verse [Q2:V222] and added: "Do everything except intercourse."[34] When the wife of the Prophet, 'Ā'ishah, was asked whether women can be "approached during their menstrual cycle," she said, "everything is allowed except her vagina." Legal scholars such as al-Shāfiʿī and Abū Ḥanīfah argued that while sexual activities with a woman in her menstrual period is allowed, "if sexual intercourse takes place, the men must atone for that by offering one *dīnār* to charity."[35]

Pre-Islamic practices relied on mythology in order to explain and enforce social practices. It is reported that the Jews of Madīnah did not like sexual intercourse wherein the man approaches the woman from behind. They argued that if they have sexual intercourse that way and the woman becomes pregnant, the child conceived during such sexual union will be cross-eyed (*aḥwal*). Muslim exegetes argue that [Q2:V222] was revealed to refute such a myth and to permit intercourse "any way and from any side they want: from behind, from the front, while she is on her knees, on her back, or on her side."[36] In a similar tradition on the authority of Umm Salmah, it is reported that the people of Madīnah used to have sexual intercourse with their wives from behind. The Jews of Madīnah discouraged such a practice arguing that sexual intercourse from the back causes the new born to be cross-eyed. But when the immigrants settled in Madīnah and married women from the Anṣār (the Supporters; people of Madīnah), they wanted to

---

[34] See the *Tafsīr* of Haymān al-Zād ilā Dār al-Miʿād (d. 1332 H) commenting on [Q2:V222].

[35] Muslim exegetes argue that the Qurʾān is explicit in prohibiting sexual intercourse in any other location but the vagina as per the segment of [Q2: V222] that says, "*fa-ʾtūhunna min ḥaythu amarakumu allāh.*" See the *Tafsīr* of Haymān al-Zād ilā Dār al-Miʿād (d. 1332 H) commenting on [Q2: V222] and *Taysīr al-tafsīr* by Aṭfīsh when commenting on the same verse. It must be noted that Sunni jurists prohibit anal and oral sex and they argue that the verse is explicit in prohibiting intercourse during menstruation because of the bleeding in the vagina (*fī al-farj*). If anal sex was allowed, the exception should be made clear in the Qurʾān. Shiʿite scholars are divided on this issue: some allow consensual anal and oral sex; others consider it undesired (*makrūh*), and a third group proscribes it. See the commentary on [Q2: V222] in al-Kāshānī's *al-Ṣāfī* and al-Ṭūsī's *al-Tibyān*.

[36] See al-Shawkānī's commentary on [Q2: V222] in *Fatḥ al-qadīr*.

have sex in a way that was new to the women of Madīnah. Subsequently, one woman refused to allow sex that way until she consulted the Prophet. When she asked him about the practice, he told her that "it is fine as long as it is in the vagina."[37]

ISLAMIC DEFINITIONS OF OBSCENITY

The Qur'ān contains thirteen references to the concept of "*fāḥishah*." Although the word is generally used to refer to illicit sexual acts, the majority of Muslim scholars argue that *fāḥishah* refers to multitudes of acts or words that are obscene,[38] the most egregious of which, in their view, is illicit sexual intercourse.[39] However, before such words gained the consistency and value they now have, it appears that these same practices and words were not judged the same way throughout historical periods. According to Muslim exegetes, the Qur'ānic revelations marked a break from past practices. Furthermore, even the Qur'ānic value system was refined in order to create a system that categorizes behavior and establishes a hierarchy that avoids contradictions. Upon close examination of the final understanding of the concept of obscenity in the Islamic discourse, it becomes clear that the definitive categorization of obscene acts is *not* the result of negotiated interpretation of authoritative texts; rather, the validation and authorization of the practices and initial understanding of the early Muslim community that lived during the formative period of Islamic law and practices. Once these practices were canonized and written down, they became absolute precedents and were labeled *ijmā'* (consensus).[40] It is shown in this study that there is no strong evidence pointing to a negotiated consensus based on the text of the Qur'ān; rather, oral traditions

---

[37] See Ibn Kathīr's commentary on [Q2: V222] in *Tafsīr al-qur'ān al-karīm*.

[38] Al-Ṭabarī defines *al-fāḥishah* as "any ugliness and excess in anything." See his commentary on [Q3: V135] in *Jāmi' al-bayān fī tafsīr al-qur'ān*.

[39] See commentaries on [Q4: V15] in *Jāmi' al-bayān fī tafsīr al-qur'ān* by al-Ṭabarī; *Tafsīr al-qur'ān* by al-Qummī; al-Ṭūsī's *al-Tibyān al-jāmi' li-'ulūm al-qur'ān*; al-Zamakhsharī's *al-Kashshāf*; al-Rāzī's *Mafātīḥ al-ghayb: al-Tafsīr al-kabīr*; and al-Qurṭubī's *al-Jāmi' li-aḥkām al-qur'ān*.

[40] There is significant evidence suggesting that "consensus" regarding certain historical claims is rather an acceptance of a written version of the story than a broad sharing of the same information or as a product of incidental spread (*tawātur*).

were transmitted from one authority to another until they were committed to writing starting in the third Islamic century; and once written down, these traditions become religious precedents that cannot be overruled by grammatical and syntactical analyses of the texts of the Qur'ān and the Sunnah.

If practice is a validation of a norm, the Qur'ān can be seen as an attempt to stop the practice by creating new categories for appropriateness. The Qur'ān first lumped unacceptable behaviors and words under the category of *faḥishah* and identified certain behaviors and words as such. Out of the thirteen verses in the Qur'ān where the term *faḥishah* is used; all but three of these verses use the word *faḥishah* in a context that is related to women and sexual behavior.[41] The most explicit of these Qur'ānic passages is the one recounting the story of Lot. In it, Lot is shown criticizing his people for committing obscene acts:

> Tell the story of Lot who said to his people that they are committing a *faḥishah* no one in the worlds before them had committed: "Indeed you engage in sexual intercourse with men, practice road banditry, and undertake wicked acts in your clubs." To this, his people replied: "bring God's punishment if you were telling the truth."[Q7:V80–4]

Commenting on the above passage, Muslim exegetes explain that, while the word *faḥishah* here refers to sodomy, the Qur'ān is also referring to other acts known to have been prevalent among the people of Lot. Ibn 'Abbās in particular lists eleven of these obscene acts and practices: (1) abusing one another, (2) cursing each other, (3) breaking wind (*yataḍāraṭūn*) during meetings, (4) Randomly picking up men from the street for sex,[42] (5) gambling, (6) face-painting, (7) cockfighting, (8) ram-fighting, (9) decorating the tips of their

---

[41] The word *faḥishah* and its derivatives used in the context of dealing with women and sexuality are verses 15, 19, 22, and 25 in chapter *al-Nisā*'; verse 80 in chapter *al-A'rāf*; verse 32 in chapter *al-Isrā*'; verse 54 in chapter *al-Naml*; verse 28 in chapter *al-'Ankabūt*; verse 30 in chapter *al-Aḥzāb*; and verse 1 in chapter *al-Ṭalāq*. The three instances where the word *faḥishah* is used without reference to women or sexuality are verse 135 in chapter *Āl 'Imrān*; verse 28 in chapter *al-A'rāf*; and verse 19 in chapter *al-Nūr*.

[42] This was done by throwing pebbles at passers-by and the one whose pebble lands on the target gets to sodomize him.

fingers with *ḥinnah* (herbal colorant), (10) cross-dressing, and (11) taxing passers-by (*maks*).[43]

Despite this "diverse" list of obscene acts, the concept of *fāḥishah* became strongly linked to what is now *Qurʾānicly* defined as improper or illicit sexual behavior to the point that *fāḥishah* and *zinā* (adultery/illicit sexual acts) are used interchangeably in most exegetical and legal works. Commenting on [Q3:V135], Muslim commentators argue that "*fāḥishah* denotes every act of disobedience [*al-fāḥishatu tuṭlaqu ʿalā kulli maʿṣiyah*]. However, it has been especially used to refer to *zinā* to the point that Jābir Ibn ʿAbdullāh and al-Sadī stated that [Q3:V135] is about illicit sexual acts."[44] Al-Rāzī (d. 606 H) writes that "*al-fāḥishah* is the obscene act and Muslim scholars concur that the word *fāḥishah* appearing in [Q4:V15] refers to *zinā* and that that word was used instead of *zinā* because the latter is more profane than any other obscenity." Anticipating the obvious challenge of his characterization of illicit sexual acts as being more obscene than even idolatry and murder, al-Rāzī adds:

> The human body is managed by three powers: (1) speech power, (2) anger power, and (3) lust power. The speech power is corrupted by idolatry and religious innovation. Anger power is corrupted by murder. Lust power is corrupted by adultery (*zinā*), sodomy (*liwāṭ*), and lesbianism (*suḥq*). The worst of all these three powers is the lust power and for this reason its corruption is the worst one; hence, its characterization as obscenity (*al-fāḥishah*).[45]

Muslim scholars claim that there is a consensus among jurists and exegetes in favor of linking *al-fāḥishah* mentioned in [Q4:V15] to illicit sexual intercourse, but Abū Muslim disagreed arguing that "*al-fāḥishah* as used in the context of this verse refers to illicit sexual acts (*zinā*) of a woman with another woman."[46] Although this view is more in line with the grammatical and syntactical language of [Q4:V15–6], it was nonetheless rejected on the basis that it is not in conformity with "the consensus of Muslim scholars." Such a claim of consensus is further challenged by other inconsistencies given that there are other verses explicitly dealing with illicit sexual

---

[43] See Ibn Kathīr's commentary on [Q7: V80–4].

[44] See Muslim exegetes' commentaries on [Q3: V135] especially Ibn Kathīr's.

[45] See the commentary on [Q4: V15] in al-Rāzī's *Mafātīḥ al-ghayb*.

[46] See the commentary on [Q4: V15–6] in al-Ṭabarsī's *Majmaʿ al-bayān fī tafsīr al-qurʾān*.

intercourse and explicitly predetermining the punishment for such an offense.[47] In order to solve this problem, Muslim jurists relied on the more controversial theory of abrogation (*naskh*), which I will explain in the next section.

In Semitic discourse, women are seen as a source of impurity; and in Jewish traditions, even the laws dealing with obscenity and sexual behavior are not to be discussed by ordinary persons for fear of weakening their religious and moral commitments. It is reported in Islamic exegetical works that the Jewish men of Madīnah used to isolate themselves from menstruating women: they did not eat with them, they did not sit with them, and they did not share bed with them. When the newcomers to Madīnah (*al-muhājirūn*) inquired about the validity of this practice, the Prophet Muhammad told them: "Muslims are allowed to associate with women and do all things with the exception of sexual intercourse."[48] However, by rescinding a standing practice of isolating menstruating women and approaching them sexually as long as vaginal intercourse is not achieved, the question of anal sex was presented as a possibility. It is reported in the works of al-Shāfiʿī, Ibn Abī Shaybah, Aḥmad Ibn Ḥanbal, al-Nasāʾī, Ibn Mājah, Ibn al-Mundhir, and al-Bayhaqī that when [Q2:V222] was revealed, "A man came to the Prophet and asked him about sexual intercourse from the back (*ityān al-nisāʾ fī adbārihinna*). He said that it is fine. As the man walked away, he called him back and asked, "What did you say? If you meant by that approaching her from behind in her vagina, then yes; but if you meant from her back in her back, then no. God is not embarrassed from the truth; so do not have anal sex with your women."[49] According to al-Shawkānī, the Prophet had warned against anal sex characterizing it as "the minor sodomy [*al-lūṭiyyah al-ṣughrā*]." Other Muslim authorities described it as "filthy (*qadhir*) even if it were permitted."[50]

---

[47] In chapter *al-Nūr*, verse 2, it is stated that "the male adulterer and female adulteress shall be flogged each one hundred time [*al-zāniyatu wa-ʾl-zānī fa-jlidū kulla wāḥidin minhumā miʾatah jaldah*].

[48] See the commentary on [Q2: V222] in Aṭfīsh's *Taysīr al-tafsīr* as well as other Sunni and Shiʿite commentaries on the same verse.

[49] See al-Shawkānī's commentary on [Q2: V222] in his *Fatḥ al-qadīr*.

[50] See his commentary on [Q2:V222] in *Fatḥ al-qadīr*. It should be noted that some Shiʿite authorities permit anal and oral sex and modern scholars, such as

FURTHER CATEGORIZATION: SPEECH, CLASS, AND THE LAW

To invent a consistent legal system, Islamic law and jurisprudence scholars relied on categories and hierarchies: categories of speech distinguishing earlier vs. later revelation and giving prominence to later revealed parts of the Qur'ān and Ḥadīth over earlier revelations; and social hierarchies distinguishing between free vs. slave, young vs. old, elite vs. public persons. Moreover, the Qur'ān itself customizes crime and punishment according to social and marital status. To be sure, for any given grievous offense (of *ḥudūd* type), the wives of the Prophet (and later the wives of the leaders of the believers') were held to higher standard by doubling their punishment.[51] Free persons were punished to the full extent of the law; whereas the punishment of slaves, former slaves, and former prostitutes was halved.[52]

Admittedly, since Muslim scholars see *zinā* and *fāḥishah* as referring to the same offense and since the Qur'ān predetermines more than one specific punishment for this same offense, it stands to reason to critique the Qur'ānic discourse as being inconsistent. In order to reconcile conflicting Qur'ānic rulings, Muslim scholars invented the theory of abrogation that allowed them to select a specific punishment for a specific offense and to dismiss other punishments as being *mansūkh* (abrogated). It ought to be mentioned that, before [Q4:V15] was revealed, Jewish and Arab practices were applied to punish those who commit illicit sexual acts. The newly established

---

Ali al-Sistani, have advised their followers of its permissibility as long as it is consensual.

[51] Although the Qur'ān explicitly warned the wives of the Prophet against immoral acts, religious and community leaders subjected their wives to higher standards as well. The Qur'ān commands the wives of the Prophet: "O wives of the Prophet, whoever among you commits an obscene act (*ya'ti bi-fāḥishah*) that is verifiable (witnessed by four people of outstanding probity), she will have her punishment doubled and that is easy for God to do." Verse 30 of chapter *al-Aḥzāb*.

[52] See [Q4:V25]: "Whoever among you is unable to marry from among free protected believing ladies (*al-muḥṣanāt*) then it is permitted for him to marry from believing slave women; God knows best the extent of your belief. Then marry them with the permission of their guardians and offer them their fair dowry so that they become protected monogamous wives. If after such marriage they (wives) commit an obscene act (*atayna bi-fāḥishatin*), then their punishment shall be half of that of *al-muḥṣanāt*. This is the recommendation for those who fear committing adultery, but if you be patient then God is forgiving and merciful.

"consensus" meant that Jewish, tribal, and even earlier Qur'ānic determinations of the law became superseded by the more recent Qur'ānic or Ḥadīthic rulings.[53]

The first instance where the Prophet is reported to have ordered the stoning of a person who committed an illicit sexual act is recorded in *al-Jāmiʿ li-aḥkām al-qurʾān* of al-Qurṭubī (d. 671 H). In it, it is said that Jābir Ibn ʿAbdullāh narrated that the Jews brought a man and a woman before the Prophet and accused them of *zinā*. The Prophet asked for two knowledgeable Jewish men and asked them about the ruling of the Torah regarding *zinā*. They told him that the punishment for such an offense is stoning provided that four reliable witnesses who actually saw the act of penetration testify to it.[54] The Prophet then verified that the four witnesses in this case were of outstanding character (people of probity) and they have witnessed the actual act; then he asked the Jewish community to apply the law of stoning.[55] There is no evidence pointing to this event as an application of any Qur'ānic law; rather, an application of Jewish law in a case that involved two Jewish offenders. Nonetheless, Muslim exegetes assert that the Qur'ān explicitly meant to uphold the Jewish law of stoning and make it applicable to Muslims as well.[56]

According to Ibn Kathīr (d. 744 H), "during the early years of Islam, when a woman was found guilty of illicit sexual intercourse,

---

[53] According to Muslim scholars, and in addition to inter-religious abrogation (a later Semitic religion abrogating earlier ones), there is what I call intra-religious abrogation wherein later parts of the religious texts abrogate earlier ones. Muslim scholars recognize three modes of abrogation: (1) the abrogation of the text and the law, (2) the abrogation of the law without abrogating the text, and (3) the abrogation of the text without abrogating the law. The law of stoning is considered an example of the third mode of abrogation wherein the text of the Qur'ān that authorized it is no longer part of the Qur'ān whereas the law is still applicable according to most Muslim jurists.

[54] It can be argued that *zinā*, in the Semitic discourse, becomes a grave and obscene act when it is done with regularity, publicity, and without shame to the point that it is easily witnessed by four or more people. As such, it is more of a challenge to public morality than it is harmful to the couple involved. This view becomes even more plausible in the Islamic discourse, given that there is more than one punishment for the same offense; hence, the categorization approach.

[55] See the commentary on [Q4: V15] in al-Qurṭubī's *al-Jāmiʿ li-aḥkām al-qurʾān*.

[56] See the commentary on [Q4: V15] in al-Shanqīṭī's *Aḍwāʾ al-bayān fī tafsīr al-qurʾān*.

she was imprisoned at home and she could not leave it until she died. The early revelation ([Q4:V15]) upheld that practice until it was abrogated by the new revelation that sanctioned stoning and flogging instead."[57] He supported this view by quoting a tradition in which the Prophet is reported to have said: "God has made the way concerning adulterers clear: the young man and young woman (*al-bikr*) are flogged one hundred times and exiled one year; whereas the elder (man and elder woman (*al-thayb*)) are flogged one hundred times and stoned."[58] In other words, this tradition abrogates the explicit verses of Qur'ān which punish *zinā* by flogging (one hundred times). However, some Muslim scholars were not certain that the above tradition abrogated verse *al-Nisa*' 4:15. Al-Zamakhsharī for instance, does not see a contradiction between [Q4:V15] and [Q24:V2] and is not certain that one abrogated the other.[59]

Arguably, none of the above explanations removes the grammatical discrepancies in [Q4:V15–6]. The use of the feminine plural in the first verse and the masculine dual in the second verse presented exegetes with a difficult challenge that exposed the disconnect and competition between the letter of the law and the practice of the early leaders and scholars. But only later scholars have acknowledged the grammatical and syntactical problem and attempted to provide an explanation. For example, the exegete al-Shawkānī (d. 1250 H) explains away the problem by further categorizing the subjects of each verse. He contends that the first verse deals with women only (young and old) while the second verse deals with men only and the dual pronoun is used to specify the two types of men: the married and unmarried (*man aḥṣana wa-man lam yuḥṣan*).[60]

---

[57] The revelation referred to here is Ḥadīth and not the Qur'ān because there is no Qur'ānic evidence in support of stoning as a punishment for illicit sexual intercourse.

[58] See the commentaries on [Q4: V15] in Ibn Kathīr's *Tafsīr al-qur'ān al-karīm*; in *Fatḥ al-qadīr* by al-Shawkānī; and in al-A'qam's *Tafsīr*. Shi'ite scholar, al-Ṭūsī, is more explicit about the fact that those found guilty of an offense punishable by stoning will be flogged first then stoned. But he argues that there is a Shi'ite minority opinion that holds that only the elder men and elder women are punished by flogging then stoning but others are only stoned. See his commentary on [Q4: V15] in *al-Tibyān al-jāmi' li-'ulūm al-qur'ān*.

[59] See the commentary on [Q4: V15] in al-Zamakhsharī's *al-Kashshāf*.

[60] See the commentary on [Q4: V15–6] in al-Shawkānī's *Fatḥ al-qadīr*.

In the Islamic discourse, sexual intercourse is not just about pro-creation, it is about satisfying an instinct.[61] As such, a person who is legally married is in one legal category, but a person who is legally married and could have sexual intercourse anytime is in a different category. To be sure, a woman who is married and who engages in sexual intercourse with her husband whenever she feels the need to do so becomes *muḥṣanah*. Similarly, a man under the same conditions becomes *muḥṣan* as well. Muslim jurists identify three aspects of the concept of *iḥṣān*: (1) qualifications of the *muḥṣan*, (2) contractual conditions for *iḥṣān*, and (3) consequences of *iḥṣān*.[62]

Regarding the requirement of qualifications, the person could be classified as a *muḥṣan* if he or she is an adult (not a minor), free (not a slave or under duress), sane, and Muslim. If a person thus described enters into a valid marriage contract, then the first con-dition for qualifying as a *muḥṣan* is met. The second condition is fulfilled when sexual intercourse is achieved wherein a man uses his penis to penetrate the woman in the vagina and wherein both man and woman are sexually satisfied upon the completion of the sexual act whenever they desire to do so. If the man or the woman, for whatever reason, is unable to reach sexual satisfaction, the con-dition of *iḥṣān* cannot be achieved.[63] However, when all the above descriptions and conditions are met, the person becomes a *muḥṣan*; a condition that causes her or him to be subjected to the harsher punishment of stoning if found guilty of illicit sexual acts. The *iḥṣān* also causes other legal actions relevant to divorce rights (such as

---

[61] Al-Ṭabarī writes about pleasuring oneself from women by marrying them, in another context he writes about enjoying their beauty. See his commentary on [Q4: V24] in *Majmaʿ al-bayān*. Furthermore, and underscoring sexual union as an act of satisfying men and women's instincts, Ibn Ḥazm argues that sexual inter-course *must* take place after each menstrual cycle. In other words, he sees inter-course as something above and beyond the need to procreate. See Ibn Kathīr's comments on [Q2: V222] in *Tafsīr al-qurʾān al-karīm*.

[62] Al-Bājī, *al-Muntaqā* (Cairo: Maktabat al-Thaqāfah al-Dīniyyah, 2004), 5:131.

[63] If a married couple dispute whether sexual intercourse took place and one of them is found guilty of illicit sexual acts, he or she cannot be punished by stoning. However, if they both agree that they have regular sexual intercourse and one of them is found guilty of illicit sexual intercourse, he or she will be sub-jected to stoning. Furthermore, if a Muslim man is married to a non-Muslim woman, he becomes *muḥṣan* and the fact that she does not qualify for *iḥṣān* does not affect his status. See Al-Bājī, *al-Muntaqā* (Cairo: Maktabat al-Thaqāfah al-Dīniyyah, 2004), 5:134–8.

dowry, waiting period, and initiation of marriage dissolution) to be reconsidered.

Subsequently, Muslim jurists defined *iḥṣān* as the condition whereby "a sane and mature person who is bound by a valid marriage contract, and who is able to have sexual intercourse whenever he or she wants to do so."[64] According to this view, sexual intercourse taking place within the legal framework becomes a means to achieving piety. As such, piety becomes the settled disposition to manage natural urges. In the case of sexual urges, piety is achieved by allowing and mandating sexual intercourse and providing the environment wherein sexual satisfaction is attained. In the Islamic discourse, marriage is the institution for encouraging and organizing sexual behavior. With that said, marriage becomes strongly recommended. In Shi'ite Islam, it is required especially from religious authorities. If marriage is not possible, Islamic law allows temporary pleasure marriages (*zawāj al-mut'ah*) or recommends extended fasting.[65] It is reported that the Prophet Muhammad said, advising young persons, "whoever is able to fulfill the obligations of marriage should marry; he who cannot, should fast; for fasting is a protection (*aḥṣan*) of the genitals."[66]

Not all unmarried individuals are unable to attain the status of a *muḥṣan*. Many Sufi figures are said to have trained themselves to avoid all pleasures of life including sexual pleasures and yet live in spiritual seclusion. The Qur'ān speaks of a number of individuals who protected their genitals and attained uprightness without having had sexual intercourse. The most intriguing of these figures is Mary:

> And God tells the story of Mary, the daughter of 'Imrān, she protected her vagina so we breathed in it from Our spirit (*rūḥinā*); she believed in the words of her Lord and His Books. She was Upright. [Q66:V12].[67]

---

[64] See M. Jawwād Maghniyyah, *Fiqh al-Imām Jaʿfar al-Ṣādiq* (Qom: Muʾassasat Anṣāriyān, n. d.), 6:255. The author also indicates that a woman who is raped will not be punished regardless of her *iḥṣān* status, but the man who commits rape shall be killed regardless of his status.

[65] Temporary or pleasure marriage is upheld in Shi'ite jurisprudence but said to be abrogated in Sunni law.

[66] *yā maʿshara al-shabāb, man istaṭāʿa minkum al-bāʾah fa-l-yatazawwaj; wa-man lam yastaṭiʿ fa-ʿalayhi bi-l-ṣawm fa-innahu aḥṣanu li-l-farj . . ."*

[67] See also chapter *Maryam* (19) of the Qur'ān.

With these references in mind, it becomes clear that the concept of *iḥsān* is ultimately an act of denial: self-denial by resisting bio-logical urges, legal denial of marriage from a woman who is already married by decree, and religious denial of continuing ancient prac-tice by divine proscriptions. *In the end, managing sexual behavior cate-gorically differentiates it from obscenity.* In doing so, women and sexuality are transformed into a subject of the discourse on public morality. Although the above examples should suffice to make the case for the dynamism of the concepts of sexuality and obscenity in the reli-gious discourse, I will nonetheless present one last piece of evidence to underscore the relationship between individual and social well being as a product of the proper management of natural urges.

In Islamic law, if a married couple were divorced for the first or second time, they are able to rescind the divorce without enter-ing into a new marriage contract. First and second divorces are categorized as revocable divorces (sing., *ṭalāq rij'ī*). If divorce is declared for the third time,[68] it becomes irrevocable divorce, which means that the couple cannot remarry unless the woman marries another man and then he divorces her (this kind of marriage is called, *nikāḥ muḥallil*). More importantly, not only must she enter into a valid marriage contract before she is allowed to marry her first husband, but she must have sexual intercourse with her second husband, a sexual intercourse that leads to orgasm for both of them. According to Ibn al-Zubayr, a woman who was married to a sec-ond man after she had been divorced for the third time from her first husband, but who did not have sex with the second one, wanted to return to her first husband. They consulted the Prophet. He told the first husband that he cannot remarry her until "she experiences orgasm"[69] while married to the second husband. Because of this tradition, Muslim jurists concluded that it is not the legal marriage contract that "removes the prohibition of remarrying; rather, it is

---

[68] Divorce, like marriage and emancipating slaves, takes effect upon the oral declaration. This stringent condition practically eliminates claims of unintention-ality and jest as a basis to withdraw the commitment in human relations. In Islamic law, most contracts can be re-negotiated and they are generally written down, but not the ones dealing with the status of human beings (which are not even written down) as doing so is considered disrespect to human dignity.

[69] "*lā taḥillu laka ḥattā tadhūqa al-'usaylah.*" See Sulaymān al-Bājī, *al-Muntaqā: Sharḥ Muwaṭṭa' Mālik* (Cairo: Maktabat al-Thaqāfah al-Dīniyyah, 2004): 69–70.

sexual intercourse (*waṭ'*) that does so." 'Ā'ishah is reported to have said that the prohibition is not removed until the second husband "has orgasm,"[70] which prompted other jurists to further argue that legal marriage contract, sexual intercourse, and ejaculation (*inzāl*) are required for the prohibition to be removed. Even the death of the second husband before sexual intercourse does not remove the prohibition.[71]

From the above example, one could argue that, if sexual intercourse with more people is obscene, one would expect the legal contract with a second husband short of sexual intercourse to be enough to remove the prohibition and maintain "sexual purity," which is usually cited as a reason for controlling sexual relations. However, requiring sexual intercourse with another man before the first husband is allowed to remarry his ex-wife shows that sexual behavior is ultimately a means and not a goal.

Conclusions

In the Islamic discourse, obscenity, like sexuality, is significant not just for what it does to the physical body of the human being, but especially to the soul.[72] As the evidence shows, in the Islamic world view, there are no acts, deeds, or words that are intrinsically obscene and absolutely profane for we have seen that some acts are encouraged (if not made obligatory) in a time and in a specific context, and the same acts are discouraged (or prohibited) depending on the time and context as well. This fluidity in the Islamic discourse is not evident only in the historical evolution of religious thought as it relates to obscenity and propriety, but also in the same act within the same timeframe. For example, sexual intercourse within the confines of a legal or social marriage is encouraged. But sexual intercourse without the framework of a legal or social contract

---

[70] "*lā, ḥattā yadhūqa 'usaylatahā.*" See Sulaymān al-Bājī, *al-Muntaqā: Sharḥ Muwaṭṭa' Mālik* (Cairo: Maktabat al-Thaqāfah al-Dīniyyah, 2004): 70.

[71] See Sulaymān al-Bājī, *al-Muntaqā: Sharḥ Muwaṭṭa' Mālik* (Cairo: Maktabat al-Thaqāfah al-Dīniyyah, 2004): 71.

[72] The idea of obscenity being a spiritual impurity is not new to early Muslim scholars. In fact, al-Rāzī used the same concept when commenting on [Q2: V222] saying, "Disobeying God is sinning, and sinning is spiritual obscenity" [*al-dhanb najāsah rūḥāniyyah*]. See his *Mafātīḥ al-ghayb*.

is proscribed. Furthermore, sexual intercourse with a slave woman is permitted according to the Qur'ānic discourse (*mā malakat aymānukum*), but sexual intercourse with the same woman once offered her freedom (upon the uttering of the words of emancipation) is taboo.[73]

In order to underscore the notion that obscenity is a disturbance of the spiritual balance of the person rather than it being only a physical pollutant, one could consider the removal of restriction on sexual intercourse with menstruating women.[74] If menstruation or blood physically defiles the person, one would expect the impurity to last until it is physically removed (washed off by water). However, according to some Muslim scholars, menstruating women could be approached (sexually) again upon the end of the period (which is estimated to range from three to ten days) even if the woman continues to bleed.[75] Other Muslim jurists argued that the restriction on sexual intercourse due to menstruation is removed with the expiry of the maximum days (10) and when the woman performs dry ablution (*tayammum*). When considering that dry ablution is not a physical purifer,[76] the notion of obscenity impacting the soul becomes evident.

Moreover, in his encyclopedic commentary on the Qur'ān, al-Janābidhī (d. 14th century H) argues that menstrual blood is defiling to the humanity (*al-insāniyyah*) and to the soul of the human being

---

[73] Contrast the idea of obscenity causing harm to the "humanity" as well as to the "machinery" of the human being unveiled in this study to modern Western take on ritual impurity developed by Mary Douglas, *Purity and Danger: An Analysis of Concept of Pollution and Taboo* (London: Routledge, 2002); Mary Douglas, *Natural Symbols: Explorations in Cosmology* (London: Cresset, 1970); Claude Levi-Strauss, *The Savage Mind, Nature of Human Society Series* (London: Weidenfeld & Nicolson, 1966); and Howard Eilberg-Schwartz, *The Savage in Judaism: An Anthropology of Israelite Religion and Ancient Judaism* (Bloomington: Indiana University Press, 1990).

[74] See al-Janābidhī's commentary on [Q2: V222] in *Tafsīr bayān al-saʿādah fī maqāmāt al-ʿibādah.*

[75] See Ibn Kathīr, *Tafsīr al-qurʾān al-aẓīm* (Beirut: Dar Iḥyāʾ al-Turāth al-Arabī, 2004), 270–7.

[76] Dry ablution (*tayammum*) is not a physical purifier because, form the way it is performed, no actually washing takes place. Rather, it is a symbolic gesture whereby the person performing dry ablution touches the ground (natural dirt that was exposed to the sun and air) or stone with his or her hands before rubbing them together once, then touches the stone again and runs hands over the face once.

"as it affects it and revives in it its savage tendencies." He refers only secondarily to its physical harm to people "as the blood affects the machinery of the body by causing it to inherit certain diseases"[77] that reduces its ability to function properly and effectively. In other words, obscenity and morality are social constructs and as such they are defined with the interest of society in mind. On the individual level, the goal of the person is to attain a mental state wherein her tranquility and psychological well being is not dependent on temporary conditions; rather, on permanent conditions that are provided by the institutions of marriage, family, and the community (as represented in mosques, churches, synagogues, and temples).

From this analysis of the concept of obscenity in the early Islamic discourse, it becomes clear that sexuality and women become the objects of public morality. The role of the elite in shaping the understanding of the scripture to reflect their interests is evident from the way sex and the woman are linked to all that is obscene and decent: the woman becomes either a symbol of decadence or an icon of uprightness. In the case of the Islamic discourse, this linkage between sex, women, and obscenity has been solidified by the sacralized practice ('amal) of the first elite of the Islamic community. Their understanding has been passed generation to generation until it was written down.

The purpose of this article is manifold. First, it is meant to shed some light on the history and development of concepts such as sexuality and obscenity in the Semitic discourse in general and Islamic civilization in particular. Second, it is an attempt to explain the way cultural norms are filtered through and incorporated into the religious worldview. In the case of sexuality and obscenity in Islam, it was shown that the earliest generation of Muslims had exerted an extraordinary role in fixing meaning and shaping later understanding. By emphasizing the role of the tradition and practice of the earliest generation of authorities, it is hoped that the religious norms are seen anew as social constructs depending on negotiated consensus not on tradition-based consensus (which became the mode of the post-recording era of Islamic tradition). Third, this article shows the variety of opinions concerning certain social values and

---

[77] See al-Janābidhī's commentary on [Q2: V222] in *Tafsīr bayān al-saʿādah fī maqāmāt al-ʿibādah*.

mores and it is hoped that the unearthing of these early texts and the unveiling of earlier debates will revive the spirit of contestations of themes of utter important to social justice issues. In learning about the often hesitant mindset of earlier Muslim thinkers when they approached topics that seem to many today as clear absolutes, it will become possible that cultural customs used to justify the brutal murder and abhorrent persecution of women in the name of "family honor" is firmly and forcefully discarded.

[12]

Gender Boundaries and Sexual Categories in the Arab World

As'ad AbuKhalil

In this brief essay, the history of Western attitudes to Islam will not be examined,[1] nor will the Orientalist legacy be scrutinized.[2] It is only the specific construction of gender and sexual images that will be covered. The discussion will switch between East and West, between past and present. Western attitudes to Islam have affected the way Islam is perceived and interpreted, and to respond to Western claims of timelessness in Muslim lives one is compelled to compare and contrast lives of Muslims. Muslims felt morally obligated to respond to the moral challenges and provocations presented to them by Western concepts. While time is not static among Muslims, as has been assumed by classical Orientalists, themes from the past may still be relevant today, not because the presence could not withstand the pressures of *Turath* (heritage) but because its themes have been forced through systematic socialization and official indoctrination. The words of Barrington Moore still resonate: "To maintain and transmit a value system, human beings are punched, bullied, sent to jail, thrown into concentration camps, cajoled, bribed, made into heroes, encouraged to read newspapers, stood up against a wall and shot, and sometimes even taught sociology. To speak of cultural inertia is to overlook the concrete interests and privileges that are served by indoctrination, education, and the entire complicated process of transmitting culture from one generation to another."[3] Western and Eastern studies of Islam are devoid of an investigation of the methods by which Islam, along with the value systems associated with it, came to be the predominant—but far from being the only—source of moral standards.

As'ad AbuKhalil is Associate Professor of political science at California State University, Stanislaus and Research Fellow at the Center for Middle Eastern Studies at the University of California, Berkeley.

A Note on Methodology

It is necessary before the subject is broached any further to define the terms of reference. How can Islam be used as a standard methodological yardstick when the diversity of Muslim lifestyles and interpretations are apparent to the researcher? The tendency to attribute all manners of sociopolitical life and systems of thought to the Islamic theological worldview has for long been a staple of Western studies of Islam. Maxime Rodinson defines this "theologocentrique" school of thought as follows: *"Les lignes de pensee selon lesquelles pratiquement tous les phenomenes observables dans les societes adherant majortairement our officiellement a la religion musulmane s'explicqueraient par cette adhesion."*[4] This methodology was perfected as an art form by the doyen of contemporary Orientalist, Bernard Lewis. In a recent edition of his *Islam and the West,*[5] he refuses to treat Islam as any other religion in the world because, he asserts, it is "the whole of life,"[6] whatever that means. It would be unfair, however, to attribute this paradigm to Bernard Lewis alone. The field of Islamocentric Orientalism began at a time when classical scholars could only study the Qur'an to understand the Muslim people. This has reinforced the emphasis in European tradition of Oriental study on the linguistic analysis of the Qur'anic word, not for purposes of the study of religion but for the analysis of Muslim behavior regardless of time and place.

The subject of Islam and sexuality has been of little interest to official religious circles in the Arab world. Not that one can find any references to sexuality and gender in Islamic writings, indeed there is an overwhelming concern—if not obsession with such issues—but the government designated clerics follow a line that was established early in the history of Western traffic with Islam. What passes as Islamic mores and conduct in much of the Islamic countries is in fact the impact of Westernization. "Puritanical Islam," which people from the past like medieval Christian polemicists or even Max Weber would never associate with the religion of Muhammad, owes much to European Protestantism. This change in Islamic treatment of the sexual question came about after centuries of Christian criticisms of Islamic moral permissiveness, just as Christian criticisms of the absence of miracles in Muhammad's life produced myths and miracles that were attributed to him after his death by Muslims put on the defensive by the severity of enemy attacks. The regularity and apparent legitimacy of homosexual relations were seen by Medieval Christians as evidence of the moral decadence of Muslims.[7] Al-Jahiz, recognizing the changes in Islamic sociosexual mores, thought that the attitude of asceticism and timidity on matters relating to sexual parts and acts is artificial and unrelated to chastity and noble behavior.[8]

It is not easy to determine why Western attitudes mattered to Muslims on those subjects relating to their private lives; it is not possible to trace with mathematical precision the sources of current Muslim behavior and values. It is realistic, however, to detect a change in the Muslim treatment of sex and gender in past and present writings. While this article will not engage in an exhaustive study of representative writings—that is not possible anyway—the discussion will select elements from the heritage and from contemporary literature in an effort to show—not the consistency, as alleged by dead and living Orientalists but—the inconsistency in what has been commonly known as "the Islamic attitude" to sex and other matters of interest to researchers.

It is important to point right at the outset that the tendency to speak about Islam is fraught with methodological hazards. First, the religion does not apply uniformly or universally to all Muslims and in all areas of the world. That Islam constitutes a closed, inflexible doctrine, or that all world Muslims form some monolithic bloc, is no more accepted by the academic community despite the efforts of stubborn Orientalists who never give up on their attempt to revive the crudest version of classical Orientalism. Second, the standard notion of an "Islam" obscures the dramatic changes that have occurred in the body of its values and even rituals throughout history when Islam was being constantly blended with local customs and cultures. The notion of change within Islam is central to any treatment of Islamic attitudes to social, economic, and political issues.

Gender Boundaries and Social Barriers in Islam

The Islamic religion still conjures up images of rigid segregation between the sexes. Male supremacy is assumed to be an integral part of the faith, nay of the moral obligation of worship. Not that Islam favors full gender equality; it does not, and the view that culture is solely responsible for the oppression and repression of women in the Middle East ignores the dynamic interaction between culture and religion over time. Elizabeth Fernea and Basima Bezirgan[9] tried to absolve Islam from responsibility in the exclusion of women from public space, and later on from what Habermas refers to as "the bourgeois public sphere."[10] Their attempt, however, fails because one cannot maintain that Islam contradicts tribal custom and culture as far as the women question is concerned. The promotion of the ostensible inferiority of women is accepted by Islam and culture of the Middle East although one may argue whether one is more guilty than the other in the deprivation of women from their rights, and whether early Islam absorbed sexist elements from the already existing cultural environment. The people who are born to the Islamic religion grow up exposed to a variety of social, cultural, economic, psychological, and political stimuli and to reduce our explanation of the gender question to one factor alone (Islam here) is to lose sight of the variety of influences in one's life.

Islam is an influence, but its role in the socialization of children and the indoctrination of adults is often exaggerated. It is yet to be proven that Muslim Arabs have some peculiar social and sexual attitudes that non-Muslim Arabs do not have. Not that there are no differences between Muslim and Christian families in, say, a place like Lebanon where many sects coexist conflictually. Those differences, however, are sometimes related to distinctions of region or variation in income levels. Another difference is that impact of state moral propaganda. A Muslim in the Middle East is in general subject to multilayered pressures; some come from one's family while others come from a state that declares itself Islamic. To be a Muslim in the Middle East is to be forcibly incorporated into a vast network of religiopolitical indoctrination that is sponsored by the state and supported by the family. The ethical identity of the state is that of the written Islam, as is portrayed in the transmitted heritage of the faith. To dissent is to risk the wrath of the penal measures of the state and to cause social discomfort to the individual.

The West today has worked into its cultural and social fabric a rigid distinction between males and females, between homosexuals and heterosexuals. It is not for this article to go into the reasons and origins of these distinctions and their socioeconomic consequences. It would be a mistake, however, to transport Western distinctions and assumptions about sexual identities to the Middle East despite recent Westernization of habits and lifestyles in that part of the world. The Qur'an does not consistently argue from an essentialist view of manhood and womanhood. There is no hint of inequality between men and women as created souls: "Oh, people have fear of your lord, who created you from a single soul, from which He created its mate, and through them He bestrewed the earth with numerous men and women."[11] In other words, this differs from that version of creationism in Genesis, which stated that a woman was created from a man's rib.

The question of the Qur'anic attitude to women will not be settled here. It is clear from the Arabic phraseology of the Qur'an, which forces one to chose gender designations, unlike Persian, that more attention is paid to men than to women in the Qur'an. Nevertheless, there are parts of the Qur'an where the language used is gender neutral (33, 35–36). On matters of sexuality, men's sexual needs are widely recognized and the references to sex between men and women contain reminders of God's gifts to men in terms of gratification.[12] The elements of gender distinctions are also found in the Qur'an; menstruation is considered "harmful,"[13] as if to condemn the biological makeup of the woman. The very nature of the woman was then held against her, especially in the misogynist writings of the Prophet's cousin and son in law 'Ali ibn Abi Talib, who declared that women were deficient in their faiths, their lots, and their minds. The deficiency of faith, he explained, is due to their inability to fulfill their religious obligation during the menstrual cycle; the deficiency of lot is due to their inheritance of half the male's share; and their deficiency of mind is due to the equation of the court testimony of one woman with that of half a man.[14] The logic of Ali punishes women, not for what they are, but for what male jurists have assumed about them.

The notion of equality of men and women in Islam is a mere invention of the apologetic school of Islam,[15] which predominates in much of the Muslim world due to its sponsorship by the ruling governments. To be sure, there are areas in the Qur'an where rewards and punishments are treated as exclusive products of one's actions, without any distinctions of race, gender, or ethnicity (99, 08). Other references in the Qur'an, however, talk about the marital unit as an advantageous arrangement that caters to the primary needs of the man. Female sexual desires are recognized but only indirectly as when the withdrawal of sexual favors by the man (banish them to bed apart)[16] in cases of *nushuz* (the juridical term of the disobedience of the wife to her husband) is mentioned. Men are also permitted to use violence (here Muslims argue about the scale but do not dispute the permission[17]) against their wives while women, who are said to subordinate to the authority of men,[18] do not have that right.

The rise of segregation needs came after the birth of the new religion, when male friends of the Prophet like 'Umar ibn al-Khattab were urging Muhammad to isolate his wives from male companions. Only then did revelation come to Muhammad, which in effect established the basis for social segregation between males and females. The Qur'anic injunction, however, was not meant to apply to all Muslim women. It has been made abundantly clear in Islamic religious writings that Muhammad's wives form a special group; they could not even be spoken to except through a curtain, and they were not allowed to marry after Muhammad's death. That restrictions (oddly, they were considered privileges by male theologians) that applied to Muhammad's wives would later apply to all Muslim women is a sign of the increasing repression of women as Islam evolved. Social status was also very much a factor in applying special designations to free Muslim women: those who veiled wanted to underline their free and upper class status while the lower class women (and especially concubines) wandered about freely in public space. Yet, it is curious that the history of Islamic women excludes the lives and experiences of the *jawari* although they were an integral part of society and polity. Classical Arabic literature is full of tales, adventures, and poetry by concubines and the suppression of their historical existence from official historiography is a sign of new modern morality that was too embarrassed about their roles.

Segregation was not consistently enforced. In the past, and the present, segregation is a claim that is made to maintain the rules of moral etiquette. It was—and is—rare for the newly wed not to have seen one another before the wedding night. Male theologians had to construct a system of social control not to establish rigid barriers on gender basis only but to ensure the monopolization over interpretation of religious texts. The inclusion of women in the clerical establishment would have produced a different Islam, and Islam that is less androcentric. The needs for segregation continued as new regimes and dynasties emerged in the Middle East. The sources of legitimacy were weak and suspect and classical ethical interpretations of Islam were always satisfying to the clerical establishment. The latter saw the indices of its power measured by its control over women's issues and education. Thus, the nature of the political recipe of Saudi Arabia is based on a delicate marriage of convenience between the Saudi royal family and the champions of Wahhabiyyah.

Homosexual Controversies

Homosexuality in Islam has generated interest on the part of Westerners. It allowed for the rendering of a region and its people as exotic and mysterious, and it also created a zone of unrestricted imagination that would not fit into the taboos of Christianity. Erotic art and literature used Islam as a background and the fascinating tales of the *Arabian Nights* were not distinguished in Western minds from Qur'anic verses. Islam was interpreted and judged through the *Arabian Nights* and not through the Qur'anic text itself, which remained—and remains today—inaccessible to Western readers. Professional translations of the Qur'an did not appear until the last century and interest in the word of God was small because the Islamic holy book made claims that Christians did not accept, and because Christian polemicists attributed false and wild ideas to the Qur'an. Any similarities between the Qur'an and the Bible were dismissed as cheap imitation by an imposter; Islam was expected not only to agree with Christianity—as it did on many issues—it had to be Christianity to be accepted. Christians were impressed that Jesus was considered a Prophet by Muslims but disappointed that his crucifixion story was rejected.

Homosexuality set the difference between the two religions; if Christianity—before and after the reformation—stood for a puritanical morality and strict ethical code, Islam was ridiculed as the religion of sexual permissiveness and ethical laxity. Short of polytheism, all is forgiven in Islam. Medieval Christians found the

God that Muslims worshipped too forgiving for their taste. Homosexuality was a central issue of polemical attacks against Islam. While homosexuality among Muslims was described in the past as a common occurrence (as it was among the Greeks, who considered young males, not women the object of male sexual desire[19]), it is now rejected as nonexistent among Arab and Muslim males. Arno Schmitt wants us to believe that even when Arab males engage in sex with other males it is not homosexuality that characterizes their behavior. He seems to imply that homosexuality is only a feature of non-Muslim Western societies.[20]

It is now said that homosexuality did not exist among the Arabs and that Arab males are more inclined toward bisexuality. This claim denies that such a thing as homosexual identities ever existed among the Arabs. What has probably led to this view is the absence of contemporary accounts by Arab homosexuals about their experiences and the focus in the studies on the subject on Western encounters with Arab men. The book by Schmitt and Sofer, which is the only full-length study of the subject, is more about Western men and their experiences in the Middle East. It reads as a tourist guide to homosexuality in Muslim lands. In the typical classical Orientalist fashion, Muslim men were not allowed to speak for themselves, to recount their experiences without having the Western judge ready to invoke rationality and objectivity on the account. It made perfect sense from the standpoint of Orientalist dogma to conclude the book with the entry by Charles Pellat; he alone can render a decisive and definitive judgment on the subject. The book has more than a tinge of prejudice to it; the experience of one Muslim man becomes the defining experience for all Muslim men. You only need to know one to know them all; diversity is a Western tribute.

Al-Jahiz disagrees; he disagrees that there is no diversity in the sexual lives of Arab men, and he disagrees that only bisexuality exists in the Middle East. The myth of Arab abstention from homosexuality was promoted most solidly this century by those clerics who insisted on providing an external (non-Arab) root to homosexuality. Adam Mez saved some Arabs from embarrassment by reporting in his classic work the claim of a Khurasanian root of Arab homosexuality. He based his statement—in his otherwise thoroughly documented volume—simply on "Muslim tradition."[21] To preserve Arab nationalism from a scandal, Hichem Djait grabs Mez's theory.[22] More serious accounts assume that homosexuality was present in the lives of the Arabs in Jahiliyyah times. Hadith deals with it in very specific terms.[23]

Al-Jahiz has left an important record of the views and perceptions of homosexuals and heterosexuals in his treatise *Kitab Mufakharat Al-Jawari wa-l-Ghilman* (A Book of the Debate Comparing the Virtues of [sex with] Women and Young Men).[24] The book can help refute two essential claims made by Schmitt, among others, about homosexuality among Muslims. First, there is no doubt—despite fashionable theories about the universality of bisexuality (Schmitt links bisexuality to peculiar sexual habits among Arab/Muslim males)—that heterosexual and homosexual identities existed in the Arab/Islamic civilization. Abu Nuwwas said: "Would I choose seas over land (in Abu Nuwwas' poetry, seas denoted love of women, and lands [barari] denoted love of men)? . . . this is what the book of God commanded us, to favor males over females."[25] Furthermore, the Caliph Al-Amin, according to As-Siyuti in *Tarikh Al-Khulafa'* simply "rejected women and concubines."[26] He refused, despite the strenuous efforts of his concerned mother, to have sex with women. "To cure her son of his passion for eunuchs the mother of the Caliph Amin smuggled among them several slender, handsome maids with short hair dressed up as boys in tight jackets and girdles. Court circles and common-folk all alike followed this fashion and similarly dressed up their slave-girls and called them *Ghulamiyyah*."[27] Abu Nuwwas sang the praises of *ghulamiyyat*: "I was tortured by the love of *ghulamiyyat* . . . and they are suitable for homosexuals (*latah*) and promiscuous heterosexuals (*zunat*)."[28] Similarly, the Abbasid Caliph Al-Wathiq devoted his life and poetry to his male lover Muhaj.[29] To dismiss homosexual identities from the lives of Muslims is to associate homosexuality with Western life and experience. Assertion of pure homosexual identities among some Muslims took extreme forms, as reported by Al-Jahiz. *Ghulat Al-Latah* (literally, ultra-homosexuals) was used to denote those homosexuals who were widely and publicly known for their homosexual preferences.

Second, Schmitt reveals the inadequacy of his linguistic skills in the Arabic language when he insists that Arabic terms for sexual acts do not contain any "form of reciprocity."[30] He is unaware that heterosexual sexual acts (*mudaja'ah* or *munakahah*), lesbian sex (*musahaqah*), and gay (male) sex (*talawwut*) all can be expressed with forms of reciprocity. It is unclear what Schmitt wishes to say with this statement, except to stress a point he makes repeatedly regarding Arab homosexual inability to give, as if selfish sexual practice is inherently Arab or Muslim. Sexual identities were clear and, in some descriptions in literature and jurisprudence, rigid. The category of *mukhannath* (effeminate)[31] was not confused with homosexuality and an Umayyad caliph once ordered a census of *mukhannathun* (plural of *mukhannath*) in Medina.[32]

The confusion in terms referring to homosexual acts are the product of this century when governments and clerics wish to stigmatize homosexuality to live up the standards of Western Christian morality, which is now assumed to apply to Islamic legal application in areas of sexual behavior. Pederasty is equated with homosexuality and both are subsumed under the word *shudhudh jinsi* (sexual perversion). The construction of a new social reality that does not recognize homosexual reality was convenient to the modern Arab state. The Arab state defines itself, at least partly, by reference—not to the groups and individuals that are allowed to exist and perform but—to those groups and individuals that are not allowed to exist and function. In the latter category, the penal code places "sexual perverts."

While the usage of the term *sexual deviance* to denote a variety of nonconformist sexual categories is prejudicial to the rights of "the other," it can be argued that the general term and its vague meaning was intended to continue the long Islamic tradition of tolerating homosexuality. Far from using the punishment of sexual deviance to deter homosexuals, the state has only rarely intervened to oppose homosexual practices. To be sure, Arabic newspapers carry occasionally news items about the prosecution of "sexual deviants" but the "crime" only rarely applies to homosexual acts. It would be erroneous to study homosexuality in the Arab world through a reproduction of legal statues applying to the practice in the countries' legal systems.[33] Furthermore, these laws are indebted to European penal codes.[34]

Some Characteristics of Present-day Sexism and Sexuality among the Arabs

Persistence of Male Dominance

Despite denials of apologetic nationalism that react strongly to any criticisms of the post-colonial state, male dominance remains a feature of Arab societies. The persistence of male domination, however, should not imply—as it has implied for classical Orientalists—the passive obedience of women, the notion that women are not only oppressed, but that they accept their oppression willingly. In the words of Martha Olcott, the doyen of American experts on Central Asia, "most women [in Central Asia] seem to philosophically accept their fate."[35]

The assumptions regarding fatalistic consequences of Islamic belief were applied to the explanation of the status of women. No attention was paid to women's resistance and opposition, not even in the writings of specialists and travelers who knew better, or should have known better. It was easier to accept the assumptions of transmitted wisdom of classical orientalists, or it was more appealing to the lazy mind. Male supremacy in the Middle East, unlike the same phenomenon in Western societies, is manifested not only socially, culturally, economically, and politically but also legally. Middle East states appease the clerical establishment by maintaining the traditional omnipotence of religious personal status laws, all of which, in the three monotheistic religions at least, preserve the domination of males over females.

The battle for legal equality has been obstructed in recent times due to the rise of Islamic fundamentalism. The movement wishes to deprive women from recent legal gains, especially in areas of job security and education. Socially, very little progress has been made. Notions of *sharaf* (honor) and *'ird* (a man's honor) still apply to enable the man to control areas of women's lives. For men, as one character in a novel by Najib Mahfouz says, "Nothing stigmatizes men."[36] The state is but a reflection of male supremacy in the family: the leader is the father figure with the privileges of the use of force and social control maintained intact.

Women and the Public Space

Fatima Mernissi once observed that the cornerstone of women's oppression in the Arab world lies in the limitations placed on a woman's ability to move freely in space.[37] In societies where measures of democratic deliberations are narrowly and restrictively permitted (like in Lebanon, Jordan, and Egypt), women are also restricted from the public sphere. Arab democratic institutions have been created to enhance the legitimacy of precarious governments; they were not intended to invite men and women to express their needs and to participate in decision making. These institutions were understood by some of the Arab leaders, like the King of Jordan, as an extension of the traditional tribal basis of their leaderships. Thus, the roles of women were discouraged; they were seen as an inconvenience that could upset the delicate alliance between the ruling elite and the clerical establishment.

Tolerated Homosexuals

In his classic *Christianity, Social Tolerance and Homosexuality*, John Boswell maintains that "most Muslim cultures have treated homosexuals with in- difference, if not admiration."[38] He generally observes a positive Islamic attitude toward homosexuals. For the strict Muslim of present-day Arab world, Islam is seen as strictly, in the juridical sense, prohibitive of homosexuality. Homosexuality is now either attributed to a historic invasion of Khurasanian morals, or to the invasion of Western values and practices. One Amin 'Abdullah Al-Gharib blames the spread of VCRs and the circulation of imported films for the existence of homosexual acts.[39] This position, as was said earlier, does not represent the original Islamic position.

The coexistence of Islam and homosexuality is related to the Islamic theory of sexuality and to the acceptance of the normalcy of sexual desires among men and women. The construction of modern masculinity in Western societies was not similar to that in Eastern societies. The rigid lines of separation and distinction between males and females, or between homosexuals and heterosexuals, were lines of qualitative moral designation. Males and heterosexuals represent the ideal social and natural roles, from the standpoint of established clerical opinion. Homosexuals do not constitute the personification of sexual violators. Islamic jurisprudence did not dwell in the past on the necessity of their punishment. Even in cases where some Arab countries have legislated strict penal measures against sodomy the state rarely enforces the law in those areas. There are cases, however, when the state chooses to punish a poor and powerless individual for a "homosexual offense" but only to send a message of moral strictness to religious leaders.

What has allowed the state to be lax in the enforcement of laws pertaining to homosexuality is the concept of masculinity in the Arab context. Arab masculinity does not negate any sexual experience with another male. Repressive sexual mores regarding males and females have normalized bisexual and homosexual experiences as a natural prelude to sex within a marriage. Not that all men cease their homosexual activities after marriage; far from that, the marriage becomes a camouflage for most Arab gay men although a few are willing to bear the social consequences of single life and in some cases ostrasization.

Furthermore, the ideology of homophobia, as an ideology of hostility against men who are homosexuals, came out of the Christian tradition and has no counterpart in the Islamic tradition despite the homophobic inclination of individual Muslims, like 'Ali or Abu Bakr in early Islam. Violence against homosexuals, which is still common in Western societies, is quite rare among the Arabs, while violence against women remains a universal phenomenon.

The Attractive Taboo

The relationship between the Arabs and sex is a strange one. Historically, early Muslims developed a healthy attitude toward the subject of sexual desire accepting its consequences in human psychology. In modern times, the Arab had to undergo a change, a change that reversed the past framework of sexuality as was established in Hadith. Sexual desires became shameful in themselves and puritanical standards prevailed to the delight of religious leaders. But discussion of sexual issues is rather confused in both Western and Arab writings. In Western writings, it is assumed that sexual issues do not figure in Arab writings, while some Arab writers may pretend that sex, like homosexuality, is a Western phenomenon. Yet, any examination of *fatawas* in Arabic or Persian illustrate the centrality of sexual matters among the religiously minded. Indeed, there is a degree of obsession with sexual concerns in the question-and-answer segments of the religious pages in Arabic and Persian newspapers.

Contemporary Islamic attitudes recognize the sexual desires of men while women's sexuality is now ignored, assumed to be nonexistent, at least among Muslim women. There is no attention in the literature to those women who practiced free love and free sex in Islamic history. It is left for the Arabic erotic literature to compile poems by lesbian women. Walladah bint al-Mustakfi, the famed poetess of Islamic Spain, remains unknown in Muslim lands. Ibn Bassam cites one line of poetry by her in his classic *Adh-Dhakhirah fi Mahasin Ahl Al-Jazirah*: "I give my cheek to whoever loves me/and I give my kiss to anybody who desires it."[40] He criticizes her for "flaunting her pleasures." Much of the poetry of Walladah (in praise of her female lover poetess Muhjah) was not saved because most authors refused to cite them due to their explicit sexual language.[41] The suppression of literary expression of free love/sex, and of free thinking in general, hinders the tasks of scholarly study of social relations in Islam. Recent attention to Waqf records in Ottoman times will solve this problem because only property owning women figured prominently in those registers.

Conclusion

The study of gender and sexual issues in the Middle East is still incomplete and preliminary. Gender studies have achieved great progress in the last two decades when Western and Eastern women have conducted empirical studies of women's lives that contrasted with literary Orientalist fantasies. Anthropologists have allowed women to speak for themselves, without having to go through the "mature" and "wise" filter of Western judgment. Most studies of the East have in the past suffered from a heavy tone of judgment. Easterners were of interest to the researcher (in the social sciences and humanities) insofar as they deviated from or approached Western lifestyles. Any signs of democratic or egalitarian aspirations were simply attributed to healthy needs for imitation of the West. It is not that the West represents, for its Western and Eastern advocates, a viable alternative to a detested reality, but that it becomes the sole answer for all social, economic, and political problems. If "Islam is the solution" summarizes the political agenda of Islamic fundamentalists, "the West is the solution" is the secular version of reductionist solutions.

The rise of Islamic fundamentalists has exacerbated social and sexual tensions in the regions. Not all of those problems can be analyzed in isolation of economic and political developments. Fixation with women's issues increases with the rise in unemployment figures; this makes it easier for strict fundamentalists to mobilize their followers behind slogans of "returning women to the home." Similarly, the popularity of the veil among new segments of the urban female population is not unrelated to the crowdedness of the street and the problems of sexual harassment. The veil then serves as a sign by women, a signal to their piety. Western attention to the veil only underlines the inability of many in the West to identify the underlying causes of Islamic fundamentalism. Not all of those causes are religious in nature.

Homosexuals remain outside of the scope of academic studies. The study of homosexuality in Middle East studies will almost guarantee a future of academic unemployment. Moreover, many heterosexuals avoid the study of homosexuality for fear of the homosexual stigma, the fear of which still afflicts Western and Eastern societies. This has enabled homophobes and journalists in the East and West to study to subject for pure ideological reasons. The works of *turath* (heritage) from the Arab/Islamic civilization remain untapped as far as the study of sexuality and gender is concerned. The exploration of those works will undoubtedly produce results that clash with the established opinions of Islamic official canons. Neither the state nor the religious establishment will permit free interpretations in those areas that now define "Islamic morality." The task, however, is not to serve this or that state's interests but to explore the ways in which gender boundaries and sexual identities developed over time. Assumptions of postmodernists regarding the rejection of metanarratives and opposition to classical social and sexual divisions are will be of help to all those who approach this subject with an open mind, and free of the taboos of religion and of the state.

Notes

1. See the classic Daniel, Norman. *Islam and the West: The Making of an Image* (Oxford: Oneworld, 1993); and Southern, R.W., *Western Views of Islam in the Middle Ages* (Cambridge: Harvard University Press, 1962).

2. Said, Edward W., *Orientalism* (New York: Vintage, 1978).

3. Moore, Barrington Jr., *The Social Origins of Dictatorship and Democracy* (Boston: Beacon Press, 1984), p. 486.

4. Rodinson, Maxime, *La fascination de l'islam suivi de Le seigneur bourguignon et l'esclave sarrasin* (Paris: La Decouverte, 1989), p. 120.

5. Lewis, Bernard, *Islam and the West* (NY: Oxford University Press, 1993).

6. Ibid, p. 4.

7. See Norman, *op. cit.*, p. 164–169.

8. Al-Jahiz. *Rasa'il Al-Jahiz* (Letters of Al-Jahiz). (Cairo: Maktabat AL-Khanji, 1965), vol. 2, p. 92.

9. See Fernea, Elizabeth W., and Bezirgan, Basima Q., *Middle Eastern Muslim Women Speak* (Austin: University of Texas Press, 1977), pp. xviii–xix.

10. Habermas, Jurgen. *The Structural Transformation of the Public Sphere* (Cambridge University Press, 1991).

11. Surat an-Nisa', Ayat 1. Translations from Arabic are all mine unless otherwise indicated.

12. Surat Al-Baqarah. Ayat 223.

13. Surat Al-Baqarah. Ayat 222.

14. See 'Ali's speech after the battle of al-Jama. In 'Ali ibn Abi Talib, *Nahj al-Balaghah* (Path of Eloquence), (Beirut: Dar Al-Andalus, 1963), pp. 133–134.

15. For a learned and sophisticated champion of this school, see As-Salih, Ash-Shaykh Subhi. *AL-Mar'ah fi-l-Islam* (Woman in Islam), (Beirut: Beirut University College, 1990).

16. An-Nisa', Ayat 34.

17. Ibid.

18. Ibid.

19. Brandt, Paul. *Sexual Life in Ancient Greece*, translated by J.H. Freese (NY: Barnes and Nobles, 1963).

20. Schmitt, Arno and Sofer, Jehoeda, eds., *Sexuality and Eroticism among Males in Moslem Societies* (NY: The Haworth Press, 1992), p. 6.

21. Mez, Adam. *Die Renaissance Des Islams*, translated by Slahuddin Khuda Bukhsh and D.S. Margoliouth (London: Luzac & Co., 1937), p. 358. This claim was supported by Charles Pellat without any further proof.

22. Djait, Hichem. *La Personalite et le Devenir Arabo-Islamiques* (Paris: Editions du Seuil, 1974), ch. 5.

23. Pellat, Charles. "Liwat." In Bosworth, C.E., et al., eds., *The Encyclopedia of Islam*, New Edition (Leiden: Brill, 1986), vol. V, p. 776. The authorship of this anonymous entry was revealed by Schmitt in Schmitt, Arno, and Sofer, J., eds., *op. cit.*, p. 151.

24. Al-Jahiz. *Kitab Mufakharat Al-Jawari wa-l-Ghilman*. In Harun, 'Abd-us-Salam Muhammad, ed., *Rasa'il Al-Jahiz* (Letters of Al-Jahiz), vol. 2 (Cairo: Maktabat Al-Khanji, 1965).

25. Abu Nuwwas. *Diwan Abu Nuwwas* (Beirut: Dar Sadir, 1962), p. 130.

26. As-Siyuti. *Tarikh Al-Khulafa'* (History of the Caliphs), (Cairo: Ahmad Al-Babi al-Halabi, 1305 A.H.), p. 118.

27. Mez, Adam, *op. cit.*, p. 357.

28. Abu Nuwwas, *op. cit.*, p. 116.

29. For a biographical sketch of him, see As-Siyuti, *op. cit.*, pp. 135–137.

30. Schmitt and Sofer, *op. cit.*, p. 10.

31. Bouhdhiba prefers "hermaphrodite" as a translation. See Bouhdhiba, A. *La sexualite en Islam* (Paris: Presses Universitaires de France, 1979), pp. 55–57.

32. Pellat, *op. cit.*, p. 777.

33. Schmitt and Sofer, *op. cit.*, pp. 131–146.

34. Ibid, p. 133.

35. Olcott, Martha. "Women and Society in Central Asia." In Fierman, William, ed., *Soviet Central Asia: The Failed Transformation* (Boulder: Westview Press, 1991), p. 236.

36. Mahfouz, Najib. *Zuqaq al-Midaqq* (Beirut: Dar Al-Qalam, 1972), p. 63.

37. See Mernissi, Fatima. *Beyond the Veil* (Bloomington: Indiana University Press, 1987).

38. Boswell, John. *Christianity, Social Tolerance and Homosexuality* (Chicago: University of Chicago Press, 1980), p. 194.

39. Al-Gharib, Amin 'Abdullah. *Nadhrat Al-Islam ila-l-Liwat wa-l-Istimna'* (The Perspective of Islam toward Homosexuality and Masturbation), (Beirut: Mu'assasat Al-A'la, 1989), pp. 16–17.

40. Ibn Bassam. *Adh-Dhakhirah fi Mahasin Ahl Al-Jazirah* (Cairo: Fu'ad I University, 1939), part I, vol. 1, p. 379.

41. On Walladah, see Hoenerbach, W. "Zur Charakteristik Walladas, Der Geliebten Ibn Zaiduns." In *Die Welt des Islams*, vol. 13 (1971). She became known as the woman who broke Ibn Zaydun's heart.

[13]

THE SHARIA, ISLAMIC FAMILY LAWS AND INTERNATIONAL HUMAN RIGHTS LAW: EXAMINING THE THEORY AND PRACTICE OF POLYGAMY AND TALAQ

JAVAID REHMAN*

ABSTRACT

This article assesses the compatibility of the Sharia and Islamic family laws with international human rights law. As a subject of enormous complexity and variation, detailed examination is restricted to two of the highly contentious subjects of Islamic family laws – polygamy and the Talaq (unilateral divorce given by the husband) within Islam. It is argued that while the Quran and Sunna remain the principal foundations of the Sharia, the formulation of a legally binding code from primarily ethical and religious sources has not been an uncontested matter. It is also submitted that the Sharia and Islamic family laws that eventually emerged during the second and third centuries of the Muslim calendar were heavily influenced by the socio-economic, political and indigenous tribal values of the prevailing times. During the development phases of the classical legal schools, the Islamic jurists frequently adopted male-centric approaches towards women's rights and family laws. As regards polygamy and the Talaq it is only recently (and with considerable reservations) that Islamic societies have allowed a debate and enquiry into the reform of established norms of the Sharia. Attempts to rectify the injustices built into the prevailing system of polygamous marriages and unilateral Talaq procedures have resulted in some, albeit limited, success through the process of directly appealing to the primary sources of the Sharia. The article concludes with the view that the Sharia and Islamic family laws are likely to remain relevant to Islamic societies as well as to English Law – a consistent review and re-interpretation of the Sharia is therefore of utmost significance.

* Javaid Rehman, Professor of International Law, Brunel University, London. email Javaid.Rehman@Brunel.ac.uk. Member of the Committee of Islamic and International Law, International Law Association, United Kingdom. This is an updated version of a paper presented to the Senior Judiciary of England and Wales at the Royal Courts of Justice, London (June 2006). I am very grateful to Mrs Justice Laura Cox and Lord Justice Keene for their generous invitation to present the paper and to the Judicial Studies Board for sponsoring the seminar; to John Eekelaar for his extremely helpful comments and for his generous encouragement. I thank the anonymous reviewer for his constructive comments on an earlier draft. I am also grateful to Professor Martha Fineman, Woodruff Professor, Law School, Emory University (USA) for her comments on the paper.

INTRODUCTION

Islam and Muslims are the subjects of considerable attention both internationally as well as within the UK (Rehman, 2000; Rehman, 2003/4). Amidst the wider debate of 'war-on-terror', differing approaches towards human rights, and a possible 'clash of civilizations', issues around divergent approaches to personal and family laws only rarely manage headline news (Rehman, 2005). Notwithstanding, the relative lack of a comprehensive understanding of Islamic family laws and social values, the subject matter is significant for the UK's legal and judicial systems. The continued relevance of Islamic family and personal laws is highlighted by the consistent invocation of the Sharia principles and the projection of diversity and religious pluralism within domestic courts (Poulter, 1986; Poulter, 1998). Requirements of the Sharia have been invoked in such contentious matters as the veil, headscarves and the wearing of Jilbab at work and in educational institutions,[1] education,[2] formalities and capacity to enter a marriage (on proxy marriages, see Poulter 1990),[3] validity of arranged or forced marriages,[4] recognition of polygamous marriages (Shah, 2003; Murphy, 2000),[5] consequence of the Talaq (unilateral divorce by the husband) (Mayss, 2000),[6] and Muslim religious obligations during employment.[7] Although the aforementioned issues have to be adjudicated by judicial and administrative officers in accordance with English law, it is often the case that elements of international law – through private international law, human rights law and application of Sharia law as foreign law – have to be factored in judicial decision-making.

The present article focuses on those aspects of Islamic Sharia that relate to Islamic family laws and in so doing assesses the question of compatibility of the Sharia with modern international human rights law. As a subject of enormous complexity and variation, detailed examination is restricted to two highly contentious subjects of Islamic family laws – polygamy and the Talaq within Islam. The article is divided into four sections. Section 1 examines the sources of the Sharia and Islamic family laws. While contextualizing the debate on issues surrounding polygamy and Talaq, sections 2 and 3 examine the reform movements within contemporary Islamic States.[8] The final section provides a number of concluding observations.

1. ARTICULATING THE SOURCES OF THE SHARIA AND ISLAMIC FAMILY LAWS

The concept of Islamic family laws encapsulates primarily those areas of the Sharia that deal with marriage, divorce, maintenance, custody of children and succession (see An-Naim, 2002; Pearl and Menski, 1998;

Mallat and Connors, 1990; Esposito, 1982). As a significant branch of the Sharia, the modern application of Islamic family laws necessitates an understanding of sources and composition of the Sharia principles. The articulation of the substance of the Sharia in the context of Islamic family laws also raises challenging questions about the apparent inconsistencies between the Sharia and modern human rights law. Examples of such discrepancies include the continuation of the institution of polygamy, criminal offences for sexual relations outside marriage and for homosexual activity, the concept of Talaq, maintenance post-divorce, succession laws, and the absence of the concept of adoption (Mayer, 1995; Weeramantry, 1988; Baderin, 2003; Afshari, 1994; Riga, 1991; Entelis, 1997; Ali, 2000. For an overlap between Islamic criminal law and sexual offences see Bassiouni, 1982).

Islamic family laws derive from two fundamental sources of the Sharia: the Quran and the Sunna. The Quran, according to Muslim belief, represents the accumulation of the verses revealed by God to Prophet Muhammad (Denny, 1994; Weeramantry, 1988; Lombardi, 1998). According to the Islamic faith, every word of the Holy Quran is divine and cannot be challenged. Neither Prophet Muhammad nor any other human being had any influence over the divine book, save for its structuring and the names of the *surahs* (chapters) which were established in the years that followed the Prophet's death. While meticulously noted down, and revealed in stages during the lifetime of the Prophet, the Quran was produced as an authentic text only during the currency of the third Caliph Hazrat Uthmān (Mahmassani, 1966; Coulson, 1964; Zweigert and Kötz, 1998). The Quran is aimed at establishing basic standards for Muslim societies and guiding these communities in terms of their rights and responsibilities. At the time of its revelation it provided a set of progressive principles. It advanced such values as compassion, good faith, justice and religious ethics with reformist ideals. The Quran, however, is not a legal document and its primarily ethico-religious revelations should not be equated to *lex lata*; in fact there is little in the Quran with strict legal content. From over 6000 verses of the Quran, strict legal content is arguably attached to only around 80 verses (Badr, 1978; Ali, 1997a; Glenn, 2000, Coulson, 1964)[9] and, 'even in these verses there are both gaps as well as doubts as to whether the legal injunction is obligatory or permissive, as indeed whether it is subject to public or private sanction' (Pearl and Menski, 1998: 3). Save for a few specific offences, there is no indication of criminal sanctions (An-Na'im, 1990). Even in the context of the most serious crimes for which penalties are prescribed, the evidential requirements are stringent to ensure that punishment is awarded only in the absence of any doubt as to the commission of the crime by the accused through requisite *mens rea* (Bassiouni, 1982: 3–54). Some regulations can be identified in relation to personal and family laws, though establishing the scope, nature and application of these norms has proved complex and complicated (Esposito, 1982). Indeed the Quran provides its own description as Huda, or guidance and not as a legally binding code. Therefore, the principal attribute of the divine book is in providing 'sublime statements of the ought to be the Holy Quran contains a comprehensive and perfect world-and-life view'(Ragi al-Fruqi, 1962: 35).

If extrapolating legal norms from the Quranic verses has proved onerous, derivation of laws based on Sunna of the Prophet has been riddled with debate and controversy. The Sunna – the second principal source of Islam – represents model behaviour and is referred to as the tradition and practices of Muhammad, the Prophet of Islam. The Sunna of the Prophet has been expanded through the practices of Prophet Muhammad's followers and other Islamic leaders (Rehman, 2005). The concept of Sunna had been in vogue long before the birth of Muhammad and was actively practised by contemporary Arab communities. While maintaining its characteristics, the application of Prophet Muhammad's Sunna took on board a more profound spiritual and religious meaning. It was to be, after the word of God, the most revered source of knowledge and legal acumen. The Sunna of Prophet Muhammad, in the words of one scholar, 'is an idea as well as a memory, and it is an ideal for Muslim behaviour. As such it is engrained in the lives of pious Muslims and handed down by example and personal teaching' (Denny, 1994: 159). The memorization and transmission of the Sunna in a literary form is characterized as *hadith*. The term *hadith* with the meaning 'occurring, taking place' represents the 'report' of Prophet Muhammad's Sunna (Weeramantry, 1988). The Sunna of Muhammad therefore is preserved and communicated to the succeeding generations through the means of hadiths (Al-Mūsawi, 1997).[10] While the Quran was recorded within a relatively short time, the recording of the Sunna took a much longer period. (Mahmassani, 1966). Several elements of the Sunna were derived from sources not readily identifiable or reliable. Over the proceeding centuries, there has developed a significant debate regarding the authenticity and accuracy of some of the Sunna, with legal scholars suggesting the possibility of substantial fabrication in the recording of the Sunna. Commenting on this subject, Coulson (1964: 22) makes the point that 'the extent of (Muhammad's) extra Qur'ānic law-making is the subject of the greatest single controversy in early Islamic legal theory'. The early jurists, attempting to establish firm legal principles of the Sharia, expressed disagreements over the validity or authenticity of a number of the apparent Sunna of the Prophet, and Islamic schools differed in their approaches towards the weight that can be accorded to particular traditions.

In understanding Islamic family laws it is important to comprehend the metamorphosis, growth and contextualization of the Sharia. The labyrinth of religious, ethical and moral raw materials derived from the two principal sources, Quran and Sunna, were given shape and direction by Islamic scholars and jurists during the second and third centuries of the Muslim calendar. The codification of the Sharia within Sunni Islam was principally the work of four jurists: Abu Hanifa (d 767/150); Malak ibn Anas (d 795/179); Muhammad ibn Idris al-Shafi (d 820/204); and Ahmad Hanbal (d 855/241). In the absence of concrete answers from the Quran and Sunna, Muslim jurists would look for analogous situations in which a decision had been made and in this process relied upon a range of secondary sources including Ijma and Qiyas (Mir-Hosseni, 1999). Ijma, meaning 'consensus', was an important secondary source providing the Islamic community essential tools to reach agreements. It also provided a powerful methodology in the interpretation of the Quran and Sunna. A useful operation was derived from Qiyas which means application by analogy or deduction (Kamali, 1991).[11] The modus operandi of deducing legal norms from the secondary sources of Qiyas and Ijma was through the process of Ijtihad. A person who engaged in Ijtihad was described as Mujtahid. In elaborating on the functioning of the doctrine, Weiss (1978: 199–200) makes the observation that 'the process of extracting or deriving (*istinbāt, istithmār*) legal rules from sources of the Law is termed, with reference to its character as a human activity, ijtihad'. Ijtihad conveyed a sense of exertion, a struggle, and has the same origins as that of Jihad. Inherent in this self-exertion and struggle were the fundamentals for reforming the society and its legal norms. (On the meaning of Jihad, see Ali and Rehman, 2005.)

Whilst unrivalled in their sincerity for developing pristine values of the Sharia, the founders of the four Sunni schools in reality established legal principles in accordance with their own subjective understanding of Islam (Rehman, 2002; Moinuddin, 1987). In the broader, pragmatic framework, the articulation of the Sharia principles and the classical Islamic family laws is therefore no more than the expression of values advanced by these jurists of the second and third century of the Muslim calendar. However, the difficulty faced by subsequent Islamic societies is that very often reviewing established norms has been treated as being tantamount to heresy. For considerable periods Muslim scholars remained reluctant to rely upon the doctrine of Ijtihad, since such an exercise implied questioning the time-honoured (though static) principles of the Sharia (Schacht, 1964; Coulson, 1964). Within Islamic jurisprudence Ijtihad, as a process and as a strategy, has retained a contested position. On the one hand it was vehemently argued that all doors towards Ijtihad were closed leading to Taqlid, 'imitation' and the acceptance of established authority (Mir-Hosseini, 2000; Vogel, 1993). On the other hand there are modern theorists such as Hallaq (1997; 2001) who have presented an aggressive rebuttal of the position that

Ijtihad was ever formally abandoned, claiming instead its continuation throughout Islamic history. The truth probably lies in the middle ground adopted by Schacht. In his classical work on Islamic law, Schacht notes that:

[t]he rule of *taklīd* did not impose itself without opposition... In later generations also there were scholars who held that there would always be a mujtahid in existence or who were inclined to claim for themselves that they fulfilled the incredibly high demands which the theory had, by then, laid down as a qualification for ijtiāhad. But these claims, as far as positive law was concerned, remained theoretical and none of the scholars who made them actually produced an independent interpretation of the Shar'īa. Other scholars did not so much claim ijtiāhad for themselves as reject the principle of taklīd (1964: 72).

2. CONTEXTUALIZING THE PRINCIPLES OF THE SHARIA AND ISLAMIC FAMILY LAWS

The principal sources of the Sharia and Islamic family laws, the Quran and Sunna, represent progressive values – the legal regulations that are extrapolated from both these sources advocate, in particular, welfare of women and children. The Quran and Sunna introduced substantial improvements in the standing of women. In Pre-Islamic Arabia, women, like slaves, did not have legal standing and were deemed to be chattels – their sale and purchase was conducted collectively by the tribal elders on behalf of the tribe (see Barlas, 2002; Pearl and Menski (1998: 4) consider women in Pre-Islamic Arabia as 'objects of sale'). In the marriage process, the sale of the wife was conducted in consideration of dower (*mahar*) provided by the husband. After the transfer, the wife was the property of the husband and the larger tribe. Women did not have any legal rights or the capacity to bring claims to change their status. Instant Talaq was a customary practice and was frequently deployed. There were other abominable institutions and practices such as (female) infanticide and unlimited polygamy.

One of the major legal innovations introduced by the Quran and Sunna was to award a legal personality to women – under the Sharia they have an independent right to enter into marriage, which is deemed a civil contract legalizing sexual relations and procreation (Mannan, 1991). As a civil contract, the only formalities that are attached to the marriage are the offer of marriage by the husband and its acceptance by the wife in the presence of two witnesses (Nasir, 1990). There are, however, issues of equality and non-discrimination – the Sharia permits polygamous marriages, a Muslim male being entitled to have valid marriages with up to four wives simultaneously. According to classical interpretations of the Sharia, while a male Muslim is allowed to marry 'woman (women) of the book' which includes Christians, Jews and Zoroastrians, a Muslim female is restricted to entering into marriage only with Muslims. A valid marriage can be contracted from the age of puberty, classical Sharia equating puberty with the age of majority. Certain Islamic schools also granted authority to the parent or the guardian (wali) to enforce child marriages, with the so-called 'option of puberty' whereby marriage is rescindable when the child attains puberty or majority. The 'option of puberty' is based on juristic interpretations of Islamic family laws and is neither stated in the Quran nor is it derived from the Sunna.[12]

Polyandry is not permitted, so that Muslim women cannot have more than one husband at the same time. While there are some differences of approach within Islamic legal schools, polygamy is legitimized both by the Quran and the Sunna. This legitimacy of polygamy is reflected in modern Islamic States practices, whereby an overwhelming majority of States authorize polygamous marriages, albeit with a variety of restrictions and sanctions. The rules relating to Islamic family law, including polygamy, have led to numerous reservations by Islamic States to the Convention on the Elimination of All forms of Discrimination against Women 1979 (Rehman, 2003; Rehman, 1997).

The permissibility of polygamy within Islamic family law raises two fundamental questions: firstly, were there any rational reasons for legitimizing polygamous marriages within the Sharia and, secondly, can polygamy be justified in the light of the prohibition in international law? An instant response is to suggest that the Sharia has been insensitive towards women's rights and that continuation of such practices as polygamy is discriminatory and contrary to modern human rights law. Without challenging the prejudicial and biased nature of contemporary polygamous unions, it is submitted that the hastiness in the condemnation of historic Islamic principles fails to take account of the contextual, and flexible nature of the Sharia and the rules of Islamic family law. In assessing the rationality of the Sharia principles it is important to have regard to the seventh century Arabian tribal customs as well as the then persisting socio-economic circumstances. The Quran and the Sunna provided a reformist and enlightened code of family values to a society engaged in substantial violation of women's and children's rights. Insofar as the institution of polygamy is concerned it is persuasive to say that, save for exceptional circumstances, the classical sources of the Sharia have perceived monogamous relationship as an ideal form of association. The following Quranic verses are often taken as legitimizing polygamy. The Quran notes:

Hand over their property to the orphans and do not exchange the bad for the good, and do not devour their property mixing it with your own. Surely, that is a great sin. Should you apprehend that you will not be able to deal fairly with orphans, then marry of other women as may be agreeable to you, two or three, or four; but if you feel you will not deal justly between them, then marry only one . . . that is the best way for you to obviate injustice (The Quran, IV: 3–5).

To invoke the above verses as an unrestricted licence for continuing the institution of polygamous marriages is contrary to the spirit of the Quran. An examination of the Quranic verses reveals the highly restrictive nature of polygamy with the Sharia. The permissibility to engage in a polygamous marriage, as Barlas (2002) has argued, 'serves a very specific purpose: that of securing *justice for female orphans*' (italics provided at 190). There are additional caveats and conditions, which form an essential precondition to entering a polygamous marriage. The *Quranic* ideal clearly is to establish monogamous union, which is also affirmed in Sura Al-Nisa, whereby the Quran notes, 'You cannot keep perfect balance emotionally between your wives, however much you desire it' (IV: 130).

Furthermore, the context in which the aforementioned Quranic verses were revealed also demonstrates their pragmatic nature. The divine ordinance was communicated to the Prophet in the aftermath of the bloody battle of Uhud (625 A.D.) which had resulted in the loss of many male warriors leaving scores of young women widowed and children orphaned. As the Sharia and Islamic family laws developed in the second and third centuries, legal scholars removed themselves from the pragmatic and reformist spirit of the Quran and the Sunna. The male dominated societies of the Arab and Muslim world entered into an abuse of the system with considerable exploitation of the rights of women and children with biased construction of 'Islamic jurisprudence where gender neutral terms have been translated and interpreted as masculine, thus creating gender hierarchies and unequal rights for men and women' (Ali, 1997b: 199).

Given the changes in the social, political and legal environment, the continuation of the practice of polygamy demands a substantial explanation. Many of the historic reasons within the Islamic world for justifying polygamous marriages (for example, the surplus of women and loss of men through battles and armed conflict) are no longer tenable. Yet, it is undoubtedly the case that there remains a huge socio-economic imbalance between the position of men and women within Islamic societies. There is also an absence of a social-security network within contemporary Islamic States to prevent the exploitation of economically dependent vulnerable divorced women. Modern constitutional and State laws must advance sufficiently to close the socio-economic gap. Until complete equality between men and women is reached, polygamy as an institution could arguably serve to protect those women who would otherwise be condemned, discarded or abandoned in that society through the operation of divorce or nullity laws.

In anticipation of a developmental stage ensuring socio-economic gender equality and a complete abolition of polygamy, various legislative and administrative strategies have been adopted by Islamic societies. Firstly, reliance has been placed upon the legal doctrine of *takhayyar* (eclectic choice) (Hallaq, 1997; Coulson, 1969). As a modern phenomenon, *takhayyar* denotes selection of the most appealing and appropriate doctrine from amongst the existing Islamic schools. Such an approach provides a more equitable solution in circumstances where insistence on the application of the principles derived from any one school would lead to injustice (Hallaq, 2004). In the context of Islamic family laws, the application of *takhayyar* has allowed the incorporation of specific clauses within the contract of marriage, prohibiting the husband to enter into polygamous marriages or other actions detrimental to the interests of the wife. Within the classical understanding of the Sunni Islamic schools of thought, such clauses were only permissible within the Hanabali school but not in the Hanafi school. However, the usage of *takhayyar* doctrine authorized Islamic jurists from all schools of thought to specifically incorporate provisions in marriage contracts prohibiting polygamous marriages. Secondly, Islamic communities have, at long last, expressed greater readiness to adopt a contextual and methodological interpretation of the Quranic provisions. This has resulted in significant limitations placed on polygamous marriages, for example in Pakistan,[13] Syria, [14] Iraq[15] or through its outright abolition, as in the case of Tunisia. [16]

Pakistan, with its unique religious-political history, presents a complicated case for the application of the Sharia and Islamic family laws (Mehdi, 1994; Ali and Rehman, 2003). In the pre-partition Indian subcontinent, Hindus and Muslims continued to determine matters of family law through the dictates of established personal laws. The British colonial rulers specifically required Muslim and Hindu religious experts to assist local courts over personal and family law matters. There thus emerged a mixed brand of law, known as 'Anglo-Mohammadan' law. A number of limited legislative reforms were nevertheless injected into customary practices and the operation of family laws. Notable amongst these were the Code of Civil Procedure 1859, the Indian Penal Code 1860, the Code of Criminal Procedure 1861, the Evidence Act 1872 and most significantly the Dissolution of Muslim Marriages Act 1939 which, as considered below, impacted upon the application of classical Hanafi grounds of granting divorce (Pearl and Menski, 1998). In its post-independence period, the most significant piece of legislative enactment, the Muslim Family Laws Ordinance 1961 has created various restrictions on polygamous marriages.

A system of compulsory registration was introduced for all marriages solemnized under Muslim law.[17] Prior to entering into a polygamous marriage, Muslim men are required to obtain the written permission of the Arbitration Council, a Council which consists of a representative of existing wife (or wives), his own representative and a neutral chairperson.[18] In addition to stating the reasons for a proposed polygamous marriage, the petitioner is also required to inform the Council as to whether the consent or agreement of the existing wife or wives has been obtained.[19] A second or further marriage is only permissible once the Arbitration Council is satisfied as to its 'necessity and just' nature in accordance with the Rules laid down in pursuance of the Muslim Family Laws Ordinance 1961. Rule 14, in defining 'just and necessary', points towards the following grounds: physical unfitness, insanity, infertility, sterility of the wife (wives) and wilful avoidance of a decree for restitution of conjugal rights on the part of the existing wife (wives).[20]

Notwithstanding this substantial move towards restricting polygamous marriages, the legislative sanctions placed are minuscule and have served as an ineffective deterrent. In practice, there are significant breaches of many of the key provisions of the ordinance, relating to registration of the marriage or obtaining the requisite permission. A marriage that is contracted without the permission of the Arbitration Council nevertheless remains valid. The limited penalties that are attached to the failure to comply with s 6 provisions – immediate payment of the dower to existing wife (wives) and imprisonment up to one year – are rarely, if ever, enforced (Farani, 1992). Furthermore, the Islamization process during the years of General Zia-ul-Haq (1977–88) reinvigorated the debate over Pakistan's credentials as an Islamic State, and the demand by the Muslim clergy for the repeal of the Muslim Family Laws Ordinance 1961. General Zia introduced several laws, such as the notorious Hudood Ordinances (1979) and the Qanoon-e-Shahadit Act (1984) which had a substantially damaging effect on the rights of women and religious communities (Jahangir and Jilani, 1990; Rehman, 2001). In contrast to Pakistan, the Tunisian legislative prohibition of polygamous marriages represents a positive and forceful assertion of the proper understanding and re-interpretation of the Sharia. The rationale behind the law is that the present social, economic and political conditions place an irrebutable presumption of monogamous Muslim marriages: the condition of justice and equity amongst wives s perceived not only in an economic and financial sense, but also from the perspective of love, affection and emotional attachment which cannot be disturbed equally in a polygamous relationship (Doi, 1984; Hinchcliffe, 1970).[21] This Tunisian legislative prohibition on polygamy epitomizes the sentiment which was adopted by an active and interventionist judiciary in Bangladesh (formerly East Pakistan) where in the case of *Jesmin Sultana* v *Mohammad Elias*[22] the High Court demanded the repeal of s 6 of the Muslim Family Laws Ordinance 1961 and the imposition of provisions banning polygamy (Pearl and Menski, 1998).

3. ISLAMIC FAMILY LAW AND THE CONTROVERSY OVER TALAQ

Both the Quran and the Sunna – the primary sources of the Sharia and Islamic family law – present negative attitudes towards Talaq (see The Quran, LXVI: 1). A number of Quranic verses discourage Talaq and deter those engaged in such practices (The Quran, LXVI: 1). In many of the Quranic verses equality is advocated between husbands and wives during their marital relationship. The Sharia principles as they developed within the Islamic schools of thought (during the second and third century) nevertheless did not translate the Quranic reservations on divorce law into legal ordinances. On the contrary, the legal schools influenced by the prevailing social, economic and political conditions granted significant advantages to husbands over wives in the process. All Islamic schools permit Talaq, with the right to divorce being regarded as 'unencumbered' within the Hanafi School (Esposito, 1982: 31). In this interpretation, a Muslim man who has attained the age of puberty has an absolute right to divorce his wife without having or citing any reasons for such an action. The Talaq can be pronounced even in the absence of, and without the involvement of, the wife in the process (Esposito, 1982).

Within the Sharia, women are granted a right to divorce, although they have (depending on the school of thought) the significantly onerous task of obtaining it, invariably by means of a judicial decree. A Khul (also known as Khula) divorce can be obtained by the wife although it requires the consent of the husband and the wife is required to forego part of (or the entirety of) the dower.[23] Reliance on Khul is less arduous as the evidentiary requirements are less exacting and the wife is not required to establish specific grounds for divorce, other than having developed irreconcilable differences with her husband (Balchin and Warrich, 1997). Dissolution of marriage is also permissible through a judicial rescission of the marriage contract. The process of rescission of the marriage by the Qadi at the behest of the wife is known as faskh (annulment or abrogation). Islamic schools have varied significantly over the grounds upon which a wife could claim annulment of the marriage. The Hanafi school, the narrowest of all four Sunni schools, allows such a dissolution of the marriage only where the marriage cannot be consummated as a consequence of a husband's impotence or a husband's desertion for a period of 90 years or where the wife can exercise the 'option of puberty'. Under the classical Hanafi jurisprudence, a wife is unable to divorce even in cases of maltreatment, cruelty or the husband's inability to support her (Carroll, 1996; Esposito, 1982). As will be shown in subsequent discussion, Hanafi law as practised within the Ottoman and Mughal empires was criticized for its highly restrictive approach and was subsequently subjected to scrutiny and reform.

The extremely restrictive and narrow grounds as contained in the Hanafi school are not followed by all schools. The Malaki school – which is the most liberal school – provides women with the right to bring judicial proceedings in instances of cruelty, refusal or inability to provide maintenance, desertion by the husband or disease or ailment of the husband. Although the initial Malaki interpretation of such concepts as cruelty, refusal or inability to maintain and desertion were rigid and biased against women, there has over time been a considerable re-evaluation to generate greater flexibility to meet the social, physical and economic needs of women. Even within schools outside the Sunni *fiqh* there has been re-interpretation and reform. Thus, for example, Iran – a State which operates predominantly under the Shia Jafari school – introduced legal amendments in 1982 whereby the wife is entitled *inter alia* to petition for divorce following the husband's failure to support her for a period up to six months (Mir-Hosseini, 2000; Mir-Hosseini, 1999).[24]

Attempts to redress the balance in favour of women have a long and enduring history. Within Sunni Islam, Egypt and Pakistan provide useful examples. The initial attempts to reform the Hanafi law in Egypt were conducted under the Ottoman tutelage through the Ottoman Law of Rights 1917. However, it was only the Egyptian law (No 25/1920 and law No 25/1929) which brought about significant reforms in the country's personal and family laws. These laws *inter alia* established additional factors (such as the husband's incurable defect or contagious disease, his desertion, failure to provide maintenance and maltreatment) as grounds for divorce petitions (Esposito, 1982). The classical Hanafi rule of 90 years of disappearance of husband was deemed extremely harsh and was replaced by a continuous absence of one year. A further more significant ground established by law 25 of 1929 opened up the possibility of divorce once the court was satisfied as to the irreconcilable differences as a consequence of the husband's maltreatment or harm (*darar*). Additional laws were introduced in 1979, which provided for compulsory registration of Talaq and the requirement that the wife be given notice of the Talaq.[25] The Talaq remained ineffective until the time of its notification to the wife. The husband was obliged to notify the wife of any of his polygamous marriages which would also entitle her to petition for divorce. Failure to obtain permission amounted to an additional basis for the wife to petition for divorce (Arabi, 2001).

The 1979 enactments introduced by President Anwar Saddat were struck down by Egypt's Supreme Court in May 1985 on the basis of their being *ultra vires* the constitution (An-Naim, 2002). Revised legislation, the Law of Personal Status 1985, whilst incorporating the key provisions from the 1920 and 1929 laws on Personal Status, nevertheless withdrew the wife's automatic entitlement to petition for divorce as a consequence of the husband's polygamous marriage. Under the 1985 legislation, the wife had to establish that she had suffered 'harm' as a result of the polygamous marriage. This law was eventually reformed by President Hasani Mubarak in 2000.[26] The 2000 legislation allows a wife to petition for divorce on the grounds of 'incompatibility' within marriage without her having to establish evidence of 'harm' (Human Rights Watch, 2004). The petitioner in this instance must nevertheless agree to forfeit any right of dowry and to return any gifts received by her at the commencement of the marriage. A significant innovation is the provision that the husband's consent to divorcing his wife is not a requirement.[27] It is instructive that the 2000 legislative reforms in Egypt were based not upon any radical modernist agenda, but can be traced through the 'rising neo-shāfism (that) started a process of reconstruction and reinterpretation of Islamic law of historic proportions affecting the whole juridical edifice' (Arabi, 2001: 7). Relying upon the Constitutional Court's decision of 1993, which placed an exclusive reliance upon the formal sources of the Sharia – with definitive origins and meaning (*qat'iyyat al thubūt wa'l dālala*) – Egypt's lawmakers were able to bypass the established Islamic schools of thought, all of which emphasize the requirement of consent on the part of the husband. The Egyptian legislature, in adopting the 2000 law, appealed directly to the sacred text of the Quran and Sunna. The re-interpretation of the so-called 'Habiba' incident in four out of the six authoritative compendia of prophetic lore, and the tenth century canonical *hadith* collections were deployed by jurists to dispense with the requirements of Khul as a consensual divorce settlement. In analysing this rationale for the 2000 Egyptian Law, Arabi makes the insightful comment that:

(t)he Egyptian lawmakers, legislating under the novel constitutional demand that no law promulgated after 22 May 1980 may be allowed to stand if it were to contravene the explicit content of any well-established (in its origin and meaning; *qat'iyyat al thubūt wa'l dālala*) sacred text, actually put this demand to profit by their reverting to the *sunna* collections. The wording in all these collections, we have seen, is very clear to the Prophet commanding Thābit to take back his garden and divorce Habība, without any indication that he sought the former's consent; and the reliability of the *hadīth* compendia in which they occur is the greatest in the Muslim normative universe. That the four schools of Islamic law interpreted the Prophet's words differently, namely in the light of the Qurān's notion of negotiated ransoming, belongs to the domain of hypothetical legal thought (*ijtihād*) which, in the opinion of the High Constitutional Court, could only issue in problematic rulings (*ahkām zaniyya*): the state legislators, however, are not bound by the results of any such legal reasoning, and may proceed to ignore any particular problematic opinion, especially when there is a textual rule of assured origin and meaning that decrees otherwise. These juridical policy rules of the 1990s provided the new principles which determined the process of lawmaking that issued in the promulgation of the Law of 2000 on *khul* (Arabi, 2001: 19).

Within the Indian Sub-continent, the first concrete initiatives affecting the application of Muslim Personal Laws were brought about by the Dissolution of Muslim Marriages Act 1939.[28] The Act continues to be operational in the three countries of the Indian Sub-continent – India, Pakistan and Bangladesh – with a number of modifications and alterations (Pearl and Menski, 1998). Injustices caused by the application of the classical Hanafi law were removed by expanding the grounds of divorce for women. The husband's desertion, failure to provide maintenance, cruelty, maltreatment, chronic illness and impotence were grounds appended to the existing provisions for seeking divorce.[29] However, unlike Egypt, desertion could only be claimed after the husband's continuous absence of four years. Reform in divorce laws was initiated through judicial activism as well as through legislative enactments. Whilst the Dissolution of Muslim Marriages Act 1939 (and more recently certain provisions of the Muslim Family Laws Ordinance 1961) has been invoked by aggrieved wives before Pakistani courts for rescission of marriages, the Muslim Family Laws Ordinance 1961 has been principally deployed to establish restrictions on the husband's hitherto unrestrained rights of extra-judicial Talaq. Within Pakistan, as in the case of reducing polygamous marriage, the Muslim Family Laws Ordinance 1961 provides for various procedural constraints during the Talaq process. Under the Ordinance, the husband is obliged to provide a written notice of the pronouncement of Talaq to the Union Council along with a copy to the wife.[30] Failure to serve notice unfortunately means that the marriage remains valid and effective. Such a situation creates substantial difficulties in cases of remarriage on the part of the wife, opening up the possibility of criminal prosecution under the current draconian law of Zina (illicit fornication).[31] The chairperson of the Union Council is required to ensure notification of divorce to the wife. Within 30 days of the notification having been sent, the chairperson of the Union Council may establish an Arbitration Council in order to bring about reconciliation. In the event of a failure of reconciliation, the Talaq becomes permanent after 90 days of its notice having been communicated to the chairperson of the Union Council.

As in the case of Egypt, in order to ameliorate the situation for women, Pakistan's judicial bodies have also made a direct appeal to the primary sources of the Sharia. Pakistan's High Court has invoked a number of charitable Quranic injunctions on women's position in society (Carroll, 1996). This allowed women the right to seek Khul divorce in situations of irretrievable breakdown of the marriage. In one case, relying upon the Quranic verse 2:29 and in accepting the wife's petition for divorce, the full Bench of the High Court noted, 'the limits of God will not be observed, that is, in their special relations to one another, the spouses will not obey God, that a harmonious married state as envisaged by Islam, will not be possible'.[32] The full Bench of the High Court:

were aware of the revolutionary nature of their decision, of the fact that they were granting the wife a right that had been denied her by Hanafi jurists and commentators for centuries. Although they were able to invoke some support from Maliki authorities, fundamentally the Court based its position on the assertion that in dealing with the interpretation of the Qur'an they were not bound by the opinions of classical jurists (Carroll, 1996: 107).

In a further reformist Judgement, the Supreme Court of Pakistan in reliance upon Quranic verses held that Khul is a right conferred by the Quran on the wife and is available to her regardless of the husband withholding his consent. The Court in granting the divorce noted:

In Islam, marriage is a contract and not a sacrament, and whatever sanctity attaches to it, it remains basically a contractual relationship between the parties. Islam, recognizing the weaknesses in human nature, has permitted the dissolution of marriage, and does not make it an unseverable tie, condemning the spouses to a life of helpless despair. The Quran'ic legislation makes it clear that it has raised the status of women. The Holy Qur'an declares in verse 2: 228 that women have rights against men similar to those that men have against them. It conferred the right of *khula* on women as against the right of *talaq* in men.[33]

The strategies and methodology of reforming the classical Sharia in its approaches towards Khul in Egypt and Pakistan provide a 'dramatic assertion of the right of *ijtiahad*' (Carroll, 1996: 108). In both these cases, whilst ensuring greater compatibility of Muslim divorce laws with international human rights law, the lawmakers were able to appeal directly to the primary sources of the Sharia. The invocation of the Quran and Sunna thus provided a significant opportunity for reform. That said it has to be conceded that whilst this innovative legislative and judicial intervention has to an extent ameliorated the position of women, in male-dominated Muslim societies, there nevertheless remains considerable violation of women's rights in the context of family laws. In the case of Pakistan, there are frequent instances of non-compliance with the statutory requirements of written notice to be served to the Union Council and to the wife, thereby leading to the significant risk of the wife being charged with *zina*, should she decide to remarry.[34]

4. CONCLUSION

In common with other great civilizations, the Islamic world has also experienced momentous changes. At its zenith, Islam was the focus of

JAVAID REHMAN   123

attention and the cradle of human civilization. In the words of one historian, Islam 'was the best social and political order the times could offer...It was the broadest, freshest and cleanest political idea that had yet come into actual activity in the world' (Wells, 1925: 613).

This article has highlighted a number of features of the Sharia as the source of Islamic family law and in so doing highlighted several controversial issues within the system. Firstly, it has been argued that, while the Quran and Sunna remain the principal foundations of the Sharia, the formulation of a legally binding code from primarily ethical and religious sources has not been an uncontested matter. Secondly, it has been submitted that the Sharia and Islamic family laws that eventually emerged during the second and third centuries of the Muslim calendar were heavily influenced by the socio-economic, political and indigenous tribal values of the prevailing times. In the development of the classical legal schools, the Islamic jurists frequently adopted male-centric approaches towards women's rights and family laws. A cardinal mistake in the subsequent history of Islam was an insistence upon Taqlid or imitation. Although not without its controversies, for centuries the dominant voices within Muslim societies continued to argue that the doors to Ijtihad had been closed. Such an argument undermined the essence of Islam, which is based on change, reform and re-interpretation. The Arabic translation of Sharia is 'the road to the watering place', signifying progression, development and freshness (Landau, 1958; Oba, 2002; Doi, 1984; Adamec, 2001). The Quran as well as the Sunna provide excellent examples of dealing with situations in a humanitarian and pragmatic manner, with reform and creativity as vital elements of the process. The generations subsequent to the Prophet appear not to have carried this message forward.

Thirdly, this article has argued that it is only recently (and with considerable reservations) that Islamic societies have allowed a debate and enquiry into the reform of established norms of the Sharia, in particular Islamic family laws. Attempts to rectify the injustices built into the prevailing system of polygamous marriages and unilateral Talaq procedures have resulted in some, albeit limited, success through the process of directly appealing to the primary sources of the Sharia. While states such as Egypt and Pakistan have introduced limited legislative and administrative constraints on polygamous marriages and extra-judicial Talaqs, in this re-interpretation of the Sharia, Tunisia has successfully been able to abolish polygamous marriages and extra-judicial and unilateral divorces.

Fourthly, it is contended that the Sharia and Islamic family laws are likely to remain relevant to English Law. The steady growth of adherents of Islamic faith in the UK – a consequence *inter alia* of proportionally higher birth rates, secondary migration through family and marriage resettlements and conversions to Islam – also necessitates a great awareness and sensitivity towards the religious, cultural and ethical values of these communities. Finally, it is submitted that a deeper, more profound meaning of religious as well as social values can be established through a proper understanding of the Quran and Sunna; these principal sources of the Sharia emphasize pragmatism and reform in accordance with demands of the society. The law-makers and judiciary in the UK may find the pragmatic message of the Sharia useful since there is a need for re-evaluation of established English family laws including a re-interpretation of such traditional concepts as family, marriage and divorce.

NOTES

[1] See *R (on the application of Begum (by her litigation friend, Rahman)) (Respondent) v Head teacher and Governors of Denbigh High School* (Appellants) [2006] UKHL 15 (wearing of Jilbal, a covering more extensive than hijab). On the veil, see the recent case of Ms Aishah Azmi (October 2006).

[2] See *Bradford Corporation v Patel* (1974) unreported. (Conviction of a Muslim father under the provisions of the 1944 Education Act for failing to send his daughter to a co-educational school on religious grounds.)

[3] On under-age marriages see *Alhaji Mahammad v Knot* [1969] 1 QB 1; [1986] WLR 1446, [1968] 2 All ER 563. See the Immigration Rules, para 277 Immigration and Nationality Directorate http://www.ind.homeoffice.gov.uk/lawandpolicy/immigrationrules/part8 (last visited 1 December 2006).

[4] See *Hirani v Hirani* (1983) 4 FLR 232 (although the particular case concerned a Hindu girl). Also note the 'primary purpose' rule, Halsbury's Law of England (1992) paras 95–7. Are arranged marriages *per se* indicative that the primary purpose of marriage is immigration to the UK? *R v Immigration Appeal Tribunal, ex parte Iqbal* [1993] Imm A.R. 270.

[5] See *Quorasishi v Quorasishi* [1983] FLR 706; See the Immigration Rules, paras 278–80 (Immigration and Nationality Directorate) http://www.ind.homeoffice.gov.uk/lawandpolicy/immigrationrules/part8 (last visited 2 December 2006). *Bibi v Chief Adjudicatiion Officer* (Gazattee 94/27, 9 July, 22) (case concerning entitlement to widow's pension in polygamous marriages).

[6] *Quazi v Quazi* [1980] AC 744; *Chaudhary v Chaudhary* [1985] FLR 476; Family Law Act 1986 (Part II); on Immigration See *R v Secretary of State for Home Department ex parte Ghulam Fatima* [1986] 2 WLR 693 (refusal of entry into UK for fiancé for non-recognition of first divorce through transnational Talaq). See UK Visas Enquires http://www.ukvisas.gov.uk/servlet/Front?pagename=OpenMarket/Xcelerate/ShowPage&c=Page&cid=1038489156801 (last visited 23 November 2006).

[7] See *Ahmad v Inner London Education Authority* [1978] QB 36, [1977] 3 WLR 396, [1978] 1 All ER 574 (Court of Appeal); *Ahmad v UK* (1982) 4 EHRR 126.

[8] The issue of identification of 'Islamic state' and its adopted interpretation of Islamic laws as 'the Islamic laws' has been problematic and highly controversial. It has been the subject of analysis elsewhere (Rehman, 2005: 26–43). Indicators may point to the proportion of Muslims in a state or the system of government that is operative. Some advocates of Islamic identity would rely upon whether Sharia is actively enforced in a state, others may acknowledge Islamic identity simply through hortatory statements in constitutional and legislative provisions. At present 15 constitutions name Islam as the 'official' religion; five states have declared themselves as Islamic Republics. For the purposes of this paper, those states are considered Islamic that are members of the Organization of Islamic Conference (OIC). The OIC identifies itself with Islam; its primary objectives are to promote Islamic solidarity and it aspires to work for the furtherance of the interests of Muslims across the globe. While the membership of the OIC is not exclusively Muslim, a huge proportion of member states do in fact have Muslim majorities. On the other hand membership does not entail any obligations to implement the Sharia or have in place Islamic political, social or ethical frameworks. For the UK, the position is also of interest: the UK has 1.6 million Muslims (2.7 per cent of the total population). The 2001 census, for the first time, inducted a voluntary question based on religious denominations – UK 2001 National Census, Religion in Britain, http://www.statistics.gov.uk/cci/nugget.asp?id=293 (last visited 13 June, 2006). All indicators are that with further immigration, increased conversion to Islam and higher levels of Muslim population growth, Muslim population will

steadily grow in the UK. Is there, then, a case for a distinct system of personal and family law for Muslims in the UK? (See Poulter, 1990: 147–66).

⁹ According to Ali the legal content can be considered to be only around 80 verses. (Ali, 1997a: 266). Glenn makes the observation that 'the Koran has some law, but not much, and it's hard to find' (Glenn, 2000: 159); 'the so-called legal matter … consists mainly of broad general propositions as to what the aims and aspirations of Muslim society should be. It is essentially the bare formulation of the Islamic religious ethic … In short, the primary purpose of the Qur'an is to regulate not the relationship of man with his fellows but his relationship with his creator' (Coulson, 1964: 11–12).

¹⁰ A Hadith consists of two parts. Isnad and Matin. Isnad refers to the link, the source or the chain of narrators of the Hadith. Hence a Hadith in its Isnad would report the person who acted as transmitters. The Matin contains the substance of the Prophets' sayings, deeds or actions.

¹¹ According to a well-recited Hadith, the role of Qiyas was confirmed at the time when Prophet Muhammad (whiling sending Mu 'adh b. Jalal to Yemen to take the position of a qadi) asked him the following question: 'How will you decide when a question arises?' He replied, 'According to the Book of Allah'. 'And if you do not find the answer in the Book of Allah?' 'Then according to the Sunna of the Messenger of Allah.' 'And if you do not find the answer either in the Sunna or in the Book?' 'Then I shall come to a decision according to my own opinion without hesitation'. Then the Messenger of Allah slapped Mu 'adh on the chest with his hand saying: 'Praise be to Allah who has led the Messenger of Allah to an answer that pleases him'. (See 'Kiyas' in Gibb and Kramers, 1953: 267.)

¹² Complications have nevertheless arisen in modern Islamic State practices whereby Classical Sharia arguments have been advanced in relation to the role and consent of the wali eg, in the marriage of adult women. According to classical Shafi and Malaki Schools (in contrast to the Hanafi School) an adult virgin needs the consent of the wali; for a recent analysis and juridical interpretation see *Hafiz Abdul Wahid* v *Asma Jahangir* KLR (1997) (Shariat Cases) 121.

¹³ Muslim Family Law Ordinance (1961).

¹⁴ Article 17 Law of Personal Status 1953 (Decree No. 59 of 1953).

¹⁵ Article 3, Law of Personal Status 1959.

¹⁶ Article 18, Tunisian Code of Personal Status 1956.

¹⁷ S 5 Muslim Family Law Ordinance 1961.

¹⁸ S 6 Muslim Family Law Ordinance 1961.

¹⁹ S 6 Muslim Family Law Ordinance 1961.

²⁰ Rule 14, Muslim Family Law Ordinance 1961.

²¹ See The Tunisian Code of Personal Status 1956.

²² (1997) 17 BLD 4.

²³ *Cf* in the exceptional Pakistani case of *Khurshid Bibi* v *Moh'd Amin* PLD 1967 SC 97, the Supreme Court held that as a matter of principle a husband's consent is not required in Khul cases.

²⁴ The Special Civil Courts Act 1979 (amending provisions of Family Protection Law, 1967).

²⁵ Law No 44 of 1979.

²⁶ See Law No 2000 on the Re-Organisation of Certain Terms and Procedures of litigation in Personal Status.

²⁷ Law No 2000 on the Re-Organisation of Certain Terms and Procedures of litigation in Personal Status.

²⁸ Act 8 of 1939, in force 17 March, 1939.

²⁹ S 2 (i)–(viii) DMMA 1939.

³⁰ S7 Muslim Family Law Ordinance 1961.

³¹ See *The State* v *Tauqir Fatima* (1964) PLD (WP) Kar 36.

³² *Mst. Balqis Fatima* v *Najm-ul-Ikram Qureshi*, PLD 1959 (Lahore) 566, para 42.

³³ *Khurshid Bibi* v *Muhammad Amin* (1967) PLD SC 97.

³⁴ *Muhammad Sarwar* v *Shahid Parveen* 1988 (SD) FSC 188.

REFERENCES

Adamec, L. W. (2001) *Historical Dictionary of Islam*, Maryland: Lanham.

Afshari, R. (1994) 'An essay on Islamic cultural relativism in the discourse of human rights', *Human Rights Quarterly* 16, 235–76.

Ali, S. S. (1997a) 'The conceptual foundations of human rights: A comparative perspective', *European Public Law* 3, 261–82.

126   POLYGAMY AND TALAQ

Ali, S. S. (1997b) 'A critical revision of family law in Pakistan:A women's perspective' in
    R. Mehdi and F. Shahid (ed), *Women's Law in Legal Education and Practice: North-South Co-operation*,
    Copenhagen: New Social Science Monographs, 198–221.
Ali, S. S. (2000) Gender and human rights in Islam and international law: Equal before Allah,
    unequal before man?, The Hague: Kluwer Law International.
Ali, S. S. and Rehman, J. (2003) 'Freedom of religion versus equality in international human
    rights law: Conflicting norms or hierarchical human rights. (A case study of Pakistan)', *Nordic
    Journal of Human Rights* 21, 404–28.
Ali, S. S. and Rehman, J. (2005) 'The concept of Jihad in Islamic international law', *Journal of
    Conflict and Security Law* 10, 1–23.
Al-Mūsawi, S. H. (1997) *Mānhājul-Fiqhil-Islam: A Course in the Islamic Jurisprudence*, Tehran: Islamic
    Culture and Relations Organization.
An-Na'im, A. A. (1990) *Toward an Islamic Reformation: Civil Liberties, Human Rights and International
    Law*, New York: Syracuse University Press.
An-Naim, A. A. (2002) (ed) *Islamic Family Law in a Changing World: A Global Resource Book*, London:
    Zed Books Limited.
Arabi, O. (2001) 'The dawning of the third millennium on Shari'a: Egypt's law No1 of 2000, or
    women may divorce at will', *Arab Law Quarterly* 16, 2–21.
Baderin, M. A. (2003) *International Human Rights and Islamic Law*, Oxford: Oxford University Press.
Badr, G. M. (1978) 'Islamic law: Its relations to other legal systems', *American Journal of Comparative
    Law* 26, 187–98.
Balchin, C. and Warrich, S. A. (1997) 'Untying the Gordian Knot: The theory and practice of
    divorce in Pakistan', in R. Mehdi and F. Shahid (ed), *Women's Law in Legal Education and Practice:
    North-South Co-operation*, Copenhagen: New Social Science Monographs, 260–75.
Barlas, A. (2002) *'Believing Women' in Islam: Unreading Patriarchal Interpretations of the Qur'ān*,
    Austin, Texas: University of Texas.
Bassiouni, M. C. (1982) (ed) *The Islamic Criminal Justice System*, London: Oceana Publications.
Carroll, L. (1996) 'Quran 2: 229: "A charter granted to the wife?": Judicial Khul in Pakistan', 3
    Islamic Law and Society 1, 91–126.
Coulson, N. J. (1964) *A History of Islamic Law*, Edinburgh: University Press.
Coulson, N. J. (1969) *Conflicts and Tensions in Islamic Jurisprudence*, Chicago: University of Chicago
    Press.
Denny, F. M. (1994) *An Introduction to Islam*, New York: Macmillan Publishing Company.
Doi, A. R. (1984) *Shariah: The Islamic Law*, London: Ta Ha Publishers.
Entelis, J. (1997) 'International human rights: Islam's friend or foe?: Algeria as an example of
    the compatibility of international human rights regarding women's equality and Islamic law',
    Fordham International Law Journal 20, 1251–1305.
Esposito, J. L. (1982) *Women in Muslim Family Law*, New York: Syracuse University Press.
Farani, M. (1992) *Manual of Family Laws in Pakistan*, Lahore: Law Times Publication.
Gibb, H. A. R. and Kramers, J. H. (1953) (ed) *Shorter Encyclopaedia of Islam*, Ithaca, NY: Cornell
    University Press.
Glenn, H. P. (2000) *Legal Traditions of the World: Sustainable Diversity in Law*, Oxford: Oxford
    University Press.
Hallaq, W. B. (1997) *A History of Islamic Legal Theories: An Introduction to Sunni usul al-fiqh*,
    Cambridge: Cambridge University Press.
Hallaq, W. B. (2001) *Authority, Continuity and Change in Islamic Law*, Cambridge: Cambridge
    University Press.
Hallaq, W. B. (2004) 'Can Sharia be restored' in Y. Y. Hadad and B. F. Stonasser (ed), *Islamic Law
    and Challenges of Modernity*, Walnut Creek: Altamira Press, 21–53.
Hinchcliffe, D. (1970) 'Polygamy in traditional and contemporary Islamic law', *Islam and the
    Modern Age* 1, 13–38.
Human Rights Watch (2004) *Divorced from Justice: Women's Unequal Access to Divorce in Egypt* http://
    hrw.org/reports/2004/egypt1204/ (December 2004), last visited 12 December, 2006.
Jahangir, A. and Jilani, H. (1990) *The Hudood Ordinances: A Divine Sanction?*, Lahore: Rhotas Books.
Kamali, M. H. (1991) *Principles of Islamic Jurisprudence*, Cambridge: Islamic Texts Society.
Landau, R. (1958) *Islam and the Arabs*, London: George Allen and Unwin Limited.
Lombardi, C. B. (1998) 'Islamic law as a source of constitutional law in Egypt: The constitutionali-
    zation of the Sharia in a modern Arab state', *Columbia Journal of Transnational Law* 37, 81–123.
Mahmassani, S. (1966) 'The principles of international law in the light of Islamic doctrine', 117
    Recueil des Cours de l'Académie de Droit International 1, 201–328.

Mallat, C. and Connors, J. (1990) (ed) *Islamic Family Law*, London: Graham and Trotman.

Mannan, M. A. (1991) *D.F. Mulla's Principles of Mohamedan Law*, Lahore: PLD Publishers.

Mayer, A. E. (1995) *Islam and Human Rights: Tradition and Politics*, Boulder Colorado: Westview Press.

Mayss, A. (2000) 'Recognition of foreign divorces' in J. Murphy (ed), *Ethnic Minorities: Their Families and the Law*, Oxford: Hart Publishing, 51–70.

Mehdi, R. (1994) *The Islamization of the Law in Pakistan*, London: Curzon Press.

Mir-Hosseni, Z. (1999) *Islam and Gender: The Religious Debate in Contemporary Iran*, London: I.B. Tauris.

Mir-Hosseni, Z. (2000) *Marriage on Trial: A Study of Islamic Family Law*, London: I.B. Tauris.

Moinuddin, H. (1987) *The Charter of the Islamic Conference and Legal Framework of Economic Cooperation Among its Member States: A Study of the Charter, the General Agreement for Economic, Technical and Commercial Co-operation and the Agreement for Promotion, Protection and Guarantee of Investments Among Member States of the OIC*, Oxford: Clarendon Press.

Murphy, J. (2000) 'The discretionary refusal of recognition of foreign marriages' in J. Murphy (ed), *Ethnic Minorities: Their Families and the Law*, Oxford: Hart Publishing, 71–86.

Nasir, J. J. (1990) *The Islamic Law of Personal Status*, London: Graham and Trotman.

Oba, A. A. (2002) 'Islamic law as customary law: The changing perspective in Nigeria', *International and Comparative Law Quarterly* 51, 817–50.

Pearl, D. and Menski, W. (1998) *Muslim Family Law*, London: Sweet and Maxwell.

Poulter, S. M. (1990) 'The claim to a separate Islamic system of personal law for British Muslims' in C. Mallat and J. Connors (ed), *Islamic Family Law*, London: Graham and Trotman, 147–66.

Poulter, S. M. (1998) *Ethnicity, Law and Human Rights*, Oxford: Clarendon Press.

Poulter, S. M. (1986) *English Law and Ethnic Minorities Customs*, London: Butterworths.

Ragi al-Fruqi, I. (1962) 'Towards a new methodology of Qur'anic exegesis', *Islamic Studies* 1, 35–52.

Rehman, J. (1997) 'Women's rights: An international law perspective' in R. Mehdi and F. Shahid (ed), *Women's Law in Legal Education and Practice: North-South Co-operation*, Copenhagen: New Social Science Monographs, 106–28.

Rehman, J. (2000) 'Accommodating religious identities in an Islamic state: International law, freedom of religion and the rights of religious minorities', *International Journal on Minority and Group Rights* 7, 139–65.

Rehman, J. (2001) 'Minority rights and the constitutional dilemmas of Pakistan', 19 *Netherlands Quarterly of Human Rights* 4, 417–43.

Rehman, J. (2002) 'Islamic perspectives on international economic law' in A. H. Qureshi (ed) *Perspectives in International Economic Law*, The Hague: Kluwer Law International, 235–58.

Rehman, J. (2003) *International Human Rights Law: A Practical Approach*, London: Longman Publishers.

Rehman, J. (2003/4) 'Islamophobia after 9/11: International terrorism, Sharia and Muslim minorities in Europe: The case of the United Kingdom', 3 *European Yearbook of Minority Issues* 217–35.

Rehman, J. (2005) *Islamic State Practices, International Law and the Threat from Terrorism: A Critique of the 'Clash of Civilizations' in the New World Order*, Oxford: Hart Publishing.

Riga, P. J. (1991) 'Islamic law and modernity: Conflict and evolution', *American Journal of Jurisprudence* 36, 103–17.

Schacht, J. (1964) *An Introduction to Islamic Law*, Oxford: Clarendon Press.

Shah, P. A. (2003) 'Attitudes to polygamy in English law', *International and Comparative Law Quarterly* 52, 369–400.

The Quran (1981) *English Translation*, London: Curzon Press.

Vogel, F. E. (1993) 'The closing of the door of Ijtihad and the application of the law', *American Journal of Islamic Social Sciences* 10, 396–401.

Weeramantry, C. G. (1988) *Islamic Jurisprudence: An International Perspective*, London: Macmillan Press.

Weiss, B. (1978) 'Interpretation in Islamic law: The theory of Ijtihad', *American Journal of Comparative Law* 26, 199–212.

Wells, H. G. (1925) *The Outline of History: Being a Plain History of Life and Mankind*, London: Cassell.

Zweigert, K. and Kötz, H. (1998) *Introduction to Comparative Law*, Oxford: Clarendon Press.

[14]

Islamic Female Sexuality and Gender in Modern Feminist Interpretation

ELIZABETH SHLALA LEO

Department of History, Georgetown University, Washington, DC, USA

ABSTRACT   *Sexuality, gender and patriarchy are modern concepts that Western feminist scholars have unquestioningly utilized in their historical inquiry into women in Islam without ample consideration of periodization or problemization. Within the revelation of the Qur'an, the sexes were gendered in relation to each other in a reflection of their physical and biological complementarity. There was not, however, the construction of sexuality and gendering that is evident in the patriarchal society of the modern world. In this essay, I will attempt to trace the historiographical evolution of female sexuality from the time of the Prophet until the Middle Ages, particularly through the development of the female gendered roles of wifehood and motherhood as found in the Qur'an, hadith and* fiqh. *Additionally, I will argue that until the present these modern constructs have been taken for granted by postmodern scholarship on the topic across many academic disciplines. This has led to scholarship that superimposes modern conceptual frameworks upon earlier time periods. Although these are modern concepts, they may be aptly applied to discourses evident in the period under review, but they must be properly clarified and situated. Furthermore, I myself will work with these concepts, but I will problematize them to show history as a process through which one can find the precursors for modern sexuality and gender construction.*

The Prophet said that women completely dominate men of intellect and possessors of hearts,
But ignorant men dominate women, because [these men] are dominated by their animal nature. (Jalaluddin Rumi)

Introduction

Sexuality, gender[1] and patriarchy are modern concepts that Western feminist scholars have unquestioningly utilized in their historical inquiry into women in Islam without ample consideration of periodization or problemization. Within the revelation of the Qur'an, the sexes were gendered *in relation* to each other in a reflection of their physical and biological complementarity. There was not, however, the construction of sexuality

---

Correspondence Address: Elizabeth Shlala Leo, Department of History, Georgetown University, 2501 Q St, Washington, DC 20007, USA. Email: ehs6@georgetown.edu

130   *E. Shlala Leo*

and gendering that is evident in the patriarchal society of the modern world, which was formulated upon misogynistic, Aristotelian reasoning during the Middle Ages. That is to say, it was not until years after the Qur'an was revealed to Muhammad that the onset of patriarchy as a system occurred. In the Arab world, patriarchy was heralded by a break with tribal culture and ensuing power struggles for leadership, which were caused by the rise of early capitalism in Mecca, the regional diffusion of Islam with a concomitant influx of slaves, and increased urbanization. In an effort to enforce the patriarchal order, the restraint of human sexuality became a means of maintaining social control and harmony in a way that appears to be significantly different from the preceding eras. In this essay, I will attempt to trace the historiographical evolution of female sexuality from the time of the Prophet until the Middle Ages, particularly through the development of the female gendered roles of wifehood and motherhood as found in the Qur'an, hadith and *fiqh*. Additionally, I will argue that until the present these modern constructs have been taken for granted by postmodern scholarship on the topic across many academic disciplines. This has led to scholarship that superimposes modern conceptual frameworks upon earlier time periods. Although these are modern concepts, they may be aptly applied to discourses evident in the period under review, but they must be properly clarified and situated. Furthermore, I myself will work with these concepts, but I will problematize them to show history as a process through which one can find the precursors for modern sexuality and gender construction.

Further justification for using the above-mentioned concepts is that feminist interpretation itself is a modern approach to understanding Islam. Feminist interpretation is aligned with the modernist approach in the following ways. *Itjihād* (personal interpretation) allows one to deconstruct women and gender through the reinterpretation of the texts, so feminists turn to the women portrayed in the Qur'an and the message of the suras concerning women to deduce a freedom and equality that is missing in the modern female gender construct. In addition, early Islamic modernists such as Muḥammad ʿAbduh posited that Islam was the first community to recognize the full equality of women with men. This argument lays the foundation for most feminist arguments today in support of a pure Islam to be found in the distant past, and to which women must return to regain their proper place beside their male counterparts in modern times. Finally, a critical point made by Ḥasan al-Bannā and Sayyid Quṭb is that Islam saves women from the exploitation of their sexuality that has been brought about by Western capitalism. This point is also important for refuting development theories that point to Muslim backwardness as a cultural product rather than a result of serious socio-economic problems endemic to some countries of the modern Arab world. Adhering to these parameters, recent feminist inquiry is by its nature a modern inquiry, and as such assumes an agenda replete with modern questionings that go back in order to inform the past; this is dangerous and may lead to linear thinking and faulty deconstruction.

I will demonstrate how time and again scholars make a theoretical leap between early Islam and modern argumentation with little to no elucidation of the concepts of sexuality and gender. Arguably, there are three main reasons for this. First, the period from the seventh century until the Middle Ages and then from the Middle Ages until the modern period is not a part of Western secondary or college curricula. Second, there is in Western academic institutions a dearth of translated sources which scholars may use to interpret these times.[2] Lastly, modern scholars insist on garnering legitimacy by relying on classical exegesis passed down from the medieval jurists instead of searching for innovative ideas inside or outside the Arab world at different times in history.

Amina Wadud, Leila Ahmed, Nawal El Saadawi and Fatima Mernissi are among the scholars I will address through their grammatical, theoretical and practical exegeses of the Qur'an by casting new light on the accepted lineage of certain *tafsīr*, hadith and *fiqh* that are patriarchal and pejorative in their treatment of women. The feminist approach they take is based on the modernist exhortation to disregard medieval *fiqh* and to return to the pure Islam of the Qur'an through *itjihād* (personal interpretation). Feminists are thus able to reinterpret the Qur'an and to extricate medieval juridical and hadith gendering of woman that is not evident in the sacred text of divine revelation.

Nonetheless, the issue remains the 'unproblematized' modern framework that they employ to do this. It is 'unproblematized' in the sense that these writers mistakenly pose modern questions that are more applicable to the lives of modern Muslim women than to the women who lived in the seventh-century world of the Prophet Muhammad. This oversight may be the more surprising given the overwhelming cultural and religious sensitivity these scholars bring to their use of Western concepts when they treat topics about Islamic women in the Middle East. In favor of such an inquiry into Islamic female sexuality, Leila Ahmed writes:

> Other worthy areas of investigation include issues of sexuality and the ways in which sexual and erotic experience, heterosexual and homosexual, shaped consciousness, and even more fundamentally the meaning of sexuality and whether the spectrum of emotional, erotic, and sexual experience within Egyptian and Arab society might be adequately or accurately captured by such modern Western terms. (Ahmed, 1992, pp. 185–186)

While Ahmed thoughtfully questions the application of modern Western concepts to modern Middle Eastern society, the greater dilemma, which she neglects to mention, is how to avoid superimposing modernity onto the past by assuming that the questions of today are applicable to yesterday. Finally, these ideas have become tangible through Michel Foucault's idea of sexuality, and the construction of the female body in relation to the greater social body through discourse.[3]

I will attempt to demonstrate that this modern idea of sexuality was not present in the Qur'ran, but through discourse was added years later through medieval *tafsīr*, hadith and *fiqh*, as demonstrated by these feminist scholars. I propose that the modern construction of woman as wife and mother is not found in the Qur'an either. That is not to say, however, that a concept of sexuality and gender specific to that time did not exist. Indeed, the modern concepts of sexuality and gender may be enlightening tools to apply towards understanding this period and defining the antecedents of modern sexuality and gender constructs in their own right. I will attempt to define and explain them in their modern forms.

Patriarchy and Islamic Feminist Historical Narratives

Patriarchy is an inherently unbalanced and unstable organizational system in which overriding social norms postulate that men are superior to women. Therefore, men hold overt power over women through the process of social construction as evident in the depiction of sexuality, the assignment of gender roles, and the social hierarchy that exists in every facet of social relations. Since patriarchy is undeniably an early modern and modern

132   *E. Shlala Leo*

organizational belief system, a lacuna exists for the portrayal and function of sexuality and gender outside of known patriarchal systems. The dawn of Islam may be an appropriate moment to initiate such an inquiry, as there is not enough academic evidence definitively to support or deny the existence of patriarchy in the seventh-century Arab world. Certainly power relations existed in society, and they seem to have stratified the sexes. However, what the dominating beliefs and social norms were remains controversial. There is no definitive proof that men were perceived as superior to women or that social relations were prioritized along those lines.[4] Feminists and misogynists alike have analyzed the Qur'an to show the efficacy of both sides of the argument, particularly through the portrayal of qur'anic female figures and suras relating to women. Furthermore, much *tafsīr* on the message of the Qur'an poses the same problem as that of sexuality: Did the Qur'an encourage or condemn patriarchy? Here again it must be reiterated that patriarchy, like sexuality, may not apply to that time period, and the question may be too modern to ask without first grappling with its position within the historical process.

Abdur Rahman I. Doi presents the popular assumption that the period of *Jāhiliyya* was one in which women were scandalously mistreated by men. This is a modernist argument widely accepted throughout the Islamic world. It is important because it attributes revolutionary change to Islam and credits the message of the Qur'an with saving women from the horrors they were experiencing during that time. Monogamy and the prohibition of female infanticide are two of the oft-cited innovations of Islam. Doi states that before Islam the Arabs would bury their female infants alive, make woman dance naked at annual fairs and treat women as cattle for sexual pleasure, giving them no rights. Islam was revolutionary because it regards women and men as created from the same soul (*nafs*), which gives women full humanity with men (Doi). Although the conditions may have existed, Doi does not use the term 'patriarchy'. Modern feminist scholars do not present a unified picture of this historical narrative, but the concept of patriarchy certainly informs their narratives.

Nawal El Saadawi postulates that the period of the Prophet was 'a cross between patriarchy and matriarchal systems where, however, man had the upper hand' (El Saadawi, 1982, p. 126). She believes that there was a matriarchy before the rise of Islam whose goddesses were conquered by the Prophet's male god. She goes on to explain that this eroded the preceding matriarchy through an influx of male control over religion and the economy. She notes that women in the towns were less free and more veiled than their desert counterparts who directly participated in the economy without the veil (*ibid.*, pp. 125–131). Like some other feminist scholars, El Saadawi records the strength and power of women during the pre-Islamic period, or *Jāhiliyya*. She notes that there were many important and socially powerful women who went to war with and against the Prophet with knives slung across their pregnant bellies. Finally, she identifies the greatest social change to be the Islamic institution of marriage. *Jāhiliyya* marriages were not restrictive for women or sexuality; children were named after their mothers. In her exposé, Islam and economic factors brought an end to this matriarchy, which was followed by the rise of patriarchy as early as the seventh or eighth century. Fatima Mernissi also claims that in the *Jāhiliyya* period tribes followed a matriarchal system. She contends that it was Islam that brought the innovation of paternity to the region through the institution of *'idda*, a waiting period of menstrual cycles to ascertain if a woman was pregnant before she was eligible to remarry (Mernissi, 1991, pp. 52–53).

Leila Ahmed proposes an extensive and more complete historical narrative of pre-Islamic patriarchy. Ahmed states that at the beginning of human history, women were not subjugated to men, as is evidenced by ancient goddess worship. She identifies the rise of urban centers, increased military competitiveness, the birth of city-states, class distinctions and economic specialization as contributing to the growth of patriarchy and the subordination of women between 3500 and 3000 BCE in the Mediterranean.[5] She posits that women were viewed for the first time as male property and as such their sexuality and reproductive capability had to be closely monitored and controlled in order for them to maintain their value. She writes that 'This led (some have argued) to the emergence of prostitution and to the enforcement of a rigid demarcation between "respectable" women (wives) whose sexuality and reproductive capability belonged to one man, and women who were sexually available to any man' (Ahmed, 1992, p. 12). Hammurabi's Code in 1752 BCE was particularly harsh towards women. At this time, 'respectable' women veiled to show who was sexually available and who was not.[6] Nevertheless, she details that women were priestesses, held jobs, entered into contracts, bought and sold property and slaves, and could modify marriage contracts. However, the influence of early Christianity on the region brought veiling, seclusion and female invisibility; it also brought the shame of sexuality to the region. Here she identifies that *circa* 300 BCE cultural exchanges among the Mesopotamian, Persian, Hellenic and Christian worlds increased patriarchy through the notion that the value of woman was related solely to her sexual and reproductive biology (*ibid.*, pp. 13–18). It is important to note what a modern argument about gender and sexuality Ahmed is putting forward here. She further expounds upon the misogyny of Zoroastrianism and Christianity that was to inform the mores, such as female infanticide, of the Arab population in the Sasanian society of the seventh century (*ibid.*, pp. 18–37). It was at the turn of the millennium that the idea of woman as thing entered into society. However, Ahmed soundly problematizes patriarchy throughout the history of the region, relying on Gilda Lerner's work. Ahmed affirms that not enough is known about the *Jāhiliyya* period to defend or deny what aspects of it were matrilineal, patrilineal, matriarchal or patriarchal, but she concludes that through monogamous, patrilineal marriage established by Islam, women's sexual autonomy was curtailed (*ibid.*, pp. 40–43). Fatima Mernissi clarifies this differentiation between Western Christian and Islamic patriarchal sexuality by positing that they took two separate paths. According to her, Western civilization divided the individual into spirit and flesh and held that the pure spirit had to conquer the debased flesh and its sexuality, while in Islam, she claims, it is not sexuality *per se* that is attacked, but women as 'the embodiment of destruction, the symbol of disorder' because, in contrast with the West, 'Muslim theory views civilization as the outcome of satisfied sexual energy' (Mernissi, 1987, p. 44).

Sexuality and Modern Feminist Inquiry

Sexuality is a reproductive and procreative power. It revolves around sex as an act and sex as a biological assignment; it is not these things themselves, but it draws its power from them. As Foucault contends, its discourses are an historical construct, although sexuality itself is not, and under certain social systems its power may be inverted or thwarted altogether. Female sexuality is a positive, universal force that derives from a woman's physical ability to birth and nourish children from her body. Under a

134   *E. Shlala Leo*

patriarchal system, this inherent female power is a threat to the social hierarchy, so discourse reveals a woman's body and abilities to be within demeaning social constructions, which posit that her body is weak and her being is overly emotional and unstable. To this end, modern 'motherhood' must be normatively regulated and empirically standardized. Overall, a great effort is made to disconnect woman's reproductive reality from her material reality through social discourse and construction. This is evident in modern societies in which pregnancy is monitored scientifically, childbirth is highly medicated and medicalized, and breastfeeding has become a commercially undesirable option. With regard to women and work, mothers are less likely to receive pay or promotion at the rate of their male counterparts. Childbirth is diagnosed in some countries as a disability, and time within the workday cannot be found for breastfeeding newborns. Female sexuality and reproduction are not ignored as they may have been in earlier times under different regimes; they are regulated into inferiority.

Despite past assumptions regarding women under patriarchy, women are not passive players in discourse and social construction. Women participate in this degradation of their sexuality by focusing their power on the discourses ascribed to them, and working towards the goals of gender success as portrayed in patriarchy—goals and success that are meaningless and remain elusive to them as they deny themselves the very real power that women embody through their sexuality. In fact, the definitions for success under patriarchy as tied to outward methods of material accumulation in capitalist systems are satisfying for neither sex.

The fruition of female sexuality has historically been a point of contention and conflict under patriarchy as regulated by the hegemonic authority. In the monotheistic faith communities, religion has worked in tandem with the state (or pre-state) to this end. This is why modern Christian cleric, Robert W. Jenson, states that 'any community that takes its own reality seriously must be ready to deal with sexuality seriously by a willingness to legislate how it is and is not to be expressed' (Jenson, 1984, pp. 46–47). Arguably, male and female sexuality are equally subjected to this legislation, although under patriarchy female sexuality is of particular concern and construct.

Although male sexuality also has a positive role to play in society, it too is demonized; it is glorified and contextualized as a negative under a patriarchal system. Men are idealized as powerful, virile and insatiable. Their sexuality, which is also procreative, is disparagingly equated with violence, anger and oppression. In this way, sexuality within the confines of patriarchy, and indeed patriarchy itself, serves the interest of neither men nor women. Nawal El Saadawi seemingly echoes this sentiment when she states that men:

> are also victims of a society that segregates the sexes, and that considers sex a sin and a shame which can only be practiced within the framework of an official marriage contract. Apart from this permitted avenue of sexual relations, society forbids adolescents and young men to practice sex in any form, other than that of nocturnal emissions.

In this way, she explains sexual assault on female relatives and children by sexually frustrated men, applying the modern paradigm of male sexual aggression in which sexual forces beyond his control impel a man to victimize a passive female or child

(El Saadawi, 1982, pp. 13–14). She confirms that patriarchy and its representation of sexuality are untenable and repressive, but she also portrays it as a fixed and limited system and in so doing conceals the dynamism and potential for change that sexuality portends.

El Saadawi also makes an important distinction between 'timeless' Western and Islamic thought about sexuality. She contends that in Islamic society sexual satisfaction for both men and women is thought to render a person more productive, whereas in Western society the repression of sexuality creates a more efficient person (*ibid.,* p. 130). Despite these seemingly divergent viewpoints, it appears that female sexuality, under the conditions of patriarchy, has been similarly oppressed in both Western and Islamic societies. Mernissi shares this interpretation of Islam's acceptance of sexuality as a part of human nature, and introduces its socially destructive potential for *fitna.* She writes:

We have seen that sexual satisfaction is considered necessary to the moral well-being of the believer. There is no incompatibility between Islam and sexuality as long as sexuality is expressed harmoniously and is not frustrated. What Islam views as negative and anti-social is woman and her power to create fitna. (Mernissi, 1987, p. 113)

Modern Western scholars have defined and situated Islamic sexuality. Islamic sexuality appears to be a monolithic concept within the sources. It is best identified in relation to the Arabic word, *fitna. Fitna* has many meanings in the various texts, such as: female desirability, female power, male weakness, social chaos and social disorder. The term is used interchangeably to mean any and all of these things. Female sexuality, *unūtha,* is based on biological, physical and mental differences from men evident in different genitalia and biological functions such as childbirth and breastfeeding. Its implications for women as a gender group are that they are quantifiably less intelligent than men, physically weaker and prone to emotional instability. In the modern Islamic world, women's bodies and beauty are seen as great temptations to weak men who cannot curb their desires. Women are temptresses who have more sexual power than men. Women are therefore burdened with the responsibility of controlling male desire, thereby saving their community from *fitna.* Men are almost powerless when it comes to female sexuality in this portrayal. Therefore, *fitna,* and not *unūtha,* is the critical social component of female sexuality.

According to Mark Swanson, this has led to modern and medieval programs of social health through veiling and the strict segregation of the sexes. In an effort to control perilous female sexuality, women are educated in Islam and marriage is the strict social norm; social chaos and female sexuality are thus equated and avoided. He also demonstrates that there were both negative views of sexuality, including the idea that it was a cause of 'unbridled chaos' and 'psychological disorders', and positive views, including associating it with 'greater intellectual power' and 'continuation of the race', although the latter were minimized in favor of the negative discourse (Swanson, 1984, pp. 187–203). In an attempt to interpret the suras of the Qur'an and their *tafsīr* with a view to their application in the modern world, he traces sexuality from the seventh to the twenty-first century with no discussion of how this modern concept can make such an ahistorical leap back and forth through time. For example, when commenting on

136   *E. Shlala Leo*

Sūrat al-Nūr (Q 24) 27–33, Swanson moves between the Qur'an, twelfth-century jurists and modern Egyptian scholars. How could one idea about sexuality span such a vast time frame? The answer is that as a fixed, static concept which exists as a social construct shaped by historical discourses, it cannot.

Female circumcision is a local cultural invention, probably pre-dating the rise of Islam, which is supported as a way of controlling female sexuality in some conservative Islamic countries. The modern feminist interpretations of the Qur'an show that it is absent from the text. Therefore, in a modern controversy spurred on by the West much like that of the veil, scholars search for its entry and acceptance into the Muslim discourse. Jonathan Berkey attempts this with the wise warning that 'modern ideas and practices may reflect medieval ones but cannot always be presumed to do so, lest we fall into the trap of abstracting and idealizing phenomena which are in fact historically contingent' (Berkey, 1996, p. 23). The same can be said for equating ancient and pre-modern ideas with medieval and modern ones. He finds that medieval jurists repeated verbatim earlier hadith both in favor of and in opposition to the practice. In general, it was perceived by medieval jurists as a ritual of religious purification for women in line with that of male circumcision. It can also be traced to ancient gendering, according to Berkey, when it was believed that men and women were born bisexual and so had male and female parts cut off in order to maintain their gender identity. Most significantly, Berkey links the medieval and modern misogynist discourses concerning females having too great a sexual appetite which therefore needed to be curbed by excising clitorises to avert sexual chaos through adultery. Furthermore, he states that these discourses are common to patriarchal societies in the Mediterranean and Near East. Thus, women had a right to sexual pleasure as long as it was a highly prescribed sexual pleasure modified by excision, while men had expansive sexual rights to these women. Although this interpretation is critical from the outset in terms of properly placing time-specific practices, it is not as thoughtful about imposing terms such as 'gender' on the ancient world, or about analyzing how the concept of female sexuality could have remained so limited in scope and argumentation over such a great period of time. To his credit, Berkey does highlight the fact that women's voices on this issue are generally absent from modern analysis from the eighth until the twentieth century.

Qur'anic representations of women and their exegeses over centuries provide another example of shifting representations of sexuality and how modern *fitna* is linearly traced throughout time. Gayane Karen Merguerian and Afsaneh Najmabadi follow the amorphous story of Zulaykha and Yūsuf from its qur'anic and biblical roots through its medieval exegesis until the modern era. It is evident that the timeless idea of *fitna* can be followed throughout history to fulfill the modern of agenda of 'destabilizing the notions of women's sexuality as a social and individual threat to the Islamic community' (Merguerian & Najmabadi, 1997, p. 503). However, is it possible that the same misogynist discourse simply continued to expand further and further over time? Were there no voices of dissent or contradictory models? Although Merguerian and Najmabadi give an excellent treatment of *fitna* through the analysis of 'female guile', it again appears as if *fitna* were an ahistorical concept. Significantly, they explain the power of female bleeding during menstruation and childbirth as an indication of female sexuality and a direct threat to male power. They also demonstrate that, although various embellished medieval accounts of the Zulaykha and Yūsuf story exist, male sexuality is always victorious.

As the frequently quoted tenth-century message of al-Ṭabarī is passed on once again, they voice his conviction that:

> Female sexual desire is a potential source of danger to men; it will cause them to sin, because it will come between them and God. It must, therefore, be punished. Only when satisfied within the bonds of marriage is female sexual desire redeemable, and, indeed, rewarded bringing happiness and sons to man. What more could a good woman want? (*ibid.*, p. 493)

Utilizing al-Ṭabarī as a source always conveys this sentiment and informs this research. However much al-Ṭabarī may have contributed to the subjugation of women in Islam, he was not employing a truly modern concept of sexuality and gender in his writings.

Gender: 'Marriage and Reproduction' versus 'Wife and Mother' Constructs

A hadith attributed to ʿĀʾisha issues this statement on marriage by the Prophet:

> Marriage is my way, and one who does not follow me is not among my followers. It is necessary for my followers to marry, so that I will be proud of my community. It is also necessary for followers who can afford to marry as well as for those who cannot afford to marry to fast, as fasting can suppress sexual desire. (Kabbani & Bakhtiar, 1998, p. 36)

The issue of marriage before the time of the Prophet among the Arab tribes is controversial. However, the consensus is that the Prophet introduced the concept of paternity through ʿidda. ʿĀʾisha recalled four types of marriage immediately prior to Islam. One was similar to Islam's concept of a man who asked a woman's father for permission to marry her and then her father received her dowry. The second kind of marriage was called al-istibdāʿ in which a husband had his wife sleep with another man in order to conceive. The third type of marriage was when a group of less than ten men had intercourse with a woman, and when she gave birth she would name one of them as the father and he would accept. The fourth form of marriage was when a woman slept with many men indiscriminately, and she decided who was the father of each of her children, as they were born, according to their physical similarities (*ibid.*, p. 220). Of course, Islam instituted its own form of legitimate marriage, which made the others illicit. If this portrayal of pre-Islamic marriages is accurate, the modern definitions of gender and sexuality may be theoretically enlightening, but they are not representative of this period. Additionally, if patriarchy can be exposed through marriage relations, it remains ambiguous in the period of *Jāhiliyya*. It implies that for the Muslim community, marriage was the communal institution towards which sexual energy should be directed.

The Qurʾan itself portrays marriage as a partnership, not the modern construct of wife and husband. Doi explains that the reason for marriage can be found in Q 30.21, which states: 'And among his signs is this, that He has created for you mates from among yourselves, that you may dwell in tranquility with them; and He has put love and mercy between you. Verily in that are signs for those who reflect' (Doi). He is not alone in this conclusion.

Amina Wadud shows that women are not very gendered or sexualized in the Qurʾan according to her own *tafsīr*. Wadud's modern exegesis provides an example of avoiding the above-mentioned methodological pitfalls by simply addressing the text in an entirely different way, which breaks with modernity and addresses the book as a living text drawn from the seventh century. Marriage, sexual desire, childbirth, menstruation and breastfeeding are referred to in the Qur'an, but not in the form of modern, or even medieval, wife and mother constructs presented by other scholars. Wadud's book is not about women in Islam, but about the Qur'an and woman in relation to each other. She avoids using the sunna and hadith because of the historical preservation and contradiction problems inherent in them as first highlighted by Fatima Mernissi. In the creation story related in the Qu'ran she finds that there is essential equality between men and women. Significantly, it is childbearing and not childcare or rearing that is assigned to women; it is obvious that the Qur'an addressed the biological function of mother, and not the cultural engendering of 'mother' (Wadud, 1999, pp. 7–22). She singles out *taqwā* (piety) as what differentiates human beings—male and male, female and female, and male and female—from each other, not gender or sexuality. At the same time, she does admit that Maryam, the mother of Jesus, is the only woman referred to by name in the Qur'an, and that the prophets were all men (*ibid.*, pp. 38–39). But what does this mean? Is it some form of misogyny? Is this a precursor or a reflection of patriarchy? Or is there some other divine meaning, as Wadud concludes? Furthermore, she finds that even in death there is no gender or sexual differentiation in the Qur'an since all experience death in the same way, on the basis not of gender, but of good and bad deeds in life. The day of judgement is similiarly ungendered, for human beings will abandon their daily reality of beings wives, mothers, husbands, fathers, sons and daughters. Hell is similarly experienced without regard to gender (*ibid.*, p. 45; Q 3.185). Wadud's interpretation calls into question the validity of the approach of other scholars who find modern sexuality and gendering in the Qu'ran.

Wadud equally attacks the assumption that the Qur'an genders women as mothers as mentioned above. Mothering is not a woman's exclusive role. However, biological childbirth is important for the propagation of the human race, and is extolled in the Qur'an as no other human function. Wadud writes: 'There is no term in the Qur'an which indicates that childbearing is "primary" to a woman.' She further states that no other gender role in the Qur'an is exclusive to one sex or the other (*ibid.*, p. 64; cf. Q 4.1). Wadud determines that household tasks and childrearing are referred to in the Qur'an as equally shared by men and women (*ibid.*, p. 91). She therefore believes that the Qur'an allows for each society to decide on its own roles and functions, which is how modern gender roles and sexuality have arisen today; they are not, despite hadith and *fiqh*, inherent in the Qur'an.

How is it then that Aliah Schleifer represents Islamic motherhood in which she espouses the modern paradigm of mother as the critical member of the Islamic family, and the harbinger of faith in the Islamic community? The truth is that she relies very little on the Qur'an and heavily on hadith and *fiqh*. The Qur'an certainly encourages children to respect and care for their parents, but it does not develop the idea of the modern mother or wife. She refers to Q 2.233, which gives the responsibility of nursing to both the mother and the father, even though it is obviously physically possible only for the mother.[7] In this way, she contradicts her own interpretation. It is not until she cites al-Ṭabarī that she declares that mothers who do not nurse their own children break their maternal bond with their children and deprive them of affection, possibly adversely affecting the child in adulthood (*ibid.*, p. 71). Furthermore, she finds nothing in the Qur'an to support her construct of woman as an important community member through her function in the family as mother based on her emotional nature (*ibid.*, pp. 47–50).

Conclusion

The concepts of sexuality, gender and patriarchy are fundamental to understanding power relations between the sexes in the modern world. However, these are modern concepts, constructed and understood within the realm of modernity and the socio-economic and hegemonic orders that characterize it. Owing to the lack of translated, popular materials dealing with periods outside of the Qur'an and the Middle Ages up to pre-modern times, these concepts, which could prove critical to our understanding of the past, have not been properly problematicized or historicized. Scholars have almost consistently insisted on using monolithic definitions that seemingly transcend time.[8] In her treatise on Foucault, Laura Anne Stoler (1995) reminds us that discourse on sexuality is a dense transfer point of power between the said of discourse and the unsaid of silence. One could argue in this case that there may be discourse that is not accessed, creating a silence that leads to faulty modern scholarship. It is imperative that more research and translation be done on potential sources ranging from seventh-century Arabia until the modern day. It is more important, however, to recognize that sexuality, gender and patriarchy are not useful concepts if they are applied backwards onto the past instead of having their evolution into our present understanding of them explored. History is a process, and its concepts and analytical frameworks are complex and dynamic too. Modern feminist inquiry is not served by artificially theorizing a linear progression of historical constructs in an effort to illegitimize the modern Muslim woman's reality.

Notes

1. Gender is a social construct, which identifies an individual with a larger social group as defined, but not limited to: genitalia (sex), behavior, social norms and prescribed abilities.
2. According to John Voll (interview November 2002), history is made by the sources that survive and are widely translated, and for this reason al-Ṭabarī, who is very problematic for women, is one of the most cited early recorders of hadith.
3. An expanded discussion of sexuality is presented later in the paper, which is informed by Foucault.
4. This is a controversial point based on historical narratives widely disseminated in the Middle East that during the pre-Islamic period of *Jāhiliyya* women were subjugated to atrocities by men but Islam was revolutionary in its egalitarian treatment of women. Ahmed and El Saadawi have very different interpretations of this period from one another, indicating the discrepancies that exist in the history. Thus, it is the age of ignorance or the age of equality depending on whose narration is read.
5. Lerner (1986) hypothesizes that formal patriarchy was pre-dated to a period of urbanization when female sexuality as reproductive capability became vital to growing male warring tribes in the Neolithic period.
6. Lerner (1986) explains that women were placed in society according to their sexual relationships with men, in contrast with men, who were related to economic modes of production.
7. Schleifer (1986, p. 68). The sura states: 'Mothers shall suckle their children for *ḥawlayn kāmilayn* [that is] for those who wish to complete the suckling. The duty of feeding and clothing the nursing mother in a seemly manner is upon the father of the child. No one should be burdened beyond his capacity ... If they desire to wean the child by mutual consent and [after] joint consultation, it is no sin for them; and if ye wish to give your children out to nurse, it is no sin for you, provided that ye pay what is due from you in fairness.'
8. Place is an additional argument to be made, as the Arab world is such a small part of the larger Muslim world.

140   *E. Shlala Leo*

References

Ahmed, L. (1992) *Women and Gender in Islam* (New Haven, CT: Yale University Press).

Berkey, J. P. (1996) Circumcision circumscribed: female excision and cultural accommodation, *International Journal of Middle East Studies*, 28, pp. 19–38.

Doi, A. R. I., *Women in the Quran and the Sunna*, http://www.usc.edu/dept/MSA/humanrelations/womeninislam/womenquransunnah.html.

El Saadawi, N. (1982) *The Hidden Face of Eve* (Boston, MA: Beacon Hill Press).

Jenson, R. W., CF (1984) The sacrament of civil righteousness, *Liturgy*, 4(2), pp. 39–63.

Kabbani, S. H. & Bakhtiar, L. (1998) *Encyclopedia of Muhammad's Women Companions and the Traditions They Related* (Chicago, IL: ABC International Group).

Lerner, G. (1986) *The Creation of Patriarchy* (New York: Oxford University Press).

Merguerian, G. K. & Najmabadi, A. (1997) Zulaykha and Yusuf: whose 'best story'?, *International Journal of Middle East Studies*, 29, pp. 485–508.

Mernissi, F. (1987) *Beyond the Veil: Male–Female Dynamics in Muslim Society*, rev. edn (Bloomington, IN: Indiana University Press).

Mernissi, F. (1991) *The Veil and the Male Elite: a Feminist Interpretation of Women's Rights in Islam* (New York: Addison-Wesley).

Schleifer, A. (1986) *Motherhood in Islam* (Cambridge: Islamic Research Academy).

Swanson, M. (1984) A study of twentieth-century commentary on Surat al-Nur (24):27–33, *Muslim World*, 74(3–4), pp. 187–203.

Stoler, L. A. (1995) *Race and the Education of Desire: Foucault's 'History of Sexuality' and the Colonial Order of Things* (Durham, NC: Duke University Press).

Wadud, A. (1999) *Qur'an and Woman: Rereading the Sacred Text from a Woman's Perspective* (New York: Oxford University Press).

[15]

Migration challenges views on sexuality

Nader Ahmadi

Abstract

The purpose of this study is to inquire into whether there are any patterns to indicate that Iranian migrants residing in Sweden have changed their views on sexuality since the time of their migration. Using qualitative research methodology, this study examines possible changes due to the transition between two cultures and how these changes may affect views on sexuality, partner choices, and so forth. The results of the study indicate that the encounter with the Swedish way of thinking and the Swedish sexual culture seems to have influenced Iranians' views on sexuality: the traditional authoritarian patriarchal sexual relationship among Iranian migrants in Sweden is giving way to more egalitarian relationships and a relatively strong tendency towards a similarity of views between the sexes regarding sexuality can be observed. The important change noted in regard to sexuality is, however, the evolving of individualism both in regard to sexual decision-making and forms of relationships.

Keywords: Islam; sexuality; migration; gender roles; marriage; ethnicity.

Introduction

Changes in gender relations due to migration have been the focus of many studies (Buijs 1993; Aswad & Bilge 1996; Akpinar 1998; Barot, Bradley & Fenton 1999; Kelson & DeLaet 1999; Ahmadi-Lewin 2001). There has been particular interest in the area of women's empowerment (Stier 1991; Gill & Matthews 1995). In Sweden cultural studies, while exploring the issue of sexuality, have mainly focused on the incompatibility of and cultural clashes between immigrants' views of sexuality, on the one hand, and the mainstream sexual culture, on the other (Månsson 1984). With the exception of a few studies, e.g. by Lewin (1991) and Frisell (1996), there has been little research to date on how sexual behaviour is changing in migrant communities in Sweden. Even fewer studies have focused on changing views on sexuality as a specific characteristic of the encounter between migrants from traditional Islamic societies and modern egalitarian cultures. The sexual reality and views of Muslim immigrants in Sweden have largely remained unexplored. Even in a nationwide study that aimed at mapping the sexual reality of contemporary Sweden, *Sex In Sweden* (Lewin 1997), migrants, although they constitute over 17 per cent of Sweden's population, are absent. The purpose of this article is to contribute towards filling these gaps in our knowledge.

A commonly held view in the research on sexuality is that sexuality is a historical, cultural and social construction (Weeks 1985, 1986; Hawkes 1996; Horrocks 1997). According to Weeks, 'Sexuality only exists through its social forms and social organization. Moreover, the forces that shape and mould the erotic possibilities of the body vary from society to society' (1986, p. 24). Thus, sexuality is constituted differently within different socio-cultural contexts, and to be a sexual being has totally different signification in different cultures and epochs. Gisela Helmius (1997) maintains that sexuality's when, where, how, why and with whom are culturally determined. Further, sexuality is related to the questions of power, (Foucault 1990) identity and view of the Self (Giddens 1992).

The purpose of this study, then, is to inquire into whether there are any indications that Iranian migrants, as the largest Muslim immigrant group in Sweden, have changed their views on sexuality since the time of their migration. Using qualitative research methodology, this study examines whether the transition from one culture to another has changed how Iranian migrants in Sweden view sexuality, virginity, partner choices, and so forth. This study is particularly relevant, as Iranian immigrants have moved from a religious society with an extremely patriarchal sexual culture to a modern secularized society where a liberal view of sexuality prevails.

An important clue to understanding the Islamic approach to sexuality is the Islamic conception of hierarchy. When discussing the relationship between God and man, or between man and nature, Islamic thought posits a sophisticated hierarchical order. According to this way of thinking, the fact that different levels of existence emanate from one and the same origin, i.e. The One or God, does not obscure the primary order of and basic difference between these different levels (Nasr 1980, p. 89). This cosmic hierarchical order is also mirrored in social life. Humankind, as a species, is regarded as the most dignified being under the heavens and constitutes the immediate link between heaven and Earth. Nevertheless, Islamic thought distinguishes between men and women regarding their place in the cosmic hierarchy; Adam belongs to the divine realm of light, whereas Eve belongs to the dark realm of matter (Nasafi 1983, p. 55). This division whereby man belongs to the superior realm of the soul and woman to the inferior realm of matter is the groundwork for the objectification, instrumentalization, and subordination of women.

686   *Nader Ahmadi*

The de facto consequence of the internal positioning of Adam and Eve in the hierarchical order is that it is man as gender, and not man as species, that is regarded as the highest being in the material universe. Man's body and soul are an entity which thereby legitimizes and sanctifies his pleasure and sexuality. In this regard, woman and the pleasure and comfort she is able to offer man are his by right. Man is entitled to benefit from woman, as he does from the whole of the material world which is inferior to him – animals, vegetation, and inorganic matter. In the Koran (Companions, XXXIX: 8; Cow, II: 183–7; Woman, III: 3) man is encouraged to find his rest in woman, to lie with her and to seek in her what God has prescribed for him (Bouhdiba 1985, pp. 8–9).

However, it should be noted that in several Koran verses women's sexuality, needs and desires are also given attention, if not to the same extent as those of men (Naseef 1995). In Islamic religious texts on marriage, the woman's right to sexual pleasure and orgasm is stressed and men are warned against egoistically ignoring the sexual satisfaction of their women (Bouhdiba 1985). Nevertheless, as we have seen from the philosophical standpoint discussed above, and because of the dominating patriarchal structure of Muslim societies in general, it is not the mutual pleasure of both genders but rather that of the male that is prioritized in reality. Men, despite their religious obligations, enjoy a privileged social position and have ignored women's sexual satisfaction. Consequently, women's individuality and personal integrity are generally ignored and women are often regarded merely as a means of satisfying man's needs. Men are regarded as possessing the right to demand sexual pleasure from their wives whenever they feel the urge.

As the title of this article suggests, this is a study about *Muslim* Iranian migrants in Sweden. Many of the Iranians currently residing in Sweden left their home country in opposition to its religious leadership and therefore might prefer to be defined as secularized persons. But one need not be religious to have internalized the most basic norms and values of a particular religion. That there exist different and more or less explicit norms about sexuality in different societies goes without saying, as is the fact that certain norms may be characteristic for a particular culture or subculture in society. In the general context of the interdependence of the social and religious realms in Islam, there is little or no distinction between 'cultural' and 'religious'. The whole of the culture is permeated by religious, ethical, and normative considerations; each institution, each pattern of behaviour is measured against religious and moral standards. In such a normative context, norms are not only regulative, but also constitutive.

Constitutive sexual norms determine our behaviour in an indirect way. We live according to these norms but seldom or never discuss them because they are so well integrated into our consciousness that we are seldom aware of them. Regulative norms, on the other hand, are explicit.

These norms are often employed consciously and are flexible and subject to change.

Hence, having received one's primary socialization in a society where Islam is the dominant cultural element leaves relatively deep traces on the person's view of the body and sexuality. Therefore, it is not an exaggeration to maintain that Islam, both as a worldview and a basis for legislation, is an integral part of the Iranian culture, or more precisely the Iranian way of thinking. Way of thinking 'refers to any individual's thinking in which the characteristic features of the thinking habits of the culture to which he belongs are revealed' (Nakamura 1971, p. 5). Way of thinking concerns the way in which we make value judgments and practical decisions, classify our experiences, and establish relationships with our surroundings (Ahmadi & Ahmadi 1998). As a way of thinking, Islam determines what place sexuality is to have in peoples' minds and dictates what is normal and desirable sexuality, which persons are regarded as legitimate sexual actors, and which forms of sexual expression are acceptable. Hence, when in this study I use the term Muslim I understand it to mean a person who has incorporated the Muslim way of thinking into his/her worldview regardless of his/her degree of religiosity.

Methods

The data collection involved making one-on-one interviews using a semi-structured questionnaire. Most of the closed-ended questions were followed by open-ended questions. This method allowed me to gather non-predictable information.

The sample

The size of the sample was not predefined, but rather was related to reaching saturation. Several respondents were recruited through local radio stations and immigrant associations and several others by means of the chain-sampling model (Patton 1990, p. 176). For practical reasons the population of the study was limited to Iranian immigrants living in Stockholm. It was easier to reach the population through one of the twenty-nine Iranian local radio stations that broadcast in this city. An additional reason for choosing Stockholm was that almost a third of all Iranians residing in Sweden live in Stockholm. Since my objective in this study was never to reach statistical representativity but rather to study mechanisms, I did not attempt to make my selection framework a straightforward reflection of the population Iranian immigrants. However, to ensure variation in social patterns, I used the broadcasting resources of different local radio stations with different political and social listener circles.

688   *Nader Ahmadi*

Selection criteria

A basic criterion was that the population include men and women between thirty and fifty years of age who have been residing in Sweden for at least ten years. This criterion confined the population to persons who are often called first-generation immigrants. The 10-year residency limit was applied to ensure that the respondents would have had enough time to learn the Swedish language, enter the job market, and settle down in their new country and acquire sufficient knowledge about its norms and values. To have a sufficient grasp of the Swedish language was a second basic criterion in the selection of the respondents. My intention was to exclude persons who lacked any direct contact with the Swedish society through the language and who would, thus, be less receptive to the Swedish sexual culture.[1]

The procedure

The 'point of saturation' for the interviews was reached after twenty-five interviews (of a total of twenty-nine interviews), each approximately one to one and a half hours long. The data were collected in 2000 and 2001 over a period of ten months.

Generalizing the results to a large number of individuals was not a main aim of the study; rather, the aim was to understand how the respondents view themselves and their surrounding world. Thus, I have collected data from subjects who have voluntarily accepted my invitation to participate in the study and who agreed to talk about their sexual culture. This has, of course, had some influence on the study. It is possible, for example, that the study reflects only the views of people who are generally interested in gender issues. And the fact that there are more single or divorced women than married women among the respondents

Table 1. *Population of the study*

	FEMALE	MALE
Total number	12 persons	17 persons
High school degree	12 persons	15 persons
Higher education	5 persons	9 persons
Employed	9 persons	13 persons
Studying	3 persons	4 persons
Grown up in large city	4 persons	2 persons
Grown up in middle range city	8 persons	10 persons
Grown up in small town/village	0 persons	5 persons
Are married/cohabit	2 persons	7 persons
Been married/cohabited	10 persons	10 persons
Total number of sexual partners until now	2–6	1–4

might indicate that married women are more reluctant to reveal their innermost thoughts on sexuality to an outsider. Furthermore, the fact that the researcher/interviewer was in this case a man might have had an inhibiting effect on some of the women respondents.

It should also be noted that the population under study does not include persons who actively practise their religion. Although it was not my intention to deliberately exclude this group, I discovered that no such person had volunteered to participate in the study. Nevertheless, several of the respondents maintained that they are believers and some even said that they follow certain religious ceremonies such as observing the fast.

Because of the sensitive nature of the topic of this research study and in keeping with the general ethical rules for research in the social sciences, a) the respondents were informed about the purpose of the study, the selection criteria, and the research methods; b) they were informed that it is their right to decide for themselves how long and under what conditions they wish to continue with the interviews; c) they were guaranteed anonymity and assured that the information they provided would be treated confidentially; d) they were given an opportunity to review those sections of the research report that included the information they provided and the interpretation I gave to that information, and they were offered a copy of the published research report if they so wished.

Analysis procedure

Five comprehensive themes (approaches to premarital sexual relationships; partner choice and forms of relationship; relationships within couples; sexual decision-making; and views on good sexuality) were chosen in advance as the initial points of departure for the interviews. However, when the transcriptions of the first ten tape-recorded interviews were analysed, a number of new themes and sub-themes emerged. The next step was to return to the original interviews to ensure that each theme and sub-theme had been treated in each of the interviews. The same procedure was repeated at regular intervals. That all relevant information in the thematic condensation was included was also checked. Following the tradition of grounded theory (Strauss & Corbin 1990), interviewing continued until pattern saturation was achieved, i.e. until subsequent interviews yielded no new categories nor new information (Bernard 1998; Patton 1990).

The answers to the open-ended questions and the discussions that evolved from them were analysed qualitatively by systematically looking for similarities and dissimilarities among the responses (Berg 1995). The analysis consisted of a broad coding of the data into general themes and sub-themes supported by interview excerpts wherever appropriate (Berg

690   *Nader Ahmadi*

1995). Particular attention was given to possible patterns in the responses, particularly with regard to the gender of the respondents. Three of the five selected themes (including their subsequent sub-themes) are presented in this article, as follows:

Approaches to premarital sexual relationships
• Sexual knowledge – before and now
• Sexual experience – before and now
• Views on young people's sexual behaviour
• Views on virginity
Partner choice and forms of relationship
Views on good sexuality

Findings

Premarital sexual relations

Sexual knowledge – before and now

To obtain background information about the respondents' views on sexuality, I prompted them by asking who or what they believe has meant most for their sexual education. In response to this question, all the respondents, regardless of gender or age, mentioned that during their growing years they had never had a dialogue with their parents, teachers, or any of their adult relatives about sexuality. Not even between older married siblings and their younger brothers and sisters has there been any kind of dialogue about sex-related issues. The study indicates that this state of affairs was as characteristic of relatively liberal and secularized families as of strongly religious ones. 'It was disrespectful to refer to sexuality; everybody pretended that the issue simply didn't exist'. (Male respondent, 40 years old)

In some instances both male and female respondents claimed that the lack of a dialogue on sexuality did not bother them since they had no interest in discussing sex-related issues or knowing more about sex. A 32-year old female respondent remarked: 'Sexuality was never an important question for me. I did not have time for it nor any reason to think about it. The question seemed premature to me since I had no plans to marry yet'.

Respondents of both genders maintained that they had no adequate knowledge about sexuality and the male/female body prior to their marriage. The only information they had acquired was the often distorted conception they had picked up in the street, from peers at school, or from obscene jokes. The sexually ignorant and inexperienced couple had often their first encounter with the reality of sexuality on their wedding night. A 43-year-old man who came from a religious family maintained:

I had never talked with a woman who was not a close relative. I didn't
know how women think, feel, or what they look like! I did not know
how to talk to women, how to express myself in front of a woman.

Another man, also 42 years old, commented:

On my wedding night I was extremely nervous, fearing I couldn't find
where to penetrate. I couldn't imagine what a vagina looked like; I
had no idea about the anatomy of female genitals.

For many female respondents their sexual experiences following upon
the wedding were characterized by pain, disgust, and shame. Some
female respondents stated that they refused to consummate their
marriage until several weeks after the wedding because they were afraid
or ashamed of having sexual intercourse. Even after the wedding there
was no dialogue about their mutual sexual needs, desires, and preferences between many of the couples. Time and practical experience
formed the basis of the respondents' knowledge about their own and
their partners' sexuality.

The study indicates that there is little dialogue about sexuality among
Iranian couples living in Sweden. On the other hand, the respondents
stated that they do have dialogues with their children about sex-related
issues. The respondents expressed their awareness of the importance and
necessity of sexual education, information, and even sexual experience
before marriage. A male respondent commented:

I regret that I had not acquired any knowledge about sexuality during
my growing years; I think that this is one [of] the reasons why my
marriage didn't last. I do not want my children to miss out on that
knowledge, like I did, or make the same mistakes I made.

Other male respondents, however, said that they had no reason to
engage in a dialogue on sex with their partners. They maintained that the
practice of sex in itself is a dialogue where the parties involved tell their
partner what they want and do not want by means of their bodies and
their actions.

The study indicates that the respondents have acquired some knowledge about the Swedish sexual culture. In general, three ways of
acquiring knowledge about Swedish sexual norms could be observed:
some respondents stated that they had acquired their knowledge via the
media and by following the public debate on equality and gender roles;
others mentioned contacts with friends and colleagues; and a small
number (especially among the women) mentioned their personal experiences of having sexual relationships with Swedes. An interesting point,
however, was that the respondents stressed that the very fact of living in

692   *Nader Ahmadi*

a Swedish cultural environment has influenced their views on sexuality. This is an interesting point in that it indicates that despite the widespread segregation of immigrants in Sweden, the very fact of residing in the Swedish society affects – in accordance with Bourdieu's understanding of the concept habitus – the immigrants' lifestyle and views on sexuality.

Sexual experience – before and now

As I mentioned before and as is illustrated by the interview excerpts above, premarital sexual relationships are not the norm in Iranian society. Many of the participants in the study stated that they seldom had an opportunity even to communicate with persons of the opposite sex outside the family circle. In fact, the following statement made by a 35-year old female respondent illustrates the dominant pattern in the responses to the question about the respondents' premarital sexual experiences: 'Nothing, nothing and nothing; that describes my sexual experiences in the best possible way'.

Nevertheless, some respondents stated that they have had some sexual experience (often petting but in no case intercourse) with their future husband/wife only while still living in Iran. A female respondent maintained:

My fiancé and I used to meet in a park where we embraced and kissed each other, but in the company of other persons we did not even look at each other or talk to one another directly.

A few of the male respondents stated that they had gained sexual experience through contacts with prostitutes. One man, coming from the urban upper-middle-class (the capital city), stated that he had had 'numerous' sexual contacts with girlfriends and prostitutes, both before and after his marriage in Iran, and even after migrating to Sweden. Nevertheless, in contrast to other studies of sexual behaviour in Islamic societies (Månsson 1984), my study does not show that young men in general are encouraged to visit brothels to acquire their sexual education. In my study the categories of persons having the least, if any, sexual experience with prostitutes are male respondents from the secularized urban middle classes, intellectuals, and males coming from religious families.

With respect to the time after their migration, there is a detectable change in the attitude of persons of both genders regarding premarital sexual relationships. My study shows a clear tendency towards an acceptance of premarital sexual relations. Furthermore, respondents of both genders stated explicitly that sexual experience before marriage was a prerequisite for establishing a serious and durable partner relationship. According to a 38-year old female respondent, premarital sexual relationships are now an essential part of the process of getting to know her future partner. There are some differences among the respondents regarding the extent of such relationships; while the men advocated more strongly and less conditionally premarital sexual relationships, some of the women expressed a more cautious standpoint and stressed that such relationships should be established in relation to plans for pair-building. A woman respondent commented:

> If I love somebody and plan to live together with him, I don't mind having sex with him before marriage. But to have sex without having feelings or future prospects . . . no . . . that is not something for me.

It is important to stress that changes regarding premarital sexual relationships are not confined merely to attitudes; the study shows that there are behavioural changes as well. Some of the respondents who formed a family or entered into a common-law relationship after their migration to Sweden maintained that they had been sexually involved with their partner between two and twelve months prior to their marriage or cohabitation. Female respondents showed a tendency to establish exogamic sexual relationships, especially with Swedes, to a larger extent than did male respondents who maintained that they would prefer to form a relationship with an Iranian woman.

Views on young people's sexual behaviour

To further elucidate their views on premarital sexual relationships, I asked the respondents to comment on sexuality among youths. As I mentioned above, all the respondents reported that they had children, although some of the children were too young for sexual relationships at the time of the interview. Regardless of their gender and age, the respondents who had teenagers or adult children stressed that they had already accepted it or would accept it if their child, whether a boy or a girl, were involved in a premarital sexual relationship. However, this acceptance did not seem to be unconditional. The prevailing pattern seemed to be to draw the line for accepting young people's sexual activities between seventeen and eighteen years of age. The most important criterion for the respondents' approval of young people engaging in sexual activities, however, was that the sexual relationship had to be based on love. Further inquiries showed that behind this reservation lay an implicit expectation that premarital sexual relationships among young people should lead to marriage, or at least to some kind of stable common-law relationship. It is worth noting that the respondents made no distinction in principle between marriage and a common-law relationship in connection with the sexual relationships of young people.

694 *Nader Ahmadi*

> My daughter (seventeen years of age) moved to her boyfriend's parents' home half a year ago, and I am fine with that, since I know that the fellow is a responsible and serious person who loves my daughter.

Some respondents maintained that their daughters, aged between seventeen and eighteen were involved in a common-law relationship or had a boyfriend. It is worth noting that the incidence of teenagers involved in sexual relationships was highest among the single parent households.

None of the respondents approved of their teenage children having more than a few sexual relationships unless it improved their future marriage prospects. Girls who have numerous sexual relationships risk being regarded as impure, and boys as irresponsible. When discussing young people's sexual behaviour, many respondents used such terms as 'being abused', 'being exploited', and 'getting hurt', which might conceal a conservative view of youth sexuality despite the respondents' approval in principle. Some respondents expressed their fear/concern about girls 'getting pregnant' prior to marriage and the risk of abortion which they regarded as inappropriate for unmarried girls but acceptable for married couples.

Views on virginity

Several respondents of both genders maintained that virginity was not a must for men or for women. Among the men who after their migration to Sweden had married an Iranian woman, several stated that their wife was not a virgin at the time of the marriage but that this did not matter to them. One man in his thirties commented that:

> To think about whether your bride is a virgin or not is the most stupid thing one can think when marrying a woman. I was not a virgin when I married my wife, so why should she be one?

Another respondent, a man in his early 40s, said that his present wife had had several sexual relationships, both in Iran and in Sweden, before she married him. She was married previously in Iran and had had a couple of 'boyfriends' in Sweden. Still another respondent, a single man in his mid-40s, said: 'If I marry again, I would prefer to marry somebody who is not a virgin and has had previous sexual experience'.

Some of the responses indicate that some male respondents consider it better to marry a woman who is a not a virgin because she was married before rather than one who is not a virgin because she has had a boyfriend. In addition, although many of the men stated that virginity was not an issue with them, some of them seemed reluctant to answer the question of whether their present wife/partner had been a virgin or had had some sexual experiences with men prior to their marriage. 'I don't know if she has had any sexual relationships'; 'I never asked'; and 'We had no reason to discuss this issue' were typical responses.

As the study shows, a more positive attitude toward the decline of the virginity imperative is observable among the female respondents. Although some of them stated that they prefer not to have premarital sexual relationships, they did not regard other women who had such relationships as being in the wrong or scandalous. However, the prevailing view among the respondents was that it is a woman's private matter whether she wants to have sexual relationships prior to marriage. A 32-year old woman commented:

> Ok, I might concede to the virginity imperative, but only if my future husband accepted it for himself, too. We must be equals, both in our rights and freedom and in our constraints.

Several female respondents commented that because of unfortunate experiences in a previous marriage they now believe that it is essential to have sexual relationships before marriage as a necessary part of getting to know one's future partner and that it is an unavoidable premarital ritual.

When asked about teenagers and adult children living at home, the most common answer was that virginity is not a factor. Nevertheless, as mentioned above, it appears that a woman should be prepared to give up her virginity only in a relationship where there are relatively good prospects of marriage or cohabitation.

Partner choice and forms of relationship

The study shows that apart from marriage, both common-law relationships and Living Apart Together relationships (LAT) occur among the respondents. Jan Trost and Irene Levin (2000, pp. 104–110) when discussing LAT relationships, which have been known in Sweden and Norway since the 80s (in Swedish, *särbo*), refer to an English term coined by the Dutch journalist Michiel Berkel in 1978 and define this kind of relationship as one existing between two people who, although they live in separate households, nevertheless consider themselves as a couple living under marriage-like conditions.

Several respondents (from both genders) stated that they are currently living in a common-law relationship. One 48-year old man said that he and his Iranian common-law partner have two children (five and eight years of age) born in the partnership. When asked whether their relatives in Iran were aware of the fact that they are not legally married, the respondent replied: 'We haven't had reason so far to tell them about the legal status of our relationship'. Although this respondent appears somewhat cautious, other respondents made no distinction in principle between marriage and common-law relationships.

> I don't believe anymore that this piece of paper [the marriage certificate] matters. If somebody wants to cheat on you, abuse you, or abandon you, he can do it regardless of whether you're married or not. Furthermore, here in Sweden, nobody would consider you a whore if you were not married to the man you are living with. So why bother getting married! (Female respondent, 37 years old)

Another female respondent (46 years old) maintained that:

> In Sweden it's so easy to get divorced. So the marriage certificate is no guarantee you'll have a long-lasting relationship. Besides, why should you want such a guarantee? Here, it's not like back home where the husband is the family's sole breadwinner and where the well-being of the wife and children depends on him. Here, everybody has to manage for themselves financially, and even if you're married you have to work outside the home and earn your own living.

The issue of love emerged as a theme in all the interviews. Respondents from both genders stressed that love is a very important factor in their choice of partner and the person with whom one is having a sexual relationship. There are some differences between men and women in this respect. While some male respondents believed that love is an inducement for sexual relations and marriage, female respondents considered it a prerequisite. Although neither of the genders excluded the possibility of having sex for its own sake, most of the respondents nevertheless pointed out that they would enter into a sexual relationship only if they had a strong feeling for that person.

Regarding LAT relationships, the interest in forming such a relationship was greater among the female respondents than among the male. Several women said that they were currently living in or had lived in a LAT relationship. One woman remarked that the advantage of a LAT relationship over other ways of forming a couple is that there is less chance of clashes between her children from previous relationships and her new partner or his children. For another female respondent, a LAT relationship was preferable because it offered her a greater chance to keep her newly won freedom and independence.

It should be noted, however, that almost all of the female respondents who reported living in a LAT relationship stressed that in the long run they would prefer to cohabit with or marry their LAT-partners. Their rationale for this preference, expressed in the interview, is that their social network and the Iranian immigrant community in general regard a relationship based on cohabitation or marriage as being more serious than one where the couple live apart.

> If I lived with my partner under the same roof I would have enjoyed a better social acceptance. Honestly, I believe that even my LAT-partner would take our relationship more seriously if we lived together. (Female 36 years old)

The question of social acceptance and the status of the couple in the eyes of others (mainly their fellow countrymen) was raised by several respondents. Their main concern was a desire to have their relationship regarded as legitimate and taken seriously by their social network, both in Sweden and in Iran. Some of the women in the study stressed that their families and relatives back home would feel more at ease in their contacts with them if they were legally married to their partners. A 35-year old woman maintained that her parents, while being aware that she was living with a boyfriend, always referred to him as her husband. Another woman, 41 years old, commented:

> We arranged a big wedding party where I wore my white bridal dress. We invited a lot of people, from Sweden and from abroad. Everyone gave us presents and congratulated us on our marriage. But in reality we never got married but were cohabiting. We did this to prevent gossip and to be legitimate in the eyes of others.

Nevertheless, several respondents reported that their relatives, after a period of resistance and rejection, had more or less accepted their common-law or LAT relationship. One woman (38 years old) described her highly religious mother's attitude as follows:

> The first time she came to Sweden for a visit, and realized that I was living in a LAT relationship, she went back home after only two days and didn't talk to me for a year. But during her second visit to Sweden, she came to the conclusion that LAT relationships are not in contradiction with Islamic thought or Islamic law!

One female respondent (33 years old) stated that she still prefers not to tell her parents in Iran about her Swedish 'boyfriend' so as not to jeopardize her 'good relationship' with them.

My study shows that marriage and cohabitation partners are generally chosen within the Iranian community. At the same time, however, there is some cross-cultural dating and sexual liaison, mainly between Iranian females and male Swedes. The male respondents generally prefer to enter into a durable relationship with Iranian females only.

To my question about the rationale for prioritizing Iranian partners, many of the respondents remarked that the most essential factor in a permanent relationship was to be able to express one's inner feelings with ease. Many respondents maintained, in this regard, that a common social and historical memory and a common knowledge of cultural codes were the most crucial factors in their choice of a life partner. Others referred, in addition, to their lack of proficiency in the Swedish language. Some female respondents maintained that their efforts to continue to live with their Swedish partners were unsuccessful and that after a while they realized that they would feel more at ease with an Iranian partner in a long-term relationship.

The respondents were also asked about their views on and experiences of sexual relationships outside marriage. The responses of both men and women indicate that extra-marital sexual relationships are rather uncommon. Some respondents stated that if such a situation were to occur in their own marriage, either for them or for their partner, they would first investigate the circumstances and not react as 'spontaneously' as they would have done prior to their immigration to Sweden. One male respondent (53 years old) stated: 'My wife had an affair with somebody a couple of years ago. Although I was devastated, I decided not to divorce her but to put it behind us and go on living with her'. Although he added, 'My feelings for my wife are not the same now as they were before this incident', he nevertheless maintained that he was happy about his decision to continue to live with her.

Good sexuality

To obtain more information about their understanding of sexuality, I asked the respondents to describe what in their view characterized an ideal sexual relationship. The rationale for this question was to learn how the respondents evaluated their own sexuality and how they wished it would be. The respondents were asked to try to look back and, in the light of their accumulated life experiences at the time of the interview, make an overall judgement of their sexuality during the different phases of their life.

In response to this question all the respondents, without exception, stressed that the precondition for a good sexual relationship was love and that what guaranteed good sexuality was reciprocity.

> Well, I have had sexual relationships without being in love, and I might have such relations in the future, too. But such relationships do not last. Sex for the sake of pleasure without love . . . no, I don't call it good sexuality. (Male, 37 years old)

The dominant pattern for the female respondents' view is expressed in the following response given by a 32-year old woman: 'I could never ever have sex with somebody I was not in love with'.

Both genders stressed that they believe that interplay and mutuality, being sensitive to and having respect for one's partner's will and desire, and seeking equality are the most important characteristics of a good sexual relationship. Even those respondents who were unable to describe their current sexual relationship as good voiced the same criteria for good sexuality. For instance, a 50-year old man who maintained that he was aware that his current sexual relationship with his wife was nothing other than his continuously raping her within the bounds of matrimony said that good sexuality should be based on mutuality!

Discussion

As the study indicates, in a traditional patriarchal society such as Iran, both men and women suffer from the lack of a dialogue on sexuality. The omnipresence of the Islamic religious norms in the Iranian society has made dialogues about sex and sexuality taboo in Iranian families. According to the respondents, prior to their migration to Sweden there was no dialogue whatsoever between adults and children about sex-related issues, neither at home nor at school. Not having had a serious discourse about sexuality, young Iranians entertained a multitude of fallacies, myths, and misunderstandings about sexuality. Respondents of both genders emphasized that their lack of sexual knowledge and experience contributed to the failure of their relationships. The negative consequences of patriarchal norms for women are self-evident. What my study indicates is that, with regard to sexuality, men, too, are oppressed in patriarchal societies where religious norms predominate. Repressing any kind of sexual relationship between persons who are not married to each other, these norms function as a double-edged sword affecting both genders, although to different extents. Dialogue and interaction with others are presumably important factors in forming our understanding of sexuality. Creating a discourse about sexuality makes sexuality a subject for discussion and scrutiny, and can lead to compromise and change. Although the study does not indicate any significant changes regarding dialogue between partners on issues relating to their sexuality, it clearly confirms that the respondents are aware of the necessity for dialogue and knowledge about sexuality for young people. This could be a consequence of the respondents' encounter with and adaptation to Swedish sexual norms.

Another tendency observed in the study is that the respondents redefine their symbols in relation to bodily functions according to their new socio-cultural context. The redefinition of the relationship between body and symbol becomes more obvious when the question of virginity is raised. According to traditional Iranian social and religious norms, a sexual relationship is reserved exclusively for married life; nevertheless, dating and some forms of premarital sexual acts are not uncommon

700 *Nader Ahmadi*

between betrothed. In the Iranian society the bride is expected to be a virgin when she marries for the first time. The groom has the right to revoke the marriage if on the wedding night he discovers that his bride is not a virgin. My study indicates clearly a tendency among the respondents to break with Iranian-Islamic sexual norms. Although the respondents show individual variations in how they interpret the relationship between body and symbol, a growing acceptance of premarital sexual relationships could be observed among both genders. The occurrence of premarital relationships can be regarded as indicating a radical liberalization of attitudes towards both sexuality and gender roles. Similar changes in the attitude of Muslim migrant women can be observed in a study that was recently carried out on young women of Moroccan descent living in The Netherlands (Buitelaar 2002).

The study clearly indicates a weakening of male dominance in sexual relationships and that there is greater individual freedom in relation to the family. Within the traditional Islamic-Iranian discourse on virginity, body and symbol are intertwined to serve men's power, interests, and privileges. Virginity is exploited by men in order to exercise control over women. The bodily function of 'losing one's maidenhead' outside marriage is, in traditional Iranian-Islamic culture, related to the symbol of bringing shame down upon the family and depriving it of honour. However, this study makes it evident that the female respondents no longer view virginity as a concern of the family, but perceive it as a personal responsibility. This attitude makes it more difficult for men to use the symbolic value of virginity as a means of exercising power.

Based on what the respondents have said about their relatives' and parents' attitude towards the respondents adapting to Swedish sexual norms and couple-building, it might be concluded that there is beginning to be a shift in the attitude of the older generation of Iranians. The findings of the study confirm the results of other studies on older Iranian immigrants (Ahmadi & Tornstam 1996). Both elder people who have emigrated to Sweden and those who still live in Iran but who have family members who have migrated, are affected by the changes in the younger generation's sexual norms and views. Some of these elderly try to re-evaluate and redefine their traditional views and to empathize with their relatives, while others just give up and accept the changes, if reluctantly. Nevertheless, the outcome may be the same: migration to Sweden might very well bring about changes in the way Iranian society views sexuality.

However, the most important change that could be observed in regard to the respondents in this study is probably the evolving of individualism. Exposed to the individualistic ideology and lifestyle of Sweden, the respondents demonstrated a clear tendency to revise their previous holistic ways of thinking. The importance of realizing one's own desires, goals, and personal life-projects has become a central issue for many migrant Iranians. As discussed earlier in this article, sexual practices reflect wider social relations. This might explain the preference among respondents for common-law and LAT relationships, i.e. relationships that grant couples more individual freedom than does traditional marriage. Many respondents stressed that in their relationship with their partner, it was crucial for them to have some 'space' for themselves, and to be on their own whenever they wished. The growing acceptance of alternative kinds of relationships can, thus, be understood as indicating the emergence of an individualistic way of thinking among the respondents.

Lastly, it should be mentioned that although all the interviews were carried out in Persian, several respondents preferred to use Swedish words when referring to intimate topics such as orgasm and sexual intercourse. According to postmodern theories of identity, personal identity changes selectively in specific settings depending on what is more beneficial to the individual (Ahmadi 2000). We define our limitations and freedom of action differently in different contexts and, depending on which identity is the more instrumental, we act and behave differently. Employing different languages in different contexts indicates a very important characteristic of the reality of the migrants in a postmodern era – that each language represents a different world, different roles, and maybe different views on life. Perhaps this is why the respondents, when referring to a topic that was not usually referred to publicly in their society, reverted to using Swedish. Understanding that dialogue about sexuality and calling genitals or sexual acts by their names is taboo and improper in the Iranian culture, the respondents shifted to the Swedish language when referring to these topics. They seem to have developed different identities that exist parallel in different contexts. They appear to step into their Swedish identities, an identity that allows them to be someone they are not allowed to be in their Iranian contexts. The fact that the researcher was of the same cultural origin as the respondents might also have influenced the interview situation and contributed to the respondents' assuming a Swedish identity. However, the fact that a number of Iranian men and women agreed to be interviewed about such an intimate and in their culture unusual topic as their views on sexuality is an obvious indication that changes have occurred in the respondents' ideas about and attitudes to sexuality. It is true that many Iranians were already exposed to modern ideas even prior to their migration; many lived a modern secularized lifestyle; and others, who although they defined themselves as Muslims, adhered to a liberal interpretation of Islam. But as I mentioned before, the influence of normative Islamic laws on the Iranian way of thinking about sexuality is substantial. I have to admit that I was concerned before starting this study whether it would be possible for me, as a male researcher, to approach women who were not used to engaging in a dialogue about sexuality and discussing sex with a

702   *Nader Ahmadi*

stranger of the opposite gender. During the interviews, the women respondents showed a surprising openness to discussing intimate sexual issues. The men, too, were willing to discuss such overtly sensitive issues as their wife's/partner's premarital sexual relationships with other men; this is rarely an open topic even in male-to-male conversations in the Iranian culture.

Conclusions

Do the results of this study indicate a change in the respondents' views, prejudices, and taboos regarding sexuality? In general, the study shows that there is a relatively surprising similarity of views on sexuality between the sexes. Iranians' encounter with the Swedish way of thinking and the Swedish sexual culture seems to have influenced their views on virginity, premarital sexual relationships, and acceptance of young peoples' sexual activities. Of course, this is quite different from asserting that to enjoy good sexuality Iranian immigrants will have to adopt Western customs, goals, and lifestyles. In the Iranian households in my study, discussion about sexuality and related subjects is no longer considered taboo, especially between parents and children. Nevertheless, the topic of sex is not addressed as overtly as in mainstream families. Traditional authoritarian patriarchal sexual relationships are giving way to more egalitarian relationships. This is, in my view, mainly a consequence of the changes brought about through migration to Sweden, which has implied appreciable changes in women's life conditions, freedom, and rights. The prevailing impression provided by this study is that changes in attitude have occurred to a relatively larger extent among women than among men. Nevertheless, men, too, have largely adapted to the sexual norms of their new social environment.

The starting point of this study has been that sexuality is a sociocultural construction and is subject to change and transformation. Sexuality is not static, unequivocal, or once and for all determined. Nor is an individual's socialization ever fully accomplished. Rather, socialization is an ongoing process through which the individual's sexuality *becomes*. As long as there exist parallel sexual realities related to different groups of people who live in one and the same society, there exists the possibility of moving into and between these sexual realities. Views on sexuality are partly determined by and altered in accordance with changes in the individual's lifestyle. According to Eva Lundgren (1993), each person is actively or passively engaged in forming and developing his/her personal project of gender and sexuality in regard to certain social, cultural, and historical dimensions. The construction of an individual's sexuality takes place therefore within many different arenas and contexts. They are different for different persons and can have different significance at different times.

Although it is not pertinent to ascribe all the changes that have occurred within the Iranian community in Sweden to their migration to this country, it is reasonable to assume that because of the change of socio-cultural context, their views on sexuality have also changed. Theoretically, one could also suggest that migration brings forth changes in the migrants' ways of thinking and living. There are several theories that support such a perspective. For example, Vattimo (1992) and Melucci (1989), from somewhat different points of departure, predict an increased capacity to overstep or transcend cultural differences in connection with moving from one society to another. Many migrant groups, such as women from patriarchal societies, welcome sexual emancipation and find it a relief from the old traditional patterns of organizing sexual relations. In this regard, migration entails a process of change in the social reality of the persons involved and reveals the dissolution of the chain of long-lived beliefs, including views on sexuality. The common approaches to the issue of migrants' views on sexuality fail to consider that people have always evaluated and re-evaluated their cultural beliefs (in this case, on sexuality) in order to manage new social conditions. Migration, with its inevitable impact on how individuals view themselves and their relationships with others, makes it necessary to revise traditional cultural views on sexuality. The experience of moving between different cultures teaches immigrants not to adhere too strongly to their cultural notions of right and wrong. The change comes with the insight that what was once The Reality has become one reality among other realties. According to Vattimo, emancipation from the chain of cultural identity lies in the 'discovery of finiteness, historicity and accidentality of our own realities and value systems' (1992, p. 66).

To see sexuality as a constructed reality leads to the recognition that the body is not an ahistoric element, nor are views of the body unchangeable. The constitution of sexuality can occur for each person individually within certain socio-historic contexts. Sexuality is, thus, both individually and socially determined. There exist different norms of sexuality within different contexts. Each individual has to follow norms that belong to one or more contexts simultaneously. Whatever we do, we contribute to the preservation, transformation, or abnegation of norms. Depending on the extent of control imposed on the individual, on the degree of freedom of choice within each context, people may choose to break with or adapt to the norms, in different ways and in different cultural contexts. The level of adaptation to Swedish sexual norms is, thus, an individual process based on numerous factors. These factors are not mutually exclusive but part of a complex web. They may involve family support and family pressure in Sweden, length of residency, altered power-relations between the genders, women's increased economic and social

704   *Nader Ahmadi*

independence, and males' vulnerable position in society because of prejudices about Middle-Eastern men. The prevalent tendency among the respondents is to break with Iranian-Islamic norms in one context and adhere to them in another. When living in Sweden and among persons who share the same values as themselves, they live according to Swedish sexual norms; when relating to their families in Iran or their more traditional compatriots, they behave according to the norms of the traditional Iranian society.

Note

1.   To help the reader to see how the sample selected corresponds to the whole Iranian immigrant group in Sweden, a comparative picture of this group is provided below (all data were collected from a survey that was carried out by the Swedish National Board of Health and Welfare (Socialstyrelsen, 1998: 1): Almost two-thirds of the total population (65% men and 35% women) were between 20 and 40 years of age at the time of their migration to Sweden (p. 27, Table 2.4); nearly 70% belonged to the middle class in their homeland (p. 22, Figure 2.3); 47% came from the capital city and 45% from other large and middle-sized cities; almost 20% had three years or more of university/college education while more than 50% of the rest of the population had a high school diploma (p. 23, Figure 2.4); today nearly 12% of men and 20% of women in the total population live on their own as singles.

References

AHMADI, F. and TORNSTAM, L. 1996 'The old flying Dutchman: Shuttling immigrants with double assets', *Journal of Aging and Identity*, vol. 1, no. 3, pp. 191–210

AHMADI, N. and AHMADI, F. 1998 *Iranian Islam: The Concept of the Individual*, London: Macmillan Press

AHMADI, N. 2000 'Kulturell identitet i gungning (Rocking cultural identities)', in C. M. Allwood, and E. Franzén, (eds), *Tvärkulturella möten (Cross-cultural encounters)*, Stockholm: Natur & Kultur

AHMADI-LEWIN, F. 2001 'Identity crisis and integration. The divergent attitudes of Iranian immigrant men and women towards integration into the Swedish society', *International Migration*, vol. 39, no. 3, pp. 121–35

AKPINAR, A. 1998 *Male's Honor and Female's Shame: Gender and Ethnic Identity Construction among Turkish Divorcées in the Migration Context*, Uppsala: Uppsala University

ASWAD, B. C. and BILGE, B. (eds) 1996 *Family and Gender among American Muslims: Issues Facing Middle Eastern Immigrants and Their Descendents*, Philadelphia, PA: Temple University Press

BAROT, R., BRADLEY, H. and FENTON, S. (eds) 1999 *Ethnicity, Gender and Social Change*, London: Macmillan Press

BERG, B. L. 1995 *Qualitative Research Methods for the Social Sciences*, Boston, MA: Allyn and Bacon

BERNARD, H. R. 1998 *Research Methods in Cultural Anthropology*, Newbury Park: Sage Publications

BOUHDIBA, A. 1985 *Sexuality in Islam*, London: Routledge & Kegan Paul Publications

BUIJS, G. (ed.) 1993 *Migrant Women: Crossing Boundaries and Changing Identities*, Oxford: Berg

Migration challenges views on sexuality   705

BUITELAAR, M. W. 2002 'Negotiating the rules of chaste behavior: Re-interpretations of the symbolic complex of virginity by young women of Moroccan descent in The Netherlands', *Ethnic and Racial Studies*, vol. 25, no. 3, pp. 462–89

FOUCAULT, M. 1990 *The History of Sexuality, Vol I: An Introduction*, New York: Vintage Books

FRISELL, A. 1996 *Kärlek utan sex går an . . . men inte sex utan kärlek. Om gymnasieflickors tankar kring kärlek och sexualitet* (Love Without Sex is Ok . . . But not Sex Without Love. About high school girls' thoughts about love and sexuality), Stockholm: Mångkulturellt Centrum

GIDDENS, A. 1992 *The Transformation of Intimacy: Sexuality, Love & Eroticism in Modern Societies*, Cambridge: Polity Press

GILL, D. S. and MATTEWS, B. 1995 'Changes in the breadwinner role: Punjabi families in transition', *Journal of Comparative Family Studies*, vol. 26, no. 2, pp. 255–63

HAWKES, G. 1996 *A Sociology of Sex and Sexuality*, Buckingham and Philadelphia: Open University Press

HELMIUS, G. 1997 'Bakgrund: tio år av planer (Background: Ten years of planning)', in B. Lewin (ed.), *Sex i Sverige* (Sex in Sweden), Uppsala: Uppsala University

HORROCKS, R. 1997 *An Introduction to the Study of Sexuality*, London: Macmillan Press

KELSON, G. A. and DELAET, D. L. (eds) 1999 *Gender and Immigration*, London: Macmillan Press

LEWIN, B. 1991 *Att omplantera sexualiteten: om latinamerikanska ungdomars sexuella socialsation i Sverige* (To Replant Sexuality: On the Sexual Socialization of Latin American Youth in Sweden), Uppsala: Uppsala University

LEWIN, B. (ed.) 1997 *Sex i Sverige* (Sex in Sweden), Uppsala: Uppsala University

LUNDGREN, E. 1993 *Det får da vaere grenser for kjönn: Voldelig empiri og feministisk teori [There Must be a Limit for Gender: Violent Reality and Feminist Theory]*, Oslo: Universitetsforlaget

MÅNSSON, S. A. 1984 *Kärlek och kulturkonflikt* (Love and Cultural Conflicts). Stockholm, Prisma

MELUCCI, A. 1989 *Nomads of the Present: Social Movements and Individual Needs in Contemporary Society*, Philadelphia, PA: Temple University Press

NAKAMURA, H. 1971 *Ways of Thinking of Eastern People: India, China, Tibet, Japan*, Honolulu: University of Hawaii Press

NASAFI, A. 1983 *Kitab al-Insan al-Kamil (The Book of the Perfect Man)*, Tehran: Institut Français d'Iranologie de Teheran and Tahuri Editions

NASEEF, F. 1995 *Droits et devoirs de la femme en islam*, Lyon: Éditions Tawhid

NASR, S. H. 1980 *Nazare motefakkerane eslami dar bareye tabiat (Conceptions of Nature in Islamic Thought)*, Tehran: Kharazmi Publishing

PATTON, M. Q. 1990 *Qualitative Evaluation and Research Methods*, Newbury Park: Sage

SOCIALSTYRELSEN 1998 *Levnadsförhällanden hos fyra invandrargrupper födda i Chile, Iran, Polen och Turkiet* (The living conditions of four migrant groups coming from Chile, Iran, Poland and Turkey), Report no. 1998-51-001, Stockholm: Socialstyrelsen

STIER, H. 1991 'Immigrant women go to work: Analysis of immigrant wives' labor supply for six Asian groups, *Social Science Quarterly*, vol. 72, no. 1, pp. 67–82

STRAUSS, A. and CORBIN, J. 1990 *Basics of Qualitative Research: Grounded Theory Procedures and Techniques*, Newbury Park: Sage Publications

TROST, J. and LEVIN, I. 2000 *Särbo: Ett par – två hushåll (Living Together Apart: One Couple – Two Households)*, Stockholm: Studentlitteratur

VATTIMO, G. 1992 *The Transparent Society*, Baltimore, MD: The Johns Hopkins University Press

706   *Nader Ahmadi*

WEEKS, J. 1985 *Sexuality and its Discontents: Meanings, Myths & Modern Sexualities,* London and New York: Routledge
—— 1986 *Sexuality,* London and New York: Routledge

NADER AHMADI is Senior Lecturer in the Department of Social Work at Stockholm University.
ADDRESS: Department of Social Work, Stockholm University, SE-10691 Stockholm, Sweden. Email: <nader.ahmadi@socarb.su.se>

Part IV
Islam and Sexuality in
Global Perspective

[16]

"He Is Your Garment and You Are His ...": Religious Precepts, Interpretations, and Power Relations in Marital Sexuality among Javanese Muslim Women

Lily Zakiyah MUNIR

Three case studies of Javanese Muslim women excavate their marital lives to unpack some of the complexities of Javanese and Islamic traditions that condition their sexual relationship with their husbands. Both these traditions in their practice underline a patriarchal society that subjugates women in sexual and marital relations. The case for women's subordinate position in Javanese Muslim society shares some common philosophical grounds with the perspective of Western radical feminists in the 1970s. However, this is not a discourse pitting Western liberalism against a restrictive Islamic orthodoxy. Instead, the discussion draws on Islamic precepts that preach equity in gender relations and examines how they can coexist with certain Islamic practices that are unfair to women. The women in these studies vary in their abilities to draw on their religious grounding to negotiate a way out of unsatisfactory matrimonial situations. Their experiences provide an opportunity to discuss how religious texts should be understood when what they prescribe is subject to conflicting interpretations.

The operating assumption for this paper is that sexuality is a cultural construct and not altogether biological and immutable.[1] Another assumption is that the teachings of the Qur'an on sexual equality and reciprocity may not always apply in Muslim society in Java. This is because there are at least two factors that determine a Javanese Muslim's attitude to sexuality. First, there is the influence of local Javanese culture which, like many other cultures, is patriarchal and has, consequently, assigned asymmetrical power relations in marriage with all its ramifications on women's sexuality. This patriarchal ideology has been sustained by Javanese stereotypical concept of womanhood, and further perpetrated by the political structure through the institutionalization of the familial ideology.[2] Second, there is the influence of how a person understands Islam and its religious texts. The religious quote referring to marital sexuality (Q.S. al-Baqarah 2:187) in the title of this paper is one of the many instances in the Qur'an and appeals to traditions traceable to the Prophet and his companions known collectively as the Hadith. It prescribes equal and complementary gender and sexual relations in marriage. Other verses or *hadith* may not be as explicit as illustrations of equity and reciprocity between man and woman; in fact, many even imply something quite the contrary.[3] This diversity in the religious texts lends itself to varied interpretations and emphasis, which results in the wide range of experiences found in Muslim communities across the world. Within the world of Javanese Muslims that my three case studies are drawn from, these differences are also evident.

Sexuality, Power, and Patriarchy

My study also seeks to understand sexuality as more than a personal issue between two partners. Articles from feminist literature epitomized by the writings of Kate Millet inform this paper, canvassing a perspective that dissects sexual relations as part of the power relationship intrinsic to human society. "Sex is political", claims the second-wave feminist Millet in her book *Sexual Politics* (1970), because the roots of women's oppression are buried deep in patriarchy's sex/gender system. The male-female relationship is the paradigm for all *power* relationships, and "unless the clinging to male supremacy as a birthright is finally foregone, all systems of oppression will continue to function" (Millet 1970, p. 25). Because male control of the public and private worlds is what constitutes patriarchy,[4] male control must be eliminated if women are to be liberated. To eliminate male control is no easy task. It must, first of all, eliminate the prevalent gender relations constructed under patriarchy.

Patriarchal ideology, according to Millet, exaggerates biological differences between men and women, ensuring that men always play the dominant role and women, the subordinate one. This ideology is particularly powerful because through conditioning, men usually obtain the

consent of the very women they oppress. The role of institutions such
as the family, the school, and religion is instrumental in sustaining patriarchy. Each of these institutions justifies and reinforces women's subordination to men with the result that most women internalize a sense
of inferiority to men. If a woman refuses to accept patriarchal ideology,
and if she manifests her mistrust by casting off her submissiveness, men
will use coercion to accomplish what conditioning has failed to achieve.
Intimidation, observed Millet, is everywhere in patriarchy (Millet 1970,
pp. 43–46).

Sexuality is a crucial issue in feminism because "aggression and the
'need' to dominate form a routine part of what is accepted as (normal)
male sexuality" (Coveney et al. 1984, p. 9). Male violence against
women is normalized and legitimized in sexual practices through the assumption that when it comes to sex, men are by nature aggressive and
dominant, whereas women by nature are passive and submissive. Because male dominance and female submission are the norm in something as fundamental as sexuality, they become the norm in other contexts as well. As most radical feminists see it, women will never be men's
full political, economic, and social equals until heterosexual relations are
entirely egalitarian — a state of affairs not likely to be achieved so long
as women's sexuality is interpreted in terms of men's sexuality.

"Sexuality is *the* locus of male power", argues Catharine MacKinnon
(1982, p. 533) because gender, the socially constructed dynamic of male
domination and female submission, is rooted in the institution of
heterosexuality. Each and every element of female gender stereotype is
sexually charged. "Softness", for example, is a gender trait associated
with women; it is sexually charged because, as MacKinnon defined it,
"softness" is "pregnability by something hard" (p. 570).

Some may dismiss these as nothing but the polemical claims of feminist activists but the feminist perspective has its historical and philosophical basis. In her book *The Creation of Patriarchy* (1986), Lerner
writes that patriarchy is a historic creation formed by men and women
in a process which took nearly 2,500 years to its completion. A review
of Western philosophical thought will support Lerner's thesis. The classical Greek theorist Aristotle was one of many philosophers who taught

that women and men were fundamentally different and asserted that woman's highest function was having children, whereas man's highest purpose was intellectual creativity (Grigsby 2002, p. 133). This was maintained by French philosopher Jean-Jacques Rousseau, who used philosophy to legitimize patriarchy. This is particularly ironic considering that he was one who preached a radical egalitarianism. "Liberty, equality, fraternity" was to be applicable only to men, both in thought and deed. In *Emile*, Rousseau is quite explicit on the position of woman: she is to be brought up as man's subordinate, to minister to his needs and to give him pleasure. He would sympathize with men who "would restrict a woman to the labours of her sex and would leave her in profound ignorance of everything else" (Figes 1986, p. 87). According to Rousseau, domination of men (by governments) was awful, but domination of women by men was natural and desirable (Grigsby 2002, p. 133).

The discourse of power and sexuality was also brought up by Foucault (1978), who views sexuality as a

> historical construct ... in which the stimulation of bodies, the intensification of pleasures, the strengthening of controls and resistances, ... are linked to one another, in accordance with a few major strategies of knowledge and power.

The influence of power in sexuality is also recognized by Giddens (1992), who contends that sexuality is "a social construct, operating within the fields of power, not merely a set of biological promptings". In his theory of structuration, he conceptualizes power as implicated at all levels of social life, from the level of "global cultures and ideologies" all the way down to the "most mundane levels of everyday interactions" (Giddens 1976, p. 113). Power can be analysed not only in social or political institutions, but also in a face-to-face encounter such as in intimate sexual relations.

The discussion of sexuality in the 1990s has found its way into an international agenda of health and women's rights. As part of reproductive health, sexual health is an intrinsic and essential component of general health. The 1994 International Conference on Population Development (ICPD) accepted sexual and reproductive health as the human rights of women which form an integral component of "human rights already recognized in national laws, international human rights documents and other consensus documents". This declaration was reaffirmed in the 1995 Fourth World Conference on Women in Beijing as articulated in the Platform for Action (PFA). However, discussing sexuality is a difficult task in Indonesia. Public discourse on sexuality has been excessively preoccupied with sexuality's negative consequences — sexually transmitted diseases (STDs), human immunodeficiency virus (HIV) — and very little attention has been given to positive sexuality,[5] despite the considerable evidence of public interest in such matters (Ford and Siregar 1998, p. 28). This paper is an attempt to make a little contribution towards redressing this imbalance.

Asymmetrical Power and Sexual Relations in Javanese Tradition

Central in the mind of the Javanese is that the cosmos consists of the micro cosmos or the human world and the macro cosmos or the universe (Beatty 1999; Ali 1989, in Machali 2001). The two levels of the cosmos coexist and it is necessary that they interact. All human relations, reflecting the hierarchy of the macro-micro cosmos relations, are hierarchical. The family, viewed as a microcosm of society, reflects the hierarchical relations of the macro structures of society. The man and woman enter marriage in a hierarchy-based relationship, as symbolized by one of the Javanese wedding rituals called the *miji dadi*, which means "the sowing of seeds". In this ritual, the bride will squat, the groom will step his foot on an egg, indicating her fertility, to break it, and she will wash his foot to symbolize her lifetime subservience to him.

Sexual relations are also a symbol of inequality. According to Beatty, the deepest meaning of an interpersonal relationship is contained in sexual reproduction. The hidden truth behind sexual intercourse in Javanese epistemology is *manunggaling kawulo gusti* — the union of servant and lord (1999, p. 173). With analogies of growth and transformation taken from plant life (the tree contained in the seed, and so forth), sex is not only an image of union, but also a fertile union (p. 167). It is therefore understandable that the Javanese would value fertile women more than barren ones.

The Javanese believe that power is not necessarily appropriated by material means. Power may be accumulated through asceticism, self-control, and meditation, but this applies more to men than women. The role of women in sex is defined in restrictive terms such as giving birth and child rearing, which are considered the "dirty" business of life. Daily chores such as kitchen work are also strictly for women and men should not get involved and "dirty" themselves. All these dynamics add up to a situation where women are viewed as less powerful than men.

The Javanese world-view on womanhood is mostly derived from the various *serat* (books) written by Javanese kings and literary writers (*pujangga*), passed down from one generation to the next by parents and society. These books deal with *piwulang* (teachings) on ethics and morals for women such as Sunan Pakubuwana IV's *Serat Wulangreh Putri* (Book on the Teachings for Women) and Ranggawarsita's *Serat Candrarini* (Book on the Beauty of Women). These books had considerable influence on the Javanese, particularly those living in mainland Java who observed the court culture. The kings were the highest authority, not only in state- and finance-related issues but also in people's daily affairs (Moertomo, in Sukri and Sofwan 2001). Nowadays, although these books are hardly known to many contemporary Javanese, the stereotypes they prescribe for women remain strongly held.

Among the stereotypes is the view that women, by nature, are weak and, therefore, need men's protection. The Javanese expression *swargo nunut neroko katut* (women follow men to paradise and to hell) implies that women's fate, good or bad, is fully in the hands of men. Therefore, women have to show their *bekti* (devotion) and respect to the husband by obeying him and serving all his needs. The Javanese term for "wife", *konco wingking* (literally, "friend at the back"), explicitly reflects the Javanese view on women, which is hardly respectful. Another stereotype is related to the sexual objectification[6] of women. Women's ideal features are related to their physical traits and their skills in satisfying men's sexual desires. In *Serat Candrarini*, for example, an ideal woman is one who is a willing party to her husband's polygamy, good at cooking, good at beautifying herself, and good at serving her husband. Those parts of a woman's body that are generally capable of arousing men's sexual drive are viewed as the most vital parts. For example, *Serat Panitisastra* (Book on the Guidance for Writing) (Sukri and Sofwan 2001, p. 92) describes that "a woman is only meaningful when she has full breasts that can be caressed in bed". Similarly, several other Javanese literary works identify women's sexual drive and power from parts of their bodies such as face, eyes, nose, neck, and so forth, including colour of skin. This identification produces a typology of women, which will enable men to predict women's sexual capacity.

The various *serat* on women's idealized sexuality were written during the Javanese kingdoms in the eighteenth to the nineteenth centuries and reflect the feudalistic culture of the society at that time. Dutch colonialism that began to hold power in the sixteenth century also helped to augment the stratified, feudalistic social relationships that exited in Javanese society then, including gender relationships (Kansil and Julianto 1986, pp. 13–14). Islam was introduced by Muslim Gujarat merchants in the thirteenth century with little upheaval to existing cultural, social, and political structures (Suseno 1997, p. 35), as well as blending itself with the already existing Buddhism and Hinduism to create a religious syncretism. This new religion was soon accepted widely through the works of the missionaries, the so-called *wali*, notably in Java. However, as Ambary (in Sukri and Sofwan 2001, p. 14) contends, the *wali*, in spite of their success in making Islam flourish, were frequently perceived as legitimizing feudalistic power and not standing up for the oppressed groups. Islamic teachings on women, unfortunately only those with gender-biased interpretation rather than those representing the liberating spirit, were simultaneously introduced in the process.

As a result, most teachings in the *serat* on women's inferior position to men can be identified with male-biased interpretations of Qur'anic verses. In *Serat Wulang Istri* (Book on the Teachings for the Wife), for example, the advice on the woman to be nice to her husband's other wives is said to derive from the Qur'an, which permits polygamy. It is obvious that the Qur'anic verse has been used for men's interest without considering the socio-historical context of its revelation. There are still many other pieces of advice to women, basically to teach them to be fully submissive to men, to worship, respect, and obey them as they would gods. The demand is for women to be good at *macak* (beautifying herself), *manak* (having sex and having children), and *masak* (cooking).

Javanese tradition and Islamic teachings share similar views on sexual relations. They are viewed as having a noble purpose: to implant the seed and obtain good offspring. A set of etiquette needs to be observed, not only for moral consideration but also to avoid mishaps befalling the child. Some of the *dos* and the *don'ts* in sexual relations are derived from the Hadith. For example, a wife's unconditional obedience in (male-biased interpretation of) Islam, is shared by the Javanese world-view. Javanese women are not supposed to express their feelings. This means that women may not speak or express their opinions openly. Women are perceived as passive sexual agents whose major task is to fulfil the needs of the male. A sexually active and aggressive woman is considered *saru* (improper). Women have to follow the culture, namely, to accept the reality and not to protest even if she is unhappy. A wife is not supposed to refuse if her husband wants to remarry, even if it is for the fortieth time. Whenever required, she even has to find him young beautiful girls if he so wishes (*Serat Wulang Estri,* in Sukri and Sofwan 2001, p. 106).

From the various prescriptions on sexuality, it is obvious that women are placed in a disadvantaged position, as a sexual object for men's satisfaction.

Fieldwork and Case Studies

This paper is based on an anthropological research conducted in mid-2000 among middle-aged and middle-class Javanese Muslim women with relatively established careers and power in the public sphere. In-depth interviews were conducted with some fourteen women, three of whom are presented as case studies in this paper. This type of study population was chosen to explore whether women of status in the public arena also exercise equal power in sexual relations with their husbands.

My main reason for selecting all women as informants was to focus on the emic[7] perspective to find out their feelings, emotions, aspirations, and expectations as they retell their life experiences. All information about the male characters in the case studies was obtained from the wives' accounts. Women's voice has been barely heard, and I think it was fair that I focused on them.

My three informants — Nur, Lisa, and Yanti (all pseudo names) — although being Javanese and Muslim, have different levels of internalization of Javanese as well as Islamic traditions. The distinction made by Geertz (1976) about *santri* and *abangan*,[8] may in some way be useful in explaining my informants; although one's level of religiosity and internalization of culture cannot be explained in such a clear-cut way. The three informants appear to blend their sense of being Muslim and being Javanese. Nur and Lisa, for example, are what Geertz would term the *santri*. Their fathers were *kyai*, religious teachers who ran Islamic boarding schools, and they were brought up to observe religious principles seriously. They internalize and believe in the liberation the Qur'an offers to women. However, they also hold on to the Javanese value on women's obedience including in sexuality, which corresponds to the male-biased interpretation of the Qur'an.[9] Yanti is what one would regard as *abangan*, one who is more fascinated with Javanese values and ritual details. However, she also observes the Islamic principle of *salat* (prayer) and she is able to read the Qur'an.

Case 1: From Obligation to Pleasure

Nur, daughter of a renowned *kyai*, was a parliamentarian and chairperson of a big Islamic women's organization. At the time she was about to enter into an arranged marriage, at the age of eighteen, she had just graduated from high school, and although she had a boyfriend, she gave him up in obedience to her parents. The first seven years of her marriage was a bitter and lonely period. Although she felt forced into the marriage, she came to accept and even derived pleasure from it. Her thirty-seven years of marriage ended when her husband died, and by then her attitude to marriage had changed tremendously. How did this change come about?

> I entered the marriage with a conviction that a wife's role is to serve and please the husband. I did not know whether it was more Islamic or Javanese, but I think it derived from both. Our religion prescribes a wife to obey her husband and to do her duties. Our Javanese culture says so too. So I just did my duties. I tried to please him. But often times, deep in my heart, I felt empty and lonely. I cried behind him. My heart was in conflict because I could not feel one with him.

Nur admitted that it was her husband's attitude that "bought" her over:

> He was very patient, caring and understanding. He knew that I could
> not forget my old boyfriend. He knew that when we were together,
> my mind was wandering elsewhere. My husband noticed and felt
> that, but he was not angry. He understood my feelings; and he even
> thanked me for my sacrifice. He said it was an honour for him that
> I accepted him as my husband. I was touched by his words. He pa-
> tiently whispered sweet nothings into my ears, giving me gentle ca-
> resses and strokes that could excite me. He never forced me if I was
> not ready. Several times he had to cancel when I said, in tears, that I
> could not do it. He said that he would wait, however long, until I was
> ready. I could only cry ...

That kind of episode recurred many times during the first seven years
of their marriage. The husband's patience finally "melted" Nur and she
realized that he really loved her. Not only that, she also felt indebted to
him for encouraging and guiding her in her self-development. Her husband knew that Nur could not be just a housewife. She was an active
woman concerned with social problems. He encouraged her to continue
her activities and even was her partner and teacher in their discussions
on social and women's issues. Later, when Nur decided to enter politics, he was still her number one supporter and teacher. Nur said:

> He was not only a husband to me, but also a teacher and a lover. He
> could make me fall in love with and admire him. Of course, I also
> observed and respected his rights as a husband. For example, I knew
> that he liked to have dinner with me at home, so I tried to be at home
> in the evening. But he could understand my situation when I was in
> the Parliament. I could not avoid being outside the house for meet-
> ings in the evenings. In this case, I usually compensated for it by hav-
> ing a long, romantic weekend, just the two of us.

Positive sexuality for Nur was crucial not only for her marriage but also
for her career. She was so thankful to God when she could finally enjoy the pleasures of sexual relations. Sex was no more felt as an obligation, but a pleasure and even a need.

> I don't believe in the Javanese myths that a woman should not be ac-
> tive in a sexual relationship. Neither did my husband. He spoke of
> the Qur'anic verse on woman-man mutuality and equality in sexual
> relations. I agreed with him. I think it is not fair if it is only the man
> who could enjoy it. Both should be fulfilled.

On the importance of sex, she said:

> You can tell from my office activities the next day. If our night (mean-ing sex) was good, I would resonate. I was in high spirit, and partici-pated in meetings enthusiastically. But if our night was not good, I would spend the day in the office in a bad mood.

Nur demonstrated a proactive attitude in sexuality when she sensed that her husband was having an affair with a young secretary at his office. She was at the peak of her career as a politician, and was often out of the house on official duties. This was how she developed her strategy.

> Instead of getting angry with my husband, I indulged him and spoiled him, especially in bed. I developed rituals before bedtime: wearing transparent sleeping dress, putting on lipstick and perfume, radiat-ing warmth and love, etc. etc. I was more aggressive than usual. Outside the bed, I did similar: making his coffee myself, and if I had time I would cook his favourite food, etc.

Nur's strategy proved to be effective. After five months, he began to realize his mistake. He was very sorry and apologized to Nur, who also felt guilty for neglecting him. They saved their marriage and earned back their happiness and sexual well-being. However, Nur had to accept her destiny when her husband died while she was still in need of him.

> I was only fifty-one, still sexually active. The world seemed to collapse on me. I missed him. I suddenly lost my confidence to face the world, especially people who knew us. I felt like those people were staring at me and despised me: "Look, that is the woman who could not re-lease her sexual desires ... She is now a widow, a lonely widow ..."

It took Nur a whole year to regain self-confidence. Now she is fully content with her education and social activities. She is back at her home-town and leads her father's *pesantren* (Islamic boarding school), which has become her full responsibility after his death. She is also actively en-gaged in developing the community around her.

Case 2: From Burning Love to Frigidity

Lisa grew up in a family with progressive parents, a *kyai* father and a politician mother, who introduced to her the Islamic values of freedom, gender equality, and justice. At a time when most *kyai* would rather arrange marriages for their daughters, Lisa's father did the opposite. He encouraged his daughters to pursue tertiary education, just as he did his sons. Although they are a Javanese family, they do not adhere strictly to Javanese values regarding gender relations. Lisa recalled her sweet memories of her late father:

> My father was a symbol of the Islamic spirit of freedom and empow-
> erment. He had a far-reaching vision of empowering the Muslims and
> enacting justice and equality for all. In spite of his academic back-
> ground in Islamic legal system, he was much influenced by Sufism
> in practising the religion. When he taught us about God through
> stories and signs in the universe, he made us feel God was so close to
> us. My childhood picture of God was sweet, loving, caring, and not
> frightening. My father was a *kyai* who could bring into light the lib-
> erating, rather than oppressive, side of the religion.

Lisa married a man of her own choice, a college friend with whom "she was madly in love". Her husband, Hadi, came from a different family culture, where male domination and material orientation prevailed, which is entirely different from the world Lisa was familiar with. In Lisa's family, daughters and sons had equal opportunities for education and everyone was involved in family discussions. In Hadi's family, fa-ther and sons were central figures and decision makers, while mother and daughters were "the others", who had to be content with kitchen-related activities. Lisa expressed her concerns about this.

> I was shocked when I first interacted with his family. I saw how
> women were discriminated against in his family. One day I witnessed
> my husband's father and brothers discussing an important family is-
> sue. Then his sister came to join, but she was turned down. "It's not
> a woman's business, it's an important decision about our family; go
> to the kitchen and make tea for us." I was hurt to hear that kind of
> male arrogance. I would have protested against such discrimination,
> if I had been her.

Only after they got married did Lisa know how arrogant and egoistic Hadi was. His male chauvinism must have been shaped by the way he was raised. His was a typical Javanese patriarchal family, where women were regarded as subordinate to men and expected to be obedient and submissive. They were nevertheless devout Muslims in the sense that they observed the religious rituals and ceremonies. But their attitude, apparently, did not reflect the Islamic mission of justice and equality for women.

> I was overwhelmed by the contradictions since the beginning of our marriage. My father, a religious leader with a large number of students and followers, knew how to respect women. Being a respectable public figure, he had no difficulty sharing responsibilities in child rearing and domestic work. Now I had to live twenty-four hours a day with an arrogant man who wanted to lord it over others in the family. We were all to obey his words and treat him as our "centre". He never touched anything in the kitchen, as it was "not his world". He argued that as head of the family he deserved special treatment because he had "bigger responsibilities". He even quoted the Qur'an that recognized men's family leadership and their being one level higher than women.

Lisa's husband used a Qur'anic verse (Q.S. al-Nisa' 4:34)[10] to justify his patriarchal attitude. This confused Lisa because her father had interpreted and implemented this same verse very differently. She said:

> My father perceived men's family leadership as empowering, supporting, and liberating. That's why men have been given certain privileges to enable them to "bring blessings" to women, the oppressed group, not the other way round. My husband was different. He perceived leadership as monopolizing, controlling, demanding rather than giving, and even repressing and exploiting, like in the case of our sexuality.

Lisa's most bitter experience was in the area of sexuality. She described her husband's sexual behaviour as "savage, insensitive, inhuman, exploitative, oppressive, and humiliating". These harsh adjectives indicate deep feelings of oppression and humiliation. This was what she said:

> I felt worse than a whore. A whore serves sex and receives money in return. I served him sex and he demanded me to work as well. He saw my big potential in earning money and, because of his materially oriented world-view, he demanded that I work. He said that everyone in the house has to be productive, including me, to earn money … He's crazy …

Lisa, with a tertiary education from a reputable university overseas, was working as a development consultant with an international agency. With bitter experiences in her marital life, she was determined to dedicate the rest of her life to advocating women's rights and promoting their status. Reflecting on the inferior status of women in the more than twenty countries she had visited, Lisa was more determined than ever to stay the course and work for equality in gender relations.

Lisa's relative success in career opportunities and financial rewards, however, did not seem to have enlightened her husband. He stuck to his culturally bound androcentrism. Sexuality, for him, appeared to be a symbol of his power over his wife and her submission to him. His egoism and self-centredness exacerbated these cruelties. He never seemed to care about his wife's sexual needs. Lisa vehemently recalled her painful memories:

> When he wanted it, he just did it, and in five minutes it could finish. For me, and maybe for other women as well, sex is not jut the act. It is very much related to the atmosphere, the romanticism, the mood, the emotions, and also the quality of your relationship in general. I explained this to him but he did not seem to understand. I often asked him to spend time, just the two of us, at the beach or in the mountains, but he did not agree. He was not romantic at all. He was insensitive. He even could not sense it when I told him that I needed small attentive gestures such as sweet words or small presents.

This so-called sexual exploitation lasted for years until Lisa could not tolerate it any longer. Bursting into tears, she boldly stated to him that she could no longer be his sexual slave. She gave him two alternatives: either to divorce her or take another wife to satisfy his sexual drive. He took neither the divorce nor the polygamy option. Lisa consulted a psychiatrist who, after examining both of them, said that Hadi could not possibly leave her. "You are his wife, his lover, and also his mother", he said to Lisa.

The marital conflict with all its ramifications lasted for many years but Lisa decided not to dissolve the marriage. Two main reasons restrained her from ending it: children and God's anger.[11] The biggest repercussion for Lisa has been the loss of her sexual desire for her husband.

Case 3: From Arranged Marriage to Lifetime Submission

Yanti was born and raised with Javanese feudalistic values where marriage is viewed as *manunggaling kawulo gusti* (the union of servant and lord). As depicted in many *serat* Yanti and her husband were very much familiar with and even internalized, the couple were a perfect symbol of the Javanese stratified marital relationship. In their daily life, Yanti and her husband demonstrated the Javanese basic principles of conflict avoidance, respect, politeness, and humility (Geertz 1961, p. 146; Magnis-Suseno 1997, p. 42; Berninghausen and Kerstan 1992, p. 34).[12] However, qualities like self-control are more readily attributed to men than women, who are considered by nature more emotional and impatient (Berninghausen and Kerstan 1992, p. 34). Furthermore, the wife-husband relationship reflects what R. Jay pointed out (R. Jay's "Javanese Villagers: Social Relations in Rural Mojokuto" cited in Berninghausen and Kerstan 1992):

> The husband is the cultural arbiter of the family, the one with some skill in the blend of traditional theology, philosophy and aesthetics that guides much of the Javanese intellectual activity. The wife responds to her husband's guidance with gentle attentiveness, while skilfully but unobtrusively managing his domestic needs, so that their detail may not distress him. (P. 36)

Yanti entered her arranged marriage when she was just sixteen, a common practice among Javanese girls then. Her marriage at that early age did not allow her to pursue formal education. But her talents in communication and writing, which she inherited from her journalist father, her perseverance in self-education, and her husband's support and guidance had enabled her to develop a career as a journalist and radio broadcaster. Despite all her tireless efforts and talents, she always humbly attributed her success to her husband.

> I am nothing compared with my husband. He is everything to me: a husband, a teacher, a father, and a protector. When I started working as journalist, he taught me how to write reports, articles, etc. Not only that. He taught me about many things in life: philosophies and practical things. When I felt restless and worried especially because of the economic hardship we used to experience, he always could make me feel secure.

As taught by the Javanese tradition, Yanti believes that talking about sex is taboo. Even when she was at the point of getting married, she had no idea what sex was like. Nobody told her what it was, and no pictures describing it could be seen. What she understood was that as a wife she had to obey her husband, serve him, and make him happy.

> I was so stupid. When my fiancée (now my husband) was holding my hand, I washed my hands immediately. I was afraid that I would get pregnant just because a man was holding my hands.

Yanti deeply internalized the Javanese values of a wife's full submission. She was taught that her role is to support her husband and to make him happy. If he is happy, she is happy as well. This teaching also applies in sexuality.

> As a Javanese woman, I never think about my own happiness in sexuality. Sex is just part of our marriage, like many other activities. I don't know if it is important or not. It's just an activity that the couple does at certain intervals. When we had sex, I never thought of happiness or satisfaction. It's a duty, you know, something that you have to do. My husband never commented about it, whether he liked it or not. It's taboo. When he wanted to do it, he simply used signs or symbols and I would understand him. My husband is a quiet person, not demanding, and never talked about it. So I never knew whether it was pleasurable or not, what orgasm was like, etc.

Despite her reluctance to talk about her intimate experiences at the beginning, Yanti was willing to share her interesting experience about the ending of their sexual episode.

> It happened one night some twenty years ago. As usual, he wanted to do it. At first, he was trying but I noticed that he was changing his mind. I felt offended and hurt. I thought he did not love me anymore and did not need me as a wife so he changed his mind [from having sex with me]. I started to cry. I was so insulted and felt useless as a wife because he did not want to do it with me. Did he have another woman? Was I boring to him?

For Yanti, a wife's main task is to serve her husband especially in sexuality. It is her main duty, and no other woman should do it. So she was hurt when her husband changed his mind after having expressed the desire to do so. She was finally relieved when he explained to her.

> He said that it was not because he did not love me anymore. It was because he could not do it. He had tried hard but he could not. He

just couldn't. I didn't believe him. I cried and asked him to take me back to my parents because I was now useless as a wife. He tried to console my heart, and said that he still loved me. Then he tried again, several times, and still failed. Finally, I was convinced that he was no longer able to do it. Maybe it was what people called "impotent." After that we never talked about that incident. That was the end of the sexual relationship in our marriage. And that was twenty years ago. ... Time had elapsed without any sex between us for the last twenty years and life went on as usual ...

Yanti ended our conversation saying that she was a happy wife in spite of the sexual drama. After all, as a "good" wife, she had done her duties by fully submitting to him.

Discussion

Despite their different family backgrounds, religious upbringing, and marriage partners with different expectations, the three women had a common view regarding who was to play the role of leader in the family. They all perceived that men should assume leadership in the family regardless of their economic status or their economic contribution to support the family.[13] For example, although Nur and Lisa, a parliamentarian and a consultant respectively, contributed more than their husbands in meeting the family expenses, they were happy to let their husbands take on the role of leader in the family. So was Yanti. These women were quite contented to be the one "led" in spite of their greater contribution financially. However, this voluntary relinquishing of power was not always properly appreciated by their husbands, who maintained their egoism as "head of the family and provider of family sustenance" and viewed the wife's financial contribution as merely something "additional and peripheral".

This sets the overall parameters for unpacking the dynamics of these marriages. The prevailing context is that of a patriarchal society with male-dominant beliefs and practice stemming from the local culture and religion. This would have conditioned the three women to a certain degree about the role they can play in shaping their marriages.

How each of these women negotiated (or were unable to) a way out of her marital problems provides an opportunity to explore the dynamics between the internalization of Islamic teachings and sexual fulfilment. Although no simple correlation has been found that suggests that deeper religious internalization brings about sexual happiness or the opposite, the experiences of the three women do point to the impact that Islamic teachings can have on a person's sexual happiness.

In Nur's case, her *santri* internalization of Islamic tradition started her on the same footing as the *abangan* Yanti when it came to marital expectations. Both expected to submit to their husbands and did not believe in taking the initiative, but the outcomes of both relationships were very different. The critical factor appeared to be Nur's husband and his belief in the Qur'anic teachings that there should be mutuality and equality in sexual relations. Yanti's husband did not or was unable to fall back on such resources provided by the Islamic faith.

However, as much as a good grounding in Islamic precepts can improve sexual relationship, it need not always be the case as illustrated by Lisa's experience. She has internalized what is open and progressive in Islam but her husband used the same Islamic teachings to oppress her. This highlights the problem of contradictions in religious texts and the diversity of interpretations that can arise from a single source.

Islam, Gender, and Sexuality: Contending Discourses

While advocating sexual equality and reciprocity as depicted in the title of this paper, the Qur'an, at the same time, contains a pivotal verse on gender (Q.S. al-Nisa' 4:34) which, in classical exegesis, illustrates sexual hierarchy, with women as sexual objects at the service of men. Although modern methodologies and paradigms currently exist,[14] which accord more justice to women, the more widely circulated interpretation appears to be the classical one. The verse in question, in al-Tabari and al-Baydawi's reading, says:

> Men are in charge of / are guardians of / are superior to / have authority over / women (*al-rijalu qawwamuuna 'ala l-nisa*) because God has endowed one with more / because God has preferred some of them over others (*bi-ma faddala Allahu ba'duhum 'ala ba'din*) and because they support them from their means (*wa-bi-ma anfaqu min amwalihim*). Therefore, the righteous women are obedient, guarding in secret that which God has guarded. As for those whom you fear

> may rebel (*nusyuz*), admonish them and banish them to separate beds,
> and beat them. Then if they obey you, seek not a way against them.
> For God is Exalted, Great. (Stowasser 1998, p. 33)

The verse legislates men's authority over their women, conferring on them the right to discipline their women in order to ensure obedience. *Nusyuz* (rebellion), according to Tabari, refers to female appropriation of superiority over the husband, undue freedom of movement, objection to sexual contact when desired by the husband, and other acts of defiance. Meanwhile, men's "superiority over" women, according to Baydawi (Stowasser 1998, p. 33) refers to the fact that men have been endowed with "a perfect mind, good management skills, and superb strength with which to perform practical work and pious deeds. To men (alone) were allotted the prophethood ... and the monopoly in the decision to divorce."

When such a hierarchical perspective on gender relations is incorporated into family laws in Muslim societies such as Indonesia, it entrenches socio-cultural norms that regard women as existing to serve men, sexually and emotionally. Another Qur'anic verse describes women as a "tilth" for their men to use when he wishes.[15] If a wife refuses her husband's sexual demands, she is to be punished.

If these Qur'anic verses were so discriminatory against women, then how do they relate to the overarching message of the Qur'an that it is God's will for humanity to create a just society and institute a variety of social reforms, including raising the status of women? The Qur'an speaks of its own mission as "to bring mercy for all creatures" (Q.S. al-Anbiya' 21:107) and "to free human beings from any oppression and discrimination due to sex, race and ethnicity" (Q.S. al-Hujurat 49:13). There are a great number of verses elucidating this mission, but the most important reform pronouncements of the Qur'an, in my understanding, are on the subjects of women and slavery. The Qur'an immensely improved the status of women, from "half or even less human" to that of a full-fledged personality. In the sixth century, in the advent of Islam, the Arabian peninsula was in a state of the so-called *jahiliyah* (ignorance) period. At that time, women were regarded as expendable. A Qur'anic verse makes an explicit reference to infanticide, apparently confined to girls (Q.S. al-Nahl 16:58–59). The Qur'an granted women the status of full human and equality to men within such a patriarchal culture where baby girls were customarily buried alive, as depicted in the verse.

Gender equality is advocated in a number of verses, guaranteeing equality in all essential rights and duties. The following verse beautifully illustrates gender equality conceptualized in the Qur'an:

> For Muslim men and women; for believing men and women; for devout men and women; for men and women who are patient; for men and women who humble themselves; for men and women who give charity; for men and women who fast; for men and women who guard their chastity; for men and women who remember Allah much — for them all has God prepared forgiveness and a great reward. (Q.S. al-Ahzab 33:35)

Equality between men and women is explicitly and implicitly mentioned in other verses such as at-Tawbah 9:71–72; Alu Imran 3:195; an-Nisa 4:124; an-Nahl 16:97; al-Mu'min 40:40; and al-Fath 48:5–6.

Another verse, inspiring the title of this paper, "*Your wives are a garment for you and you are a garment for them*" (Q.S. al Baqarah 2:187), points to the ideal sexual relations. Annemarie Schimmel (in Murata 1992, p. ix) posits that the term "garment", according to ancient religious ideas, is a reference to the alter ego of a human being. The garment can function as a substitute for the person, and with a new garment one gains as if it were a new personality. Furthermore, it hides the body, blocks private parts from the eye, and protects the wearer. Husband and wife are, according to this interpretation, so to speak, each other's alter ego, and each of them protects the partner's honour. This seems to show the proper functioning of the *yin-yang* principle of the Far Eastern tradition. The husband and wife are equal and complement each other in their perfect togetherness.

A secondary source of Islamic laws and thoughts is the Hadith. Like the Qur'an, which contains seemingly contradictory verses, the Hadith too is made up of various *hadith* that appear controversial. While some *hadith* uphold positive sexuality and sexual pleasures for both men and women, others, which are widely disseminated and internalized by the Muslim are just the reverse as can be seen, for example, in al-Ghazali's

Book on the Etiquette of Marriage,[16] part of *Ihya Ulum al Dien* (The Revival of the Religious Sciences). In this classical book, al-Ghazali weaves together threads of etiquette and Islamic law on marriage which, in many cases puts women in a subjugated position. Al-Ghazali, in spite of his reputation as a renown *sufi* and Islamic scholar, fully maintains the Christian marital affirmation for the woman to "honour and obey" (Farah 1984, p. 41). Farah further explicates:

> He stresses this throughout by emphasizing that a woman should not feed anyone, unless the food is about to spoil, without the permission of her husband; that she should not go out of the house or to the mosque for prayer without his permission; that she should be discreet in dress and manner, and careful about to whom she speaks when on the streets or in the markets; that she should not emphasize the obvious, that is, as al-Ghazali puts it, in case she be beautiful and her husband ugly; and that she should be conservative in spending and not wasteful of the husband's money.

In al-Ghazali's *Book of Counsel for Kings*, he devotes chapter 7 to "Describing Women and Their Good and Bad Points", wherein he states:

> A wife will become dear to her husband and gain his affection, firstly by honouring him; secondly by obeying him when they are alone together; and (further) by bearing in mind his advantages and disadvantages, adorning herself (for him only), keeping herself concealed (from other men) and secluding herself in the house; by coming to him tidy and pleasantly perfumed, having meals ready (for him) at the (proper) times and cheerfully preparing whatever he desires; by not making impossible demands, not nagging; keeping her nakedness covered at bedtime, and keeping her husband's secrets during his absence and in his presence. (As quoted in Farah 1984, p. 41)

There is a *hadith* which brings severe repercussions to the life of Muslim women, including those of the three women in the case studies. It is retold by Bukhari and Muslim, two most reliable *rawi* (transmitter) as follows: "*Idha da'a rajul imra'atahu ila firashih fa abat wa huwa ghadlban la'anatha al-mala'ikah hatta tusbiha*" (If a husband wants to have sex with his wife and the wife refuses him and the husband is angry, the angels will curse her till morning). In my in-depth interviews during the fieldwork, most of my informants referred to this *hadith* as a reason for submitting to their husbands' sexual demands. Not only were they familiar with the Hadith, but they were also frightened and felt threatened by the "curse of the angels". So, in spite of their being unprepared for a sexual intercourse, they suffered it anyway, just to avoid "being cursed by the angels".

There are, however, a number of *hadith* that feature the positive side, pleasures, and reciprocity of sexuality. For example, a *hadith* illustrating the Prophet who forbade husband to pursue only his own pleasure without paying attention to the wife. It is retold by Ibn Majah as follows: "*idza jama'a ahadukum ahlahu, falyusaddiqha, faidza qadha hajatuhu qabla an taqdiya hajatahu fala ya'zalha hatta inqadha hajataha*" (If one of you are in the company of your wife, do pay complete attention to her needs; if the husband has fulfilled his desires [reached orgasm] before his wife, he should not leave her in haste but stay until she reaches her orgasm). Still, in order to ensure the wife's pleasure which is often denied her because of her husband's premature ejaculation, the Prophet forbade the practice of *coitus interruptus* (*'azl*) without the wife's consent: "*Naha rasul Allah an yu'zala an al-mar'ah illa bi idhniha*" (The Prophet forbade a husband to practice *coitus interruptus* without the wife's consent), as retold by Ibn Majah.

The importance of mutual pleasures for both partners is illustrated in the following *hadith*: "*Idha jama'a ahadukum ahlahu fala yatajarradani mujarrad al 'irayn, fal yuqaddim al-talattuf wa al-taqbil*" (If one of you would like to have sexual relations with your wife, do not do it as two camels or donkeys would; instead, be with her, whispering sweet nothings and showering her with kisses). Another *hadith* retold by Ibn Abbas illustrates the importance of mutual pleasures: "*uhibbu an tazayyana li imra'ati kama uhibbu an tatazayyana li*" (I like to adorn myself to attract my wife, as much as I would like her to make herself pretty so as to seduce me).

How can one explain these arguments for, and against, gender and sexual equality and reciprocity in the Qur'an and the Hadith, especially when related to the Qur'an's mission of human and woman freedom and elimination of discrimination?

A prominent Muslim feminist, Fatima Mernissi (1985, 1987), wittingly and courageously opens our eyes about the tradition of misogyny among Muslim societies. She convincingly argues that neither the Prophet Muhammad nor Allah as the source of the holy law desired anything other than equality between the sexes; but these teachings are reversed in reality. Muslim societies, in general, appear to be more concerned with trying to control women's bodies and sexuality than with supporting them in achieving their rights. Another Muslim feminist, Riffat Hassan, makes a similar observation. While the Qur'an, because of its protective attitude towards all oppressed classes, appears to be weighted in many ways in favour of women, many of its women-related teachings have been used in patriarchal Muslim societies against, rather than for, women. She criticizes Muslim scholars, including Al-Maududi and Al-Jullundhri with their writings on human rights in Islam, for "either not speaking of women's rights at all or are mainly concerned with how a women's chastity may be protected" (p. 25). Afkhami (1995, p. 1) shares a similar concern, that for Muslim fundamentalists "every domestic issue is negotiable except women's rights and their position in society".

The above reality poses us with hermeneutic questions to ponder. Have God's messages on gender and sexual equality been properly understood by the human? Is our understanding of the Qur'an in line with what God intends to express? What do gender and sexuality signify in the world-view of Islam? What are the theological roots of gender distinctions? Can we capture Prophet Muhammad's ideas through pieces of sentences compiled in the Hadith? Such hermeneutic questions, according to Murata (1992, p. 3), cannot be addressed on the level of the *shari'a* (Islamic jurisprudence), which simply presents human beings with a list of *dos* and *don'ts*. Nor can they be addressed by *Kalam* (theology), which is locked into an approach that places God the King and Commander at the top of its concerns. But they can be addressed and are addressed by the sapiential tradition, which attempts to explore the deeper reasons, the *why* and not just the *what*, for an Islamic world-view and is interested in the structure of reality as it presents itself to us.

The language of religion is not just a medium of communication; it has ontological and eschatological dimensions; and, therefore, a textual and structural approach in understanding religion is not sufficient to capture these dimensions (Hidayat 1995). The Qur'an, historically, is a product of an oral discourse between the transcendental subject of Angel Gabriel, representing God's heavenly interests, and Prophet Muhammad, representing the earthly realm of human beings with all their social dynamics. It is a complex discourse, rich in meanings and nuances. When a Qur'anic text is understood separately from its socio-historical contexts, it runs the risk of losing the socio-psychological aspects of the discourse and may lead to distortion of information and even misunderstanding.

The Qur'an itself speaks of God's infinite signs and commandments that cannot be expressed "even if all the trees were made into pens, and all the wide Oceans, multiplied seven times, were made into ink" (Q.S. Luqman 31:27). Ali (1989, p. 1041) comments on the verse by writing "there are mysteries beyond mysteries that man can never fathom. Nor would any praise that we could write with infinite resources be adequate to describe His power, glory, and wisdom." Murata and Chittick (1994, pp. xv–xvi) quote the Prophet that "every verse of the Qur'an has seven meanings, beginning with the literal sense, and as for the seventh and deepest meaning, God alone knows that". The Qur'an, notwithstanding its specific Arabic form, is a universal guidance sent to all the world's inhabitants. Its language, not only language of the tongue but also language of the heart and mind, is synthetic and imagistic. People naturally understand different meanings from the same verses. This richness of Qur'anic language and its receptivity towards different interpretations, according to Murata and Chittick, help explain how this single book of the Qur'an could have given shape to one of the world's great civilizations.

By looking into its socio-historical contexts, one will understand why certain Qur'anic and Hadith texts appear to be biased, not reflecting the fundamental mission of Islam as a liberating religion. Riffat Hassan observes that

> the cumulative (Jewish, Christian, Hellenistic, Bedouin and other) biases which existed in the Arab-Islamic culture of the early centuries of Islam infiltrated the Islamic tradition and undermined the intent of the Qur'an to liberate women from the status of chattels or inferior creatures and make them free and equal to men. (1995, p. 25)

Conclusion

After studying the myriad conventions in Islamic and Javanese traditions regarding gender and sexuality, we may infer that the two traditions, in some way, show similarities. The context of Qur'anic revelation, the Middle East of the seventh century, and Javanese culture share a similar feature of patriarchy, where masculine epistemology and misogynist traditions prevail. One major mission of the Qur'an was to liberate the oppressed group, and promote women's status to one of equality with men, as depicted in the title of this paper. However, this vision of gender and sexual equality was and has been challenged by misogynist and patriarchal attitudes in Muslim societies. The Qur'an itself is, in fact, not free from cultural biases as shown in a number of its verses which appear contradictory to its grand mission. So are the teachings of the Hadith. This reality has prompted some hermeneutic questions as to the method of understanding God's messages. Textual understanding of the Qur'an and Hadith, as widely practised, may lead to misunderstanding. Without taking into consideration the social-historical context of revelation, one's understanding of religious texts may be partial and static. Furthermore, the formal legalistic approach to the Qur'an, the *shari'a*, is only interested in the *what* and deals with the *dos* and *don'ts*, and thus may not be able to capture the deeper side of God's messages. The sapiential approach, which attempts to explore the deeper reasons and is interested in the structure of reality as it presents itself to us, may be able to address these issues of *why*.

The three cases share similar features of hierarchical gender and sexual relations although they were manifested differently and to varying degrees. This reality has brought to our attention the male's "politics of the ego" coined by the early radical feminists. Developing de Beauvoir's emphasis on the psychological dynamics occurring between lovers, the radical feminists argue that men's power over women is seen to rest on the culturally developed ability of the male ego[17] to have power over the female ego (New York Radical Feminists 1971, in Langford 1996, p. 25). She continues that the "politics of the ego" are based, not in any direct desire on the part of men to hurt women, but through men's need to derive their own strength and self-esteem by overriding women's independent sense of self (Langford 1996, p. 25). This results in one-way emotional relationships underpinning the system of sexual inequality, as contended by Firestone (1979, p. 122) that "(male) culture is parasitical, feeding on the emotional strength of women without reciprocity".

In patriarchal Muslim societies, the Qur'anic spirit of gender and sexual equality portrayed in the title of this paper is inevitably challenged. The key to its realization, in my opinion, lies in the success of educating Muslim men and women on the authentic meaning of the Qur'an and its mission to liberate women. Efforts to socialize women's rights in Islam and the equality between man and woman need to be enhanced to reconstruct equitable Muslim societies idealized by the Qur'an. Otherwise, male-biased interpretations of the Qur'an and misogynist influence of local cultures will continue to impede the realization of the Qur'anic mission, among others, as depicted in the title of this paper.

NOTES

1. The term "sexuality" used in this paper refers to its narrow meaning, that is, feelings and actions connected with erotic desire of sexual relations.
2. This ideology assumes that women as wives and mothers contribute significantly to nation building through their unique roles and participation in development. However, they were constantly reminded that their primary roles should be as loyal supporter of their husbands and caretaker of the household and children.
3. Consider, for example, Q.S. al Baqarah 2:223 and several *hadith* that may appear contradictory to the egalitarian verse in the title. Further discussion follows later.
4. I use the term "patriarchy" in the same sense as that provided by the second-wave feminist Adrienne Rich in her book *Of Woman Born: Motherhood as Experience and Institution* (1986, pp. 57–58). She defines "patriarchy" as the power of the fathers: a familial — social, ideological, political system in which men — by force, direct pressure, or through ritual, tradition, law, and language, customs, etiquette, education, and the division of labour, determine what part women shall or shall not play, and in which the female is everywhere subsumed under the male. She points out that patriarchy assumes the omnipotence-impotence relationship existing in all men-women dealings and this becomes imprinted as a paternalistic

image. Rich further illustrates with examples: "Under patriarchy, I may live in *purdah* or drive a truck ... I may serve my husband his early-morning coffee ... or march in an academic procession. ... fundamentally masculine assumptions have shaped our whole moral and intellectual history."

5. Positive sexuality is the positive concept of sexual health, which is defined as "sex that is pleasurable and free from emotional, physical and social problems for the persons practising it, and free from unwanted pregnancy and infections" (IPPF 1991, in Ford and Siregar 1998, p. 8).

6. Sexual objectification is a concept associated with the work of MacKinnon and Dworkin on pornography, in which women are "dehumanized as sexual objects, things, or commodities". Still pejoratively, the term has later been used in ordinary social discussions of people and events (Nussbaum 1999, p. 213).

7. The terms "emic" and "etic" (derived respectively from "phonemic" and "phonetic") are widely used in anthropology to designate two contrasting levels of data or methods of analysis. An emic model is one which explains the ideology or behaviour of members of a culture according to the indigenous definitions. An etic model is one which is based on criteria from outside a particular culture. Etic models are held to be universal; emic models are culture-specific (Barnard and Spencer 1996, p. 180).

8. *Santri* is the root word of *pesantren*. In *pesantren*, students live in dormitories within the complex owned by the *kyai*. The students are called *santri*, Muslims who follow Islamic principles seriously. An *abangan*, on the other hand, is a nominal Muslim, fairly indifferent to Islamic laws but fascinated with Javanese values and ritual details.

9. Gender and sexual relations in Islam have been a major debate among Muslim feminists. A major portion of this paper will be specifically devoted for this topic.

10. The substance of Q.S. al-Nisa' 4:34 will be discussed in greater detail later.

11. Islam takes a middle path regarding divorce; it neither prohibits it nor makes it too easy. Divorce is recognized when a marriage becomes impossible to sustain and to materialize its goal of creating a peaceful and loving home (*mawaddah wa al-rahmah*), as specified in the Qur'an (QS. al-Rum 30:21). For further details on divorce, consult books on Islamic law (*shari'a*) or women's rights such as Jawad 1998; Engineer n.d.; Engineer 2000; An-Na'im 2002; Esposito 1982; Do'i 1992.

12. The principle of conflict avoidance requires Javanese people to avoid open confrontation in every situation; while the principle of respect requires the "observance in speech, demeanour of and behaviour of respect towards all those whose position in society demands it" (Magnis-Suseno 1997, p. 42).

13. The relationship between economic contribution to the family and family leadership is clearly stated in Q.S. al-Nisa' 4:34.

14. Among others, those introduced by the Egyptian theologian and jurist Muhammad Abduh (d. 1905), who called for the education of men "in the true

meaning of Islam", which would make them give up all selfishness, material greed, power hunger, and love of tyranny, so they would begin to deal with their wives in the spirit of love, compassion, and equality that the Qur'an enjoins (Muhammad Abduh, n.d., p. 117). The Pakistani scholar Fazlur Rahman in his book *Islamic Methodology in History* (1965) brought into light a new epistemology for the Qur'an by taking into consideration the historical sociological contexts when the Islamic traditions were formed. Without this, our understanding of Islam and the Qur'an tends to be partial and static. The context and outcome discourse is also brought up by another Islamic scholar, An-Na'im (1990, 2000), who believes that "the Qur'an has to be understood, and its guidance implemented, through human reason and action".

15. The verse is Q.S. al-Baqarah 2:223, and it reads: "Your wives are as a tilth to you, so approach your tilth when or how you will."

16. Farah identifies the weakest aspect of the *Book on the Etiquette of Marriage* as al-Ghazali's quotation of Hadith that was not deemed reliable, or quoting reliable traditions along with the unreliable to bolster his arguments for or against marriage.

17. "Ego" is used here in the sense of a people's image of themselves, especially in terms of self-importance.

REFERENCES

Abduh, Muhammad. *Al-Islam wa-al-Mar'ah fi Ra'y al-Imam Muhammad Abduh* [Islam and women in the view of Muhammad Abduh]. Cairo: Muhammad 'Imara, n.d.

Afkhami, Mahnaz. *Faith and Freedom: Women's Human Rights in the Muslim World.* London: I.B. Tauris, 1995.

Ali, Abdullah Yusuf. "The Holy Qur'an: Texts, Translation and Commentary". Brentwood, Maryland: Amana Corporation, 1989.

An-Na'im, Abdullahi. *Toward an Islamic Reformation: Civil Liberties, Human Rights and International Law.* Syracuse, NY: Syracuse University Press, 1990.

———. "Islamic Foundation for Women's Human Rights". In *Islam, Reproductive Health and Women's Rights,* edited by Anwar and Abdullah, pp. 33–57. Kuala Lumpur: Sisters in Islam, 2000.

———. *Islamic Family Law in a Changing World: A Global Resource Book.* London: Zed Books, 2002.

Barnard, Alan and Jonathan Spencer. *Encyclopedia of Social and Cultural Anthropology.* London: Routledge, 1996.

Beatty, Andrew. *Varieties of Javanese Religion: An Anthropological Account.* Cambridge: Cambridge University Press, 1999.

Berninghausen, Jutta and Birgit Kerstan. *Forging New Paths: Feminist Social Methodology and Rural Women in Java.* London: Zed Books, 1992.

Coveney, Lal, Margaret Jackson, Sheila Jeffreys, Leslie Kay, and Pat Mahoney. *The Sexuality Papers: Male Sexuality and the Social Control of Women.* London: Hutchinson, 1984.

Do'i, Abdur Rahman I. *Women in Shari'ah (Islamic Law).* Kuala Lumpur: A.S. Noordeen, 1992.

Engineer, Asghar Ali. *The Qur'an, Women & Modern Society.* Kuala Lumpur: Synergy Books International, n.d.

_____ . *Hak-Hak Perempuan Dalam Islam (Women's Rights in Islam).* Yogyakarta: LSPPA, 2000.

Esposito, John L. *Women in Muslim Family Law.* Syracuse, NY: Syracuse University Press, 1982.

Farah, Madelain. *Marriage and Sexuality in Islam: A Translation of al-Ghazâlî's Book on the Etiquette of Marriage from the Ihyâ'.* Salt Lake City: University of Utah Press, 1984.

Figes, Eva. *Patriarchal Attitudes: Women in Society.* New York: Perseus Books, 1986.

Firestone, S. *The Dialectic of Sex: The Case for Feminist Revolution.* London: Women's Press, 1979.

Ford, N.J. and K.N Siregar. "Operationalizing the New Concept of Sexual and Reproductive Health in Indonesia". Mimeographed. 1998.

Foucault, Michael. *The History of Sexuality: An Introduction,* vol. I. Harmondsworth: Penguin, 1978.

Geertz, Clifford. *The Religion of Java.* Chicago: University of Chicago, 1976.

Geertz, Hildred. *The Javanese Family: A Study of Kinship and Socialization.* New York: Free Press of Glencoe, 1961.

Giddens, Anthony. *New Rules of Sociological Method.* London: Hutchinson, 1976.

_____ . *The Transformation of Intimacy: Sexuality, Love & Eroticism in Modern Societies.* California: Stanford University Press, 1992.

Grigsby, Ellen. *Analyzing Politics: An Introduction to Political Science.* Belmont, CA.: Wadsworth and Thomson Learning, 2002.

Hassan, Riffat. "Women's Rights in Islam: From the I.C.P.D. to Beijing". Mimeographed. 1995.

Hidayat, Komaruddin. *Memahami Bahasa Agama: Suatu Pendekatan Hermeneutika* [Understanding the language of religion: a Hermeneutics approach]. Bandung: Mizan, 1995.

Jawad, Haifaa A. *The Rights of Women in Islam: An Authentic Approach.* London: Macmillan Press, 1998.

Kansil, C.S.T. and Julianto. *Sejarah Perjuangan Kebangsaan Indonesia* [History of Indonesia's national struggle]. Jakarta: Erlangga, 1986.

Langford, Wendy. "Romantic Love and Power". In *Women, Power and Resistance:*

An Introduction to Women's Studies, edited by Cosslett et al., pp. 23–34. Buckingham: Open University Press, 1996.

Lerner, Gerda. *The Creation of Patriarchy*. Oxford: Oxford University Press, 1986.

Machali, Rochayah. "Women and the Concept of Power in Indonesia". In *Love, Sex and Power*, edited by Blackburn, pp. 1–15. Melbourne: Monash Asia Institute, 2001.

MacKinnon, Catharine. "Feminism, Marxism, Method, and the State: An Agenda for Theory". *Signs: Journal of Women in Culture and Society* 7, no. 3 (Spring 1982): 515–44.

Magnis-Suseno, Frans. *Javanese Ethics and Worldview: The Javanese Idea of Good Life*. Jakarta: PT Gramedia Pustaka Utama, 1997.

Mernissi, Fatima. *Beyond the Veil: Male-Female Dynamics in a Modern Muslim Society*. New York: Halsted Press Book, 1985.

_____ . *The Veil and the Male Elite: A Feminist Interpretation of Women's Rights in Islam*. Massachusetts: Perseus Books, 1987.

Millet, Kate. *Sexual Politics*. New York: Doubleday, 1970.

Murata, Sachiko. *The Tao of Islam: A Sourcebook on Gender Relationship in Islamic Thought*. New York: State University of New York, 1992.

Murata, Sachiko and William C. Chittick. *The Vision of Islam*. Minnesota: Paragon House, 1994.

Nussbaum, Martha C. *Sex and Social Justice*. New York: Oxford University Press, 1999.

Rahman, Fazlur. *Islamic Methodology in History*. Karachi: Central Institute of Islamic Research, 1965.

Rich, Adrienne. *Of Woman Born: Motherhood as Experience and Institution*. New York: Norton, 1986.

Stowasser, Barbara. "Gender Issues and Contemporary Qur'an Interpretation". In *Islam, Gender and Social Change*, edited by Haddad and Esposito. New York: Oxford University Press, 1998.

Sukri, S. and Sofwan. *Perempuan dan Seksualitas Dalam Tradisi Jawa* [Women and sexuality in the Javanese tradition]. Yogyakarta: Gama Media, 2001.

Suseno, Frans Magnis. *Javanese Ethics and World-View: The Javanese Idea of the Good Life*. Jakarta: PT Gramedia Pustaka Umum, 1997.

Lily Zakiyah Munir is a medical anthropologist who studied at the University of Amsterdam. She is based in Jakarta and currently working as an activist and researcher on issues of gender and Islam.

[17]

SEXUALITY IN CONTEMPORARY ARAB SOCIETY

Abdessamad Dialmy

Abstract: Arab scholarship of sexuality is currently emerging against many obstacles. This article provides a suggestive introduction to the current state of knowledge in the area. After briefly sketching an archetype of Arab sexuality, especially its peculiar form of phallocracy, new sexual trends are reviewed, some of which adapt current practices to Shari'a law (e.g., visitation marriages), while others break with it altogether (e.g., prostitution). The article then discusses three distinctive areas of public and policy concerns in the region, namely, honor killings, impotence and Viagra use, and sex-education programs that are precipitated by concerns over HIV/AIDS. The essay concludes with an assessment of some of the main challenges still facing research into the topic in the Arab Islamic world.

Key words: Arab world, health, honor crimes, Islam, social research, sexuality

Introduction: The Meaning of Sexuality

Arab public and scientific discourses about sexuality have shifted considerably over the centuries, from a broad scientific, legist, and cultural engagement in earlier centuries (Al Munajjid 1958) to a silence in modernity. Ben Salama (1985: 155) argues that what does not exist as a concept does not exist at all, and is forced to express itself in pathological linguistic and behavioral forms, such as humor, provocation, repression, or fantasy.

Modern Arab discourse has, in fact, lost the appropriate terminology to deal with the topic. Ben Salama points out that the Qur'anic concept of sex—the word *farj*—denotes merely 'vagina' in modern usage. Woman has become the totality of *farj* because *farj* is an opening and signifies fragility, that is, a lack. Evidently, this negative meaning became mechanically linked to the woman as a result of the subjection of the Arab mind to a patriarchal logic that is predicated on considering the female a lacking being, and therefore on diminishing the woman and belittling her. Furthermore, the reduction of *farj* to the woman, and to her sexual organ at that, expresses this negative diminution that the concept of sex has undergone in Arab and Islamic history, namely, its movement from the status of scientific concept and from a valuable status into what is without meaning and without value. In attempting to rehabilitate the Qur'anic concept of *farj* as the Arabic equivalent to the Western concept of sex, Ben Salama ignores the supersession of the concept of sex in Western thought itself and the appearance of the concept of sexuality.

Naturally, Arab scholarship in this area must construct an Arab equivalent to the concept of sexuality that contains the biological dimension and transgresses it at the same time through melding the personal and social dimensions in the intellectual construction of the matter. In this respect, we suggest the concept of *jinsaniyya* as a translation for the word 'sexuality', based on the common Arabic usage of the concept of *jins* as a translation for the word 'sex'.

Sexuality is a rich and complex phenomenon, especially in the contemporary Arab world. An example of this intricacy is the body of the Muslim woman, which becomes a tool for resistance to the globalization of dress and the individual, liberal sexual values it symbolizes. The feminine body becomes entrusted with Arab culture and identity more than ever before, so that the movement of Islamization of Arab society begins initially with the Islamization of the woman's body through the call for the veil. In addition to the inherent complexity of the topic, the constant interventions by stakeholders—including ideologues, clinicians, and activists, most notably feminists—inevitably affect the academic researcher's study of sexuality by complicating the researcher's task and, moreover, by preventing the field from easily being turned into a subject of dispassionate, objective study.

In view of the complex nature of the phenomenon and its versatility, and in view of the impossibility of treating all the themes of sexuality within an article such as this, one must inevitably narrow down for discussion some of the topics that typify Arab sexuality. Three major axes have therefore been chosen: the Arab construction of sexual identities, recent developments in social frameworks for a new Arab sexuality, and some substantial social-sexual problems.

The Arab Construction of Sexual Identities

All traditional Arab cultural regimes concur in considering the sexual order both binary and hierarchical at one and the same time. This order revolves around two poles: one pole, which is superior, active, and dominating, is made up of men, and the other pole, which is inferior and passive, is made up of wives, children, slaves, homosexuals, and prostitutes. One of the fundamental characteristics of this asymmetrical polarity between the single sexual active and the multiple sexual passives is the construction of all sexual passives in the image of the woman. The woman is the distinct archetype of the sexual passive; she is the second sexual identity in the foundational myth of Adam and Eve, the secondary in the Arab-Islamic political economy, and the inferior in the management of and access to political power. The secondary position of woman and her inferiority is applied to all other sexual passives, for they share with her the reception of the phallus and subjection to its domination—phallocracy.

Indeed, the basic stake in the cultural regime of sexuality in traditional Arab societies has been precisely the construction of two sexual genders—man and not man—emanating from biological sexual identity without being restricted to it in an absolute fashion. The Arabic language itself points in that direction by providing two distinct expressions: 'maleness', which applies to the biological given, and 'manliness', which indicates the construction of man as social domination. As for woman, the term 'femininity' refers at one and the same time to the female and to the woman, that is, to the biological and to the (subordinate) social gender. In its turn, the Arabic language linguistically reifies the domination of maleness over femininity, as Tahar Labib (1973) has pointed out. But the maleness of the boy or the maleness of the homosexual is not enough to construct man, for man is not only male; he penetrates and is not penetrated.

In order to achieve this distinction between man and not man, and between maleness and manliness, it is inevitable that social initiation would be achieved through a basic rite of passage by means of which masculine identity is constructed in Arab societies, namely, circumcision. And since the masculine identity is prized and glorified, the circumcision of the boy is an opportunity to celebrate and take pride, in contrast with the circumcision of girls, which takes place silently and in secret. The circumcision of the boy is the subject of pride precisely because it rids the boy of the membrane of femininity—the foreskin—according to the patriarchal perspective, and it is therefore a break between the boy and femininity. Circumcision is a symbolic and practical transition for the boy from the world of women to the world of men. In it there is an achievement for the boy of a measure of control and the beginning of supremacy over all the women of the family (Labidi 1989).

The dichotomy of active/passive is predicated, then, on a masculinist definition of the sexual act as penetration, in the sense that man penetrates all the elements of the other pole. This dichotomy is located within a regime that is typified by "the general importance of male dominance, the centrality of penetration to conceptions of sex and the radical disjunction of active and passive roles in male homosexuality" (Rowson 1991: 73). Transsexual man is at the bottom of the social ladder, for he plays the role of the passive woman in the sexual relation. Thus, medieval Arab society accepted transsexual men only as musicians, dancers, and singers.

Following this logic, the penetrating man becomes the sole sexual active. He is the only element that should be considered sexually active by virtue of his penetrative act, for penetration is the act, and the act is penetration, and both mean and secure his domination and control. Around this penetrating active man and beneath him hover dependent sexual passives, "wives, concubines, boys, prostitutes (male and female) and slaves (male and female)" (Dune 1998: 10). All passives are equal in their lack, and it does not matter whether the passive is male or female. The multiplicity of sexual partners means the fragmentation of active man's desire so that man does not become a dependent sexual passive to anyone. In the multiplicity there is a sort of independence for man from the sexual passive, and especially from woman.

Mauritanian society constitutes the only Arab exception that is not based on the spatial segregation of the two sexes, on the seclusion of women, and on patriarchal jealousy. Tauzin (2002: 7) goes as far as to suggest that men's courting of a married Mauritanian woman is a source of pride to her husband. But courting never reaches sexual consummation; it remains a confined act that casts the woman/lady as saintly and godly.

The active/passive dichotomy is central in the traditional Arab organization of sexuality. It is a dichotomy that equates manhood essentially with virility. Virility encompasses the power of (sexual) desire, the length of intercourse and its repetition, and the ability to sexually satisfy women in order to ensure their sexual loyalty. It also means multiple sexual partners, as well as fertility.

Moreover, masculinity hides itself in its control of female sexuality through the rite of defloration, which is one of the most important rites of passage for both genders. In most Arab societies, this rite testifies to the virginity of the bride and the virility of the groom. But the defloration by finger in rural Egypt makes the rite a means to ascertain the virginity of the bride alone, for the use of the finger of the groom or the traditional midwife leaves no scope for the groom to demonstrate his virility at that moment of the nuptial rites. But most important is the confirmation of the honor of the family through the confirmation of the virginity of the bride. Virginity is the basis of family honor, and interference with it constitutes interference with the family honor, especially the honor of its men who failed to protect it, since the sexual penetration of a girl before marriage means, patriarchally, the sexual penetration by the penetrator of all the males of the sexually penetrated woman. Put differently, this sexual penetration entails a symbolic transformation of all men of the sexually penetrated group into women, that is, into males without virility (Moussaoui 2002: 12), into passives. Masculinity is seen as the capacity to act, and the capacity to act is not only the ability to sexually penetrate but also the ability to prevent sexual penetration.

Within the Arab epistemology of sexuality that reduces sexual activity to penetration, this act becomes a fundamental condition for the construction and empowerment of the Arab male ego and for securing his mental health (Chelli 1986: 93). This pattern in the integration of sexuality into the personality of the Arab man makes sexuality the basic determinant of the masculine personality and, moreover, turns sexuality into a pivotal meaning of life for the Arab man.

The situation is different for woman. Compared with man, sexual activity does not have the same significance for the Arab woman's sense of femininity. Childbirth has a greater significance in determining the feminine identity and the sense of that identity. The Arab patriarchal regime has thus distinguished between the respectable woman—the wife and mother—and loose women (songstresses, prostitutes, lovers), who are linked to sexual pleasure. These images can be seen in popular proverbs such as "She moves, she is divorced" in the dialect of Fez. The meaning of this proverb is that if the wife were to move during intercourse, she would be divorced, because her movement would indicate the presence of desire and pleasure, something that does not become a respectable wife. The sexuality of the respectable wife is confined to satisfying her husband's desire and producing a large number of male off-spring. Few indeed are the Arab wives and mothers who insist on their Shar'i right to sexual pleasure.[1] This is the result of an imposition of a kind of identity between woman and wife, that is, the focus on the image of the wife in describing the ideal woman, which means the elimination of feminine sexual desire. The tenets of patriarchy turn woman into a creature that was created of man and for man to satisfy his sexuality.

But the Arab masculine unconsciousness contains a different image of feminine sexuality, an image that turns her into the stronger sexuality (Ait Sabbah 1982) and a continuous challenge to the virility of man. For this reason, erotology developed special categories of sexual enhancers made up of plants and medicines that the man takes in order to extend intercourse and to sexually satisfy the woman. This demonstrates that feminine sexuality is regarded as a potential cause of discord (Tucker 1993: 66). In order to ensure that it does not become a cause of discord in practice, feminine sexuality requires constant surveillance, the patriarchal presupposition being that it is insatiable—an ogre that never refrains from devouring the male member.

This masculine depiction of feminine sexuality justifies the necessity to marry off the woman early, to seclude her in order to avoid discord, and, more generally, to subject her to a firm hierarchy that denies her freedom of movement and instills in her contempt toward sexual pleasure. This depiction also gives men the right to dominate the patterns, norms, and repetition of the sexual act. Furthermore, woman stands accused of diverting man from God's worship. This is what Yemeni poetry has pointed out, as do stories known in Mauritania as 'women's trickery' (Tauzin 1991: 60–71; cf. Ibn 'Arabi n.d.: 201).

Naturally, the situation differs in relation to what Abdelwahab Bouhdiba (1975: 131–133) has called the anti-spouse—the songstress, the prostitute, the lover. The anti-spouse is the object and true site of lust, for she "not only incites to depravity or debauchery, but also emasculates the man and deprives him of his freedom by placing him under the power of desire and subjects him to her control" (Bencheikh 1988: 104). Notwithstanding the legal ban, prostitution was regulated and taxed in medieval Arab societies (Raymond 1973: 508–509).

The ideological separation between the respectable woman, that is, the wife, and sexual pleasure is not the sole means of protecting man from the worry engendered by the fear of feminine sexuality. There are other defense mechanisms in the psycho-analytical sense, such as platonic love, which is predicated on keeping woman in the position of God, that is, outside marriage and outside sex altogether. Platonic desire spares the man feelings of castration, deficiency, and annihilation.

But female circumcision remains the technique most expressive of the Arab man's fear of the (fantasized) feminine sexual force and of his desire to dominate and control it. Nonetheless, female circumcision is a phenomenon that does not exist in all the countries of the Arab world, and its historical origins are difficult to determine (Meinhardus 1967). The *Egypt Demographic and Health Survey* (DHS 1995) confirmed that 97 percent of single Egyptian women have been circumcised and 82 percent of women support the practice. Female circumcision is carried out by the traditional midwife on girls between the ages of 6 and 12 (Kamran 1996: 97). Egyptian society considers circumcision a proper, traditional practice that is religiously required—a manifestation of cleanliness and purity.

Hind Khattab (1996: 20) shows that female circumcision has multiple functions, including the consolidation of feminine difference and the establishment of feminine identity; reducing physical desire ('clipping the girl's wings') and protecting virginity; preventing masturbation; the beautification of the vagina and the seduction of the man; a greater preparation for marriage and allowing the husband greater pleasure; and preventing the wife from marital infidelity during the husband's absence. The Egyptian woman herself shares this positive image of female circumcision, its maintenance, and its reproduction. We thus find her seeking circumcision for herself and her female relatives, and feeling a lack if it does not occur. Most Egyptian women who were interviewed in Khattab's study asserted that female circumcision does not negatively affect their capacity for sexual pleasure.

But the Egyptian feminist movement, led by Nawal Al Saadawi, has strongly criticized female circumcision. In her book *Woman and Mental Struggle*, Al Saadawi (1977) has described female circumcision as mutilation and a detrimental practice to a girl's mental health that negatively affects her future capacity to reach orgasm. This issue has fueled a continuing debate concerning the sexual satisfaction of the Arab woman (see, for example, Khair Badawi 1986).

This analysis of the Arab masculine unconscious, the Arab sexual mind, and the Arab man's need for domination synthesizes some of the characteristics of traditional masculinity. But this synthesis is merely a provisional approximation because Arab sexuality, like all social phenomena, unfolds in specific historical and social conjunctures and is always contingent and contestable, that is, historical. Thus, a recent study has shown that programs of sexual and reproductive health play an important role in helping the Arab man to accept a new masculine identity (Dialmy 2000c). This is but one example of an increasing number of studies that highlight ongoing transformations in contemporary Arab sexuality.

Social Frameworks for a New Arab Sexuality

While Arab society continues to be based, to a large extent, on a masculinist (oppressive/hierarchical) interpretation of Islamic Shari'a law (Dialmy 2000d, 2002b), there has been a noticeable change at the level of sexual conducts toward openness, occasionally in contravention of religious values. Such developments in sexual conducts in the Arab world have been motivated by various factors, such as the improved standards and increased duration of education among girls (and hence the drop in rates of early marriage), women's joining the paid labor force, the increase of contraception outside the confines of family-planning programs (that is, outside marriage), the spread of the ideology of sexual consumerism (through the media), and the crises of housing shortages and unemployment (hence the drop in marriage rates). These factors have brought about the appearance of 'new' forms of nuptial associations (de facto marriages, visitation marriages), the increase in prostitution, and the emergence of non-commercial pre-marital feminine sex (Dialmy 2003b: 77).

The New Forms of Marriage

One observable phenomenon throughout the Arab world is an increase in average age at first marriage. For Moroccan women, for instance, this average rose from 17.3 years in 1960 to 26.4 in 1997. This phenomenon involves a continuous increase in the ratio of single women as the following table shows. Under the pressure of demographic changes new forms of marriage have appeared, of which we shall discuss the visitation marriage and the de facto marriage.

TABLE 1   Ratio of Single Women in the Age Groups 20–24 (per 1,000 women)

Year	Tunisia	Algeria	Kuwait
1966	270	112	161
1975	360	310	320
1984	590	534	391

Visitation Marriage. Saudis practice in their kingdom what is called visitation marriage (Kamal 1997: 65–73). The main reason for the emergence of this type of marriage is the rise in the cost of marriage. Kamal argues that the essential function of the visitation marriage is the ending of abstinence that the Saudi youth must undergo. The lengthening period of schooling and the increasing investments in careers delay marriage and enhance the temptation of non-marital affairs. In order to avoid this downward slide, the visitation marriage has become a legitimate alternative. In a visitation marriage, the wife is visited by the husband. Often it functions as a softened form of polygyny, whereby a man can visit a new wife without the knowledge of his co-resident wife (ibid.: 68–70).

De Facto Marriage. De facto marriage involves a conjugal settlement without documentation and in some instances without public announcement or common residence. De facto marriage is to some extent the Sunni equivalent of the Shi'a temporary marriage, except that it is normally contracted on a permanent basis.

It is possible to observe three situations in which de facto marriages are practiced. The first situation is of Arab youth who feel the pressure of sexual need yet face the impossibility of marriage for economic and religious reasons.

De facto marriages are often conducted among youths in secret in order to avoid the anger of their parents.

The second situation is a recourse to de facto marriages—which are legitimate according to Shari'a law but not according to state law—to express a lack of political recognition in the legitimacy of the state. The Islamist group al Takfir wal Hijra became famous for such practices. The heads of such groups may marry more than one woman. As for the wife of the ordinary holy warrior, she becomes an organizational ticket, as it were, as she is one of the daughters of the organization, "often the daughter of a superior commander of the new recruit, and she guarantees to the leadership the loyalty of this recruit, as she forces upon him the bonds of recruitment" (Kamal 1997: 54).

The third situation is the use of de facto marriage to confer Shar'i legitimacy on the sexual relations of sex tourists from the oil-rich Arabian peninsula. Sexual tourism, which became prominent in the early 1980s as a result of the increasing Arabian petroleum revenue, indicates the harvesting of sexual fruit within the Arab world, both in licit and illicit ways. As with prostitution, it involves the exploitation of the poverty of villagers and of residential suburbs, but unlike prostitution, Shar'i legitimacy is conferred upon the sexual relations. And to the extent that the verbal settlement is fixed in time, for a period of five days or a week (in return for bride wealth), de facto marriage quite clearly comes close here to temporary marriage.

The Increase in Prostitution

Current Arab prostitution is linked to the increasing poverty in oil-poor Arab countries. However, it is impossible to isolate the economic factor because the impetus to consume has become in its turn a driving force for many Arabs to commodify both body and sex. No longer confined to the economically vulnerable strata, prostitution has also extended to individuals from middle social classes who strive to live at a level that is above their objective material means.

Prostitution may be either a permanent or temporary occupation, and includes both young women and men, children of both sexes, married and divorced women, school and university students, blue-collar and white-collar workers, so much so that some have started talking about the economy of prostitution. Sex work has also become a means for some homosexuals to pursue their same sex desires, behind the pretext of earning a living. Through sex work the homosexual is better able to confront the social persecution to which he is exposed in Arab society (Amnesty International 1997: 7).

The authorities themselves are conscious of the economic role of prostitution and the inevitability of the social crisis that would be precipitated by the elimination of prostitution. It is for this reason that there is practical, though not legislative, toleration of prostitution. Most of the time, this toleration hides behind a pretence of lack of knowledge and awareness, though from time to time the authorities initiate cleansing drives to pressure some of the people active in the field of prostitution, to remind all that the authorities are capable of interfering, and to make a show of defending Islamic values and of combating debauchery.

24 | *Abdessamad Dialmy*

Pre-marital Sexuality

Notwithstanding the existence of 'new' forms of marriage, non-marital sexual activity has increased in scope, oftentimes beginning at an early age (Dialmy 2000a: 80, 114–124). The first regional study—"Woman and Sex in Morocco" (Dialmy 1985: 134–135)—has shown that by the end of the 1970s, only 9 percent of Moroccan male youth adhered to the Islamic ban on pre-marital sexual activity, while 68 percent of young men practiced sex as a goal in its own right, compared with 45 percent of young women. In the 1980s, 65 percent of young women confirmed that they had practiced sex at least once before marriage (Naamane Guessous 1987: 44).

Of course, the pre-marital practice of sex does not always mean full and complete intercourse, as the wish to retain the hymen intact leads to alternative sexual practices: non-penetrative, anal, and oral (Dialmy 2000a: 85–90). Should the hymen break, some women resort to its artificial restoration by means of a simple surgical procedure. In the Moroccan cities of Rabat and Casablanca, the cost of this surgery ranges from US $60 to US $500 (Dialmy 2000b: 43).

In a Tunisian study (Nasraoui 1986), 80 percent of young, unmarried male workers stated that they had engaged in sexual activity as opposed to only 2 percent of female workers. Clearly, such statements reflect the prevalent double standard of patriarchal morality. The study also found that 72 percent of the sexual relations involving workers occurred with prostitutes.

At the University of Tunis, Angel Foster (2001) recorded the appearance of patterns of sexual activity among female university students. In a study of students of secondary education in Beirut, 30 percent of young men had reportedly experienced at least one sexual relationship, as opposed to 2 percent of young women. At the American University in Beirut, 24 percent of new students had entered into sexual relationships (Major 2001).

But in all Arab states—with the exception of Tunisia, where female prostitution is regulated—there is a religious prohibition and/or a legal ban on pre-marital and extra-marital sexual relations. Some Arab intellectuals have begun criticizing the legislative tenacity in criminalizing some sexual practices that society no longer considers a vice. But this positive attitude toward some of the appearances of non-marital sexuality has not yet been adopted by political or social forces in those Arab societies that allow a measure of relative sexual openness. The intellectual's criticism of penal law in the area of sex remains both an individual and a preliminary criticism. Some of the human-rights activists, in their turn, live a contradiction between a sexually liberal personal position and a conservative collective position (Dialmy 2000b: 81–84).

Against the proliferation of non-marital sex and calls for its liberalization, the emergence of de facto marriage and the appearance of the visitation marriage are phenomena that reflect the defensive, conservative response. This response opposes the modernization and secularization of sexual activity. Its paramount concern is to continue the organization and control of sexuality according to established essential and substantial Islamic laws.

Social-Sexual Problems

This section discusses three topics that are pivotal and representative, both socially and sexually, at one and the same time. These are the issues of honor crimes, Viagra consumption, and the spread of HIV/AIDS in Arab societies.

Honor Crimes

In parallel with the relative normalization of pre-marital sex among some Arab social circles, we find that honor crimes continue to typify most Arab societies. Moreover, the two phenomena may occasionally co-exist, notwithstanding their contradictory nature. Honor crimes are widespread in Jordan, Palestine, Lebanon, Egypt, Iraq, and Morocco. It stands to reason that Article 340 of the Crimes Act in Jordan, by exonerating the person (invariably a male) who commits an honor crime or reducing his penalty, encourages the commission of this type of crime. The woman alone is made responsible for morality and for any violation of sexual mores. Such a clause exists one way or another in all Arab criminal codes without exceptions (Abu Odeh 2002: 366). The tolerance toward honor crimes is also expressed toward young unmarried mothers who kill their natural children with the intention of saving the family honor. It is clear from this that the woman carries the burden of family honor: it is her body that has been soiled, whatever the circumstances and regardless of whether the sexual activity was consensual or forced.

These laws differ only with regard to the person who stands to benefit from the extenuating circumstances. While the Jordanian and Libyan legislation benefit the father, the brother, and the husband, the Egyptian and Algerian legislation benefit the husband alone. Lama Abu Odeh concludes from this difference that the restriction of the list of beneficiaries to the person of the husband alone implies a transition from the concept of honor to the concept of passion, and is a transition in the direction of modernizing crime in the sense of its individualization, that is, in the sense of liberating it from the group logic. The husband benefits from the extenuating circumstances upon catching his wife in the act of marital infidelity as a consequence of jealousy and anger.

These crimes appear to be more widespread in the lower classes (Droeber 2003: 45). This sociological link is the basis of an economic hypothesis according to which honor crimes fulfill an economic function. The argument is that the young woman constitutes an economic burden on the poor family and thus is being dispensed with under the pretext of saving honor. In some instances, the authorities lock up these 'guilty' young women in order to protect them from the fury of their relatives (Husseini 2001–2002: 40–41). This 'protective' imprisonment usually lasts decades because the desire to wash away the shame dies out only with the killing of the young woman when she is released from prison. In some cases, the family pays a sum of money to the state to have the young woman discharged so that she can be killed. This refutes the economic hypothesis because the imprisoned young woman does not constitute an economic burden on her family. The issue is one of honor; that is, it is an issue of masculinity at its core.

In Palestine, such crimes are often ignored by the justice system and are listed as suicides or as natural deaths (Shalhoub-Kevorkian 2001). According to the estimation of one judicial authority, 70 percent of the crimes committed in Gaza and the West Bank are honor crimes (Ruggi 1998: 12–13). Surveys indicate the existence of judicial tolerance toward the perpetrators of these crimes. From among 35 cases of killings between March 1998 and April 2000, the court issued 27 custodial sentences for less than five years (three years on average).

In Iraq, faith in secularism was shaken when in April 1990 a law was issued to allow any man to kill any woman in his family if it could be established that she had fornicated. According to Sonia Dayan-Herzburn (1991: 52), this is an adaptation to the Islamist trend. In Lebanon, it became clear that legal reform alone is not sufficient to end the phenomenon. In 1999, Article 562, which prevented the criminalization of honor killing, was stricken from the Crimes Act. Notwithstanding this deletion, the judicial treatment of those crimes is still characterized by a measure of leniency and understanding (Serhan 2001: 25).

This issue has become bitterly politicized. Feminist organizations that attempt to help rape victims or pregnant women receive constant threats and accusations of rebelling against traditions and of corrupting society (as happened to the Solidarité Féminine association in Morocco). National authorities do not normally respond to feminist political demands, notwithstanding the fact that government social agencies prepare shelters and that the police recognize these feminist organizations and the legality of their services. The struggle has subsequently turned toward legislation to achieve parity between the two sexes and toward raising society's consciousness by debating honor crimes in the media.

Erectile Dysfunction and Viagra

Two and one-half million Egyptians, it has been reported, suffer from sexual impotence ('Abdullah 1998: 3), but the journal *Al 'Arabi* goes much further and insists that between 25 and 30 percent of married men in Egypt, which amounts to 12 million men, are suffering from impotence (Al Qassas 1998: 13). In Morocco, according to Viagra manufacturer Pfizer Corp., a million men complain about erectile dysfunction. An unpublished epidemiological study by the census bureau of the Casablanca district has found that 53.6 percent of men suffer from erectile dysfunction. The study recommends that erectile dysfunction should be considered a public-health issue, given its negative effect on family stability (Qadri et al. 1999: 27).

The consumption of Viagra in Egypt has grown to such an extent that women now consider it a danger to the stability of married life. While the essential concern of the man is to show his virility and protect it at all costs, the woman's basic goal is the preservation of her social status as a wife, a status that she feels is threatened by Viagra. Indeed, many women have admitted to fear of Viagra because it reinforces the man's ego by strengthening his virility, a fact that exposes the wife to the double danger of divorce or of having to co-exist with a second wife. Therefore, women are inclined to prefer sexual

impotence over Viagral virility because the husband's impotence allows the
woman to dominate the marriage and also protects married life.

In Morocco, it is invariably private physicians who are consulted about this
complaint, not only because Morocco does not provide a hospital that special-
izes in male diseases (as is the case in Egypt with the International Adam Hospital), but also because the private sector guarantees a measure of discretion
and intimacy, something that is highly sought after in cases of erectile dysfunction. Psychological consultations to diagnose and treat erectile dysfunction
continue to pose a social threat to the sufferer (Harakat 2001), in that the sufferer is exposed to the accusation of lack of masculinity, that is, to humiliation
and shame. Even in instances in which the patient seeks a medical consultation, he does not declare his erectile dysfunction spontaneously and naturally
but waits for the physician to discover it himself (cf. Dialmy 2000b: 50).[2]

The few studies on the matter indicate that not only the ill consume Viagra,
but also healthy males who do not complain of erectile dysfunction at all. This
phenomenon points to the Arab man's permanent fear of the inability to achieve
erection and his desire for a continuous guarantee of virility—that elementary
dimension of the Arab definition of masculinity. Viagra provides a sense of security and extends the traditional Arab concern with sexual aphrodisiac, a concern
that translates into a desire for sexual control and domination out of fear of
the tyranny of the woman. This issues goes back to the promotional image of
Viagra. The newspaper '*Al Ousbou*' ('Abdullah 1998) discussed what it called
"Viagra freaks"—men who were taken by the drug's distorted and exaggerated
promotional image, which implies that it enhances the libido, lengthens the
duration of intercourse, increases its repetition, and turns the old man into a
young one. This image coincides with the special mental needs in the emotional
make-up of today's Arab man to produce the Viagra freak. The economically
vanquished Arab male—who is unable to justify his patriarchal control and
privileges by rights of what he spends on his wife—requires something through
which he can compensate for his economic incapacity. Intensified sexual activity becomes a means of compensation as well as a way to strengthen control.

HIV/AIDS and Sex Education

Compared with the states of sub-Saharan Africa, Europe, and North America,
the Arab world is characterized by a low spread of HIV/AIDS (*SidAlerte* 1995:
2). Notwithstanding the low level of infection in the Arab world and the great
secrecy that surrounds those who are infected, both of which turn HIV/AIDS
into an invisible and absent phenomenon in Arab daily life, some responsible
bureaucrats have been persuaded of the need to establish preventive educational programs to ensure that sexual behavior is conscious and cautious. In
Lebanon, sex education programs were developed to allay fears by providing information about AIDS and to disseminate an educational message that
encouraged both abstinence from sex as well as responsible decision-making
about pre-marital sex. These programs faced resistance from religious authorities and have since been scrapped (Beydoun 2001: 15).

But Aaraj (2001: 30) demonstrates that preventive sensitization campaigns outside educational institutions did not produce reassuring results: only 20 percent of young men (15–24 years old) changed their sexual conduct in response to the danger of AIDS, and just 23 percent settled on using condoms. In Palestine (West Bank), 66 percent of young men believed that abstinence is the ideal prophylactic. Only 1 percent mentioned condoms (Shaheen 2001: 31).

The emerging association between the condom and non-marital sexuality, which is stigmatized in the Islamic/Arab unconscious, makes the condom inherit all of the negative images that are associated with that sexuality. Furthermore, the condom meets with a threefold opposition, according to Dialmy (Dialmy 2002a, 2003a). It is the subject of a popular rejection, of Islamic juridical condemnation, and of medical instrumentation. As for the sexually active, the condom is rejected because in hindering arousal and erection, it threatens the basis of virility (Dialmy and Manhart 1997). Among its other negative attributes are its high cost and the embarrassment experienced during its purchase, in addition to the fact that it causes doubt among sexual partners.

As far as the jurists are concerned, there is no scope for legal innovation that would allow the use of condoms in non-marital relations for prophylactic purposes because such relations are primordially banned (Dialmy 2000a; see especially the chapter "Islam et Prévention"). One should point out here that Muslim jurists do make new rules in this area when they are in countries where Islam is not the state's religion, especially in European countries. The AIDS and Mobility Association has been able to persuade imams of Swiss mosques to offer condoms for free to visitors and worshipers (Van Duifhuizen 1995: 33). For his part, the imam of the Paris mosque, Dalil Boubakeur (1993), would advise young Muslim men to use condoms in cases of inability to maintain pre-marital sexual abstinence.

The source of all this is the lack of an integrated public policy on sexuality that recognizes, even implicitly, the right to sex as one of the basic human rights (Dialmy 2003a). Such a policy could establish a civic morality that would break the linkages between sex and marriage, and between sex and heterosexuality.

Conclusion

Obviously, the scope of the article, the breadth of the topic of sexuality, and the vastness of the geographical area covered have combined to limit the depth of this analysis and to curtail detailed descriptions. Moreover, the analysis is hindered by the rarity of regional and survey data and by their insufficient distribution within Arab countries.

Up until the appearance of HIV/AIDS in the Arab world, the subject of family-planning programs constituted the main, indirect introduction to Arab sexuality, that is, the intellectual veil that hides the true intellectual topic, by which we mean precisely sexuality. Following the spread of HIV/AIDS, some Arab governments were compelled to conduct sociological and anthropological studies of sexuality with the intention of identifying the cultural and social factors that surround sexual practices. The aim was to use these factors in developing suitable educational and media programs that encourage people to avoid practices that may expose them to the danger of the virus.

These studies have found that Arab sexuality continues to be predicated on domination and hierarchy between men and women, between the older and the younger, between the normal and the 'queer', and between the clients and the sex workers. It became clear that the dominating, hegemonizing nature of sexual relations in most cases turns sexual conduct into coercive conducts, that is, conducts that are products of necessity, fear, obligation, or opportunism.

Notwithstanding the need for studies of sexuality, the Arab researcher in this field still suffers from lack of recognition, regardless of the exhaustive effort and trouble taken in collecting and interpreting the data. The researcher also feels isolated and is often subjected to rejection, threats, and persecution, for when the researcher lays bare the sexual reality, this disturbs all sorts of social activists, be they technocrats, politicians, or feminists alike. Sexuality in and of itself continues to be semi-banned in teaching. It is an intellectual taboo for the various Arab peoples and a political taboo for the ruling Arab regimes and, moreover, for the Arab feminist movements themselves.

The ruling regimes continue to find the study of sexuality annoying to a great extent. Inevitably, these studies have led to the recording of sexual conducts and practices that are illegitimate from the point of view of Islamic jurisprudence, a fact that leads the fundamentalist movements to condemn political regimes for not being vigilant in respecting Islamic sexual morality and not carrying out the Shari'a requirements in the area. The ruling Arab regimes' avoidance of the study of sexuality aims to deprive political rivals, especially fundamentalists, from scientific proof demonstrating the reality that Arab sexuality is incompatible with what it should be, from an Islamic point of view. In other words, the reality of Arab sexuality might bring about accusations that the ruling regimes have failed to provide employment to youth, thereby making it impossible for them to marry (Dialmy 1998: 17), and that they have turned a blind eye to sex work, or even organized it—accusations, in brief, that they are engaged in moral corruption. Since the Arab political regimes themselves link their legitimacy to the Islamic nature of their sexual regimes, and to Islam in general, they prefer not to produce sociological studies of sexuality that will inevitably expose them to many fundamentalist criticisms.

The Arab feminist movement has become the basic channel through which flow the values of gender equity and equality in the Arab world. But in matters that relate to pre-marital sex or to gay and lesbian sexual practices, we find a quasi-universal tendency toward silence. Sexual rights still constitute one of the taboos of Arab feminist movements. These movements hide their political and intellectual coyness in this area behind the logic of priorities—the priorities of education, employment, and health for women. This enables Arab feminism to suspend and postpone the purely sexual demands that are unique to the woman as woman, and to the woman as human. There is not a single Arab feminist movement that demands explicitly the right of the young woman to sexual pleasure. Moreover, we find that the sexuality of the married Arab woman herself remains to a large extent the object of silence and timidity inside this movement. Arab feminism still presents the woman in an image of a social being without a sex life and without sexual needs.

The strategic goal of the feminist movement, namely, to share in political authority, explains to a large degree its avoidance of sexuality as a demand and a topic of research. Seeking political authority imposes upon the movement the acceptance of the patriarchal rules of the game of sexuality—rules that turn sexuality into a means of controlling the feminine body.

The stake that emerges from this vagueness is the necessity to establish an Arab sexual democracy that moves sexuality from a religious order to a civil order without this shift meaning a rejection of the prevailing creed in the Arab world at an individual level. Here exactly is the direction in which the Arab feminist movement must proceed, a direction that will make it clear to Arab politicians and Muslim jurists that the secularization of sexuality does not necessarily mean the rejection of religious values. Those values will become, for the individual, a free choice from among a variety of possibilities. At the same time, this direction will enable Arab researchers to reintroduce sexuality into the Arab discourse and liberate it from the various forms of patriarchal bureaucracy.

— Translated from the Arabic by Allon J. Uhlmann

Abdessamad Dialmy is Professor of Sociology, Head of the Inter-Disciplinary Laboratory for Studies of Health and Population (LIDESP), Faculty of Arts and Humanities, Fez University, Morocco.

Notes

An earlier version of this article appeared in Arabic in *al Mustaqbal al Arabi* (2004, issue no. 299: 138–167), a journal published in Beirut by the Center for Arab Unity Studies.

1. According to Lutfi (1991: 101, 109–118), it seems that in Egypt during the Ottoman period, many women took legal action to gain this right.
2. But one must point here to the appearance of an embryonic retreat from the mechanical link between masculinity and virility that emerges in Dialmy's study (2000c) concerning masculine identity and reproductive health. Perhaps this indicates that the Arab man is becoming aware of the dangers posed to his mental stability and to his relationships with women by this blind link between masculinity and virility.

References

Aaraj, Elie. 2001. "Lebanese Youth, Knowledge and AIDS-Related Risky Behavior." P. 30 in *Sexuality in the Middle East* (Conference Report), ed. Angel M. Foster. Oxford: American University of Beirut and University of Oxford.

'Abdullah, Mohamed. 1998. "Viagra Freaks." [In Arabic.] *'Al Ousbou'*, 25 May.

Abu Odeh, Lama. 2002. "Crimes of Honor and the Construction of Gender in Arab Societies." Pp. 363–380 in *Women and Sexuality in Muslim Societies*, ed. Pinar Ilkkaracan. Istanbul: WWHR/New Ways.

Ait Sabbah, Fatna. 1982. *La femme dans l'inconscient musulman* [Woman in the Muslim Unconsciousness]. Paris: Le Sycomore.

Al Munajjid, Şalaah 'Aldin. 1958. *Sex Life among Arabs* [In Arabic.]. Beirut: Dar 'Alkitaab.

Al Qassas, Akram. 1998. "Viagra Falls." [In Arabic.] *'Al 'Arabi*, 25 May.

Al Saadawi, Nawal. 1977. *Woman and Psychological Struggle*. [In Arabic.] Cairo: 'Almu'assasa 'Al'arabiyya Liddiraasaat Wannashr.

Amnesty International. 1997. *Breaking the Silence: Human Rights Violation Based on Sexual Orientation*. London: Amnesty International.

Ben Salama, Fethi. 1985. "L'énigme du concept de sexe dans la langue arabe" [The Enigma of the Concept of Sex in the Arab Language]. *Peuples Méditérranéens*, no. 3: 155–162.

Bencheikh, Jamal Eddine. 1988. *Les mille et une nuits ou la parole prisonnière* [One Thousand and One Nights, or The Imprisoned Talk]. Paris: Gallimard.

Beydoun, Azzah Shararah. 2001. "School Curriculum for Sexual Education in Lebanon." P. 15 in *Sexuality in the Middle East* (Conference Report), ed. Angel M. Foster. Oxford: American University of Beirut and University of Oxford.

Boubakeur, Dalil. 1993. "L'Islam, la sexualité et la prévention du Sida" [Islam, Sexuality, and the Prevention of AIDS]. *Le Journal du Dimanche*, 9 May.

Bouhdiba, Abdelwahab. 1975. *La sexualité en Islam* [Sexuality in Islam]. Paris: PUF.

Chelli, Mounira. 1986. "Est-il vrai que la femme se libérera en libérant sa sexualité?" [Is It True That Woman Will Liberate Herself When Liberating Her Sexuality?]. Pp. 77–104 in *Psychologie différentielle des sexes*, ed. CERES. Tunis: Université de Tunis.

Dayan-Herzburn, Sonia. 1991. "Women: Political Stake." [In Arabic.] *Mawaaqif*, no. 64: 49–57.

DHS (Demographic and Health Survey). 1995. *Egypt Demographic and Health Survey*. Cairo: National Population Council.

Dialmy, Abdessamad. 1985. *Woman and Sex in Morocco*. [In Arabic.] Casablanca: Dar 'An Nashr 'Almağribiyya.

———. 1998. "Moroccan Youth, Sex and Islam." *Middle East Report*, no. 206: 16–17.

———. 2000a. *Jeunesse, Sida et Islam au Maroc*. Casablanca: Eddif.

———. 2000b. "Sexualité et politique au Maroc: Rapport final." Rabat. FNUAP. (Non-published.)

———. 2000c. "Identité masculine et santé reproductive au Maroc: Rapport final" [Masculine Identity and Reproductive Health in Morocco: Final Report]. Beirut. LCPS/MERC/Ministry of Health.

———. 2000d. *Toward an Islamic Sexual Democracy*. [In Arabic.] Fez: Dar 'Anfu-Print Linnashr.

———. 2002a. "Sexuality and Sexual Health in Morocco." Paper presented at symposium, "Technical Consultation on Sexual Health." World Health Organization.

———. 2002b. "Regarding the Connection between Islamic Law and International Law against the Discrimination between Women and Men in Rights and Obligations." [In Arabic.] *Prologues*, Hors série, no. 4: 68–88.

———. 2003a. "L'usage du préservatif au Maroc" [The Use of the Condom in Morocco]. Pp. 50–59 in *L'approche culturelle de la prévention et du traitement du VIH/SIDA* (Colloque Régional UNESCO/ONUSIDA Fès 2001), Etudes et Rapports, Série Spéciale, No. 13, Division des Politiques Culturelles, UNESCO 2003. http://unesdoc.unesco.org/images/0013/001303/130320f.pdf (accessed 19 May 2003).

———. 2003b. "Premarital Female Sexuality in Morocco." *Al Raida* 20, no. 99: 75–83.

Dialmy, Abdessamad, and Lisa Manhart. 1997. *Les maladies sexuellement transmissibles au Maroc* [The Sexually Transmitted Diseases in Morocco]. Temara: Ministère de la Santé/ Université de Washington/USAID.

Droeber, Julia. 2003. "Harassment, Honour, Gossip, and the Reputation of Young Women in Jordan." *Al-Raida* 20, no. 99: 44–48.

Dune, Bruce. 1998. "Power and Sexuality in the Middle East." *Middle East Report*, no. 206: 8–11.

Foster, Angel M. 2001. "Sexual Knowledge among Tunisian University Students." Pp. 16–17 in *Sexuality in the Middle East* (Conference Report), ed. Angel M. Foster. Oxford: American University of Beirut and University of Oxford.

Harakat, Abou Bakr. 2001. "Troubles érectiles et consultation sexologique" [Erectile Dysfunction and Sexological Consultation]. *Espérance médicale*, no. 70: 117–119.

Husseini, Rana. 2001–2002, "Imprisonment to Protect Women against Crimes of Honor: A Dual Violation of Civil Rights." *Al-Raida* 19, no. 95–96: 40–41.

Ibn 'Arabi, Mohayyi Eddine. n.d. *Settings of the Wisdoms*. [In Arabic.] Beirut: Dar al Fikr.

Kamal, Abdallah. 1997. *The licit prostitution*. [In Arabic.] Beirut: al Maktaba at Taqafiya.

Kamran, Ali Asdar. 1996. "Notes on Rethinking Masculinities: An Egyptian Case." Pp. 89–110 in *Learning about Sexuality: A Practical Beginning*, ed. Sondra Zeidenstein and Kirsten Moore. New York: The Population Council/International Women's Health Coalition.

Khair Badawi, Marie-Thérèse. 1986. *Le désir amputé: Le vécu sexuel des femmes libanaises* [The Amputee Desire: The Sexually Lived of Lebanese Women]. Paris: L'Harmattan.

Khattab, Hind. 1996. *Women's Perceptions of Sexuality in Rural Giza*. Giza: The Population Council.

Labib, Tahar. 1973. "Langue arabe et sexualité" [Arab Language and Sexuality]. *L'homme et la société*, no. 28: 11–22.

Labidi, Leila. 1989. *Cabra hacham: Sexualité et tradition* [Patience and Shame: Sexuality and Tradition]. Tunis: Dar Annwras.

Lutfi, Huda. 1991. "Manners and Customs of Fourteenth-Century Cairen Women: Female Anarchy versus Male Shari' Order in Muslim Prescriptive Treatises." Pp. 99–121 in *Women in Middle Eastern History*, ed. Nikki R. Keddie and Beth Baron. New Haven, CT: Yale University Press.

Major, Stella. 2001. "Clinician's Experiences Counseling Young Adults Seeking Information and Assistance in Their Sexual Development." Pp. 15–16 in *Sexuality in the Middle East* (Conference Report), ed. Angel M. Foster. Oxford: American University of Beirut and University of Oxford.

Meinhardus, Otto. 1967. "Mythological, Historical and Sociological Aspects of the Practice of Female Circumcision among the Egyptians." *Acta Ethnographica Academiae Scientarum Hungaricae*, no. 16: 387–397.

Moussaoui, A. 2002. "La légitimation des transgressions: Violences au féminin. Le viol entre sacrifice et sacrilège" [The Legitimity of Transgressions: Female Violences. The Rape between Sacrifice and Sacrilege]. Paper presented at symposium, "Islams et Islamités." Centre Jacques Berque de Rabat.

Naamane Guessous, Soumeyya. 1987. *Au delà de toute pudeur* [Beyond All Modesty]. Casablanca: Eddif.

Nasraoui, Mustapha. 1986. "La vie sexuelle des jeunes ouvriers tunisiens célibataires" [The Sexual Life of Young Tunisian Workers]. Pp. 105–132 in *Psychologie différentielle des sexes*, ed. CERES. Tunis: Université de Tunis.

Qadri, Abdellah, Mohammed Berrada, Abbas Tahiri, and Chakib Nejjari. 1999. "La prévalence de la dysfunction érectile au Maroc" [The prevalence of erectile dysfunction in Morocco]. Casablanca. Département des Statistiques. (Non-published.)

Raymond, André. 1973. *Artisans et commerçants au Caire au XVIIIe siècle* [Craftsmen and Merchants in Cairo in the Eighteenth Century]. Cairo: IFAO.

Rowson, Everett K. 1991. "The Categorization of Gender and Sexual Irregularity in Medieval Arabic Vice Lists." Pp. 64–81 in *Body Guards: The Cultural Politics of Ambiguity*, ed. Julia Epstein and Kristina Straub. New York and London: Routledge.

Ruggi, Suzanne. 1998. "Commodifying Honor in Female Sexuality: Honor Killings in Palestine." *Middle East Report*, no. 206: 12–15.

Serhan, Randa. 2001. "Honour Crimes in Lebanon: The Significance of Change in Legal Stipulations." Pp. 25–26 in *Sexuality in the Middle East* (Conference Report), ed. Angel M. Foster. Oxford: American University of Beirut and University of Oxford.

Shaheen, Mohammad. 2001. "Knowledge and Attitudes of Palestinian Youth toward Health-Related Issues with a Focus on AIDS/STDs." P. 31 in *Sexuality in the Middle East* (Conference Report), ed. Angel M. Foster. Oxford: American University of Beirut and University of Oxford.

Shalhoub-Kevorkian, Nadera. 2001. "Femicide: Woman-Killing in Palestinian Society." P. 25 in *Sexuality in the Middle East* (Conference Report), ed. Angel M. Foster. Oxford: American University of Beirut and University of Oxford.

SidAlerte. 1995. "Sida: Le Soudan est le pays le plus touché de la région arabo-musulmane" [AIDS: Soudan Is the Most Affected Country in the Arab-Muslim Region]. *SidAlerte*, no. 49: 2.

Tauzin, Aline. 1991. "The Torture of Desire." [In Arabic.] *Mawaaqif*, no. 64: 58–73.

———. 2002. "Du hiatus entre loi religieuse et tradition: L'exemple de la Mauritanie" [The Cut between Religious Law and Tradition: The Mauritania Example]. In *Sexualité et Religion*. Paris: Association Française de Sciences Sociales des Religions. (Non-published.)

Tucker, Judith. 1993. *Gender and Islamic History*. Washington, DC: American Historical Association.

Van Duifhuizen, Rinske. 1995. "Les besoins et les possibilités de la collaboration internationale: L'expérience du projet 'AIDS and Mobility'" [Needs and Possibilities of International Cooperation: The Experience of the "AIDS and Mobility" Project]. Amsterdam: AIDS and Mobility. (Non-published.)

[18]

Zina and the moral regulation of Pakistani women

Shahnaz Khan

abstract

From 1998 to 1999, I interviewed women who had been incarcerated under the *Zina* Ordinance (*zina* means illicit sex) in Pakistan. This led me to an examination of women's moral regulation by their families, a process in which I maintain the state is complicit. I argue against relativist explanations of this process, which view Pakistani culture or notions of timeless Islam as the reason for women's incarceration. Instead, I examine the interconnection of morality with the legal/judicial structures, the relationship between the state and patriarchy within families, and the plight of impoverished women in Pakistan within an era of globalization. In my analysis, I link economic development and human rights to globalization and the continuing costs of militarization. Such connections allow feminists to target the structural conditions that sustain the laws in Pakistan and help create an environment that will bring about the repeal of the laws while contributing to trans-national feminist solidarity.

keywords

Zina; women; morality/sexuality; Islam; imprisonment

introduction

I married my neighbour. My parents were against the marriage although my husband had come with a formal proposal and asked for my hand. My parents said they wanted one *lakh*[1] before they gave him permission to marry me. Then my husband sold his land and was willing to give them the one *lakh* they had asked for. But they still said no. This time they said that he is Punjabi and we are Sindhis[2] and we are of a different *biradi* [community]. So I ran away with him and we got married anyway. My parents found us eventually and charged us with *zina* and both of us are in jail. Now they say give us the one *lakh* we asked for and then we will withdraw the charges. But the money has been spent on hiding from my parents and on lawyers. Now we have no more money. I am afraid that when we are released, that is my son, my husband and I, my parents will find us and kill us.

These comments were made by twenty-five-year-old Naheed[3] who has had no formal education. She was charged under the *Zina* Ordinance (also known as *zina* laws) and was an inmate of *Kot Lakpat* prison in Lahore, Pakistan where I interviewed her in December of 1998.

Zina refers to sex outside of marriage–both adultery and fornication. In Pakistan, the *Zina* Ordinance suggests and regulates what constitutes ethical behaviour in sex, and, more generally, within the family and the social institution of marriage in ways in which women's fundamental rights under the constitution, and some argue in Islam, are violated. Specifically, *zina* laws are part of the *Hadood* Ordinances[4] promulgated in 1979 by General Zia-ul-Haq, the self-proclaimed president of Pakistan, as a first step in his Islamization policies. Drawing upon the sacred texts of Islam, the *zina* laws seek to define and reinforce the notion of a 'pure and chaste' Pakistani citizen. The text states:

> Whereas it is necessary to modify the existing law relating to zina so as to bring it in conformity with the injunctions of Islam as set out in the Holy Quran and the Sunnah...
>
> (Mahmood and Shaukat, 1994: 3).

The *Zina* Ordinance covers, among other things, adultery, fornication, rape and prostitution under the rubric *zina* and treats them as offences against the state. Critics of the law (Mehdi, 1991; Jahangir and Jilani, 1988) point out that the ordinance makes no distinction between the level of proof required to sentence someone for rape or for adultery. Under the terms of the law, victims of rape have been convicted of adultery (because they acknowledge intercourse) and the accused, who denied that he had intercourse, released for lack of evidence of rape. Men can also be convicted of adultery. If convicted under the ordinance, the rape victim is sentenced to one hundred lashes if unmarried and death by stoning if married (Shaeed and Mumtaz, 1987). To date, no woman or man convicted under these laws has been stoned in Pakistan, largely due to pressure exerted on the government by national and international human rights organizations. The Nigerian

1 One lakh is 100,000 rupees, the equivalent of $2,500 Canadian

2 Sind and Punjab are two different provinces in Pakistan. Naheed's parents are conflating provincial regional groups with ethnicity as is often done in Pakistan.

3 The women's names have been changed to ensure that my research does not affect them in any way.

4 The *Hadood* Ordinances include laws dealing with property offences, prohibition against alcohol and drugs, *zina* Ordinance and *Qazaf* (the law of false accusation of *zina*). For a broader discussion of the *Hadood* Ordinances, see Jahangir and Jilani (1988).

5 See 'Death By Stoning Sentence Draws Verbal Lashing' (2002), *The Globe and Mail*, 21 August, p. A10.

government also faced pressure to stay the execution of a woman convicted under similar laws in that country.[5]

Although 95 percent of the prisoners charged for *zina* are released upon trial, they face years of incarceration before trial. Moreover in the 'lock-up', they are vulnerable to custodial rape and other forms of physical, emotional and sexual torture (HRCP, 1997; HRW, 1992). So much so that Benazir Bhutto passed a law in 1996 that no woman can spend the night in a police lock-up; instead, she is sent directly to jail. Conditions in the urban jails are under the scrutiny of non-governmental organizations (NGOs) and charity organizations that work there, and the women that I interviewed for this study stated that they were treated better by jail officials than by their families on the outside. However, rural jails are another matter. There are few NGOs operating in rural areas, and many of the jails have no separate section for women with female staff. Abuse of prisoners could likely occur in such circumstances.

Research documents that thousands of women have been charged and jailed under the *Zina* Ordinance and that the interpretations and repercussions of the laws are class based. Although meant to be applied to all Pakistani citizens, *zina* laws are unevenly exercised, and the most vulnerable members of society — impoverished and illiterate women — are the most affected. That is, women who cannot afford lawyers are most likely to be charged and jailed (Jahangir and Jilani, 1988; Sumar and Nadhvi, 1988). Furthermore, my data supports the view that many of the women incarcerated under *zina*-related charges are not there because of sex crimes but because their families or former husbands used the *zina* laws to jail the women when they went against their families' wishes. The *zina* laws were promulgated to help bring about a just and moral society in Pakistan. Critics of the ordinance (Rouse, 1998; Shaheed, 1997; Toor, 1996; Mehdi, 1991; Jahangir and Jilani, 1988), however, argue that these laws allow families to draw upon the power of the state to help regulate the morality and sexuality of 'their' women and reclaim family honour. This contributes to the growing incidence of state-sanctioned violence against women.

Notwithstanding the complexities of the context which led to the promulgation of the *Hadood* Ordinance and the pressures that continue to sustain it, narratives of experience such as that of Naheed risk a particular reading in the West. Their accounts are often trivialized as human interest stories or the women are portrayed as victims of their cultures and their men (Khan, 2001; Mohanty, 1991; Min-Ha, 1989). As Gayatri Spivak (1999) and Lata Mani (1986) have stated so forcefully in other contexts, such notions often serve to further demonize and stereotype third-world peoples, reinforcing a view that, Spivak reminds us, seeks to free brown women from brown men. These views are also supported by some feminists who, Angela Miles (1996: 99) argues, have not questioned the prevailing stereotypes about third-world women (or 'two-third world women' as she calls them) 'as more passive, powerless, and oppressed than [f]irst [w]orld women'.

Western women, largely excluded from power themselves, often perpetuate these prejudices through the exclusion of women of colour, thus reinforcing the East/ West binary (Yegenoglu, 1998). Although binary thinking no longer dominates feminist theory, these ideas continue to circulate at the fringes and to structure popular perceptions about the third-world woman. Contemporary theorists (Spivak, 1999; Hall, 1997; Bhabha, 1994a) suggest that we move away from culturalist explanations of such events towards an examination of the local and global forces which help shape people's lives. Indeed, Naheed's comments about her incarceration for *zina* could easily be seen in the West as yet another example of third-world women's oppression rather than as an incident with a wider connection. In interrogating her account, it is crucial to locate her comments in a geo-political context. I have examined the politics of representation of the third-world woman in the West more extensively elsewhere (Khan, 2002). In this discussion, I am more interested in understanding the ways in which discourses of morality, sexuality, nation and religion conflate with those of law to create the conditions that influence Naheed's life.

moral regulation

Phillip Corrigan and Derek Sayer (1985: 4) define moral regulation as 'a project of normalizing, rendering natural, taken for granted, in a word 'obvious', what are in fact ontological and epistemological premises of a particular and historical form of social order'. State practices, moreover, promote a common experience of individuals, which denies differences including race, ethnicity, class, gender and sexuality. Corrigan and Seyer (1985: 6) argue that this idea of a common collective consciousness of the nation is not a free-floating signifier. It is grounded in relations of domination and subordination. The ways in which the state promotes the collectivity reinforces specific notions of what is morally permissible, distinguishing between the licit and illicit. These socially produced notions, Corrigan and Seyer claim, 'are simultaneously descriptive and moral' (1985: 6).

Furthermore, Jeffery Weeks (1995: 47) has pointed to the connection between notions of morality and sexual behaviour 'to the extent that 'immorality' in the English language almost invariably means sexual misbehaviour'. This appears true in Pakistan as well. State prescriptions of morality help sustain an eternal Islam not grounded in a geo-political context. Policies and practices influenced by such determinations regulate gendered and classed bodies into docile citizens in ways that serve capitalist and patriarchal interests. Such a process facilitates sex to be transferred from the sphere of 'family matters' to sexuality in the public sphere, where it can be shaped to coincide with 'national interests'. In other words, *zina* laws allow the state to identify and regulate sexual conduct as a crucial element of creating a just society. Moreover as Anne McClintock (1995) has noted elsewhere, female respectability appears linked to the middle-class woman. The disease of poverty was especially dangerous in the female body and served to rationalize the policing of boundaries between the ruling class and the immoral poor. These comments are certainly applicable to the women I interviewed. Class is an important factor in regulating immorality for the women that I found in prison and in the *Darul Amans* were all impoverished. Their accounts suggest that many of them are young and deemed immoral by virtue of defying parental wishes. The older women charged with *zina* on the other hand are often constructed as disobedient and therefore immoral wives; at the same time their accounts suggest that their current or former husbands are attempting to extort money from them.

Although women's kin groups and families are the primary agents of the process of moral regulation, the practices associated with *zina* laws confirm state complicity. This complicity, I argue, is not incidental. As individual bodies become the focus of the regulating gaze, discourse promoting morality in Pakistan remains limited to containing illicit sex. At the same time, attention is deflected away from structural issues such as increasing indebtedness and rising militarization, practices that might implicate politicians and state officials. The women charged with *zina* have resisted these claims on their bodies and, as I will demonstrate, have found themselves entangled in a complex web of state incompetence and corruption. I suspect there are tens of thousands of others who have been intimidated by the threat of similar charges and complied with family wishes. What then are the conditions that have brought about this law and continue to influence its existence?

Liberal intellectual traditions, including those of liberal feminism, focus on the abstract universal citizen rendering the body irrelevant to the social order. Other feminist theorists, however, believe that the body, particularly the female body, is central to thought processes (Shildrick and Price, 1999). For example, radical feminists (Rich, 1992; MacKinnon, 1989) have examined the ways in which the institution of heterosexuality regulates and constrains women so that their sexuality services the nation through culturally and biologically reproducing new generations of citizens. Socialist feminists (Yuval-Davis, 1997; Brah, 1996) have spoken of the means through which bodies of impoverished classes have been excluded from sites of power in ways in which their fundamental citizenship rights are violated. Nira Yuval-Davis (1997) also comments that the state is not the only entity demanding loyalty and exercising power over women. Kin groups often function in the same way as families in this regard. For example, women are members of national collectivities where they are granted constitutional rights of equality and liberty, but, unlike men, they are also subject to special rules as laid out by their community groups. These rules may deny them rights guaranteed by the state. Although many of these challenges to the abstract individual have drawn upon Western traditions, Fatna Sabah (1988) has identified a similar trend in muslim societies. According to Sabah, Islamic legal de-contextualized discourse defines reality, as it dismisses and devalues all others, including the erotic discourse.

79

The constitution of Pakistan too has a liberal tradition in that it grants rights to all citizens, giving Naheed the liberty to marry whomever she wishes. However, the practices associated with the *Zina* Ordinance override that right and allows her family to intimidate her and have her incarcerated. I do not wish to reinforce a male/female dichotomy and argue that only women are victimized through this process or that it is men alone who inflict charges of *zina* on women. Indeed, in this case Naheed's husband was also incarcerated for *zina*. Furthermore, women's narratives identify instances where mothers have initiated *zina* charges against daughters. Through their connections with their sons, and other male family members, menopausal women frequently have significant status in their families and communities. These arrangements help identify the ways in which women and men strategize within a set of concrete constraints that reveal and define the blueprint of what Deniz Kandiyoti (1988) has termed as 'a patriarchal bargaining' in a society. I want, however, to identify Naheed as more vulnerable than her husband in this process because of the gender bias in Pakistani law (Shaheed, 1997; Mehdi, 1991; Jahangir and Jilani, 1988), a bias also present in other countries (Comack, 2000; Hazarika, 1988).

The ways in which middle- and upper-class women negotiate *zina* is beyond the scope of this paper. My concern is with those women who have found themselves incarcerated, formally in prison or more informally in state-run shelters, the *Darul Amans*.[6] All the women whom I have interviewed have been without financial and other resources suggesting that women with such resources, are able to post bail and are now free. Moreover, several well-publicized cases suggest that things happen differently in more influential families. Particularly, Saima Waheed's court challenge helped construct the legal definition of an adult *sui juris* female capable of entering into the marriage contract.

The Saima case, as it was popularly known, illustrates the extent to which a woman with material resources can pose legal challenges when faced with ambiguity about her status in the law (Sardar Ali, 2000). The common understanding of the Hanafi school of Islamic law, to which the majority of Pakistanis belong, is that a muslim woman has the right to enter a marriage of her own accord. It is not lawful for a guardian to force into marriage an adult woman against her consent. However, this view does not always translate into legal practice for Pakistani courts have given contradictory rulings on this matter. At times they have sided with the woman and her right to make her own marriage choices, and at other times they have sided with the parents and stated that her *wali's* (guardian's) right supersedes her own. Saima married against her family's wishes while her father stated that as *wali* he had the right to forbid the match. When she took up residence in a women's shelter managed by an NGO, her father filed criminal charges against the refuge and accused them of abducting his daughter. Saima petitioned the court stating that she, as an adult woman, could enter into a marriage contract on her own without the approval of her *wali* and requested a declaration upholding her marriage. Her

6 *Darul Amans* are women's shelters sponsored by the state and funded by *Anjuman-i-Himayat -Islam*, a religious organization. Women who seek refuge here find that they are in an informal prison. They cannot leave and except for their immediate family, other people cannot visit them without permission from the courts. Further, they are also subject to discretionary 'judging' by officials in charge. The *Darul Amans* do not have structured proce- dures and policies that provide any significant protec- tion to the resi- dents. This likely places the residents at greater risk than in prison. See 'Locating a Feminist Voice: *Zina* Laws in Pakistan', an article written and held on file by the author.

case raised several important issues: Is marriage indeed a civil contract in Islam? If yes, then in order to enter into this contract does she have to be *sui juris*? Moreover, how does the will of her *wali* enter into this contract? Although Saima was finally deemed an adult capable of entering into a marriage contract, Justice Ihsan-ul-Haq Chaudhary, in a dissenting opinion, argued that 'although the full and free consent of a woman forms an essential element of a valid marriage, this consent is qualified by the overriding right of the *wali* or marriage guardian to withhold or accord assent' (Sardar Ali, 2000: 161). In a more recent court challenge, Humaira Mahmood raised these issues again and the Pakistani women's ability to contract marriages as an adult was re-validated through a unanimous court ruling in 1999.[7]

Saima Sarwar and Uzma Talpur also came from wealthy families whose influence with authorities denied them the relative safety of institutions. Saima was murdered in her lawyer's chambers in front of witnesses for the 'crime' of seeking a divorce from a brutalizing husband against the wishes of her family. Her murderers have as yet not been charged. Instead her father, a member of the Peshawar Chamber of Commerce, has used his influence to have a *fatwa* (religious decree) issued against her lawyer Hina Jilani. The second woman, Uzma Talpur, married against her family's wishes and has since disappeared, a disappearance popularly believed to have been orchestrated by her family. Both cases illustrate how wealthy families are able to keep their daughters out of prison and thus within the reach of their vengeance.[8]

I met about 150 women at *Kot Lakpat* prison in Lahore, and at Karachi Central Jail, as well as women in the *Darul Amans*, in Karachi and Lahore, during the course of my research visits to Pakistan beginning in 1998. I have, however, been unable to locate any woman who had been incarcerated under the *Zina* Ordinance and who is now out of prison and free to speak about her experiences. Hina Jilani, a lawyer with the Human Rights Commission of Pakistan, claims that we are unable to locate the women because of the destructive process of incarceration. Some of the women go back to their families after they are released from prison and the families protect/prevent them from outside contact.[9] More frequently, however, the women are afraid to return to their families. They disappear and make their lives anew in whatever way they can. As I was unable to find former women prisoners who were relatively free to speak about the process of incarceration, several areas were left unexplored. What were their experiences in the lock-up and in the prison? What kinds of contact did they have with their families upon release? Were they able to connect with and regain custody of their children? What strategies did they employ to rebuild their lives? These unanswered questions suggest some of the limitations of my investigation. They do, however, partially explain why the victims of *zina* laws do not offer resistance to the state. They do not, for instance, organize against the law or agitate against the process that treated them so unjustly. Their families silence them, or they purposely vanish.

7 Humaira Mahmood vs State LID 494, Lahore High Court, 1999.

8 For a further discussion of these cases, see Amnesty International (2002).

9 I tried to locate two women whose families had accepted them back and whose address I had. I was, however, given the run around by their relatives, who were suspicious of me and my motives.

Their disappearance hands the state a clean slate in which there are no victims demanding restitution, just activists who can be dismissed as being contaminated by the West.[10]

10 For a larger discussion of this topic, see Khan (2002).

The culture of the jails and the shelters denies visits with women alone. An institutional official is always present. So I chose to start the interviews with the question 'What events led you to this place?'. In this manner, each woman could answer with what felt safe for her. I only interjected to clarify what she had said. It is very possible that they wanted to say more but did not feel safe in front of the official or with me, the newcomer. They told their stories without hesitation or doubt, as if they had narrated them before. Their comments suggest that they are not passive victims of the *Zina* Ordinance but actively negotiate discourses of gender, ethnicity and class. It is to an examination of those negotiations that I now turn.

the enforcement of zina laws

Drawing upon the work of Claude Levi Straus, Gayle Rubin (1975) has pointed out in another context that marriages are a form of exchange between kin groups, and women are seen as a precious gift. This gift allows kin groups to build alliances and become related by blood. Women are not partners in these exchanges and cannot realize the benefits of their circulation. Families are the beneficiaries of the exchanges, Rubin points out. Comments from women I interviewed suggest that similar transactions have taken place. Members of women's families frequently use the *zina* laws to dictate to women and to intimidate them into marrying and having children with whom they want. Families with little means to cope with increasing inflation and chronic unemployment often find that their daughter's sexuality is a valuable asset, a commodity commanding a high price. Marrying her to the highest bidder in exchange for a 'gift' frequently becomes one method of paying off debts. Furthermore, many women are 'sold' into marriage to sustain alcohol and drug habits of their male relatives. Indeed, the women whom I spoke to cited increasing poverty and family violence as the reason for their plight.

> My father's relatives were against his marriage to my mother. But he married her anyway. This cut him off from his own relatives. Now father married me to a man who I like and am happy with. He is close in age to me: he is twenty-two years old. Father and mother used to fight. He left the family and the country. I don't know where he is. No one knows where he is. Now mother wants me to divorce my husband. She says that I am only fifteen and a minor and that she has authority over me. She wants me to marry someone who has promised her money. So my mother has charged us with *zina* and my husband with abduction. My marriage has been registered and my husband has the *nikahnama* [marriage certificate].
>
> I am happy with my husband and I do not want to leave him. Twice I have been to court where I was told that I am a minor and should go with my mother and do as she says. But I

refused. Finally I came to *Darul Aman* for I am afraid. Next week I will appear before the court again, I will tell them that I want to stay married to my husband. My mother beats me a lot. She beats my siblings less. My in-laws are good to me and send me money from time to time. But as yet neither my husband nor my in-laws have been allowed to visit me here.

(Gulbano, age 15 Years)

Gulbano's account challenges the notion put forward by some feminist theorists that it is only men who control women and deny them their rights. Instead, her narrative makes a case for an analysis identifying the complexities of the patriarchal bargain. In this instance, Gulbano's mother does not have a nurturing relationship with her; instead, she attempts to commodify her daughter's body. Several of the women commented that their mothers had sided with their fathers in oppressing them, although a few pointed out that it was out of fear.

Gulbano is Pathan and the money promised to her mother in exchange for her is the bride-price, a common practice among Pathans living in rural areas, where as Shaheen Sardar Ali (2000: 176) points out 'a woman's consent and/or participation in drawing up of her marriage contract is considered of no consequence. She is bartered away at a suitable bride-price'. However, both Sardar Ali and Esposito (1982) argue that this practice is in contradiction with the Islamic requirement that dower (bride-price) be paid to the woman. Many rural Pathans have migrated to larger urban centres of Lahore and Karachi, the locales where I interviewed the women. Also, rural women are frequently transferred to urban prisons where they have special facilities for females. This has occurred in response to allegations of abuse in rural prisons. Through the payment of bride-price to parents, women become property to be bought and sold. Young girls are socialized into this practice. Many do not resist and those who do frequently face accusations of *zina*.

Although *zina* laws have an enormous impact on the lives of those impoverished women who resist, religion appears to provide them with only a tenuous legitimacy. Historically, religious scholars and jurists have drawn largely upon the *Qur'an* and the *Sunnah* to formulate *sharia* (religious law). Regional and customary laws also influence these formulations (Shaheed, 1997). For example, under the *Hanafi* version of *sharia* law commonly used in Pakistan, fathers and grandfathers can contract marriage for minors that cannot be annulled at puberty. John Esposito (1982) argues that this power is not supported by any verse in the *Qur'an* or by the *Sunnah*. However, should the minor's marriage have been contracted through fraud or by someone other than the father or grandfather (including the minor's mother), Esposito points out, the minor can repudiate the marriage upon attaining puberty. The *Hanafi* reading of the sacred in Pakistan then allows parents to contract marriages for minor daughters, whose sexuality becomes a commodity that can be sold. Many women resist this practice. Their resistance brings them into greater contact with the police force and legal system known for their corruption. Indeed,

83

a recent survey found that out of 12 selected government agencies, the police were deemed the most corrupt followed by the lower courts, the two agencies that women will likely come into contact with in the process of incarceration (Ghausi, 2001).

The use of *zina* laws to intimidate with the threat of imprisonment those daughters who have married without their permission suggests that parental right overrides men's right/claim to their wives. Often young men are as powerless as young women in deciding their destiny.

> I married against my parents will and they accused my husband of abducting me. Both of us are now in jail. My husband is my cousin [son of mother's brother]. I had asked my parents for permission to marry him but they said no. I got married anyway. And my parents registered a case of *zina* against me.
>
> (Nausheen, age 20 Years. She has been at *Kot Lakpat* three months and is expecting her first child this month.)

Nausheen's situation suggests that having a *nikhanama* (marriage certificate) is insufficient. She claims that her father as *wali* has refused to sanction the marriage. Moreover, her parents have bribed the officials who performed and registered the marriage to say that no marriage exists. They insist that her marriage certificate as well as her marriage is a fraud. Now Nausheen and her husband have to appear in court to argue their case before the judge. This is hampered by the fact that they have little money with which to pay for a lawyer. Court dates are notoriously difficult to get in the overburdened system. The couple may have to wait in jail for months before they appear before a magistrate. Had they been charged in a rural court, their situation might have been worse as was the case with Rubina. Although she is fortunate to have a legal aid lawyer, Rubina's case has been registered in Thatta, where there are no jail facilities for female prisoners. I met her in the Karachi jail where she had been transferred and where she was awaiting a court date. Rubina has a certificate to prove that she is indeed divorced from her first husband who charged her with committing *zina* with her current one. In order to present this evidence in court before a judge, she has to deal with several factors. She has to wait for a female guard to come and escort her to Thatta. Many times these guards do not appear at the appointed time; Rubina has missed two court dates, six months apart. When the guard finally arrived to escort Rubina to the court in Thatta, the judge did not show up due to illness. Sixteen-year-old Gurmat, faced with similar circumstances commented, 'What a nonsense system this is, first we wait for the female guard, then we wait for the judge, all to show them our papers. Who designed this system?'.

The women that I interviewed are well aware of the challenges they face. They are conscious of being painted as immoral, loose and promiscuous. Fifteen-year-old Saima pointed out that the only immorality she is guilty of is going against her family wishes. At the same time she commented 'My religion allows me to marry who I want'. Saima and many of the other women want relationships of love and romance and disobey familial demands. They believe that they are being punished for their disobedience. Many turn to the law for protection, however, their lack of resources makes their access to the law limited.

Moreover, religion, custom and illiteracy interconnect to further exacerbate the situation. In Islam, marriage is a civil contract and the *Qur'an* recommends that contracts be put in writing. 'Disdain not to reduce the writing of [your contract] for a future period...it is more just in the sight of God, more suitable as evidence, and more convenient to prevent doubts among yourselves' (Qur'an, 1968 II: 282). This does not often happen in Pakistan, particularly in the case of illiterate women with few material resources (Jilani, interviewed in 1998). Frequently, the husband repudiates his wife, as allowed by *sharia*, but does not register the divorce with the district council as required by civil law. Since the divorce is not registered, it is invalid. The woman, however, often believes that she is indeed divorced. Should she remarry, her first husband can and frequently does blackmail her with the threat of *zina*.

> My husband, Ahmad, used to come late at night and sometimes he never came home at all. When I asked him about it, he beat me. He told me that he did not like me and beat me. One day he beat me so badly that I had to have stitches on my forehead and my nose. Then he pronounced *talaq* (divorce by repudiation) three times and said 'You are no longer my wife. I have divorced you. If I see you in my house again I will kill you'. So I took my three children and went home to my parents.
>
> My parents are old and they do not have much money. In the house only my brother was working and he has four children. So they all began to pressure [me] to marry again. And eventually I married again to a man they found for me. Amin, my new husband, he was good to me and my children. And for a while I was happy. Then my first husband, Ahmad, came back and said that we are not divorced, he has not registered our divorce with the local council and [that] I am committing *zina* with Amin. He went to the police and launched an FIR [First Investigative Report] against us and now we are all in jail, Amin, the children and I too. Ahmad wants money before he withdraws his case. He wants one *lakh*. We are poor people, where will we get that kind of money? I do not understand why we are in jail. I did everything Ahmad wanted. I even left the house when he told me to go. I did everything my parents wanted, I married the man they found for me when Ahmad divorced me. I do not understand why we are in jail.
>
> (Nussrat, age 26 Years. She had been in Karachi Central Jail for one year).

Husbands find that these laws work in their favour. Paradoxically, they use the threat of *zina* to intimidate their wives as well as compel them to commit *zina* as a source of income. Rashida Bibi, like Naheed, is also from Sindh where they practice bride-price.

> Father owed money to an old man. And he married me to the old man. My new husband not only slept with me but also made me commit *zina* with six other men in exchange for money, which he kept. And he also beat me and broke my arm. He had a first wife who was also

involved in prostituting me and she also beat me. I registered a case of rape against the old man and his wife with the police. I am in *Darul Aman* because the old man's son-in-law has threatened me. My father also used to beat me.

(Rashida Bibi, age 18 Years. She had been at *Darul Aman* for four months).

Impoverished women with few resources provide ideal victims for the police. Jilani (interviewed in 1998) argues that once a case has been initiated and an FIR launched, police are 'under pressure to tie up the investigation and send the case for prosecution.' (Jilani, 1998). Police performance is evaluated annually. Since unresolved cases reflect poor police performance, Jilani points out that they are often looking for a victim who will provide a tidy conclusion for the case. At other times, the police conduct random raids looking for victims to extort money from.

My husband's younger brother was getting married. I had come to Lahore on my way to Islamabad for the wedding. I was at the Lahore station waiting to take the coach to Islamabad. I sat down at a table to have tea and a man sat down at the same table to have tea. The police came and accused us of *zina*. They said that 'You have booked a room at the hotel for zina'. And I said that 'I have never even thought of this'. They arrested me and also arrested the man. We are both in jail. I have five children, their ages are one, two, four, six and eight years. The youngest one is with my mother and the rest are with my husband. My husband believes me and thinks of me as a *gharaloo* [domesticated] woman. But we have no money and no property to register. We can't pay bail.

(Amina, age 35 Years She is from Kasur District and had been in prison for twenty-two days)

Amina's account reveals the middle-class bias in the law. She does not have bail money and neither does she have property she can register in lieu of bail money. She and her family will have to rely on an inadequate legal aid system to secure their release.

Application of *zina* not only provides docile daughters, mothers and wives, but also promises to provide docile workers who will accept difficult and poorly paid working conditions without organizing for change. These are exactly the kind of workers that multinational corporations are looking for when they invest in a country. The moral regulation of women at the intersection of class, gender and ethnicity suggests that docile middle-class women are considered moral while agentive, impoverished women are then deemed immoral. These constructions are also influenced by everyday verbal and textual conversations of middle-class women regarding 'the loose sexual promiscuous lower class woman' whose sexuality is running wild and needs to be controlled. Feroza Bibi's account suggests that employers draw upon conventional occupational stereotypes of the domestic servant as immoral and unreliable to sanction and persecute those considered undesirable. Feroza is fifty years old and her crime is not that of committing *zina* but of helping to facilitate in the immorality of a younger woman.

I used to work as a sweeper...a young girl also worked for the mistress and she ran away. When her parents came with the police to question the mistress about the girl's disappearance, she told the police that I had helped her run away. They registered a case of *zina* against my husband and I. The police came to our village and brought us to jail. Now my husband and I are both in jail. No one comes to visit us. The mistress and master have also implicated my older children and they are afraid to come and see their parents. Who will be my *vakil* (lawyer)? Allah is my *vakil*. Maybe Allah will have pity on me; it is *Ramazan* (the muslim holy month of fasting and prayer).

(Feroza Bibi, age 50 Years. She had been in prison for over a year)

There is another aspect to women's confinement. Najma Parveen (interviewed in 1998), the superintendent, pointed to an informal segregation within the Karachi Central Jail. A barrack has been set aside by the police and authorities for those known to be sex workers. These women frequently have resourceful connections that post their bail and secure their release. When the authorities identify a young woman among the sex workers, there is an assumption that she ought to be 'saved' from sex work. Needless to say, the authorities do not provide substantive alternative life choices for those women who are so saved. Twelve-year-old Sajida was one such young girl. She was screened out of the barracks reserved for sex workers and put into a barrack reserved for regular prisoners charged under *zina*. Unlike other inmates of her barrack however, her bail was posted within two months of her incarceration and she left the prison shortly after I met her. Sixteen-year-old Ghazala, another sex worker, who had also been screened into the barracks for 'regulars', has no such connections. She has been in prison one and a half years.

I was in a hotel with a man. I have been to hotels with men before. My mother is sick and my father is dead. I charge twenty-five rupees for *zina*. The first time I was fifteen. When my father died we had a lot of debt and creditors would come to our house and threaten us. Ami [mother] said 'Don't prostitute yourself'. But I don't know where else to get the money so the creditors will not bother us. A friend of mine also does *zina* for money and she showed me how to get clients. The man I was with is in jail as well. We were eating in a hotel and the police caught us. My mother has come to visit me in jail and she is trying to get bail money. But we have no money.

Ghazala's poverty, lack of education and lack of alternative options to earn a living are some of the reasons why she is in jail. She is not alone. At least 50 percent of the women in prison in Pakistan are there because of the *zina* laws (HRCP, 1997). Most women are illiterate and do not have the financial resources to post bail. Even if they did have the resources, bail has to be posted by a male: their father, their brother or their husband. Often, these are the people who are responsible for their being in jail in the first place. In a sense, the *zina* laws are used to sweep the streets clean of women, particularly poor unwanted and rebellious women.

87

The laws are supposed to stop women and men for having sex outside of marriage, but unlike Sajida and Ghazala who are sex workers, there is little conclusive proof that the women in jail had sex in the first place. Many of them were accused of merely aiding and abetting abductions. A report by the Commission of Inquiry on the Status of Women (1997) suggests that the police have used the pretext of investigating *zina* to break into homes. Also that they have arrested and locked up married couples for having illicit relations, widows for being suspect, and wives and daughters for not being compliant enough to the men in their families.

The police, as agents of the state, are delegated to protect the rights of citizens against violence. Yet frequently, it is the police who become perpetrators of violence. Women running from family control and coercion find the police to be another violent and corrupt adversary. At the hands of the police, they face sexual, physical and emotional violence and extortion. Impoverished women have nothing with which to buy their way out of the situation, and they are the ones who suffer the most. The state's treatment of the *zina* victims puts into question the nation's commitment to protect the interests of all its citizens. Women are born into a national symbolic order that treats them as chattels to be bartered. The nation needs morality, and women and lower-class citizens are sacrificed to provide a moral face for the nation.

The notion of Pakistan, literally the land of the pure, evokes a desire for a national community of moral citizens. I argue that this morality is expressed in discourse suggesting the ideal citizen as a moral disembodied male. Women's narratives disrupt this ideal. Their accounts suggest a hidden side of the nation. Yet in their desire to present themselves as *gharaloo* (domesticated), they too desire to be part of the national narrative. As Pakistan narrates its past and present and tries to imagine its future, there is a struggle over ideology and particularly which interpretations of Islam will help construct the guiding force of the nation. These struggles are indicative of the conflicts within the larger social context. It is to an examination of this that I now turn.

locating the context which sustains *zina* laws

Pakistan was imagined as a homeland for muslims of British India. In the process of the partition of India (into India and Pakistan), over ten million people were displaced in 1947 as they moved (both ways) across the newly created national border between India and Pakistan. This border was erected across British India on the basis of a two-nation theory (hindu/muslim). Although the founder of Pakistan described the state as secular, he also used religious symbols and imagery when it suited his political purposes. The process of lobbying for and finally securing the state of Pakistan linked nationalism to religion, both of which were important in helping to construct the identity of millions of displaced persons pouring across the border from India. This early linking of nationalism and religion continues to be a significant element of how the nation imagines itself (Jalal, 1991). The concept of nation, as Homi Bhabha (1994b: 139) has persuasively argued, 'fills the void left in the uprooting of communities and kin'. This connection of religion to nationalism persists, even though in Pakistan's fifty-five year history of existence, not one politician of national significance has come into power through a religious platform.[11] Invoking Islam has, however, been an important aspect in mobilizing a nationalist consensus, particularly for the frequent wars with India, which in turn have justified military spending. Ayesha Jalal (1994) calls this a political economy of defence, which helps sustain the army as a major power broker in Pakistan. The connection was strengthened in 1979 with the promulgation of the *Hadood* Ordinances, of which *zina* laws form a part, and more recently with the endorsement of *sharia* (Islamic religious law) in 1991 by the Nawaz Sharif regime.

There is another dimension to this increasing interconnection between nationalism and religion. Kum-Kum Sangari and Sudesh Vaid (1990) note that the politicization of communal and religious identities around ideas of the nation in South Asia has accompanied the impoverishment of women. This has significant implications for the ways in which *zina* laws are enforced. The Pakistani state appears to lack the means and/or the political will to enforce the laws for any except the most vulnerable citizens: poor women. As more and more women suffer the effects of poverty, their bodies marked through exclusionary practices of class and gender are rendered the most vulnerable to *zina* laws.

Normative judgements about morality and immorality inform state practices and policies of the police, as well as the judicial and penal systems, that women suspected of *zina* will come into contact with. These judgements are used to assess and monitor actions and attitudes of the victims. As women are made to tell their stories in the process of incarceration, many prison officials as well as legal and medical personnel claim that their accounts are lies. Yet lies and manipulation of events might be a necessary response to discourses, ideologies, institutions, prohibitions and practices to which they have been subjected. Powerful signifiers of nation and religion render ideas about *zina*, or illicit sex, a significant regulator of normative morality. Challenging them means not only questioning religion but also the symbolic force that created and continues to sustain the state of Pakistan.

General Zia's military regime promulgated the *Hadood* Ordinances as a component of the new moral order in Pakistan in 1979. Critics of the Ordinances (Shaheed, 1997; Jahangir and Jilani, 1988), however, argue that the regime brought in the *zina* laws to bolster its political base through alliances with right-wing religious parties. Subsequent weak regimes have allowed it to continue to wreak havoc in society at the expense of the most vulnerable members of society, lower-class women. All of these regimes have had Western financial and political support. In the West, few questions have been raised concerning the misuse of religion or lack

11 Indeed, many observers point out that anti-American-ism due to American bombing of Afghanistan and the presence of American troops in Pakistan are responsible for the religious parties winning 51 seats in the 2002 election. Where these trends lead us, it appears, depends on American foreign policy as much as it does on local struggles.

of human rights in Pakistan. The United States in particular has seldom used its influence with Pakistani regimes to press for an end to human rights violations.

Generally, intellectual debate in Pakistan is against the laws, yet they still remain in effect. Why? There is no clear answer to this question, however, I will attempt to approach it in several ways. I will argue that economic and political conditions play a part in sustaining the *Hadood* Ordinance. Moreover, national and international alliances between the military and religious groups to maintain the status quo appear to disregard the rights of the most vulnerable members of society.

The forces of globalization have affected economies worldwide, causing retrenchment of government services such as health care, primary education and state subsidies for essential goods (Bello, 2000; Chakravarthi, 1990). These structural adjustments are connected to access to international aid. They have helped integrate economies of the south into the north-dominated markets and have also increased poverty and violence in third-world societies (Bello, 2000). Cultural devaluation of the third world, another significant factor, stems also from the colonial periods and is reinforced by the new forms of colonialism linked to globalization. Dislocation due to urbanization generates insecurities among the peoples of the south and exacerbates the situation. Economic and cultural crises lead even those regimes that define themselves as secular to identify religion as a significant organizing principle of society and to seek greater legitimacy through political alliances with religious forces in their regions. Iraq after the Gulf War is one such example. In a country where much of the infrastructure has been destroyed during the war, Saddam Hussein fostered alliances with Islamists and passed a series of anti-women laws, including laws that focused on keeping women 'moral'. Gema Martin Munoz's comments support my argument, 'Whereas at one time the most pressing concern was to achieve modernization, now introducing morality into the political and socio-economic order has come to the fore as a result of the corruption and the marginalization that the state has generated' (Munoz, 1999: 10). She argues that this desire for morality appears connected to a reassertion of Islamic identity.

This is certainly so in Pakistan where reassertion of Islamic identity has not replaced nationalism but remains connected to nationalism. Indeed, there is an urgency to reassert Islam in a context of recurring political and economic crises. Edited memories of past glory fuel the national imagination while at the same time the general population is suffering the effects of globalization. Moreover, as Aijaz Ahmad (2000) points out, both India and Bangladesh have larger muslim populations than Pakistan. The latter's reason for existence has begun to shift from being a homeland for muslims in the subcontinent to being the home of the pure muslims of the region. The pure muslim, the one connected to the imperial past, is an ideal most realised by those Pakistanis who are male and propertied. Most Pakistanis, by virtue of their gender and class, have only a tenuous claim to

90

this ideal. Yet his past is violently enforced on the nation, and de-contextualized religious laws including the *zina* laws are often used as mechanisms of enforcement.

There is another aspect of this process. Pakistan is a heavily indebted country, and it continues to borrow every year. Consequently, the priorities of the Pakistani government include making payments on the national debt and submitting to restructuring directives such as devaluing the rupee, raising the price of essential goods, and cutting back on infrastructure including health care and education (Burki, 1994). Additionally, the state is committed to military spending due to its long-standing dispute with India over Kashmir (Schofield, 2000). Indeed, military spending was up 11 percent in the year 2000. The Pakistani state also needs to keep the multinational investors happy by providing a docile labour force. This means keeping down the societal violence resulting from the rising price of basic foods and high unemployment due to restructuring.

The state juggles these contradictory demands and maintains a delicate balance. The repeal of the *zina* law threatens this balance. Pakistani nationalism is integrally connected to religion. *Zina* laws are seen as religious laws, and dispensing with them would pose a symbolic challenge to the nation. Their repeal has the potential to ignite a fuse within an unhappy and increasingly impoverished populace that has not been included in the benefits of globalization; instead, they are the victims of globalization.

Zina laws invoke a desire for moral purity in a context of societal corruption. They examine and identify embodied morality focusing on illicit sexuality. Paradoxically, notions of embodied purity, absence of illicit sex, render invisible the societal impurity of the nation. This impurity comes out of the economic and political corruption of the state. The moral regulation of impoverished women through *zina* laws, however, rhetorically cleanses the symbolic impurity of the country. Although recent court proceedings have largely ruled in favour of the *zina* victims, these decisions reinforce class and gender relations. Women who are incarcerated in prison or more informally in the *Darul Amans* cannot claim constitutional rights of liberty, equality and citizenship. They are granted these rights through the judicial process dominated largely by middle- and upper-class males.

A further reason why the laws still exist is that the victims of *zina* laws are not considered an important constituency. They are often illiterate with few material resources. Moreover in what appears to be an elitist idea of enfranchisement, it is commonly believed that they do not vote. Often middle-class ideas of elections are removed from the needs of the 'poor and illiterate', and deny that impoverished women can also determine the needs of the day despite not being educated. Such determinations render the human rights of *zina* victims a low priority with Pakistani regimes, particularly since it is felt that they will be released upon trial anyway, as was noted by eminent Pakistani jurist Khalid Issaq

(1999). There are several problems with this reasoning. Even though the women are released upon trial, their lives are often destroyed as a result of their imprisonment. Moreover, it is commonly believed that within the prison system they are often recruited into prostitution and the drug trade (although I found no evidence to substantiate this claim). Even if they escape the recruiters in the prison, they become susceptible to these offers upon release. Frequently they are fleeing their families and have no place to go. Pakistan has a weak rehabilitation programme, and there is little assistance available to women after they leave. Many pointed out that their worst worry was where they would spend the first couple of nights after release.

Zina laws do not wreak havoc within Pakistan without resistance. Women who are victims of the laws are contesting control of their sexuality and morality and indeed commodification of their bodies, particularly those women at the *Darul Amans*, where, despite the restrictive and oppressive conditions, many have chosen to find refuge. They are running away and seeking shelter from the domination and violence of fathers, husbands, brothers and, at times, mothers who beat them and sell them in marriage to the highest bidders. They are choosing their own marriage partners, knowing that their choices place them at considerable risk. Despite the tremendous odds they face, many of the women are rejecting claims of their families as they try to take control of their lives. Seventeen-year-old Gulbaden Bibi's voice describes the struggles she was up against.

> My father sold me in marriage for 20,000 rupees when I was fifteen to Akram who is 50 years old and a *zamidar* (landowner). He used to beat me and yell at me, and call me names. So my father helped me obtain a divorce and paid back the 20,000 to Akram. Then I married my cousin and father consented. Father drinks alcohol and gambles and takes opium, and has a lot of debt. So he now wants me to divorce my cousin and marry a man in Karachi who is willing to pay for me. This way father can pay off his debt. I refused. I want to stay with my husband Qamar. Father said that there is no marriage between my cousin and myself as I no longer have his permission to be married to Qamar. So he charged me with *zina*. I want to stay married to Qamar. The police brought me to prison and I am safe here. Outside I was afraid of what my father would do to me. I am Muslim. Allah gave me the right to marry who I want. I want to stay married to Qamar.

Gulbaden Bibi is also a Pathan. Married at the age of 15 years and charged with *zina* at the age of 17 years, she has never been to school or voted in an election. She fears her father and has no support from her mother because she claims 'my mother is also afraid of my father, he beats her. [Moreover] I do not want to end up like my mother'. Her resistance to her family's attempts to control is a political act. She had been in Karachi Central Jail for eleven months when I interviewed her in 1999. The discursive practices surrounding *zina* label Gulbaden as a participator in illicit sex. Prison has become a site of her moral regulation while *zina* laws are one of the instruments used to put her there. Although the state is not the only

92

agent of Gulbaden's regulation, in the *Zina* Ordinance, the state provides a mechanism for her family to control her. So in effect the state colludes in the process of pressuring rebellious Gulbaden back into her family's fold.

Deniz Kandiyoti's (1991) analysis helps us understand the ways in which women and some men challenge what she calls classical patriarchy found in North Africa, China, India and the Muslim Middle East including Pakistan. These challenges reveal a variety of ways in which they accommodate, acquiesce, as well as contest and renegotiate community and familial rules. The perspectives of the men incarcerated due to *zina* will likely be of great significance in understanding how women charged with *zina* bargain with patriarchy. Such an examination however is not the subject of this investigation but identifies an important area of research for future studies.[12]

12 This insight came from one of the anonymous reviewers of *Feminist Review.*

Although the state invokes Islam to legitimize *zina* laws, the women's narratives suggest that it is not religion but the state, along with their families, that is responsible for their plight. In rejecting the laws and the system that spawned them the women also embrace the spirituality associated with religion. Thus, propriety becomes important even to resisting women. They frame their resistance in religious terms for many invoke the mercy of Allah or resign themselves to the will of Allah as they turn to religion to make sense of the situation. In so doing they often become recruits for the Women Aid Trust (WAT), an organization of the *Jamat-i-Islami* doing rehabilitative work in the jails.

Kandiyoti (1991) has argued that classical patriarchy is based on male authority with a material base. Increasing emmiseration under globalization appears connected to shaking this material base. I argue that through the practices associated with *zina* charges, a particular economics gets transferred into symbolic idioms of sexuality and morality. At the same time the patriarchal myth about the protection of women in exchange for feminine ideals of docility provides an opening for renegotiation. While women's contribution to the familial economy is essential, the women who I interviewed were not skilled workers. They cannot make significant contributions to their family economies and have to contribute in other ways. Fifty-year-old Fatima begged in order to support the drug addiction of her husband. When she no longer brought enough to pay for his habit, he suggested that she prostitute and charged her with *zina* when she refused.

For many women, *zina* is operationalized in ways that connect the process to monetary exchanges, highlighting the material predicaments of their families and suggesting that their economic situation is driving them to take recourse to repressive *zina* laws. Moreover, it leads us to speculate that control of morality and sexuality through *zina* might be used as a facade for material sustenance. What happens if we do away with the *zina* laws, would the women still suffer? The violence that women face is coming out of social and political attitudes. Religion acts as an ideology that pressures women to accept particular norms. These norms were regulated through community pressure. However, communities are not as isolated as they have been in the past. Indeed, many of the women fleeing their families have found anonymity in the cities where they can only be regulated through *zina* charges. This leads many to speculate that the women who actually commit *zina* are murdered in 'honour killings'. The ones charged with *zina* are innocent women and the families know that they are innocent. The primary purpose of these charges is to bring them into line with family wishes. The women's comments substantiate these commonly held beliefs. Many point out that their families have indicated that if they initiate charges of abduction against their husbands and comply with family wishes, their families would post bail on their behalf and help secure their release. They are in jail, they stated, because they refused, leading me to speculate that there are likely thousands who took up these offers of 'help'. We only know of those who resist, and are in prison. In prison, resisters find a space where they can negotiate a better bargain with patriarchy. They frequently take advantage of the literacy and skill development programmes available to them. These patriarchal bargains open up new arenas of struggle and negotiations.

I do not want to negate the agency of women. Their narratives are a testimony to their poverty and to their endurance in the face of tremendous odds. However, those without resources are also frequently without legal services. They do not know the justice system and need lawyers. The NGOs provide this invaluable service, although not enough to help all the women. These organizations include Shirkat Gah, Applied Socio-Economic Research (ASR), Lawyers for Human Rights and Legal Aid (LHRLA), and the legal aid cell AGHS connected to the private watchdog organization the Human Rights Commission of Pakistan (HRCP). These agencies have successfully posed legal challenges to the laws, with the result that the government has brought fewer charges against women than in the past, and the courts have shown greater leniency to women charged with *zina*.

My conversations with members of the WAT suggest that even Islamists are aware of the excesses of the *zina* laws. Sabiha Razi of WAT works with women in prison where she organizes and delivers basic literacy and religious education. Razi (2001) pointed out that although the *Hadood* laws were part of a larger plan to build a moral society in Pakistan, some members of the *Jamat* want to see changes in the laws. She indicated that the *Jamat* has requested the government for a national debate on the laws. In order to prepare for this debate, they have begun a consultative process in the hopes of proposing a reformulation of the laws. The process includes deliberations of religious scholars acceptable to the *Jamat*, Razi claimed. She did not think feminist scholars, activists or other human rights groups such as LRHLA and HRCP would be invited to participate in this process. Pakistan society is deeply contested. Razi's comments, however, suggest that Islamists are likely not open to input or alliances with other stakeholders. In fact, members of NGOs in Pakistan have shared the concern with me on numerous occasions that

94

religious organizations do not want to work in collaboration with those they consider secular. How this issue resolves itself, given the growing visibility of religious influence in Pakistan, will shape the struggles of the future.

Myron Weiner and Ali Banuazizi (1994) identify a commonly held belief in Pakistan: there is an innocent and virtuous private sphere in need of protection from the corruption of the state. The narratives of women whom I interviewed disrupt the state (public) and family (private) binary and identify the contradictory forces that oppress and support women. At times, the state is a willing partner in the families' desire to control their women. At other times, the state rules against the families and provides a place of refuge for women either in prison or in state-endorsed shelters. Unfortunately, many activists believe that this process also helps to criminalize an already impoverished female population.

Recently however there have been some state attempts at changing gender discrimination in policies and practices. In 1994 the executive branch of the Pakistani government, the Senate, created a Commission of Inquiry for Women (CIW). Its terms of reference included a review of all existing laws that discriminate against women or affect their rights to equal citizenship in Pakistan. The Commission was mandated to suggest amendments in the existing laws or rules and to bring the laws into accord with the injunctions of Islam as enshrined in the Holy *Qur'an* and *Sunnah*.

Even though not all commission members could be classified as 'feminist activists', they all reached consensus on several critical points. The report of the CIW noted that the high incarceration rate, along with low convictions of *zina* victims, suggests widespread misuse of the *Zina* Ordinance. Moreover the Commissioners stated that these laws were not in conformity either with Islam or with the Constitution of Pakistan. They recommended that the *Hadood* Ordinances, including the *Zina* Ordinance, be repealed. Notwithstanding the Commissions recommendation, the Ordinances remain in effect.

Comments made by officials of the current regime of General Pervez Musharraf suggest that they may be willing to go further than previous regimes on this issue. Musharraf's inaugural address to the Convention on Human Rights and Human Dignity on 21 April 2002 in Islamabad provides an example. At that time General Musharraf said 'It shall be the endeavour of my government to facilitate the creation of an environment in which every Pakistani can find an opportunity to lead his life with dignity and freedom' (AI, 2002: 4). Musharraf's regime has also taken some steps in this direction by expanding the country's National Assembly to 350 seats, 60 of which were reserved for women (BBC News, 7th March 2002). Furthermore, a National Commission on the status of Women was set up by Ordinance on 17th July 2000. Its mission included a determination to examine laws related to women with a view to identifying those that are discriminatory (AI, 2002: 5). This mandate was echoed in statements made by the Interior Minister that 'all discriminatory laws against women should be repealed or amended to remove discrimination against women' (AI, 2002: 6). However by early 2002 none of these pronouncements had led to any substantive action (AI, 2002: 7).

Although there appears to be a shift at least in the stated priorities of the current government, the material reality of women's rights in Pakistan remains largely unchanged. Budgets and five-year plans continue to reveal a high priority to the military while a low priority is given to poverty alleviation and to development. There is little institutionalization of democracy and a dismal human rights record. As for women's rights, few in Pakistan would say that women do not have rights under Islam or under the Constitution. Yet the rights of women, particularly lower-class women, are systematically denied in political forums, institutional practice and family traditions.

conclusion

I draw upon Nira Yuval-Davis and Pnina Werbner's (1999) comments that differences among citizens impact on their citizenship. This comment is certainly relevant in Pakistan where gender and class determine the extent to which individuals can claim the full benefits of citizenship. State practices do not provide impoverished women equality of rights or protection. Their vulnerability to the *zina* laws helps deflect attention away from societal corruption and a political economy of defence towards an embodied immorality of the individual.

Phillip Corrigan and Derek Sayer (1985) argue that capitalism require moral workers who participate in unequal relations. To facilitate this process, state practices often mark a particular behaviour normal while distinguishing it from the abnormal. In Pakistan, the state evokes an eternal Islam to justify prosecution for *zina*. Women's stories articulate particular local and national arrangements. The promulgation and continuance of *zina* laws appear rooted in a particular economic and political expediency. At the same time, continuation of state practices associated with the *zina* laws renders the incarceration and detention of women natural and normal. Women are intimidated into becoming docile bodies and participating in unequal relations with their families, their husbands and their employers. Through the *zina* laws the state lays the groundwork for new forms of 'traditions' which can be used to control future generations of women both at home and at work. At the same time the effects of state practices help render women more vulnerable to prostitution and drug trafficking, thus potentially criminalizing impoverished women.

Women are biological and cultural reproducers of the nation. As such, their sexuality is a valuable resource that is utilized to service their families and the nation. Should they decide to enter associations of romance and love, they frequently face the wrath of their families. In this refusal to submit to parental pressures and pressures of former husbands, many women find themselves incarcerated in prison or more informally in the *Darul Amans*. Paradoxically, the state both helps families intimidate the women and helps the women escape the grip of their families by providing them shelter in state-run institutions. During the course of their confinement the women learn to be independent of their families and some acquire basic literacy and life-sustaining skills such as embroidery and sewing. They are however traumatized by the process. At the same time, regulation of women's sexuality helps build a case for national morality on a base of societal corruption and injustice. The state considers lower-class women expendable, and their liberty is sacrificed for the moral health of the nation. Increasing structural inequality and growing societal violence can then be explained away as a lack of individual morality, rendering the cost of globalization and military spending invisible.

In terms of the current capitalist structure within which Pakistan is embedded, market value determines why things are done. There is no market value in giving women the choice to make decisions about their lives or to the repeal of *zina* laws. In contrast to such determinations of worth, Angela Miles (1996) proposes an integrative feminist approach which values life rather than profit. Within this approach the lives of victims of *zina* laws are not considered expendable in the pursuit of globalization and militarization. Moreover, in bringing back the structural issues into a discussion of individual morality, this analysis moves away from a cultural relativist position to identify the effects of the capitalist system that helps create the conditions sustaining *zina* laws.

Jeffery Weeks (1986: 12) believes that 'the increasing politicization of sex in the past century offers new possibilities and consequently challenges: not just of moral control ... but [also] of political analysis, opposition and of change'. In Pakistan, competing interests create the conditions for sustaining *zina* laws as well as possibilities for change. While women have equality with men under the constitution, state policies surrounding the *zina* laws produce conditions through which women, particularly lower-class women, are rendered less equal than men. There are also state and civil interests that promote the *zina* law as Islamic or that allow it as a matter of political expediency. At the same time, there are forces that oppose the laws and activists who support women in their struggles. These contradictory forces in society allow women to move out of the helpless victim position and give them room to manoeuvre.

The women whom I interviewed are clear in this desire to control their bodies and opposed to those who lay claim to them. By seeking refuge in *Darul Aman* and by risking incarceration, they are asserting their agency even as the state-sponsored space of the shelter attempts to neutralize their efforts. Feminist social action can support these women in their struggles and support the struggles of other activists in Pakistan by imagining and promoting solidarity through which we identify and challenge how the local and global are connected to produce systems of injustice in Pakistan and elsewhere.

author biography

Shahnaz Khan is Assistant Professor of Global Studies and Women's Studies at Wilfrid Laurier University, Canada. She is the author of *Aversion and Desire: Negotiating Muslim Female Identity in the Diaspora*, Women's Press, 2002. She has also published articles on muslim women and representation in *Signs: Journal of Women in Culture and Society*, and the online journal *Genders*.

acknowledgements

This analysis has benefitted by comments made by Maureen Moynagh and the anonymous reviewers of *Feminist Review*. This research was funded by the Social Science Humanities Research Council (SSHRC).

references

Ahmad, A. (2000) 'Of dictators and democrats: Indo-Pakistan politics in the year 2000' in A. Ahmad (2000) editor, Lineages of the Present: Ideology and Politics in Contemporary South Asia, London: Verso Press, 301–324.

Amnesty International (AI) (2002) *Pakistan: Insufficient Protection of Women*, AI Index ASS 33/006.

Anzaldua, G. (2000) *Interviews: Edited by Ana Louise Keating*, New York: Routledge.

Bello, W. (2000) 'Building an iron cage: Bretton Woods institutions, the WTO and the South' in S. Anderson (2000) editor, *Views from the South: The Effects of Globalisation and the WTO on Third World Countries*, Chicago, Illinois: First Food Books, 54–90.

Bhabha, H. (1994a) *The Location of Culture*, London: Routledge.

Bhabha, H. (1994b) 'Dissemination: Time, narrative and the margins of the modern nation' in H. Bhabha (1994b) editor, *The Location of Culture*, London: Routledge, 139–170.

Brah, A. (1996) *Cartographies of Diaspora: Contesting Identities*, London and New York: Routledge.

Burki, S.J. (1994) 'The state and the political economy of redistribution in Pakistan' in M. Weiner and A. Banuazizi (1994) editors, *The Politics of Social Transformation in Afghanistan, Iran, and Pakistan*, Syracuse, New York: Syracuse University Press, 270–332.

Chakravarthi, R. (1990) *Recolonisation*, Penang: Third World Network.

Comack, E. (2000) 'Women and crime' in R. Linden (2000) editor, *Criminology: A Canadian Perspective*, Toronto: Harcourt, 137–175.

Commission of Enquiry on the Status of Women (1997) *Report (CIW)*, Islamabad, Pakistan: Government of Pakistan publication.

Corrigan, P. and Seyer, D. (1985) *The Great Arch*, Oxford, UK: Basil Blackwell.

Esposito, J. (1982) *Women in Muslim Family Law*, Syracuse, New York: Syracuse University Press.

Ghausi, S. (2001) 'Police top 'dirty dozen chart'' *Dawn* 31 May.

Grewal, I. and Caplan K. (1994) 'Introduction' in I. Grewal and C. Kaplan (1994) editors, *Scattered Hegemoies*, Minneapolis: MN: University of Minnesota Press.

Hall, S. (1997) 'The local and the global: Globalizatiaon and ethnicity' in A. King (1997) editor, *Culture, Globalization and The World-system: Contemporary Conditions for the Representation of Identity*, Minneapolis, MN: University of Minnesota Press, 19–40.

Human Rights Commission of Pakistan (HRCP) (1997) *State of Human Rights in Pakistan in 1997*, Lahore, Pakistan: Maktaba Jadeed Press.

Human Rights Watch (HRW) (1992) Double Jeopardy: Police Abuse of Women in Pakistan, USA.

Hazarika, S.(1988) 'For women in Indian prison, a 'grim picture'' *The New York Times*, February 29.

Jahangir, A. and Jilani, H. (1988) *The Hadood Ordinances: A Divine Sanction?*, Lahore: Rhotas Books.

Jalal, A. (1991) 'The convenience of subservience: Women and the state of Pakistan' in Deniz Kandiyoti (1991) editor, *Women, Islam and the State*, Philadelphia: Temple University Press.

Jalal, A. (1994) 'The state and political privilege in Pakistan' in M. Weiner and A. Banuazizi (1994) editors, *The Politics of Social Transformation in Afghanistan, Iran, and Pakistan*, Syracuse, New York: Syracuse University Press, 152–184.

Kandiyoti, D. (1988) 'Bargaining with patriarchy' *Gender and Society*, Vol. 2, 274–290.

Kandiyoti, D. (1991) 'Islam and patriarchy: A comparative perspective' in N. Keddie and B. Baron (1991) editors, *Women in Middle Eastern History: Shifting Boundaries in Sex and Gender*, New Haven, London: Yale University Press.

Khan, S. (2001) 'Between here and there: Feminist solidarity and Afghan women', *Genders Issue*, Vol. 33, Spring.

Khan, S. (2002) 'Performing the Native Informant: Doing Ethnography from the Margins', *Canadian Journal of Women and the Law*, Vol. 13 No. 4: 266–284.

Kaplan, C., Alarcon N. and Moallem M. 'Introduction' in C. Kaplan, N. Alarcon, and M. Moallem editors, *Between Woman and Nation: Nationalisms, Transnational Feminisms, and the State*, Durham: Duke University Press, 1–16.

MacKinnon, C. (1989) *Toward a Feminist Theory of the State*, Cambridge, MA: Harvard University Press.

Mahmood, S. and Shaukat N. (1994) *Hadood Laws (Muslim Penal Laws)*, 2nd edition, Lahore, Pakistan: Legal Research Center, Noor Villa.

Mallick, R. (1988) *Development, Ethnicity and Human Rights in South Asia*, New Delhi: Sage Publications.

Mani, L. (1986) 'Contentious traditions: The debate on sati in colonial India', *Cultural Critique*, Vol. 7, 119–156, (originally printed in *Feminist Review*, No. 35).

McClintock, A. (1995) *Imperial Leather: Race, Tender and Sexuality in the Colonial Context*, New York: Routledge.

Medhi, R (1991) 'The offence of rape in the Islamic law of Pakistan' in *Women Living Under Muslim Laws*, Dossier 18, B.P. 23, 34790 Grabels, France, 98–108.

Miles. A. (1996) *Integrative Feminisms: Building Global Visions 1960s–1990s*, New York: Routledge.

Min-Ha, T. (1989) *Woman Native Other*, Bloomington, Indiana: Indiana University Press.

Mohanty, C. (1991) 'Under Western eye: Feminist scholarship and colonial discourses' in C. Mohanty, A. Russo and L. Torres (1991) editors, *Third World Woman and the Politics of Feminism*, Bloomington and Indianapolis: Indiana University Press, 51–80, (originally printed in *Feminist Review*, No 30).

Munoz, G.M. (1999) 'Islam and the West, an intentional duality' in G.M. Munoz (1999) editor, *Islam Modernism and the West*, London: I.B. Tauris, 3–24.

Qur'an, Text Translation and Commentary (1968) AbdullahYusuf Ali (1968) editor, Beirut: Dar al-Arabia.

Rich, A. (1992) 'Compulsory heterosexuality and lesbian existence' *Signs Reader*.

Rouse, S. (1998) 'Sovereignty and citizenship in Pakistan' in P. Jeffery and A. Basu (1998) editors, *Appropriating Gende*, New York: Routledge, 53–70.

Rubin, G. (1975) 'The traffic in women' in R. Reiter (1975) editor, *Toward an Anthology of Women*, New York: Monthly Review Press.

Sabah, F. (1988) *Woman in the Muslim Unconscious*, translated by Mary Jo Lakeland, Oxford, UK: Pergamon Press Inc.

Sangari, K-K. and Sudesh, V. (1990) *Recasting Women: Essays in Indian Colonial History*, New Brunswick, NJ: Rutgers University Press.

Sardar Ali, S. (2000) *Gender and Human Rights in Islam and International Law: Equal Before Allah, Unequal Before Man?*, The Hague: Kluwer Law International.

Schofield, V. (2000) *Kashmir in Conflict: India, Pakistan and the Unfinished War*, New York: I.B. Tauris.

Shaheed, F. (1997) 'Woman, state and power: the dynamics of variation and convergence across East and West' in N. Hussain, S. Mumtaz and R. Saigol (1997) editors, *Engendering the Nation-State: Volume I*, Lahore, Pakistan: Simorgh Women's Resource and Publication Centre, 53–78.

Shaeed. F. and Mumtaz, K. (1987) *Women in Pakistan: Two Steps Forward One Step Back*, London: Zed Press.

Shildrick, M. and Price, J. (1999) 'Introduction' in J. Price and M. Shildrick (1999) editors, *Feminist Theory and the Body: A Reader*, New York: Routledge, 1–14.

Spivak, G. (1999) *A Critique of Post-Colonial Reason*, Cambridge, MA: Harvard University Press.

Sumar, S. and Nadhvi, K. (1988) 'Zina: The Hadood ordinance and its implications for women (Pakistan)', *Women Living Under Muslim Laws Dossier #3* International Solidarity Network, 34980 Combaillaux (Montpellier).

Toor, S. (1996) 'The state, fundamentalism and civil society' in N. Hussain, S. Mumtaz and R. Saigol (1997) editors, *Engendering the Nation-State: Volume I*, Lahore, Pakistan Simorgh Women's Resource and Publication Centre, 111–146.

United States Department of State (USDS) (2000) '1999 Country Report on Human Rights Practices in Pakistan', Bureau of Democracy Human Rights and Labour, February 25.

Weeks, J. (1995) *Invented Moralities: Sexual Values in an Age of Uncertainty*, Cambridge, UK: Polity Press.

Weeks, J. (1986) *Sexuality*, London, UK: Routledge.

Weiner, M. and Banuazizi, A. (1994) 'Introduction' in M. Weiner and A. Banuazizi (1994) editors, *The Politics of Social Transformation in Afghanistan, Iran, and Pakistan*, Syracuse, New York: Syracuse University Press, 1–34.

Yegenoglu, M. (1998) *Colonial Fantasies: Towards a feminist reading of Orientalism*, Cambridge, UK: Cambridge University Press.

Yuval-Davis, N. and Werbner, P. (1999) 'Introduction' in N. Yuval-Davis and P. Werbner (1999) editors, *Women, Citizenship and Difference*, London: Zed Books, 1–38.

Yuval-Davis, N. (1997) *Gender and Nation*, London: Sage Publications.

doi:10.1057/palgrave.fr.9400111

[19]

SEXUALITY AND THE MORAL "CONSTRUCTION" OF WOMEN IN AN ISLAMIC SOCIETY

JANET L. BAUER

Tufts University

Gender differences in the Middle East lead to discussion of the relationship between the individual self and social expectations for behavior. In the case of Iran, women learn to adapt to what is acceptable and morally appropriate within their social class. As in other societies, constructs of sexuality are more important in communicating the moral standing and regulating the conduct of women than of men in working-class Iran. While women may have little opportunity to operationalize other choices, they are able to discuss and show preference for alternative moral interpretations of situationally-necessitated behavior. These findings are taken beyond the discussions of honor and shame in anthropology to illuminate recent discussions of gender and moral development.

The religious stories told in the working-class neighborhoods of Tehran and the villages of Iran frequently focused upon the *khejalat* (shame, propriety) of Fatima, the Prophet's daughter, and the hospitality of Muhammad's male relatives, Ali and Husayn, as examples of behavior to be emulated. The contrasting images produced by these examples suggest the local importance placed upon women's *use of their bodies* (or sexuality) and men's *social graces* in constructing moral behavior and concepts of self.

In Iran moral judgments about poor urban and rural women were made in terms of the social context in which conduct was interpreted, irrespective of the women's own judgments of whether the expected behavior was appropriate, equitable, or moral. Transgressing preferred status norms or values was viewed in terms of *sexual misconduct* and judged as immoral regardless of actual conduct; talking to an unfamiliar person might be seen as indicative of "loose" behavior. Thus women had to take into consideration the thoughts and impressions of kin, neighbors and friends and to view themselves in terms of how others demand that they act and behave. While women often conformed their actions to social expectation, their expressed thoughts on morality and their ability to manipulate their actions highlight the difficulties of doing cross-cultural research on morality and identity.

Recent literature on morality and culture has raised questions about the relationship between social context, gender identity, and moral conceptions (cf. Rosaldo 1984; Gilligan 1977; Ferguson 1984). Historically and cross-culturally there appear to be similarities in the social significance of sexuality in judging women's morality, especially in state societies with class divisions. For analyzing the role of social contingencies in determining morality and self conception, Middle Eastern ethnography already provides extensive discussions of shame and honor in the determination of social persona and self,[1] and the situation of Middle Eastern women seems to offer a paradigmatic case for the linkage of family honor to female morality and sexuality (cf. Youssef 1973; Rassam 1980). This literaure, which suggests the complexity of social relations and ways in which a family's honor is supposed to be contingent upon the virtuous behavior of its females, provides a good case for investigating the moral construction of women.

I first relate women's knowledge of their bodies and the responsibility assigned to them for control of their bodies to the conditions under which they might exhibit some control in acceptable ways. I look at how women learn what is appropriate moral behavior in different situations in terms of visibility and the familiarity of the others present. I draw particular attention to the way in which observed transgressions of approved social behaviors are judged in sexual terms and labeled as immoral.

The women in this study came primarily from working-class, migrant and some of the religious, middle-class neighborhoods of Tehran (and a few regional cities) and four different rural areas of Iran. A total of 286 women were interviewed along with significant male relatives in their households, just prior to the institution of the Islamic Republic of Iran. These women's thoughts about what was acceptable or desirable conduct for women often contrasted with both social judgments and perceived Islamic prescriptions. An account of their construction of moral selves depends as much on understanding the contrast between their behaviors and their verbalizations as on understanding either verbalizations or conduct alone.

The kinds of behavior considered to be morally acceptable, in engagement practices and norms for contact with the opposite sex for example, varied across class and geographical regions. Class and individual differences in conceptions of morality reflect differences in access to religious and other education as well as differences in social and material conditions. Folk sayings about women, especially in rural areas, emphasized their unimportance—"It doesn't make any difference whether a woman makes *nazr* (vows) or not because she won't get to heaven anyway," said one woman.[2] Most of the stories told to women in working-class or rural areas, especially religious ones, focused upon the female relatives of important religious figures and emphasized modesty and chastity, although not necessarily in the specific behavioral terms of women's own lives. The implementation of perceived *prescriptions* became a matter of interpretation. In the urban areas, women had access to other stories and other role models—like educated career women—through personal contact and media representations, and were privy to different interpretations of Islamic codes and different social environments.

Defining the focus of moral behavior and moral thinking has been problematic in the existing literature. In some discussions, emphasis is placed analytically on autonomy to choose behaviors; in others, attention is focused on whether *responsibilities to others* or *individual rights* underlie moral judgemnts.[3] In either case, social relations are not given sufficient attention. Theoretical discussions do not usually distinguish between normative constraints and circumscription by social others on the one hand, and the abstract principles of caring for others that might motivate one's hypothetical choices (even when one cannot act on them) on the other. Obligations to others in need, and feelings of social responsibility are important domains of Iranian women's moral decision-making. Women did recognize obligations to others and make choices about

whom to aid and assist. Here I focus on conduct with sexual implications that is used to define the morality of women since this is recognized as important in the distinctions between women's verbalization about choices that affect their moral standing and their constraint by social circumstances.

Women's Ritual Control and Responsibility for Their Bodies

Women were responsible for the care and use of their bodies through *ritual* means for maintaining purity and honor. In fact, they were deemed incapable of real control and given little explicit instruction in the use of the body, but learned through experience to define socially accepted limits. Women were responsible for the fluids that emanated from their vaginas and for ritual control over them. They were also responsible for semen and milk. Since menstruation was *najes*, or unclean, and could prevent women from entering religious places, many women had pills they believed stopped menstruation for seven days so that they could make religious pilgrimages with their families. Women were taught to observe *xoslay* (prayers of purification) after menstruation and intercourse.

Women came to their marrriage beds with some terms for body parts but very little exact knowledge of sexual relations or the way their bodies worked. They attempted to control intercourse, virginity, abortion and pregnancy mostly through ritual means. Although they overheard and sometimes saw adults engaging in intercourse during the nights, social convention prevented married women from talking of such subjects within earshot of unmarried women. They were customarily prepared for their wedding nights just prior to consummation; two older family members (a representative of the groom's family and one from the bride's family) explained what they were supposed to do. "It's hard," said one woman, "not knowing what to do or what to expect." They were treated specially during the night of consummation and for some days following first intercourse. The event itself was very embarrassing for most young women—foisted upon someone they did not know well while family and neighbors waited outside for the consummation. "It is very embarrassing. But what can we do?"

Women *did* speak of sexual desires and interests. One day during a Quran class for young girls in the South Tehran neighborhood where I lived, the haggard old teacher suddenly asked me, "How do you say *vagina* and *penis* in English?" Then the thrice-married lady pointed between her legs and said "*Vagina,* that's what life is all about," leaving ambiguous whether she was referring specifically to the pragmatics of reproduction or to the pleasure of sexual relations. Women who had been married for some time expressed sexual feelings which they felt were unacknowledged by their husbands. One woman said of marital relations, "The first year is best. After that, it is all very disappointing." The Quran and *hadith* (reported events from the prophet's life), they said, admonished men to attend to the sexual needs and desires of their wives; however, "our husbands think we only have these 'openings' to urinate from; they don't realize we have sexual desires as well." Women (especially unattached ones) were seen by men as dangerous because of their sexuality. While women suggested that it was their responsibility to be sexually attractive to their husbands within the confines of the household (so that husbands would not "stray"), men did not pay as much attention to the sexual interests of their wives. As a result, women sometimes fantasized about more romantic relationships with other men. One woman who had resisted the courting attempts of a stranger many years before often looked for him on the streets; "I imagine what it would be like to be married to him." Women who felt secure in their marital relationships (middle-aged married women) could use intercourse as political leverage when angry with their husbands. Other women could ridicule male sexual ineptness in all-female *baziha* (playful dramatizations) that usually occur during marriage celebrations.

Women were expected to reproduce. In fact, many men stated that a woman without children was like a fruit tree that had dried up without producing fruit—useless. Becoming pregnant was an important part of Islamic identity for women. However, women did use birth control and abortion, primarily as means of childspacing. Contraceptive aids

were more available in urban areas; the extent to which these were used depended upon age, number of children already conceived, relationship to spouse, and education. Several women whom I interviewed had had abortions. In the rural areas this was achieved primarily through jumping up and down or beating one's stomach. In the urban areas women went to clinics or doctors to have abortions performed, often with the secret financial assistance of a sister or even a sister-in-law.

Women were expected to maintain their virginity until their first marriage, although they were considered to be incapable of preserving it by themselves. Women were thought to reach sexual maturity by the age of seven (sometimes nine), according to local interpretations of Islamic hadith. Some families felt obligated to marry off their daughters very young to avoid the familial responsibilities of protection. In south Tehran and the villages, bloody handkerchiefs were still demanded as proof of virginity. However, many women in villages, recounted how chicken blood could be substituted and "hymen repair" was one of the most sought-after procedures according to both Tehran gynecologists and the young divorced women I interviewed.

Some had new ideas about contact and familiarity before marriage. Others felt it was not respectable or morally acceptable to even show one's face to a prospective spouse before marriage. In Quranic classes in some working-class neighborhoods of south Tehran the question, "Is it sinful for a woman to show her face to her fiancé or is this a part of getting to know one another?" was debated endlessly. While it was no longer acceptable there for women to admit they had contact with fiancés in the past—and many in the city and countryside demanded a "no-contact" period of engaged couples—older village women would admit that they had clandestine meetings with their fiancés and boyfriends in the furrows at night. "Talk, that's not all we did," said one illiterate village woman. In several village homes with engaged daughters, young women received their fiancés at night, all night, in private corners of the house, particularly after the part of the marriage rituals involving the signing of the contract had been negotiated and performed, but before the official consummation of the marriage.

Women were more likely to be instructed, however vaguely, about modesty in the presentation of one's body—hair was especially provoking and justified wearing the *chador* or veil—than in the workings of their bodies. Women were taught to control where they walked, how they talked and how they sat. Lying on the floor in a prone position in the presence of unfamiliar or high-status individuals could be interpreted as immodest and sexually inviting. Etiquette came to be every bit as important for a woman's position as her reproductive conduct in defining her as a moral agent. More attention was given to what kinds of persons in whose presence one could display certain behaviors or uncover parts of the body than to understanding the processes of the body.

The Visibility of Women's Behavior and Their Control Over It

In discussing women's obligations in the handling of their bodies, I began to see differences between explicitly stated normative moral behavior (especially in women's talk about Islamic prescriptions) and women's own feelings about the correctness of their conduct. Women realized that they had to adjust to the social circumstances in which they lived even though they might hold other views of appropriate behavior. "If we could only move to another neighborhood we would not be penalized for going out of the house or going without the veil." The extent to which women could actually behave in ways which they valued or preferred and found morally acceptable to themselves depended upon the social restraints placed upon that behavior. The extent to which they could demonstrate control over their conduct was related to its *visibility* and context.

Women could actually control the physical but private aspects of sexuality—fertility regulations, body secretions and premarital contact, irrespective of (perceived) Islamic prescriptions on these matters—more easily than conduct which was more open to public scrutiny such as manner of dress or gait. Women were responsible for aspects of dress, conversation, movement and travel

that might place them in situations where they were seen with unrelated men or strangers. These situations had just as many sexual implications as actual physical contact. The ability of others to view and morally judge their behaviors was extremely important to choices women made. It was harder to ascertain what might be going on behind closed doors—whether there was actual sexual contact or not—although this was often surmised.

The key to the *immorality* of certain behaviors was not so much their religious objectionability or personal objectionability, but whether or not women could keep them from public purview. Women showed less disparity between their own judgments of acceptability and the behaviors they engaged in when behaviors were less visible. Only 28 percent of the women interviewed showed any disparity between their beliefs about birth control and their reported use of contraception. However, for conduct which was more visible they showed more disparity between their reasoning on these behaviors and their engaging in them—52 percent on talking to men, 58 percent on going without a veil, 71 percent on working outside the home, 48 percent in riding in a car with males whether related or not, 68 percent on traveling alone.

Women's own conceptions of when various uses of their bodies were allowed depended upon the extent to which such behavior was visible to those with whom they were *not* so familiar. Therefore women could select to have an abortion or engage in a relationship with a man depending partly upon who might have access to that information and pass judgment upon it.

Many men and women admitted that integrity and chastity were not in fact indicated by superficial behaviors ("Even prostitutes wear a veil") but that social sanctions demanded these measures of morality. One man said, "It is unfortunate but true, a woman's reputation and morality is bound up in how she wears her veil." To travel alone, talk to men, or not wear the veil in the city when in public streets or among people one did not know very well placed a woman's character in question and implied sexual misbehavior and questionable morals.

Women who worked in offices were also thought to engage in sexual misbehavior. One young woman in south Tehran worked in an office in the northern part of the city. Her father was approached by neighbors and asked to curtail his daughter's activities since she would serve as a bad role model for other girls in the neighborhood who might be encouraged to follow her shameful behavior.

To be seen going places alone or with certain people was indication enough of shameful, probably *immoral,* behavior. Another woman, Hadejeh, worked at the women's center and often had to ride in the van with the male driver on errands; people talked about her, using similar immoral terms. "I don't have to do anything," she said, "the gossips will 'choose my clothes' for me." I used pictures and stories of such events to evoke judgments. When women themselves did not know the woman or the woman was not known to others in the story, interviewees did not see anything wrong or *sexual* with being in the same car with men or talking to men. However, if the woman was in the presence of those to whom she was known but who weren't close friends or family, the same behavior became suspect, sexual, shameful, and immoral. Women themselves reinforced these judgments. One woman whose brother-in-law had just married a widow with several children after the death of his own wife, talked disapprovingly about the voracious sexual appetite of her new sister-in-law. Respectable widows did not remarry, but devoted themselves to the raising of their children. "She has the [sexual appetite] of a dog," she said. When I asked women under what circumstances they could engage in a variety of behaviors, they noted that when unfamiliar individuals were around, they had to assume the normative standards of their own group until their status was established. So even if an unfamiliar female were in their presence they would have to don the veil in order to avoid moral reproof. However, if this stranger-woman did not have any connection to their own social group, they could then relax their veils. Thus, degree of familiarity of those around, in addition to gender, helped to determine the *public* nature of any social

setting.[4]

Young women found some ways to make their behavior less visible. Many went out of their houses in the cities to meet with or pass notes to young men, even though such behavior, if observed, would result in much gossip with overtones of sexual misbehavior. One found ways to go with a young man on weekend excursions outside of the city with the collaboration of her cousins. Many young women found ways of manipulating the opinions of others around them by disguising their actions where possible. This kind of manipulation was not considered immoral if it did not inflict hurt on others.[5] Thus one woman encouraged her divorced co-worker to have her hymen repaired and purchase a revised birth certificate in order to more easily secure a new husband as an untouched woman.

Women's rationalizations for transgressions of what was considered normatively acceptable were couched in practical terms. A woman might have to travel to visit a sick relative alone if no one else could accompany her. "What can we do, " they would say. "I have no choice." Any retribution they suffered depended upon their reputations and the extent to which others considered them weighty or respectable or generally moral already. Women's judgments of other women indicate the extent to which their own conduct was determined by social constraints rather than personal choices in many instances. More educated women and women of slightly higher class standing were often perceived to be more respectable and therefore exceptions were allowed in their behavior. One young woman who wore a veil and showed concern and compassion for others in her neighborhood was not penalized for often traveling outside of the neighborhood by herself. "She is *sangine* [indicating respectable]," one neighbor told me.

Women's Judgments and Choices Within the Context of Islamic Prescriptions

Women were able to distinguish their preferences and judgments from what was demanded of them, even though they pragmatically adjusted their behavior to immediate situations. While understanding of proper Islamic conduct was extremely important to women, their own thoughts on moral behaviors (and even their actual behaviors) sometimes contrasted with accepted interpretations of Islamic prescriptions. It is instructive to contrast women's own judgments (and acceptance) of some behaviors with those they attributed to Islam.

Fifty-two percent of the women I interviewed thought women could use birth control, although they thought Islam deemed it sinful. Most declared that "it is even more sinful and immoral to have children one cannot afford." A few indicated that they would need their husband's permission, but many also discovered that they could use contraception without their husband's knowledge.

More women believed that abortion was sinful in the eyes of Islam. "It is like killing someone," many said. Only 30 percent could justify abortion, while still believing it to be sinful in Islam. Women did have abortions although they would not always admit this in certain company, just as they did not admit practices of contact with fiancés before marriage in certain company. More urban women than rural women considered abortion sinful.[6]

Despite customs of modesty, women did go to male doctors, and they did not show a great deal of concern over whether or not the doctor performing an abortion was male or female—especially since it was a private affair unknown to others except a selected few—even though many *stated* that in Islam one should not associate with strange males. Again few people had access to knowledge about this. Women were not overly concerned either with whether others said ritualized xoslay (purification prayers) before entering a mosque, or for that matter whether I did. That was something that could not easily be determined publicly anyway, just as premarital contact was not always easy to verify.

As already noted, opinion differed over whether Islam permitted women to show their faces or speak to their fiancés in the city; but in the countryside, exploration with fiancés, especially when initial engagement ceremonies had been held, was allowed through night visits to the fiancee's home. (The young man might arrive secretly by night and leave the sequestered spot of the house before morning.) Some women in the city were able to arrange a rendezvous with male friends in other neighborhoods.

Many urban and rural women considered viewing television to be immoral in Islam. Most felt that television was not as harmful as the *mahit* (neighborhood or social environment) and that they could watch it in the home without much social retribution. "It is the mahit which corrupts our male children." Supposed Islamic prescriptions on traveling alone or talking to males or receiving education (which the *MULLAS* taught was the "work of the devil") likewise contrasted with many women's own judgments on these behaviors.

Social Context and the Moral "Construction" of Women

Women's choices for behavior and the way in which they made moral decisions about behavior were determined largely through a specific reinforcement of cultural expectations for appropriate behavior and the social and material circumstances under which women lived. As a matter of sexual politics, women in this study learned to be concerned with social contingencies and with *appearances* in making judgments of moral import. Their assessments of the consequences and rightness of their behaviors were not lodged in their assessment of the act itself (or religious assessments of morality), but in social implications and repercussions, not in individual judgment of behavior but in motivation from existing contingencies.

Women by definition had more occurrences to be judged impure than did men. Women, especially working- class women, had many occasions to be considered unclean: mensturation and contact with urine and feces of infants were considered particularly unclean. The same was not true for men; men were not judged on the *sexual* nature of their conduct. Women knew that their moral position depended as much upon how they were viewed by others as upon any abstract principles. The repercussions of social judgments of morality were much more severe for women than for men. In one village a young woman was known to have been seduced by her brother when the parents were out of the house. She suffered irreparable damage to her status and was unable to marry within the village, while her brother had no problem in finding a bride and did not suffer any consequences.[7] In another case, a mullah even suggested that it was not immoral to kill a woman found in adultery but that it was immoral for a wife to kill a husband in similar circumstances because a man can have more than one wife—something the first wife might not know of.

How do women come to think about themselves and their capabilities as defined by or independent of these circumstances? Women felt efficacious about doing those things they thought justified and reasonable in terms of structural and social conditions. Some women did describe men as more capable, intellectually competent and rational, especially in the public sphere. Many women were unwilling to discuss career options for their children, but then so were some men of the same social class. Sometimes "naturalness" arguments[8] used by others were adopted by women to justify why, for example, men were in *need* of more than one wife. "Men are more sexually driven—they need more women," they said. Some women lost confidence in themselves after experiencing little success in acting on the basis of their preferences. Others could verbally seperate these conditions from their own abilities. They rationalized transgressions in terms of the social and practical constraints which they faced, not in terms of their deficiencies. "Sure, men are more capable in making family decisions because they have more experience and/or education." Men could comment on appropriate careers for offspring because they had more information about such things. Sometimes women said, "Yes men are more capable of intellectual conversation; they are smarter than women because they have more experiences to talk about." While a few did suggest that "women are *more* capable than men," social conditions and the way these entered into assessments often made it necessary for women to present themselves as *less* capable than their husbands. One married woman told me, "You are lucky that you have no one [husband] over you, to act like they're

giving you guidance."

Many young women who hoped to have some control over their marriage choices accommodated their expectations about their futures to family preferences. Some even discussed careers and other activities which would postpone marriage although adulthood was still defined by marriage and reproduction. Some expected to find someone who shared their philosophies of life, who would "think like" they did, and who would be friends. Before marriage, Cobra hoped to take up an occupation and to travel and planned to marry only after finding a man with whom she felt intellectually compatible. However, during the spring and summer she was reported by neighbors to be flirting with boys in the streets, so her father entertained suitors in early fall. When her father found a suitable partner, she acquiesced and married him within two-weeks' time. Said Cobra, "If I do not accept the advice of my parents in this matter, I will not be able to go to them for support if I am having trouble with my husband."

Conclusion

The case of women in Iran makes clear the importance of social context in the construction of gender and morality. General discussions on gender and morality by Rosaldo, Gilligan and others draw attention to the importance of social context and social relations in women's negotiation of feelings of selfishness and of responsibility to others, but the implications of these contexts are not fully explored. What results is an ambiguous portrayal of social "responsibilities" and their importance in motivating behavior either in the normative or in the personal, cognitive dimensions—an ambiguity between being tied to normative constraints and using responsibility to others as an abstract ethical principle.

There is a need to clarify women's thinking about social responsibilities as opposed to their being bound by what others think about women's behavior or morality, because these notions are central to concepts of gender discrepencies in moral development. The highest valuations have been given to the use of "abstract" moral principles in decision-making, and assertions are made that men are more likely to reach a stage where they rely on moral principles that emphasize individual rights in making decisions, while women continue to respond to social responsibility (cf. Gilligan 1977). It is conceivable that women will feel constrained to conform to socially accepted standards (as these vary over classes) and yet will abstractly discuss principles of morality and moral standards in making actual decisions. This work on women in Iran certainly suggests that women are socialized to pay more attention to social constraints than men are, yet there is evidence that they cognitively make moral decisions based on more abstract principles that may be independent of specific social expectations.

It is also feasible that women may independently agree with the normative assessment whatever it may be. So agreement with the normative assessment in a particular time or place may not indicate accomodation to social constraints alone. Social responsibility to others may constrain choice *or* it may be used as a principle of moral decision-making. Furthermore, it is not clear that social constraints and abstract moral principles are mutually exclusive. Both accepted norms and individual decision-making may involve principles that emphasize individual rights or those that emphasize obligations to others. It is very difficult to see these differences unless individuals are asked for the reasons behind their choices, behavioral or cognitive.

Ethnographic studies of women contribute to these debates. Previous work on the Middle East has investigated at length the individual's relationship to society through notions of honor and shame (cf. Peristiany 1966). This work relates to sorting normative aspects (and cultural ideals) of behavior from cognitive and personal ones—or social constraint (shame/honor) versus individual moral judgments (guilt) with specific implications for moral thinking. Several authors follow Pitt-Rivers (1976;1966) in discussing gender and class differences in standards of honor and the use of aspects of shame/honor as part of social control.

Citing this tradition of investigation, Rosaldo contrasts individual guilt with socially circumscribed notions of honor—specifically in the sphere of emotion and feeling—and suggests that the appropriate relation between the social and personal self in emotion (or in the present case, morality) is socially and culturally specific (cf. D'Andrade 1984; Rosaldo 1984). I have followed her example in examining women and morality in Iran to gain initial insight into ambiguitites in conceptions of social constraint and social obligations. Women in essence were defined by others, especially male others around them; but women also in some sense let those around them continue to define the limits of their abilities and their self-perceptions. If men were seen as better prepared for many things, women sometimes had a different conception of what they could do. In this way social contingencies become important for understanding how body conceptions "motivate" or influence behavior—as well as how conceptions of self and morality are constructed—and for trying to understand the difference between social constraints on behavior and variation in abstract judgments. In Iran women could talk abstractly of moral behavior that differed from normative generalizations. Women could make judgments about actions and relationships but were constrained publicly from acting on them by what was considered moral behavior in their social class. The contradiction between their own judgments and my observation of what they did (as well as their own accounts of these contradictions) underscores that the construction of women's personal and moral identities can be independent of socially located decision-making. Women rarely had the opportunity to make decisions that affected their own morality given class and other constraints on behaviors, but they could and did when their actions were less visible. Moreover, their abstract moral thinking sometimes focused on principles of individual rights and sometimes on responsibilities; sometimes women agreed with interpretations of Islamic prescriptions and sometimes they didn't.

While this paper focused on how sexuality and sexual behavior are bases for the moral construction of women, women themselves made specific moral judgments regarding behavioral obligations to others, sometimes on the basis of kinship or social relations and sometimes on the basis of more universal principles of need and concern. Rural women were more likely to see a moral obligation to assist anyone who was sick, old or unemployed because of their need; urban men and women were more likely to feel these obligations were based on kinship relations to those afflicted. These examples of women's thinking on social responsibilities are based on abstract considerations of obligation, sometimes related to religious prescriptions and sometimes to personal interpretations.

Women's notions of selfhood and their ability to talk abstractly about self or about relations to others were also affected by region and class differences because of variations in individual exposure to and education in religious and secular knowledge. The degree to which women could make abstract choices and conceive of things that did not seem possible under current conditions was partly reflected in degree of education and class circumstances. Presented with hypothetical situations for moral behavior or decision-making, more rural (and nonliterate) women than urban (and more educated) women were unable to conceive of possible scenarios—to say to whom one could talk or what they could do under certain circumstances. When choices were put in terms of concrete and immediate situations, these women deliberated and delivered judgments. Access to information and education may prepare people to abstract themselves from situations and to consider the abstract motives of action, although not all researchers believe education is so pivotal in the process (Street 1984).

There has been a call for new frameworks to understand the development of gender differences in moral thinking and action as well as self-identity, to which the present discussion has been tied (Young 1984). Any such framework must consider both developmental aspects and contingency aspects of moral thinking in a way that (a) takes into account class and cultural differences, especially in normative conceptions of morality,[9] and (b) clarifies the role of social relations in women's morality, in both normative constraint and cognitive, individual selection of behavior. Although much of the debate on women and morality has developed outside of anthropology, these debates may be informed by anthropological approaches to understanding the complex relationship between individuals and society. Anthropologists, especially those working in the Middle East, have a tradition of investigating the negotiation of cultural ideals and individual acceptance of these within social and economic contexts.

NOTES

Acknowledgments: This analysis is based on 18 months of anthropological research in Iran (1977-1978). An earlier version of this paper was presented at the 1984 American Anthropological Association meetings in Denver, CO. I am grateful to Jon Anderson for very helpful editorial comments on the final draft.

[1] Rosaldo draws attention to the material on guilt and shame in discussing the social negotiation of emotion and self. This is one area where Middle Eastern ethnography has made significant contributions (e.g. Meeker 1976).

[2] For more extensive discussion of these differences in stories and role models for behavior, see J. Bauer (1983).

[3] Gilligan (1982:67) suggests that the "essence" of moral decisions is autonomy to choose and taking responsibility for that choice. Others like Frigga (1984) present morality as normative in nature.

[4] I have provided extensive discussion of the importance of familiarity in the social negotiation of behaviors elsewhere (Bauer 1981, 1979). Those accounts go beyond the stranger/familiar person or kin/nonkin dichotomies in explaining social distance and behavior.

[5] This type of concern with or responsibility toward others in the negotiation of behavior cannot be said to reflect concern for others' normative opinions since this is a way of allowing escape from those normative concerns, under the principle of not inflicting hurt or harm.

[6] The rural sample reflected an age bias toward older females.

[7] In the telling of this tale by other villagers, note is made of the killing and burial of the infant born of this union, but with much less moral disapproval than was directed toward the sister who bore the child.

[8] That is, arguments which explain things as natural or as part of nature (cf. Pierce 1971).

[9] See the debates over the social learning approach, which focuses on contingencies, and the cognitive development approach of Kholberg, which explores stages of moral development, in *Ethics* 92(3) [Flannigan 1982].

REFERENCES CITED

BAUER, J.
  1983 — Women and social consciousness in revolutionary Iran. *In* Women and Revolution in Iran. G. Nashat, ed. Colorado: Westview Press, pp. 141-169.

  1981 — Changes in the behavior and consciousness of Iranian women. Ph.D. Dissertation. Stanford University

  1979 — Women, the use of space and social change in Iran. Paper presented at the 78th Meeting of the American Anthropological Association, Cincinnati, Ohio.

D'ANDRADE, ROY
  1984 — Cultural meaning systems. *In* Culture Theory. Essays on Mind, Self, and Emotion. Shweder and Levine, eds. New York: Cambridge University Press.

FERGUSON, ANN
  1984 — On conceiving motherhood and sexuality: A feminist-materialist approach. *In* Mothering. Treblicot, ed. Rowman and Allenheld, pp. 153-182.

FLANNAGAN, OWEN
  1982 — Virtue, sex and gender. Some philosophical reflections on the moral psychology debate. Ethics 92(3):499-512.

HAUG, FRIGGA
  1984 — Morals have two genders. New Left Review 143:51-68.

GILLIGAN, CAROL
  1982 — In a different voice. Psychological theory and women's development. Cambridge, MA: Harvard University Press.

  1977 — In a different voice: Women's conception of self and morality. Harvard Educational Review 47(4):481-517.

MEEKER, MICHAEL
  1976 — Meaning and society in the Near East: Examples from the Black Sea Turks and the Levantine Arabs (I and II). International Journal of Middle Eastern Studies 7:243-270 383-422.

PERISTIANY, J. G.
  1966 — Introduction. *In* Honour and Shame. The Values of Meditterean Society. J. G. Peristiany, ed. Chicago: University of Chicago Press, pp. 9-18.

PIERCE, CHRISTINE
  1971 — Natural Law language and women. *In* Women in a Sexist Society. Gornick et al., eds. New York: Basic Books, pp. 160-172.

PITT-RIVERS, JULIEN
  1977 — The fate of schechem or the politics of sex. Essays in anthropology of the Mediterranean. New York: Cambridge University Press.

  1966 — Honour and social status. *In* Honour and Shame. The Values of Mediterranean Society. J.G. Peristiany, ed. Chicago: University of Chicago Press, pp. 21-77.

RASSAM, AMAL
  1980 — Women and domestic power in Morocco. International Journal of Middle Eastern Studies 12(2): 171-179.

ROSALDO, MICHELLE
  1984 — Toward an anthropology of self and feeling. *In* Culture Theory. Essays on Mind, Self and Emotion. Shweder and LeVine, eds. New York: Cambridge University Press, pp. 137-157.

STREET, BRIAN
  1984 — Literacy in theory and practice. New York: Cambridge University Press.

YOUNG, IRIS
  1984 — Is male gender identity the cause of male domination. *In* Mothering. Treblicot, ed. Rowman and Allenheld, pp. 129-146.

YOUSSEF, NADIA
  1973 — Cultural ideals, feminine behavior and family control. Comparative Studies in Society and History 15:326-347.

[20]

Negotiating space with family and kin in identity construction: the narratives of British non-heterosexual Muslims

Andrew K.T. Yip

Abstract

This paper highlights significant moments, strategies, and themes in British non-heterosexual Muslims' management of familial and kin relations. Significant socio-cultural and religious factors constitute the framework within which they negotiate such relations. These factors are: the strict religious censure of non-heterosexuality (specifically homosexuality) based on various Islamic written sources, the pervasive cultural censure of homosexuality as a 'western disease', the expectation of marriage as a cultural and religious obligation, the respect for parents, and the maintenance of family honour (*izzat*) particularly in the close-knit kinship network. These factors, which significantly inform the participants' responses and experiences, also reflect the social position of this religious and ethnic minority in British society. Specifically, the participants highlighted the complexity of secrecy, silence and discretion in balancing individualism (ie expression of sexuality) and socio-religious obligations. In general, the data demonstrate the intricate inter-relatedness of structure and agency, and the cultural embeddedness of the production and management of identity and social relations.

Introduction

In recent years, sociologists have argued that the family has undergone significant changes in contemporary western society. Processes such as de-traditionalization and individualization have transformed the family from an institution with fixed roles and hierarchical relations to 'practices' which are flexible and negotiable. It is argued that this has empowered agency in individual family members' negotiation of role, rights and relations (eg Morgan, 1996; Silva and Smart, 1999; Bauman, 2001; Beck-Gernsheim, 2002). This is an outcome of the democratization of emotions that is increasingly characteristic of contemporary intimate relationships (eg Giddens, 1992; Bauman, 2003), a reflection of the risk-laden, contingent and pluralistic society where individual and social life is a calculated product of reflexivity, rather than conformity to traditional behavioural blueprint (eg Giddens and Pierson, 1998; Adam, Beck and von Loon, 2000). Nevertheless, this dominant discourse of family is based exclusively on the white population of Judeo-Christian heritage, using the nuclear family as the referential framework for charting such transformation. Ethnic and religious minorities are often excluded in such discourse, or assumed to follow the same trajectory in due course (Chamberlain, 1999; Ramji, 2003; Ribbens, McCarthy, Edwards and Gillies, 2003). This dominant discourse underpins the analysis of non-heterosexuals' accounts of 'coming out' (revealing their sexuality) to their families of origin (eg Bernstein, 2003). In the face of intolerance or rejection, non-heterosexuals, with sexuality as 'master status' of their identity, distance themselves from their families, and construct their own support networks. This discourse is informed by expressive individualism that is much assumed in the western construction of identity.

It is undeniable that powerful socio-cultural changes in contemporary society do have far-reaching impacts on all aspects of individual and community life. However, such impacts are filtered and mediated through significant social factors such as ethnicity and religion. It is therefore imperative to take into serious consideration socio-cultural and religious specificity while studying how individuals, as late modern social actors, manage their lives.

In this paper, I highlight the significant meanings, issues and themes pertaining to British non-heterosexual[2] Muslims' (primarily of South Asian origin) negotiation and construction of space in their familial and kin relations, as part and parcel of their identity management. The socio-cultural framework within which British Muslims live significantly informs such efforts. Therefore, the significant issues and themes in this respect reflect the socio-cultural and religious specificity of this religious and ethnic community. In view of this, I want to set the scene by exploring the religious and socio-cultural framework within which they construct, contest and negotiate their identities, with specific reference to familial relations. As I shall demonstrate, this structural framework reinforces hegemonic heterosexuality, thus constructs non-heterosexuality (specifically homosexuality) as the problematic 'other'.

Islam, culture and homosexuality

The 2001 British Census puts the number of British Muslims at 1.6 million (National Statistics Online, 2003), which some consider a conservative estimate. The majority of British Muslims are of South Asian origin. Like their counterparts across Europe, British Muslims are not a monolithic and homogeneous community (Berns McGown, 1999; Hasan, 2001; Ahmed, 2003). Nevertheless, there are certain well-documented prominent characteristics specific to this community. One of these characteristics is the intensity of religious identification. Indeed, empirical studies have shown that, in comparison to their white and Afro-Caribbean counterparts, British Muslims reported significantly stronger adherence to religious beliefs (Modood, 1997, 2003).

Andrew K.T. Yip

Furthermore, religious values are also integral to this community (Werbner, 1990; Modood, Beishon and Virdee, 1994). This is common among ethnic minorities, where religious identification is heightened as a form of cultural defence in a religiously and ethnically different society. Religion, in this case, plays a pivotal role in ethnic formation and identification (Soysal, 1997; Yang and Ebaugh, 2001; Bruce, 2002).

On the whole, scholars agree that Islam is about orthodoxy, placing great importance on tradition. Ideally, Islam is more than a religion to individual believers. It is a meaning system that permeates all aspects of their life, as Norcliffe states: 'For the Muslim all of a person's life is for God and any division of life into secular and religious aspects has no warrant. . . . Islam is a total system, an ideology, which guides the Muslim through every aspect of life, both as an individual and collectively' (1999: 2; See also Bouhdiba, 1998).

The Islamic worldview is that of 'bivalence' and 'dual relations', which upholds the 'opposition of contraries'. In terms of sexuality, it emphasizes the complementarity and unity of the sexes (*zawj*), which is creative and procreative. Outside this framework, all sexual activities (eg *zina* [adultery] and homosexuality) are considered not only sexual deviation, but also revolt against God. Thus, the Islamic worldview of sexuality accords hegemonic status to heterosexuality within marriage. Homosexuality, therefore, is censured in the *Qur'an* (eg *suras* [chapters] 7 and 26), the *Shari'ah* (Islamic laws) and the *Hadith* (Sayings of the Prophet Muhammad) (Bouhdiba, 1998). In short, the dominant Islamic discourse of sexuality constructs homosexuality as a violation of nature and deviation from the primary purpose of sexuality, namely procreation (Green and Numrich, 2001).

Islam is a scriptural religion, and Muslims place great emphasis on its written sources. The *Qur'an*, for instance, is widely believed by Muslims to be the literal word of God, not open to change, compromise and abridgement (Norcliffe, 1999). The uncompromisingly negative view of homosexuality in such sources underpins the religious and social censure of it, and this poses significant challenges to non-heterosexual Muslims in all areas of their lives (Naz Project, 1999, 2000; Safra Project, 2002). This is further compounded by the fact that, unlike their Christian counterparts in the west, non-heterosexual Muslims currently have very limited alternative theological resources that affirm their sexuality and challenge the censorious dominant Islamic discourse of sexuality (eg Jamal, 2001; Nahas, 2001; Hekma, 2002).

Family honour and social obligations

The British Muslim community prides itself on its close-knit family and kinship network, which generates high cultural expectation of integration and conformity (Naz Project, 1999, 2000). This is particularly true for the first generation, who were economic immigrants and secondary immigrants to Britain primarily in the latter half of the 20th century[3]. To Muslims, family[4] is imperative to social stability. Maintaining family honour (*izzat*) is therefore a responsibility of paramount importance (Norcliffe, 1999; El-Hadi, 2000; Roald, 2001).

Altruism, care and respect towards parents and elders, strong family ties and loyalty are inextricably linked to one's expression of religious faith. For instance, the *Qur'an* (eg 2: 83; 47: 22; 92: 177), the *Shari'ah*, and the *Hadith* emphasize the rights of parents and relatives, and idealize familial duties and hierarchical relations (Basit, 1997; Modood and Berthoud, 1997; Husain and O'Brien, 2000; Zokaei and Phillips, 2000). The cultural values most primed in the Muslim community are not independence and individuality that characterize western society, but inter-dependence and inter-connectedness (El-Hadi, 2000).

Another important social obligation for Muslims is marriage, which is also considered a religious duty through which one's religious faith is deepened. Marriage is a contractual framework involving rights and duties in relation to personal, family and community life (Green and Numrich, 2001). It is also deemed the sole legitimate means for the propagation of life (Bouhdiba, 1998). One-third of legal injunctions of the *Qur'an* relate to marriage, the family, and how they should be properly managed and regulated (Norcliffe, 1999; El-Hadi, 2000). Not surprisingly, many more families with children in Muslim (ie South Asian) community have formally married parents, compared to white and Afro-Caribbean families (Modood and Berthoud, 1997).

Beyond the nuclear family, kinship network, such as the *biradari* among Pakistanis, is another significant element of the Muslim community. Kinship network is important particularly to first-generation economic immigrants, as it serves as a support network and a safe environment for the reinforcement of socio-cultural practices from their countries of origin. This generates a strong sense of kin ties and obligations (Anwar, 1995; Werbner, 1995; Kathane, 2000; Khan, 2000). External conflict with the host society only serves to heighten internal solidarity and integration, and concomitantly, heightened expectation for conformity, leading to a process of 'encapsulation', underpinned by an 'in-group' and 'out-group' mentality. Among younger generations of Muslims, however, this 'us and them' boundary is more blurred and contested, as their identity draws upon a wider cultural repertoire that incorporates their own culture and that of the host society.

The research and the sample

The qualitative data presented in this paper are drawn from an exploratory study of 22 male and 20 female British non-heterosexual Muslims. The study aims to examine their life circumstances and lived experiences on three analytic levels. These levels are: individual (eg how they reconcile cognitively the seeming contradiction between their sexuality and religious faith), interpersonal (eg how they manage information about their sexuality in familial rela-

Andrew K.T. Yip

tions), and intergroup (eg how they access support networks). This paper, however, focuses on the interpersonal level (for a detailed discussion about the other two levels, see Yip, 2004a, 2004b).

A representative sample of hidden populations such as this is unobtainable (Heaphy, Donovan and Weeks, 1998). Thus, the study employed a variety of sampling methods in order to construct a convenience sample. These methods are: support group networks (eg *Al-Fatiha UK* and *KISS*), lesbian and gay Press (eg *Gay Times* and *Diva*), personal networks, snowballing, and publicity in non-heterosexual events (eg women's meetings).

Each participant completed a brief postal questionnaire, with open- and closed-ended questions on their biographical characteristics. They were then interviewed for approximately two hours each, based on an interview guide designed along the above-mentioned analytic themes. The interviews primarily took place at the participants' homes. In addition, two focus group interviews were also conducted with two support groups (one mixed and one women-only), involving five participants in each case.

The majority of the participants (71%) lived in Greater London and the Southeast of England. Some 88% of the sample was of South Asian (Pakistani, Indian, and Bangladeshi) descent. The participants were relatively young, with 64% under the age of 30. They were also highly-educated (52% have at least a first degree), and the majority (76%) were in full-time employment.

Since this is a non-random convenience sample, it is of paramount importance that the findings should not be generalized to the entire non-heterosexual Muslim population. Nevertheless, the findings offer illuminating insights into the lives of this sexual minority within a religious/ethnic minority.

Homosexuality as a 'western disease'

The participants reported that homosexuality is widely perceived within their community as a 'western disease'. Indeed, the dominant discourse of homosexuality is inextricably linked to their religious/ethnic minority social position. This constructs homosexuality as an appendage of the permissive and immoral western 'other'. To be homosexual and Muslim, therefore, is being a victim of 'westoxication' (being intoxicated by secular western culture), as Jamal explains:

> My mother thinks I'm homosexual and that I have like two men in my arms all the time! And I'm always having sex. . . . in these seedy places and drinking and dancing with nude men! I think when it comes to homosex, she thinks it's a western disease and I'm in that cult! I think the majority of the Asian, Pakistani mothers or fathers, or brothers or sisters think that way.

340

This typical narrative testifies that homosexuality is perceived as moral decadence in the mainstream culture characterized by secularity, permissiveness
and individualism. In the view of many parents, declaring oneself as non-
heterosexual not only reflects the defilement of one's moral character, but
also, symbolically, the defilement of the community's collective religious and
cultural purity. Arifa explains:

> I think that the main issue between gay Asians, gay Muslims and gay white
> people is that there is a definable cultural identity for western gay people.
> There is a gay culture. In our countries [of origin], there isn't a definable
> gay culture. So that's probably why our parents say it's a western idea, and
> you have learnt it from them. I think it's easy to blame the west because it
> is so in your face . . . So that's their main concern.

The dualistic construction of moral purity (ie Islamic sexuality) and moral profanity (ie western homosexuality) renders non-heterosexual Muslims traitors
of not only their religion, but also their collective ethnic and cultural heritage.
To many parents, sexual morality (specifically in *not* being non-heterosexual)
becomes a 'boundary indicator' of one's morality, and therefore religious and
cultural commitment. This boundary is often rigid, serving as a significant
marker of contrast between the moral and the immoral. Indeed, as discussed,
the social position of Islam in Britain as a minority religion heightens the
believers' religious commitment as a form of cultural defence. This produces
a socio-cultural context that is not conducive to the emergence of internal pluralism and dissident identities. As I shall demonstrate below, this structural
backdrop has significant impacts in the participants' management of familial
and kin relations.

The complexity of secrecy and silence

The participants acknowledged that the prominent socio-cultural and religious characteristics already discussed have a significant impact on the way
they managed their sexuality. Certain that their families were likely to subscribe to the pervasive Islamic view of sexuality that problematizes homosexuality, they emphasized the importance of discretion, as the following
narrative illustrates:

> Being a Muslim, your sexuality does interfere with your religion a lot. [This
> is] because in Islam there's so much stress on brotherhood, on the family,
> on the rights [of] and respect for neighbours and parents. Talks about family
> issues and homosexuality will get like, connected. Other religions may not
> give that much emphasis on society or social values. Islam is a very com-
> munity-oriented religion . . . [so] when you talk about community you can't
> hide your sexuality. (Faruq)

Andrew K.T. Yip

On the whole, 10 female (50%) and 12 male (55%) participants have come out to their parents. More have come out to their siblings – 15 female (75%) and 18 male (82%) participants. There seems to be no significant gender differences in terms of the extent of coming out to parents and siblings. The primary reason for the higher rate of coming out to siblings compared to parents is the participants' perception that their siblings, being of the younger generation, were more open to dialogue and tolerant of sexual diversity. Indeed, most siblings responded with cautious tolerance, or even support. In the case of parents, the mother was more likely to be the target of coming out than was the father. This is because the father, occupying the highest position in the family hierarchy, is the most revered member of the family. He also has the greatest power to effect significant impacts on the participants, in response to their coming out. Thus, both generation and gendered parent roles significantly shape the participants' disclosure strategies.

The majority of participants who had come out to family members met with tolerance. Nevertheless, parents generally responded by pressurizing the participants to get married. Underpinning this response is the perception that marriage could 'cure' homosexuality (this is discussed in great detail in the next section). However, the research has also come across a minority of extreme cases where such disclosure met with rejection, and even persecution. In the case of Muhammad from the north east of England, his coming out was considered such a shame to the family that he was persecuted and asked to leave his family and hometown. He was so scarred by the experience that he resorted to substance abuse and even attempted suicide. He even went as far as adopting officially an English name as a symbolic gesture to renounce his cultural and religious heritage. In another case, Jafar, a bisexual man in his late 20s, was attacked by his older brother and hospitalized:

> My family's reaction when I came out was really hard, because I was actually attacked by my middle brother. I was hospitalized for about three months ... He beat me up really badly. He just wanted to get it [homosexuality] out of me [as if] it's just like a phase kind of thing ... That's why I'm not communicative with my family that much now.

Some participants decided to conceal their sexuality, citing two primary reasons for this management strategy – fear of rejection and respect of parents, and therefore the importance of maintaining family honour (*izzat*). Coming out could exact high social and psychological costs, as evidenced by the accounts above. These participants therefore emphasized the importance of silence, as the following focus group exchanges demonstrate:

Shabid: I think the fear we do have is the rejection of the family. That's something I always worried about, that my mum and dad will kick me out, and I'll never be able to visit. You think, oh no, no one is going to talk to me and that's it, that's the end of life.

Zareena: That's the main difference between Asian Muslim and [white
           English] gay people. We're very close to our families. They're a
           lot more important to us than [to] white people.
Jamal: The ties are stronger.
Zareena: If you're white English you are expected to leave home at 16,
           17, 18. In our cultures we maintain a relationship, a strong
           contact with them all of your life. So that's family. Families are
           more important to us.

Participants also cited respect for parents as a major reason for concealment.
Here, individual expression is outweighed by social obligation. Coming out,
to them, not only exact personal costs, but would also tarnish family honour
in the close-knit community. This consideration reflects the participants'
refrain from self-expression in this specific context not only due to fear of
rejection, but also out of a sense of familial duty and obligation. The physical
and emotional proximity among family and kin in such a close-knit community makes this a prominent issue for consideration, as expressed in the
following narrative:

> My parents are extremely important to me. I'd rather sacrifice that [sexu-
> ality] for them. All my friends said it's your life, you should do what you
> want to do. But I find that an extremely selfish viewpoint . . . What's the
> point in telling my parents and going through all this hassle and stress? It
> would virtually kill them. They would never be able to show their face in
> the community. They would rather be dead. (Zahid)

Silence is sometimes a strategy employed by the participants *and* their parents
in order to maintain space and boundary. Some participants reported that they
suspected their parents or even siblings had some inkling about their sexuality. However, the issue was never discussed, so that they did not have to face
the consequences. The participants rationalized that their sexuality is a private
matter, thus using the private and public divide as a management strategy, as
Jamila testifies:

> They know about it [her sexuality] but they don't want to break that thin
> line of talking about it. They all thought it was a phase . . . I find it hard to
> talk to them about it. I think being quiet about it makes it easier for all of
> us. Once it's in the open, you can't put it back.

Negotiating marriage

Parents often consider it their responsibility and religious duty to ensure that
their children get married at an appropriate age. Parental pressure to get
married, therefore, becomes a significant moment when the participants

343

needed to decide either to comply or reveal their sexuality, particularly if other delaying tactics (eg education, work) have proved ineffective. Some participants reported that this significant moment precipitated their coming out to their parents. In return, the disclosure often heightened the pressure to get married. Many parents view marriage as a 'cure' through which their children's 'deviant' sexuality could be 'normalized'. This view is buttressed by the perception that marriage is a rite of passage sanctioned and blessed by religion, thus enhancing its 'healing power' and sanctity, as Yasser's account illustrates:

> You tell them that you are gay, the pressure [to get married] increases because they think, oh, if he's gay, let him get married and he will be all right. He'll be healed. When my parents started having these inklings that I'm homosexual, the pressure increases.

It is clear from the parental response that marriage is more than just a socio-religious duty. Parents also perceived marriage a 'saving device' to re-align their non-heterosexual children's morality. Four female (20%) and 7 male (32%) participants succumbed to the pressure to perform this religious and social duty. At the point of interview, only three remained married. Imran, who is now divorced, recounts his experience:

> In my interpretation [of Islam], it makes marriage compulsory. I would say marriage was very much instilled in us from a very young age . . . I thought, as a gay man, I was not fulfilling a stipulation of what Islam expects of me . . . And this whole thing about family unity, and community involvement, it's something that you just can't do [as a gay person] because you are seen as different. I think you have two options. You either pull away from that particular community and that faith, and make it a very personal thing within yourself, or you lead a life that is a lie. (Imran)

Imran's narrative illustrates the enormous complexity and difficulty in negotiating the pressure of marriage with oneself and the family. He complied with such social expectation and got married, and led 'a life that is a lie'. The marriage only lasted ten months, before he decided that the fulfilment of his sexuality outweighed the compliance with this duty.

While some participants entered into marriage with the confused hope that they could be 'healed', some used marriage as a convenient cover to construct space for their sexuality which they were determined to explore in private, as Zafar, who is now divorced, asserts:

> I think it is very important to do what was publicly expected of you. I'm sure had I chosen to have stayed married and led a double life, and seen at various events and functions and presented a very united front, then no

one would suspect anything. I think it [Islam indirectly] gives permission for men to lead double lives, as long as publicly they are married.

Some parents who knew about their children's sexuality proposed a compromise that they were willing to tolerate their children's (particularly the sons') presumably occasional homosexual activity, as long as they got, and remained, married. This is a compromise that some participants accepted, in order to balance individual freedom, family honour and social obligation. Such is the negotiated 'safe' space within which all parties concerned got something, though not everything.

Resisting marriage could have significant impacts on familial relations. While the majority who were not married used education and work to deflect such pressure, some participants had resorted to more drastic measures. Shazia, for instance, ran away from home primarily due to her mother's pressure of marriage (her father had passed away). She was empowered to take this action by a well-paid job, which gave her financial independence. On the other hand, Faiza used the pursuance of university education as a convenient time to distance herself from home, without any intention of maintaining contact. When her family insisted on contacting her, Faiza had to apply for a court injunction against them:

> I had really difficult experiences in my family . . . I was being controlled in different ways . . . I couldn't see myself surviving really, if I had stayed. . . . I'd left secretly and then they found me and took me back, and then I had to leave again. I actually had to get a court injunction in the end so that they leave me alone. That was the last time I saw them. I was relieved, although I do miss them.

Managing kin relationships

As discussed earlier, kinship network is featured prominently in Muslim community life. This factor therefore plays a significant role in the participants' and their families' management of social information about their sexuality. On the whole, 8 female (40%) and 8 male (36%) participants had disclosed their sexuality to selective relatives. Two factors appear to inform their responses. First, the participants' fear of rejection by community. As the following narratives illustrate, kinship network is of paramount importance, so is its approval of one's lifestyle.

> I've always felt that God made me how I was, that has to be accepted. This is not against Islam . . . My problem was with facing the community and having them reject me. And being in a white society where you are not the majority, where you are the minority, it's really important to have that community support and if they reject you, where are you going to have

the support against the racism that you might face. That was my fear. (Azlin)

I think it's important that you get on well with your relatives. In my culture, they play a very important role. We support one another when things get sticky, like racism. . . . I won't tell them [about his sexuality]. What's the point? They won't understand anyway. Within the Muslim community, it's a nono subject. I would probably be rejected. (Muhammad)

Another significant factor is the maintenance of family honour. Many parents who were themselves tolerant insisted that the participants did not disclose any information beyond the boundary of their nuclear family. This is a compromise that some participants were willing to accept, in exchange for a certain degree of tolerance within their own family. The following narratives illustrate this.

On the individual level, people might accept their son or daughter as lesbian or homosexual, but they would not like the extended family or neighbours to find out about that. And I understand because the social network is like this . . . They would think it is just another attack on their cultural and ethnic heritage or their identity. (Deepak)

My mum . . . supports me. But she has specifically said to me, if I could just keep it to ourselves. She did say, 'Don't tell my sisters and don't tell your extended family. They will have nothing but bad comments to make.' I respect that. (Tabassam)

The targets of disclosure are generally younger members of the kinship network. As with younger members of their own families to whom they were more likely to come out, this is again a reflection of their confidence that younger members of the community were more open-minded to the issue.

Conclusion

In this paper, I have presented narratives of non-heterosexual Muslims which demonstrate how they engaged with significant socio-cultural and religious factors in managing their sexuality in the context of familial and kin relations. The prominent issues and themes highlighted reflect not only socio-cultural and religious specificity, but also the structural position of British Muslims as a religious and ethnic minority. This structural framework constitutes a cultural base pattern that sets the boundary for acceptable sexuality and behaviour.

The data have showed that, against a backdrop of cultural and religious censure of non-heterosexuality – complicated by the emphasis of family honour, marriage and close-knit kinship – non-heterosexual Muslims devised

a variety of strategies to construct safe space to manage their dissident identity. Specifically, the management of secrecy and silence is particularly
complex. The concealment of their sexuality, in most cases, was motivated by
the fear of rejection and conformity to the cultural norm of respecting elders
(particularly parents), thus the maintenance of family honour.

On the other hand, participants who were at least partially 'out' to their
family and kin were more likely to have come out to younger members. This
is primarily due to the perceived generational differences in responses to
counter-normative sexuality. This response is indicative of the generational
shift in the integration with the western cultural base that is more open to
sexual diversity. The younger generations, being more integrated into the host
society, straddling well between the western cultural base and their own. Their
wider cultural repertoire opens up more space and possibilities for the discourse of sexuality and identity in general (eg Samad, 1998; Roald, 2001). In
the main, the participants' coming out was met with cautious tolerance.
However, some experienced threat of or actual physical violence, and had to
distance themselves from their families.

In the participants' negotiation of space, marriage emerged to be a significant issue. Parental pressure to get married sometimes led to the disclosure of sexuality. This in turn led to the increase of parental pressure, as they
saw marriage as a 'cure' to the perceived transitional phase of non-
heterosexuality. Marriage can also act as a convenient cover for all parties
involved. The fulfilment of this cultural and religious obligation ironically
opened up some space for the participants to explore their sexuality in private.

Few participants had come out to members in their kinship, generally for
fear of rejection and the tarnishing of family honour. While some parents
tolerated their children's sexuality, such information was kept strictly from
relatives, once again highlighting the importance of family honour. On the
whole, their coming out strategies and experiences are culturally-embedded,
and their identity other-informed and socio-centric (Phellas, 2002).

In general, the narratives illustrate the intricate inter-relatedness of structure and agency. There is no denying that the participants, as social actors in
late modern society, demonstrated the capacity to construct space within the
structural framework in their attempt to balance individualism, social responsibility and religious duty. Nevertheless, structure – in the form of cultural and
religious norms – exerts its impact on this process. Traditions are still prominent in the structural framework within which they construct their identities.
Their experiences seem to challenge the dominant sociological discourse of
the construction of personal identity in contemporary society, which gives
undue prominence to the freeing of agency – vis-à-vis de-traditionalization
and individualization – in the construction of individual social biographies,
underpinned by radicalized reflexivity (eg Giddens and Pierson, 1998). This
ideological framework, what Adams (2003: 222) calls 'the extended reflexivity thesis', prioritizes agency in the form of an over-rationalized and highly
calculating self, free from the shackles of culture and tradition. The narratives

Andrew K.T. Yip

presented here illustrate the nuanced engagement of agency and structure, demonstrating cultural situatedness in the construction and management of identity and social relations. This supports the 'co-existence thesis' (for more details see Heelas, Scott and Morris, 1996) that recognizes the continued prominence of structure (ie tradition) despite the ascendance of agency. Thus, sociological discourse must continue to be sensitive to the cultural embededness of identity and social relations (Adams, 2003).

Nottingham Trent University   Received 3 October 2003
                                                                 Accepted 7 April 2004

Notes

1 This paper is based on an ESRC-funded project entitled *A Minority within A Minority: British Non-heterosexual Muslims* (Award No. R000223530; May 2001–October 2002). The author gratefully acknowledges the support from the ESRC, various support groups, and all the participants.
2 'Non-heterosexual' is a contentious term. Some consider it pejorative because it labels people against the perceived norm of heterosexuality. They prefer 'lesbian, gay, and bisexual'. This phrase itself is unsatisfactory, as others insist on prolonging it, in the name of inclusivity, by adding 'transgendered', 'queer', and more recently, 'intersex'. I decided to use 'non-heterosexual' throughout the text (expect where there is a need to specify) primarily because it embraces all the labels used by participants in contrast to 'heterosexual'.
3 For a detailed discussion of their migration history, see Yip (2004a).
4 To Muslims, 'family' does not exclusively refer to 'nuclear family' (or its derivative forms, such as single-parent family), as current dominant discourse on family uncritically uses as the baseline. Generally, this term is used more widely by Muslims to embrace family structure bigger than the nuclear family (ie extended family members and kin).

References

Adam, B., Beck, U. and von Loon, J., (2000), *The Risk Society and Beyond*, London: Sage.
Adams, M., (2003), 'The Reflexive Self and Culture: A Critique', *British Journal of Sociology*, 54 (2): 221–238.
Ahmed, A., (2003), *Islam under Siege*, Cambridge: New Century Polity Press.
Anwar, M., (1985), *Pakistanis in Britain*, London: New Century Publishers.
Anwar, M., (1995), 'Social Network of Pakistanis in the UK: A Re-evaluation', in Rogers, A. and Vertovec, S. (eds), *The Urban Context*, Oxford: Berg.
Armstrong, E., (2002), *Forging Gay Identities*, Chicago: Chicago University Press.
Basit, T., (1997), '"I Want More Freedom, but Not Too Much": British Muslim Girls and the Dynamics of Family Values', *Gender and Education*, 9 (4): 425–439.
Bauman, Z., (2001), *The Individualized Society*, Cambridge: Polity Press.
Bauman, Z., (2003), *Liquid Love*, Cambridge: Polity Press.
Beck-Gernsheim, E., (2002), *Reinventing the Family*, Cambridge: Polity Press.
Berns McGowan, R., (1999), *Muslims in the Diaspora*, Toronto: Toronto University Press.
Bernstein, R., (2003), *Straight Parents, Gay Children*, New York: Thunder's Mouth Press.
Bouhdiba, A., (1998), *Sexuality in Islam*, London: Saqi Books.
Bruce, S., (2002), *God is Dead*, Oxford: Oxford University Press.

Chamberlain, M., (1999), 'Brothers and Sisters, Uncles and Aunts: A Lateral Perspective on Caribbean Families', in Silva, E. and Smart, C., (eds), *The New Family?*, London: Sage.

El-Hadi, A., (2000), 'The Muslim community: Beliefs and Practices', in Lau, A., (ed.), *South Asian Children and Adolescents in Britain*, London: Whurr.

Giddens, A., (1992), *The Transformation of Intimacy*, Cambridge: Polity Press.

Giddens, A. and Pierson, C., (1998), *Conversations with Anthony Giddens*, Cambridge: Polity Press.

Green, M. and Numrich, P., (2001), *Religious Perspectives on Sexuality: A Resource Guide*, Chicago: The Park Ridge Center.

Hasan, A.G., (2001), *American Muslims: The New Generation*, New York: Continuum.

Heaphy, B., Donovan, C. and Weeks, J., (1998) ' "That's Like My Life": Researching Stories of Non-heterosexual Relationships', *Sexualities*, 1: 453–470.

Heelas, P., Scott, L. and Morris, P., (1996), *Detraditionalization*, Oxford: Blackwell.

Hekma, G., (2002), 'Imams and Homosexuality: A post-gay Debate in the Netherlands', *Sexualities*, 5 (2): 237–248.

Husain, F. and O'Brien, M., (2000), 'Muslim Communities in Europe: Reconstruction and Transformation', *Current Sociology*, 48 (4): 1–13.

Jamal, A., (2001), 'The Story of Lot and the *Qur'an*'s Perception of the Morality of Same-sex Sexuality', *Journal of Homosexuality*, 41 (1): 1–88.

Kathane, R., (2000), 'Roots and Origins: Ethnicity and the Traditional Family', in Lau, A., (ed.), *South Asian Children and Adolescents in Britain*, London: Whurr.

Khan, Z., (2000), 'Muslim Presence in Europe: The British Dimension – Identity, Integration and Community Activism', *Current Sociology*, 48 (4): 29–43.

Modood, T., (1997), 'Culture and Identity', in Modood, T. and Berthoud, R. (eds), *Ethnic Minorities in Britain*, London: Policy Studies Institute.

Modood, T., (2003) 'New Form of Britishness: Post-immigration Ethnicity and Hybridity in Britain', in Sackmann, R., Peters, B. and Faist, T., (eds), *Identity and Integration: Migrants in Western Europe*, Aldershot: Ashgate.

Modood, T. and Berthoud, R., (1997), *Ethnic Minorities in Britain*, London: Policy Studies Institute.

Modood, T., Beishon, S. and Virdee, S., (1994), *Changing Ethnic Identities*. London: Policy Studies Institute.

Morgan, D., (1996), *Family Connections*, Cambridge: Polity Press.

Nahas, O., (2001), *Islam en Homoseksualiteit*, Amsterdam: Bulaaq.

National Statistics Online, (2003), *Religion in Britain*. <http://www.statistics.gov.uk/cci/nugget.asp?id=293>

Naz Project, (1999), *Hard to Reach, Hard to Teach*, London: Naz Project.

Naz Project, (2000), *Emerging Sexualities: Ten Testimonies*, London: Naz Project.

Nielsen, J.S., (2000), 'Muslims in Britain: Ethnic Minorities, Community, or Ummah', in Coward, H., Hinnells, J. and Williams, R., (eds), *The South Asian Religious Diaspora in Britain, Canada and the United States*, New York: State University of New York Press.

Norcliffe, D., (1999), *Islam*, Brighton: Sussex Academic.

Phellas, C., (2002), *The Construction of Sexual and Cultural Identities*, Aldershot: Ashgate.

Ramji, H., (2003), 'Engendering Diasporic Identities', in Puwar, N. and Raghuram, P., (eds), *South Asian Women in the Diaspora*, Oxford: Berg.

Ribbens McCarthy, J., Edwards, R. and Gillies, V., (2003), *Making Families: Moral Tales of Parenting and Step-parenting*, Durham: Sociologypress.

Roald, A.S., (2001), *Women in Islam*, London: Routledge.

Safra Project, (2002), *Identifying the Difficulties Experienced by Muslim Lesbian, Bisexual and Transgender Women in Accessing Social and Legal Services*, London: Safra Project.

Samad, Y., (1998), 'Media and Muslim Identity: Intersections of Generation and Gender', *Innovation*, 11 (4): 425–438.

Silva, E.B. and Smart, C., (1999), *The New Family?*, London: Sage.

349

Andrew K.T. Yip

Soysal, Y.N., (1997), 'Changing Parameters of Citizenship and Claims-making: Organised Islam in European Public Spheres', *Theory and Society*, 26: 509–527.

Werbner, P., (1990), 'Manchester Pakistanis: Division and Unity', in Clarke, C., Peach, C. and Vertovec, S., (eds), *South Asian Overseas*, Cambridge: Cambridge University Press.

Werbner, P., (1995), 'From Commodities to Gifts: Pakistani Migrant Workers in Manchester', in Rogers, A. and Vertovec, S., (eds), *The Urban Context*, Oxford: Berg.

Yang, F. and Ebaugh, H., (2001), 'Transformations in New Immigrant Religions and Their Global Implications', *American Sociological Review*, 66 (1): 269–288.

Yip, A.K.T., (2002), 'Same-sex Relationships', in Goodwin, R. and Cramer, D. (eds), *Inappropriate Relationships*, Mahwah, NJ: Lawrence Erlbaum.

Yip, A.K.T., (2004a), 'Embracing Allah and Sexuality?: South Asian Non-heterosexual Muslims in Britain', in Kumar, P. and Jacobsen, K., (eds), *South Asians in the Diaspora*, Leiden, The Netherlands: EJ Brill.

Yip, A.K.T., (2004b), 'Minderheit in der Minderheit: nicht Heterosexuelle Britische Muslime', in Berlin-Brandenburg e.v. (Hg.), (ed.), *Muslime unter dem Regenbogen: Homosexualitat, Migration und Islam*, Berlin: Queverlag GmbH.

Zokaei, S. and Phillips, D., (2000), 'Altruism and Intergenerational Relations among Muslims in Britain', *Current Sociology*, 48 (4): 45–58.

350

Name Index